SEVENTH EDITION

Classroom Assessment

Principles and Practice that Enhance Student Learning and Motivation

James H. McMillan

Virginia Commonwealth University

 Pearson

330 Hudson Street, NY, NY 10013

Director and Publisher: Kevin M. Davis
Content Producer: Janelle Rogers
Development Editor: Jill Ross
Content Project Manager: Pamela D. Bennett
Media Project Manager: Lauren Carlson
Portfolio Management Assistant: Anne McAlpine
Executive Field Marketing Manager: Krista Clark
Executive Product Marketing Manager: Christopher Barry

Procurement Specialist: Carol Melville
Cover Designer: Cenveo® Publisher Services
Cover Photo: Getty Images/Caiaimage/OJO+
Full-Service Project Management: Katrina Ostler, Cenveo Publisher Services
Composition: Cenveo Publisher Services
Printer/Binder: LSC, Crawfordsville
Cover Printer: Phoenix Color
Text Font: 10/12pt Palatino LT Pro

This book was previously published under the title *Classroom Assessment: Principles and Practice for Effective Standards-Based Instruction.*

Library of Congress Cataloging-in-Publication Data

On file with the Library of Congress.

ISBN 10:   0-13-452330-X
ISBN 13: 978-0-13-452330-9

20 2019

I remember it well: When I took my first "tests and measurements" course in graduate school at Michigan State University, I was fairly apprehensive—what would this class have to do with teaching and learning? Would I be using complex mathematics and learning about the technical aspects of "standardized" testing that really had little to do with what I wanted to do day in and day out in the classroom? Well, the course met some of my negative expectations! It was interesting, but not as helpful as I hoped when applied to teaching. I have written this book to address this shortcoming, to be directly relevant to instruction so that student learning and motivation are enhanced.

The premise of this book is that classroom assessment is the most important element in evaluating students that has a direct and powerful impact on student learning and motivation. It is through everyday interactions with students, as well as quizzes, unit tests, papers, and assignments, that teachers communicate what is important in learning, the standards that indicate proficiency and more advanced levels of understanding and skills, and communicate with students about what they understand and what needs further learning. While much recent emphasis has been placed on large-scale accountability testing, classroom assessments, from what I have seen in classrooms, show what is really being learned, as well as what influence teachers have had on student achievement and motivation. Classroom assessment is the most direct, specific, and helpful indicator of what students know, the depth of their understanding, and the nature of their dispositions.

Over the past two decades the field of classroom assessment has changed considerably. There is now more emphasis on how *student assessment is an integral part of teaching that effects student learning and motivation*, not just something that is done after instruction to measure what students have learned. Much attention is now focused on *formative assessment*—what is also called assessment *for* learning. In recent years, there has also been a dramatic change in curriculum throughout the United States that has led to standards-based instruction and assessment at every level of education and nearly every subject. The Common Core State Standards and accompanying "national" and state tests of those standards reinforce the emphasis on assessing students' levels of proficiency, which will have direct implications for what you do for your classroom assessments. Finally, there is continued high interest in the importance of "scientific" research and "empirical data" as sources of knowledge about what works in education (*evidence-based*). These three influences—assessment as part of instruction to improve student learning and motivation, standards-based education, and data-driven evidence—form the foundation for this book. All are essential factors in understanding how classroom assessments can improve targeted student outcomes.

This book, then, is designed to provide prospective and practicing teachers with:

- a concise, nontechnical, and engaging presentation of assessment principles that clearly and specifically relate to student learning and motivation;
- current research and new directions in the classroom assessment field; and
- practical and realistic examples, suggestions, and case studies.

The approach I have taken to meet these goals is to build assessment into the instructional process, focusing on assessment concepts and principles that are essential for effective teacher decision making, and integrating principles of learning and motivation. The emphasis throughout is on helping teachers to understand the importance of establishing credible performance standards (learning targets), communicating these standards to students, and providing feedback to students on their progress. There is much less emphasis on technical measurement concepts that teachers rarely find useful, though there is extensive discussion of aspects of assessment that result in high quality and credibility, such as accuracy, fairness, matching assessment to clearly and publicly stated standards, positive consequences, and practicality.

For previous users of this book, you have probably noticed a new subtitle for this edition. This change is important because it represents the evolution of the emphasis from integrating assessment with instruction to assessment that enhances student learning and motivation. This is important because the examples and explanations have been revised and updated with student learning and motivation at the forefront.

With three exceptions, the basic organization of the text is unchanged from the sixth edition. Chapters 1 through 3 present the fundamental principles of assessment and instruction, with an emphasis on the importance of the teacher's professional judgment and decision making as integral to making useful and credible assessments that enhance learning and motivation. Chapters 4 and 5 cover formative assessment, but here I've made a significant change. These chapters are now divided so that each one captures the essential elements of two types of formative assessment. Chapter 4 examines *embedded* formative assessment, the type that occurs "on the fly" during instruction, and Chapter 5 presents formative assessment that occurs after students take a more formal summative assessment, such as chapter or unit tests. Both Chapters 6 and 7 focus on summative assessment—Chapter 6 for summative assessments like tests and quizzes that occur weekly or monthly, and Chapter 7 for externally designed, large-scale tests tied to accountability. The types of standards-based tests included in Chapter 7 are now commonplace for teachers (this content is moved from later in the book in the previous edition). The next few chapters (8–11) are organized by type of assessment, beginning with selected-response item formats. Each of these chapters shows how to assess different types of learning targets.

Chapter 12 presents so-called "noncognitive" assessments that are used to measure attitudes, values, interests, beliefs, self-efficacy, student self-reflection, and other dispositional traits, as well as many 21st-century skills. Chapter 13 reviews the assessment of students who have special needs and are included in the regular classroom. The new Chapter 14 presents assessment practices that are needed for culturally and linguistically different students, an increasingly important segment of the student population. The final chapter examines grading and reporting the results, with a strong emphasis on standards-based grading.

New to This Edition

There have been several significant additions for the seventh edition.

- Introductory case studies of teacher decision making are included at the beginning of each chapter to engage and focus readers, with answers at the end of the chapters.
- The chapter on assessment of students with special needs was extensively revised.
- A new sequence of chapters allows students to better incorporate the expanding influence of high-stakes accountability testing on classroom assessment.
- Learning Outcomes are specified at the beginning of each chapter and are aligned with new digital content that is available within the Pearson MyEdLab with Pearson Etext, including interactive self-check quizzes and application exercises.
- A new chapter on assessment of culturally and linguistically diverse students was added.
- New *Teacher's Corner* features provide updated examples of how National Board Certified teachers practice assessment.
- Chapters on formative assessment are reorganized to show the entire process separately for embedded and summative-based types.
- More emphasis on the role of student perceptions of assessment, which influences motivation, is provided.
- There is greater coverage of the role of technology in assessment, grading, and reporting of information. This includes coverage of computer-enhanced–type test items, eportfolios, digitally formatted test items, and electronic grading systems.
- A new appendix includes an example of a complete Individualized Education Program (IEP) for a student with special needs.
- The self-instructional review exercises that were included at the end of each chapter in previous editions are now moved to Appendix C along with the answers.

Other significant improvements in this edition include:

- Updating of research on key concepts and practices.
- Incorporation of newly adopted test standards.
- Expanded emphasis on the influence of externally developed standards-based tests and test items.
- Changes in writing style to be more engaging and concise.
- New figures and diagrams to organize information and show steps needed to implement recommended practice.

- New design elements to enhance the clarity of presentation of information that facilitates understanding.

Throughout the book there is a unique blend of educational psychology with principles of assessment. This approach to assessment is unique and helps teachers understand how good assessment is critical to enhancing student learning and motivation.

Several instructional aids are included to facilitate understanding and applying the material. These include *cognitive maps* at the beginning of each chapter to provide graphic overviews; *boldface key terms*; *quotes from National Board Certified and state-recognized teachers* throughout to illustrate practical applications; *chapter summaries* to review essential ideas; *interactive MyEdLab Self-Check Quizzes and Application Exercises at the end of each chapter (see the following section for more on this)* to provide opportunities for practice and application; *suggestions for conducting action research*; extensive use of *examples, diagrams, charts,* and *tables; case studies for reflection*; and a *glossary* of key terms.

MyEducationLab® with Pearson Etext

The most visible change in this edition (and certainly one of the most significant) is the expansion of the digital learning and assessment resources that are now embedded in the etext. The online resources in the MyEdLab with Pearson Etext include:

Self-Checks. MyEdLab: Self-Check Quizzes. These quizzes are meant to help you assess how well you have mastered the chapter learning outcomes. These self-checks are made up of self-grading multiple-choice items that not only provide feedback on whether questions are answered correctly or incorrectly, but also provide rationales for both correct and incorrect answers.

Application Exercises. Also tied to specific chapter learning outcomes, these exercises can challenge you to use chapter content to reflect on teaching and learning in real classrooms. The questions you answer in these exercises are usually constructed-response items. Once you provide your own answers to the questions, you receive feedback in the form of model answers written by experts.

These new digital resources are located in a MyEdLab box at the end of each chapter.

Acknowledgments

Throughout the development and writing of this book, I have been fortunate to have the support and assistance of classroom teachers who have provided quotations, practical examples, and suggestions. I am very grateful for their willingness to help, for their patience in working with me, and, most of all, for keeping me grounded in the realities of teaching. They include Brian Letourneau, Rachel Boyd, Jamie Mullenaux, Susan Pereira, Marie Wilcox, Carole Forkey, Beth Carter, Tami Slater, Arleen Reinhardt, Patricia Harris, Ann Marie Seely, Andrea Ferment, Terri Williams, Steve Myran, Suzanne Nash, Steve Eliasek, Daphne Patterson, Craig Nunemaker, Judy Bowman, Jeremy Lloyd, Marc Bacon, Mary Carlson, Michelle Barrow, Margie Tully, Rixey Wilcher, Judith Jindrich, Dan Geary, Joshua Cole, Christy Davis, Elizabeth O'Brien, Beth Harvey, Rita Truelove, Rita Driscoll, Dodie Whitt, Joe Solomon, Stephanie Stoebe, Elizabeth Shanahan, Dan Leija, and Leslie Gross. I am very fortunate that Dr. Amy Hutton, a former doctoral student in education here at Virginia Commonwealth University, assisted me extensively in many ways for this seventh edition—editing, checking references, researching topics and offering suggestions, always doing exceptional work, and for taking the lead on first drafts of two chapters.

I am deeply grateful for the essential contributions of Dr. Heather Bumgarner, a practicing National Board Certified teacher. Dr. Bumgarner authored the introductory case studies, made arrangements for new Teacher's Corner excerpts, and provided much-needed editorial suggestions for all chapters. In particular, she worked tirelessly to construct the introductory case studies as realistic examples of assessment situations facing teachers that reinforce major points in the relevant chapter. I know her inputs have helped to keep the book grounded in reality, better organized, and more accurate.

I am also fortunate that Dr. Serra De Arment was able to provide excellent revision work on the chapter focused on assessment of students with exceptional needs, and that Dr. Divya Varier contributed to the chapter on grading and reporting.

I would also like to express my appreciation to the following college and university professors who offered insightful and helpful comments and suggestions. For the first edition, thanks go to Cheri Magill, Virginia Commonwealth University; H. D. Hoover, University of Iowa; Kathryn A. Alvestad, Calvert County Public Schools; John R. Bing, Salisbury State University; John Criswell, Edinboro University of Pennsylvania; George A. Johanson, Ohio University; Catherine McCartney, Bemidji State University; and Anthony Truog, University of Wisconsin, Whitewater; for the second edition, Lyle C. Jensen, Baldwin-Wallace College; Cathleen D. Rafferty, Indiana State University; Gerald Dillashaw, Elon College; Daniel L. Kain, North Arizona University; Charles Eiszler, Central Michigan University; and Betty Jo Simmons, Longwood College; for the third edition, Gyu-Pan Cho, University of Alabama; Saramma T. Mathew, Troy University; E. Michael Nussbaum, University of Nevada; and Kit Juniewicz, University of New England; for the fourth edition, Sally Blake, University of Texas at El Paso; Roberta Devlin-Scherer, Seton Hall University; Carla Michele Gismondi Haser, Marymount University; and Saramma T. Mathew, Troy University. For the fifth edition, thanks go to Rondall R. Brown, Eastern Oregon University; Carolyn Burns, Eastern Michigan University; Candyce Chrystal, Mount Marty College; Stephanie Kotch, University of Delaware; Alan L. Neville, Northern State University; and

Tasha Almond Reiser, The University of South Dakota. For the sixth edition, thanks go to Kristen Bjork, University of Nevada–Las Vegas; Patricia Lutz, Kutztown University; Linda Fortune-Creel, Troy University; and Alton Corley, Texas State University. For the current edition, appreciation is extended to Nelson J. Maylone, Eastern Michigan University; Shambra Mulder, Kentucky State University; Christopher Palmi, Lewis University; Amy Lynn Rose, University of North Carolina-Greensboro; and Bo Zhang, University of Wisconson Milwaukee.

I am very grateful for the encouragement and direction of my editor, Kevin Davis. In addition, many thanks to others at Pearson, especially Jill Ross, Pearson developmental editor and Katie Ostler of Ostler Editorial, Inc.

On a more personal note I continue to be amazed at the support provided by my wife, Jan—for putting up with all that has been required to complete the book editions over the years.

BRIEF CONTENTS

CONTENTS

CHAPTER **3**

High-Quality Classroom Assessment 70

CHAPTER **4**

Embedded Formative Assessment 107

CHAPTER **7**

Summative Assessment II: Using Large-Scale Standards-Based and Standardized Tests   187

CHAPTER **8**

Selected-Response Assessment: Multiple-Choice, Binary-Choice, and Matching Items   215

CHAPTER **12**

Assessing "Noncognitive" Dispositions and Skills   326

CHAPTER **13**

Assessment for Students with Exceptional Needs   365

CHAPTER **14**

Assessment for Culturally and Linguistically Diverse Students   398

The Role of Assessment in Teaching and Learning

Integrating Instruction and Assessment

- Realities of teaching
  — fast paced
  — hectic
  — complex
- Teacher decision making
  — before instruction
  — during instruction
  — after instruction

Factors Influencing

- 21st-century knowledge, skills, and dispositions
- Technology
- Principles of cognitive and sociocultural learning and motivation
- Standards-based education
- High-stakes testing

Research on Learning, Motivation, and Instruction

- Cognitive theories
  — meaningful
  — self-regulated
  — active construction
- Thinking skills
- Motivation
  — feedback

Types of Assessment

- Preassessment
- Formative assessment
- Summative assessment

ROLE OF ASSESSMENT IN TEACHING

Students' perceptions of assessment

Classroom Assessment

- Four components
  — purpose
  — measurement
  — interpretation
  — use

Assessment Standards for Teachers

Assessment and Grading Decision Making

- Internal beliefs and values
- External factors

Recent Trends

- Alternative assessments
- Assessment integrated with instruction
- Student self-evaluation
- Authenticity
- Public standards and criteria
- Student involvement with assessment
- Formative assessment

CHAPTER 1 Concept Map

Learning Outcomes

After reading this chapter, you should be able to:

1.1 Understand the nature of classroom assessment, its purposes and characteristics, and how classroom assessment differs from other types of assessment.

1.2 Understand and be able to give examples of how classroom assessment *of*, *for*, and *as* learning can be integrated with instruction.

1.3 Know how different contextual factors, such as high-stakes accountability testing and theories of learning, influence teacher decision making about how classroom assessments are designed and implemented in a specific classroom.

Introductory Case Study

What Should Abby Do?

When John walked into the math teachers' workroom, Abby was thinking about her upcoming unit on fraction computation and the changes this year she wanted to make in assessing student learning. She wasn't happy with the end-of-unit summative test that her peers and administration suggested be given to students. Her belief that assessments should help her understand her students' strengths, misunderstandings, and learning errors simply didn't merge with the current assessment. The assessment was computerized and contained 30 questions that were multiple-choice, fill-in-the-blank, and technology-enhanced items similar to those on the end-of-year high-stakes test.

Instead, Abby wanted to ask her administration if she could give a constructed-response assessment with fewer items that followed recent assessment trends and learning theories. Her proposed assessment would provide a scenario involving cooking pizzas at the new pizzeria in the neighborhood and allow student choice for which eight of ten teacher-created open-ended problems students wanted to complete. Students would also create and solve two of their own fraction problems. Throughout the fraction unit, students had completed these types of tasks and Abby had provided feedback to students on their progress in mastering the learning targets. Abby knew her assessment would allow students to apply their knowledge within an authentic task. Additionally, by using a rubric for scoring, she could emphasize student effort, which she knew would encourage her students to stay motivated for learning.

Abby explained her idea to John, a teacher with whom she had collaborated in designing most of the math unit's real-world applicable lessons, and asked John if he wanted to codevelop the assessment and give it to his students. John looked at Abby with questioning eyes. He declined her offer and suggested she stick with the current computerized assessment. Abby bantered with John telling him that she believed the traditional summative assessment was solely for providing students with a grade, that this test didn't align with their teaching methods, and that the end-of-unit assessment lacked impact on student learning and motivation.

John's response was that he believed the current assessment provided reliable standardized feedback to teachers and parents on students' mastery of learning targets. Additionally, teachers could use the efficient computer data analysis to drive immediate remediation efforts. He also believed it was important for students to be exposed to assessments similar to the end-of-year high-stakes test so students would have practice in preparing for it.

To encourage Abby and show his support of her assessment beliefs and values, John suggested that Abby give the computerized summative assessment and instead incorporate her assessment ideas throughout the unit of study.

As you read this chapter, think about what Abby should do. Should she follow John's advice and give the computerized assessment or ask permission to give her end-of-unit assessment? If she follows John's advice, how can Abby integrate her assessment beliefs and values throughout the unit?

Allow me to begin with two stories that are directly relevant to the importance of classroom assessment. When my daughter, Ryann, was 11, she was heavily into gymnastics, working out most days of most weeks. During this particular year, the gym where she worked out hired new coaches, both from Russia. Immediately, the review of her work (performance) changed dramatically. What she was once praised for now received detailed, critical feedback (e.g., "No, put your hands in this position, not like this"). When the girls were "tested," doing their routines, they were judged with higher expectations and only received praise when well deserved. Instead of hearing "good" all the time, they heard "wrong" most of the time. Negative comments, though, were accompanied by suggestions for doing something different and practice that would help them. The gym and training assessment environment changed, and with it, eventually, the level of performance. The acceptance of mistakes and honest feedback changed the "assessment" culture in the gym. The end of the story is a happy one. As a team, they were the best in the state, and Ryann made positive contributions!

Consider as well my son, Jon, who decided to be an art major in college. He gravitated toward ceramics, sold his work as a potter after graduation, then enrolled in a master of fine arts program. His experiences in graduate school impressed me from an assessment perspective. His work was continually and publicly subjected to criticism from both his professors and other students. It was as if this method of instruction, which could be brutally honest, fostered a perspective that what might seem to be "negative" feedback was what was needed to learn. As with my daughter, mistakes and errors were pointed out. They were an integral part of the assessment process and helped him advance in his craft. Another happy ending. Jon is now a ceramics professor!

These stories illustrate how important assessment is for learning, whether in the gym, the studio, or the classroom. It shows how the right kind of assessment, and the manner in which it is integrated with instruction, can have dramatic effects on how much is learned and how well something is performed.

The Bigger Picture Context of Classroom Assessment

OK, so it's clear that as a teacher you will be responsible for assessing what students in your classroom have learned, essentially gathering evidence of student learning and using that evidence to document and, hopefully, promote student motivation and achievement. But more than that, you instruct, follow a curriculum, and influence students in a multitude of ways. All of these occur in a larger context that has changed considerably in recent years. Essentially, there are a number of powerful influences now that affect everything you do in the classroom, including assessment, and understanding these factors is essential in developing and using effective assessments. That's because of something I'll be talking a lot about in this text—alignment. **Alignment** simply means that things are configured so that they reinforce and support each other. In science, for example, it's important to have alignment between research questions and methods; in gymnastics, it's critical to align music to the floor routine.

Teaching, which includes the use of student assessment, is most effective when these powerful contextual forces are aligned with what the teacher is doing in the classroom. For example, when the curriculum and your instruction are aligned with state standards, it's likely that students will achieve well on state tests. When your teaching and assessment are aligned to what we know about how students learn, achievement and motivation are enhanced. What, then, are these contextual influences? I've laid them out in Figure 1.1 to emphasize their impact on classroom assessment.

21st Century-Knowledge, Skills, and Dispositions

You have probably heard much about what students need to know and be able to do to function effectively in life in the 21st century, and what high school graduates need to do to be ready for college and/or careers. From many levels, including national and state government, business, and educational policy wonks, there is an almost endless series of high-profile calls to action for changes in education to meet the new demands of an information-based, interconnected world. We'll consider these in more detail in the next chapter, but here is a short summary of what is now considered "essential" for students:

- Deep understanding of fundamental concepts of important content areas and disciplines
- Cognitive skills such as problem solving, decision making, critical thinking, and metacognition
- Creativity and innovative thinking
- Effective communication skills
- Effective social skills
- Global understanding and perspectives
- Dispositions such as responsibility, flexibility, self-direction, determination, perseverance, risk taking, and integrity

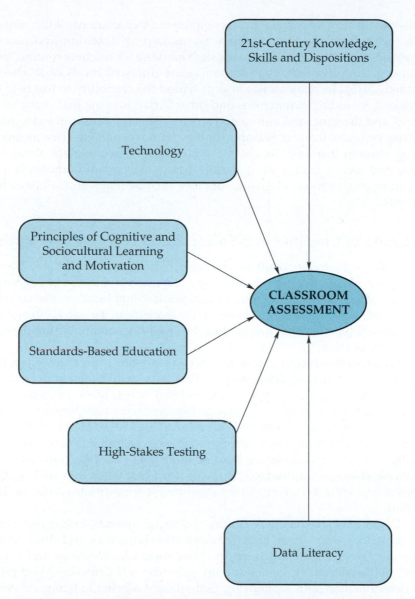

FIGURE 1.1 Significant Factors Influencing Classroom Assessment

Your challenge is to develop and use assessments to foster the development of all of these 21st-century skills, not just to assess the subject you are teaching.

Technology

The prevalence of technology has significant implications for classroom assessment. Not only are we teaching postmillennial digital natives (though careful here—not all students are!) with accompanying expectations, skills, and comfort with technology, we also use new technology in teaching and assessment. Improved technology has now made item banking for teachers routine, including the use of adaptive tests that accommodate different levels of student ability (Bennett, 2015). Technology has also provided the capability to use new types of test items, including simulations and other active formats that demand student actions and thinking, and automated scoring. This is a huge influence and, as we will see, provides many new opportunities for novel and effective means of evaluating student learning. Teachers are now able to access data about students online and record grades electronically. Many teachers now routinely use apps and other programs on electronic devices such as iPads and iPhones to assess students.

Principles of Cognitive and Sociocultural Learning and Motivation

Here is where the rubber really meets the road. If you want to achieve 21st-century knowledge, skills, and dispositions, you must teach and assess in alignment with what we know about how children and adolescents learn and what motivates them. There has been a flood of research, especially in the areas of cognitive and sociocultural theories, that has led to solid, well-documented principles of learning and motivation.

We know that learning must be built on students' prior knowledge, life experiences and background, and interests. That is, new information needs to be connected to existing knowledge in meaningful ways. More than accumulating knowledge, students need to actively construct new and deeper understanding by integrating knowledge, skills, and procedures to solve problems, and by developing metacognition to monitor learning strategies. Learning progressions and scaffolding show how thinking can become more sophisticated. Transfer of learning to new situations is emphasized. Students learn best when they self-regulate their progress and enhance their self-efficacy through appropriate causal explanations to effort.

Cognition is mediated by culture and social contexts, influenced extensively by interactions with others. Effective motivation is intrinsic and students are especially engaging when challenged to revise misunderstandings and solve problems. Self-assessment is needed to provide self-direction, self-reflection, self-determination, and monitoring. Self-efficacy, a belief in being able to be successful, is essential for motivation and engagement in learning.

Good instruction provides an environment that engages the student in active learning, which becomes an ongoing process in which students actively receive, interpret, and relate information to what they already know, understand, and have experienced. Effective assessment, in turn, promotes this process by documenting the attainment of progressive levels of more knowledge and understanding that eventually lead to mastery.

Research on motivation suggests that teachers must constantly assess students and provide feedback that is informative. By providing specific and meaningful feedback to students and encouraging them to regulate their own learning, teachers encourage students to enhance their sense of self-efficacy and self-confidence, important determinants of motivation (Brookhart, 2008). Meaningful learning is intrinsically motivating because the content has relevance. The implication here is that assessment does not end with scoring and recording the results. Motivation is highly dependent on the nature of the feedback from the assessment. Thus, in keeping with the integration of assessment with instruction, feedback is an essential component of the assessment process.

There have also been significant recent changes in curriculum theory that have clear implications for classroom assessment. Due in part to the standards-based movement, curriculum is now based on the premise that all students can learn, that standards for learning need to be high for all students, and that equal opportunity is essential. Curriculum needs to show students how learning is connected to the world outside school.

The research from cognitive learning and curriculum theories has laid the foundation for significant changes in classroom assessment (Penuel & Shepard, 2016). As we discover more about how students learn and what motivates them, we realize that assessment practices, as well as instructional practices, need to change to keep pace with this research. The list of principles is long and I can't do them justice here, but in Table 1.1 many of them are listed with implications for assessment. I've done this to again emphasize the importance of alignment of assessment with the principles.

Over the past 20 years or so, research on teacher decision making, cognitive learning, student motivation, and other topics has changed what we know about the importance of assessment for effective teaching. For example, one finding is that good teachers continually assess their students relative to learning goals and adjust their instruction on the basis of this information. Another important finding is that assessment of students not only documents what students know and can do but also influences learning. Assessment that enhances learning is as important as assessment that documents learning. As a result of this research, new purposes, methods, and approaches to student assessment have been developed. These changes underscore a new understanding of the important role that assessment plays in instruction and learning.

Standards-Based Education

Essentially, we have a "standards-based" educational system in America. *Standards-based*, using commonly accepted objectives for student learning, is now a ubiquitous buzzword in education, if ever there was one. As we'll see in detail in Chapter 2, standards frame what students should know and do—they formalize and standardize what gets taught and assessed. Every state has learning standards, with corresponding pacing guides and curriculum at the district level for implementation. While mostly content-driven, standards have become the benchmarks for evaluating students, schools, and very recently, teachers.

TABLE 1.1   Implications for Assessment from Cognitive Learning Theories

Theory	Implications for Classroom Assessment
Cognitive Theory Knowledge is constructed; learning involves creating personal meaning that connects new information with prior knowledge.	• Use multiple modes of assessment that allow flexibility in how students demonstrate knowledge and understanding. • Assess current state of knowledge to target instruction and subsequent assessments. • Use assessments that require application of knowledge. • Individualize feedback so that it is meaningful for each student.
Differentiation There is variety among students on learning styles, language, memory, aptitudes, attention, and developmental pace.	• Provide choices in how to show mastery/competence. • Provide sufficient time for all students to demonstrate knowledge. • Provide students opportunities to revise and retest. • Use multiple modes of assessment.
Goal Setting Students perform best when they know the goal, see examples or exemplars, and know how their performance compares with established standards of mastery.	• Make standards explicit before beginning instruction. • Give students examples of performance at different levels. • Provide specific feedback that links performance with standards. • Use assessment during instruction. • Use student self-assessments.
Self-Regulation Students need to know when to use knowledge, how to adapt it to new situations, and how to monitor and manage their own learning.	• Use performance assessment with actual "real-life" problems and issues. • Use student self-assessment. • Use assessment during instruction. • Limit objectively scored assessments. • Provide progress monitoring feedback.
Self-Efficacy Motivation and effort are important components of learning and performance that shape perceptions of capability to succeed.	• Use "real-life" tasks and examples. • Use assessment during instruction. • Provide individualized feedback to see the connection between effort and performance. • Provide feedback that encourages internal attributions, especially effort.

High-Stakes Testing

Like it or not, it is abundantly clear that externally mandated high-stakes account-ability tests have a profound impact on teaching and classroom assessment. For most teachers, there is no escaping this reality. What you do in the classroom will be influenced by both the content and the nature of these tests.

Students, teachers, and administrators have always been held accountable, primarily at a local school or district level, and sometimes at the state level. In the last two decades unprecedented federal and state accountability testing policy ini-tiatives have increased the pressure on schools to show positive test results, as well as to evaluate teachers on the basis of their students' test scores. **High-stakes tests** are ones that have important consequences. This is the case for tests that determine whether a student can graduate from high school, when school accredi-tation is tied to test scores, or when teacher evaluation is determined by how their students perform on tests.

In 2002 the No Child Left Behind (NCLB) Act was passed, with federal-level pressure for demonstrating consistently improving student test scores. The heart of NCLB was to ensure that states had "challenging" content standards and exten-sive testing of the standards to hold schools accountable. By the 2005–2006 school year, all states tested reading and mathematics annually in grades 3–11 (once in grades 10–12). Science tests were required in 2008–2009. To hold schools account-able with these tests, each state was required to establish a "starting point" target for the percentages of students that need to be classified as "proficient" in 2002. Then, using a concept called **adequate yearly progress (AYP)**, states established increasingly high percentages of students reaching the proficient level at each grade each year. The Race to the Top initiative, launched in 2009, was focused on national standards and testing in major subject areas. The Every Student Succeeds Act (ESSA) was signed in 2015 to address increasingly unworkable and unrealistic prescriptive requirements from earlier legislation. ESSA places much less empha-sis on a one-size-fits-all federal process, allowing states more flexibility in testing and standard-setting. For teachers, this means some easing of pressure in one sense but introduces new testing demands that can also be onerous. Regardless, there is little doubt that some kind of federal and/or state pressure will ensure that large-scale accountability tests will have high stakes and negative sanctions for low-achieving schools, resulting in some cases with state takeover of schools. It is also clear that administrators and local boards of education, as well as state-level policy makers, want these measures of student performance to be as strong as possible.

Now the stakes attached to accountability tests are set to go even higher. Our profession has entered a new era of teacher evaluation, with student performance on high-stakes and what are called "common" tests (those given every quarter rather than at the end of the year), a primary measure of teacher effectiveness. Can you imagine that your evaluation as a teacher will depend on how well your stu-dents do on high-stakes tests? (This has happened in many cities, including Los Angeles and New York, which have seen publicly available rankings of teachers based on student test scores). Actually, the idea of judging your perfor-mance as a teacher based on student achievement has some merit, but there is much that influences these test scores that you can't control, and much harm that occurs in the form of teaching the test (more about that in Chapter 7). You can probably imagine the dynamics that get set in place when these assessments are used for teacher evaluation. One thing is for sure—the pressure is on, and teachers are reacting.

With these new accountability requirements, large-scale and common test-ing has significantly influenced what teachers do in the classroom, including what they do in the selection, construction, and use of their student assessments. Today, in certain tested subjects such as math and English, there is much more selection of possible test items from online databases than teacher construction of items. There is a great amount of emphasis on "test prep," on "teaching to the test," on aligning classroom tests with large-scale tests, and on using classroom test for-mats that are like the ones used in the state accountability tests. Almost all high-stakes tests use multiple-choice and technology-enhanced questions, and teachers are increasingly asked to use the same item formats in their classroom assessment.

Clearly, classroom assessment must be considered in the current climate that emphasizes high-stakes testing. One purpose of this book is to incorporate these accountability and large-scale testing demands and influences with classroom assessment procedures that we know can enhance student learning. Unfortu-nately, for many, teaching to external standards and high-stakes tests conflicts with classroom assessment methods that have changed to be more consistent with contemporary theories of learning and motivation (though this is now beginning to change). But here is the silver lining: It turns out that classroom assessments that are selected and implemented on the basis of promoting student learning, rather than just showing student performance, will result in higher accountability test results. The key is focusing on *how classroom assessments will maximize student motivation and learning*, rather than on what will result in the highest percentages of students judged at least "proficient."

Data Literacy

There is no question that we have entered the world of big data, whether called data-driven decision making, data dashboards, or more pessimistically though perhaps accurately data-deluged, resulting in data-diving, data delirium, and sometimes being data doped. Big data are everywhere, and there are recent calls for teachers to be "data literate." In various forms the need for data literacy skills for all educators has been strongly promoted, and is now included in standards adopted by professional organization, including the Council for the Accreditation of Educator Preparation (CAEP), the Council of Chief State School Officers (CCSSO), and the National Board of Professional Teaching Standards (NBPTS), as well as increasingly present in state certification requirements for teachers and administrators. A key feature of the call for improving educators' capacities to use data is the emphasis on multiple sources of data, habits of mind (Bocala & Boudett, 2015), data properties, transformation of data, data management, data transformation, and communication (Mandinach, Friedman, & Gummer, 2015). A very important consequence of the emphasis on big data that directly impacts teaching and assessment is a renewed emphasis on understanding and using quantitative analyses related to standardized and other large-scale and common testing. This includes the need to understand with greater depth more technical concepts such as reliability/precision, standard error, pretest-posttest analyses, accurate graphic presentations, validity, and a host of other complex topics that are typically given little space, especially in teacher preparation.

Assessment is typically portrayed as one, relatively small, component of data literacy. Some use the term "assessment literacy" to convey what assessment knowledge and skills are needed by teachers, but the new press on data literacy puts new pressures on teachers' use of assessment. Since data literacy includes the interpretation of all types of data (including, e.g., classroom climate, attendance records, behavioral, family information, extracurricular activities), you will need to integrate these data into what is needed for assessment. At this point this is uncharted territory, but the train has left the station.

If you are still wondering why these six factors in Figure 1.1 are important, here's my take on classroom assessment and what I stress throughout this text. Assessment is an integral part of teaching and learning, not something just done after instruction to document student achievement. It happens all the time during teaching, in informal and anecdotal ways, as well as in the form of tests, papers, and projects. The simple fact is that what and how you assess, on a continual basis, will directly influence your teaching and student learning and motivation in the broadest sense, and that process is influenced by these six factors.

Integrating Instruction and Assessment

The Realities of Teaching

Classroom life is fast paced, hectic, and complex. To illustrate this reality, I summarize here some of what Michelle Barrow does during a typical day in her first-grade classroom. She has 10 boys and 11 girls in her class, four of whom are from racial minority groups and six of whom are from single-parent families. As many as four of her students will participate in the gifted/talented program, and four students were retained from the previous year. See how easy it is for you to get through this list of disparate tasks.

Before school begins in the morning, Michelle:

- Reviews what was learned/taught the previous day
- Goes over student papers to see who did or did not grasp concepts
- Prepares a rough agenda for the day
- Speaks with aide about plans for the day
- Puts journals on student desks

As soon as students enter the classroom, Michelle:

- Greets students at the door
- Reminds students to put away homework
- Speaks with Brent about his expected behavior for the day
- Reminds Anthony about what he is to do if he becomes bothered or frustrated by others

During the morning, Michelle:

- Calls students to the table to go over the reading assignment
- Has Dawn read a column of words and then goes back and randomly points to words to see whether Dawn knows them or simply has them memorized
- Comments to Lucy that she has really improved since the first day of school
- Discusses with Kevin the importance of doing homework every night
- Listens as Tim attempts to sound out each word and gradually blends them together
- Reminds Maggie that she is to be working in her journal rather than visiting and talking with others
- Gives Jason, Kory, and Kristen a vocabulary sheet to do because they have completed their journals
- Observes students in learning centers before calling reading groups to tables
- Verbally reinforces correct answers, gives each student a copy of the week's story, goes through the book, and points out action words
- Calls up the low reading group and focuses on letters m and f
- Notices that Kevin has poor fine-motor skills and makes a mental note to send a message to his parents telling them that he should practice his handwriting
- Checks on Anthony to see how many centers he has completed
- Notices that students in the writing center are not doing as they were instructed
- Walks beside Anthony down the hall, verbally praising him for following directions
- Notices that Sarah has some difficulty answering higher-level thinking questions
- Makes a mental note to split gifted group up into two smaller groups

After lunch, Michelle's day continues as she:

- Starts math lesson on beginning addition with hippo counter
- Walks behind Scott and gives the next problem to the class
- Punches cards of students who have followed directions
- Notices that another table immediately stops talking and starts paying attention
- Tells students to rewrite sloppy copies

- Reminds Kevin and Brent to use guidelines on the paper
- Praises and gives punches on cards to Sarah and a few other students for good handwriting and concentration
- Notices that Tim is watching others, asks him if he needs help
- Gives 5-minute warning for music time, notices students working more intensely
- While students are in music, looks over their writing, arranges the papers into groups

After students leave for the day, Michelle continues by:

- Grading student papers
- Making sure materials are ready for the next day
- Making notes in her gradebook about notes sent home and how the day went
- Checking portfolios to see progress
- Calling some parents

And so it goes for most classrooms. There is a hectic immediacy while multitasking. Many decisions are made continuously about students, instruction, and assessment. What is represented here is just a small sample of Michelle's actions, all of which are based on decisions that in turn depend on how well she has assessed her students. How did she decide to discuss with Kevin the importance of homework? What evidence did she use to decide that she needed to check Dawn's reading? In each of these cases, Michelle had to conduct some kind of assessment of the student before making her decisions. The role of an effective teacher is to reach these decisions reflectively, based on evidence gathered through assessment, reasoning, and experience.

Each decision is based on information that Michelle has gathered through a multitude of student interactions and behavior. Research indicates that a teacher may have as many as 1,000 or even 1,500 interactions with students *each day* (Billups & Rauth, 1987; Jackson, 1990). Often these interactions and decisions occur with incomplete or inaccurate information, making the job of teaching even more difficult.

Consider how the following aspects of Michelle's and other teachers' classrooms affect decision making (Doyle, 1986).

1. *Multidimensionality:* Teachers' choices are rarely simple. Many different tasks and events occur continuously, and students with different preferences and abilities must receive limited resources for different objectives. Waiting for one student to answer a question may negatively influence the motivation of another student. How can the teacher best assess these multiple demands and student responses to make appropriate decisions?
2. *Simultaneity:* Many things happen at once in classrooms. Good teachers monitor several activities at the same time. What does the teacher look for

and listen for so that the monitoring and responses to students are appropriate?

3. *Immediacy:* Because the pace of classrooms is rapid, there is little time for reflection. Decisions are made quickly. What should teachers focus on so that these quick decisions are the right ones that will help students learn?

4. *Unpredictability:* Classroom events often take unanticipated turns, and distractions are frequent. How do teachers evaluate and respond to these unexpected events?

5. *History:* After a few weeks, routines and norms are established for behavior. What expectations for assessment does the teacher communicate to students?

It is in these complex environments that teachers must make some of their most important decisions—about what and how much students have learned. Accurate and appropriate student assessment provides the information to help teachers make better decisions. In the classroom context, then, **classroom assessment** *is gathering, interpreting, and using evidence of student learning to support teacher decision making in a variety of ways*:

- Diagnosing of student strengths, weaknesses, misunderstandings, and learning errors
- Monitoring of student effort and progress toward proficiency
- Documenting student learning
- Improving student learning, motivation, and 21st-century skills and dispositions
- Assigning grades
- Providing feedback to parents
- Improving instruction

Assessment is an umbrella concept that encompasses different techniques, strategies, and uses. It is much more than simply "testing."

Instructional Decision Making and Assessment

It is helpful to conceptualize teacher decision making by *when* decisions are made—before, during, or after instruction—and then examine how assessment affects choices at each time. Preinstructional decisions are needed to set learning goals, select appropriate teaching activities, and prepare learning materials. As instructional activities are implemented, decisions are made about the delivery and pace in presenting information, keeping the students' attention, controlling students' behavior, and making adjustments in lesson plans. At the end of instruction, teachers evaluate student learning, instructional activities, and themselves to know what to teach next, to grade students, and to improve instruction.

Thinking about teaching as phases that occur before, during, and after instruction is aligned with three major types of classroom assessments—*preassessment*, *embedded formative assessment*, and *summative assessment*. **Preassessment** is what you will do before instruction to ascertain students' knowledge, attitudes, and interests. This information is then used as a starting point for designing instruction (Chapman & King, 2009). For example, a government teacher who wants to begin a unit on the 2009 recession might want to know how well students are prepared by examining scores on a previous test that demonstrate their knowledge of supply and demand. If students show weak understanding, these concepts need to be reviewed. **Embedded formative assessment** occurs during teaching. It is a way of assessing students' progress, providing feedback, and making decisions about further instructional activities. (You've probably heard about formative assessment; it's everywhere in the literature, but you may not have heard about *embedded* formative assessment. As we will see in later chapters, there is an important distinction.) **Summative assessment** is conducted after instruction, primarily as a way to document what students know, understand, and can do, but also as providing information that can be used to provide feedback and guide subsequent teaching and learning.

Table 1.2 presents examples of the types of questions teachers ask themselves at these different points in the instructional process. Table 1.2 also offers examples of the type of assessment information needed to make these decisions.

Figure 1.2 illustrates further how assessment is involved in each stage of the instructional process. This figure shows how preassessment is used to provide information to transform general learning goals and objectives into specific learning targets. You will usually be provided with general state, district, or school learning standards for a particular grade level or subject. These standards are used as a starting point to develop more specific learning targets that take into account the characteristics and needs of the students and your style and beliefs.

The next step in instructional decision making is to specify the evidence that is needed to evaluate student learning. This evidence is identified up front, *before* determining instructional plans, because it should influence the nature of instruction. This approach to planning is known as "backward design" (McTighe & Wiggins, 2004; Wiggins, 1998; Wiggins & McTighe, 2005; Wiggins & McTighe, 2011). It is called "backward" because conventional instructional planning typically considers assessment an activity that is done after instruction. But it is very helpful to think like an assessor before planning learning activities. This helps accomplish a true integration of assessment and instruction.

Once acceptable evidence is identified, the teacher selects instructional strategies and activities to meet the targets. This is often operationalized as a lesson plan or instructional plan. It consists of what teachers will do and what they will have their students do for a specific period of time. During instruction, there is interaction between the teacher and students that constantly involves making assessments about how to respond to students appropriately and keep them on

TABLE 1.2 Examples of Questions for Decision Making and Assessment Information

When Decisions Are Made	Questions	Assessment Information
Preassessment		
Before Instruction	How much do my students know?	Previous student achievement; test scores; observations of student performance
	Are my students motivated to learn?	Observations of student involvement and willingness to ask questions
	Are there any exceptional students? If so, what should I plan for them?	Student records; conference with a special education teacher
	What instructional activities should I plan? Are these activities realistic for these students?	Overall strengths and needs of students; comments from previous teachers; evaluations of previous teaching
	What homework assignments should I prepare?	Student progress and level of understanding
	What is acceptable evidence that students have attained desired proficiencies?	Determine which assessment methods will provide needed evidence
Embedded Formative Assessment		
During Instruction	What type of feedback should I give to students?	Quality of student work; type of student
	What question should I ask?	Observation of student understanding
	How should a student response to a question be answered?	Potential for this student to know the answer
	Which students need my individual attention?	Performance on homework; observations of work in class
	What response is best to student inattention or disruption?	Effect of the student on others
	When should I stop this lecture?	Observation of student attention
Summative Assessment		
After Instruction	How well have my students mastered the material?	Achievement test results in relation to a specified level
	Are students ready for the next unit?	Analysis of demonstrated knowledge
	What grades should the students receive?	Tests; quizzes; homework; class participation
	What comments should I make to parents?	Improvement; observations of behavior
	How should I change my instruction?	Diagnosis of demonstrated learning; student evaluations

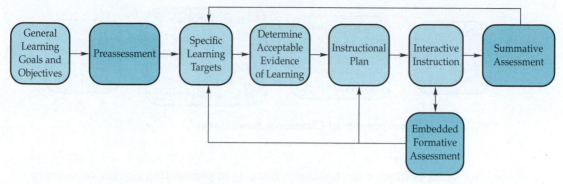

FIGURE 1.2   Relationship Between Instruction and Assessment

task, embedded formative assessment information is used to monitor learning, check for progress, diagnose learning problems, and apply instructional adjustments.

After instruction, more formal summative assessment of learning targets is conducted, which loops back to inform subsequent learning targets, instructional plans, and interactive instruction. Assessment at the end of an instructional unit also provides information for grading students, evaluating teaching, and evaluating curriculum and school programs.

The point is that assessment is not only an *add-on* activity that occurs after instruction is completed. Rather, assessment is integrally related to all aspects of teacher decision making and instruction. Michelle Barrow did assessment *before* instruction by reviewing the performance of students on the previous day's work to see who did and who did not grasp the concepts. She used this information to plan subsequent instruction. *During* instruction Michelle constantly observed student work and responded to provide appropriate feedback and to keep students on task. *After* instruction she graded papers, checked student progress, and made decisions about the focus of instruction for the next day.

With this introduction, we will now consider in more detail what is meant by such terms as *test* and *assessment* and how current conceptualizations enhance older definitions of *measurement* and *evaluation* to improve teaching and learning.

Components of Classroom Assessment

Classroom assessment is a multifaceted process that includes the collection, interpretation, and use of information to help teachers make decisions that both document and improve student learning. Conceptualized in this way, assessment is more than *testing* or *measurement*, which are familiar terms that have been used extensively in discussing how students are evaluated.

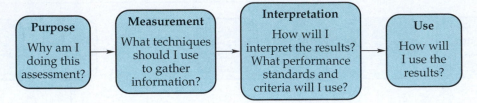

FIGURE 1.3   Components of Classroom Assessment

There are four essential components to implementing classroom assessment: purpose, measurement, interpretation, and use. These components are illustrated in Figure 1.3, with questions to ask yourself at each step. The figure shows the sequence of the components, beginning with identification of purpose.

Purpose

Whether done before, during, or after instruction, the first step in any assessment is to clarify the specific purpose or purposes of gathering the information. A clear vision is needed of what the assessment will accomplish. Why are you doing the assessment? What will be gained by it? What teacher decision making is enhanced by the information gathered through the assessment process?

There are many reasons for doing classroom assessments, some of which are traditional (such as the first four listed next [Popham, 2014]), and others that have become important with changes in learning and motivation theory, curriculum alignment, and the current context of high-stakes testing:

- To diagnose students' strengths and weaknesses
- To monitor student progress toward achieving objectives
- To assign grades
- To determine instructional effectiveness
- To provide students feedback
- To prepare students for high-stakes tests
- To motivate students

Knowing the reason for the assessment is crucial because this will determine what the assessment should look like, how it is administered and scored, and how the results will be used.

Measurement

The term *measurement* has traditionally been defined as a systematic process of assigning numbers to behavior or performance. It is used to determine how much of a trait, attribute, or characteristic an individual possesses. Thus, **measurement** is the process by which traits, characteristics, or behavior are *differentiated*. The process of differentiation can be very formal and quantitative, such as using a thermometer to measure temperature, or can consist of less formal processes, such as observation ("It's very hot today!"). Typically, measurement is used to assign numbers to describe attributes or characteristics of a person, object, or event. A variety of techniques can be used to measure a defined trait or learning target, such as tests, ratings, observations, and interviews. Among these many methods, the one that stands out is classroom assessment; it's the most powerful type of measurement that influences learning and motivation.

Interpretation

Once measurement is used to gather information, you will need to place some Tleve of value on different numbers and observations. This process is identified in Figure 1.3 as *interpretation*, the making of judgments about quality that determine how good the behavior or performance is. Interpretation involves an evaluation of what has been gathered through measurement, in which value judgments are made about performance. For example, measurement often results in a percentage of items answered correctly. Evaluation is a judgment about what each percentage-correct score means. That is, is 75% correct good, average, or poor? Does 75% indicate "proficiency"?

Teachers' professional judgments play a large role in interpretation. What is a "good" student paper to one teacher may be only an "adequate" paper to another teacher. Assessment is more than *correctness*; it is also about evaluation.

Use

The final stage of implementing assessment is how the evaluations are used. The use of test scores and other information is closely tied to the decisions teachers must make to provide effective instruction, to the purposes of assessment, and to the needs of students and parents. As indicated in Figure 1.2, these decisions depend on *when* they are made; they can also be categorized into three major classroom uses: diagnosis, grading, and instruction.

Diagnosis.   Diagnostic decisions are made about individual students as well as about group strengths, weaknesses, and needs. Typically, information is gathered that will allow the teacher to diagnose the specific area that needs further attention or where progress is being made. The diagnosis includes an assessment of *why* a student may be having difficulty so that appropriate instructional activities can be prescribed. For example, teachers use homework diagnostically to determine the extent of student understanding and to identify students who do not understand the assignment. A pretest may be used to diagnose specific gaps in student knowledge that need to be targeted. Students are closely monitored to check motivation, understanding, and progress.

Grading.   Grading decisions are based on measurement-driven information. Although most teachers must adhere to grading scales and definitions, there is a great amount of variability in what teachers use to determine grades, how they use the process of grading to motivate students, and the standards they use to judge the quality of student work. Some teachers, for example, use grading to control behavior and motivate (e.g., "This assignment will be graded"), and often teachers use completed work as a basis for giving privileges and otherwise rewarding students (e.g., "good" papers are posted). Grades and associated oral and written comments also provide *feedback* to students and parents.

Instruction.   Teachers constantly make instructional decisions, and good teachers are aware that they must continuously assess how students are doing to adjust their instruction appropriately. One type of decision, termed a *process* instructional decision, is made almost instantaneously, such as deciding to end a lecture or ask a different type of question. *Planning* instructional decisions are made with more reflection; they might include changing student seating arrangement or grouping patterns, spending an extra day on a particular topic, or preparing additional worksheets for homework. It is hoped that teachers will use credible measurement information with clear standards to evaluate student behavior accurately.

Finally, assessment processes can be used *as* instruction. For example, performance and authentic assessments are long term and provide opportunities for student learning. As we will see in later chapters, such assessments are useful as teaching tools as well as methods to document student learning. As such, they educate and improve student performance, not merely audit it (Wiggins, 1998).

Recent Trends in Classroom Assessment

In the past decade, some clear trends have emerged in classroom assessment for better alignment with the need to focus on 21st-century knowledge, skills, and dispositions, and year-end accountability testing. More established traditions of assessment that relies on "objective" testing at the *end* of instruction, promoted heavily as preparation for similarly formatted high-stakes tests, are being supplemented with other assessments that are better for measuring important outcomes. These have been called "alternative" assessments. **Alternative assessments** include authentic assessment, performance assessment, portfolios, exhibitions, demonstrations, journals, technology-enhanced items, simulations, and other forms of assessment that require the active construction of meaning rather than the passive regurgitation of isolated facts. These assessments engage students in learning and require thinking skills, and thus they are consistent with cognitive theories of learning and motivation as well as societal needs to prepare students for an increasingly complex workplace. In addition, teachers are starting to use more extended-type and interpretive-type objective items. Finally, as I have already emphasized, formative assessment is quite the rage.

Another trend is the recognition that knowledge and skills should not be assessed in isolation. Rather, it is necessary to assess the application and the use of knowledge and skills together. More emphasis is now placed on assessing thinking skills and collaborative skills that are needed to work cooperatively with others. Newer forms of assessment provide opportunities for many "correct" answers, rather than a single right answer, and rely on multiple sources of information.

At the same time that assessment is embracing new kinds of assessment that are based on solid theories of learning and motivation, and as previously mentioned, what and how teachers assess in the classroom is now influenced significantly by year-end, high-stakes accountability testing. We'll discuss this much more, but suffice it to say now that there is a trend toward for classroom tests and other assessments to mimic accountability tests.

An intriguing and very recent trend is to involve students in all aspects of assessment, from designing tasks and questions to evaluating their own and others' work. Engaging students in developing assessment exercises, creating scoring criteria, applying criteria to student products, and self-assessment all help students understand how their own performance is evaluated. This understanding, in turn, facilitates student motivation and achievement. Students learn to confidently evaluate their performance as well as the performance of other students. For example, if students are taught to internalize the key elements of what should be included in comprehending a short story, they are better able to monitor their progress toward achieving learning targets. Likewise, when students generate lists of the ways good essay answers differ from weak ones, they learn the criteria that determine high student performance. Thus, there is a change of emphasis from the teacher providing all assessment tasks and feedback to promoting student engagement in the assessment process. This is best accomplished when there is "a continuous flow of information about student achievement . . . to advance, not merely check on, student learning" (Stiggins, 2002, p. 761). That is, assessment *for* learning becomes as important as assessment *of* learning.

The distinction between assessment *of* learning and assessment *for* learning is critical for understanding the influences of recent theories of learning and motivation on the one hand (*for* learning), and external accountability testing on the other (*of* learning). These differences are summarized in Table 1.3. Note, too, that assessment *as* learning is also important.

In the first of many Teacher's Corner inserts, Susan Pereira makes a strong case for the integration of assessment with instruction. Note how she uses assessment to know "where" students are in their learning so that she can decide what subsequent instruction will be most effective.

These and other recent trends in classroom assessment are summarized in Figure 1.4. In presenting these trends, I do not want to suggest that what teachers have been doing for years is inappropriate or should necessarily be changed. Much of what we have learned about evaluating students from previous decades

TABLE 1.3 Characteristics of Assessment *of* Learning, *for* Learning, and *as* Learning

Assessment *of* Learning	Assessment *for* Learning	Assessment *as* Learning
• Summative	• Formative	• Nature of assessment engages students in learning
• Certify learning	• Describes needs for subsequent learning	• Fosters student self-monitoring of learning
• Conducted at the end of a unit; sporadic	• Conducted during a unit of instruction; ongoing	• Conducted during a unit of instruction
• Often uses normative scoring guidelines; ranks students	• Tasks allow teachers to modify instruction	• Emphasizes student knowledge of criteria used to evaluate learning
• Questions drawn from material studied	• Suggests corrective instruction	• Student selects corrective instruction
• General	• Specific	• Specific
• Used to report to parents	• Used to give feedback to students	• Fosters student self-monitoring
• Can decrease student motivation	• Enhances student motivation	• Enhances student motivation
• Highly efficient, superficial testing	• In-depth testing	• Testing teaches students
• Focus on reliability	• Focus on validity	• Focus on validity
• Delayed feedback	• Immediate feedback	• Immediate feedback
• Summary judgments	• Diagnostic	• Diagnostic

Source: Adapted from Earl, L. M. (2003). *Assessment as Learning: Using Classroom Assessment to Maximize Student Learning.* Thousand Oaks, CA: Corwin Press; and LeMahieu, P. G., & Reilly, E. C. (2004). Systems of coherence and resonance: Assessment for education and assessment of education. In M. Wilson (Ed.), *Toward Coherence between Classroom Assessment and Accountability. 104th Yearbook of the National Society for the Study of Education.* Chicago: National Society for the Study of Education.

is very important and useful. For example, properly constructed multiple-choice tests are excellent for efficiently and objectively assessing knowledge of a large content domain. What is needed is a *balanced* approach to assessment, in which appropriate techniques are administered and used in a credible way for decision making. Just because the assessment focuses on complex thinking skills or uses portfolios does not mean it is better or more credible. Assessment technique need be matched to purpose and must be conducted according to established quality standards, and must be relevant to your teaching style and context. Some of the recent trends, such as making standards and criteria public, are helpful procedures regardless of the assessment employed, and they will improve traditional as well as newer types of measurement by engaging students in the entire assessment process.

FIGURE 1.4   Recent Trends in Classroom Assessment

From	To
General praise	Specific feedback
Assessing outcomes	Assessing process and metacognition
Isolated skills	Integrated skills
Isolated facts	Application of knowledge
Artificial tasks	Authentic tasks
Decontextualized tasks	Contextualized tasks
A single correct answer	Many correct answers
Secret standards	Public standards
Secret criteria	Public criteria
Individuals	Groups and peer assessments
After instruction	During instruction
Little feedback	Considerable feedback
"Objective" tests	Performance-based tests
Standardized tests	Informal tests
External evaluation	Student self-evaluation
Single assessments	Multiple assessments
Sporadic	Continual
Conclusive	Recursive
Assessment *of* learning	Assessment *for* and *as* learning
Summative	Formative
Emphasis on ability	Emphasis on effort
Learning successes	Learning errors
Recall of facts	Thinking skills

Teachers' Classroom Assessment and Grading Practices Decision Making

Every teacher makes many decisions about the types of assessments that will be used, when these assessments are used, and grading. These decisions result in highly individualized and idiosyncratic practices. Despite policies and electronic grading programs that attempt to standardize assessment practices, each teacher does his or her own thing. This suggests that you, too, will develop your own assessment and grading practices.

To better understand the decision-making process teachers use, I partici-pated in a study in which in-depth, individual interviews were conducted with

Teacher's Corner

Susan Pereira

National Board Certified Elementary Teacher

In my classroom, instruction and assessment are always integrated. In fact, it's difficult for me to even think about them as separate entities. Assessment happens prior to any teaching, during teaching, and after teaching. Before the learning, sometimes this is done formally through standardized testing. Other times, it occurs informally in discussions with my students. Through both informal and formal assessments, I gather a "picture" of their previous learning and where they currently are in the learning process. After this initial data is gathered, I can analyze the group as a whole and organize the students into learning groups according to where they are in their learning. I can also use the data I have gathered to sit down and plan appropriate, engaging lessons for each small group of students. During the actual teaching, more assessment occurs. This assessment can look different—it may be a pencil-and-paper task, or it may be information gathered through questioning my students, watching their body language, noticing how often they volunteer to answer questions, and how they communicate their learning to me and to others. Quality assessment during the teaching guides me in how long I need to spend on a topic, when I need to reteach, and when students need enrichment activities. My ongoing assessments drive the lesson, not me as the teacher.

28 teachers to investigate the reasons teachers gave for the assessment decisions they made (McMillan, 2003; McMillan & Workman, 1999). The results have interesting implications because of the strong connection between this decision-making process and instruction.

We found that two major sources of influence affect assessment and grading practices decision making. One source lies within the teacher and consists of beliefs and values about teaching, and learning more generally, that provide a basis for explaining how and why specific assessment and grading practices are used. A second source lies external to the teacher, consisting of pressures that need to be considered, such as high-stakes testing. We found that these two sources of influence are in constant tension. Although internal beliefs and values that reflect a desire to enhance student learning are most influential, external pressures cause teachers to engage in certain practices that may not be in the best interests of student learning.

These influences are depicted in Figure 1.5 to show the nature of the internal and external factors and how these factors are in tension. Internal beliefs and values include a philosophy of teaching and learning, and assessment practices are consistent with that philosophy (Bonner, 2016). For example, if teachers believe that all students can succeed and that individual differences among students should be accommodated, then the teacher uses multiple types of assessment to allow sufficient opportunities to show success. If teachers believe it is important to

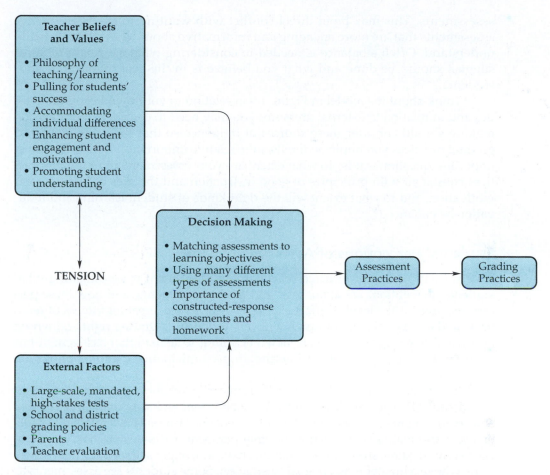

Teacher Beliefs and Values

- Philosophy of teaching/learning
- Pulling for students' success
- Accommodating individual differences
- Enhancing student engagement and motivation
- Promoting student understanding

TENSION

Decision Making

- Matching assessments to learning objectives
- Using many different types of assessments
- Importance of constructed-response assessments and homework

Assessment Practices

Grading Practices

External Factors

- Large-scale, mandated, high-stakes tests
- School and district grading policies
- Parents
- Teacher evaluation

FIGURE 1.5   A Model of Assessment and Grading Practices Decision Making

get students involved, engaged, and motivated, they may use performance assessments and give points for student participation and effort. To better understand how much students know and can do, most teachers rely on assessments in which students show their work.

External pressures include school or school district assessment and grading policies that must be followed; parental demands; large-scale, high-stakes testing; and 21st-century skills and dispositions. Teachers want to collect assessment information that will show parents why specific grades were given. Externally mandated accountability testing of students can be very influential, as well as in direct contradiction to teachers' internal beliefs and values. For example, if statewide testing consists of multiple-choice items covering a great amount of material, and student performance will have important consequences, teachers feel pressure to use the same kinds of tests for classroom assessments. This may be in direct conflict with wanting to use performance assessments that are more engaging and informative about what students really understand. Often a balance is needed in considering what external pressures suggest should be done and what you believe is in the best interests of your students.

Think about the model in Figure 1.5 in relation to your own beliefs and values and in relation to external pressures you may need to consider. Your decision making should consider these sources of influence so that the assessment and grading practices you implement reflect the relative importance of each. The most important question is this: To what extent are your assessment and grading practices consistent with principles of good instruction and theories of learning and motivation, and to what extent will the right kinds of student learning and motivation be enhanced?

Students' Perceptions of Assessment

A new, exciting area of research on classroom assessment is investigating what students' perceptions are about tests and other assignments, and how these perceptions impact the level of effort exerted, performance, meaningfulness of feedback, and emotional reactions to doing well or poorly, to getting right and wrong answers. Long neglected, we are now beginning to realize that assessment has meaning to students, and their interpretations, anticipations, and emotions are important.

In a recent review of literature of students' perceptions toward assessment (McMillan, 2016), it was clear that there are both *trait* and *state* characteristics that students bring to each assessment event. A *trait* characteristic is a relatively stable emotion, motivational disposition, or other personality dimension that lies within each student. Some students, for example, have a stronger self-efficacy than others or may have a greater mastery goal orientation. Some students see assessments as challenges, others are fearful. *States* are established more on the basis of what an assessment event looks like. These vary from situation to situation, as well as with different subjects. That is, some assessments are long, some are short; some contain mostly multiple-choice questions, others are mostly essay; some assessments are easy, some are hard. Students know pretty quickly whether assessments are for accountability or for helping them learn.

These traits and states affect motivation, effort, anxiety, and expectations. Obviously, for example, most students are more worried if they view the assessment as extremely difficult or something that they have had problems with in the past. They are more confident and focused when they bring a strong sense of capability, when they have exerted appropriate effort to succeed, and when they have done well in the past on similar tests.

Following an assessment event students display a wide range of emotions and thinking, and these reactions feed into subsequent actions and the development of motivational dispositions. After a generally positive outcome there may be a sense of pride, relief, and happiness, or when wrong, there may be a sense of hopelessness, confusion, or puzzlement. Attributions to success or failure are made typically either to effort, ability, or some outside factor, such as poor health or unfair test items. When students attribute success to effort and failure to lack of effort (internal attributions), the outcome is generally positive; when attributions are more external, the consequence is a lack of responsibility, often with negative implications for motivation.

A particular interest of mine is how students think about and deal with being wrong (McMillan, forthcoming). While it is no secret that students are often told that being wrong is helpful for learning, the reality in most schools is that being right trumps being wrong every time. The rewards are for getting high scores, "mastery," and correctness, not for making mistakes or learning errors. This has led to a culture where the norm is that being wrong is somehow undesirable, bad, or negative, and should be avoided. Rather than seeing "wrongness" as a vehicle for learning, students learn to fear it. What is unfortunate is that there is a significant amount of research from several fields confirming that being wrong leads to more effective learning, as well as to the positive development of self-regulatory skills, persistence, and resilience. Dweck (2008) suggests that the development of persistence depends on being wrong and attributing the lack of complete success to one's effort, having what she terms a *growth mindset*. Dweck has demonstrated that children praised for their ability to do well made them less likely to persist when facing difficulties or challenges, while children praised for effort showed greater persistence, even though mistakes were being made.

In some interviews I did with elementary and middle school students (McMillan & Turner, 2014), there was a clear difference between making "careless mistakes" and "not understanding." When talking about careless mistakes students generally attributed their careless mistakes to what they thought of as "accidents," like forgetting to check over their work or circling the wrong answer when they knew the correct one. They took responsibility for their actions, but they clearly did not dwell on them (e.g., "like I misread the question, like it said NOT and I didn't see, and I put the wrong answer," "sometimes it just slips out of your mind"). The consequences of making careless errors entailed actions such as double-checking their work before submitting it or managing their time better during the assessment. Their cognition, in other words, was about reminding themselves to be more careful. Emotionally, students voiced that they experienced brief negative affect, such as disappointment or frustration (e.g., "ugh," "darn," "rats"), though this quickly subsided because they understood that, as one student said, "everyone makes mistakes."

Some further comments related to careless mistakes include the following:

- "I don't feel bad. I feel disappointed in myself but I mean, usually if it's like a silly mistake, I mean, yeah, I don't feel bad."
- "Sometimes I get a little aggravated with myself, especially if I already had the right question, I mean, the right answer, and then I'm like I don't know and change it, I get kind of mad."

- "I get a little bit frustrated because I'm like, I knew the answer to that, but I got it wrong."
- "I get a little bit frustrated because I'm like, knew the answer to that, but I got it wrong. And then I like realize I didn't put a period at the end, didn't capitalize the beginning of my sentence or something, so I'm like, oh, wow, can't believe I did that."

When students were asked how they felt when they realized they did not know the content or were unable to perform the skill, the affective response was negative though muted, more serious than when making careless errors. They may have been "disappointed," "not happy," or "frustrated," "upset," or "kind of mad," but more severe emotions such as shame, despondency, and hopelessness were rarely mentioned. Rather, perceptions were not overly negative (e.g., "It's okay, just try harder next time," "I would be a little disappointed"). As would be expected, the level of negative emotion was tied to the resultant grade, for example, "When I answer them wrong, it all depends on how many I get wrong. If I get one wrong, I'm just going to be like a little disappointed because I got a good grade, but if I got a lot wrong, then I'm going to be really disappointed because I got a really bad grade." Notably, with the students we interviewed, there were healthy perspectives about being wrong:

- "If I have a bad grade, I feel like I didn't try hard enough or I didn't study hard enough."
- "It just means I didn't study long or hard enough."
- "I feel like when you pay attention in class, that's when you really know what you're doing."
- "It shows me that I didn't study enough."
- "I should have listened better, or you know I should have not talked."
- "It means you have to try harder."
- "Once I get it back and I know I've studied and I see that I got it wrong . . . I know that I need to study that more."
- "Any lower than that, I'm just like what did I do wrong?"
- "I just know that I need to study that more."
- "Well, if I don't get that god of a grade, that means that I didn't do the best I could in studying and I didn't really study that hard."

These student reactions, generally positive, show the importance of the reactions. To the contrary, one student voiced when he didn't do well, "[it means] that I'm a loser and that I didn't know." It is easy to see the implications. The question for you as a teacher is how to structure your assessment environment and process to enable and encourage positive outcomes, not negative ones. From the research on student perceptions, as summarized in Table 1.4, there are several implications for positive practice. One thing is for sure, students take assessment very seriously, trust the results, and hope to do well. My hope is that you are as serious about assessment as they are.

TABLE 1.4   Implications from Research on Students' Perceptions of Assessment

Implications for Practice	Explanation
Consider students' varied perceptions toward assessment.	When teachers know the full range of their students' perceptions of assessment, essentially emphasizing with students, they will be better able align instruction, assessment, and feedback. Attention needs to be paid to reactions at each phase of assessment (before, during, and after), following up with students as needed to facilitate positive reactions and consequences.
Take time to understand students' trait characteristics.	Knowing students' general dispositions enables teachers to directly address misconceptions about ability, dysfunctional levels of anxiety, and unrealistic expectations.
Stress assessment relevance and value.	Students can tell the difference between assessments that are relevant from those that aren't, those that have value and those that are meaningless, and they react much more positively when they belief the assessment is to help them learn. Being wrong needs to be addressed so that students see it as a way to enhance learning.
Use a variety of moderately challenging, untimed, relatively short assessments.	Moderately challenging assessments tend to produce good motivation and effort. Assessments that are either too easy or too hard result in lack of effort, hopelessness, or anxiety. Long, timed assessments lead to anxiety, fear, and other negative emotions.
Involve students in assessment.	When students believe they are partners in assessment, they are much more positive and serious about being engaged. As students identify targets, evaluate their performance, and determine next steps, self-regulation is enhanced.
Focus attention on effort and test preparation.	The right level of preparation effort is essential for making appropriate attributions.

Classroom Assessment Knowledge and Skills for Teachers

One of the perplexing, long-standing trends about classroom assessment is that most teachers receive very little training in it (Campbell, 2012). There have been several attempts to come up with standards for what teachers should know about assessment but, by and large, these haven't been adopted as professional standards in either teacher training programs or professional development programs. The standards that have been developed are good, in my opinion, in helping you understand the breadth of assessment and how it integrates with teaching. They represent serious efforts by major educational organizations to come up with specific areas of assessment knowledge and skills that teachers should possess to perform assessment roles and responsibilities (some of which concern large-scale testing). The standards also include responsibilities of the teacher for involvement in school and district decision making and involvement in the wider professional roles of teachers. The four major documents that summarize these competencies include the following:

- *Standards for Teacher Competency in Educational Assessment of Students* (1990). American Federation of Teachers, National Council on Measurement in Education, National Education Association.
- *Code of Professional Responsibilities in Educational Measurement* (1995). National Council on Measurement in Education.
- *Principles and Indicators for Student Assessment Systems* (1995). National Forum on Assessment.
- *Student Evaluation Standards* (2003). Joint Committee on Standards for Educational Evaluation. (These standards are set to be updated as this text is being published.)

Many of the standards from these four sources were prepared more from a psychometric than from a teaching perspective, with reliance on technical principles that have relatively little relevance to the classroom. Brookhart (2011) has updated the 1990 *Standards for Teacher Competency in Educational Assessment of Students* to reflect more contemporary issues concerned with formative assessment, high-stakes testing, and standards-based education. As such, they represent what I think is a very nice set of competencies that provide a foundation for what you should know and be able to do to develop and use assessments effectively. See if you can justify why each of these is important!

   I. Teachers should understand learning in the content area they teach.
  II. Teachers should be able to articulate clear learning intentions that are congruent with both the content and depth of thinking implied by standards and curriculum goals, in such a way that they are attainable and assessable.
 III. Teachers should have a repertoire of strategies for communicating to students what achievement of a learning intention looks like.
  IV. Teachers should understand the purposes and uses of the range of available assessment options and be skilled in using them.
   V. Teachers should have the skills to analyze classroom questions, test items, and performance assessment tasks to ascertain the specific knowledge and thinking skills required for students to do them.
  VI. Teachers should have the skills to provide effective, useful feedback on student work.
 VII. Teachers should be able to construct scoring schemes that quantify student performance on classroom assessments into useful information for decisions about students, classrooms, schools, and districts. These decisions should lead to improved student learning, growth, or development.
VIII. Teachers should be able to administer external assessments and interpret their results for decisions about students, classrooms, schools, and districts.

IX. Teachers should be able to articulate their interpretations of assessment results and their reasoning about the educational decisions based on assessment results to the educational populations they serve (student and his/her family, class, school community).

X. Teachers should be able to help students use assessment information to make sound educational decisions.

XI. Teachers should understand and carry out their legal and ethical responsibilities in assessment as they conduct their work. (p. 7)

Summary

This chapter introduced assessment as an integral part of teacher decision making and instruction. As a systematic method of collecting, interpreting, and using information, good assessment improves student learning. Major points in the chapter are the following:

- Classroom assessment consists of gathering, interpreting, and using information.
- Six important factors influencing classroom assessment include 21st-century knowledge, skills, and dispositions; technology; cognitive and sociocultural learning and motivation theory; standards-based education; high-stakes testing; and data literacy.
- Assessment includes four major components: purpose, measurement, interpretation, and use.
- Measurement consists of quantitatively differentiating behavior and performance.
- Interpretation involves professional judgment of the value or worth of the measured performance.
- Recent research on learning, motivation, and instruction suggests the need to use more alternative forms of assessment, such as performance assessments, simulations, portfolios, and interpretive items.
- Student involvement in assessment promotes student engagement and achievement.
- The current trend is for more emphasis on formative assessment and assessment *for* learning rather than *of* learning.
- State and federal accountability requires high-stakes objective testing, which influences classroom assessments.
- Teacher assessment and grading decision making is influenced by internal beliefs and values and external factors.
- Students' perceptions of assessment are important determinants of subsequent learning, performance, and motivation.
- Professional standards have been developed to provide a framework for what teachers need to know about classroom assessment.

Introductory Case Study Answer

Abby should give the computerized assessment because balance is needed between external pressures of high-stakes tests and teachers' notions of what they believe are in the best interest of their students. If Abby gives the computerized summative assessment, she can incorporate her assessment beliefs and values throughout her teaching unit. In doing so, Abby will have a balance in types of assessments that will give her a variety of data that she can use to:

- diagnose student strengths, weakness, misunderstandings, and learning errors;
- monitor student effort and progress toward proficiency;
- document student learning;
- improve student learning, motivation, 21st-century skills, and dispositions; and
- provide feedback to students and parents.

Abby can use her beliefs and values regarding assessment to guide her creation of multiple formative assessments. The assessments could be integrated with her instruction, and by giving them on a continual basis, the assessments would directly influence her instructional plan, as well as her students' learning and motivation.

Suggestions for Action Research

At the end of each chapter are suggestions for action research. The intent of these suggestions is to help you apply what you are learning from the text to practical situations. By conducting this type of informal research, the principles and ideas presented will have greater relevance and meaning to you.

1. Investigate the time that is taken for assessment in the classroom by observing some classes. Compare your results to how much time the teacher believes is devoted to assessment. Also note in your observations the nature of teacher decision making. What kinds of decisions are made? How, specifically, does information from assessment contribute to this decision making?

2. Conduct an interview with two or three teachers and ask them some questions about assessment. For example, you could take Figure 1.4 and ask the teachers if they believe the so-called recent trends are actually evident. You could ask about the relationship between assessment and teaching/learning to see the extent to which assessment and teaching are integrated. Use Figure 1.5 to ask about "internal" and "external" factors that affect their assessment, grading practices, and decision making.

3. Interview a school administrator about what teachers need to know about assessment. Ask about the assessment standards to get a perspective on the reasonableness of the standards.

4. Talk with some students about assessment. Ask them what they think about different types of assessment, how motivated they are to perform well, and their reactions to doing well or doing poorly. See if they have any suggestions for how teachers should do assessment to be more helpful for their learning.

MyEdLab Self-Check 1.1

MyEdLab Self-Check 1.2

MyEdLab Self-Check 1.3

MyEdLab Application Exercise 1.1   Integrating Instruction and Assessment

MyEdLab Application Exercise 1.2   Assessment *of* and *for* Learning

Standards and Cognitive Learning Targets

Standards
- State and Common Core
- Content
- Performance
- Developmental
- Grade-level
- Deconstructing standards

Sources of Learning Targets and Standards
- Bloom's taxonomy
- Bloom's revised taxonomy
- New taxonomy
- National standards
- State standards
- District standards

Outcomes
- Goals
- Objectives
- Standards
- Expectations
- Criteria
- Learning targets

STANDARDS AND COGNITIVE LEARNING TARGETS

Learning Targets
- Knowledge and simple understanding
  — declarative
  — procedural
  — comprehension
  — application
- Reasoning and deep understanding
  — analyze
  — evaluate
  — create
- Criteria

Criteria for Selecting Learning Targets and Standards
- Right number
- Comprehensive
- Reflects school goals
- Challenging yet feasible
- Consistent with learning

21st-Century Knowledge, Skills, and Dispositions
- Cognitive skills
- Core subject area knowledge
- Global understanding
- Communicating
- Collaborative skills
- Technology skills
- Dispositions

CHAPTER 2 Concept Map

Learning Outcomes

After reading this chapter, you should be able to:

2.1 Understand the differences between goals, objectives, standards, and learning targets, and be able to identify when it is appropriate to use each type of outcome.

2.2 Distinguish between various types of standards and know how different sources of standards can be helpful in stating outcomes that are appropriate for your teaching.

2.3 Be able to write learning targets that include appropriate types of cognitive skills and some indication of criteria for evaluating student performance.

2.4 Demonstrate a clear understanding of differences between knowledge, deep understanding, and reasoning.

Introductory Case Study

What Are Eli's Misconceptions?

Eli was so excited. This morning his mentor, Zoe, was coming to observe his English 10 class in the library. Eli had been collaborating with the librarian and he was proud that he had designed a unit where students were learning about three English 10 standards (using electronic resources for research, writing persuasive pieces, publishing digitally) and showing their mastery through an authentic assessment. Eli knew students were enjoying the learning process and he was proud of their progress towards completing their products. Today, the students would get a quick mini-lesson on how to add voice to their persuasive writing and then be allowed to work independently.

When Zoe entered the library, she quickly noticed the students were fully engaged. Students were on-task talking with their peers and the librarian was helping two students using a search-engine. Eli was conversing with a student about revising her editorial piece for publishing on a local newspaper's website. Zoe walked around asking students about their projects and each student was excited to tell her about their topic and publishing ideas. Clearly, students were having fun while learning. She asked two students how they would know if they met the project's requirements. The students replied that Mr. Johnson had given general guidelines, but not specific grading criteria because he wanted students to be creative in their projects.

Later that day, Zoe and Eli met. Zoe asked Eli to tell her about his specific learning targets and how they related to assessing students' learning through the project. Eli animatedly talked about his learning targets: He wanted his students to develop their 21st-century communication, collaboration, English content, and technology skills. In regards to assessing students, he wanted to develop students' dispositions for self-direction and foster innovation, so he had decided to remove the boundaries of clear guidelines regarding the final product. He provided students with a sheet of general guidelines that explained the project. Eli told Zoe that he had a rubric he would use for grading their products, but he didn't give it to students because he felt it would lead students to direct their efforts towards what he wanted and not in the direction of their ideas.

As you read this chapter, reflect on Eli's misconceptions regarding learning targets and their link to assessment. What are Eli's misconceptions about learning targets? What advice can Zoe, as Eli's mentor, give him in regard to developing future learning targets? What are Eli's errors in his assessment practices?

Good classroom assessment begins with appropriate standards and learning targets, the right outcomes. How else will you know what to teach, what to assess, and how to judge student performance? In recent years there has been much controversy about what the standards and learning targets should be and who should set them, evidenced most visibly by standards-based school reform. In this chapter you will learn about the nature of standards and cognitive learning targets, as well as a framework that will help you to determine them for your students so that they are aligned well with instruction and assessment. Affective, product, skill, disposition, and motivational targets will be covered in later chapters.

Knowing Where Your Students Are Going

No, this isn't about going to the movies, park, river, or beach. Here we are concerned about how sound assessment begins with a clear description of intended student competencies that result from student learning, a clear statement of student outcomes. Although there is much history and established practice in the labels that are used to identify these outcomes (e.g., goals, objectives, standards, or "what students should know and be able to do," benchmarks, proficiencies, competencies), the exact terminology used in a given setting may indicate something somewhat different, and could very well vary from one locality to another. It is important to review these differences because we need to be precise in our descriptions. I favor the term "learning target" because it conveys a specific outcome that can be used with relatively short instructional units. In the end, though, the label is not as critical as making sure the outcomes are clear, appropriate, and drive effective instruction and assessment.

Revisiting the Big Picture

While I know you will be teaching a specific subject or perhaps several subjects, I emphasized in Chapter 1 that it's very important to have the "bigger picture" in mind. What we want our students to learn goes way beyond subject-area knowledge and skills, and your instruction and assessment need to be aligned with these larger purposes of schooling.

The relatively new catchphrase, "21st-century knowledge, skills, and dispositions," has literally "caught" on everywhere (Pellegrino & Hilton, 2012). Policy makers have realized that to be successful in college and the workplace students need to be prepared with many different skills and attitudes, not simply subject-area knowledge. This emphasis has become a driving force in education, and it is now explicitly addressed in state and school division goals for student learning. Of course, much of this has always been the focus of schooling to some extent. For example, most teachers have always wanted to instill responsibility in their students, but the repackaging of many outcomes has led to an increased emphasis on many traits given less attention in the past two decades.

I have created Figure 2.1 to show you the breadth of 21st-century knowledge, skills, and dispositions. As you can see, there is much to be done and many expectations! How do you address all these areas when teaching math, science, or English? It becomes a matter of how you instruct and assess your students, get students involved, and set the right climate for learning. And you will find that

FIGURE 2.1   21st-Century Knowledge, Skills, and Dispositions

Teacher's Corner

Daniel Leija

Texas State Teacher of the Year

My role is to prepare students to compete in a globalized market by becoming critical thinkers, problem solvers, and team players. I stimulate learning with lessons that are authentic, relevant, and challenging. I meet regularly with my team members and campus content specialists to review data, identify problem areas, and plan follow-up support for students who are struggling in identified areas. This element is especially critical for students at a Title-1 campus because it provides the background knowledge needed to successfully navigate the curriculum. I find my students are much more successful when provided a myriad of learning opportunities rather than forced to memorize rules and formulas to pass a state-mandated test.

there are ways of classroom assessment that address many of these skills and dispositions. For example, if you encourage student self-assessment, you are developing metacognitive and self-regulation skills. If you use enhanced multiple-choice test items, you develop thinking skills. Peer assessment fosters collaboration. There is much you can do in your daily assessments and feedback that will influence perseverance in the context of students' learning errors. Notice how Daniel Leija addresses these needs in his instruction.

Looking forward, subsequent chapters of the text will examine ways of assessing many of these 21st-century skills and dispositions. For now, just keep the big picture in mind. Remember your students' futures depend on it!

A good illustration of how standards are changing is what is now used in many states to teach science, the Next Generation Science Standards (NGSS). What is unique about these standards is that the intent goes beyond what students should know: "These standards give local educators the flexibility to design classroom learning experiences that stimulate students' interests in science and prepares them for college, careers, and citizenship." (Retrieved May 19, 2016, from http://www.nextgenscience.org). There is an emphasis in the science standards on thinking skills, not just knowledge, and meaningful connections across four science domains (physical science, earth and space science, life science, and engineering design). The change in focus for both instruction and assessment is nicely summarized by middle school math teacher Megan Szabo. Megan, who was awarded Delaware State Teacher of the Year in 2015, recently said the following about the Next Generation Science Standards:

What I love about the NGSS, and how they are moving science education in this country, is that the focus is no longer on just teaching students science, but rather, teaching them how to think like scientists. Instead of just focusing on a list of standards and vocabulary words that students should know, these new science standards focus on teaching students how to be thinkers, how to be problem-solvers, and to use what they learn in science class to explain how the world around them works. (Retrieved May 20, 2016, from http://www.nextgenscience.org/sites/default/files/news/files/Op-Ed%20-%20Delaware%20-%20New%20Science%20Standards%20turn%20Students%20into%20Thinkers.pdf)

Notice the emphasis on thinking skills, problem solving, and explanations, and connections to actual life. This has clear implications for assessment—what type of assessment will best promote and capture these skills?

Educational Outcomes

It's pretty clear that the language that is used to identify different educational outcomes is varied and often confusing. Consider these possible terms, all of which are commonly used:

Goals
Objectives
Aims
Competencies
Outcomes
Standards
Targets
Dimensions
Expectations

How do you keep them all straight? The most important way is to be keenly attuned to what is used in your state, district, school, and discipline, being aware that the same terms could mean something somewhat different, depending on the source. What makes most sense to me is to think about how outcomes transition from being very general to very specific. My use of the terms to show this is illustrated in Figure 2.2. The key is to understand how assessment is connected to each one of these stages. For goals, which are typically divided into three types (cognitive, affective, and psychomotor), there is rarely a measure in each of the three domains. State standards or general objectives are assessed by end-of-year accountability tests and address the cognitive domain. Common tests align with state tests but are given every few weeks. Specific objectives and learning targets are related closely to instructional units and relate to quizzes, tests, projects, and other assessments that are used day-to-day or week-to-week. It is the learning target that forms the foundation for achieving proficiency on standards and goals.

Educational Goals

Educational goals are very general statements about desired student outcomes, the overall purpose or main intention. They cover in broad terms what will be

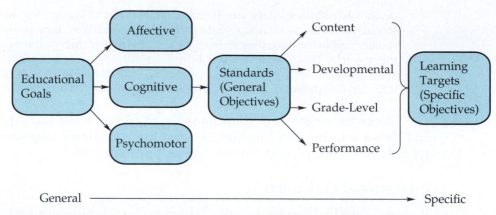

FIGURE 2.2   **Relationship Between Goals, Standards, Objectives, and Learning Targets.**

emphasized during extended learning times, typically over a year or more, often what is emphasized throughout all school years. Goals are mostly intangible and abstract, which makes them very hard to measure. Here are some examples of educational goals:

- Understand and appreciate scientific knowledge
- Learn to think and study independently
- Become good citizens
- Understand the founding principles of our country
- Develop sophisticated mathematical reasoning skills
- Develop a positive attitude toward mathematics and science
- Enhance communication skills

Goals are a necessary beginning point to determine what should be taught and assessed. They have historically been communicated as part of the mission of school districts, but are too broad to be of much use in the classroom. And today, the focus is less on "goals" and much more on 21st-century learning outcomes, skills, and dispositions.

Standards

During the 1990s the idea of "standards" became ubiquitous and powerful, fueling reform by advocating specific "high-level" student outcomes. Although the standards movement mostly concerned what have been traditionally been called general student outcomes or objectives, the reframing of how these outcomes would be judged was needed to stress three points: (a) this is not business as usual, not like "outcome-based" education; (b) standards apply to *all* students; and (c) the student achievement expectations are much higher than what has been used in the past. The intent was to frame the idea of standards in such a way that few could reasonably refute its importance. This is how Popham (2008) delightfully describes it:

> *Standards*, of course, is a warmth-inducing word. Although perhaps not in the same league with *motherhood*, *democracy*, and *babies*, I suspect that "standards" ranks right up there with *oatmeal*, *honor*, and *excellence*. It's really tough not to groove on standards, especially if those standards are *high*. Everyone wants students to reach high standards. (p. 109)

It seems everything is based on "standards" of one kind or another. So what, exactly, are they? **Standards** are statements about what students should know and be able to do in major content areas, typically stated for different grade levels. Standards identify the knowledge and skills students need to have for a particular level, course, or curriculum. As such, standards are pretty much synonymous with general (long-term) objectives. The term "objective" has a storied history, and the ideas associated with general objectives apply to standards (specific objectives are very similar to learning targets).

All major subject-matter associations have standards, as do all states, and de facto "national" standards have been established. This has led to a dizzying array of many different standards from which to choose, though the most important ones, the ones tested by the state, are set by the state. Different types of educational standards are illustrated in Table 2.1, but you'll be most affected by whatever terms are used for your state and district.

TABLE 2.1   Types of Educational Standards

Type of Standard	Description	Examples
Content	Desired outcomes in a content area	• Students will demonstrate an understanding of the Constitution. • Students will understand how immigration has influenced American society.
Performance	What students do to demonstrate competence	• Students will compare the contributions of Socrates, Plato, and Aristotle to Greek life. • Explain in two paragraphs what makes matter sink or float when put in water.
Developmental	Sequences of growth and change over time	• Grades 3–5: Apply knowledge of common English morphemes in oral and silent reading to derive meaning from literature and texts in content areas. • Grades 6–8: Apply knowledge of word relationships, such as roots and affixes, to derive meaning from literature and texts in content areas.
Grade-level	Outcomes for a specific grade	• The student, given a decimal through thousandths, will round to the nearest whole number, tenth, or hundredth. • The student will investigate and understand that matter is anything that has mass and takes up space; and occurs as a solid, liquid, or gas.

State Standards

Because accountability testing is based on state standards, these are the ones that you'll be most concerned about. Some examples of state standards will help you understand what they are and what they mean for your instruction and classroom assessments. Let's start with some from my home state, Virginia.

In Virginia, the Standards of Learning (SOL) describe the Commonwealth's expectations for student learning and achievement in grades K–12 in English, mathematics, science, history/social science, technology, the fine arts, foreign language, health and physical education, and driver education. The SOL are organized by grade level, or individual courses at the secondary level, and by subject. For second-grade math, for example, there are 22 different standards, divided into six categories (number and number sense; computation and estimation; measurement; geometry; probability and statistics; and patterns, functions, and algebra). Each standard states what proficiency students are expected to demonstrate by the end of the year. Here is one of the measurement standards:

> The student, given two whole numbers whose sum is 99 or less, will (a) estimate the sum; and (b) find the sum, using various methods of calculation.

For grade 10 English there are eight standards divided into four categories (communication [speaking, listening, media literacy], reading, writing, and research). Here is one of the writing standards:

> The student will develop a variety of writing to persuade, interpret, analyze, and evaluate with an emphasis on exposition and analysis.
> A. Generate, gather, plan, and organize ideas for writing to address a specific audience and purpose.
> B. Synthesize information to support the thesis.
> C. Elaborate ideas clearly through word choice and vivid description.
> D. Write clear and varied sentences, clarifying ideas with precise and relevant evidence.
> E. Organize ideas into a logical sequence using transitions.
> F. Revise writing for clarity of content, accuracy, and depth of information.
> G. Use computer technology to plan, draft, revise, edit, and publish writing.

Note that in the Virginia standards there is an emphasis on performance. The use of words such as *interpret*, *analyze*, and *estimate* give an indication of what students need to do to be successful. It is not a simple content standard (e.g., students will know the steps to critique a persuasive essay). Virginia also provides extensive information for each standard, including an indication of "essential" understandings, knowledge, skills, and processes to be able to show proficiency, as well as suggested activities, resources, and even classroom assessment methods, including teacher observation, oral exams, conferences, journals, objective tests, and student self-assessments. More detail about the SOL is given on the Virginia Department of Education website.

Texas takes a slightly different approach. The Texas standards are set out in TEKS (Texas Essential Knowledge and Skills). As in Virginia, the standards are organized by subject and grade level. But in Texas there are many more standards for each level in each subject. For example, in second-grade mathematics there are 50 standards in 10 different areas (e.g., data analysis, geometry and measurement, number and operations). Here are two of the six standards for number and operations:

> The student applies mathematical process standards to understand how to represent and compare whole numbers, the relative position and magnitude of whole numbers, and relationships within the numeration system related to place value. The student is expected to:
> A. use concrete and pictorial models to compose and decompose numbers up to 1,200 in more than one way as a sum of so many thousands, hundreds, tens, and ones;
> B. use standard, word, and expanded forms to represent numbers up to 1,200;

The TEKS take a different approach to organizing standards at the high school level. There are 13 different areas that are covered throughout high school. Within English Language Arts and Reading there are four areas (English I, English II, English III, and English IV). Each of these four areas has general statement about what is expected. This is what is indicated for English I:

> Reading/Comprehension Skills. Students use a flexible range of metacognitive reading skills in both assigned and independent reading to understand an author's message. Students will continue to apply earlier standards with greater depth in increasingly more complex texts as they become self-directed, critical readers. The student is expected to:
> A. reflect on understanding to monitor comprehension (e.g., asking questions, summarizing and synthesizing, making connections, creating sensory images); and
> B. make complex inferences about text and use textual evidence to support understanding.

Within each area are many more specific standards. For English I, for example, there are 26 areas of emphasis with a total of more than 50 standards. The following are the specific standards for one of the 26 areas, Writing/Persuasive Texts:

> Students are expected to write an argumentative essay to the appropriate audience that includes:
> A. a clear thesis or position based on logical reasons supported by precise and relevant evidence;
> B. consideration of the whole range of information and views on the topic and accurate and honest representation of these views;
> C. counter-arguments based on evidence to anticipate and address objections;
> D. an organizing structure appropriate to the purpose, audience, and context; and
> E. an analysis of the relative value of specific data, facts, and ideas.

You will notice in reading the Texas standards that, similar to Virginia's standards, there is emphasis on what students will do, not simply the nature of the knowledge or skill.

In Massachusetts, the standards are contained within what are called Curriculum Frameworks, also organized by grade level and subject. The Curriculum Frameworks use the heading Content Standards (though they are actually performance standards). Like Virginia, there are major categories for each subject and grade level, but there are also subcategories. In second-grade mathematics there are 26 standards organized into four major areas (operations and algebraic thinking, number and operations in base 10, measurement and data, and geometry). As an example, here is one subcategory under measurement and data with two standards.

Represent and interpret data.

9. Generate measurement data by measuring lengths of several objects to the nearest whole unit, or by making repeated measurements of the same object. Show the measurements by making a line plot, where the horizontal scale is marked off in whole-number units.

10. Draw a picture graph and a bar graph (with single-unit scale) to represent a data set with up to four categories. Solve simple put-together, take-apart, and compare problems, using information presented in a bar graph.

For high school English Massachusetts's standards are similar in organization and specificity to those of Virginia. Here is one of 10 standards for grade 8 writing:

Gather relevant information from multiple print and digital sources, using search terms effectively; assess the credibility and accuracy of each source; and quote or paraphrase the data and conclusions of others while avoiding plagiarism and following a standard format for citation.

Often state standards will include introductory information that provides further clarification of the nature of what student outcomes are expected. For example, Virginia's grade 5 Mathematics Standards of Learning introduction includes the following:

Problem solving has been integrated throughout the six content strands. The development of problem-solving skills should be a major goal of the mathematics program at every grade level. Instruction in the process of problem solving should be integrated early and continuously into each student's mathematics education. Students must be helped to develop a wide range of skills and strategies for solving a variety of problem types.

Obviously it is important for Virginia mathematics teachers to include problem-solving and reasoning targets. The actual standards make this more specific. The following is one of 22 Virginia mathematics grade 5 standards:

Computation and Estimation Strand

5.3. The student will create and solve problems involving addition, subtraction, multiplication, and division of whole numbers, using paper and pencil, estimation, mental computation, and calculators.

In the last decade state standards have improved considerably and become increasingly specific. Because they are the foundation for high-stakes accountability testing, you'll need to take them very seriously. Each standard and the accompanying text tell what student competencies are tested. Here is another example of state standards, from high school history in Missouri:

> Examine the relevance and connection of constitutional principles in the following documents:
>> Mayflower Compact
>> Declaration of Independence
>> Articles of Confederation
>> U.S. Constitution
>> Federalist Papers
>> Amendments to Constitution, emphasizing Bill of Rights

As a final example, in Missouri each standard is characterized by a "depth-of-knowledge" indicator based on a four-point continuum: recall, skill/concept application, strategic thinking, and extended reasoning. This history standard is identified as requiring complex reasoning.

What has been presented for these four states gives you a good indication about the variety of schemes, labels, descriptions, and language used in standards-based education. State and local guidelines are critical. If you teach in Missouri, for example, you need to study carefully what is meant by the different types of reasoning.

So what is to be learned from these various state standards? First, there are more differences in terminology than anything else. They tend to be organized in a similar fashion and all communicate expected proficiency at the end of the year. But there are also many "outcomes" that must be achieved along the way! Second, state standards represent the essence of what is now being taught in schools, so you will need to be very familiar with them. Third, many state standards are now aligned with 21st-century knowledge and skills. Fourth, state standards drive assessment, not just year-end accountability testing, but also classroom assessment. We now turn to an effort that has generated much excitement as well as concern, the Common Core State Standards.

Common Core State Standards

Over the past two decades there has been an effort to establish essentially the same standards for all states. Since education policy is primarily a state-controlled endeavor, however, this is no small task. In 2009, governors and state education officials from across the country decided to establish a single, common set of national standards, mostly in response to the fact that each state and professional association had somewhat different standards, even for the same subject and grade level, so everyone was focused on something somewhat different (whether this is good or bad is another question). According to some, there was too much content in the existing state standards (Kendall, 2011), with too little emphasis on 21st-century learning and skills. Enter the Common Core State Standards Initiative, or what is often just called the Common Core.

The Common Core State Standards (CCSS) were released in 2010 as a set of "agreed-upon" standards for English/language arts and mathematics. The standards were developed by the states, to "provide a consistent, clear understanding of what students are expected to learn . . . designed to be robust and relevant to the real world, reflecting the knowledge and skills our young people need for success in college and careers" (www.corestandards.org). It is claimed that the standards:

- Are aligned with college and work expectations;
- Are clear, understandable and consistent;
- Include rigorous content and application of knowledge through high-order skills;
- Build upon strengths and lessons of current state standards;
- Are informed by other top-performing countries, so that all students are prepared to succeed in our global economy and society; and
- Are evidence-based.

Since most states have signed on to use the standards (though some states are having second thoughts), and states that haven't align their standards to the Common Core, they are essentially becoming de facto national standards. They are intended to bring together many different state standards by providing a single set of high expectations for learning (Rothman, 2012). Like many states, Massachusetts's Curriculum Framework is explicitly and formally aligned with the Common Core. Hence, in mathematics the Common Core has 26 standards for grade 2, using the same categories as Massachusetts and nearly the same wording for the standards. As a further example, the Common Core uses five categories for grade 6 mathematics (ratios and proportional relationships, the number system, expressions and equations, geometry, and statistics and probability). Within each of these are subcategories with standards under each subcategory. Two of three standards for Develop Understanding of Statistical Variation, one of two subcategories of probability, are the following:

Understand that a set of data collected to answer a statistical question has a distribution which can be described by its center, spread, and overall shape.
Recognize that a measure of center for a numerical data set summarizes all of its values with a single number, while a measure of variation describes how its values vary with a single number.

What is interesting about these particular standards is that the words *understand* and *recognize* are used, compared to more action verbs in the Virginia and other state standards. These Common Core standards are mostly about content, not performance, though throughout the Common Core the phrase "students will understand and be able to do" is used extensively, which implies performance as well as content. At the high school level probability standards are more action-oriented:

> Use the mean and standard deviation of a data set to fit it to a normal distribution and to estimate population percentages. Recognize that there are data sets for which such a procedure is not appropriate. Use calculators, spreadsheets, and tables to estimate areas under the normal curve.

For English/language arts the Common Core uses five categories (reading, writing, speaking and listening, language, and media and technology) with subcategories under each. For grade 3, one subcategory under reading literature is:

Craft and Structure

- Determine the meaning of words and phrases as they are used in a text, distinguishing literal from nonliteral language.
- Refer to parts of stories, dramas, and poems when writing or speaking about a text, using terms such as chapter, scene, and stanza; describe how each successive part builds on earlier sections.
- Distinguish their own point of view from that of the narrator or those of the characters.

Overall, the state and Common Core State Standards represent major efforts to clarify student outcomes, and because they form the basis of accountability tests they are important. But remember that these are student outcomes at the end of the year, so they often are not that helpful for deciding what to teach and assess on a daily and weekly basis. To do that it is necessary to "unpack" the standards and align their overall intent with lesson plans and assessments. This is sometimes systematically achieved through what are called pacing guides, which at least gives teachers a standardized set of guidelines for covering certain content at specified times.

The problem with all these standards is that generally there is so much content that not everything can be covered, and often there is no provision for depth of understanding and reasoning. As we will see later in this chapter, these elements are central to what you will teach and assess. So while state- and national-level standards are influential, you can't use them without much more work on what should be included in instruction and assessment.

One very important point about state standards is that they often express "minimum" levels of competency. As expressed in the following Teacher's Corner, it is wise not to depend solely on state standards, even if they are the ones that are tested on high-stakes tests. Your best guide is to use whatever levels of

Teacher's Corner

Marie Wilcox

National Board Certified Middle School Mathematics Teacher

Standards-based education has changed the look of education. An accomplished teacher knows what skills need to be mastered in order for the students to be prepared for higher-level learning in future years. Teaching just to the standards shortchanges students' education. If teachers teach concept and application rather than just procedure and state standards, students will pass the standard tests (SOL in Virginia). The SOL test is a minimum proficiency assessment; educating students for their future is clearly more important. I charge all teachers to teach to a higher level and preparedness for SOL testing will fall in place.

competency are appropriate to enhance student learning. This is often reflected in teacher standards and learning targets that go beyond state standards.

Deconstructing Standards

Once you know what standards you'll be responsible for teaching and assessing, you will need to make sense of them, to "unpack" them so that you know more specifically what to target in instruction and what your assessments should look like. A deconstructed standard shows what it means by providing further description and details by breaking out different parts. This is usually accomplished by distinguishing knowledge and understanding from reasoning and skills. For example, one of the North Carolina Essential Standards for grade 4 social studies is "analyze the chronology of key historical events in North Carolina history." Table 2.2 shows how the standard is unpacked. Note how there are specific examples of what students should understand and know, and how there are verbs that indicate how they should demonstrate that learning (e.g., summarize and explain). If students need to summarize content knowledge, such as the change in cultures, this suggests being able to recall the information. This would be best assessed with a constructed-response type test item.

Deconstructing could also show whether there is a progression among different standards, and how standards relate to each other. This information is very helpful in teaching math and English language arts where sequence is critical. This requires an in-depth understanding of what is meant by "knowledge," "reasoning," "skills," or other ways of describing the nature of the proficiency. The next two sections of this chapter will help you develop this in-depth understanding.

TABLE 2.2   Deconstructing Standards.[1]

Essential Standard:
4.H.1 Analyze the chronology of key historical events in North Carolina history.
Concept(s): Movement, Change, Colonialism, Cultural Diffusion, Conflict

Clarifying Objectives	Unpacking What does this standard mean a student will understand, know, and be able to do?
4.H.1.1 Summarize the change in cultures, everyday life and status of indigenous American Indian groups in NC before and after European exploration.	The student will understand: • When new groups move into an area, existing groups may experience change. • Interactions between indigenous and migrant groups often result in cultural transformation. The student will know: • The types of government, language, food, shelter, and cultural traditions of various American Indian groups (e.g., Algonquian, Iroquois, Siouan, Tuscarora, Occaneechi, Tutelo, the Waxhaw, Catawba, and Cherokee). • How the culture, everyday life and status of American Indian groups changed after the arrival of Europeans. For example: American Indians were displaced as Europeans arrived and cleared land to build settlements.
4.H.1.2 Explain how and why North Carolina was established.	The student will understand: • Colonies may be established for political, social, or economic reasons. • A nation's desire for new opportunities for trade and the need for new areas of settlement may encourage the migration of people into different regions. The student will know: • The English monarchy sponsored attempts at colonization along the North Carolina coast (Roanoke Island and The Lost Colony). • The contributions of key individuals to the establishment of North Carolina (e.g., Sir Walter Raleigh, Queen Elizabeth, John White, Ralph Lane, King Charles II, Lords Proprietors).

[1]North Carolina Department of Education, retrieved May 23, 2016, from http://www.dpi.state.nc.us/docs/acre/standards/support-tools/unpacking/social-studies/4th.pdf

Educational Objectives

Educational objectives are statements of student performance that should be demonstrated at the end of an instructional unit. There is a long history of using the term "objectives" to describe student outcomes. However, over the years, the term has been used in many different ways, depending on words that indicate the type of objective, the intent of the user, and degree of specificity. Gronlund (1995) used the term *instructional objective* to mean "intended learning outcomes" (p. 3), though in my mind use of the term "instructional" suggests something that the teacher does, not the student. Objectives for student learning are sometimes referred to as *behavioral*, *performance*, or *terminal* objectives. These types of objectives are characterized by the use of action verbs such as *add*, *state*, *define*, *list*, *contract*, *design*, *categorize*, *count*, and *lift*. Action verbs are important because they indicate what the students actually do at the end of the unit. Here are some examples of specific behavioral objectives.

The student will:

- Summarize the main idea of the reading passage
- Underline the verb and subject of each sentence
- Write a title for the reading passage
- List five causes of the Civil War
- Identify on a map the location of each continent
- Explain the process of photosynthesis

Proponents of behavioral objectives emphasize that teachers should learn to write them at an appropriate level of generality—not so narrow that it takes much too long to write and keep track of each piece of knowledge or skill, and not so general that the objectives provide little guidance for instruction. Ideal objectives are stated in terms that are specific enough to inform teaching and assessment but not limit the flexibility of the teacher to modify instruction as needed. Also, it is best to focus on *unit* rather than daily lesson plan objectives. These intermediate-level objectives help keep the focus of student learning on the main understandings, learning processes, attitudes, and other learning outcomes of the unit as a whole. Writing objectives that are too specific results in long lists of minutiae that are time consuming to monitor and manage. Some examples of behavioral objectives that are too specific, too broad, and about the right level of specificity (intermediate) are shown in Table 2.3.

Whether you focus on general or specific objectives, the main point is to describe what students will know and be able to do, not what you will do as a teacher to help students obtain the knowledge and skills identified. What you plan to do as a teacher may be called a **teaching objective** or *learning activity* and may include such things as lecturing for a certain amount of time, asking questions, putting students in groups, giving feedback to students individually, conducting experiments, using a map to show where certain countries are located, asking students to solve math problems on the board, having students read orally, and so on. These teaching objectives describe the activities students will be engaged in and what you need to do to be sure that the activities occur as planned.

Taxonomies of Educational Objectives

Several popular taxonomies of educational objectives are used by teachers to categorize the nature of the content that is learned and the mental processes that are used to learn the content. These taxonomies are widely used because they use a

TABLE 2.3 **Specificity of Behavioral Objectives**

Too Specific	About Right	Too Broad
Given a two-paragraph article from the newspaper, the student will correctly identify 10 statements that are facts and 5 statements that are opinions in less than 10 minutes without the aid of any resource materials.	Students will state the difference between facts and opinions.	Students will learn how to think critically.
Based on reading the content of Lincoln's and Douglas's debates over 1 week, the student will, without any aids, write four paragraphs in 1 hour that summarize, with at least 80% accuracy, their areas of agreement and disagreement.	Students will identify areas of agreement and disagreement in the debates between Lincoln and Douglas.	Compare and contrast the Lincoln/Douglas debates.
The student, given grid paper, will analyze data on the frequency of student birthdays in each month and construct a bar graph in 1 hour in teams of two of the results that show the two most frequent and two least frequent months.	Given frequency data and grid paper, students will construct bar graphs of selected variables.	Students will construct bar graphs.

systematic approach to defining the nature of what is learned, and they provide a common language for describing student learning. Although three major taxonomies are summarized in this chapter, remember that they don't need to be followed exactly as presented. You need to use the taxonomies to categorize different learning outcomes that make the most sense, given your overall goals for students and state and district standards. Many states use features of taxonomies to deconstruct their standards.

Bloom's Taxonomy of Objectives. Perhaps the best-known source for educational objectives is the *Taxonomy of Educational Objectives I: Cognitive Domain* (Bloom, 1956). As implied in the title, this initial taxonomy covered cognitive learning objectives. Later publications of the taxonomy focused on the affective and psychomotor areas. Thus, "Bloom's taxonomy," as it has become known, consists of three domains—cognitive, affective, and psychomotor.

Bloom's taxonomy of the cognitive domain has received considerable attention and has been used to specify action verbs to accompany different types of cognitive learning (see Table 2.4). The cognitive domain contains six levels. Each level represents an increasingly complex type of cognition. Although the cognitive domain is often characterized as having "lower" and "higher" levels, only the knowledge level is considered by authors of the taxonomy to be lower; all other levels are higher. The first level describes several different types of knowledge. The remaining five levels are referred to as "intellectual abilities and skills."

Bloom's taxonomy can be very helpful when formulating specific objectives, even though this categorization of cognitive tasks was created more than

TABLE 2.4   Bloom's Taxonomy of Educational Objectives: Cognitive Domain

Level	Illustrative Verbs
Knowledge: Recalling and remembering previously learned material, including specific facts, events, persons, dates, methods, procedures, concepts, principles, and theories	Names, matches, lists, recalls, selects, retells, states, defines, describes, labels, reproduces
Comprehension: Understanding and grasping the meaning of something; includes translation from one symbolic form to another (e.g., percent into fractions), interpretation, explanation, prediction, inferences, restating, estimation, generalization, and other uses that demonstrate understanding	Explains, converts, interprets, paraphrases, predicts, estimates, rearranges, rephrases, summarizes
Application: Use of abstract ideas, rules, or generalized methods in novel, concrete situations	Changes, demonstrates, modifies, produces, solves, constructs, applies, uses, shows
Analysis: Breaking down a communication into constituent parts or elements and understanding the relationship among different elements	Distinguishes, compares, subdivides, diagrams, differentiates, relates, classifies, categorizes
Synthesis: Arranging and combining elements and parts into novel patterns or structures	Generates, combines, constructs, assembles, formulates, forecasts, projects, proposes, integrates
Evaluation: Judging the quality, worth, or value of something according to established criteria (e.g., determining the adequacy of evidence to support a conclusion)	Justifies, criticizes, decides, judges, argues, concludes, supports, defends, evaluates, verifies, confirms

50 years ago. Since that time, there have been significant changes in the educational and psychological theories that formed the basis for the taxonomy. The taxonomy reflected a strong behaviorism emphasis. More recently socioconstructivist theories have dominated. The taxonomies are still valuable, however, in providing a comprehensive list of possible learning objectives with clear action verbs that operationalize the targets, and many educators still refer to the taxonomy.

Bloom's Revised Taxonomy of Objectives.   A revision to Bloom's original taxonomy was proposed in 2001 "to refocus educators' attention on the value of the original *Handbook* . . . and to incorporate new knowledge and thought into the framework" (Anderson & Krathwohl, 2001, pp. xxi–xxii). The revised taxonomy uses a two-dimensional model as a framework for identifying and writing learning objectives. The knowledge dimension includes four levels that describe different types of knowledge with a number of subcategories (see Figure 2.3). The cognitive process dimension includes six major categories and numerous

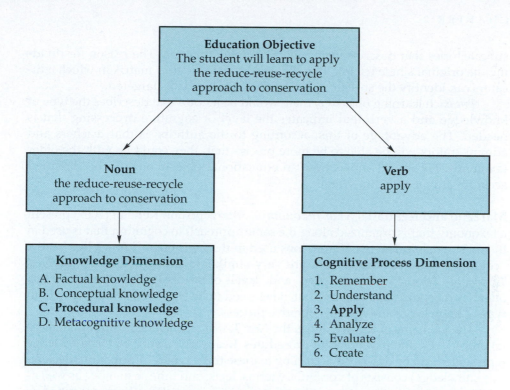

Education Objective
The student will learn to apply the reduce-reuse-recycle approach to conservation

Noun
the reduce-reuse-recycle approach to conservation

Verb
apply

Knowledge Dimension
A. Factual knowledge
B. Conceptual knowledge
C. Procedural knowledge
D. Metacognitive knowledge

Cognitive Process Dimension
1. Remember
2. Understand
3. **Apply**
4. Analyze
5. Evaluate
6. Create

The Knowledge Dimension	Cognitive Process Dimension					
	1. Remember	2. Understand	3. Apply	4. Analyze	5. Evaluate	6. Create
A. Factual						
B. Conceptual						
C. Procedural			✗			
D. Metacognitive						

The student will learn to apply the reduce-reuse-recycle approach to conservation

FIGURE 2.3   How an Objective (the Student Will Learn to Apply the Reduce-Reuse-Recycle Approach to Conservation) Is Classified in the Taxonomy Table

Source: Anderson/Krathwohl/Airasian/Cruikshank/Mayer/Pintrich/Raths/Wittrock, *A Taxonomy for Learning, Teaching, and Assessing: A Revision of Bloom's Taxonomy of Educational Objectives*, Abridged Edition, 1st Ed., © 2001. Reprinted and Electronically reproduced by permission of Pearson Education, Inc., Upper Saddle River, New Jersey. Adapted by permission of Pearson Education, Inc., Upper Saddle River, NJ.

subcategories that describe increasingly complex thinking. The reason for dividing the original single list into two dimensions is to create a matrix in which educators can identify the specific nature of the learning that is targeted.

For each learning objective, there would be a noun that describes the type of knowledge and a verb that indicates the level of cognitive processing that is needed. The advantage of this, according to the authors, is that teachers and administrators will be able to be more precise than they could be with the older taxonomy. Figure 2.3 shows how an educational objective could be classified according to the two dimensions.

Marzano and Kendall's *New Taxonomy.*   Marzano and Kendall (2007) present a taxonomy that is organized along the same approach to cognition that is used in Bloom's revision. The two dimensions used in the revision, a "knowledge" and a "cognitive process" dimension, are very similar to the two used in the *New Taxonomy*—"domain of knowledge" and "levels of processing." Both of these taxonomies recognize that learning outcomes need to be classified according to both type of knowledge and type of cognitive process.

The Domains of Knowledge in the *New Taxonomy* include information, mental procedures, and psychomotor procedures. In any given subject, the knowledge represented can be described according to these three types. Information (declarative knowledge) consists of vocabulary terms, facts, and time sequences, as well as principles and generalizations. Mental procedure is what has been described as "procedural knowledge." It is knowledge that is needed to carry out an action or solve a problem. Psychomotor procedures include physical activities such as finger dexterity, posture, and strength.

The *New Taxonomy* Levels of Processing includes a "cognitive system" consisting of a hierarchical set of four cognitive operations—retrieval, comprehension, analysis, and knowledge utilization. Retrieval is simple recall or recognition. Comprehension is a type of understanding in which knowledge may be translated, classified, and interpreted. Analysis involves elaboration of and extension of knowledge, generalization, and application. Knowledge utilization consists of decision making, problem solving, experimenting, and investigating. The *New Taxonomy* also includes metacognition and self-system thinking as additional levels of processing.

A graphic representation of the *New Taxonomy* is presented in Figure 2.4. Like Bloom's revision, a matrix results to show how learning consists of different types of knowledge across various cognitive operations that begin with retrieval and extend to knowledge utilization. Thus, it would be possible to select procedural knowledge that is simply retrieval or is used to solve problems (knowledge utilization).

Both Bloom's revised taxonomy and Marzano & Kendall's *New Taxonomy* have had mixed success. While the notion that nouns and verbs can be isolated into knowledge and thinking skills is very helpful for deconstructing standards, most approaches to standards use a more simplified approach (e.g., just knowledge, understanding, reasoning, skills).

FIGURE 2.4   **Representation of Marzano & Kendall's** *New Taxonomy*

	Domains of Knowledge		
Levels of Processing	Information	Mental Procedures	Psychomotor Procedures
Retrieval			
Comprehension			
Analysis			
Knowledge Utilization			
Metacognitive System			
Self-System			

Learning Targets

Now we finally come to what you will use daily in your teaching—learning targets. A **learning target** is defined as a statement of student performance for a relatively restricted type of learning outcome that will be achieved in a single lesson or a few days. Thus, compared to what we have already discussed concerning outcomes, this is the most specific and is what will suggest explicit instructional activities and assessments.

What is unique about learning targets, from my perspective, is that they can contain *both* a description of what students should know, understand, and be able to do at the end of instruction, similar to a specific behavioral objective, *and* something about the criteria for judging the level of performance demonstrated (see Figure 2.5).

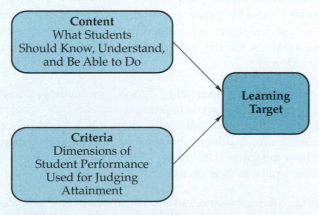

FIGURE 2.5   **Components of Learning Targets**

Can you recall being in a class in which you thought you knew what was expected, only to find out *after* the teacher graded the work what was really important? It's one thing to set a learning standard, outcome, or objective. What is also important is how the work is evaluated, how it is determined that the standard is achieved. This is where criteria come in, and standards are just statements until the criteria are added.

One of the most frustrating experiences for students is not knowing "what the teacher wants" or "how the teacher grades." Perhaps you can remember being in a class in which you did an assignment with little guidance from the teacher about how he or she would grade it. Once your assignment was returned with comments, your reaction might well have been, "If I had only known what the teacher was looking for, I could have provided it!" Essentially, this issue is concerned with the criteria the teacher uses for evaluating student work and whether students know, *in advance*, what those criteria are. Here is a poignant illustration of how a lack of clear criteria can be unfair. The following actually happened to a sixth grader:

> [The student] was given the following problem to solve: "Three buses bring students to school. The first bus brings 9 students, the second bus brings 7 students, and the third bus brings 5 students. How many students in all do the buses bring?" The student answered "21 kids," and the answer was marked wrong. After encouragement by my colleague the student asked the teacher "Why?" The reason was that the student said "kids" instead of "students." (Arter, 1996, p. VI-1:1)

Criteria, then, are clearly articulated and public descriptions of facets or dimensions of student performance that are used for judging the level of achievement. As pointed out in Chapter 1, criteria may be called *scoring criteria*, *rubrics*, *scoring rubrics*, or *scoring guidelines*. (The term *performance criteria* may also be used.) Although criteria have been promoted most for more recent alternative and performance assessments, the issue of how student responses will be evaluated lies at the heart of any type of assessment. The key component of criteria is making your professional judgments about student performance clear to others. All methods of assessment involve your professional judgment. If you use multiple-choice testing, judgment is used to prepare the items and decide which alternative is correct. In an essay test, judgment is involved in preparing the question and in reading and scoring answers. Clearly articulated criteria will help you in many ways, including the following:

- Defining what you mean by "excellent," "good," or "average" work
- Communicating instructional goals to parents
- Communicating to parents, students, and others what constitutes excellence
- Providing guidelines for making unbiased and consistent judgments
- Documenting how judgments are made
- Helping students evaluate their own work

When specifying criteria, it is necessary to summarize the dimensions of performance that are used to assign student work to a given level. The dimensions are what you consider to be essential qualities of the performance. They can be identified by asking yourself some questions: What are the attributes of good performance? How do I know when students have reached different levels of performance? What examples do I have of each level? What do I look for when evaluating student work? Criteria are best developed by being clear on what constitutes excellence as well as proficiency in the performance area of interest. By identifying and prioritizing key elements, the most important aspects of the performance will be utilized.

Once the dimensions have been identified, you can develop a quantitative or qualitative scale to indicate different levels of performance. Label each level as "good," "excellent," "poor," and so on. Examples are presented in Chapters 10 and 11.

Although it is very helpful for students to know the criteria as communicated in a scoring rubric, it is even more beneficial if students can see an example of a finished student product or performance and your evaluation of it. These examples are called **exemplars** or **anchors**. For example, if you have established four levels of performance, an exemplar of work at each level will make the criteria more clear. To emphasize once again, you should share the exemplars with students *before* they begin their work. This will help students internalize the standards that you use and know what constitutes excellence. The exemplars could be as simple as giving students examples of the type of math word problems that will be on a test and how their answers will be graded. Of course, you don't want to give students something that they will memorize or copy, but you do need to give them a sense of the difficulty of the task.

Think for a moment about a target at which one would shoot an arrow. The performance might be stated as "the student will hit the target with an arrow." But you need to communicate more than simply "hit the target." How far away is the target? How large is the target? Does it matter where the arrow hits the target? In other words, you need to indicate something about the dimensions of the performance that translate into qualitatively different levels of performance. Two teachers can state the same learning objective, but if different criteria are used to evaluate the performance, then in reality students in each class are learning something different.

A similar case can be made for learning subjects in school. The outcome "students will know state capitals in the United States" means something different if the student has to recall all 50 capitals from memory rather than if the student can correctly match half of the names of capitals with states. You must be able to articulate, as part of the target, the criteria you will use to judge performance, and remember, students should know these criteria *before* instruction. This does not need to be done in a single sentence. It is easier, in fact, to think about targets as a description of what will be assessed and how it will be judged. These two aspects of the target can be separated into different sentences. For example, this describes what students need to know:

Students will demonstrate an understanding of the effect of the sun on seasons, length of day, weather, and climate.

Information about criteria could be added with another sentence:

Students will demonstrate their understanding by correctly answering short-answer questions about each relationship.

If a matching test is used, try this description:

Students will demonstrate their understanding by correctly matching all effects with the four elements discussed.

In practice, you would not be so wordy in describing the target. It is understood that "students will demonstrate" so you can simply say "understand effect of sun on seasons, length of day, weather, and climate." The information about criteria can be shortened by simply referring to "matching" or "short answer."

What I am suggesting about targets is akin to what was promoted many years ago by those enchanted with behavioral objectives—including the behavior (knowing or doing), the conditions under which the behavior is performed, and the criteria for determining acceptable performance. But behavioral objectives were too specific. They would often begin with the condition (e.g., given a map of Virginia, students will have 40 minutes to answer six short-answer questions without use of notes or conversation with others . . .) and continue so that to use them was overwhelming. But criteria, in my mind, can't be separated from content or skill, so at least that component needs to be in your thinking about learning targets.

Let's return for a moment to the earlier discussion about educational outcomes. As I've emphasized, don't be too worried about all the different terminology around outcomes—objectives, standards, targets, expectations, etc. Whatever your setting, you'll soon learn what is most used and what it means. Regardless of the terms used, the most important outcomes you will need to distinguish are the various types of cognitive learning outcomes, what I call cognitive learning targets. We now turn to these types of targets.

Types of Cognitive Learning Targets

As we have seen with the taxonomies of objectives, cognitive targets essentially divide into three major categories: knowledge, understanding, and reasoning. But, of course, there are different types of knowledge, different levels of understanding, and many different reasoning skills. It makes the most sense to me to use two major categories in the cognitive domain: knowledge and simple understanding, and deep understanding and reasoning. Each of these can then be broken into more specific types. (See Figure 2.6.)

Knowledge Representation

Until recently, Bloom's taxonomy provided a definition of *knowledge* for many educators. In this scheme, *knowledge* is defined as remembering something. All that is required is that the student recall or recognize facts, definitions, terms, concepts, procedures, principles, or other information.

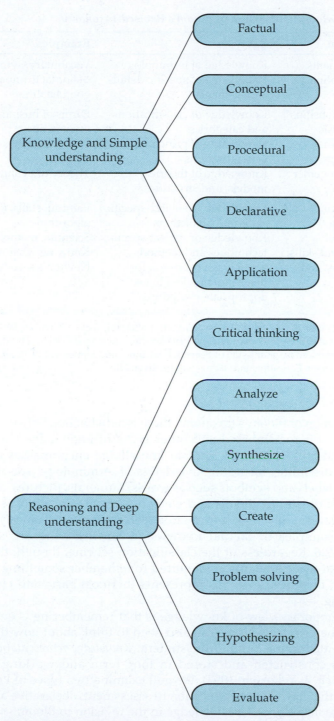

FIGURE 2.6   Major types of cognitive learning targets.

TABLE 2.5   Part of the Knowledge Dimension of *Bloom's Revised Taxonomy*

Major Types	Definition	Subtypes	Examples
Factual Knowledge	Basic elements of a discipline	Knowledge of terminology Knowledge of specific details and elements	Vocabulary; symbols Major facts important to good health
Conceptual Knowledge	Interrelationships among basic elements that enable them to function together	Knowledge of classifications and categories Knowledge of principles and generalizations Knowledge of theories, models, and structures	Forms of business ownership Law of supply and demand Theory of evolution
Procedural Knowledge	How to do something, methods of inquiry, and skills, algorithms, and methods	Knowledge of subject-specific skills and algorithms Knowledge of subject-specific techniques and methods Knowledge of criteria for determining when to use appropriate procedures	Painting skills; division algorithm Scientific method Knowing when to apply Newton's second law

Source: Anderson/Krathwohl/Airasian/Cruikshank/Mayer/Pintrich/Raths/Wittrock, *A Taxonomy for Learning, Teaching, and Assessing: A Revision of Bloom's Taxonomy of Educational Objectives,* Abridged Edition, 1st Ed., © 2001. Reprinted and Electronically reproduced by permission of Pearson Education, Inc., Upper Saddle River, New Jersey. Adapted by permission of Pearson Education, Inc., Upper Saddle River, NJ.

In the revision of Bloom's taxonomy there is a distinction between "factual knowledge" that is remembered and other types of knowledge (conceptual, procedural, and metacognitive). Factual knowledge encompasses basic elements about a discipline, including knowledge of terminology (specific verbal and nonverbal labels and symbols such as words, numerals, pictures, and signs) and knowledge of specific details and elements (events, locations, sources of information, dates, and other information pertaining to a subject). Further details with examples of factual knowledge remembering are shown in Tables 2.5 and 2.6. Regardless of the classification scheme, though, the important point is that when students are required to remember something, whether facts, concepts, or procedures, this represents the most basic and elementary form of learning.

The contemporary view of knowledge is that remembering is only part of what occurs when students learn. You also need to think about how the knowledge is represented in the mind of the student. *Knowledge representation* is how information is constructed and stored in long-term and working memory (Gagne, Yekovich, & Yekovich, 1993). We will examine two types of knowledge representation that have direct application to assessment: declarative and procedural. These are major types of knowledge in the revision to Bloom's taxonomy (Table 2.6).

TABLE 2.6 **Part of Cognitive Process Dimension of** *Bloom's Revised Taxonomy*

Major Types	Definition	Subtypes	Illustrative Verbs	Examples
Remember	Retrieval of knowledge from long-term memory	Recognizing Recalling	Identifying Retrieving	Recognize dates of important events Recall dates of important events
Understand	Construct meaning from oral, written, and graphic communication	Interpreting Exemplifying Classifying Summarizing Inferring Comparing Explaining	Representing, translating Illustrating Categorizing, subsuming Abstracting, generalizing Concluding, predicting Contrasting, mapping Constructing models	Paraphrase meaning in important speeches Give examples of painting styles Classify different types of rocks Write a summary of a story Draw a conclusion from data presented Compare historical events to contemporary events Show cause-and-effect of pollution affected by industry
Apply	Carry out a procedure	Executing Implementing	Carrying out Using	Divide whole numbers Apply procedure to an unfamiliar task

Source: Anderson/Krathwohl/Airasian/Cruikshank/Mayer/Pintrich/Raths/Wittrock, *A Taxonomy for Learning, Teaching, and Assessing: A Revision of Bloom's Taxonomy of Educational Objectives*, Abridged Edition, 1st Ed., © 2001. Reprinted and Electronically reproduced by permission of Pearson Education, Inc., Upper Saddle River, New Jersey. Adapted by permission of Pearson Education, Inc., Upper Saddle River, NJ.

Declarative Knowledge and Simple Understanding. *Declarative knowledge* is information that is retained about something, knowing that it exists. The nature of the information learned can be ordered hierarchically, depending on the level of generality and degree of understanding that is demonstrated (Marzano & Kendall, 2007) and the way the knowledge is represented. At the "lowest" level, declarative knowledge is similar to Bloom's first level—remembering or recognizing specific facts about persons, places, events, or content in a subject area. The knowledge is represented by simple association or discrimination, such as rote memory. At a higher level, declarative knowledge consists of concepts, ideas, and generalizations that are more fully understood and applied. This type of knowledge involves *simple understanding* in the form of comprehension.

Knowledge, then, moves from rote memorization and association of facts to generalized understanding and usage. This is a critical distinction for both learning and assessment. As pointed out in Chapter 1, constructivist views contend that students learn most effectively when they connect new information meaningfully to an existing network of knowledge. Constructivists believe that new knowledge is acquired through a process of seeing how something relates, makes sense, and can be used in reasoning. This notion is quite different from memorized learning that can be demonstrated for a test. Although I don't want to suggest that some rote memorization is not appropriate for students, I do want to point out that your learning targets can focus on recalling or understanding types of declarative knowledge and that your choice of assessment method and test items will be different for each of these.

Let's look at an example of different types of declarative knowledge. One important type of information students learn about is geometric shapes. Each shape is a concept (mental structures that use physical characteristics or definitions to classify objects, events, or other things into categories). If students learn the concept of "rectangle" at the level of *recall* or *recognition*, then they simply memorize a definition or identify rectangles from a set of different shapes that look like the ones they studied in class. If students *understand* the concept of rectangle, however, they will be able to give original examples and identify rectangles of different sizes, shapes, and colors they have never seen before. Each of these levels of learning is "knowing something," but the latter is much closer to true student mastery and what constructivists advocate. Also, because these levels are hierarchical, understanding requires recall. Thus, it may be better to state learning targets that require understanding but teach and test for recall as well because one is a prerequisite to the other.

Procedural Knowledge and Simple Understanding.   *Procedural knowledge* is knowing how to do something. It is knowledge that is needed to carry out an action or solve a problem. What is demonstrated is knowledge of the strategies, procedures, and skills students must engage in; for example, how to tie shoes, how to divide fractions, the sequence of steps for using a telescope, or how to check out library books. Like declarative knowledge, procedural knowledge can be demonstrated at different levels. At the level of recall, students simply identify or repeat the needed steps. Simple understanding is indicated as students summarize in their own words (comprehension) and actually use the steps in executing a solution (application).

Reasoning and Deep Understanding

Like other taxonomies, *Bloom's Revision* separates simple cognition such as remembering and conceptual understanding from "higher-level" cognition with which students analyze, evaluate, and create. These "higher levels" are generally regarded as reasoning skills, in which students mentally manipulate information to solve a problem or come up with an answer. With knowledge and comprehension you are able to make sense out of something, and with further involvement and more detailed information, you deepen your understanding to eventually use information in new ways; to think about what is known in a systematic, integrated, holistic manner; and to explain relationships. This continuum is

FIGURE 2.7 The Knowledge/Understanding Continuum

Remembering	Simple Understanding	Deep Understanding and Reasoning
Fragmented	Comprehend	Penetrating
Ritualized	Apply	Elegant
Fragile	Rudimentary	Sophisticated
Literal	explanations	Explanations
Superficial	Think about	Justify
Surface	Interpret	Compare and contrast
Temporary	Illustrate	Construct
Recall	Describe	Expert
Recognize		Critical thinking
Novice		Reasoning
Inflexible		Grasp structure
Formulaic		Rethinking
		Revising
		Reflective
		Enduring
		Infer

represented in Figure 2.7 with terms that are associated with knowledge and different levels of understanding. The terms are meant to describe the nature of knowledge and the relative degree of understanding that is demonstrated, showing the spectrum from shallow to sophisticated.

Deep understanding implies that students know the "essence" of something, that they can think about and use knowledge in new and sophisticated ways, and that they can grasp the idea of relativity and significance (McTighe & Wiggins, 2004; Wiggins, 1998; Wiggins & McTighe, 2005); they can discover and interpret new relationships, construct novel explanations, and reason with what they comprehend. They are able to understand the complexity of knowledge. When we initially learn about something, our understanding is undeveloped and not very sophisticated. As we have more experience with it, our understanding deepens. For example, you may have had a surface or simple understanding of the meaning of the term *performance assessment* before reading this text. Initially, you may be able to provide a definition and simple understanding by recognizing performance assessments. Your understanding will be richer and more developed after you study performance assessments, use some in the classroom, and discuss their strengths and weaknesses with others.

It is important to realize that deep understanding targets are needed to help students internalize what they are able to do with their knowledge and construct meaningful connections with what they already know. At the very least, distinguish between surface recall and recognition knowledge, and deep understanding. As we will see, the implication for assessment is significant. Assessments that work well with knowledge and simple understanding are different from those that should be used for deep understanding.

Reasoning is something students do with their knowledge, a kind of cognitive or mental operation that employs their understanding to some end. Of course, knowledge and simple understanding, like reasoning, involve some type of thinking skill. Thinking occurs in the most fundamental process of remembering something, just as it does in demonstrating understanding and reasoning. It is in the nature of the thinking, however, that knowledge and simple understanding is distinguished from deep understanding and reasoning.

Reasoning, as I have conceptualized here, involves some kind of mental manipulation of knowledge. The task is to *employ* knowledge to interpret and draw inferences, solve a problem, make a judgment or decision, or engage in creative or critical thinking. Thinking is not normally content-free. Thus, I find it helpful to identify three ingredients to reasoning. One is the mental skill needed to perform the task; a second is the declarative or procedural knowledge or simple understanding needed; and the third is the task itself. These ingredients differentiate cognitive skills such as analysis, comparison, and discrimination from the problem-solving or interpretation task (see Figure 2.8). The mental skills are used in conjunction with knowledge to perform the task. Even though we are sometimes interested in teaching and assessing students on their ability to perform certain types of mental operations, such as analysis or deductive logic, we don't normally test these skills directly. Rather, we are usually interested in the *use* of

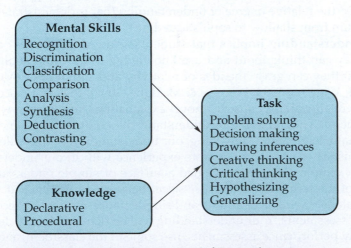

FIGURE 2.8   Major Components of Reasoning

these skills to demonstrate deep understanding or to perform a problem-solving task in subject-matter domains.

In the revision of Bloom's taxonomy, three cognitive processes apply to deep understanding and reasoning: *analyze*, *evaluate*, and *create*. Analyze is essentially the same as *analysis* in other frameworks, whereas evaluate is similar to critical thinking and problem solving. The create process is similar to *inquiry* and emphasizes synthesis of information and problem solving. The three cognitive processes, with definitions and examples, are summarized in Table 2.7.

TABLE 2.7   Deep Understanding and Reasoning Parts of the Revision of Bloom's Taxonomy

Cognitive Process	Definition	Subtypes	Illustrative Verbs	Example
Analyze	Break material into its constituent parts and determine how the parts relate.	Differentiating	Discriminating, distinguishing, focusing, selecting	Distinguish between relevant and irrelevant numbers in a math word problem.
		Organizing	Finding coherence, integrating, outlining	Structure historical evidence for and against a particular historical explanation.
		Attributing	Deconstructing	Determine the point of view of an author based on his or her political perspective.
Evaluate	Make judgments based on criteria and standards.	Checking	Coordinating, detecting, monitoring, testing	Determine if conclusions follow from observed data.
		Critiquing	Judging	Judge which of two methods is the best way to solve a problem.
Create	Pull elements together to form a whole; reorganize elements into a new structure or pattern.	Generating Planning Producing	Hypothesizing Designing Constructing	Generate hypothesis to account for observed phenomenon. Plan a research paper. Build habitats for a specific purpose.

FIGURE 2.9 Checklist for Selecting Learning Targets

✓ Are there too many or too few targets?
✓ Are all important types of learning included?
✓ Do the targets reflect school goals and 21st-century knowledge, skills, and dispositions, as well as state standards?
✓ Will the targets challenge students to do their best work?
✓ Are the targets consistent with research on learning and motivation?
✓ Are the targets established before instruction begins?

Criteria for Selecting Learning Targets

After you have consulted existing sources of standards and objectives and begun the task of selecting your learning targets, you will need to make some choices about which targets to keep, which need revision, and which may not be feasible to teach and/or assess. The following criteria will help you judge the adequacy of your learning targets. They are summarized in Figure 2.9 in the form of a checklist.

1. **Establish the right number of learning targets.** The number of different learning targets will vary, depending on the length of the instructional segment and the complexity of the target. Obviously, the longer the instructional period, the more targets are needed. Also, more complex targets, such as those requiring reasoning, take more time. I have found the following general rules of thumb appropriate: 40–60 targets for a year; 8–12 for a unit; 1–3 for a single lesson. Hundreds of targets for a year are clearly too many.

2. **Establish comprehensive learning targets.** It is essential that the targets represent all types of important learning from the instructional unit. Be careful not to overemphasize knowledge targets. Try to maintain a balance among the five areas (knowledge and simple understanding, reasoning and deep understanding, skills, products, and affect). Higher priority may be given to targets that integrate several of these areas. Do not rely too heavily on textbook objectives or teacher's guides.

3. **Establish learning targets that reflect school goals and 21st-century skills.** Your targets should be clearly related to state standards as well as more general school, district, and state learning goals. Priority may be given to targets that focus on school improvement plans or restructuring efforts, as well as both skills and dispositions needed for college and career.

4. **Establish learning targets that are challenging yet feasible.** It is important to challenge students and seek the highest level of accomplishment for them. You will need to develop targets that are not too easy or too hard. It is also important

to assess the readiness of your students to establish these challenging targets and standards. Do they have the necessary prerequisite skills and knowledge? Are they developmentally ready for the challenge? Do they have the needed motivation and attitudes? Will students see the standards as too easy? As we will see in the next chapter, these questions need to be answered through proper assessment before your final selection of learning targets, standards, instructional activities, and your assessment of student learning.

5. Establish learning targets that are consistent with current principles of learning and motivation. Because learning targets are the basis for learning and instruction, it is important that what you set as a target will promote learning that is consistent with what we know about how learning occurs and what motivates students. For example, will the targets promote long-term retention in a meaningful way? Do the targets reflect students' intrinsic interests and needs? Do the targets represent learning that will be applicable to life outside the classroom? Will the targets encourage a variety of instructional approaches and activities?

After you identify the targets, it is best to write them out before teaching. This will allow a ready reference throughout the lesson and free you to concentrate on the fast-paced and complex activities in the classroom. From year to year you will find it necessary to revisit your targets and make appropriate modifications depending on changes in your students, curriculum, textbooks, and state requirements. It will also be helpful to identify performance standards as well as criteria, with examples of student work that illustrate different levels of performance. This doesn't mean, however, that you should start teaching by stating the learning targets. This often results in a listing of objectives each day, with students writing them down. This can be a devastating way to begin instruction! It turns into what students find pretty boring—telling them what will be learned, how they will learn, and how they will be assessed. It's good for students to know generally where they are going, and certainly as the teacher you need to have specific learning targets clearly identified. But remember, you want your students engaged and motivated, curious, challenged, and questioning. When students get drilled on "standards" or learning targets, that is what gets emphasized—drilling students! Others may disagree with me about this, but it is something to consider. Without student enthusiasm and effort, instruction is much less effective, as is the usefulness of assessment.

Summary

Learning targets—what students should know and be able to do and the criteria for judging student performance—are contrasted in this chapter with other ways of identifying outcomes using concepts such as *goals*, *standards*, and *objectives*. The major points include the following:

- Goals are broad statements about student learning, manifested most recently in statements that identify 21st-century knowledge, skills, and dispositions.
- States have established grade-level standards that have ubiquitous implications for teachers, instruction, and classroom assessments.
- Common Core State Standards identify de facto national standards in mathematics and English/language arts for many states.
- Behavioral objectives are specific statements that indicate what students should know and be able to do at the end of an instructional period.
- Learning targets need to contain as much about criteria as possible and be feasible, because criteria are critical in establishing the standards on which performance toward the learning target is judged.
- Criteria are clearly stated dimensions of student performance that the teacher examines in making judgments about student proficiency. These criteria should be public and explained to students before each instructional unit.
- Exemplars and anchors are important examples that help students understand how teacher evaluations are made.
- Five types of learning targets are introduced: knowledge and simple understanding, reasoning and deep understanding, skill, product, and affect.
- Criteria to be used in selecting targets and standards were indicated. You should strive for the right number of comprehensive, challenging targets that will reflect school goals and will be consistent with current principles of learning and motivation.

Introductory Case Study Answer

Eli didn't start the project with clear learning targets to guide his assessment. His "learning targets" were really goals or objectives that did not describe what students should know and be able to do or contain the criteria for judging student proficiency.

Zoe should help Eli understand the difference between goals, objectives, standards, and learning targets. She should also explain the difference between the five types of learning targets (knowledge and simple understanding, deep understanding and reasoning, skill, product, affect) and help Eli understand the following criteria he should use when selecting learning targets.

- Establish a right number of learning targets.
- Establish comprehensive learning targets.
- Establish learning targets that reflect school goals and 21st-century skills.
- Establish learning targets that are challenging yet feasible.
- Establish learning targets that are consistent with current principles of learning and motivation.

Eli should have open transparency about the rubric. Additionally, he should provide the rubric at the beginning to the unit and provide exemplars so students know the criteria for judging their performance.

Suggestions for Action Research

1. Obtain some examples of student work from teachers that demonstrate different levels of performance on the same assessment. How easy is it to see how the examples are different? See if the criteria you use to differentiate the examples are the same as the criteria the teacher used.

2. In small groups, generate some examples of student performance on the same learning target that would demonstrate qualitatively different levels of achievement concerning the content of this chapter or Chapter 1.

3. Examine state and national standards in your area of expertise. How are they similar, and how are they different?

4. Interview a teacher and ask about using state standards. How useful are these standards? What determines whether the teacher will use them?

5. In a group of three or four other students, develop a scoring rubric that could be used for judging the performance of a student on an assignment, project, or test that was used in a school setting. Find or generate examples of student work that illustrate different levels of performance.

MyEdLab Self-Check 2.1

MyEdLab Self-Check 2.2

MyEdLab Self-Check 2.3

MyEdLab Self-Check 2.4

MyEdLab Application Exercise 2.1   Learning Targets

MyEdLab Application Exercise 2.2   Reasoning

High-Quality Classroom Assessment

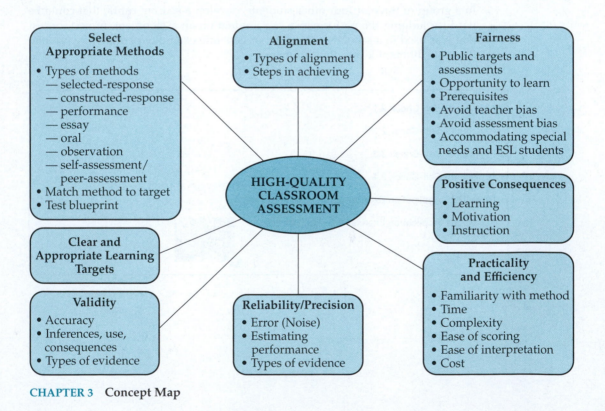

CHAPTER 3 Concept Map

Learning Outcomes

After reading this chapter, you should be able to:

3.1 Know how different types of assessment match with different types of learning targets, understanding that some assessment methods are best for measuring knowledge and understanding and other types for measuring reasoning skills.

3.2 Understand the nature of evidence for validity and reliability/precision as characteristics of obtained scores—how they are different and why they are important for obtaining credible assessment data.

3.3 Know what is needed for fair assessment, including how to avoid bias and how to make assessment appropriate to special student populations.

3.4 Understand what makes assessment practical and efficient and why this is an important consideration in determining how to measure student outcomes.

Introductory Case Study

Which Assessment Should Keona Use?

After nine snow days during her unit on cells, Keona, a sixth-grade life science teacher, was frustrated. Her learning targets surrounded students acquiring knowledge of cellular parts and a simple understanding of their functions, but the snow days limited her teaching time. Keona had been lucky her students had completed their interactive notes on cell parts, watched a Discovery video on cell parts' functions, completed a matching-sort of parts to definitions, looked at cells under a microscope, and made paper diagrams of both types of cells. While Keona had plans for an interactive WebQuest and making 3-D plant and animal cells out of shoe boxes and Jell-O, there simply was no time.

With the snow, there were only two days left in the unit and having students use technology to make cell diagrams was important. It would allow Keona to assess her students' learning. So tomorrow students would have a choice: Students would pick whether to use the iPad drawing app or the computer program Pixi to make a cell diagram. No matter which option was chosen, students had to label, define, and provide a sentence about each part's cellular function. Since the project would take two days, the downfall to having such little time left in the unit was that students would be able to complete only a diagram of an animal cell.

Since every non-snow day, Keona had focused on teaching and she now had no assessments to demonstrate students' learning about cells. She had formatively assessed her students' learning through her questions and their work in class, but Keona lacked graded quizzes or projects. She knew the value of grades since they provided a way of communicating with students and their parents about a student's progress in mastering concepts, so she wanted to be sure to have at least two grades: One regarding students' learning on plant cells and the other on animal cells. The animal cells grade could come from the diagram students were completing, but she didn't know what to do about assessing students' learning on plant cells.

Keona decided she could (a) give a quiz that had students demonstrate their learning about plant cells by matching definitions, labeling cell parts, and completing multiple-choice items regarding functions, or (b) give an at-home project with a grading rubric that required students to build a model of a plant cell with parts labeled, defined, and functions explained. She was torn since both assessments aligned with her format of in-class learning activities and state standards of students knowing cellular parts and their functions.

As you read this chapter, think about which assessment Keona should use. What should be Keona's overall concern when deciding between the assessments? Should she give the quiz or project? What should Keona's specific criteria be for making her decision, and using the criteria, in what ways is each assessment strong and weak?

C lassroom assessment consists of determining purpose and learning targets related to standards, systematically obtaining information from students, interpreting the information collected, and using the information. In Chapter 2, establishing learning targets was identified as the first step in conducting assessments. Once you have determined *what* to assess, you will need to think about *how* to assess it. That is, what methods of data collection will you use to gather the information? At this point it is important to keep in mind several criteria that determine the quality and credibility of the assessment methods you choose. In this chapter, we review these criteria and provide suggestions for practical steps you can take to keep the quality of your assessments high. High quality is of paramount importance! Weak assessments are dismissed by students, lead to inaccurate conclusions about student proficiency, and are not helpful in designing more effective instruction.

What Is High-Quality Classroom Assessment?

Traditionally, the quality of large-scale and standardized tests has been determined by the extent to which specific psychometric standards, such as validity, reliability/precision, and fairness, were met, using highly technical, statistically sophisticated procedures. For most classroom assessments these complex technical qualities have little relevance. This is not to say that the *ideas* of validity, reliability/precision and fairness are not important for classroom assessment. High-quality classroom assessment involves many other criteria as well, substituting statistically substituted evidence of validity and reliability/precision with concerns about how the assessments influence learning and provide fair and credible reporting of student achievement. For you, a key determinant of quality is how the information influences students. Thus, the focus is on the *use* and *consequences of the results* and what the assessments get students to do.

High-quality classroom assessments, then, provide results that verify and promote targeted student learning and motivation. High-quality classroom assessments also inform instructional decision making. As pointed out in Chapter 1, our understanding of learning and motivation, our realization that much more is demanded of students than demonstrating simple knowledge, and the

FIGURE 3.1　**Criteria for Ensuring High-Quality Classroom Assessments**

- Clear and appropriate learning targets
- Alignment of assessment methods and learning targets
- Validity
- Reliability/precision
- Fairness
- Positive consequences
- Alignment
- Practicality and efficiency

introduction of 21st-century knowledge, skills, and dispositions has changed how we define high-quality classroom assessments. My experience suggests that there are eight criteria of high-quality classroom assessment (Figure 3.1). They are all important and can be addressed for each assessment that is planned and implemented.

Clear and Appropriate Learning Targets

As discussed in Chapters 1 and 2, sound assessment begins with clear and appropriate learning targets. Are the targets at the right level of difficulty to motivate students? Is there adequate balance among different types of targets? Are the targets consistent with your overall goals and the goals of the school and district? Are the targets comprehensive, covering all major dimensions that you hope to change and need feedback about? Are the criteria for judging student performance clear? Answers to these questions help ensure high-quality assessment. Clear targets mean that both students and teachers understand the nature of learning that is expected, and what student proficiencies will result. Appropriate targets are those that are reasonable and aligned with student characteristics, instruction, and standards.

Alignment of Assessment Methods and Learning Targets

As you are well aware, a number of different types of assessment methods can be used in the classroom. Although your ultimate choice of an assessment method will depend on how well all the criteria in Figure 3.1 are met, the match between type of target and method is very important. Even though most targets may be measured by several methods, the reality of teaching is that certain methods measure some types of targets better than other methods do. Thus, once you have identified the targets, one of next steps is to match them with methods. That is, which method of assessment best matches the nature of the learning target?

Types of Assessment Methods

I have categorized different types of assessments in Figure 3.2 according to the nature and characteristics of each method. A brief description of the methods is presented here to facilitate an understanding of how the methods should be matched to targets. They are covered in much more detail in later chapters.

Figure 3.2 divides different methods of assessment into four major categories: selected-response, constructed-response, teacher observation, and student self-assessment. The major distinguishing characteristic of most classroom assessments is whether the items use selected-response or constructed-response formats. In the **selected-response** format students are presented with a question that has two or more possible responses. Students then select an answer from the possible choices. Common selected-response items include multiple-choice, true/false, and matching. These kinds of items may also be called *objective*, referring to the way the answers are scored without judgment. A single correct or best answer is identified for each item, and scoring is simply a matter of checking to determine whether the choice was correct.

A **constructed-response** format requires students to create or produce their own answer in response to a question or task. Brief constructed-response items are those in which students provide a very short, clearly delineated answer, such as filling in a blank at the end of a sentence, writing a few words or a sentence or two, or answering a mathematics problem by showing how they arrived at the answer. Although many constructed-response assessments require considerable subjectivity in judging an answer, brief constructed-response items are objectively scored in one sense because there is typically a single correct answer that is easily identified.

Performance (or performance-based) assessments require students to construct a more extensive and elaborate answer or response. A well-defined task is identified, and students are asked to create, produce, or do something, often in settings that involve real-world application of knowledge and skills. Proficiency is demonstrated by providing an extended response. Performance formats are further differentiated into products and performances. The assessment may result in a product, such as a painting, portfolio, paper, or exhibition, or it may consist of a performance, such as a speech, athletic skill, musical recital, or reading.

Essay items allow students to construct a response that would be several sentences (restricted-response) to many paragraphs or pages in length (extended-response). Restricted-response essay items include limits to the content and nature of the answer, whereas extended-response items allow greater freedom in response.

Oral questioning is used continuously in an informal way during instruction to monitor student understanding. In a more formalized format, oral questions can be used as a way to test or as a way to determine student understanding through interviews or conferences.

Teacher observations, like oral questions, are so common that we often don't think of them as a form of student assessment. But teachers constantly observe

FIGURE 3.2 Classification of Assessment Methods

Selected-Response	Constructed-Response			Teacher Observation	Student Self-Assessment
	Brief Constructed-Response Items	*Performance Tasks*	*Essay Items*	*Formal*	*Self-Report Inventories*
• Multiple-choice	• Short answer	*Products*	*Skills*	• Informal	• Attitude survey
• Binary-choice (e.g., true/false)	• Completion	• Paper	• Speech		• Sociometric devices
• Matching	• Label a diagram	• Project	• Demonstration	*Oral Questioning*	• Questionnaires
• Interpretive	• "Show your work"	• Poem	• Dramatic reading	• Informal questioning	• Inventories
• Technology enhanced		• Portfolio	• Debate	• Examinations	
		• Video/ audiotape	• Recital	• Conferences	*Self-Evaluation*
		• Spreadsheet	• Enactment	• Interviews	• Ratings
		• Web page	• Athletics		• Portfolios
		• Exhibition	• Keyboarding		• Conferences
		• Reflection	• Dance	*Essay Items*	• Self-reflection
		• Journal	• Readings	• Restricted-response	• Evaluate others' performances
		• Graph		• Extended-response	
		• Table			
		• Illustration			

75

students informally to assess student understanding and progress (formative assessment). Teachers watch students as they respond to questions and study, and teachers listen to students as they speak and discuss with others. Often nonverbal communication, such as squinting, inattention, looks of frustration, and other cues, is more helpful than verbal feedback. Observation is used extensively as well in performance assessments, and other formal observational techniques are used to assess classroom climate, teacher effectiveness, and other dimensions of the classroom.

Student self-assessment refers to students' reporting on or evaluating themselves. In *self-evaluation of academic achievement*, students rate their own performance in relation to established standards and criteria. In *self-report inventories*, students are asked to complete a form or answer questions that reveal their attitudes and beliefs about themselves or other students. A related type of assessment occurs when peers rate or evaluate each others' demonstrations of learning. Peer-assessment can be effective but is fraught with difficulties.

Matching Targets with Methods

Figure 3.3 presents the Matching Targets with Methods Scorecard. This figure summarizes the relative strengths of different methods for measuring different targets. Notice that the same types of targets can be assessed very well by several methods. This is good for providing more flexibility in the assessments you use (it's always good to use a variety of assessments), but it also means there is no simple formula or one correct method.

FIGURE 3.3 Matching Targets with Methods Scorecard

Targets	Assessment Methods					
	Selected-Response and Brief Constructed-Response	Essay	Performance	Question	Oral Observation	Student Self-Assessment
Knowledge and Simple Understanding	5	4	2	4	3	3
Reasoning and Deep Understanding	2	5	4	3	2	3
Skills	1	3	5	2	5	3
Products	1	1	5	2	4	4
Affect/Dispositions	1	2	4	4	4	5

Note: Higher numbers indicate better matches (e.g., 5 = excellent, 1 = poor).

The scorecard gives you *general* guidelines about how well particular assessment methods measure each type of target. The numbers (1 = poor, 5 = excellent) represent the relative strength of the method to provide a high-quality assessment for specific targets. Variations to what is presented in the figure should be expected. For example, good selected-response items *can* provide a high-quality measure of reasoning, but such items are difficult and time consuming to prepare. What I have considered in assigning the numbers are both technical strengths and practical limitations. When each method is described in greater detail in later chapters, the variations will become more obvious. For now, however, the scorecard will give you a good overview and provide some preliminary information to use in selecting methods that are appropriate.

Knowledge and Simple Understanding.   Well-constructed selected-response and brief constructed-response items do a good job of assessing subject matter and procedural knowledge, and simple understanding, particularly when students must recognize or remember isolated facts, definitions, spellings, concepts, and principles. The questions can be answered and scored quickly, so it is efficient. These formats also allow you to adequately sample from a large amount of knowledge. Asking students questions orally about what they know is also an effective way to assess knowledge, but this takes much more time, and the results are difficult to record. It also takes advance planning to prepare the questions and a method to record student responses. Thus, assessment by oral questioning is best in situations in which you are checking for mastery or understanding of a limited number of important facts or when you are doing informal diagnostic assessment. This is usually done during instruction as formative assessment to provide feedback about student progress.

Essays can be used effectively to assess knowledge and understanding when your objective is for students to learn large chunks or structures of knowledge that are related.

Using performance assessments presents some difficulties for determining what students know. Because performance assessments are time intensive for teachers and students, they are usually not the best choice for assessing vast amounts of knowledge. Much of the preparation for the performance often takes place out of class, and the final paper or product typically does not provide opportunities for demonstrating that the student has mastered specific facts.

Reasoning and Deep Understanding.   Reasoning and deep understanding skills are best assessed in essays and performance assessments. Essays can focus directly on specific reasoning skills by asking students to compare, evaluate, critique, provide justification for, organize, integrate, defend, and solve problems. Time is provided to allow students to use reasoning before answering the question. When oral questions require deep understanding and reasoning for an answer, they are excellent, though inefficient, for systematic assessment of all students at the end of a unit.

Performance assessments are also effective in measuring reasoning skills and deep understanding. For example, by observing students demonstrate how to go about planning a budget for a family of four, you can draw inferences about how the student used all the information provided and balanced different priorities. Science projects illustrate the ability to interpret results and make conclusions.

Selected-response and brief constructed-response questions *can* be a good method for assessing certain aspects of deep understanding and reasoning. When the item demands more than simply recalling or recognizing a fact, reasoning may be needed. For example, if an item requires the student to interpret a chart, analyze a poem, or apply knowledge to solve a problem, thinking skills can be measured.

Student self-evaluations of the reasoning they used in answering a question or solving a problem can help you diagnose learning difficulties. Students can be given sample-graded answers and then asked to compare these to their responses. Students can also be involved in scoring teams to provide peer-based evaluations of answers.

Skills.   Performance assessments are clearly the preferred method to determine systematically whether a student has mastered a skill. Whether the student is demonstrating how to shoot a basketball, give a persuasive speech, sing a song, speak in a foreign language, or use a microscope, the skill is best assessed by observing the student perform the task. On a more informal basis, teachers use observation extensively to assess progress in demonstrating skills.

Selected-response and brief constructed-response tests and oral questioning can be used to assess student procedural knowledge of the skills, such as knowing the proper sequence of actions or recognizing the important dimensions of the skill. But this represents prerequisite knowledge and is not the same as measuring the extent to which the student can actually *do* it.

As with essays, student self-evaluations can be used to focus students on how well their demonstration of skill meets stated criteria. Student evaluations of others' demonstrations are also useful.

Products.   The best way to assess student products is to have students complete one through a performance assessment (e.g., to write persuasively, write a letter that argues for something; if you want students to be able to act, have them participate in a play).

Like skills, objectively scored items, essay items, and oral questions can be used to determine whether students know the components of the product or to evaluate different products. But there is no substitute for actually creating the product.

Student self-evaluations are very effective with performance assessment because students need to focus on the performance criteria and make judgments about their own performance in relation to the criteria. It is also effective to have students judge one another's performances.

Affect/Dispositions.   Affective and dispositional outcomes are best assessed by either observing students or using student self-reports. The most direct and efficient way to assess affect is to ask the students directly through self-report surveys and questionnaires. Direct oral questioning can be revealing if the right relationship exists between teacher and student and if the atmosphere is conducive to honest sharing of feelings.

Observation can be effective in determining, informally, many dispositional traits (e.g., motivation and attitudes toward subjects and student self-concept are often apparent when the student shows negative feelings through body posture, a reluctance to interact with others, and withdrawal). Some performance assessments provide ample opportunities for teachers to observe affect and dispositions, though like other observations, this is usually nonsystematic, and considerable inference is required.

Validity

What Is a Validity?

Validity, reliability/precision, and fairness are the three criteria that form the pillars of good assessment (Figure 3.4). If you focus on these three, you will be well on your way to high-quality assessment. The first two are especially critical because they address the accuracy and appropriateness of the scores you get from each assessment. I like to think of these two in the context of the *signal* and the *noise*, a metaphor sometimes used to examine the level of precision achieved in

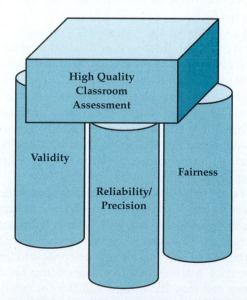

FIGURE 3.4   Three pillars of high-quality classroom assessment

research. The signal is what you want to assess with as much accuracy and clarity as possible. It represents the actual or true nature of what students know and can do. For example, when you want to know if students are able to add three-digit numbers with carryover, you want the score on the test to show the actual or real competence of the student, not something else. *Noise* gets in the way of accuracy, and this is where validity and reliability/precision come in. If your test items use three-digit number problems without carryover, the result will not be accurate (this is a validity problem). If your test items are poorly constructed and confuse students, or if students are ill and can't concentrate, error is introduced (a reliability/precision problem). What you want in high-quality assessment is to get as close as you can to finding the signal. This occurs to the extent that noise is eliminated. For example, if your test of French language comprehension contains words that haven't been studied, that's noise (validity). Likewise, if the audio message is filled with static and hard to hear, that's also noise (reliability/precision). Both sources of noise would mean that the actual test scores would not very accurately represent achievement of the target, the signal, which in this case is French vocabulary recognition. So, my admonition is to always remember the signal and the noise. It will help you immensely in your quest to have high-quality assessment. Now we'll turn to validity in more detail, then reliability/precision and fairness.

Validity is a characteristic that refers to the appropriateness of the inferences, uses, and consequences that result from the assessment. It is concerned with the soundness, trustworthiness, or legitimacy of the claims or inferences that are made on the basis of obtained scores. In other words, is the interpretation made from the scores or ratings reasonable? Is the information gathered the right kind of evidence for the decision that needs to be made, or the intended use? How sound is the interpretation of the information?

Validity has to do with the quality of the inferences you make from the scores, not just the test itself. That is, it is an inference or use that is valid or invalid, not the test, instrument, or procedure that is used to gather information. Often the phrase "validity of the test" is used, but it is more accurate to say "the validity of the interpretation, inference, or use of the results." For instance, it is common to use test scores to determine proficiency (e.g. rating students as needs improvement, proficient, advanced). When these labels are used, validity is a judgment about whether the designations are accurate. That is, is a student labeled "proficient" really proficient? When the interpretations are accurate, *with little noise*, you'll have good validity and get a *clear signal*.

You probably have or will come across a somewhat different definition of validity, something like "the extent to which a test measures what it is supposed to measure." Although this notion is important to many decisions and uses, it suggests that validity is a characteristic that the test or instrument always possesses. In reality, the same test or instrument can be valid for one purpose and invalid for another. Actually, validity is always a matter of degree, depending on the situation. For example, a social science test may have high validity for inferring that students know the sequence of events leading up to the American Revolution, less validity for inferring that students can reason, even less validity for inferring that students can communicate effectively in writing, and virtually no validity for indicating a student's mathematical ability. An assessment is not simply valid or invalid; it is valid to some degree in reference to specific inferences, uses, or consequences.

For classroom assessments one of the important consequences to consider for validity is the impact of the assessment on student learning (Bonner, 2013). That is, you need to think about whether the assessment is reasonable in its effect on student motivation and learning within the context in which you are teaching. In this sense, validity is what has meaning and value within your specific situation. Because it is a local issue, then, you need to consider the unique perspectives of students, parents, and other stakeholders.

How Is Validity Determined?

Validity is determined primarily by professional judgment. For classroom assessment, this judgment is often made by the teacher, though increasingly assessments that have purportedly been "vetted" are provided. (I say "purportedly" because you need to be your own best judge—I've seen many poor supposedly "vetted" tests and test items.) An analysis is done by accumulating evidence that would suggest that an inference or use is appropriate and whether the consequences of the interpretations and uses are reasonable and fair. That is, close to the signal!

The process of determining validity is illustrated in Figure 3.5. We will consider how classroom teachers can use three types of evidence to make an overall judgment about the degree of validity of the assessment (see Table 3.1).

Content-Related Evidence. One feature of teaching that has important implications for assessment is that often a teacher is unable to assess everything that is taught or every objective or target. Suppose you wanted to test for everything sixth-grade students learn in a 4-week unit about insects. Can you imagine how

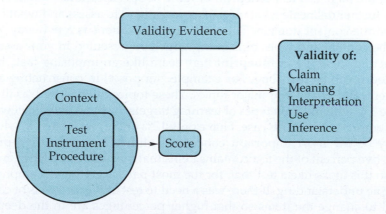

FIGURE 3.5 Determining Validity

TABLE 3.1   Sources of Evidence for Classroom Assessment Validity

Content-Related Evidence	The extent to which the assessment is representative of the domain of interest
Criterion-Related Evidence	The relationship between an assessment and another measure of the same trait
Consequential Evidence	The extent to which the assessment leads to reasonable expected and unexpected outcomes

long the test would be and how much time students would take to complete the test? What is done in these situations is to select a *sample* of what has been taught to assess, and then use student achievement on this sample to make inferences about knowledge of the entire domain of content. That is, if a student correctly answers 85% of the items on your test of a sample of the unit on insects, then you infer that the student knows 85% of the content in the entire unit. If your sample is judged to be representative of the larger domain, then you have **content-related evidence** for validity (or *evidence based on test content*). The inference from the test is that the student demonstrates knowledge about the unit.

Adequate sampling of content is determined by professional judgment. This judgment process can range, from being rather haphazard or casual, to very systematic. In a superficial review of the target, objectives, and test, validity is based only on *appearance*. This is sometimes referred to as face validity. *Face validity* is whether, based on a superficial examination of the test, there seems to be a reasonable measure of the objectives and domain. Does the test, on the face of it, look like an adequate measure? Although it is important to avoid face *in*validity, it is much better if the evidence is more structured and systematic.

Once the complete domain of content and targets is specified, the items on the test can be reviewed to be certain that there is a match between the intended inferences and what is on the test. This process begins with clear learning targets. Based on the targets, a **test blueprint** or **table of specifications** is sometimes prepared to further delineate what objectives you intend to assess and what is important from the content domain. The table of specifications is a two-way grid that shows the content and types of learning targets represented in your assessment. Constructing this type of **blueprint** may seem like an imposing task, but once completed it can be revealing. For example, suppose I'm constructing a test on assessment, and I have four major topics. These topics can be listed, as illustrated in Figure 3.6, with different types of learning targets to get an overall view of what is being emphasized. In this case, I have only 12% of the test related to what could arguably be the most important concepts, validity and reliability/precision. Seventy-five percent of the test contains items that measure knowledge and application, so this looks like a test that, for the most part, is getting at comprehension and simple understanding. If there was a need to test at higher levels of cognition, I'd need to change the items so that higher percentages are in the deep understanding and evaluate categories.

FIGURE 3.6   Table of Specifications for a Test on Assessment Showing Number and Percentage of Items

Major Content Areas	Types of Learning Targets				
	Knowledge	*Application*	*Deep Understanding*	*Evaluate*	*Totals*
Validity	4/(12%)	2/(6%)	2/(6%)	0	8/(24%)
Reliability/precision	2/(6%)	1/(3%)	1/(3%)	0	4/(12%)
Fairness	6/(18%)	2/(6%)	2/(6%)	2/(6%)	12/(35%)
Practicality	2/(6%)	6/(18%)	2/(6%)	0	10/(29%)
Totals	14/(41%)	11/(32%)	7/(21%)	2/(6%)	34/(100%)

I want to emphasize that the goal of a blueprint is to systematize your professional judgment so that you can improve the validity of the assessment. As illustrated in Table 3.2, your judgment is used to determine what types of learning targets will be assessed, what areas of the content will be sampled, and how the assessment measures both content and type of learning. At this point, you are making decisions about the importance of different types of targets, the content assessed, and how much of the assessment is measuring each target and area of content. If the assessment does, in fact, reflect an actual or modified table of specifications, then there is good content-related evidence of validity.

You will also want to align your assessments with state standards. This can be done by simply listing standards that are addressed by the targets, or by making a table of specifications with standards on one dimension and targets on the other. You can use superscripts to indicate within the table the level of learning (e.g., knowledge or deep understanding).

Another consideration related to this type of evidence is the extent to which an assessment can be said to have *instructional* validity. **Instructional validity** is concerned with the match between what is taught and what is assessed. How closely does the test correspond to what has been covered in class and in assignments? Have students had the opportunity to learn what has been assessed?

TABLE 3.2   Professional Judgments in Establishing Content-Related Evidence for Validity

Learning Targets	Content	Instruction	Assessment
What learning targets will be assessed? How much of the assessment will be done on each target area?	What content is most important? What topics will be assessed? How much of the assessment will be done in each topic?	What content and learning targets have been emphasized in instruction?	Are assessments adequate samples of students' performance in each topic area and each target?

Again, *your* professional judgment is needed to ensure that what is assessed is consistent with what was taught. One way to check this is to examine the table of specifications after teaching a unit to determine whether the emphasis in different areas or on different targets is consistent with what was emphasized in class.

Criterion-Related Evidence.   Another way to ensure appropriate inferences from assessments is to have evidence that a particular assessment is providing the same result as another assessment of the same thing. **Criterion-related evidence** (or evidence based on relations with other variables) provides such validity by relating an assessment to some other valued measure (criterion) that either provides an estimate of current performance (concurrent criterion-related evidence) or predicts future performance (predictive criterion-related evidence). Test developers and researchers use this approach to establish evidence that a test or other instrument is measuring the same trait, knowledge, or attitude by calculating a correlation coefficient to measure the relationship between the assessment and the criterion (see Appendix A for a discussion of correlation).

Classroom teachers rarely conduct formal studies to obtain correlation coefficients that will provide evidence of validity, but the *principle* is very important for teachers to employ. When you have two or more measures of the same thing, and these measures provide similar results, then you have established, albeit informally, criterion-related evidence. For example, if your assessment of a student's skill in using a microscope through observation coincides with the student's score on a quiz that tests steps in using microscopes, then you have criterion-related evidence that your inference about the skill of this student is valid. Similarly, if you are interested in the extent to which preparation by your students, as indicated by scores on a final exam in mathematics, predicts how well they will do next year, you can examine the grades of previous students and determine informally if students who scored high on your final exam are getting high grades and students who scored low on your final are obtaining low grades. If a relationship is found, then an inference about predicting how your students will perform, based on their final exam, is valid. Based on this logic, an important principle for obtaining high-quality assessment is to conduct several assessments of the learning targets; try not to rely on a single assessment.

Figure 3.7 shows how different assessments suggest consistency of evaluations for each of the students.

FIGURE 3.7   Criterion-Related Evidence for the Validity of Classroom Assessments

Source of Evidence	Jack	Jim	Jon
Teacher observation	A–	C+	B+
Quiz	90%	77%	84%
Student self-assessment	Advanced	Proficient	Proficient
Overall Grade	A–	C	B

An excellent illustration of the need to give a variety of assessments is voiced in the following Teacher's Corner. Note how Carole uses different methods of instruction. She also matches targets with methods of assessment and stresses the importance of using a variety of assessment tools.

Consequential Evidence.   Evidence based on the consequences of giving an assessment and providing feedback to students is critical because it lies at the heart of the purpose of education—to enhance student motivation and learning. Consequences consist of both intended and unintended effects on students, teachers, and instruction. Consider the effect of using multiple-choice tests on how students study and learn. To the extent that the questions get at surface knowledge, students will tend to memorize facts and figures and will not engage in deep understanding. Also, what is the consequence of using this type of assessment for providing students with feedback about their level of knowledge? Teachers often indicate right and wrong answers without much further feedback. In contrast, more extensive and individualized comments can be made on student answers to open-ended questions.

Consequences for student motivation and effort are also very important. When you administer assessments that challenge students, you are more likely to engage them. Your assessments should not be too difficult or too easy. They need to elicit mistakes and errors in understanding to promote motivation for further learning. When assessments are designed to encourage student engagement, their efforts are more likely to enhance their self-efficacy, their belief that they are capable of learning.

When assessment results are valid, the findings are meaningful with respect to the next instructional steps. Invalid assessment leads to bad decisions about

Teacher's Corner

Carole Forkey

National Board Certified High School Biology Teacher

I believe that the essential elements that would make an assessment high quality are varied and need to include 21st-century learning skills of all students. In designing assessment questions, I will ask myself, "Will learning be achieved?" I use a combination of questions in my assessments including knowledge-, comprehension-, application-, and synthesis-level questions. In addition, it is important to note that not all assessments need to be a traditional test or quiz. To increase student achievement using 21st-century skills, assessments should incorporate the use of a variety of skills such as critical thinking, creativity, communication, and collaboration. These skills can be achieved through project-based learning, laboratory activities, as well as a variety of other assessment tools.

FIGURE 3.8　**Checklist for Enhancing Classroom Assessment Validity**

✓ Ask others to judge the clarity of what you are assessing.
✓ Check to see if different ways of assessing the same thing give the same result.
✓ Sample a sufficient number of examples of what is being assessed.
✓ Prepare a detailed table of specifications.
✓ Ask others to judge the match between the assessment items and the objective of the assessment.
✓ Compare groups known to differ on what is being assessed.
✓ Compare scores taken before to those taken after instruction.
✓ Use different methods to assess the same thing.
✓ Use *only* for intended purposes.

what students need. For example, a test of history that does not sample all areas adequately leaves the teacher with an incomplete picture of student learning, with accompanying insufficient knowledge whether additional instruction in specific areas is needed.

How will the assessments impact attainment of 21st-century dispositions? Will student responsibility and perseverance be enhanced? Will students learn that mistakes, errors, and obstacles are part of learning and should be embraced rather than avoided? Will the assessment affect whether students develop a positive attitude toward what they are learning? What is the effect of the nature of the assessments on how you teach? If you give mostly objective tests, are you more likely to stress recall and recognition levels of knowledge? If you give essay tests, are you more likely to stress deep understanding and reasoning?

The consequences of classroom assessments are many and varied, and you can't consider them all each time you assess your students. They are so important that more consideration of consequences is summarized later in this chapter. But you can keep consequences in mind, and you can conceptualize validity in part in terms of the effects of what you do on students, yourself, and instruction. I hope you will!

The checklist in Figure 3.8 summarizes what you can do to enhance the validity of your assessments.

Reliability/Precision

What Is a Reliable/Precise Score?

Like validity, the term *reliability* has been used for many years to describe an essential characteristic of sound assessment. For classroom assessments, what is now called **reliability/precision** is concerned with the extent to which the scores are free from error (noise). Suppose Mrs. Calder is assessing her students' addition and subtraction skills. She decides to give the students a 20-point quiz to determine their skills. Mrs. Calder examines the results but wants to be sure about the level of performance before designing appropriate instruction, so she gives another quiz 2 days later on the same addition and subtraction skills. The results for some of her students are as follows:

Student	Addition		Subtraction	
	Quiz 1	Quiz 2	Quiz 1	Quiz 2
Rob	18	16	13	20
Carrie	10	12	18	10
Ryann	9	8	8	14
Felix	16	15	17	12

The addition quiz scores are fairly consistent (consistency is often used as a descriptor for reliability/precision). All four students scored within one or two points on the quizzes; students who scored high on the first quiz also scored high on the second quiz, and students who scored low did so on both quizzes. Consequently, the results for addition are reliable. For subtraction, on the other hand, there is considerable change in performance from the first to the second quiz. Students scoring high on the first quiz score low on the second one, and students scoring low on the first quiz score high on the second. For subtraction, then, the results are unreliable because they are not consistent. The scores contradict one another.

So, what does Mrs. Calder make of the mathematics scores? Her goal is to use the quiz to accurately determine the defined skill. She cannot know the *exact* level of the skills, but, as in the case of addition, she can get a fairly accurate picture with an assessment that is reliable. For subtraction, on the other hand, she cannot use these results alone to estimate the students' real or actual skill. More assessments are needed before she can be confident that the scores are reliable and thus provide a dependable result. But even the scores in addition are not without some degree of error. In fact, *all* assessments have error; they are never perfect measures of the trait or skill. Let's look at another example to illustrate this point.

Think about the difference between a measure of attitude toward science and time required to run a mile. The measure of attitude will have a relatively high degree of error, but the measure of time will be precise with little error (highly reliable). This is because there are many more influences on how students answer questions about their attitudes (such as the student's mood that day, the heat in the room, poorly worded items, and fatigue) than there are on a timekeeper's ability to press the stopwatch and read the time elapsed. This is not to say that the measure of time is without any error. It's just that measuring time will have much less error than measuring attitudes.

Assessment Error

The concept of error in assessment is critical to our understanding of reliability/precision. Conceptually, whenever we assess something, we get an *observed* score or result. This observed score is a product of what the *true* or *real* knowledge, ability, or skill is (the signal) *plus* some degree of *error* (the noise):

Observed Score = True Score (Signal) + Error (Noise)

Reliability/precision is directly related to error. It is not a matter of all or none, as if some results are reliable and others unreliable. Rather, for each assessment there is some *degree* of error. Thus, we think in terms of low, moderate, or high reliability/precision. It is important to remember that the error can be positive or negative. That is, the observed score can be higher or lower than the true score, depending on the nature of the error. Sometimes you will know when a student's score is lower than it should be based on the behavior of the student at the time of the assessment. For example, if the student was sick, tired, in a bad mood, or distracted, the score may have negative error and underestimate the true score.

Figure 3.9 shows how different sources of error influence assessment results. Notice how reliability/precision is influenced by noise factors within the student (internal sources of error), such as mood and physical condition, as well as

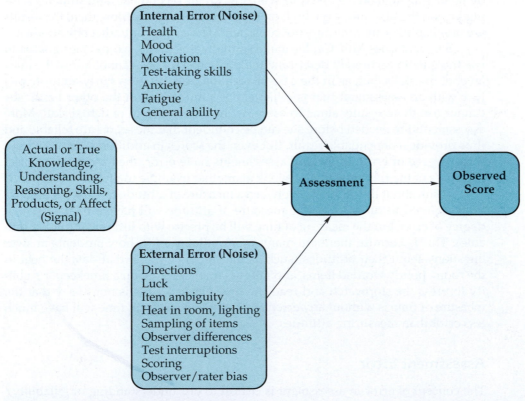

FIGURE 3.9   **Sources of Error in Assessment**

external noise factors, such as the quality of the test, scoring errors, and test directions. The actual or true knowledge, reasoning, skill, or affect, the signal, is captured to some extent by the assessment, but the internal and external sources of error also contribute to the score. In the end, you get an *observed* score that is made up of the actual or true performance plus some degree of error (noise).

An important practical implication of knowing about error in testing is that small differences between scores of different students should be treated as if they were the same. Typically, your interpretation of a score of 75 should be the same as your interpretation of a score of 77. These observed scores are so close that, when we consider error that can be positive or negative, the true scores of the students should be considered equal (e.g., 75, plus or minus 3, or 77, plus or minus 3).

How Is Reliability/Precision Determined for Classroom Assessments?

Reliability/precision in classroom assessment is unique because teachers use results from the assessments to make instructional decisions. Thus, classroom assessment reliability/precision is a combination of measurement error, as previously described, and instructional decision making (Parkes, 2013). While traditional, psychometric ideas of reliability/precision focus on measurement error, in classrooms teachers need to consider the dependability of their decisions about student learning. Thus, reliability/precision for classroom assessment is estimating the influence of various sources of error within the context of decision making about student learning. The primary focus is on the decision.

Generally, if there is little error, decisions are more reliable. Sources of possible error are determined logically and through professional judgment (see Figure 3.8),

Teacher's Corner
Elizabeth O'Brien

National Board Certified Secondary Mathematics Teacher

In determining if classroom assessments are high quality, I take several factors into consideration. First, I work collaboratively with the other teachers in my department who teach the same subjects that I do. By working together, we are able to check one another and offer suggestions and feedback on questions that each of us creates. Second, I look at each of the objectives that I have taught and match questions accordingly. Not only do I make sure that each objective has been assessed, but I also make sure that it has been assessed at several different levels of difficulty. For example, I want to ensure that students not only recall material but also can apply it and even evaluate others' work in some situations. Finally, over time I have determined that some questions are unfair and not suitable based on students' responses.

unlike the statistical estimates of error obtained for large-scale tests. They are considered by observing the consistency with which students answer questions on the same topic. If one subgroup of students always scores well each time a quiz is given that measures the same target, whereas another subgroup always scores low, this consistency is logical evidence of good reliability/precision. That is, when responses to the same types of questions or problems are consistent, the responses tend to be reliable. This occurs when you have two separate measures of the same thing, several similar items in a single test, or two or more observers who agree on their ratings.

How to Improve Classroom Assessment Reliability/Precision

There are a number of factors to keep in mind to enhance the reliability/precision of your classroom assessments. In general, we know from much research that teachers may not always agree about how to answers to extended constructed-response items, performance assessments, or portfolios. (Parkes, 2013). The issue is that well-intentioned, excellent teachers can differ in their professional judgments about student learning, and what is needed is a set of guidelines to reduce this variation to make reliable decisions. The most important factor is to have clear and relatively specific directions for how students should answer questions, guidelines for scoring results, and exemplars of performance at different levels. This often means that teachers have rubrics for scoring constructed-response answers. For objective tests, other things being equal, more items will result in higher reliability/precision.

The number of students taking an assessment also makes a difference—the higher the number of students, the stronger the reliability/precision for making decisions about the group. This is important for making instructional corrections for small groups or the entire class. Difficulty of items also affects reliability/precision. The best reliability/precision is often obtained when items are not too easy or too hard (as I've already emphasized, moderately difficult items are best). Items that are carefully constructed will improve reliability/precision, while poorly worded or unclear items result in greater noise. The more objective the scoring, the greater the reliability/precision. Typically, multiple-choice tests obtain better estimates of reliability/precision than do constructed-response, performance, or portfolio assessments.

Finally, it is *really* important for you to consult with other teachers about your assessments and decisions. A team approach is excellent. Together with others, collaboratively, you can consider various sources of possible noise and examine the evidence that leads to decisions. In a formal sense, you can have others actually rate student performance to provide a direct comparison with your own rating, but that's difficult from a practical standpoint. But you do need verification from others that your assessments do not contain much error and that your decisions are sound.

Figure 3.10 summarizes suggestions for developing and implementing classroom assessments that will produce highly reliable/precise scores. The degree of reliability/precision needed is dependent on the type of decision that will be

FIGURE 3.10 Checklist for Enhancing Classroom Assessment Reliability/Precision

✓ Provide clear guidelines for answering and scoring assessments.
✓ Use a sufficient number of items or tasks. (Other things being equal, scores from longer tests are more reliable.)
✓ Use independent raters or observers who provide similar scores for the same performances.
✓ Construct items and tasks that clearly differentiate students on what is being assessed.
✓ Make sure the assessment procedures and scoring are as clear and objective as possible.
✓ Continue assessment until results are consistent.
✓ Eliminate or reduce the influence of extraneous events or factors to limit the extent of error.
✓ Use shorter assessments more frequently than fewer long assessments.

made on the basis of the results. Higher reliability/precision is needed when the decision has important, lasting consequences for individual students (e.g., placement to receive special education services). When the decision is about groups and is less important, the reliability/precision does not need to be as high (e.g., whether to repeat a part of a unit of instruction).

Fairness

A *fair* assessment is one that provides all students an equal opportunity to demonstrate achievement. This is achieved with transparency about learning expectations, clear criteria for judging student performance, and the absence of bias (Tierney, 2013). All students need a fair opportunity to show us what they have learned. If some students have an advantage over others because of factors unrelated to what is being taught, then the assessment is not fair. Fair assessments are *unbiased* and *nondiscriminatory*, uninfluenced by irrelevant or subjective factors. That is, neither the assessment task nor scoring is differentially affected by race, gender, sexual orientation, ethnic background, handicapping condition, or other factors unrelated to what is being assessed. Fairness is also evident in what students are told about the assessment and whether they have had the opportunity to learn what is being assessed. The following criteria, summarized in Figure 3.11, represent potential influences that determine whether an assessment is fair.

Transparency: Student Knowledge of Learning Targets and Assessments

How often have you taken a test and thought, "Had I only known the teacher was going to test *this* content, I would have studied it!"? A fair assessment is one in which it is clear what will and will not be tested. Your objective is not to fool or

FIGURE 3.11   Key Components of Fairness

- Student knowledge of learning targets and assessments
- Opportunity to learn
- Prerequisite knowledge and skills
- Avoiding student stereotyping
- Avoiding bias in assessment tasks and procedures
- Accommodating special needs students and ESL learners

trick students or to outguess them on the assessment. Rather, you need to be very clear and specific about the learning target—what is to be assessed and how it will be scored. And this is very important: Both the content of the assessment and the scoring criteria should be *transparent*. Being transparent means that students know the content and scoring criteria *before* the assessment is administered, and often before instruction begins. When students know what will be assessed, they know what to study and focus on. By knowing the scoring criteria, students understand much better the qualitative differences the teacher is looking for in student performance. One way to help students understand the assessment is to give them the assessment blueprint, sample questions, and examples of work completed by previous students and graded by the teacher.

When students know the learning targets and scoring criteria in advance, it is likely that they will be more intrinsically motivated and involved to obtain true mastery, rather than mere performance. It helps to establish a *learning goal orientation* for students, in which the focus is on mastering a task, developing new skills, and improving competence and understanding. In contrast, when a *performance goal orientation* is established, in which students perform to get a grade, recognition, or reward, motivation is extrinsic and less intense, and students are not as engaged or involved.

Opportunity to Learn

Opportunity to learn is concerned with sufficiency or quality of the time, resources, and conditions needed by students to demonstrate their achievement. It concerns the adequacy of instructional approaches and materials that are aligned with the assessment. Fair assessments are aligned with instruction that provides adequate time and opportunities for all students to learn. This is more than simply telling students, for example, that a test will cover certain chapters. Ample instructional time and resources are needed so that students are not penalized because of a lack of opportunity.

Prerequisite Knowledge and Skills

It is unfair to assess students on things that require prerequisite knowledge or skills that they do not possess. This means that you need to have a good understanding of the level of knowledge and skills your students bring to an instructional unit.. It also means that you need to examine your assessments carefully to know what prerequisites are required. For example, suppose you want to test math reasoning skills. Your questions are based on short paragraphs that provide needed information. In this situation, math reasoning skills can be demonstrated only if students can read and understand the paragraphs. Thus, reading skills are prerequisites. If students do poorly on the assessment, their performance may have more to do with a lack of reading skills than with math reasoning.

Avoiding Student Stereotyping

Stereotypes are judgments about how groups of people will behave based on characteristics such as gender, race, socioeconomic status, physical appearance, and other characteristics. It is your responsibility to judge each student on his or her performance on assessment tasks, not on how others who share characteristics of the student perform. Although you should not exclude personal feelings and intuitions about a student, it is important to separate these feelings from performance. It is difficult to avoid stereotypes completely because of our values, beliefs, preferences, unconscious biases, and experiences with different kinds of people. However, we *can* control the influence of these prejudices.

Stereotypes can be based on groups of people, such as "jocks have less motivation to do well," "boys do better in math," "students from a particular neighborhood are more likely to be discipline problems," and "children with a single parent need extra help with homework." You can also label students with words such as *shy, gifted, smart,poor, learning disabled, leader,* and *at-risk.* These labels can affect your interactions and evaluations by establishing inappropriate expectations. The nature of teacher expectations is discussed in greater detail in the next chapter.

Avoiding Bias in Assessment Tasks and Procedures

Another source of bias can be found in the nature of the actual assessment task—the contents and process of the test, project, problem, or other task. Bias is present if the assessment distorts performance because of the student's ethnicity, gender, race, religious background, or cultural background. Popham (2017) has identified two major forms of assessment bias: offensiveness and unfair penalization.

Offensiveness occurs if the content of the assessment offends, upsets, distresses, angers, or otherwise creates negative affect for particular students or a subgroup of students. This negative affect makes it less likely that the students will perform as well as they otherwise might, lowering the validity of the inferences. Offensiveness occurs most often when stereotypes of particular groups are present in the assessment. Suppose a test question portrays a minority group in low-paying, low-status jobs and white groups in high-paying, high-status jobs.

Students who are members of the minority group may understandably be offended by the question, mitigating their performance. Here is an example of a biased mathematics test question that may result in offensiveness:

> Juan Mendez gathers lettuce for his income. He receives 15 cents for every head of lettuce he picks. Juan picked 270 heads of lettuce on Tuesday. How much money did he make?

Unfair penalization is bias that disadvantages a student because of content that makes it more difficult for students from some groups to perform as compared to students from other groups because of gender, socioeconomic status, race, language, or other characteristic. Suppose you take an aptitude test that uses rural, farm-oriented examples. The questions deal with types of cows and pigs, winter wheat, and farm equipment. If you grew up in a suburban community, do you think you will score as well as students who grew up on a farm? Do test items containing sports content unfairly advantage boys? Here is a reading comprehension test question that is biased with unfair penalization:

> Write a persuasive essay about the advantages of sailing as recreation. Include in your essay comparisons of sailing with other types of recreation such as hiking, swimming, and bowling.

Teachers don't *deliberately* produce biased assessments. It is most often unconscious and unintended. For these reasons, bias can be minimized by having others review your assessments, looking specifically for the types of bias presented here and, of course, by your own sensitivity to bias when creating the assessments. Keep in mind that assessment tasks are not necessarily biased solely on the basis of differential performance by separate groups (e.g., Latinos compared to Caucasian).

Cultural differences that are reflected in vocabulary, prior experiences, skills, and values may influence the assessment. These differences are especially important in our increasingly diverse society and classrooms. Consider the following examples of how cultural background influences assessment:

- Knowledge from the immediate environment of the student (e.g., large city, ethnic neighborhood, rural, coastal) provides a vocabulary and an indication of the importance or relevance of assessment tasks.
- Depending on the culture, rules for sharing beliefs, discussion, taking turns, and expressing opinions differ.
- Respect and politeness may be expressed differently by students from different backgrounds (e.g., not looking into another's eyes, silence, squinting as a way to say no, looking up or down when asked a question).
- Learning style differences—which are exhibited in preferences for learning alone or in a group, for learning by listening or reading, for reflective or impulsive responses, and in the ability to think analytically or

globally—influence a student's confidence and motivation to complete assessment tasks.

The influence of these differences will be minimized to the extent that you first understand them and then utilize multiple assessments that will allow all students to demonstrate their progress toward the learning target. If an assessment technique or approach advantages one type of student, another technique may be a disadvantage to that type of student. By using different types of assessments, one provides a balance to the other. Students who are unable to respond well to one type of assessment will respond well to another type. This reinforces the admonition that you should *never rely solely on one method of assessment*. This does not mean, however, that you should arbitrarily pick different methods. You need to select your assessments on the basis of what will provide the fairest indication of student achievement for *all* your students. More about culturally different children, with implications for assessment, is presented in Chapter 14.

Accommodating Special Needs and English Language Learners

Another type of assessment task bias that has received a lot of attention recently is the need to accommodate the special abilities of exceptional children. An assessment is biased if performance is affected by a disability or other limiting characteristic when the student actually possesses the knowledge or skill being measured. In other words, when assessing exceptional students, you need to modify the assessment task so that the disabling trait is not a factor in the performance. For example, students with hearing loss may need written directions to complete an assessment that you give orally to other students.

With the increasing number of students with different languages teachers need to be aware of how these ESL (English as a second language) students (English language learners [ELL]) may make it difficult to obtain fair assessments. Teachers should consult with appropriate ELL specialists to ensure fair assessment. More about special needs and ELL students is presented in Chapters 13 and 14.

A Model of Fairness in Classroom Assessment

In Figure 3.12, a model of fairness in classroom assessment is illustrated (McMillan & Tierney, 2009). The model captures important aspects of fairness, organized by the sequence of steps teachers take in their instruction and assessment. At each step, there are factors teachers should consider, given the context and teacher understanding of fairness. Note the importance of confidentiality. This issue has become more important in recent years.

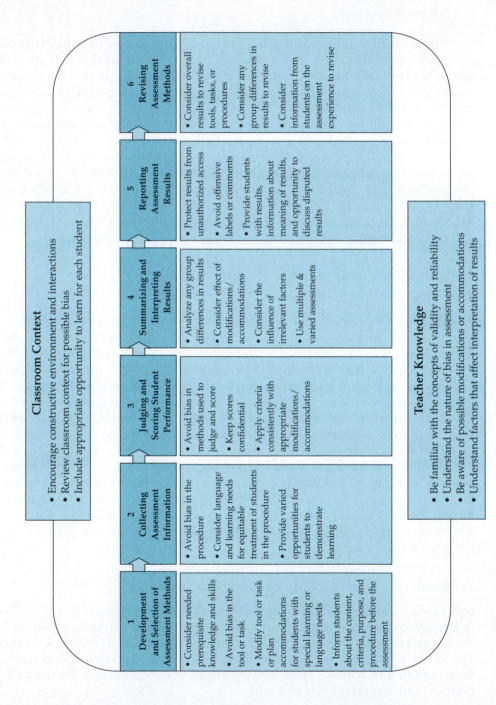

FIGURE 3.12 Model of Fairness in Classroom Assessment

Positive Consequences

High-quality assessments have positive consequences for yourself, instruction, and your students. Here we'll consider in more detail how your classroom assessment consequences will be beneficial.

Positive Consequences for Students

As I have emphasized, the most direct consequence of assessment is that students will learn and study in a way that is consistent with your assessment task. If the assessment is a multiple-choice test to determine the students' knowledge of specific facts, then students will tend to memorize information. If the assessment calls for extended essays, students tend to learn the material in larger, related chunks, and they practice recall rather than recognition when studying. Assessments that require problem solving, such as performance-based assessments, encourage students to think and apply what they learn. A positive consequence, in this sense, is the appropriate match between the learning target and the assessment task.

Assessments also have clear consequences for student motivation (McMillan & Hearn, 2008). Student motivation is best conceptualized in the context of student learning as a "process whereby goal-directed activity is instigated and sustained" (Schunk, Meece, & Pintrich, 2014, p. 5). Defined in this way, motivation involves three key elements: goals, making a commitment to put forth effort to learn, and putting forth continued effort to succeed. Students are motivated when they believe that their effort will result in meaningful success. In relation to assessment, think about how these factors are influenced. Does the nature of learning targets determine whether success is meaningful? (yes!) Do the types of test items influence student effort in studying and trying to learn? (yes!) Does teacher feedback to students affect their conceptions of whether they can succeed? (yes!) Does the structure of the assessment determine whether students are able to show their best performance? (yes!) Table 3.3 shows the positive and negative effects of classroom assessment practices on motivation. Obviously we want positive motivational consequences. It is clear that the nature of the assessments affects this motivation. If students know what will be assessed and how it will be scored, and if they believe that the assessment will be fair, they are likely to be more motivated to learn.

Motivation also increases when the assessment tasks are relevant to the students' backgrounds and goals, challenging but possible, and structured to give students individualized feedback about their performance. What good is a high score on an easy test? Authentic assessments provide more active learning, which increases motivation. Giving students multiple assessments, rather than a single assessment, lessens fear and anxiety. When students are less apprehensive, risk taking, exploration, creativity, and questioning are enhanced.

TABLE 3.3   **Motivational Consequences That Result from Different Assessment Practices**

Motivation *Decreased* by Assessments That:	Motivation *Increased* by Assessments That:
Are irrelevant to students' lives	Are relevant to students' lives
Are summative	Are designed around student interests
Are closed-ended	Are open-ended
Use feedback to manage students	Use immediate and specific feedback
Disclose or display student performance publicly	Are aligned with learning goals set by students
Emphasize quantity rather than quality	Show how mistakes are essential to learning
Compare students to one another	Use learning goals that incorporate specific performance standards
Are artificial and abstract	Are meaningful and authentic
Use tasks at which only some students can be successful	Use tasks that are challenging but attainable
Use long-term goals	Use short-term goals
Provide little and/or inaccurate attributional feedback (why they succeeded or failed)	Provide credible attributional feedback
Emphasize end products	Emphasize progress
	Include student self-assessment

Finally, the student–teacher relationship is influenced by the nature of assessment. When teachers construct assessments carefully and provide the right kind of feedback to students, the relationship is strengthened. Conversely, if students have the impression that the assessment is sloppy, not matched with course objectives, designed to trick them (like some true/false questions we have all answered!), and provides little feedback, the relationship is weakened. How quickly do you return papers or tests to students? What types of comments do you write on papers or projects? Assessment affects the way students perceive the teacher and gives them an indication of how much the teacher cares about them and what they learn.

Positive Consequences for Teachers and Instruction

Like students, teachers are affected by the nature of the assessments they give their students. Just as students learn depending on the assessment, teachers tend to teach to the test. Thus, if the assessment calls for memorization of facts, the teacher tends to teach lots of facts; if the assessment requires reasoning, then the teacher structures exercises and experiences that get students to think. The question, then, is how well your assessments promote and encourage the teaching you want and what you want your students to learn.

Alignment with Standards

One of the most important influences of high-stakes testing is much greater emphasis on the "alignment" of standards, tests, curriculum, and instruction. **Alignment** in this case is the degree of agreement among these different components. There is usually a concerted effort to align the state standards with the local curriculum. It makes sense, obviously, that what is taught is about the same as what is tested (instructional validity). But "degree of agreement" and "about the same" are matters of professional judgment. Although such judgments can be made reliably, the process is far from standardized because there are different types or levels of alignment.

In considering alignment with Common Core State Standards four important questions can be asked (American Educational Research Association [AERA], 2003, p. 3):

- Does the test's content match the content (topics and skills) in the standards?
- Do the tests and standards cover a comparable "range" or breadth of knowledge, and is there an appropriate "balance" of knowledge across the standards?
- Does the level of cognitive demand or challenge called for in the standards match that required for students to do well on the assessment?
- Does the test avoid adding material that is irrelevant to the standard supposedly being assessed?

The first two questions are concerned primarily with whether test items correspond to a standard and whether the number of items in different areas matches with the emphasis of different areas in the standards (content-related evidence for validity). Cognitive demand is a judgment about the nature of the mental skill required to answer the test item. For instance, does the item require knowledge or deep understanding? Is it primarily a function of recall or application? The cognitive level is determined by the standard; then the item is matched to that level. Of course, what is simple understanding to one teacher might be deep understanding to another teacher. That's the nature of professional judgment, so some level of agreement among your colleagues is desirable.

For the purpose of aligning your instruction and classroom assessments with state standards, it is critical to examine the standards and determine the nature of the cognitive skill demanded. It is also good to examine sample test items, if they are available, but the standard is the most important source of information. Once the cognitive skills embodied in the standard are identified, you can begin the process of judging alignment with your curriculum, instruction, and classroom assessments. The type of judgment you make is represented in Figure 3.13. This continuum shows that the more easily made judgment (*primitive*) is not nearly sufficient to inform you about what to teach, how much to teach, and how to assess each area. This is because the alignment is based on

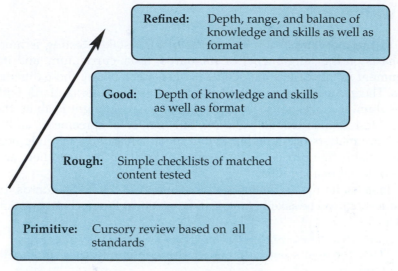

Refined: Depth, range, and balance of
knowledge and skills as well as
format

Good: Depth of knowledge and skills
as well as format

Rough: Simple checklists of matched
content tested

Primitive: Cursory review based on all
standards

FIGURE 3.13   Continuum of Alignment Judgments

a cursory review of the standards and assessments as a whole. *Rough* alignment adds a systematic way of simply checking for the presence of each standard and matching assessment. *Good* alignment includes judgments about depth of knowledge and understanding. It also incorporates the item formats of state tests. Ratings would be more sophisticated and show the alignment by degree, rather than making a yes/no judgment.

The *refined* approach includes matching the cognitive demand (*depth*) with the standards, whether the *range* of what is covered in the standards is consistent with your instruction and assessment, and whether the degree of emphasis of different areas (*balance*) is appropriate. And, of course, you also need to have your classroom assessments align with your learning targets, theories of learning and motivation, instructional tasks given to students, assignments, questions asked, and criteria for scoring student work. Yes, this is a *lot* of alignment!

If you teach in a grade level and subject area that is assessed with a state accountability test, you will need to align, at a minimum, your coverage of content and classroom assessments with the state standards. Many districts have developed pacing guides that all teachers follow. These guides outline what is taught and for how long. It is also common for teachers to key classroom tests to the state standards. But doing so at the wrong cognitive level will not help students nearly as much as making sure that your teaching and assessments demand the right cognitive skills. Simply covering content as directed and matching classroom test items to content areas is comparatively superficial and often results in superficial coverage of many areas.

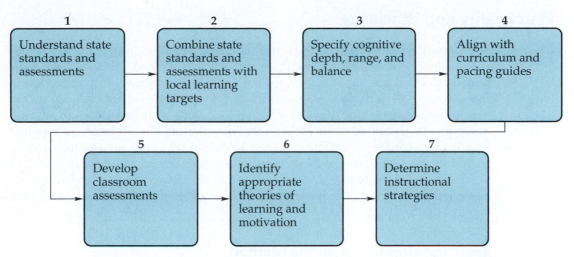

FIGURE 3.14   Steps in Achieving Alignment

Figure 3.14 shows a series of steps that you can use to approach alignment with standards in a systematic way. Because of the pervasiveness of state accountability tests, the first step is to understand the state standards and then combine them with local learning targets. It is helpful to use simple ratings at each step so that the alignment is clear and in a format that can be shared with others. The goal is to plan and implement instruction and classroom assessment that will document the attainment of important targets, including state standards, and provide feedback to promote instructional correctives needed for students to meet state standards.

Another kind of alignment that teachers are increasingly asked to do is to make the format of their classroom assessments like the high-stakes tests. This typically means using multiple-choice items for classroom assessments, and more recently computer-enhanced items. There are two important issues with this. First, it is difficult to develop multiple-choice test items that measure advanced cognitive skills (more about this in Chapter 8). Second, there may be an ethical issue if your classroom assessments are practically the same as those on the state accountability tests. There is nothing wrong with using the same item format for both classroom and high-stakes tests; actually this is desirable. You want students to be familiar with the format. But it is not appropriate to use classroom test items that essentially mimic items that are used in the high-stakes tests. This is closer to teaching the test, rather than teaching *to* the test. Also, remember that your ultimate goal is increasing student learning, not just achieving high test scores. These two outcomes do not necessarily go hand in hand. It would be unethical to drill students to get high scores while simultaneously decreasing their learning, especially when many of your learning targets may not correspond to state standards.

Practicality and Efficiency

High-quality assessments are practical and efficient. It is important to balance these aspects of assessment with previously mentioned criteria. As I have already pointed out, time is a limited commodity for teachers. It may be best to use extensive performance assessments; but if these assessments take away too much from instruction, it may be better to think about less time-consuming assessments. Essentially, ask yourself this question: Is the information obtained worth the resources and time required to obtain it? Other factors to consider include your familiarity with the method of assessment, the time required of students to complete the assessments, the complexity of administering the assessments, the ease of scoring, the ease of interpretation, and cost. We'll consider each briefly.

Teacher Familiarity with the Method

You need to have a good understanding of the assessment methods you select. This includes knowledge of the strengths and limitations of the method, how to administer the assessment, how to score and properly interpret student responses, and the appropriateness of the method for given learning targets. Teachers who use new or unfamiliar assessment methods risk time and resources for questionable results.

Time Required

Other things being equal, it is desirable to use the shortest assessment possible that provides credible results. In other words, gather only as much information as you need for the decision or other use of the results. The time required should include how long it takes to construct the assessment, how much time is needed for students to provide answers, and how long it takes to score the results. The time needed for each of these aspects of assessment is different for each method of assessment. Multiple-choice tests take a long time to prepare but a relatively short time for students to complete and for teachers to score. Thus, if you plan to use this format over and over for different groups of students, it is efficient to put in considerable time preparing the assessment as long as you can use many of the same test items each semester or year (be sure to keep objective test items secure so you don't have to construct an entirely new test each time). Essay tests, on the other hand, take less time to prepare but take a long time to score. Performance assessments are probably most time intensive (in preparation, student response time, and scoring). For all types of assessments, reuse questions and tasks whenever possible.

Another consideration in deciding about time for assessment is reliability/ precision. In general, assessments that take at least 20 minutes provide reliable/ precise results for a single score on a short unit. If separate scores are needed for subskills, more time may be needed. A general rule of thumb is that 3 to 5 objective items are needed to provide a reliable assessment of a specific concept or skill.

Complexity of Administration

Practical and efficient assessments are easy to administer. This means that the directions and procedures for administration are clear. Assessments that require long, complicated directions and setup, like some performance assessments, are less efficient and may, because of student misunderstanding, have adverse effects on reliability/precision and validity.

Ease of Scoring

It is obvious that some methods of assessment, such as objective tests, are much easier to score than other methods, such as essays, papers, and oral presentations. In general, use the easiest method of scoring appropriate to the method and purpose of the assessment. Objective tests are easiest to score and contribute less scoring error to reliability/precision. Scoring performance assessments, essays, papers, and the like is more difficult because more time is needed to ensure reliability/precision. For these assessments, it is more practical to use rating scales and checklists rather than writing extended individualized evaluations.

Ease of Interpretation

A single score from an objective test is easy to interpret with respect to overall success; individualized written comments are more difficult to interpret. Many subjectively evaluated products, for example, from performance assessments, are given a score on a rubric enhance ease of interpretation. It is necessary to provide sufficient information so that whatever interpretation is made is accurate. Often grades or scores are applied too quickly without enough thought and detailed feedback to students. This can be partially remedied by sharing a key with students and others that provides meaning to different scores or grades. Interpretation is easier if you are able to plan, before the assessment, how to use the results.

Cost

Because most classroom assessments are inexpensive, especially with access to online examples and test banks, cost is relatively unimportant (except perhaps for the district as a whole). Some performance assessments are exceptions because the cost of materials can be an important factor. Like other practical aspects, it is best to use the most economical assessment, other things being equal. But economy should be thought of in the long run, less-expensive tests may eventually cost more in further assessment.

Summary

High-quality classroom assessments provide reliable/precise, valid, fair, and useful measures of student performance. Quality is enhanced when the assessments meet these important criteria:

- It is best to match the method of assessment to learning targets. Knowledge and simple understanding targets are matched best with selected-response and brief constructed-response items, reasoning and deep understanding targets with essays, and affective/dispositional targets with observation and student self-reports. Performance assessments are best for measuring deep understanding, skills, and products.
- Validity and reliability/precision are concepts that can be applied to identify noise that distorts the signal.
- Validity is the degree to which a score-based inference is appropriate, reasonable, and useful in a specific context. Inferences and decisions are valid or invalid—not tests.
- Different types of evidence are used to establish the validity of scores from classroom tests, the most important of which is content-related evidence.
- Whether based on face validity, a test blueprint, or instructional validity, the teacher's professional judgment is needed to ensure that there is adequate content-related evidence.
- Consequential validity involves an understanding of the effects of the assessment on students and instruction.
- Reliability/precision is used to estimate consistency and the amount of error in scores, ratings, and decisions.
- Different sources of error should be taken into consideration when interpreting test results.
- Reliability/precision is improved with a sufficient number of items that are clear and have medium difficulties, clear scoring guidelines, verification by others, and limited sources of error.
- Assessment is fair if it is unbiased and provides students with a reasonable opportunity to demonstrate what they have learned.
- Fairness is enhanced by student knowledge of learning targets before instruction, sufficient opportunity to learn, possessing prerequisite knowledge and skills, unbiased assessment tasks and procedures, teachers who avoid stereotypes, and accommodating special needs, ESL, and culturally different learners.
- High-quality assessments are aligned with standards, learning targets, and instruction.
- Positive consequences for both teachers and students enhance the overall quality of assessment, particularly the effect of the assessments on student motivation and study habits. Assessments need to take into consideration the teacher's familiarity with the method, the time required, the complexity of administration, the ease of scoring and interpretation, and the cost to determine the assessment's practicality and efficiency.

Introductory Case Study Answer

Keona should be concerned with how the assessment will (a) influence learning and motivation and (b) also provide fair and credible reporting of student achievement. High-quality assessments promote targeted student learning and motivation while providing verified results of the learning.

Both assessments will influence student learning because students will need to demonstrate the same knowledge. While the motivation for learning may be higher with the at-home project, it may not provide fair and credible reporting of student learning. Thus, Keona should give the in-class quiz.

Keona should use the eight criteria for ensuring high-quality classroom assessments.

- Keona has **clear appropriate learning targets** that center on knowledge and simple understanding of cellular parts, so either assessment **aligns with her learning targets**. While the performance task of a product seems more involved, the content is simple. There is no reasoning or critical thinking involved with the product. Additionally, both assessments are **aligned with her state standards** on knowledge of cellular parts and functions.
- Both assessments provide **positive student consequences** in regards to learning and motivation. For both, students will be inclined to review material so as to ensure a successful demonstration of student learning and thus a positive grade. The difference in student learning is that one allows for student reference throughout the assessment process, the other requires student recall without reference.
- Thus, the criteria for which the assessments differ are in **fairness, validity, and reliability/precision**. For the product, parental influence may influence fairness and validity (Is it the student or parents' knowledge?). The reliability/precision of student learning decreases since students have access to reference materials. For the quiz, these issues are eliminated.
- With respect to **practicality and efficiency**, the quiz will be faster to score and allow Keona to provide quicker remediation.

Suggestions for Action Research

1. Interview a teacher and ask about the types of assessments he or she uses. See if there is a match between the assessment methods and targets consistent with Figure 3.3. Also ask about validity and reliability/precision. How does the teacher define these concepts, and how are they determined informally, if at all, by the teacher? How does the teacher account for error in testing? Finally, ask about additional criteria for making assessments fair and unbiased. Does the teacher make it clear to students what they will be tested on? Do all students have the same opportunity to do well?

2. Prepare a table of specifications for a test of this chapter. Include all the major target areas. Compare your table with those of other students to see how similar you are with respect to what you believe is most important to assess. Also include examples of test items.

3. Ask a group of high, middle, or elementary school students, depending on your interest in teaching, about what they see as fair, high-quality assessment. Ask them to generate some qualities that they believe contribute to good assessments, and then ask them specifically about each of the criteria in the chapter. Also, ask them how different kinds of assessments affect them; for example, do they study differently for essay and multiple-choice tests?

MyEdLab Self-Check 3.1

MyEdLab Self-Check 3.2

MyEdLab Self-Check 3.3

MyEdLab Self-Check 3.4

MyEdLab Application Exercise 3.1   Different Types of Assessment

MyEdLab Application Exercise 3.2   Assessment Practicality and Efficiency

---

Embedded Formative Assessment

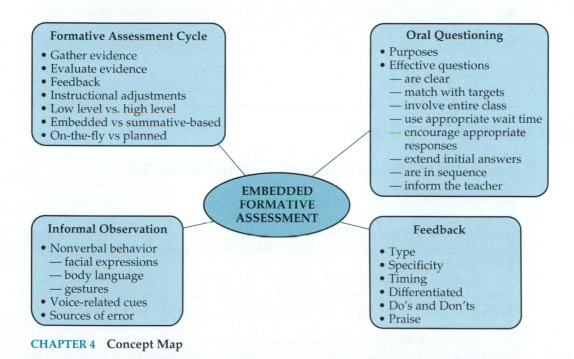

Formative Assessment Cycle
- Gather evidence
- Evaluate evidence
- Feedback
- Instructional adjustments
- Low level vs. high level
- Embedded vs summative-based
- On-the-fly vs planned

Oral Questioning
- Purposes
- Effective questions
  — are clear
  — match with targets
  — involve entire class
  — use appropriate wait time
  — encourage appropriate responses
  — extend initial answers
  — are in sequence
  — inform the teacher

EMBEDDED FORMATIVE ASSESSMENT

Informal Observation
- Nonverbal behavior
  — facial expressions
  — body language
  — gestures
- Voice-related cues
- Sources of error

Feedback
- Type
- Specificity
- Timing
- Differentiated
- Do's and Don'ts
- Praise

CHAPTER 4 Concept Map

Learning Outcomes

After reading this chapter, you should be able to:

4.1 Know the key components of formative assessment; understand the differences between embedded and summative-based formative assessment; and distinguish low-level formative assessment from high-level formative assessment.

4.2 Understand how observation of student behavior, vocal cues, nonverbal cues, facial and bodily gestures, and eye contact can be used to interpret student engagement and understanding. Know the limitations of observation and how it should be combined with other sources of information to verify conclusions about student understanding.

4.3 Be able to ask questions that effectively elicit appropriate student responses to engage students and show understanding.

4.4 Know and understand how to apply feedback to students during embedded formative assessment periods. Be able to give examples of different types of feedback. Know the differences between effective and ineffective feedback practices.

Introductory Case Study

How did Madison Use Embedded Formative Assessment?

On Thursday, Madison had just started her fifth-grade math block when Randy, her assistant principal, entered her room. Madison wasn't surprised to see John, as unannounced observations by school administrators were regular and short in duration. During each observation, data were collected on a single instructional practice.

Madison had already divided her students into two math groupings. The groups were flexible; today's groups were based on Madison's observations of student performance from the previous day. Madison had noticed some students were accurately measuring angles with a protractor while others needed more assistance.

In the Guided Math center, Madison was meeting with small groups of students. For the struggling learners, Madison began by reminding them of their learning target and then modeled how to use a protractor. For this group of students, she had prepared five note cards with an angle drawn on the front and the measurement answer on the back. Students worked independently to measure and check each angle. When students were incorrect, Madison used questions to help students find and describe their error. Madison wanted to ensure that she and the student understood their error. Madison then made a decision for whether to remodel, measure the next angle collaboratively with the student, or allow the student to measure the next angle solo. When the other groups of students, those who appeared yesterday to have a good grasp of how to use a protractor came to the center, Madison did not model nor have students do the angle note card angles. She instead told students their learning target and then had the students work to measure angles in pictures that she had cut from magazines. She knew this was more challenging. As with the other group, Madison used questions to provide guidance as students made errors.

As you read this chapter, think about Madison's embedded formative assessment practices. What positives do you believe Randy, the assistant principal, will give Madison regarding his observation on her use of embedded formative assessment? What strengths will Randy highlight about Madison's feedback to students?

I n this chapter and the next, we will examine formative assessment in some depth. I'm pretty sure you've heard about formative assessment. It's clearly a much-ballyhooed buzzword in education, but a significant issue is that it has taken on many meanings. First, we need to examine these various connotations because there are different ways formative assessment is described and implemented. These days it's not whether or not you use formative assessment, you will because in one sense, as we will see, formative assessment is what good teachers have always done. It just wasn't called formative assessment. It is now important to understand what *kind* of formative assessment you are using, and how to use it effectively. When formative assessment, in whatever its nature, *is used correctly*, there is good evidence that it will have positive benefits on student learning and motivation (Wiliam & Leahy, 2015). What has also been documented is that in practice what is called "formative assessment" may not embody what makes it truly effective. After briefly considering different types of formative assessment, we'll dig deeper into one of the most efficacious types, what is embedded in ongoing instruction and teacher–student interactions.

What Is Formative Assessment?

Formative assessment is a package deal. It's not only a type of assessment with respect to how and when evidence of student learning is gathered, but it also consists of a number of components that work together to effect student motivation and achievement. A good starting definition is the following:

> Formative assessment is the process of gathering evidence of student learning, providing feedback to students, and adjusting instructional and learning strategies that enhance achievement.

There is emphasis on the function that is served with formative assessment—the idea that evidence of student learning is "fed back" into students' and teachers' decision making about what and how to learn. In other words, assessment *forms* instruction and learning experiences (Wiliam & Leahy, 2007). It is a purposeful process in which the teacher is consciously and continuously absorbing evidence of student learning in relation to identified learning targets, and then using the information for teacher decision making, to give feedback to students, and to make instructional adjustments (Wiliam, 2010). The intent is to close the "gap" between what students need to know and their current level of knowledge by establishing a path to facilitate student learning (Furtak, 2009). As such, it is the clearest and most powerful way assessment is integrated with instruction.

As I have pointed out, the term "formative assessment" actually has taken on multiple meanings. For some, it refers primarily to an instrument, tool, or procedure, while for others it is a process that describes how data are used to improve student learning. In fact, some experts have even stopped using the term "formative assessment" because it has been adopted by the commercial testing industry to refer simply to a test that gives diagnostic information. Often the term "assessment *for* learning (A*f*L)" is used, rather than formative assessment. Actually, any assessment event that produces evidence of student learning can be *used* formatively to improve student learning. This is what's most important— formative assessment is not complete unless the results are used to improve student learning and motivation.

The Process of Formative Assessment

Formative assessment is a circular, continuing process involving evaluations of student work and behavior, feedback, and instructional/learning adjustments (sometimes called "instructional correctives") (Figure 4.1). Initially, of course, the first step in any good assessment, including formative assessment, is to establish and communicate clear learning targets.

After teachers gather evidence of students' knowledge, understandings, and skills, that evidence is interpreted to identify gaps between what is known and what still needs to be learned, accompanied by appropriate feedback. This feedback, which either supports and extends proper understandings or targets deficiencies, is followed by instructional/learning adjustments that will build on

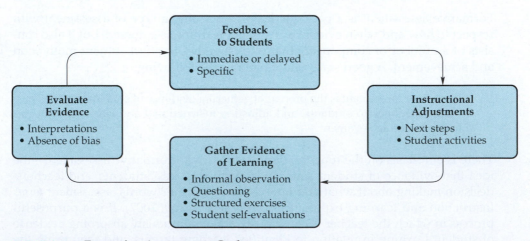

FIGURE 4.1 Formative Assessment Cycle

understandings to broaden and expand their learning or correct misconceptions (Guskey & Bailey, 2010; Shepard, 2004). Instructional/learning adjustments may be determined by the teacher. It is important that instructional correctives contain new strategies and approaches. It is also possible for students to determine how they need to change their learning. When students' judgments about what more is needed are used, the process is particularly helpful in motivating students (Brookhart, 2007; Harlen, 2003; Moss & Brookhart, 2009).

Feedback informs and helps guide these changes, ideally including the message that *making errors or being wrong is a part of learning*. It doesn't do too much good to simply repeat what was already an unsuccessful activity. Rather, correctives and new learning strategies need to be qualitatively different from the initial teaching or study. Following instructional/learning correctives, new evidence of student learning is gathered, and the cycle is repeated if necessary.

Teachers have always had to determine how well students are doing. Formative assessment formalizes an approach to that role by providing a more organized structure in which decisions about next steps (instructional/learning adjustments) are based on carefully gathered and interpreted evidence. This process is consistent with cognitive theories that emphasize the importance of actively constructing meaning with what is learned. As students relate new ideas and knowledge to existing understandings, formative assessment helps them see the connections and clarify meaning in small, successive steps.

Characteristics of Formative Assessment

In practice, formative assessment is more complex than the four components in Figure 4.1. Table 4.1 summarizes 11 possible characteristics of formative assessment and shows how each can be defined and put into practice. What is called formative assessment can differ with respect to which characteristics are emphasized. For example, teachers may provide meaningful feedback with little emphasis on student self-evaluation or may provide feedback without instructional adjustments, but both could be called formative assessment.

These differences are reflected in the continuum that ranges from *low-level* to *high-level* (McMillan, 2010). *Low-level* formative assessment is rudimentary or primitive. The process could be as simple as students taking a test, getting their scores back, and receiving simple feedback about what they answered correctly and incorrectly, with a general suggestion for further learning. *High-level* formative assessment fully integrates ongoing gathering of evidence, feedback, and instructional/learning adjustments, and also includes additional important characteristics. For example, within a supportive and trusting environment, high-level formative assessment may be implemented so that both teachers and students are invested in improved achievement, or there may be an emphasis on developing student self-assessment and self-regulatory skills, mastery goal orientation, effort attributions, and independent learning.

TABLE 4.1   Formative Assessment Characteristics[1]

Characteristic	*Low-Level* Formative		*High-Level* Formative
Evidence of student learning	Mostly objective, standardized	Some standardized and some anecdotal	Varied assessment, including objective, constructed response, and anecdotal
Structure	Mostly formal, planned, anticipated	Informal, spontaneous, "at the moment"	Both formal and informal
Participants involved	Teachers	Students	Both teachers and students
Feedback	Mostly delayed (e.g., give a quiz and give students feedback the next day) and general	Some delayed and some immediate and specific	Immediate and specific
When done	Mostly after instruction and assessment (e.g., after a unit)	Some after and during instruction	Mostly during instruction
Instructional adjustments	Mostly prescriptive, planned (e.g., pacing according to an instructional plan)	Some prescriptive, some flexible, unplanned	Mostly flexible, unplanned
Choice of task	Mostly teacher determined	Some student determined	Teacher and student determined
Teacher–student interaction	Most interactions based primarily on formal roles	Some interactions based on formal roles	Extensive, informal, trusting, and honest interactions
Role of student self-evaluation	None	Tangential	Integral
Motivation	Extrinsic (e.g., passing a competency test)	Both intrinsic and extrinsic	Mostly intrinsic
Attributions for success	External factors (teacher; luck)	Internal, stable factors (e.g., ability)	Internal, unstable factors (e.g., moderate student effort)

[1]Adapted from McMillan (2010).

Types of Formative Assessment

A useful way to conceptualize formative assessment is to think of two kinds—*embedded* and *summative-based*. **Embedded formative assessment**, the focus of the rest of this chapter, is conducted in the context of day-to-day, ongoing, real time instruction. It occurs as instruction and learning take place, continuously woven

TABLE 4.2   Characteristics of Embedded and Summative-Based Formative Assessment

	Embedded	Summative-Based
Descriptive terms	On-the-fly, at-the-moment, real-time, immediate, unstructured, informal	Structured, formal, delayed,
Nature of evidence	• Student dialogue, answers to oral questions, and results on short in-class assignments and activities	• Results from planned assessments such as homework, unit tests and quizzes, common assessments, and large-scale assessments
Gathering of evidence	• Spontaneous • Ongoing • Close monitoring	• Planned • Follows instruction
Feedback	• Immediate	• Delayed
Instructional/learning adjustments	• Immediate	• Delayed

into instruction through teacher observation, questioning, timely feedback, and immediate instructional/learning correctives. The distinguishing characteristic is that it is literally "embedded" with instruction (see Table 4.2).

As illustrated in Figure 4.2, embedded formative assessment includes two types, on-the-fly and "planned." *On-the-fly* embedded formative assessment occurs spontaneously as teachers interact with students, usually by using questions, seatwork or group work to gather evidence of learning, essentially creating "teachable moments." *Planned* embedded formative assessment involves

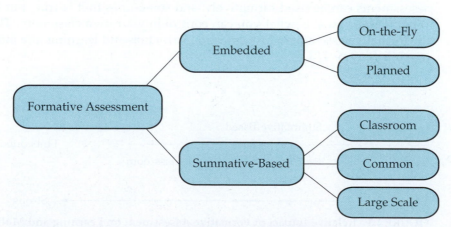

FIGURE 4.2   Different Types of Formative Assessment.

the use of prepared questions and tasks that are employed at particular points in instruction. Either way, the evidence gathered is used immediately to assess and determine next steps. For example, teachers may plan to use a seatwork task half way through a lesson to check for student understanding. This is different from circulating among students, hearing comments, and then giving feedback or asking questions. The challenge is knowing what to ask students to do that will elicit the right kind of evidence that you can use to improve learning.

Summative-based formative assessment is when a more formal or traditional measure of achievement, such as a test, quiz, paper, project, or homework, is used to provide the evidence of learning, then the evidence is used later to provide feedback. This is essentially using summative assessment, with the primary purpose of documenting and reporting what students know, to also provide feedback to improve learning. These are formal, structured assessments that all teachers use, with an added purpose—to enhance student learning. As shown in Figure 4.2 there are essentially three types of summative-based formative assessments—classroom, common, and large-scale. Classroom summative-based formative assessments are teacher-designed and implemented, typically focused on units, chapters, and relatively short durations of learning (e.g., a few days or weeks). Common assessments (developed by teachers in a department, school, or district) are used across classes or schools to assess achievement over six or more weeks, in intervals during the year. Large-scale tests are typically standards-based accountability assessments given at the end of a year or as benchmark or interim tests every nine or so weeks.

An important difference between these different types of formative assessment is what research says about how much each is able to impact student learning and achievement. It is clear that embedded formative assessment has the greatest documented positive benefit for increasing student achievement (Wiliam & Leahy, 2015), and large-scale assessments have the least impact (often none). There are many claims from testing companies that large-scale assessments can be used formatively, and sometimes that is true, but be wary. What matters most is what you can control in your own classroom. The closer the formative assessment process is to instruction and learning, the more effective it is (Figure 4.3).

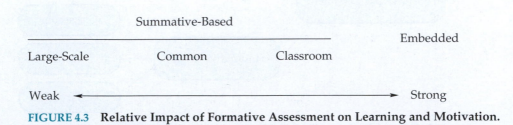

FIGURE 4.3   Relative Impact of Formative Assessment on Learning and Motivation.

Gathering Evidence for Embedded Formative Assessment

A key element in the process of effective instruction is continuous monitoring by teachers to ascertain their students' reactions to instruction and students' progress toward understanding the content or accomplishing the skill. Heritage (2013) refers to this as "evidence collecting strategies . . . information about how learning is developing while instruction is underway" (p. 179). How is the flow of activities? How are students responding to the activities? Are they interested and attentive? Should I speed up or slow down? Should I give more examples? Here is where good formative assessment is essential to effective teaching, and where assessment drives successful instruction. You need to know what to look for in your students while you deliver instruction, how to interpret what you see and hear, how to respond to the students, and then how to adjust your teaching.

On-the-fly formative assessment can occur at any time during the school day as a result of teacher–student and student–student interaction. It can involve individual students, small groups, or the entire class. Evidence is gathered constantly by the teacher during instruction and as students learn. The evidence can be verbal or nonverbal, and it has a spontaneous, "at-the-moment," or "real-time" character.

With both on-the-fly and planned embedded formative assessment, it is critical for the teacher to use diverse learning opportunities with a variety of tasks to provide evidence of student understanding, to closely monitor student behavior, and to provide immediate, specific feedback. The emphasis is on eliciting information from students that demonstrates their understanding, interpreting this information immediately, and providing feedback quickly (Ruiz-Primo & Furtak, 2007).

The mainstays of embedded formative assessment are teacher observation and questioning. Students also have a role in gathering evidence, primarily through self-assessments. This process is addressed in Chapter 12.

Observation

No embedded formative assessment activity is more pervasive for teachers than observation of student behavior. These observations are made to assess such factors as:

- The nature of student participation in class discussion
- The interpersonal skills used in cooperative groups
- The correctness of student responses to questions
- The verbal skills demonstrated in expressing thoughts
- Whether more examples are needed
- Which students to call on
- The interest level of the students
- The degree of understanding demonstrated in student answers
- Emotional and affective responses of students

This list could go on and on. Observation for embedded formative assessment is "unstructured" in the sense that there is no set format or procedure, but it is not random (Nilsen, 2008). For example, effective teachers learn to observe key students in each class who show their reactions more clearly than others. Some of these students are vocal and stand out, and others are quiet leaders.

Assessing Nonverbal Behavior.   Teachers rely greatly on students' body language, facial expressions, and eye contact for accurate observation. These actions are called *nonverbal* because the message is communicated by something about the student other than the content of what he or she says. These nonverbal cues are often more important than what is said, largely because they are usually unintentional and uncontrollable (Mottet & Richmond, 2000). According to Mehrabian (1981), as much as 90% of the emotion conveyed in a message is communicated by nonverbal factors. Some of this is through general appearance and behaviour, such as body language, gestures, and facial expressions, and some is communicated by vocal cues that accompany what is said, such as tone of voice, inflection, pauses, and emphasis.

Nonverbal behaviors help you to assess both meaning and emotion. For instance, we rely on facial and bodily expressions to determine the intent of the message. Nonverbal cues punctuate verbal messages in much the same way that exclamation points, question marks, boldface, and italics focus the meaning of written language. Knapp and Hill (2013) suggest that this punctuation occurs in the following ways:

- *Confirming or Repeating.* When nonverbal behavior is consistent with what is said verbally, the message is confirmed or repeated. For instance, when Sally gave the correct answer to a question, her eyes lit up (facial expression), she sat up straight in her chair, and her hand was stretched up toward the ceiling (body motion). She indicated nonverbally as well as verbally that she knew the answer.
- *Denying or Confusing.* Nonverbal and verbal messages are often contradictory, suggesting denial or confusion. For example, Ms. Thomas has just asked her class if they are prepared to begin their small-group work. The students say yes, but at the same time look down with confused expressions on their faces. The real message is that they are not ready, despite what they have said.
- *Strengthening or Emphasizing.* Nonverbal behavior can punctuate what is said by adding emotional color, feelings, and intensity. These emotions strengthen or emphasize the verbal message. Suppose Mr. Terrell suggested to Teresa that she take the lead in the next school play. Teresa responds by saying, "No, I wouldn't want to do that," while she shakes her head, avoids eye contact, and becomes rigid. Teresa doesn't just mean no, she means NO! If she really wanted to take the lead, her nonverbal behavior would deny her verbal response.

Because most nonverbal behavior is not consciously controlled, the messages are relatively free of distortion and deception. It is not difficult, when you consciously attend to appropriate nonverbal behavior, to determine mood, mental state, attitude, self-assurance, responsiveness, confidence, interest, anger, fear, and other affective and emotional dispositions. This is especially helpful when the nonverbal message conflicts with the verbal one. That is, *how* students say something, through their nonverbal behavior, is as important, if not more so, than *what* they say. Think about a student who answers a question but does so with a slow, low voice, looking away. Even if the answer is correct, these nonverbal cues may tell you something important about the student's level of confidence. Your interpretation would be different for a student who looked directly at you, spoke with authority, and whose face displayed excitement. In this section, we look at how specific nonverbal behaviors communicate different meanings and emotions and how teachers respond to these cues.

Facial Expressions.   The face is the most important source of nonverbal information because it is the primary outlet for emotions and it rarely distorts meaning (Hill, 2007). The face projects a great variety of messages. To know what to look for it is best to focus on three areas: the brows and forehead; the eyes, lids, and nose; and the lower face. The upper portion of the face is more likely to indicate feelings of concern and anger (e.g., the brows are lowered and drawn together in anger). The lower area, particularly the mouth, will communicate happiness and amusement. Smiles, frowns, twisted lips, a raised chin, a clenched mouth, and other expressions are also fairly clear in what they communicate.

Let's see how you do with a short "test" of facial meaning. Figure 4.4 shows seven photographs of different facial expressions.

Match the following emotions with the pictures *before* looking at the correct answers:

Facial Meaning	Photograph # (from Figure 4.2)	Facial Meaning	Photograph # (from Figure 4.2)
Distrust	_____	Surprise	_____
Happiness	_____	Anger	_____
Sadness	_____	Determination	_____
		Fear	_____

The correct choices are distrust = 5, happiness = 6, sadness = 4, surprise = 1, anger = 3, determination = 7, and fear = 2.

For the purposes of teaching, you need to be especially careful to attend to facial expressions of bewilderment and interest. Teachers use these emotions extensively to gauge student understanding and motivation. Emotions similar to bewilderment are confusion, doubt, frustration, and puzzlement. Obviously these cues suggest that the student is not understanding or is not progressing. Interest

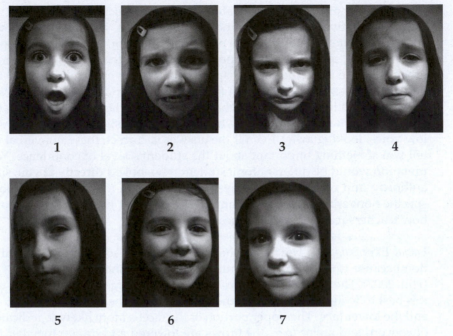

FIGURE 4.4   Facial Expressions

conveys anticipation, excitement, and attention. These emotions are important as an indication of attention.

The most informative aspect of the face is the eyes and the nature of eye contact. Eye contact indicates a readiness to communicate, and continued direct eye contact signifies confidence and competence. Students who use positive eye contact, who look directly at you and watch your movements, are probably attentive and interested. Longer and more frequent eye contact suggests trust and respect.

Averted eyes often suggest an unwillingness to respond, a lack of confidence, or a general sense of apathy. For example, if a student looks down before responding, looks away from teachers when interacting with them, keeps eyes downcast, or looks at the ceiling, a reasonable interpretation is that the student may lack confidence, knowledge, or skills. When most of the students in a class start looking around the room, at each other, and out the window, they have lost interest and are not involved. This may mean that students do not understand well enough, or it may mean they are bored (in some cultures the lack of eye contact may indicate respect for an authority figure or older person, and not a lack of self-confidence or other negative feeling).

The pupils of the eyes convey the intensity of emotion shown more generally in the face. They tend to enlarge as we become more interested in something, more emotionally aroused, and happier with positive anticipation. Eye pupils contract as we become less interested and have more negative emotions such as sadness, sorrow, and indifference.

Body Language and Signals.   Like facial expressions and voice, body language, movement, and posture communicate messages. The meaning associated with different bodily cues is best understood by considering four categories of nonverbal behavior, each of which is based on a different function or purpose: emblems, illustrators, affect displays, and regulators (Ekman & Friesen, 1969).

An *emblem* is a body cue that has a direct one- or two-word verbal translation. Emblems are used to consciously communicate a particular message, such as holding up your hand with your palm facing the other person (which means "wait"), putting your finger to your puckered lips ("quiet"), and waving toward yourself ("come over"). Most of these emblems are substitutes for words. In observing emblems, be aware of possible cross-cultural differences. For example, nodding your head in the United States means that you agree, but in Japan it acknowledges only that you have received the other person's message.

An *illustrator* is used to increase clarity and awareness and to augment what is being said. It reinforces the strength of the emotional message. For example, holding your fingers close together augments "small," and pointing to an object clarifies what you intend to communicate about. If a student's fist is clenched, it may indicate anger in association with what the student has verbalized.

The third type of bodily communication is the *affect display*. These cues show emotion through the position and posture of the body and certain gestures. If the student has a rigid, tense, slumped body with arms and legs crossed, the affect is negative and defensive. Students with open, relaxed bodies who lean toward the teacher and do not fidget or tap something communicate positive affect, attention, and confidence.

Regulators are used to indicate the initiation, length, and termination of verbal messages. Students use these cues to inform the teacher about whether they want to initiate a response, are finished with a comment or thought, or want to continue speaking. An obvious initiation regulator is to raise the hand or index finger. Other initiation regulators include eye contact, head nodding, smiles, and raised eyebrows. When students do not want to make a comment, they may use such "turn-denying" behaviors as staring at something (especially looking down at the desk) and slumping in the chair. Students who want to continue speaking may lean toward you, use gestures to punctuate their thoughts, and display an enthusiastic, expectant face. Regulators are vital for teachers as they observe students' signs about whether they understand something or are ready to move on. These are given in response to teacher questions and consist of response cards, clickers, stickers, and other methods of receiving quick and often confidential feedback from students (more on these in the next section).

Gestures.   Gestures are hand and arm movements that individuals use to communicate, either supplementing verbal messages or acting as the sole means through which meaning is conveyed. Gestures clarify, contradict, or replace verbal messages and play an important role in child development and learning. For example, young children often point to answers or use some kind of gesture to indicate understanding. Students often use gestures as part of an explanation of something or as an answer. Gesturing allows students to express learning in a simple and direct way, often demonstrating understanding that is not apparent through language. By paying attention to gestures, teachers are able to confirm whether students have a complete or partial understanding of something. Understanding is partial when there is discord between gestures and speech. It is more complete when gestures and speech are in concurrence. Some research suggests that gesture–speech mismatches indicate a readiness for learning (Roth, 2001).

Assessing Voice-Related Cues.   Voice-related cues include tone of voice, loudness, intensity, pauses, silences, voice level, inflection, word spacing, emphases, and other aspects of voice that add color to the content of what is said. The potential of vocal cues to provide information about a student's level of understanding, confidence, and emotional state is exceeded only by facial expressions.

A summary of research on the relationship between vocal cues and messages is presented in Table 4.3 (Leathers & Eaves, 2008). Although this research has not been conducted with teacher–student dyads or groups, the findings do have important implications. For example, on the basis of vocal cues, with some exceptions due to cultural background, you would expect students who are confident in their knowledge or skill to be relatively loud rather than quiet, to speak in a high pitch, to have a rather rapid speaking rate, and to speak fluently with few pauses, "ahs," sentence changes, throat clearings, word repetitions, and incomplete sentences. Students who are unsure of their knowledge or ability to perform a skill are likely to speak quietly, in a low pitch with little variety, and to speak slowly with many pauses and frequent throat clearings. The student who lacks confidence will speak nonfluently, the voice will be flat, more like a monotone rather than showing variety in pitch and rate. Research has also determined that persons who demonstrate little variation in pitch and rate tend to be

TABLE 4.3   Vocal Cues and Messages

Vocal Cue	Message
Loudness	*Loud*—competent, enthusiastic, forceful, self-assured, excited
	Quiet—anxious, unsure, shy, indifferent
Pitch (musical note voice produces)	*High*—excited, explosively angry, emotional
	Low—calm, sad, stunned, quietly angry, indifferent
	Variety—dynamic, extroverted
Rate	*Fast*—interested, self-assured, angry, happy, proud, confident, excited, impulsive, emotional
	Slow—uninterested, unsure, unexcited, unemotional
Quality (combination of attributes)	*Flat*—sluggish, cold, withdrawn
	Nasal—unattractive, lethargic, foolish

viewed as introverts, lacking assertiveness and dynamism. Voices that are clear, articulate, and confident are viewed as positive.

You will need to be careful not to infer lack of knowledge, confidence, anxiety, or motivation *solely* on the basis of vocal cues. Like nonverbal behavior, voice is one of many pieces of evidence that you need to consider to make an accurate assessment.

The challenge is being able to observe these nonverbal and verbal cues, make appropriate interpretations, and then take corrective action when needed. To help you with this, I have prepared a table that combines different types of nonverbal behaviors and vocal cues in relation to particular messages students send (Table 4.4).

TABLE 4.4 **Messages Students Convey Through Nonverbal Behavior and Vocal Cues**

Message	Facial Expressions	Body Language	Vocal Cues
Confident	Relaxed, direct eye contact; pupils enlarged	Erect posture; arms and legs open; chin up; hands waving; forward position in seat	Fluent; few pauses; variety in tone; loud
Nervous	Tense; brows lowered; pupils contracted	Rigid; tense; tapping; picking	Pauses; "ah" sounds; repetition; shaky; soft; fast; quiet
Angry	Brows lowered and drawn together; teeth clenched; eyes narrow	Fidgety; hands clenched; head down	Loud or quiet; animated
Defensive	Downcast eyes; pupils contracted; eyes squinted	Arms and legs crossed; leaning away; leaning head on hands	Loud; animated
Bored	Looking around; relaxed; pupils contracted	Slumped posture; hands to face	Soft; monotone; flat
Frustrated	Brows together; eyes downcast; squinting	Tense; tapping; picking; placing fingers or hands on each side of head	Pauses; low pitch
Happy	Smiling, smirking; relaxed; brows natural; pupils enlarged	Relaxed; head nodding; leaning forward	Animated; loud; fast
Interested	Direct eye contact; brows uplifted	Leaning forward; relaxed; opening arms and legs; nodding; raising hand or finger	Higher pitch; fast
Not Understanding	Frowning; biting lower lip; squinting eyes; looking away	Leaning back; arms crossed; head tilted back; hand on forehead; fidgeting; scratching chin; leaning head on hands	Slow; pauses; "ah," "um," "well" expressions; low pitch; monotone; quiet; soft

I have asked teachers to summarize the nonverbal behavior and vocal cues they attend to, how they interpret what they see and hear, and the action they take following their observation and interpretation. Some examples of their responses include the following:

Nonverbal Behavior	Interpretation	Action
Students start to look around the room and at each other.	Some students are not understanding; some may be bored.	Refocus students; review previous lesson; reteach lesson; regroup students.
Room quiets; students are writing in their notebooks.	Students are motivated and on task.	Keep going—it may not last long!
Students squint and adjust the focus of their eyes.	Indicates a lack of understanding, frustration, or boredom.	Rephrase the question or ask the students what it is that they do not understand.

Note how these observations occur during instruction, and how teachers use the information to make instructional adjustments. In some cases, teachers don't provide feedback to students, but still use the information to gauge student learning and engagement.

Sources of Error in Moment-by-Moment Observation.   In a busy classroom, it's difficult to make continuous observations that are accurate, whether of individual students or of groups. Some of the more common errors that teachers make in their moment-by-moment observations and interpretations are presented in Table 4.5. To make accurate, reliable observations, it is best to first learn what to look for and listen to. Next, you need to be aware of the types of errors that are possible and consciously monitor yourself so that these errors are not made. Finally, it is helpful if you are able to use a few simple procedures, some of which are used after the instructional segment:

- Ask yourself, is the verbal message consistent with the nonverbal behavior? Is this behavior normal or unusual?
- Plan time to do informal observation while not actively teaching a lesson to the entire class (e.g., during seatwork, small-group work, and individual interactions).
- Keep a list of possible errors from Table 4.5 in a place that is easily referred to, such as in your desk. Make a habit of referring to the list frequently.
- When possible during the school day, write down informal observations, your interpretations, and the action you took during the instructional segment. Be sure to keep the interpretations separate from the observations. The brief, written descriptions of behavior are essentially **anecdotal observations** or *notes*. These notes will provide accurate records of what transpired and will improve the accuracy of the observations. In addition, anecdotal records can be used to document personal insights and student reactions that otherwise are easily forgotten or distorted. (See Hill, Ruptic,

TABLE 4.5 **Observation Sources of Error**

1. Leniency or generosity	Tendency to be lenient or generous.
2. Primacy effects	Initial impressions have a distorting effect on later observations.
3. Recency effect	Interpretations unduly influenced by his or her most recent observation.
4. Halo effect errors	Assumptions that some nonverbal behavior generalizes to other areas (e.g., lack of confidence in math means lack of confidence in English).
5. Biased sampling	Observations do not occur frequently enough to provide a reliable measure, or may be skipped.
6. Observer bias	Teachers' preconceived biases and stereotypes distort the meaning of what is observed.
7. Hawthorne effect	Some students get nervous or uneasy when observed by teachers (e.g., students would behave differently if the teacher were not present).
8. Student faking	Students may fake (e.g., eye contact and nodding does not always indicate engagement); as students become more sophisticated, they develop strategies to make themselves appear to be on task.

& Norwick, 1998, and Nilsen, 2008, for a more extensive discussion of anecdotal notes.)

- At the end of the day, set aside a few minutes to record, briefly, important informal observations. Refer to your notes each week to look for patterns and trouble spots that need attention.
- If you are unsure about what a nonverbal behavior may mean, and the implications may be serious, check them out with the student during another activity. For example, if you are picking up from nonverbal behavior that a student does not understand a procedure, even though the student's answers are correct on worksheets, ask the student directly about how he or she felt about the procedure and inquire about his or her confidence. You may discover that the student was concerned with other things at the time, and this affect was being displayed.
- Consciously think about informal observations of behavior in relation to student understanding and performance of learning targets. Those that directly relate to the targets are most important.
- Don't be fooled by students who appear to be on task and interested but aren't.

Informal Oral Questioning

Along with observations, teachers rely heavily on how students answer questions during instruction to know if students understand what is presented or can perform targeted skills. You may well spend up to one-third of your instructional time asking questions. (The average teacher asks 400 questions a day!

[Moss & Brookhart, 2009].) Good questioning is flexible because it can be used with individuals or groups of students and can be customized based on specific student answers (Green & Johnson, 2010).

Questioning typically occurs in four formats: whole-class, teacher-led reviews of content, discussions, recitations, and interactions with individual students and small groups of students. The review may be a fast-paced drill that is designed to cover specific knowledge, and many of the questions may be planned in advance. Discussions are used to promote student questioning and exchange ideas and opinions to clarify issues, promote thinking, generate ideas, or solve a problem. Typically, both planned and unplanned questions are used. In a recitation, the teacher asks questions as part of the presentation of material to engage students in what they are learning. These are usually planned. Teachers question students individually and in small groups on-the-fly to obtain information that is specific to the students. This allows teachers to individualize assessment and target feedback and suggested next steps.

Questions can efficiently grab students' attention and engage them in the lesson. Questions can challenge beliefs and get them to think about the topic under discussion by creating a sense of cognitive dissonance, imbalance, or disequilibrium. McTighe and Wiggins (2004) describe "essential" questions as those that provoke and engage students in inquiry and argument about plausible responses. Second, questions can promote student reasoning and comprehension by helping them think through and verbalize their ideas. By actively thinking through answers to questions, student understanding is enhanced. Learning is also enhanced by listening to the answers of other students because these answers may represent a way of expressing ideas that makes more sense to the student than the way the teacher explains things.

Questions signal to students important content to be learned and provide an opportunity for students to assess their own level of understanding in these areas. The types of questions asked also indicate how the students should prepare to demonstrate their understanding. For instance, asking questions that compare and contrast (e.g., How were presidents Carter and Clinton alike?) will cue students that they need to learn about how these presidents were similar and different, not just characteristics of each one. If you ask simple recall questions (e.g., What three major legislative initiatives occurred during the Obama presidency?), you are communicating to your students that they need to memorize the names of these initiatives.

Questions are also used to control student behavior and manage the class. Questions asked at random of different students—and that require brief, correct answers—maintain student attention. Teachers often ask a specific question of a student who is not paying attention to stop inappropriate behavior. Conversely, questions can be used to reinforce good behavior. Questions are also used to refocus students and to remind them of the classroom rules and procedures. Through your use of good questions, students will keep actively involved in learning, preventing opportunities for student misbehavior.

Most important for formative assessment, questioning is used to obtain information about student understanding and progress. This is accomplished if the questions are effective and elicit information that will help you understand the depth of knowledge of your students and what follow-up will help them learn. The elements of good questions and questioning skills for this purpose are presented next.

Characteristics of Effective Questioning for Embedded Formative Assessment

Your goal is to ask questions during instruction that will provide you with accurate information about what students know and can do, and that will provide insights into students' depth of understanding and thinking processes. With this goal in mind, the following suggestions and strategies will help you:

1. State Questions Clearly and Succinctly So That the Intent of the Question Is Understood. Students understand the question if they know how they are to respond. Questions are vague to students if there are too many possible responses or if the question is too general. With such a question, students wonder, "What does he mean?" Because they are unsure of what is intended, they are less willing to answer the question, and you are less likely to find out what they know. This occurs for a single vague question and for run-on questions (those in which two or more questions are asked together). For example, if a fourth-grade teacher wants to determine current student understanding of noun–verb agreement in sentences, an inappropriately vague question might be:

What is wrong with the sentences on the board?

It would be better to ask:

Read each of the three sentences on the board. In which sentence or sentences is there agreement between the noun and the verb? In which one or ones is there disagreement? How would you correct the sentence(s) in which the verb and noun do not agree?

Other questions that are too vague:

What did you think about this demonstration?
What about the early explorers of America?
Can you tell me something about what you learned?
What do you know about the solar system?

As emphasized by Green and Johnson (2010), design brief, succinct questions that are directly related to students' understanding of the task. Here are some examples:

What cause of the Vietnam War do you believe was most misunderstood by the media?

What was the primary reason for Columbus to come to the Americas?

Why did the leading character in this story decide to leave his home?

2. **Match Questions with Learning Targets.** The questions you ask should reflect your learning targets, the emphasis on different topics that will be assessed more formally in a unit test, and the difficulty of learning targets. Ask more questions and spend more time questioning with difficult learning targets. This will give you sufficient information to make sure students understand. Try to ask questions in rough proportion to how you will eventually test for student learning. We have all been in classes where much class time was spent discussing something that was covered only lightly on the test. Try to avoid this!

Matching questions to learning targets requires that the questions be phrased to elicit student responses that are needed for the learning target. For this purpose, most oral questions will correspond to either knowledge or understanding targets. Knowledge targets focus on remembering and understanding. Questions that assess knowledge targets often begin with *what, who, where,* and *when*. For example, "What is the definition of *exacerbate*?" "When did Columbus discover America?" "Who is Martin Luther King?" These are examples of knowledge questions that generally require factual recall or rote memorization of dates, names, places, and definitions.

Other knowledge questions assess student understanding and comprehension. Students are required to show that they grasp the meaning of something by answering questions that require more than rote memory, for example, "What is the major theme of this article?" "What is an example of a metaphor?" "Explain what is meant by the phrase 'opposites attract,'" and "How do you find the area of a parallelogram?" These types of questions are effective when you want to assess more than one student in whole-group instruction because each student uses his or her own words for the answer. If there is only one way to state the correct answer, only one student can answer it correctly.

More time is needed to respond to reasoning questions. These questions are generally *divergent* in that more than one answer can be correct or satisfactory. In a reasoning question, the teacher asks students to mentally manipulate what they know to analyze, synthesize, problem solve, create, and evaluate. Reasoning questions will include words or intents such as *distinguish, contrast, generalize, judge, solve, compare, interpret, relate,* and *predict,* such as "Relate the causes of the Civil War to the causes of World War I. How are they the same and how are they different?" "What was the implication of the story for how we live our lives today?" "What would happen if these two liquids were mixed?" As you might imagine, reasoning questions are excellent for promoting student thinking and discussion.

An effective approach to engaging students in reasoning is to have a one-on-one conversation with the student in which questions can be specific to that student. Asking students to "think out loud" when responding or when solving a problem can reveal their ability to employ appropriate thinking strategies and steps (Stiggins, 2008).

3. **Involve the Entire Class.** You will want to stay clear of questions that result in a few students answering most of them. Balance is needed between students who volunteer and those who don't, high- and low-ability students, males and females, and students near and far from you. It is easy to call on the same students most of the time, so it's best to be aware of who has and who has not participated. If you are judging the progress of the class as a whole, it is especially important to obtain information from different students, although normally if your better students are confused or having difficulty, chances are good that this is true for the rest of the class as well.

Involvement will be enhanced if everyone's responses are supported. One technique for engaging most students is to address the question to the class as a whole, allow students time to think about a response, and then call on specific students. This encourages all the students to be responsible for an answer, not just a single student if you call the name first, and will result in a better understanding of overall student progress. An effective variation is to have students answer individually, then share with a partner and discuss why each is correct or incorrect. Avoid the strategy that many teachers use—ask a question, have students raise their hands to answer, then call on one of those students. This tends to disenfranchise many students who aren't completely confident about the answer. Often it's the same few students. It's better to call on students randomly, even though they probably won't like that until they get used to it.

4. **Allow Sufficient Wait Time for Student Responses.** Students need to have sufficient time to think about and then respond to each question. Students use this time to process their thoughts and formulate their answers. Research shows that some teachers have difficulty waiting more than a second or two before cuing a response, calling on another student, or rephrasing a question. It has been shown that when teachers can wait three to five seconds, the quality and quantity of student responses are enhanced. It follows from these findings that longer wait time will result in better assessment, but only if the questions are such that students will be engaged in thinking. A longer wait time for a simple recall question is not nearly as effective as a question that engages students to deepen their understanding. This point is illustrated nicely by the following teacher comments (Black & Wiliam, 2004, p. 26).

> Not until you analyze your own questioning do you realize how poor it can be. I found myself using questions to fill time and asking questions which required little thought from the students . . . it is important to ask questions which get them thinking about the topic and will allow them to make the next step in the learning process. Simply directing them to the "correct answer" is not useful.

It may be difficult for you to wait more than a couple of seconds because the silence may seem much longer. It's helpful to tell students directly that such wait time is not only expected, but required, so that immediate responses do not take opportunities away from students who need a little more time. This will help alleviate your own insecurity about having so much "silence" during a lesson.

5. Give Appropriate Responses to Student Answers. Your responses to student answers will be very important for gathering valid information about student progress because your style and approach—the climate and pattern of interaction that is established—will affect how and if students are likely to answer your questions. Ideally, each student's response should be acknowledged with some kind of meaningful, honest feedback. Feedback is part of ongoing assessment because it lets students know, and confirms for you, how much progress has been made. You will also want to think about providing nonverbal support, even when answers are wrong or there are mistakes. Take the same body position as students, maintain eye contact, keep appropriately close to all students, and match your facial expressions to your words. This is where taking a video of yourself teaching is invaluable. Often we just aren't aware of our nonverbal behavior.

6. Avoid Closed Questions. Closed questions are answered by a single response, usually one word. These include questions that elicit a simple "yes" or "no" (e.g., Is this word an adjective in this sentence? Is this animal a mammal?). Other closed questions could be asked as true/false, or other simple choices of possible responses. These types of questions are common, but they don't help much in the formative assessment process, mostly because they don't reveal much about students' depth of understanding. They are simply not very diagnostic, and after all, with binary-choice questions, there is a 50% chance of guessing the right answer. If you want to use such questions, do so sparingly and as a warm-up to questions that are better able to assess student learning. Adding a simple *why* after an answer to a yes/no question will increase its diagnostic power considerably.

Open questions communicate much more about what students know and allows them to personalize answers and be more engaged. This is not difficult to accomplish. By changing key words such as "what" and "is" into "why" and "how," you can make dramatic changes in classroom dynamics and formative assessment. See examples in Table 4.6.

TABLE 4.6   Examples of Reframing Closed to Open Questions

Closed	Open
Is this spider an insect?	Why or why not is this spider an insect?
Is this a question or a statement?	Why is this sentence a question or statement?
What is the distance traveled between three cities?	How do you calculate the distance traveled between three cities?
Is ice a liquid?	Explain why ice is or is not a liquid.
Was the threat of the use of weapons of mass destruction a reason the United States went to war against Iraq?	Why did the United States go to war against Iraq?

7. Use Probes to Extend Initial Answers. Probes are specific follow-up questions. Use them to better understand how students arrived at an answer, their reasoning, and the logic of their response. Examples of probes include phrases such as

- Why did you think that was the correct answer?
- How did you arrive at that conclusion?
- Explain why you think you are correct.
- Explain how you arrived at that solution.
- Give another example.
- Could you argue that that is not the best solution?
- Tell me more about your conclusion.
- How did you come up with that answer?
- How would you explain the solution to someone else?

Essentially you are asking students to extend their understanding, to think about what they have learned. When students are asked to explain their answers, their learning improves (Black & Wiliam, 1998). Also, a benefit of this technique is that it shows students that thinking about what they are learning is as important as giving the right answer.

8. Avoid Tugging, Guessing, and Leading Questions. Asking these types of questions makes it difficult to obtain an accurate picture of student knowledge and reasoning. Tugging questions ask a student to answer more without indicating what the student should focus on. They are usually vague questions or statements that follow what the teacher judges to be an incomplete answer. For example, "Well? . . . " "And? . . . " and "So? . . . " are tugging questions. It is better to use a specific probe. For example, if the question is "Why were cities built near water?" and a student answered, "So the people could come and go more easily," a tugging question would be "And what else?" A better probe would be "How did coming and going affect the travel of products and food?"

Guessing questions obviously elicit guessed answers from students, for example, "How many small computer businesses are there in this country?" This type of question is useful in getting students' attention and getting students to think about a problem or area, but it is not helpful in assessing progress.

Leading questions, like rhetorical questions, are more for the teacher to pace a lesson than for obtaining information about student knowledge. Therefore, these types of questions ("That's right, isn't it?" or "Let's go on to the next chapter, okay?") should be avoided.

9. Avoid Asking Students What They Think They Know. It is not usually helpful to orally ask students directly if they know or understand something. The question might be, "Do you know how to divide fractions?" or "Is everyone with me?" Students may be reluctant to answer such questions in class because of possible embarrassment, and if they do answer, the tendency is to say they know and understand when the reality is that they don't. If your relationship with your students is good, asking them if they understand or know something may work well.

TABLE 4.7   Do's and Don'ts of Effective Questioning for Formative Assessment

Do	Don't
State questions clearly and succinctly.	Ask closed questions.
Match questions with learning targets.	Ask tugging questions.
Involve the entire class (all students).	Ask guessing questions.
Allow sufficient wait time for students to respond.	Ask leading questions.
Give appropriate responses to student answers.	Ask students what they know.
Extend initial answers with probes.	
Sequence questions appropriately.	
Ask questions of all students, not just those you know will answer correctly.	

10. Ask Questions in an Appropriate Sequence. Asking questions in a predetermined sequence as a type of planned embedded formative assessment will enhance the information you receive to assess student understanding. Good sequences generally begin with knowledge questions to determine if students know enough about the content to consider reasoning questions. Consider the following situation. After having her students read an article about the U.S. military involvement in Haiti in 1994, Mrs. Lambiotte asks the question, "Should the United States stay in Haiti and enforce the local laws until a new government is formed?" Students give some brief opinions, but it's clear that this reasoning question is premature. She then asks some knowledge questions to determine whether students understand enough from the article to ask other reasoning questions, such as "What was the condition of Haiti before the U.S. involvement?" "Historically, what has happened in Haiti the last two times a new government has taken control?" "How did the people of Haiti receive the American soldiers?" Such questions also serve as a review for students to remind them about important aspects of the article. Once students show that they understand the conditions and history, then divergent questions that require reasoning would be appropriate. A summary of what to do and what to avoid doing when using questions for formative assessment is presented in Table 4.7.

Table 4.8 shows a number of practical techniques that will be useful in eliciting student understanding and thinking.

Providing Effective Feedback for Embedded Formative Assessment

One way teachers use assessment information is to know how to respond to students after they demonstrate their knowledge, reasoning, skill, or performance. The teacher's response is called **feedback**—providing information to the student

TABLE 4.8   Practical Techniques for Eliciting Student Understanding and Skills

Technique	Description	Example
Response or Voting Cards	Index cards or other items (e.g., sticky notes back to back) held up simultaneously by all students to indicate their response to a question. Can be preprinted with responses or a constructed response, such as with small whiteboards.	Math teacher uses preprinted responses "positive correlation" and "negative correlation." Students are given examples orally and hold up one of the cards to indicate their answer.
Hand Signals	Use of thumbs up, sideways, or down, or showing a number of fingers to indicate understanding.	A science teacher asks students to use the "thumb" technique when pausing after each stage of the Krebs cycle is explained.
Electronic Audience Response	Handheld devices that give immediate, electronically messaged answers. Also called clickers.	After presenting a history lesson the teacher presents multiple-choice questions and asks all students to select the best answer.
Retelling	Ask students to orally summarize, in their own words, what they understand.	After a discussion of why cities were historically built by rivers, the teacher asks students in small groups to share their understanding of factors influencing the location of cities.
Think-Pair-Share	A cooperative learning technique in which students share their understanding with each other before presenting to a larger group.	Following an example provided of a written paragraph, students are paired, asked to think about the main idea, then share their thinking with each other.
Line Up	Students with different stages in a sequence are asked to line up in order.	Students are given Maslow's hierarchy of needs and asked to line up from lower to higher.
Bump in the Road	Students are asked to write down a point, issue, or confusion about what is being learned.	Following a unit on personal economics students are asked to write down any bumps in the road to understanding how to do a budget.
Sticky Note Sorting	Use of sticky notes to classify or organize information.	Students are asked to use labeled sticky notes to identify verbs and nouns in sentences put on the board.
Traffic Signal	Use of color-coded props to signal "go on," "go slower," or "stop."	Students use different colored cups to indicate to the teacher if they are ready for the next math problem.

following an assessment about his or her achievement. The nature, purpose, and types of feedback teachers give to students based on academic work has been extensively researched, with initial studies of positive reinforcement published nearly 100 years ago. More recently, several reviews of literature on feedback provide a strong case about what works and what doesn't when teachers respond to student answers and products in particular ways (Brookhart, 2008; Hattie, 2008; Hattie & Timplerly, 2007; Kluger & DeNisi, 1996; Ruiz-Primo & Li, 2013; Shute, 2008).

A primitive type of feedback is simply confirming the correctness of an answer or action, that is, whether it is right or wrong. This is what we do during instruction with observed seatwork—tell students what they got right and what they missed; it is also the extent of the feedback teachers often give to students' answers to oral questions—"Good," "That's right," "Close," and so on. Feedback of this nature is only part of what students need to improve their learning. Such statements are actually more evaluative judgments than feedback, and they provide very limited usefulness for the student. Students also need to know how their performance compares to learning targets, what can be done to close the gap between their performance and these targets, and when they commit learning errors. When feedback is presented as information that can guide the student's meaningful construction of additional knowledge and understanding, learning and intrinsic motivation are enhanced (Mayer, 2002).

Because ongoing, real-time teaching is complex, depending on the nature of students, the context, and the subject being taught, effective feedback that needs to be given at the moment is also no simple matter (nor is it simple for summative-based formative assessment). There are many choices about what kind of feedback to give, how much to give, and when to give it, depending on the learning targets and student characteristics. As Brookhart (2008) says, "In the final analysis, feedback is always adaptive. It always depends on something else" (p. 112). Effective feedback, then, is more than keeping in mind a few important principles, such as "keep feedback specific and individualized," or "keep it positive and brief." Rather, good feedback depends on appropriate teacher decision making and responses to students contingent on several important variables. That is, effective feedback is *differentiated*—what works for one student may not be effective for another student.

That said, there are well-researched, essential characteristics of effective formative feedback that provide a foundation for what you'll decide to do in a specific class, with individual students, as teaching and learning occur (Brookhart, 2013a; Chappuis, 2012; Ruiz-Primo & Li, 2013) (see also Table 4.3). The following list is also useful for summative-based formative assessment:

- Focus on evidence of learning connected to progress toward achieving specific learning targets, using appropriate success criteria.
- Actively engage students in generating and using feedback.
- Focus feedback so that it positively impacts self-regulation, self-efficacy, and goal orientation.
- Make sure feedback is descriptive about students' work, the task, not about the student more generally.

- Make feedback timely when needed for immediate use.
- Differentiate feedback as appropriate.
- Provide opportunities for students to use the feedback—make it *actionable*.
- Consider how students will react to the feedback (e.g., will it increase or decrease effort?).
- Limit feedback to information the student can act on.
- Highlight student errors in understanding.
- Make sure feedback is honest and accurate.
- Be positive but don't use too much sugarcoating.

Overall, your goal is to use feedback to establish a classroom climate in which students anticipate and value feedback, where being wrong and making mistakes are viewed as opportunities to learn and not failure, where students are willing to admit their lack of understanding and ask for help, and where students are involved as self-assessors who reflect on their learning and responsibility for further learning. Finally, feedback must be acted on—something must occur after feedback that moves the student toward greater learning (Wiliam & Leahy, 2015).

Types of Feedback

There are many different types of feedback. Some of these are summarized in Table 4.9, which shows feedback based on complexity, as either simple (verified feedback) or more complex (elaborated feedback). Interestingly, the research on

TABLE 4.9   Types of Feedback Based on Complexity

Feedback Type	Description
Verification	Informs students of the correctness of their answers
Correct response	Acknowledges student's correct answer with no additional information
Try again	Acknowledges student's incorrect answer and allows attempts to relearn in the same way
Error flagging	Highlights errors in response without giving the correct answer or suggestions for improvement
Elaboration	Includes explanation about why an answer was correct or incorrect; may allow for additional time to relearn
Attribute isolation	Presents central attributes of what is being learned
Response contingent	Describes why an incorrect answer is wrong and why a correct answer is right
Hints	Prompts or cues guiding the student in the right direction to learn the correct answer
Bugs	Misconceptions are explained with error analysis and diagnosis
Informative tutoring	Includes verification feedback, error flagging, and strategic hints on how to proceed without providing the correct answer

Source: Based on Shute, 2008, p. 160.

whether increased complexity is better for learning than simple feedback is mixed (Shute, 2008). The inconclusive findings suggest that other factors in the nature of feedback may be more important than complexity, and that what matters most is what you *do* with the feedback to improve learning. In addition to these, four other types of feedback are important for formative assessment—goal-referenced, scaffolded, self-referenced, and standards-referenced.

Target-Referenced.   Feedback for embedded formative assessment that is *target-referenced* provides immediate information about your students' progress toward achieving a specific learning goal or objective (Wiggins, 2012). It is important that the targets are challenging yet attainable, and that the student has an expectation that he or she can, with sufficient, moderate effort, achieve the goal. Moderately difficult, attainable targets also result in greater student motivation and engagement. This is especially true if the feedback is directed toward greater mastery and understanding, rather than simply obtaining a right answer. It has been well established that individuals with a *mastery* or *learning goal orientation* will be more motivated than individuals with a *performance orientation*, demonstrating greater persistence despite failure and choosing more challenging tasks. A performance orientation, in contrast, results in a tendency to disengage with failure, show less interest in challenging tasks, and select tasks that are easy. Providing feedback that stresses mastery and connects effort to success helps to develop a mastery goal orientation. If a target is too easy and performance exceeds standards, feedback can actually lower motivation and subsequent performance (Wiliam, 2011). It turns out that positive feedback for success on easy tasks is less meaningful than feedback focused on partial success. In other words, don't strive for constant student success as they learn, and don't ask questions for which students always answer correctly!

Scaffolded.   Scaffolding is an approach to instruction in which the teacher provides support to enhance learning by breaking a task down into smaller parts and interacting with students to help them learn each part sequentially to reach a learning target (like what my daughter experienced in gymnastics). Typically, teachers give tips, strategies, new materials, and cues to students as "supports" that allow students to gradually develop autonomous learning strategies. Supports are removed as students progress in their learning and understanding.

Although there are many levels and types of instructional scaffolding, the elements of scaffolding that are important for immediate feedback include the emphasis on manageable, sequential steps and the goal of gradually shifting responsibility for learning from the teacher to the student. Feedback is focused on skills that are just beyond the student's capabilities and efforts, with guidance to pursue additional learning. This principle is based on Vygotsky's *zone of proximal development,* in which teachers identify and focus on skills that are within student capabilities and also challenge them to move them to higher learning (Horowitz et al., 2005). Teachers guide students' attention by giving them ideas and directions to enhance performance without giving correct answers.

Self-Referenced. This type of feedback compares student work or expectations with previous performance. Showing students how they progressed from what they did previously helps them see the improvement they made. The focus is on how work builds on or is better than previous performance (e.g., "Pat, your writing today shows a better understanding of noun–verb agreement than what you handed in last week"). This encourages students to believe that they are capable of subsequent learning and helps students define what needs to be done next; for example,

> "Maria, your division has improved by showing each step you used in your work. Now you need to be more careful about subtraction."

When students complete a learning task, they often think about *why* they were successful or unsuccessful. These messages are called *attributions*, and it is important for teachers to help students internalize appropriate reasons for success and failure as they learn. Motivation will be enhanced if students believe they were successful because of the effort they put forth (Pintrich & Schunk, 2013). Effort attributions are helpful because they communicate an ability to do the work successfully, which helps establish a positive self-efficacy that. That is, teachers can point out how students' specific effort was responsible for being correct. Effort attributions are especially important for low-performing students. Too often these students develop external attributions that when they are successful, it is for some reason that is not under their control (e.g., luck or teacher help), rather than an internal attribution such as effort. These attributions should emphasize a moderate amount of effort.

Standards-Referenced. Comparing student performance to identified standards of performance and exemplars is generally the most important and effective type of feedback to move students to higher learning. This type of feedback is goal referenced, with an emphasis on helping students understand how their current performance relates to criteria that demonstrate targeted learning on established standards. The emphasis is on showing students how their work compares with the criteria and standards, rather than to their previous work or how others performed.

As previously emphasized, it is important for students to know the criteria their performance will be judged against before attempting an answer to a question or task. This makes it much easier for you to show students how their performance compares to the criteria and for students to self-assess their work. You can show students exemplars of student work and reinforce the meaning of scores and grades to make this process more efficient. Word your feedback to refer to the criteria. For example, "Jon, your paper did not include an introductory paragraph, as shown here in our exemplar" or "Your answer is partially correct but, as I said in my question, I am looking for an example of a sentence with both adjectives and adverbs."

Determining the Nature of the Feedback

Feedback can differ on a number of dimensions. In keeping with our emphasis on how feedback needs to be tailored to the context, these few factors are important in determining the nature of effective feedback that you will use in your teaching.

Amount.   Generally, feedback that is specific and descriptive is better than making general comments. A specific, descriptive statement specifies in exact terms the nature of the performance, though this may be difficult to provide in the context of ongoing instruction. Furthermore, it is not practical to provide specific feedback to every student. You will need to make some choices about what to focus on. It best to determine where the most errors occur or what changes will be most helpful to the student. For example, it is relatively easy to comment on misspellings and grammatical errors while students are engaged in a writing assignment, but are these the most important aspects of the paper the student needs feedback about?

Timing.   It is generally recommended that feedback should be given during or immediately following student performance, or given with as small a delay as possible. By giving immediate feedback to students, they are able to use the information while they have time to act on it to improve their learning. If there is a significant delay, the feedback may not be as meaningful. Giving feedback during a performance is especially effective. When Ryann did her gymnastics, her coach gave her feedback on her performance as she did her routine, not just after she finished ("straighten your legs, point your toes, lift your chin, smile").
You provide more frequent, immediate feedback when you:

- Develop or select activities with built-in opportunities for feedback.
- Circulate to monitor individual work, making comments to students.
- Use examples of ongoing student work to show all students' mistakes and corrections.
- Use techniques during recitations to monitor the progress of all students.

It should be noted, however, that there is evidence that some kinds of delayed feedback are as or more effective than immediate feedback (Shute, 2008). Immediate feedback is clearly more effective than delayed feedback in learning simple cognitive tasks and for less-able or struggling students, whereas delayed feedback may be more effective for more complex tasks and higher-ability students. In any event, it is generally better to return student work promptly. Feedback given weeks later is typically not very helpful.

Mode.   There are three modes of delivering feedback—oral, written, and demonstration. Oral feedback is needed for on-the-fly formative assessment when the teacher is circulating and monitoring student seatwork, sees opportunities for effective feedback, and then provides it. For planned embedded formative assessment feedback is also typically oral, though some brief written comments can be used.

Audience.   Feedback is given to either individuals, small groups, and large groups. Often embedded formative assessment feedback is given individually. When the same message or information is helpful to many students, group feedback is appropriate and more efficient. When teachers observe many students struggling with a seatwork task they will interrupt students' efforts with an explanation or feedback for the entire group.

Type of Task. Feedback typically focuses on either *what* was learned or *how* it was learned. In giving feedback about what was learned, the focus is on knowledge and understanding, on content that needs to be mastered. The emphasis is on what was successfully understood, what still needs work, and actions to improve knowledge and understanding.

An emphasis on how performance improved can also focus on the skills, strategies, and procedures students used as they were learning. Here the emphasis is on procedural targets, how well they are applying specific thinking strategies or steps. Feedback is directed toward important skills and strategies, noting which were used well and which need further work, and explaining how students can improve these skills and strategies; for example, "Gerald, your answer to the problem is correct. I can see that you used the right three steps in solving the problem."

For relatively simple learning tasks (e.g., simple recall and recognition, knowledge, as determined by the student's capabilities), it is generally best to use immediate feedback. For difficult new tasks, it is better to give immediate feedback, at least initially. When the task is a thinking skill or strategy, delayed and elaboration feedback are most effective. Elaboration feedback provides cues to the student to identify the correct answer, rather than verifying the right answer.

Differentiated Embedded Formative Feedback

It has been stressed that effective feedback is differentiated, that it depends on matching the type and nature of the feedback with contextual variables. We'll now consider three of these variables—learner level of ability, grade level, and subject.

Learner Level of Ability. Higher-ability students tend to benefit more from delayed feedback, especially for complex learning tasks. Some research suggests that low-ability students may need more immediate, specific feedback and might benefit more from receiving both verification and elaboration feedback and knowing they are on track, rather than something like, "Try again," without knowing the correct response. Norm-referenced comparisons should be avoided; instead, scaffolded feedback should be emphasized. With struggling students, it is also helpful to check to make sure they understand the feedback. Because they are performing poorly, they may not want to ask clarification or explanation questions about the feedback.

Lower-ability students need to know specifically how their performance relates to effort. This encourages a hopeful and positive approach to further learning. They need self-referenced feedback that stresses the importance of their effort in making progress. However, lower-ability students may need instruction in self-referenced feedback first, which is important to not be demoralized by what is judged to be continual failure.

Finally, feedback must be honest for lower-ability students without unjustified praise, but there is also a need to avoid a self-fulfilling prophecy in which poor work is continually expected and produced. For low-ability students who are reluctant to learn, feedback needs to be sensitive to their tendency to think that any kind of feedback is "critical" and affirms their self-perception of being inadequate, inferior, or even stupid. According to Brookhart (2008), it is important to deal with the negative feelings about feedback first, then to provide scaffolded feedback so that students are able to understand and use it. It is best to select one or two suggestions. It is also important to avoid constant "negative" feedback (e.g., this is wrong, this is wrong, and this is wrong!). Although you need to be honest with students about their performance, too much negativity only reinforces their poor self-efficacy. It is best to use self-referenced feedback for these students and to set goals that provide initial success before moving on to more difficult goals.

Higher-ability students benefit more by being challenged, as well as by questioning that takes them to higher learning. To the extent that these students have a larger base of knowledge from which to draw, feedback that enables them to examine errors in thinking is effective. Higher-ability students are often more receptive to feedback, especially in messages that not only improve their understanding but also extend it to further learning. These students are more receptive to critical comments because they see these as needed to improve, as an integral aspect of learning. They need elaboration feedback that challenges them to learn more and feedback that emphasizes processes such as cognitive skills and strategies. Higher-ability students may also be more receptive and skilled at self-referenced feedback.

Grade Level.   At the elementary level, where teachers are primarily responsible for one class, it is much easier to give immediate feedback, to scaffold, to check student understanding of feedback, and to use elaborative feedback compared to the secondary level. Elementary teachers have more opportunities to work individually with students to guide their thinking and efforts. Elementary-level instruction tends to be more teacher directed than student directed, with more control over feedback resting with the teacher and opportunities for continual use of feedback.

Subject.   To what extent would or should feedback vary, according to the subject matter that is taught? We know that feedback is not a single process for every context, and there are differences for different subjects. Math and science have relatively clear paths of progression for learning and understanding. Typically, a predetermined sequence of knowledge is taught and learned, promoted by external standards-based accountability tests. Scaffolded feedback is relatively easy with math and science, as is an emphasis on fairly structured patterns of thinking, skills, and strategies in these subjects.

In contrast, English and humanities tend to be taught in a more meandering, less-planned manner, with an emphasis in English on ideas, imagination, and creativity. Continual questioning and feedback are used to enhance students' thinking skills and deep understanding, initiated by impromptu, varied, and unpredictable student comments and questions. In these classrooms, much feedback is immediate, designed to fit the nature of what is happening in a specific classroom at a specific time. Even two classes with the same learning targets can stimulate different types of feedback, based on what occurs in each class. Although it is more difficult to scaffold feedback in English, social studies classes, with an emphasis on content knowledge, lend themselves to scaffolded feedback. The emphasis on content also encourages a verification type of delayed feedback.

Table 4.10 shows key do's and don'ts for effective feedback.

What About Giving Praise?

Most teachers use praise ubiquitously in the classroom. It can be thought of as a type of feedback to the student, but it is also used frequently to control student behavior and for classroom management. In general, research shows that teachers use too much praise and use it inappropriately as positive reinforcement (Good & Brophy, 2008).

Like effective feedback, praise can be helpful to students if it draws attention to student progress and performance in relation to standards. It is also a good type of message to accompany other types of feedback. This is especially true when the praise focuses on student effort and other internal attributions so that students know that their efforts are recognized, appreciated, and connected to their performance.

TABLE 4.10   Key Do's and Don'ts for Effective Feedback

Do	Don't
Use challenging yet attainable goals.	Use goals that are too high or too low.
Emphasize mastery goal orientation.	Emphasize performance goal orientation.
Ensure that feedback is clear, transparent, and easily understood.	Use feedback that is unclear and/or difficult to understand.
Compare student performance to standards, criteria, cognitive strategies, and previous performance.	Compare student performance to the performance of other students or emphasize the person rather than the task.
Use a moderate amount of specific, individualized, and descriptive feedback.	Use general or vague feedback.
Give feedback as soon as possible, especially for simple cognitive tasks, tests, and other assignments.	Give delayed feedback, except for slightly delayed feedback for cognitively complex tasks, especially for high achievers.
Use both verification and elaboration feedback.	Use only verification feedback.
Match feedback to student ability.	Use the same feedback for all students.
Focus on key errors and misunderstandings.	Ignore key errors.
Emphasize effort attributions.	Emphasize external attributions.
Give feedback as students learn.	Give feedback only after performance.
Anticipate probable feedback messages.	Rely on unplanned or unanticipated feedback.

Praise is most effective when it is delivered as a spontaneous, genuine, and accurate message, and when it is accompanied by a description of the commended skill or behavior.. You should praise students simply and directly, in natural language, without gushy or dramatic words. A straightforward, declarative sentence is best. For example, say: "Good; you did a wonderful job of drawing the vase; your lines are clear and the perspective is correct," not "Incredible!" or "Great!"

You definitely want to avoid praising how smart or intelligent kids are. That's because if success is then attributed to ability it can actually have deleterious consequences (Dweck, 2008). For example, if Susan keeps hearing "wow, you are so smart," she may think she doesn't need to study very hard. If students focus on being good at something, for example, "you are really great with math," there is some evidence that there is less resilience to making mistakes than when you say "you really did well solving that math problem."

Try to use as many different phrases as you can when praising. If you say the same thing over and over, it may be perceived as insincere with little serious attention to the performance. This is especially true if the phrase is a vague generality such as "good" or "nice job." It is also best to keep your verbal praise consistent with your nonverbal behavior. Students quickly and accurately pick up teachers' nonverbal messages. So, if the performance really is good and progress is demonstrated, say your praise with a smile, using a voice tone and inflection that communicates warmth and sincerity.

In the end, as I have already pointed out the reaction of the student to the feedback is what matters most. Wiliam and Leahy (2015) make the point this way (p. 107): "Feedback—no matter how well designed—that the student does not act upon is a waste of time." This means that just giving at-the-moment feedback, hopefully focused on the task and not the person, isn't sufficient. You also need to pay attention to how the student reacts to it and what is done with the information.

Summary

This chapter focused on how to implement embedded formative assessment. Key points in the chapter include the following:

- Formative assessment provides ongoing feedback from students to teachers and from teachers to students; summative assessment measures student learning at the end of a unit of instruction.
- Formative assessment consists of a teacher monitoring students and their academic performances to inform instructional and learning decision-making and the nature of feedback given to students.
- Formative assessment occurs while instruction occurs, as embedded, or after a more formal assessment, as summative-based.
- Embedded formative assessment occurs on the fly, at the moment, spontaneously, as well as at planned points in an instructional sequence.

- Observation for embedded formative assessment includes teacher "reading" nonverbal behavior such as facial expressions, eye contact, body language, and vocal cues. These behaviors indicate student emotions, dispositions, and attitudes.
- Emotion is communicated best through facial expression. Eye contact is key to assessing attentiveness, confidence, and interest.
- Body language includes gestures, emblems, illustrators, affect displays, regulators, body movement, and posture.
- Voice-related cues such as pitch, loudness, rate, and pause indicate confidence and emotions.
- Informal observation consists of observing student behavior, interpreting it, synthesizing, and naming the trait or characteristic.
- Errors in informal observation are often associated with when the observations are made, sampling of student behavior, and teacher bias.
- Teachers use oral questioning during instruction to involve students, promote thinking, review, control students, and assess student progress. Effective questions are clear, matched with learning targets, involve the entire class, and allow sufficient wait time. Avoid closed, tugging, guessing, and leading questions, and keep questions in the proper sequence.
- Effective feedback relates performance to standards, progress, and corrective instructional procedures. It is timely and given frequently, and it focuses specifically and descriptively on key errors.
- Effective feedback is varied and actionable.
- Effective feedback involves the student and affects self-regulation, self-efficacy, and goal orientation.
- Effective feedback is honest and accurate.
- Effective feedback is tailored to individual students and teacher preferences.
- Different types of feedback include verification, elaboration, goal-referenced, scaffolded, self-referenced, and standards-referenced.
- Feedback should be differentiated based on learner level of ability, grade level, and subject.
- Effective praise is sincere, spontaneous, natural, accurate, varied, and straightforward. It focuses on progress, effort attributions, specific behaviors, and corrective actions.

Introductory Case Study Answer

Madison used multiple embedded formative assessment practices. She used her *observations* from the previous day to drive her decision regarding her flexible grouping of students, and she decided to differentiate the Guided Math center activities based on her observations. She used *questions* in her Guided Math center to understand her students' errors and to make decisions on whether to remodel, collaboratively work with the student, or allow the student to try again independently. Students were getting *timely feedback* regarding whether they were measuring angles correctly and Madison was providing *immediate and instructional corrective measures*.

In the Guided Math center, Madison ensured that

- the feedback was directly linked to her learning target;
- she actively engaged students in generating the feedback on their error;
- the feedback positively impacted students' self-regulation, self-efficacy and goal orientation;
- her feedback focused on the task;
- she provided immediate opportunities for students to use the feedback;
- she and the student worked together to highlight errors in understanding; and
- she made sure the feedback was accurate.

Suggestions for Action Research

1. While in a classroom, informally observe students' nonverbal behavior. It would be best if another observer could also observe in the class so that you could compare notes. Take a sheet of paper and draw a line down the middle. On the left-hand side, record a description of the nonverbal behavior—such as a facial expression, body language, or vocal cue—and on the right side, summarize your interpretation of each one. It would be interesting to check these out with the teacher for accuracy.

2. Ask a teacher about the kinds of questions he or she asks and what kinds of student responses are typical. Compare the teacher's comments to the suggestions for effective questioning presented in Table 4.7. If possible, observe the teacher and record examples of effective and ineffective questioning.

3. Ask a teacher if it makes sense to conceptualize formative assessment as embedded or summative-based, and whether he/she uses both on-the-fly and planned embedded formative assessment.

4. Observe how teachers in two or three different classrooms use praise. What kind of praise is given by each teacher? What is the effect of the praise on the students? How could the praise you observe be improved?

5. Explore some online websites that focus on providing formative feedback to students you may one day teach. Match the suggestions on the websites with the keys to effective feedback in this chapter. What is overlap?

MyEdLab **Self-Check 4.1**

MyEdLab **Self-Check 4.2**

MyEdLab **Self-Check 4.3**

MyEdLab **Self-Check 4.4**

MyEdLab **Application Exercise 4.1**   Questioning for Embedded Formative Assessment

MyEdLab **Application Exercise 4.2**   Embedded Formative Assessment

Summative-Based Formative Assessment

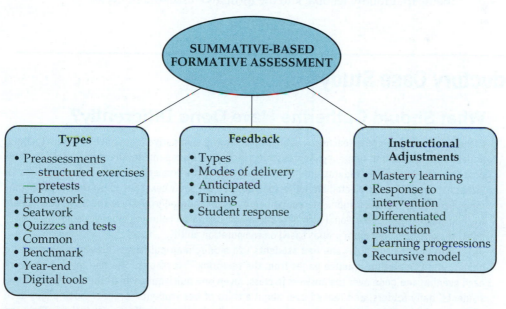

CHAPTER 5 Concept Map

Learning Outcomes

After reading this chapter, you should be able to:

5.1 Understand and be able to explain how preassessments (structured exercises and pretests), homework, and seatwork are used for gathering information about what students know and can do prior to determining appropriate instruction.

5.2 Identify advantages and disadvantages to using different types of summative-based assessments to provide results that will be used formatively, including tests, quizzes, interim and year-end large-scale assessments.

5.3 Distinguish effective from ineffective student feedback that can be provided to students from tests, quizzes, and other forms of summative-based formative assessments.

5.4 Identify and be able to show how to apply different instructional adjustments that follow feedback in the formative assessment cycle.

Introductory Case Study

What Should Catherine Have Done Differently?

Catherine, a second-grade teacher, was home scoring the summative assessment on her students' understanding of counting money. As she scored each child's assessment, she started getting nervous: The majority of her students did not have mastery of the concept. She started asking herself, "What happened?" and reflected on her lessons for the past two weeks. She knew that at the beginning of the unit, she had forgone pretesting her students' knowledge because she believed students weak in computation skills would also be weak when working on counting money. Using this knowledge, she organized her math groups based on computation ability.

Throughout the unit, she had students use money manipulatives, play money counting games, and completing practice pages from the textbook's workbook. She had given homework each evening and gone over the answers in class, given one quick quiz, which she sent home in the students' daily folders, and looked over about a third of her students' practice book pages each afternoon. By looking at students' workbook pages, she had an idea of misconceptions. She used this information to start math instruction the following day with an additional practice problem. Students completed the problem and she looked at the results during her planning period later in the day.

Catherine had used the same set of lessons this year as she had last year because her previous students had demonstrated success. Yet, this year, the students' summative results were very different. Catherine wondered where she had gone wrong with her instruction.

As you read this chapter, think about what Catherine should have done differently. What is the overarching problem with Catherine's use of summative-based formative assessment? How would you advise Catherine to improve her summative-based formative assessment practices?

This chapter has a seemingly contradictory title. Summative and formative assessment together? As explained in the previous chapter, formative *purposes* are often achieved with what are first and foremost summative assessments. This chapter focuses on these so-called "summative-based" formative assessments, from actually gathering data to providing feedback and instructional adjustments. While much from the previous chapter is relevant to this use of summative assessments, key differences are noted. Summative-based formative assessment, or what some would call "formal" formative assessment, is a planned, structured activity, usually for the entire class or groups of students, that generates results that are used after some time has elapsed, rather than immediately. It is different from embedded formative assessment by virtue of being done either *before* or *following* instruction, rather than occurring *during* instruction. Student knowledge, understanding, and skills are assessed, and the results are used by teachers to give feedback and plan instruction. These assessments are used prior to beginning instruction, as a preassessment, during seatwork, following a unit of instruction (e.g., a quiz, chapter test, or semester exam), or as common, interim, or benchmark tests that are given every few weeks or quarterly to assess progress toward achievement of state standards. We'll consider each of these types and discuss how the results from them are used formatively.

Preassessments, Homework, and Seatwork

As indicated, a **preassessment** (or *early* assessment) is given prior to instructing students, before they study and learn. It is set up in advance and administered as planned, with some amount of time between the gathering of data and interpretation that allows teachers to reflect on the results and determine the next most appropriate instructional activities. It's used to "size up" students. Typically, there would be hours, days, or even weeks between the assessment and feedback to students and instructional adjustments. For example, it could be a unit test covering several weeks' instruction to see what students did not understand, with further small-group instruction focused in specific areas in subsequent weeks.

Preassessments are important for several reasons. First, they help teachers identify where in learning progressions instruction should be focused, avoiding redundancy and moving students ahead. Second, preassessments can help teachers determine the appropriate level of challenge and difficulty students need to motivate them, making instruction more intrinsically interesting, relevant, and engaging. Third, preassessment helps students understand learning targets and the sequential process of learning that is needed. We will consider two types of preassessments: structured exercises and pretests, as well as two other planned types of formative assessment that are used following instruction—homework and seatwork.

Structured Exercises

A good approach to evaluating current student knowledge and skills is to design structured exercises that will provide you with an opportunity to observe students in the context of specific performance situations. These exercises are not like a formal pretest, but they are more structured than informal observation.

One approach is to design an activity for all students. This could be a writing assignment, an oral presentation, or group work. For example, asking students to write about their summer vacation, in class, can help to identify language arts skills. Students can interview each other about their summer vacations and make short presentations to the class. Digital games can be used to observe students' math skills. Students can be asked to read aloud. A common technique is to ask students to write information about themselves on cards, such as names of family members, hobbies, and interests. Any one of these demonstrations of knowledge or skills alone would not be sufficient for instructional planning, but as you build a portrait of your students from many such observations—and combine this information with previous test scores, student records, and comments from other teachers—you will have a pretty accurate idea of the strengths and weaknesses of your students.

It is best to keep structured exercises nonthreatening. This is important because you want to minimize student anxiety. Also, it is best not to grade the exercise. Arrange the conditions for engaging in the structured activity to be as comfortable as possible. Having a student read orally to a small group or only to you is probably less threatening than reading to the entire class. If students are able to work at their own pace, without strict time constraints, they are more likely to be relaxed. Avoid comparisons of students.

Pretests

It is becoming more common for teachers to administer a formal pretest of the content that will subsequently be covered. The pretest would supposedly indicate what students know and don't know or what they can or cannot do. The operative word here is "supposedly." For several reasons, pretests often will not be very helpful for planning instruction. First, at least at the beginning of school in the fall, students have returned from vacation and have probably thought little about world history, algebra, or other school subjects. Their actual or true knowledge may not be reflected on a "surprise" test. Second, it is hard to motivate students to do their best on such tests. What do they have to gain by trying hard to answer the questions? This is especially true for older students. Third, to be helpful diagnostically, the pretest would need to be fairly long and detailed. Finally, presenting students with a pretest right away in the fall may not be the best way to start a class. Testing students what they know about something they will learn may be intimidating and create anxiety about the class (on the other hand, a pretest can communicate to students that the teacher is serious about learning). For these reasons, formal pretests are not used very often for formative assessment. The validity of the information is questionable, and the effect on the classroom environment and teacher–student relationships may be negative. What will students think if they do poorly on the pretest? How will they react and what will it mean?

A more recent and controversial use of pretests is for setting a baseline of student proficiency that can be tested weeks later to determine "progress" in learning. A "pretest/posttest" logic is used to assess student growth. Sometimes these are "common" tests prepared by the school or school district so that all teachers are using the same pretest, but in many schools, teachers prepare their own pretests. Either way, the process is prone to corruption since the results are typically used to evaluate teachers. If teachers need to show growth from pre- to posttest, why not assure growth by making the pretest difficult and the posttest easy? Why not grade strictly on the pretest to give low scores and leniently on the posttest? This issue gets at validity—what the test scores are used for and if it's reasonable to use the scores to evaluate your teaching.

If a pretest (other than common test) is to be used successfully, it needs to be short and targeted to specific knowledge and skills. Students need to be motivated to do their best work, and you need to make clear to students that the purpose of the test is to help them learn more and help you plan more effective instruction. The results may suggest the need for further diagnostic assessment, especially if students do very well. In that case, more difficult questions are needed to find the "sweet spot" for effective instruction. After all, it may do more harm than good to teach students something they already know! Most of us have firsthand experience with that.

Homework

The primary purpose of homework for most teachers is to provide extra practice in applying knowledge and skills. Homework is also used to extend, expand, and elaborate student learning. A third purpose is to check on student learning, which acts primarily as way for teachers to determine whether students, individually and as a group, have reached or exceeded proficiency. In this sense, homework can be used diagnostically to determine which specific areas of knowledge and skill need further instruction, and to give students specific feedback. The information can be used to give further assignments, group students, and provide individualized help. You'll need to be prepared in advance when certain percentages of students do very well. What will you do with the 25% of students who "master" the homework, while you provide additional instruction to another 25% who didn't get it at all?

There are well-known limitations with homework, most importantly uneven and unknown input and assistance from parents, siblings, and friends. Because of this, homework that provides good diagnostic information should require students to complete, in their own writing, answers to constructed-response questions and assignments that show, where appropriate, work that led to their answers (e.g., with math problems). By reviewing students' work in small steps, you will be able to provide greater specificity in the feedback you give as well as with the instructional correctives to help students. Simply giving correct answers and having students check their work, without any prescriptive information, is not very helpful. Students need to know why they do not understand or have not correctly applied a skill.

Seatwork

Through the use of a variety of in-class student summative tasks, teachers are able to obtain feedback about student learning from multiple perspectives. With seatwork and other individualized activities, teachers can circulate, monitor student performance, and provide immediate, specific feedback as students work to complete a task or question. Often, digital games and apps are used to engage and "test" students. Seatwork can be used to provide formative information as long as there is close monitoring, frequent feedback, and opportunities for students to self-assess according to rubrics and criteria that have been provided. Many apps provide immediate feedback to students. Typically now, students use iPads or other digital devices to use the apps. To use seatwork as formative assessment, you need to be actively engaged with students, interacting frequently. It is not a time to simply allow students to be on their own. At the very least, students should be required to come to the teacher to have their work checked and to receive meaningful feedback. Seatwork is similar to embedded formative assessment. The difference is that seatwork is planned, with predetermined questions and tasks.

The advantages and disadvantages of using different types of preassessments, homework, and seatwork for formative purposes are summarized in Table 5.1.

TABLE 5.1   Advantages and Disadvantages of Using Preassessments, Homework, and Seatwork for Formative Purposes

Type of Assessment	Advantages	Disadvantages
Structured Exercises	Comfortable, less "test" oriented with less accompanying stress	Does not provide a common, standard result or finding More prone to being incomplete
Pretests	Provides a standard baseline for all students Provides a starting point for more specific diagnostic assessments Provides results teachers can analyze	Formal test structure can be intimidating Students may react negatively if they do poorly May not discriminate well for high-achieving students
Homework	Relatively low stakes Can be individualized Useful for detecting common misconceptions, struggles, or errors	Not always the result of student work Difficulty knowing what to do with students who do not complete the work
Seatwork	Digital versions engage students and provide immediate feedback Tasks can be individualized Teachers can monitor and respond to individual questions	Not systematic and prone to errors Relies on students to be motivated Easy for students to be off task Technical difficulties with apps and digital games

Quizzes and Unit Tests

Even though quizzes and unit/chapter tests are summative, to document what students know, teachers often do or should use quizzes and unit tests formatively. From a formative standpoint the quiz is a structured procedure to check on student learning of specific skills, standards, or relatively specific learning targets that are part of more general goals for major units of instruction. Typically objective in nature, the purpose is to provide the teacher with an indication of current knowledge or skills quickly, and to be able to give fairly immediate feedback to students. Helpful feedback is best provided when quizzes are graded in class, right after they are completed. With this procedure students learn right away what they know and what they missed. With just a few questions on the quiz, it's easy for them relate their performance to how they learned the material, and to see what they do not know or misunderstand. This information is then used to individualize instruction, form small groups, and provide instructional correctives that will address learning deficits and move students as appropriate to the next level of proficiency. Keep in mind that the results must be used to give students feedback that they act upon, and for instructional correctives. That's the kicker. All too often students only know what was right or wrong, without any individualized feedback, or, even more likely, have no opportunities for more instruction to improve their understanding.

With tests that cover weeks of content, what would be called unit, chapter, or semester tests, using the results formatively is challenging. This type of assessment is primarily summative in purpose. Students take the test one day and receive results at a later point—maybe the next day, but often the next week or even longer. The time interval between when students take the test and when the results are available is important for several reasons. First, the student has to "think back" about their performance, and the longer the time interval, the more difficult it is for the student to connect the result with how they studied. Second, students will focus mostly on the overall result (e.g., score, rating, or grade) and tend to pay less attention to feedback. Third, feedback is often general, if it's provided at all, and harder to act upon as the time interval increases. We've all experienced this! You take a chapter test and receive the results a week later with a score and grade, and not much else.

For constructed-response tests and papers, feedback can be more specific, but it can take significant time to individualize comments. Sometimes rubrics can be used effectively, as will be described in upcoming chapters, but my experience is that students anticipate individualized feedback and pay attention to it. Teachers often wonder if their comments are even read! Sometimes I'm sure they aren't, but if the right assessment climate and expectation is established students will indeed pay attention to your comments. The most common, most personalized approach is to write comments throughout the paper or after selected constructed-response question answers. Because efficiency is important, shorthand can be established, or brief comments can cue students to probe further about what they missed or did not fully understand.

Digital Tools

The use of digital tools for formative assessment is now ubiquitous and quickly replacing physical classroom response systems that use sticky notes, exit tickets, or clickers. Digital tools involving free online sites, laptops, iPads, iPhones, tablets, and other devices allow students to record responses electronically. The tools allow students to complete a task with an app, game, or prompt. Either the instructor presents material to students, then poses a question or quiz, or, more likely, students simply engage in the digital program that contains the questions.

For most digital tool systems students respond to the question at the same time, which helps you to immediately gauge student understanding. Often teachers will ask students to discuss the results in small groups and retest. With many systems, the teacher can tabulate and graph student responses, which can be immediately displayed to students (e.g., how many students selected each alternative in a multiple-choice question). Many systems automatically provide feedback to students. What digital tools you use for summative-based formative assessment may be prescribed, or, you may have the freedom and support to select what works best for your students and teaching style. Either way, there is much to

Teacher's Corner

Jamie Mullenaux

National Board Certified Teacher, Elementary

As a technology resource teacher, teachers often talk with me about how to incorporate technology and formative assessment. My first question is always, "What do you want to accomplish?" There are great technology tools available and free to use, but teachers need to know their purpose in using a tool. Every tool has different purposes.

For example, does the teacher want to increase student engagement when formatively assessing? If so, using a technology tool that provides a game or competition environment may be a great choice. Does the teacher want students to give students immediate feedback regarding their knowledge on a topic so students know what to review for a unit test? If so, using a tool that provides students with individual feedback regarding their responses is timelier than the delay

in feedback from a paper-pencil quiz. Does the teacher want to use technology to help drive her future instruction? If so, tools that provide disaggregated data can be beneficial. Does the teacher want to use technology to evaluate students' thinking when the teacher can't be present and talk with the students while they are working? If so, tools that allow students to take a picture of their work and do voice-over annotations or create a video of their work as they complete it can be beneficial.

The key to using technology for formative assessment is to know what you want to formatively assess and why you want to use technology as a platform. Then teachers can pick a tool that will align with the content and purpose so that the use of technology enhances their formative assessment practices.

choose from. If you enter something like "formative assessment apps" on a browser, many possibilities will pop up. Many are free or very inexpensive (see https://www.nwea.org/blog/2014/33-digital-tools-advancing-formative-assessment-classroom/). Central office personnel may have a repository of apps and other systems that have been used successfully. An important caveat, however, is that if someone else is designing test items, you'll need to review those items carefully for validity, reliability/precision, and bias.

Common Assessments

In the past few years a new type of summative-based formative assessment has developed—what is called a **common assessment**. As mentioned in Chapter 4, common assessments are prepared collaboratively by a team of teachers and/or others (e.g., district supervisors) to measure student progress toward shared standards-based learning targets and goals. Usually a few weeks of learning is assessed, similar in some ways to benchmark tests, but because the tests are the same for all students and teachers, there are great opportunities for teachers to review and discuss results, and suggest instructional adjustments. While common tests usually have good evidence that they are closely related to content and instruction, other technical aspects concerned with reliability/precision and fairness could be weak. More recently, teachers are able to select from prewritten items, which usually (but not necessarily!) improves technical quality.

Interim Assessments

High-stakes accountability demands have led to widespread implementation of periodic testing during the school year (e.g., every 9 weeks) to determine student progress toward meeting standards that will be assessed on the end-of-the-year high-stakes tests. These assessments are called **benchmark** or **interim tests**. What is pertinent to this chapter is that many in the commercial testing industry, as well as others, contend that these tests are also formative. However, this claim and the nature of the testing usually results in *low-level* formative assessment, at best. There is often little feedback to students and little use of the data to influence subsequent instruction, especially when compared to assessments prepared and administered by teachers for their classes (Goertz, Olah, & Meggan, 2009; Marsh, Pane, & Hamilton, 2006). On the other hand, testing companies have developed new types of items and reporting systems that more effectively than in the past address formative assessment (Bennett, 2015).

The primary purpose of interim tests is summative, to document what students have learned over a 9-week period. Using the results in a formative manner is not straightforward for several reasons. First, the amount of material covered by these tests, which typically have 30–50 multiple-choice test items, is considerable. This rarely provides more diagnostic information that would suggest specific deficiencies. Typically, there is insufficient detail to suggest specific instructional correctives. Feedback to students is spotty at best. Often there is no feedback to students. Finally, when these tests are prepared by the school districts, the technical quality of the items may be low. The result is that many teachers find them restrictive, burdensome, and unnecessary, especially if little new information about what students can do is provided.. This is consistent with the more generalized finding that it is difficult to use the results from summative tests formatively (Perie, Marion, & Gong, 2009).For students, these assessments tend to interrupt instruction and contribute to what many believe is a serious overtesting of students.

On the positive side, interim tests give teachers immediate results, usually broken out by student and item, with options for graphing trends (for secondary teachers, though, this creates a mountain of data). Some teachers have reported using interim test results to identify student strengths and weaknesses, to set subsequent instructional priorities, and to differentiate instruction (Abrams, Wetzel, & McMillan, 2010). There have also been reports of increased collaboration among teachers (Wayman & Cho, 2009). Some research suggests that positive formative uses of interim tests depend on a supportive culture that expects use of test data, having high-quality test items, and conditions in which teachers can discuss together the meaning of results (Abrams & McMillan, 2012). If interim test results suggest deficiencies, it will be best for you to confirm with other evidence and discuss results with others to identify trends and reasons for poor performance. Often students are not motivated to do their best work for these tests, with obvious implications for interpretation.

Interim testing may have some formative value, but be wary. It is insufficient to simply administer a test after several weeks of learning, give teachers results, and call it formative assessment. There is a need to structure the interim testing process so that instruction is actually affected and student learning improved. Because the level of resources school districts invest in what they may think is "formative" is significant, especially when the tests are purchased from commercial testing companies, there needs to be careful consideration of the factors to be addressed so that the "return on investment" is high.

Teacher's Corner
Rachel Boyd

National Board Certified Teacher, Elementary

One of the ways I use interim assessments formatively is to look in-depth at the data and use it to drive my math daily reviews. I make daily reviews that contain four questions which students complete at the end of the block. The topics covered on the reviews are based on the interim data. I check students' work daily during class so I can immediately fix misconceptions and to determine when students have repeatedly mastered a topic and I can eliminate that concept from the daily reviews. The students also complete their work in a notebook so both the students and I can see their progress.

Year-End Large-Scale Assessments

Since using assessment to improve student learning is all the rage, it's not surprising that companies and states that develop tests intended for wide usage for assessing proficiency on end-of-year standards have pivoted to formative assessment. Two efforts in this regard that are based on the Common Core competencies are the Smarter Balanced Assessment Consortium and the Partnership for Assessment of Readiness for College and Career (PARCC). Both of these organizations boast "next generation" summative year-end assessments that focus on cognitive skills as well as content knowledge, and use innovative item-types and alignment to standards to promote a new type of assessment. Both also emphasize formative assessment. For example, on the Smarter Balanced website, the promotion is that their tests are "more than just a test," and can be used to support high-quality teaching, improved learning for all students, and assessment of 21st-century skills (see www.smarterbalanced.org). Interim assessments may be purchased to check student progress toward proficiency on the standards assessed at the end of the year. Also, many states develop their own year-end large-scale accountability tests, and most hope the results from these tests will be used formatively.

The issue is that the promise of using large-scale test results formatively does not match well with the reality of how these tests are designed and the level of detail provided that can be used either for feedback or instructional adjustments. Typically, these tests have 35–50 items to measure learning that has occurred over an entire school year. This provides a general, overall score for each student on all the standards (though the standards are sampled, not comprehensively assessed), and sometimes subscale scores. Even though results are now reported immediately, it is difficult to give students fine-tuned, helpful feedback on the basis of a general score. Any instructional adjustments are likely to be implemented the following year, if at all. Consequently, large-scale summative assessments, at least those administered at the end of the school year, are not effective summative-based formative assessments. The interim tests that derive from them and associated digital resources are much more useful.

Feedback Reconsidered

As you have hopefully now been thoroughly convinced, feedback is heart and soul of formative assessment. We've discussed feedback extensively in the previous chapter and inserted feedback principles as appropriate throughout this chapter. Some further application of principles of feedback for summative-based formative assessment is needed, but before venturing into that information, allow me to tell you another short story about my daughter, Ryann. As a gymnast, Ryann's goal was to earn a score of 10 on each of her routines. After she completed a routine, the judges gave her a score of, say, 8.5 or 9.2. This is analogous to a teacher giving a student a score or grade. But simply *knowing* the score didn't help Ryann know what she needed to do to *improve* her score. When the judge immediately indicated, specifically, why certain points were deducted, then she knew what to work on. Furthermore, if the judge or coach told Ryann how she could improve the skill, corrective procedures were suggested. Similarly, a student who receives a 70% on a test knows that he or she has not done well, but this information alone does not tell the student what to do next. Or, suppose you just started to learn golf. You swing and miss the ball (as I have). Your skill level is obviously low. But knowing that is not enough. You need to get feedback about *why* you missed it. Is it because of your stance, your hand grip, the position of your head, your backswing, or some other aspect of your swing? When the teacher tells you precisely what you did wrong, what you need to correct, how you can correct it, and how you can advance, effective feedback has been provided.

Now, on with more about summative-based formative assessment feedback.

Feedback Types and Modes of Delivery

In Chapter 4, different types of feedback were described, with suggested delivery modes for differentiation as needed. Table 5.2 shows types and modes as applied to summative-based formative assessment, with examples. You will see an emphasis on student engagement, specific actionable information, and follow-up. As emphasized in Figure 5.1, a key component is knowing how students respond to the feedback that is provided. Is the information helpful? What is there emotional response? What does it mean to them? Will they follow up as hoped? What you need to do is ask students about the feedback they receive, addressing these kinds of questions. This will show to students that you are very serious about how assessment helps their learning, and that their feedback about your feedback is valued. This helps establish a positive assessment climate and appropriate student expectations.

To be used formatively, results from summative assessments must include feedback that is actionable. With an objective test students know questions they answered correctly and incorrectly, but additional feedback is needed. There needs to be further information that can help the student understand why an answer is incorrect, why there has been a misunderstanding or misconception. For example, after a student gives a speech, you will provide feedback. Note how the following is specific and actionable, helping the student know what to do differently the next time: "Your speech was delivered too quickly. It will help you to pronounce each word more slowly and to pause between each sentence." Similarly: "I really liked the way you read your story this morning. You pronounced the words very clearly and spoke enthusiastically." How often have you received feedback like "good work," "nice job," "excellent," "awkward," "OK," and "try harder"? What do vague messages like these convey? There is only verification of correctness, with little or nothing that helps students understand in greater detail the particular aspects of their work or behavior that are appropriate or that need improvement.

There are limits, however, to specificity. It is possible to provide so much specific, narrow feedback that it is overwhelming or difficult to understand. Helpful feedback is not too general and not too specific. It is something in between that

TABLE 5.2 Summative-Based Formative Assessment Feedback Types and Modes of Delivery

Type/Mode	Description	Example
Verification	Indicates wrong answers, with or without correct answers flagged or retakes permitted.	Test is returned with wrong answers indicated; students have an opportunity to retake a parallel form of the test.
Elaboration	Includes explanation of why answers are incorrect; may provide cues to correct answers and/or error analysis.	Test is returned with a key that shows students why incorrect alternatives are wrong.
Target-Referenced	Provides fine-tuned feedback related to a specific learning target.	Quiz is returned with specific comments about why the answer did not reflect a complete understanding.
Scaffolded	Indicates where in a learning sequence or progress understanding is incomplete.	Tests designed to capture each step in sequential learning is used to show where in the sequence there is misunderstanding.
Self-Referenced	Shows how current performance has progressed from previous performance.	Test is returned with comments about what specific progress has been demonstrated since a previous assessment.
Standards-Referenced	Compares performance to criteria used to demonstrate proficiency in meeting standards.	Chapter test results are accompanied by rubrics that show performance in relation to criteria or aspect of the standard.
Amount	Amount of feedback.	Providing comments on key components of writing skill on a paper.
Timing	When feedback is provided.	Providing feedback to students on a digital test or quiz immediately.
Mode	How feedback is provided.	Digital scoring of a test that shows which questions were missed and the correct answers with explanations.
Audience	Feedback recipients.	The whole class discusses questions most students missed.
Type of Task	How the complexity of the task affects feedback.	A test intended to measure "higher-order" thinking focuses feedback on examples that show adequate and inadequate skills.
Differentiated	Providing different types of feedback to different students, taking into account student ability, grade level, and subject area.	High-ability students receive feedback focused on what they need to do to progress toward more in-depth understanding; struggling students' feedback helps achievement of basic proficiency.

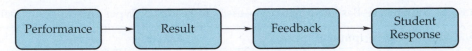

FIGURE 5.1   Feedback and Student Response.

can help the student move forward. For example, if you return a paper with comments about every paragraph or most sentences, the student may not be able to internalize the more important points. Not only does it take the teacher a long time to give this kind of feedback, but also it is not as effective as selecting key paragraphs or sentences and making specific comments. Also, you don't want to do the students' work for them.

Written feedback is most effective when there is a need to provide specific comments for each student on completed papers, projects, and tests. Written feedback also provides comments that students can save and use at a later time. For psychomotor learning targets, when many students are struggling to learn, demonstrations of correct procedures with the whole class will the helpful. Keep in mind, though, that the research on whether oral or written feedback is most effective is unclear. It turns out that the timing, specificity, and connections to further improvement are more important (Wiliam, 2010).

With older students feedback is often delayed and more planned. Limited class time and high numbers of students limit what can occur in a short time frame, especially individually. Secondary teachers can depend more on student initiative and responsibility for letting teachers know their confidence that they understand. and is often the best way for teachers to identify current understanding (e.g., rather than giving a quiz). Older students are also more adept at using scoring rubrics and criteria and using self-assessment.

Word your feedback to refer to the standards. For example, "Jon, your paper did not include an introductory paragraph, as shown here in our exemplar" or

Teacher's Corner
Tami Slater

National Board Certified Elementary Reading Specialist

Feedback is important to give to students during any unit of study. I try to give feedback on an every other day basis. Feedback can come in the form of one-to-one conferences, small-group conversations, or comments written on papers. A simple percentage or letter grade does not help the students learn from their mistakes or revise their work to make it better. When giving feedback, I give them one positive comment about their work or performance. Then I give them feedback in one area for improvement. Feedback is given on both their product and their effort. I also always ask them to do some self-evaluating and ask them for their interpretation of their product and performance.

"Your answer is partially correct but, as I said in my question, I am looking for an example of a sentence with both adjectives and adverbs."

Anticipating Feedback

As you may be thinking, the variables affecting summative-based formative feedback can make giving it effectively a very challenging task. Good teachers are able to anticipate the nature of the feedback they provide (Furtak, 2009). Through their understanding of the subject, student knowledge, and typical barriers to learning, they are able to informally plan out feedback. Although seemingly cumbersome, this teaching task is far more effective than waiting for each opportunity for feedback during the class.

To anticipate the nature of the feedback to provide, using three steps will be helpful (Furtak, 2009):

1. Understand the learning target.
2. Know probable student errors.
3. Establish feedback ideas.

Use of these steps is illustrated in Table 5.3 for a unit on density. The learning target is stated in terms of what students will know. Probable student errors consist of typical alternative explanations and conceptions. In the third step, feedback ideas are summarized. With this information, it is much easier and efficient for the teacher to identify thinking errors and provide feedback that will move students toward achievement of the learning target.

Skill in anticipating and responding to student misconceptions is a key attribute of effective teaching, one that develops with experience and in-depth

TABLE 5.3   Example of Steps in Anticipating Feedback

Learning Target	Students will understand that density is an independent property of shape or size of a material.
Probable Student Errors	Students believe that density changes when the size and/or shape of the material is changed.
Feedback Ideas	Ask students to explain their thinking to focus on either shape or size or both.
	Ask students to think about the fundamental idea of density.
	Tell students that density is independent of size and shape.
	Show students what happens to different pieces of soap in water, and use the demonstration to help them understand that size is not a factor in density.
	Have students cut different shapes of the same material, measure mass and volume, then calculate density.

knowledge of the subject being taught. You may also be able to identify sources of information that suggest possible misconceptions and can use these clues to arm yourself with what to look for. Misconceptions are often identified with multiple-choice items. Good distractors focus on specific misconceptions, so that when students select a particular distractor, the teacher has knowledge of how student thinking is inaccurate. Once the error is identified, appropriate feedback and instructional adjustments can be provided. In addition to knowing if students are correct in their answers, an analysis of the wrong choices is key to how teachers take the next steps toward greater student understanding. Some digital tools will do this electronically, providing students with feedback based on which wrong answer was selected.

Instructional Adjustments

An essential component of formative assessment is to include instructional adjustments that will help students reach learning targets. These adjustments, or correctives, are needed to help students understand what is needed to close the gap between current performance and what is specified by the learning target.

Effective corrective action is pragmatic and possible. It gives students specific actions in which they can engage to improve, and typically these actions use instruction that is different from what was initially used for student learning. (If it didn't work the first time, why use it again?) For example:

"You have made seven errors in the use of commas in your paper. Please refer to Chapter 3 in your text and generate three sentences that follow the rules for using commas."

"Your understanding of how to use adverbs can be enhanced if you work through a special computer program that is now available."

When an entire class shows similar progress, the teacher can decide to slow down, speed up, review material, or try new instructional approaches for the entire class, small groups of students, or individual students. The professional judgment of the teacher is used continuously as students learn to adapt instruction to meet student needs.

Students who have mastered the learning target can still benefit from feedback that tells them what actions are required to extend and deepen their understanding. This feedback is not "corrective" in the sense that there is a deficit to be addressed, but such feedback keeps students on task and furthers their learning.

In Table 5.4 a number of possible instructional adjustments are listed with examples. Which of these or others you use will depend, of course, on the students, context, nature of the content or skill, and your own preferences. But you need to have these tools internalized, ready to go, for immediate use following feedback. While there is little research on the nature of specific instructional adjustments, let alone which are most effective (Heritage, 2013), there are several systematic approaches that are appropriate for summative-based formative

TABLE 5.4   **Types of Instructional Adjustments**

Type	Example
Further reading	Read an additional article on the nature of free enterprise.
Individual tutoring	Work with another student to generate additional examples of obtuse triangles in real life.
Small-group work	Work with three other students cooperatively to solve an additional math problem.
Modeling	Show how to think through the steps to take in solving math word problems.
Whole-class oral questioning	Ask additional questions about the consequences of tight monetary policy.
Re-explanation	Provide a different explanation, using different words, about why some objects float and some sink.
Worksheets (paper or digital)	Give student additional math problems.
Peer tutoring	Pair students to generate additional examples of randomized design science experiments.
Clarifying criteria	Reteach criteria to use in evaluating writing with further detail.
Changing sequence	Reteach procedure to analyze arguments by changing the sequence of steps.
Online exploration	Ask students to research online the meaning of freedom of religion.
Concept mapping	Ask students to sketch the components of an argument for increasing coal production.
New digital tool	Provide students with a new digital tool that can reteach and use questions to check for student proficiency.

assessment. We will look briefly at each of these, beginning with mastery learning. Mastery learning was the first major theory on individualizing teaching to students based on feedback from assessment.

Mastery Learning

As noted by Guskey (2007, 2010), a major change in education occurred with the work of Benjamin S. Bloom, who, in the 1960s, introduced a concept he initially called *learning for mastery*, which was shortened to *mastery learning* in the 1970s. The goal of mastery learning was to change the prevailing view of education in which teaching was essentially the same for all students, resulting in variation in student achievement. In mastery learning, instruction would vary to result in similar achievement. This would be accomplished by initial assessment, feedback, corrective instruction based on the results of this assessment, and "second-chance" opportunities for student performance (formative assessment!).

The purpose of the initial assessment in mastery learning was to show what students had accomplished and what was not yet learned. With this knowledge, additional instruction was designed to close the gap between what was learned and what needed to be learned. Each assessment was paired with additional instructional opportunities (e.g., additional sources of information, use of different textbooks, or videos, as well as additional practice). Following this additional instruction, students were reassessed to verify "mastery" of the material. Thus, each student could theoretically have a detailed prescription of what needed to be done following the initial assessment. As students show mastery, enrichment activities could be provided.

While mastery learning is not typically applied in a formal sense, it is clear that many of the principles foreshadowed formative assessment. The essential elements are there—a clear learning outcome, assessment, feedback, and further instruction to reach proficiency. A major contribution of mastery learning was the idea that the time and supports for learning should vary, depending on each student's progress, rather than keeping time and supports constant for all students, resulting in variability of achievement. Formative assessment represents a middle ground, with the realization that time and supports, as well as continuing testing, are limited.

Differentiated Instruction

Differentiated instruction is essentially an updating of mastery learning, incorporating new research and a more comprehensive approach to teaching. It has emerged as a way of providing students alternative approaches to learning, often in digital formats, and has integrated assessment as a main tenet.

Differentiated instruction involves five elements: (1) classroom environment, (2) curriculum, (3) assessment, (4) instruction, and (5) management. Each of these elements contributes to a systematic approach for tailoring instructional adjustments to individual students (Tomlinson & Moon, 2013a, 2013b). It is a theory of teaching, learning, and assessment in which student needs are used in planning and executing lessons tailored to small groups of students. Student needs include interests, abilities, prior achievement, and other factors that define readiness to learn and receptivity to engagement. Different instructional options are provided, based on assessment, for students who are behind, in the middle, or advanced in their proficiency. Instruction is not individualized to such an extent that each student has a separate lesson plan. Rather, heterogeneous and homogeneous groups of students are given different instructional paths with the goal of having all students at an appropriate level of challenge. The idea is that learning is maximized when students are challenged to move slightly beyond what they are able to do on their own (zone of proximal development).

Teachers are encouraged to differentiate three key elements of instruction—content, process, and products. Content refers to what parts of subject matter are emphasized. Using pretests and other assessments, teachers determine where students need to begin to study a topic or unit. Process is concerned with how students learn and what learning strategies are used. Here teachers match student learning styles and strategies with how material is presented. Differentiation based on products means how students demonstrate what they know and understand. The intent is to use whatever summative-based formative assessment techniques at key points providing the best opportunity for success, including the use of student choice of assessments. In addition, teachers are urged to use a variety of assessment strategies for all students.

Differentiated instruction takes into account different ways of learning for students who bring a variety of talents, interests, and readiness to the classroom. It is organized yet flexible, changing as needed to maximize learning of all students. A toolbox of both physical and digital techniques and approaches is needed by the teacher to adequately differentiate instruction. Based on assessments of important student values, interests, learning styles, and previous achievement, the "data literate" teacher provides the best-matched instruction to enhance student motivation and learning.

Assessment is an ongoing, diagnostic aspect of differentiated instruction. It occurs prior to learning to identify student interests as well as prior knowledge and skills. A proficiency baseline is established to determine which instructional activities will best match existing knowledge, interests, and learning styles. During instruction students need different ways of showing what they know and can do. Assessments following instruction also can be differentiated (e.g., hand or computer-based writing; selected-response or constructed-response items; written tests or teacher interviews), and provide further information to determine the best instructional adjustments for each student.

Response to Intervention

Response to intervention (RTI or RtI) integrates assessment with instructional adjustments within a multi-tier intervention system of support (Jimerson, Burns, & VanDreHeyden, 2015; National Center on Response to Intervention, 2010). Typically, struggling students are closely monitored with ongoing, frequent summative-based formative assessments (progress monitoring), provided systematic instructional interventions, and continually monitored with increasingly focused intervention as needed. While often targeted to students at risk of failure and student with disabilities, RTI is effective with all students who have been identified as needing more targeted resources to improve low achievement.

RTI uses different levels of intensity in the interventions, beginning with all students at level 1, moving to small group instruction for level 2, and providing the most focused intervention at level 3. Teams of teachers and other professionals use monitoring data, including summative-based formative assessment, to determine subsequent instruction. Often the steps used with RTI provide a basis for evaluating eligibility for referral to special education services (see Chapter 12).

Learning Progressions

Learning progressions (or *competency-based pathways*) describe in successive steps or building blocks increasingly sophisticated understandings of core concepts and principles in a domain (Achieve, 2015; Heritage, 2013). These steps and enabling knowledge form a coherent sequence of learning, and as such, can form the basis of effective questioning. As noted by Black, Wilson, and Yao (2011),

> one essential ingredient that the teacher needs is to have in mind an underlying scheme of progression in the topic . . . [to] . . . guide the ways in which students' contributions are summarized . . . and the orientation which the teacher may provide by further suggestions, summaries, questions, and other activities (p. 74).

Learning progressions are relatively new and hold great promise as instructional correctives for summative-based formative assessment. Here are two definitions of learning progressions:

> (1) descriptions of successively more sophisticated ways of thinking about an idea that follow one another as students learn; they lay out in words and examples what it means to move toward more expert understanding. (Wilson & Bertenthal, 2005, p. 3)

> (2) a carefully sequenced set of building blocks that students must master en route to a more distant curricular aim. The building blocks consist of sub skills and bodies of enabling knowledge. (Popham, 2017, p. 285

Learning progressions provide a "road map" over an extended time period for knowing what information needs to be gathered about student understanding and corresponding instructional adjustments that are needed. This makes it possible to match learning activities to the progression and to know criteria for evaluating successful performance with each step. Once a teacher confirms that a student is at a specific point in the learning progression, using summative-based formative assessment, appropriate instruction can be implemented. The goal is to promote more sophisticated ways of reasoning and thinking within a content domain.

Learning progressions are integral to summative-based formative assessment because they show when teachers need to be sure students understand a "step" before moving to the next level in the learning sequence. They define the points at which you need to plan for sufficient time in your instruction to provide students with additional practice, discussion, feedback, or other activities that will ensure mastery.

For most instruction there is a trajectory or sequence of how knowledge and understanding develops, a series of sequential steps that students take in moving from an initial level of proficiency to a more sophisticated understanding (Alonzo

& Gearhart, 2006; Heritage, 2007; Heritage & Anderson, 2009). Essentially, these progressions lay out how students go from point A to point B. By being aware of the steps that need to be taken, teachers are able to focus their formative assessment on these steps to inform them about further instruction. They are able to plan potential feedback and instructional correctives that are based on the progression (Heritage, 2008).

An important contribution of learning progressions is that it provides more detailed information than a standard about how learning should progress. Standards are endpoints, but typically they do not help teachers know how to get there. By instituting intermediate "substandards" along a continuum of progress, teachers have a much improved curriculum guide to help them focus summative-based formative assessment on these important steps.

Part of a learning progression for attainment in history is illustrated in Figure 5.2. Note the increasing complexity and depth of understanding that develops as students move from level 1 to level 2. It is readily apparent how to match instruction to these steps. Teachers attend to key words and concepts, such as from "recognizing" to "understanding" to "increasing depth." These outcomes suggest particular ways of doing assignments, giving feedback, and using instructional correctives matched to each level.

A Model of Instructional Adjustments Using Summative-Based Formative Assessment

Figure 5.3 shows how instructional adjustments are used with summative-based formative assessment. Based on an initial summative-based assessment, the teacher considers what content and process targets need attention and provides appropriate feedback to students. Then, based on ongoing assessments of student needs, different instructional approaches are selected and implemented. After the instruction, more formative assessment is used to repeat the process of matching learning tasks, activities, assignments, and assessments to student needs.

Whether based on mastery learning, differentiated instruction, RTI, learning progressions, or other theories and approaches to teaching, the important point is that instructional correctives are used to complete the formative assessment process. This results in assessment that is truly integrated with instruction and shows that both are needed to maximize student learning.

A final important point about instructional adjustments is that they need not be determined by the teacher (or the digital program). The process of identifying next steps is sometimes most effective if the student is involved in deciding what these steps should look like (Harlen, 2003). Teachers can give students alternative approaches or ask them directly how they think they can obtain a better understanding; they are not treated as passive recipients of feedback and provided prescriptions for further learning. Rather, students become partners with teachers. This is also effective in improving students' self-efficacy and feelings of internal control of their learning.

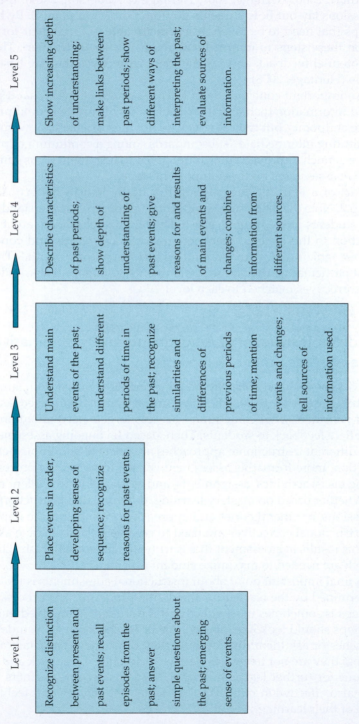

Level 1

Recognize distinction between present and past events; recall episodes from the past; answer simple questions about the past; emerging sense of events.

Level 2

Place events in order, developing sense of sequence; recognize reasons for past events.

Level 3

Understand main events of the past; understand different periods of time in the past; recognize similarities and differences of previous periods of time; mention events and changes; tell sources of information used.

Level 4

Describe characteristics of past periods; show depth of understanding of past events; give reasons for and results of main events and changes; combine information from different sources.

Level 5

Show increasing depth of understanding; make links between past periods; show different ways of interpreting the past; evaluate sources of information.

FIGURE 5.2 Learning Progression for History

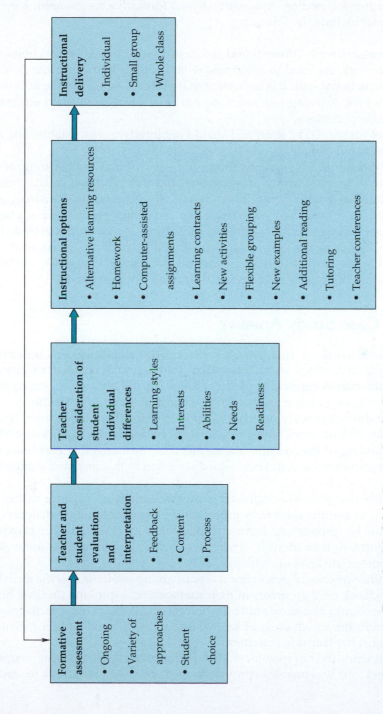

FIGURE 5.3 **Recursive Model for Instructional Adjustments**
Source: Based on Tomlinson (1999) and Guskey (2007).

Summary

This chapter focused on summative-based formative assessment. Key points in the chapter include the following:

- Preassessments (pretests and structured exercises), as well as homework and seatwork, are used to determine what students know and can do prior to an instructional unit. It is important that pretests, especially those covering considerable learning outcomes, do not create a negative class environment or low expectations.
- Pretests should be short and should not interfere with establishing a positive classroom climate.
- Instructional adjustments, through the use of mastery learning, response to intervention, learning progressions, and differentiated instruction, provide students specific activities, different from the original instruction, to aid them in closing their knowledge gap and achieving the learning target.
- Homework, in-class assignments, and quizzes can be used effectively for formative assessment as long as they are sufficiently specific, targeted, and diagnostic.
- What are the do's and don'ts for effective use of homework, in-class assignments, and quizzes to be effective formative assessments?

Introductory Case Study Answer

Catherine needs to use summative-based formative assessment practices that provide individualized feedback to students and can lead to specific instructional changes.

Catherine's overarching problem is that she did not use her summative-based formative assessments effectively to make instructional adjustments. She gathered data, but did not provide students with effective feedback on their learning nor did she make instructional adjustments based on students' knowledge, skills, and understanding of the concept. She assumed her students this year were similar to last year's students and did not tailor instruction to this group of students.

- Catherine should administer a preassessment in advance of her teaching unit to use the data to appropriately differentiate her instruction to determine her groups and instructional sequences. It would have provided more information to identify where her instruction should be focused and the appropriate level of challenge.
- Catherine should determine a way of giving students specific individualized feedback on their errors in their mathematical thinking on their homework. She should also view students' homework so she can use it diagnostically to determine which areas of knowledge and skill need further instruction and adjust her learning activities.
- Catherine did not monitor student performance while students completed their work. She was unable to provide immediate, specific feedback to students.

- Catherine gave a review problem each day; however, she looked at the results after math class. Catherine should instead create a system in her class that allows her to work with students on the review problem, immediately determine student mastery, and provide feedback.
- It would be better to go over the quiz in class and provide students more than right/wrong verification of their learning. She needs to elaborate on why answers may be incorrect and provide error analysis, and to use the quiz information to make instructional adjustments to help her students reach their learning targets. Using last year's plans was not very helpful.

Suggestions for Action Research

1. Go to the Internet and identify two apps that could be used for summative-based formative assessment. Choose apps that you might be likely to use. Try it out. How well do you think it would work for students? What seem to be its strengths and weaknesses?

2. Ask a teacher about how they use summative-based formative assessment and compare their description to characteristics of effective formative assessment.

3. With two other students, prepare a report that shows how unit tests an interim tests could be used formatively. What are the advantages and limitations of each one?

4. Ask a group of students, those about the age you would like to teach, about the kind of feedback they get from teachers after they take a test. Question them about how the feedback affects them.

5. Identify a standard in your grade level and subject and prepare a learning progression that would take students from their initial understanding at the beginning of the year to the standard. Trade your progression with others in the same subject and grade level and compare answers.

MyEdLab Self-Check 5.1

MyEdLab Self-Check 5.2

MyEdLab Self-Check 5.3

MyEdLab Self-Check 5.4

MyEdLab Application Exercise 5.1   Feedback Reconsidered

MyEdLab Application Exercise 5.2   Mastery Learning

Summative Assessment I: Planning and Implementing Classroom Tests

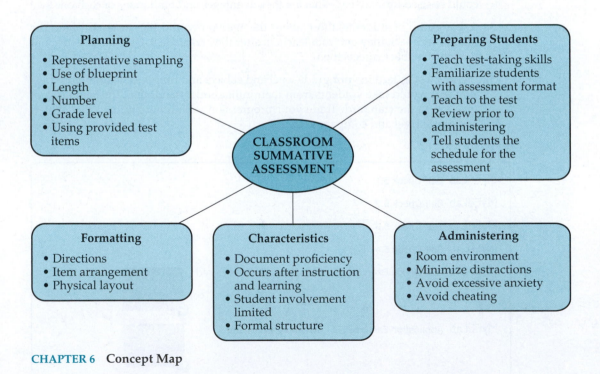

Planning
- Representative sampling
- Use of blueprint
- Length
- Number
- Grade level
- Using provided test items

Preparing Students
- Teach test-taking skills
- Familiarize students with assessment format
- Teach to the test
- Review prior to administering
- Tell students the schedule for the assessment

CLASSROOM SUMMATIVE ASSESSMENT

Formatting
- Directions
- Item arrangement
- Physical layout

Characteristics
- Document proficiency
- Occurs after instruction and learning
- Student involvement limited
- Formal structure

Administering
- Room environment
- Minimize distractions
- Avoid excessive anxiety
- Avoid cheating

CHAPTER 6 Concept Map

Learning Outcomes

6.1 Be able to apply the essential elements of planning sound classroom summative assessments, including sampling of content, constructing items, and determining appropriate test length.

6.2 Understand the appropriate test-taking skills students need to use, as well as how excessive test anxiety can be minimized.

6.3 Know what is needed for good summative test directions, item arrangement, and physical layout, as well as principles of appropriate test administration.

Introductory Case Study

How Can Jalen Defend Her Assessment?

Jalen, an American history teacher, turned in her last week of lesson plans, the review sheet, and her unit assessment on the Great Depression to Suzy, the history department chair. She was planning to give the end-of-unit review sheet a week in advance of the test date that she had announced at the beginning of the unit. The sheet had an outline explicitly telling students what they should know, gave a sample of questions demonstrating the different styles of questions students would be required to complete on the test, and stated guidelines for how to write a solid compare-and-contrast short-answer response.

Jalen also included with her plans a copy of the end-of-unit assessment. The assessment was one Jalen had created, opting to design the assessment herself instead of giving students the one provided by the textbook publisher. Jalen had used the textbook to teach the state's standards, but she had also introduced students to additional images and authentic pieces of literature, and shown two video biographies about people who lived during the Great Depression. Jalen felt the supplemental materials were necessary to ensure students mastered her five learning targets, one of which included comparing and contrasting people's viewpoints on a historical event. So, while Jalen used some questions from the textbook publisher, she decided that creating her own summative assessment allowed her to assess students' learning more appropriately. She adjusted the number of selected-response questions from 50 to 25 and added four constructed-response questions, one that asked students to compare and contrast the video autobiographies by creating a Venn diagram.

When Suzy reviewed the materials, she questioned Jalen on why she created her own test rather than using the one provided by the textbook publisher. She also questioned Jalen about her reasoning for giving students the detailed study guide. Suzy's opinion was that the textbook publisher test should be preferred since it was created by authorities on the standards and comprehensive review materials and allowed students to minimize their studying.

As you read this chapter, decide how Jalen can defend her summative assessment. Was it correct that Jalen opted to create her own summative assessment? How can she support her use of a detailed review sheet?

A s described in Chapter 1, summative assessments are used primarily to doc-ument student performance; it is assessment *of* learning. Summative assess-ments are used to monitor and record student proficiency, to give students grades, to report to parents, for selection into special programs, for conferring of honors, for establishing a record of performance used by colleges for admissions and hiring by employers, accountability, and recently, as evidence of student learning to evaluate teachers. Examples include chapter and unit tests, semester tests, common tests, final papers, reports, and presentations. They are also used by teachers to plan instruction. Actually, some formative assessment during instruction, such as seatwork assignments, could be thought of as a "mini" sum-mative assessment in the sense that there is evidence of student proficiency in relation to learning targets. The primary difference between summative and formative assessment is in the use of the evidence. Summative assessment infor-mation can be used formatively, as pointed out in the previous chapter, but the primary purpose is to establish a score or grade to represent what students know and can do. In this chapter planning and formatting summative assessments that have traditionally been constructed by teachers for use with their students are discussed. In the following chapter standardized and standards-based assess-ments (large-scale rather than classroom/teacher-based) complete our coverage of summative assessment.

Key characteristics of summative assessment are summarized in Table 6.1. Keep in mind that these characteristics vary, depending on the amount of learning that is measured (see Figure 6.1). Quizzes, for example, assess very short lessons and can be targeted to specific student misunderstandings or competencies. Unit or chapter tests are more comprehensive assessments of learning that occurs over several weeks. As such, the assessment is broader and tends to sample student proficiency in certain areas. Year-end accountability tests, those designed to meas-ure many months of learning, are still more general. They are more comprehen-sive in what is covered but typically sample only part of what was learned to

TABLE 6.1   Characteristics of Summative Assessment

Purpose	To document student proficiency
When Conducted	After instruction
Teacher Role	To plan, administer, and record performance
Student Involvement	Limited
Student Motivation	Typically, performance-oriented
Learning Emphasized	Knowledge, comprehension, and application
Level of Specificity	General, group-oriented
Structure	Rigid, structured, formal

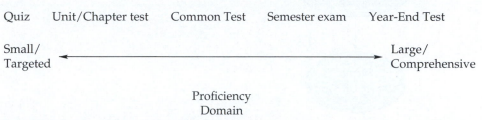

FIGURE 6.1   **Relationship Between Types of Summative Assessments and Proficiency Domain**

generalize to a larger domain of knowledge and/or skills. The reason it is important to consider what amount of knowledge is assessed is that you may well be asked to use test items that align with what is measured in large-scale accountability tests. More than ever, teachers are pressed into this type of alignment, which as emphasized in the case study that introduced this chapter, has both strengths and weaknesses.

Planning Summative Assessment

The first step in constructing a classroom summative assessment is to review initial ideas in light of the criteria for ensuring high-quality assessments that were presented in Chapter 3:

- Do I have clear and appropriate learning targets?
- What method of assessment will match best with the targets?
- Will I have good evidence that the inferences from the assessments will be valid?
- How can I construct an assessment that will minimize error?
- Will my assessment be fair and unbiased? Have students had the opportunity to learn what is being assessed?
- Will the assessment be practical and efficient?
- Will my assessment be aligned with instruction?
- Are consequences of the assessment positive?

Additional considerations include how you will obtain a representative sample of what has been learned, the length and number of assessments, whether you should use tests provided by publishers, how students should be prepared for the assessment, when the assessment should be scheduled, and when you should construct the assessment.

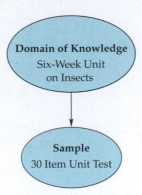

FIGURE 6.2   **Sampling from a Domain to Obtain Test Items**

Representative Sampling

Most summative assessments, with the exception of quizzes, measure a *sample* what students have learned in the larger domain of knowledge (see Figure 6.2). It is rare, except for quizzes over short lessons, that you will assess with a unit or chapter test everything that is included in the domain. There simply is not enough time to assess each fact or skill. Rather, you will select a sample of what students should know and then assume that the way they respond to a sample of items is typical of how they would respond to additional items of the entire domain.

Use Assessment Blueprint

As pointed out in Chapter 3, an important step in representative sampling is preparing an assessment blueprint or outline. This set of specifications is helpful because it indicates what students are responsible for learning. When assessment items are based on this outline, there is a greater likelihood that the sampling will be reasonable. You will literally be able to look at the blueprint to see how the sampling came out. Without a test blueprint or some type of outline of content, there is a tendency to oversample areas that you particularly like and to overload the assessment with a disproportionately large number of questions about simple facts (mainly because these questions are much easier to write). Figure 6.3 shows a blueprint in which the sampling of content is about the same across all topics.

Number and Length of Assessments

The next step is to decide how many separate assessments will be given and the length of each one. This decision will depend on several factors, including the age of the students, the length of classes, and the types of questions. One rule of thumb, though, is that the time allocated for assessment should be sufficient for all students to answer all the questions, within reason (allowing some students hours when others finish in less than an hour is not reasonable). We generally do not

FIGURE 6.3 **Example of a Well-Balanced Test Blueprint for Items on Assessment of Experimental Design**

	Knowledge	Application	Total
Control of extraneous variables	4	2	6
Control of the intervention	3	4	7
Random assignment	3	4	7
Control group	4	2	6
Internal validity	5	2	7
Total	19	14	33

want to use *speeded* tests. This is because **speeded tests**, which require students to answer as quickly as possible to obtain a high score, increase the probability that other factors, such as anxiety and test-taking skills, will influence the result.

Suppose you are preparing a test for a six-week social studies unit on early civilizations, and you want to assess how much knowledge the students retained. How many items will be needed? Thirty? Sixty? Eighty? In the absence of any hard-and-fast rules, a few rules of thumb will help determine how many items are sufficient. First, 5 to 10 items are needed to assess each knowledge learning target that is included within the unit. Thus, if one learning target is that "students will identify the location of 25 ancient cities on a map," preparing a test that asks them to identify 5 to 10 of the 25 would be reasonable. Which 10, you may be thinking? You can select randomly if all the cities are equally difficult to locate. Normally, however, your sampling will be purposeful so that a good cross section of difficulty is selected (in this case, different types of cities). With more specific learning targets, as few as three items can provide a good assessment. For example, you can get a pretty good idea if a student knows how to multiply three-digit numbers by requiring students to supply answers to three such problems. And, of course, difficulty counts here as well. Missing one or two hard questions isn't as revealing as missing a couple of easy ones.

There is an obvious relationship between the number and length of assessments. Many short assessments can provide the same, if not better, information than a single long assessment. It will help you to focus on length first without regard to the number of assessments. This will indicate what is needed to obtain a representative sample. Then you can decide whether what is needed is best given in one large block of time - three smaller tests, weekly assessments, or whatever other combination is best. If you wait until the end of a unit to begin constructing your assessment, you may find that there is insufficient time to administer the test so that other high-quality criteria are met.

Grade Level

The age of students and the length of their classes are important considerations. Kindergarten and first-grade students have relatively short attention spans, so summative assessments usually last only 5 to 10 minutes. As attention spans and stamina increase with age, testing time can be lengthened. Thus, in later elementary grades, summative assessments typically last between 15 and 30 minutes, and for secondary students 30 to 50 minutes.

Ironically, when students are old enough to have longer attention spans, they are in middle or high schools where the length of the class usually determines the maximum length of the assessment. Consequently, most teachers plan unit and other summative assessments to last one class period, or approximately 45 minutes in many schools. In this situation, you need to provide time for directions and student questions to be careful not to end up with a speeded test. With block scheduling and other innovations, more time is available for assessment. Generally, upper elementary students can handle 20 to 30 selected response items; secondary students 30 to 50 such items. Younger students will take much longer than older ones to complete extended-response open-ended items.

Type of Item

Another important influence on the length of time it takes students to complete an assessment is the type of item used and the cognitive level of thinking needed to answer the question. Obviously, essay items require much more time to complete than objective items. It also takes students longer to complete short-answer items than multiple-choice or true/false questions. For example, in a test of simple knowledge in a content area, secondary students can generally answer as many as 2 to 4 objective items per minute. For more difficult items, one per minute is a general rule of thumb. In math, students may need as long as 2 or 3 minutes for each constructed-response item. Experience will be your best guide. Initially, try some assessments that are short so you can get an idea of how long it takes students to complete each item. Using practice questions will also give you an idea about the number of items that would be reasonable in a unit test. Table 6.2 summarizes factors that should influence the length of your assessments.

TABLE 6.2   Factors Affecting Assessment Length

Factor	Assessment Length	
	Shorter	**Longer**
Grade level	Elementary	Secondary
Cognitive level	Higher, more sophisticated	Lower, less sophisticated
Item type	Constructed-response; performance	Selected-response and brief constructed-response
Class period	Short	Extended

Use of Assessments Provided by Textbook and Test Publishers and School Districts

You will receive ready-made test items from textbook and instructional packages, typically provided in digital format, that can be used for your classroom summative assessments. School district central offices and school department offices often provide banks of items. These items are usually prepared for chapter and unit assessments, and now are often aligned with year-end accountability tests. Some of these items are adequate and may be useful if you remember a few key points. First, you can't assume that just because the items are provided, the results will be reliable or valid. You need to review the items carefully to make sure that fundamental principles of good assessment are followed. Second, a decision to use *any* type of assessment—whether provided in instructor's materials, by other teachers, or by yourself—is always made *after* you have identified the learning targets that you will assess. The prepared items may be technically sound, but if there is not a good match between what it tests and what you need tested, it should not be used in its entirety. Also, because prepared items are often constructed by someone other than the textbook author(s), or accountability test publisher, or someone in a different grade level in the district, some areas may be stressed much more than others. Third, check the items carefully to make sure the language and terminology are appropriate for your students. The author(s) of the items may use language that is not consistent with the text or the way you have taught the material. The vocabulary and sentence complexity may not be at the right level for your students.

As pointed out in Chapter 4, test publishers are now heavily in the business of preparing assessments for teachers. The companies can literally customize a test for you once you have identified the state standard or target. But there is no guarantee that the test items will be of high quality, or whether they necessarily match well with your instruction. However, test company items are probably of higher quality than items prepared by textbook publishers.

The obvious advantage of using these "prepared" test items is that they can save you a great deal of time, especially when the test is provided in a format that can be simply copied. Feel free, however, to modify individual questions if you have permission to do so. Often the best use of prepared items is to get ideas that provide a good starting point for you to prepare your own test. The best advice I can give you, if there are resources to access test banks provided by others, is to do so with caution.

Preparing Students for Classroom Summative Assessments

Your objective in summative assessment is to obtain a fair and accurate indication of student learning. This means that you need to take some simple steps to prepare your students so that they will be able to best demonstrate what they know, understand, and can do (see Figure 6.4).

✓ Teach assessment-taking and testwiseness skills.
✓ Familiarize students with test length, format, and types of questions.
✓ Teach *to* the test (do not teach *the* test).
✓ Share the assessment blueprint.
✓ Review before the assessment.
✓ Tell students when the assessment is scheduled and how long it will take to complete.
✓ Make sure students have the technical skills needed to be proficient with digitally administered tests.

Assessment-Taking Skills and Testwiseness

The first step is to make sure that all your students have adequate assessment-taking skills (also called *test-taking* skills). The notion here is that there are legitimate skills students should know to be able to show their best work. This is not cheating! My belief is that these skills should be explicitly taught to all students. The skills include paying attention to directions, being adept at using computer programs, reading each item in its entirety before answering it, planning and outlining responses to essay questions, using clear writing for answers, pacing themselves while answering the questions, eliminating wrong alternatives, and checking responses. (As one teacher told me, "When I first gave math tests, students would include the item number with the problem; for example, if item 2 was 3 + 4, they would answer 9—incorrect answer, but they knew how to add!") Students should be directed to answer all questions (guessing is rarely penalized in classroom tests, though you don't want to encourage mindless guessing). If there is a separate sheet for recording responses, teach students to check the accuracy of their answers.

It is also helpful to teach test-wise skills. **Testwiseness** is the ability to identify clues in poorly written items that make it easier to obtain the right answer—often without any knowledge of the content! Consider the following test item:

The independent variable in an experimental study is

a) intervening variable as well
b) manipulated by the researcher
c) outcome of the study
d) compound variable

Your knowledge of grammar allows you to get the answer correct, even if you know very little about experimental design! Here is a list of some testwiseness skills (usually used for selected-response test items):

- Grammatical clue
- Same words used in the stem and correct alternative

- Longer alternative the correct one
- One alternative includes all the others
- Pattern of placing correct choice second or third
- Use of "always" for incorrect alternatives

Of course, these hints also tell you what to avoid in writing test questions.

Item Type and Format

A second step is to make sure students are familiar with the format and type of question and response that will be needed on the test. This is accomplished by giving students practice test items. If time is available, it is very instructive to have students practice writing test items themselves. This is good for review sessions. Familiarity with the type of question lessens test anxiety. Of course, you don't want to teach the test—that is, use examples in class that are identical to the test items—or give students practice on the test items before they take the test. It's fine to teach *to* the test, in the sense that you want to instruct students about what they will eventually be tested on. It's also helpful to students if they know the length of the test and how much the test will count in their grade. One effective way to accomplish this is to give your students the test blueprint.

It is likely that you will be asked or required to use test item formats that match the ones in state accountability tests. This typically comes down to two formats—multiple-choice and writing in response to prompts. But it is easy to overuse multiple-choice formats. Remember, your primary objective is to accurately record student proficiency and increase student learning. This will rarely be achieved if only one type of test item is used. *Use the type of item that is best for maximizing student engagement and learning.* Students need to demonstrate their knowledge and understanding in different ways, and constructed-response items are often the best kind of assessment for detecting errors.

Finally, you will want to tell students, as soon as possible after beginning the unit, when the test is scheduled. This gives students an adequate period of time to prepare for the test. Try to avoid giving a test on days that make it difficult for students to perform to their capability (e.g., prom day, right after spring vacation, after a pep rally). Also, try to schedule the test when you know you will be present and not when the class has a substitute.

Assessment Anxiety

We've all experienced assessment (test) anxiety. The emotional tightness and difficulty in thinking with high levels of anxiety can sometimes be debilitating, and should be avoided. A little anxiety, though, is a good thing. It motivates and facilitates good performance. Excessive anxiety can be a real problem for some students, both high and low achievers. So, it's best to mitigate it with a few procedures:

1. Give students feedback on their performance to help them realize the assessment will foster further learning (mastery goal orientation).
2. Arrange test items from easy to hard.
3. Give plenty of time to complete the assessment.
4. Minimize interruptions and other distractions.
5. Avoid threatening students if they do poorly.
6. Avoid unrealistically high expectations or expecting perfect performance.
7. Avoid severely negative consequences if students perform poorly.
8. Provide students with the test blueprint or outline of the assessment.
9. Avoid walking around the room, looking over shoulders.
10. Avoid making comparisons with other students.
11. Provide for optional retesting.

When to Construct Summative Assessments

Summative assessments need to be planned well in advance of the scheduled testing date. A good procedure is to construct a general outline of the test before instruction, based on your learning targets and a table of specifications. At least identify the nature of the evidence needed to provide a fair indication of student learning. This does not necessarily include the development or selection of specific items, but it provides enough information to guide you in instruction. As the unit proceeds, you can make decisions about the format of the test and begin to construct individual items. The final form of the test should be determined no later than the review session. But don't try to finalize the test too soon. You will find that as you teach, your learning targets will most likely change somewhat or that the emphasis you place on certain topics did not turn out as planned. These expected instructional variations should be reflected in the test. Consequently, you want to allow the test and instruction to influence each other while teaching the content or skills.

Table 6.3 summarizes key considerations in planning for summative assessments. Figure 6.5 shows a map that indicates a helpful sequence to know when to construct summative assessments. The overall learning target, understanding components of high-quality assessment, leads first to the nature of validity, for which a quiz is used to check learning, followed by a retest of validity. Instruction then moves to reliability, after which a unit test could be given on both validity and reliability. Using a quiz for validity provides an important pause in learning and assurance that students understand this concept (and the three aspects indicated) before moving on to reliability. The unit test would include both because it is important to show understanding about how they are related and distinguished from one another.

TABLE 6.3   Key Considerations in Planning Classroom Summative Assessments

Consideration	Key Elements
What will result in high-quality assessments?	• Appropriate learning targets • Assessment methods matched with learning targets • Reliability/precision • Validity • Fairness
Will the sampling of content be appropriate?	• Test blueprint • Use a sufficient number of items
Will the number and length be appropriate?	• Avoid speeded tests; give too much rather than too little time • Age of students • Many short assessments or few long assessments
Should textbook/publisher/testing company assessments be used?	• Check quality of items • Check match to instruction • Check cognitive levels assessed • Use with caution • Combine with teacher-made items
How should students be prepared?	• Teach test-taking skills • Familiarize students with examples of item formats • Review before the test
When should the assessments be scheduled?	• Avoid distracting days • Construct instructional/assessment map • Announce test date in advance
When should assessments be constructed?	• Well in advance of testing date • Identify needed evidence before teaching • Finalize just before administering

Putting Summative Assessments Together

Once you have developed items, they need to be put together in the form of an assessment (test). Following a few guidelines, which include suggestions for directions, arranging items, and the physical layout of the assessment, will result in a better assessment.

Preparing Assessment Directions

According to Miller, Linn, and Gronlund (2013), assessment directions should include the following:

1. Purpose
2. Time allowed for completing the test

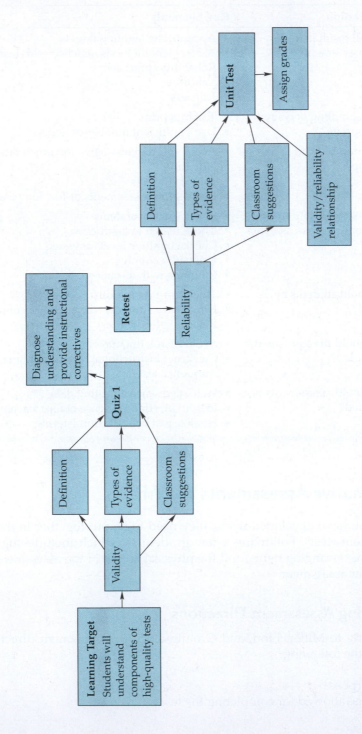

FIGURE 6.5 Instruction/Assessment Map

3. Basis for responding
4. Procedures for recording answers
5. What to do about guessing
6. How constructed-response items will be scored

The purpose of the test should be made clear to students well in advance of the testing date. This is usually done when the test is announced. Students need to know why they are taking the test and how the results will be used.

Students need to know *exactly* how much time they will have to complete the test, even if the test is not speeded. It is helpful to indicate to students how they should distribute their time among various parts of the test, and to allow plenty of time for students so that they do not feel rushed. As indicated earlier, students can be expected to complete at least one multiple-choice and two binary-choice items per minute, but the actual time will depend on the difficulty of the items and student preparation. Your judgments about how many items to include will improve with experience. In the beginning, err on the side of allowing too much time.

The basis for responding simply refers to what students are to do to answer the question, that is, how to respond. This should be a simple and direct statement (e.g., "Select the correct answer," or "Select the best answer"). The procedure for responding indicates how students show their answers, whether they circle the answer, write the answer next to the item, write the word in the blank, and so on. If computations are to be shown, tell the students where they should write them.

In a test containing selected-response items students may ask about whether there is a penalty for guessing. In classroom tests it is very rare to find a correction for guessing. The best practice is to be very clear to students that they should try to answer each item (e.g., "Your score is the total number of correct answers, so answer every item").

The final suggestion for directions concerns the scoring criteria for constructed-response items. For these items it is important to clearly indicate the basis on which you will grade the students' answers *before* they study for the test. We will explore this in Chapter 9.

Item Arrangement

Arranging items by level of difficulty (e.g., easy items first, then difficult ones) has little effect on the results. If you think your students gain confidence by answering the easiest items first, it's fine to order the items by increasing difficulty. The most important consideration in arranging questions is item type. *Keep all the items that use the same format together.* Keep all the multiple-choice items in one section, all the matching items in another, and so on. This reduces the number of times students need to shift their response mode. It also minimizes directions and makes scoring easier. Generally, it is best to order items based on how quickly students can answer. Items answered more quickly, such as completion and binary-choice, would generally come first, followed by multiple-choice and short-answer items.

FIGURE 6.6 Checklist for Putting Summative Assessments Together

✓ Include complete directions.
✓ Arrange items from easiest to hardest.
✓ Put the same item formats together in separate sections.
✓ Customize to the age of the students.

If possible, it is best to group the items according to learning targets and keep assessments of the same target or content together.

Physical Layout

Items need to be formatted so that they are easy to read and answer. A few commonsense suggestions help to achieve this goal. First, all the information needed to answer an item should be on the same page. Avoid having part of an item on one page and the rest of the item on another page. Second, do not crowd too many items onto a page. Although we all need to be careful about wasting paper, a test that is crowded is likely to contain more errors than one that has reasonable spacing and white space. This means that multiple-choice options should not be listed horizontally on the same line. Rather, it is best if the options are listed vertically below the item.

Finally, the format of the test should enhance scoring accuracy and efficiency. For older students (upper elementary and above), taking a paper test, it is best to use a separate answer sheet that can be designed for scoring ease or use online tests. Students circle or write in their answers or select the answer online. If you have students answer on the same piece of paper that contains the questions, leave blanks to the left of each binary-choice, multiple-choice, or matching item and blanks on the right-hand side of the page for completion items. For younger students, it is best to minimize transfer of answers by having them circle or underline the correct answer, write the answer in the space provided in the item, or answer on the same screen if online.

Figure 6.6 shows a checklist for how to put together effective summative assessments.

Administering Summative Assessments

When administering classroom summative tests, several procedures are desirable. First, the environment during testing needs to be conducive to maximizing student performance. This means that there is sufficient light, the temperature is appropriate, and efforts are made to ensure quiet, with no interruptions. Put a sign on your door—Testing, Do Not Disturb. Appropriate arrangements will need to be made for students with special needs (see Chapter 13). In essence, the physical environment should not interfere with students' demonstrating what they know, understand, and can do.

Teacher's Corner

Brian Letourneau

National Board Certified Teacher, High School History

At the beginning of each unit, I provide my Advanced Placement United States History students with a unit plan that will cover about 3 to 4 weeks of teaching time. The plan provides students with important dates, including the end-of-unit test date, the content to be covered in the unit, and 7 to 10 essential questions students should be able to answer at the end of the unit. Students can use this guide to prepare for the unit test by deciding if they can answer each essential question fully, provide a general answer without details, or are unsure of how to answer. Their self-evaluation provides guidance for their studying.

As for the test format, I mirror the style of the Advanced Placement exam by including multiple-choice and short-answer questions along with an essay question. Since students take the Advanced Placement test at the end of the year and the test has college credit potential, I want to be sure my students have practice and are comfortable with the test format. Thus, I include one set of 2 to 3 stimulus-style multiple-choice questions for each essential question, a few short-answer questions that combine information covered in 2 to 3 essential questions, and 1 essay question that has students demonstrate a larger understanding of the unit by covering material from 3 to 4 essential questions.

When deciding on the unit test's specific questions, I look at my overall unit plan. In determining what essential questions to cover in the short-answer and essay potion of the assessment, I look at other activities and assessments I conducted during the unit so I don't duplicate assessed information. For instance, during our unit that includes Andrew Jackson, I have students write an essay on Andrew Jackson and conduct a debate during the unit. So, for the final test, I only include multiple-choice questions on Andrew Jackson. When creating the test, I also think about the amount of time spent on each essential question and mirror it to the percentage of points on the test. For instance, if 25% of class time is spent on one essential question, I want 25% of the test's points to be on that essential question.

With respect to writing multiple-choice questions, I make some of my own, but I'm also fortunate to have colleagues willing to share questions they've made. Together we have a "bank" of questions for each unit. I evaluate the questions based on the appropriateness of the stimulus, wording of the corresponding set of questions, and reading comprehension level of the stimulus to ensure a good fit for my students before including on my unit test. I do have and use a textbook for the course; however, I find the unit tests don't align with my learning targets. The tests are good at assessing a student's knowledge of reading the book, but I have more learning targets. So, the textbook unit tests aren't a good fit.

Second, you want to arrange an assessment to both discourage and prevent cheating. Research summarized by Cizek (1999, 2003) indicates that many, if not most, students cheat or know that others cheat. This includes looking at other students' test answers, using crib notes or a cheat sheet, plagiarizing, getting others to do the students' work, obtaining copies of a test or correct answers, colluding, and using prohibited materials (Cizek, 2003). Of special note is plagiarism.

With the Internet, students have access to prepared text on just about any topic. In addition to the issue of simply using such text, students may claim that they did not understand what constitutes plagiarism.

Cheating can be prevented by making sure there are clear guidelines for students regarding cheating and the importance of providing honest answers for improving student learning, by formatting tests and answer sheets to make it difficult to cheat, by careful and continuous close monitoring of students when they are completing the test, by using special seating arrangements, and by using more than one form of the test (e.g., different item order; Miller, Linn, & Gronlund, 2013). If plagiarism is possible, special precautions should be made, including providing examples to students and explaining how the information could be presented so that it is not plagiarized. It is also good to let students know how you can use the Internet to detect language in term papers that has been purchased or otherwise obtained from the Internet.

Use of Summative Assessments

The results of summative assessments need to be analyzed with other sources of data to provide evidence for validity. The technical aspects of these assessments, especially reliability/precision and fairness, may not be stellar, which only increases the need for other sources of information about performance related to the learning target. Sometimes the results will indicate that the assessment was not fair because of a mismatch between planned and actual instruction. Achievement of the best students may indicate an instructional problem if their responses are incorrect. Even so, the results can be used for whole-class, small-group, and/or individual student remediation.

Whole-class analysis is used to understand how the students, as a group, are performing. The results for the whole class can be reviewed to search for overall patterns of understanding and misunderstanding. Once trends and patterns are identified for the whole class, the teacher can "zoom in" on homogeneous subgroups. Subgroup analysis helps teachers answer the following questions (DiRanna et al., 2008):

- How did each group of students perform?
- Are there differences between different groups?
- Are students within the group showing similarity of responses?
- Are there differences among high-, medium-, and low-achieving groups?
- Do students who tend to be more global in their learning style achieve differently from students who have an analytic learning style?
- Are there any differences among students based on race/ethnicity, gender, and socioeconomic status?

Individual student performance allows teachers to group students for further instruction and, when needed, to provide individualized remediation. It's also helpful to compare individual performances of students expected to do best to students expected to perform poorly. This is a check on validity, providing evidence of a match between achievement leading up to the test and performance on the test. Often "target students," those identified before testing who will receive focused analysis, will help the teacher design differentiated further instruction.

Summary

This chapter has summarized characteristics of classroom summative tests. It included presentation of characteristics of such assessments, how to plan them, what the tests should look like, and how they should be implemented. Major points include the following:

- Summative assessment *of* learning documents student performance.
- Classroom summative assessments are taken after an instructional unit.
- Poorly prepared summative assessments tend to discourage student involvement, promote extrinsic motivation, and emphasize testing of knowledge.
- Well-planned summative assessment consists of representative sampling of learning targets, the appropriate number of items, and skeptical use of items provided by test publishers.
- Students should be prepared for taking summative tests by having adequate test-taking and testwiseness skills, knowledge of the format and types of questions, and an adequate review of material.
- Include appropriately complete assessment directions.
- Arrange and format items to be together by type, not continue to next pages, and to provide adequate white space.
- When administering summative tests, it is best to establish an appropriate physical environment and amount of student anxiety and to prevent cheating.
- Avoid excessive assessment anxiety by providing sufficient time, minimizing distractions using a blueprint, and litigating overly negative consequences.

Answer to Introductory Case Study

Jalen can support her decision to create her own summative assessment because the textbook assessment did not align with her learning targets. She also felt that 50 items were too many for the allotted testing period and that the textbook test contained only multiple-choice items, no constructed-response items.

When preparing students for summative assessments, Jalen believes you should

1. familiarize students with the test length, format, and types of questions;
2. share the assessment blueprint;
3. provide a review before the assessment; and
4. tell students when the assessment is scheduled.

Suggestions for Action Research

1. Identify test items that are available from instructional packages that could be used for a unit or chapter test. Review the items for representativeness. Are there about the right number of items? Is there a table of specifications? If possible, compare the items to a test prepared by a classroom teacher.

2. Ask five other students in your class about summative assessments they have taken recently in a course. See if suggestions for planning and administering the tests meet those identified in the chapter.

3. Ask several teachers about how they prepare and administer their summative assessments. Compare their answers to suggestions contained in the chapter.

4. Conduct a review of research on the differences between formative and summative assessment. Compare what you find with what is presented in Table 6.1.

MyEdLab Self-Check 6.1

MyEdLab Self-Check 6.2

MyEdLab Self-Check 6.3

MyEdLab Application Exercise 6.1   Planning Summative Statements

MyEdLab Application Exercise 6.2   Preparing Students for Summative Assessments

---

Summative Assessment II: Using Large-Scale Standards-Based and Standardized Tests

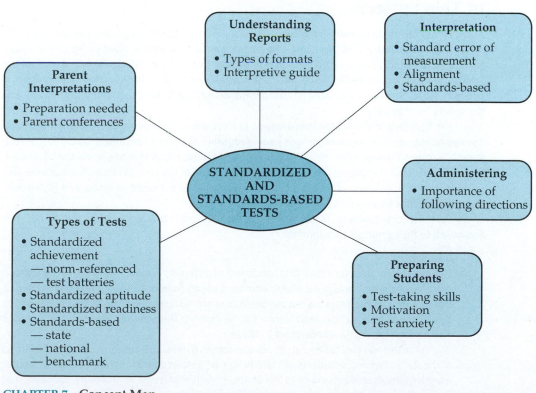

Understanding Reports
- Types of formats
- Interpretive guide

Interpretation
- Standard error of measurement
- Alignment
- Standards-based

Parent Interpretations
- Preparation needed
- Parent conferences

STANDARDIZED AND STANDARDS-BASED TESTS

Administering
- Importance of following directions

Types of Tests
- Standardized achievement
  — norm-referenced
  — test batteries
- Standardized aptitude
- Standardized readiness
- Standards-based
  — state
  — national
  — benchmark

Preparing Students
- Test-taking skills
- Motivation
- Test anxiety

CHAPTER 7 Concept Map

Learning Outcomes

After reading this chapter, you should be able to:

7.1 Understand the essential characteristics of large-scale standards-based and standardized tests, and how they differ from classroom assessments.

7.2 Know how to use scores from standards-based and standardized tests both formatively and summatively.

7.3 Understand how to interpret standards-based and standardized test scores, including provisions for score error, for informing parents, for making instructional adjustments, and for conclusions about student proficiency.

7.4 Know how to appropriately prepare students to take standards-based and standardized tests, and to create the best environment for testing.

Introductory Case Study

What Are the Strengths and Weaknesses of This Letter?

At the end of the previous year, Graceville Elementary School students in grades 3 to 5 took benchmark assessments for the first time. Since the process was new, parents received various communications or no communication at all from teachers regarding the benchmark assessment, and much of the information that was shared was incorrect. This year, as part of the school improvement process, a goal was set to increase parent–teacher communication regarding standards-based testing and how the results could be used.

The first step in the school improvement process was to provide teachers with professional development to ensure they were properly knowledgeable about the benchmark test. Then, before Parent–Teacher Conference Day, the principal reminded teachers they should discuss the benchmark test with parents so that parents understood (a) the purpose of the test, (b) how students were prepared for taking it, (c) conclusions about student performance that could be made, and (d) instructional adjustments that would be made based on the scores.

For those parents who could not conference, the third-grade teachers wrote the following letter and gave it to their principal for approval:

Dear parents,

This month your child took their first benchmark assessments in reading and math. The purpose of these assessments was to determine whether students have mastered our first grading period learning targets. Students are not compared to other students, but instead are determined to be proficient or advanced in their learning of the content. This assessment is a standards-based achievement test, not a standardized ability test.

The test was created by district representatives to mimic as closely as possible the format of the state assessment students will take in May. While the test was not in the state's computer adaptive format, students did complete computer-enhanced items. Additionally, the content of the benchmark matched content previously taught and there were enough items on the test to accurately measure student learning. Thus, student performance on this assessment can predict an *approximate* student performance on these items on the end-of-year assessment. Your child scored _____ % on this assessment.

Our third-grade team has reviewed each item's results on the test, and using this data, we will adapt our instructional sequence to help students obtain the learning targets. Please also note that we will look at other assessments, class work, and student conferences to supplement the benchmark data when determining student performance for report card grades.

Sincerely,
The third-grade team of teachers

As you read this chapter, think about the strengths and weaknesses of this letter. What category of information did the team appropriately convey to parents? What category of information is missing from the letter? What two categories of information did the letter attempt to explain, but in doing so, provided only partial information leading to parent questions?

Education in the United States has become saturated with testing. The dramatic increase in the use of standards-based accountability testing is noteworthy for many reasons, not the least of which is that this movement has significant impacts on your teaching and classroom assessments decision making (see Chapter 1). In the previous edition of this book the chapter on standardized testing was the last one, an add-on to classroom assessment that had some but limited influence on teachers and instruction. The accountability testing movement is now so pervasive that it clearly influences not only what you do with your daily and weekly assessments, but also your instruction and attitudes about teaching (Nichols & Harris, 2016). Consequently, I've moved the chapter to this location for this edition of the book. In addition, since end-of-year standards-based tests are being used to evaluate teachers, the stakes have increased. For some teachers, the scores may determine whether they continue to have a job. So, it's really important for you to understand these kinds of tests and know how to interpret results. In addition, you will be involved in administering these tests, and in preparing your students to take them. You may also need to interpret results to parents. In this chapter, different types of standardized-based and standardized tests will be reviewed briefly, along with your role in interpreting and using results. The emphasis will be on state standards-based tests, including those being developed to assess the Common Core State Standards.

What Are Standardized-Based and Standardized Tests?

In contrast to classroom assessments, what you use daily and weekly in your teaching, there are many large-scale, externally developed assessments that are used to document student learning, and, increasingly, are purported to be useful as formative assessment. In fact, there are hundreds of such assessments. They have been used worldwide for decades. **Standards-based** and **standardized tests** are assessments that are administered and scored in a set or "standard" manner. The questions, procedures for administration, and reporting of scores are consistent each time it is used. In other words, it is a test that is given the same way for test-takers, and the results are calculated and reported in the same way, regardless of when the test is administered or who takes it. While there are many different types of standards-based and standardized tests, they share some essential characteristics:

- Fixed or equivalent set of test items
- High technical quality (e.g., good evidence of validity, reliability/precision, and fairness)
- Set directions for administration
- Set procedures for scoring student responses
- Norms or criteria for interpreting results

We'll consider two major types of large-scale assessments—state standards-based tests used for accountability, and more traditional standardized achievement and aptitude tests. Not to confuse, but with respect to terminology, it is possible and even desirable to have classroom assessments aligned to standards, so in one sense they too could be thought of as "standards-based." However, more broadly in the profession, the term "standards-based test" has been used primarily to refer to the large-scale type, which is the focus of this chapter.

Standards-Based Tests

Standards-based tests are now clearly the most common type of large-scale assessment used in schools. You will become very familiar with them! As we have discussed, such assessments drive instruction and learning as well as your classroom assessments.

Standards-based tests are designed to determine whether students have attained targeted knowledge, understanding, and skills that have been identified by policy makers as important. As discussed in Chapter 2, each state has lists of standards for different subjects and grade levels. As a result, what is tested is public and common for all students at each grade level. There are no secrets about the learning outcomes tested, and the standards are the same for all students. But a caveat here is very important: State standards typically describe what proficiency should be demonstrated after an entire year of learning. Consequently, it's impossible to have enough items to measure everything that was learned. Rather, there is sampling of all the standards, which introduces some degree of unreliability when making conclusions about proficiency. Furthermore, it is a snapshot at one point in time, and does not necessarily show progress or improvement over the year.

There are levels of performance, or benchmarks, that indicate proficiency. This is very similar of assessments that were called **criterion-referenced tests**, in the sense that predetermined criteria set the levels of expected performance. In contrast to norm-referenced tests, then, standards-based tests are all about placing students in categories, for example, proficient or advanced, in relation not to other students, but to the standards that are set for learning.

The idea that students are compared to preestablished criteria suggests that all students can perform at the highest level, or conversely, all students can score at the lowest level. While this sounds reasonable theoretically, in practice it doesn't work out that way. Whenever and wherever you see reports of student achievement, there will be some students at every level in the overall results, say, for a state or large school district. The reasons for this are both technical because of how the tests and test items are developed, and related to the fact that it is very difficult to measure achievement without also measuring ability, which tends to be normally distributed across a large population of students.

State Standards-Based Tests.   At the state level, standards-based tests are used to measure levels of performance as reflected in the specific bodies of knowledge and skills developed and approved by state officials. Each state has its own set of content standards and corresponding tests.

By going to your state education agency website you can learn all about your state's standards-based tests. There are typically helpful materials to facilitate your understanding of the standards and the nature of the tests. There is usually a test blueprint, which will tell you the number of items in each standard and substandard, and released tests and test items that give you a sense of the difficulty, scope, and depth of understanding needed.

The nature of the items in state standards-based tests continues to evolve. Once made up of mostly traditional multiple-choice items and short writing exercises, newer formats that take advantage of technology are being used. These computer-enhanced items are both selected and constructed-response, and I suspect that as they become more common, you'll find them in classroom assessments as well. Most are interactive items that require students to apply their knowledge and skills. In my state, Virginia, the Standards of Learning Tests now include four types of computer-enhanced items:

- Drag and drop: Answer options are dragged to bays to answer the question.
- Hot spot: Answer options are part of a graphic, art, numbers, or text that are selected as answers. More than one answer may be correct.
- Bar graph or histogram: Requires students to graph data.
- Fill-in the-blank: Answers are typed into boxes.

Figure 7.1 is an example of a "drag-and-drop" item; Figure 7.2 shows an example of constructing a bar graph. These are for fourth-grade math (easy for you!).

Another advancement in standards-based testing is the use of the computer adaptive format. A **computer adaptive test** (CAT) is electronically administered to essentially provide each student with a test that is customized to ability level. The actual items each student answers are based on responses to previous questions.

For item 15, drag the correct place value for each individual digit.

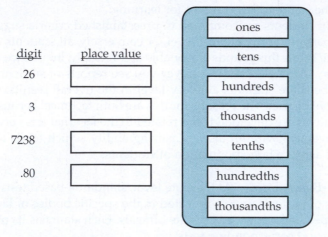

FIGURE 7.1   **Example of Drag-and-Drop Item**

Starting with easier items, as long as students answer correctly, more difficult items are presented. As a result, students typically take a different number of items. Computer adaptive tests are most effective in subjects such as math, where there is a clear sequence of increasingly difficult skills. Regardless of the number of items answered correctly, students are still categorized according to preestablished standards (e.g., proficient, advanced).

I also want to point out that many state standards-based tests are developed in partnership with large testing companies. While this provides testing expertise and results in strong test score reliability/precision, it also limits to a certain

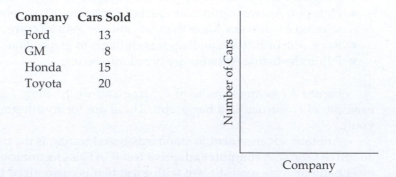

FIGURE 7.2   **Example of Constructing a Bar Graph Item**

degree what the state is able to deliver. With the trend toward more formative uses, the companies are trying very hard to produce tests that can be used diagnostically. This is a tall order for a year-end test!

National Standards-Based Tests.   As you may know, the United States doesn't really have any national tests that all students take (the National Assessment of Educational Progress [NAEP] tests national samples with standardized tests, and there are international tests that also use national samples). That has now changed, at least for many states. Two large consortia of states obtained significant federal funding to come up with assessments that measure the Common Core State Standards beginning in the 2014–2015 school year, and at least three other groups are also working on tests. Not surprisingly, these assessments will be anchored in 21st-century knowledge and skills—what is needed for success in higher education and the workplace. The assessments utilize computer-enhanced items as well as performance tasks, and include interim assessments as well as summative assessments.

The two major consortia that provide Common Core tests are the Smarter Balanced Assessment Consortium and the Partnership for Assessment of Readiness for College and Careers (PARCC). Both of these organizations have developed assessment systems aligned to Common Core standards, including both year-end summative tests, practice tests, and formative assessments. Smarter Balanced boasts that "our tests and resources support teaching and learning," (Smarter Balanced Assessment Consortium, 2016); PARCC utilizes formative tasks, diagnostic tools, and other services and products to promote student learning (Partnership for Assessment for College and Careers, 2016). A tremendous amount of work has been invested in these efforts, and what is provided is technically sound and focused on using technology-enhanced formats to assess "higher-level" cognitive skills. This is illustrated in Figure 7.3, which shows sample items from Smarter Balanced fifth-grade tests.

Benchmark Assessments.   Benchmark, or *interim*, assessments were introduced in Chapter 5 as tests that are given every 6 or 9 weeks, based on what has been taught during these weeks, hopefully aligned to standards that will be assessed on end-of-year accountability tests. The purpose of using these tests is to determine student status on achieving year-end standards to design appropriate instruction, such as remediation for certain students or whole-class review of specific content, and to predict performance on end-of-year tests (Perie, Marion, & Gong, 2009). But as pointed out by Abrams and McMillan (2012) and Shepard (2009), the utility of benchmark assessments is not well established. The quality of items is sometimes poor, and there may be no estimates of reliability/precision or evidence for validity. This is especially true for benchmark test items that are written by district personnel. Although having district teachers develop test items does contribute to validity, it is still likely that there will be weak items and sometimes inaccurate "correct" answers. Items from test publishers, from private companies, and from released items from state assessments will probably have better quality.

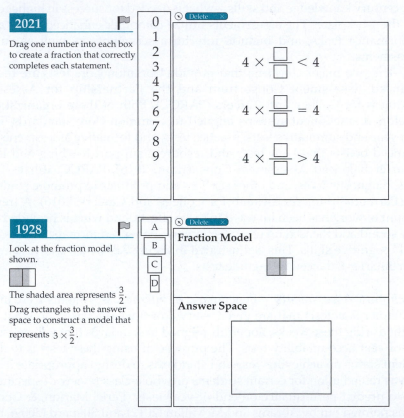

2128

Complete the chart to show which building materials caused the Tower of Pisa to lean and which fixed the leaning. Click in the boxes next to each material that matches the categories in the top row.

	Caused leaning	Fixed leaning
cathedral bells	☐	☐
steel	☐	☐
marble	☐	☐
lead weights	☐	☐
bell room	☐	☐

To complete this task, students must be able to identify errors in punctuation to separate items in a series and in the use of a comma to set off the words yes and no.

2021

Drag one number into each box to create a fraction that correctly completes each statement.

0
1
2
3
4
5
6
7
8
9

Delete ✕

$$4 \times \dfrac{\Box}{\Box} < 4$$

$$4 \times \dfrac{\Box}{\Box} = 4$$

$$4 \times \dfrac{\Box}{\Box} > 4$$

1928

Look at the fraction model shown.

The shaded area represents $\frac{3}{2}$.

Drag rectangles to the answer space to construct a model that represents $3 \times \frac{3}{2}$.

A
B
C
D

Delete ✕

Fraction Model

Answer Space

FIGURE 7.3 **Examples of Formats Used in Smarter Balanced Computer-Enhanced Items**

You will typically get benchmark test results immediately, by item for each student. They could be part of a "data dashboard" that is organized to help interpret the results. These kinds of data require careful consideration when examining the results for your class. It is very helpful for teachers to get together and discuss their results. When students do poorly, you need to probe quality and difficulty of the item and to determine if the content was taught (Abrams & McMillan, 2012; Abrams, Wetzel, & McMillan, 2010). Then, tentative conclusions about students, individually and for groups, need to be verified with other sources of evidence about student knowledge and skills.

Standardized Tests

I'm sure you have taken many standardized tests, so you're familiar with them—tests like the SAT, ACT, Iowa Test of Basic Skills, Otis–Lennon School Ability Test, Stanford–Binet, or Differential Aptitude Test. Typically, you take the test in a room with others and there are specific directions about how to answer—everyone is treated the same way.

Standardized tests have been much criticized as having few positive implications for teaching. The argument is made that because of broad coverage and infrequent testing, heavy reliance on selected-response formats, encouragement to "teach to the test," cultural bias, and inappropriate ranking and comparing students, the information from these tests is not very helpful. Despite these criticisms, however, standardized tests can be very helpful in tracking student progress, selecting students for special programs (or highly selective colleges), providing an external check on learning, and for instructional planning. Recently, both the SAT and ACT have been approved as measures of high-school student competence. The key is being able to understand the scores that are reported, as well as the limitations on how scores should be interpreted. As long as results from these tests are used in conjunction with other data and achievement information, much can be gained by their use.

Norm-Referenced Achievement Test Batteries.   Norm-referenced **achievement test batteries** (or *multilevel survey batteries*) contain a series of individual tests of different areas with common *norms*. When standardized tests are **norm-referenced**, national samples of students have been used as the *norming group* for interpreting relative standing. Because of the norms, you will be able to compare different areas of achievement to discern strengths and weaknesses.

Each type of norm differs with respect to the characteristics of the students who comprise the norm group. The most commonly used types are *national norms*. These norms are based on a "nationally representative" sample of students. Generally, testing companies do a good job of obtaining national samples, but there is still variation from one test to another based on school cooperation and the cost of sampling. Also, most testing companies oversample minorities and other underrepresented groups. Thus, one reason that national norms from different tests are not comparable is that the sampling procedures do not result in equivalent norm groups. For example, you should never conclude that one student with a reading score on the Stanford Achievement Test at the 90th percentile is a better reader compared to a student who scored at the 80th percentile on the reading subtest of the Metropolitan Achievement Test (there would also be differences in the content of the items). On the other hand, most testing companies use the same norm group for their tests for both achievement and aptitude batteries, which allows direct achievement/aptitude and subtest score comparisons within aligned tests from the same company.

There are also many different *special group norms*. These types of norms comprise subgroups from the national sample. For example, special norms are typically available for large cities, high- or low-socioeconomic-status school districts, suburban areas, special grade levels, norms for tests given at different times of the year (usually fall and spring), and other specific subgroups. Whenever a special group norm is used, the basis for comparison changes, and the same raw score on a test will probably be reported as a different percentile rank. For instance, because both achievement and aptitude are related to socioeconomic status (higher socioeconomic status, higher achievement), school districts that contain a larger percentage of high-socioeconomic-status students than is true for the population as a whole (and hence the national norm group) almost always score above the mean with national norms! Conversely, districts with a high percentage of low-socioeconomic-status students typically have difficulty scoring above the mean. However, if the high-socioeconomic-status district is compared to suburban norms, the percentile ranks of the scores will be lower; for low-socioeconomic-status districts, the percentiles will be higher if the norm group is low-socioeconomic-status districts. Understandably, then, suburban districts almost always want to use national norms!

Another type of norm is for a single school district. These are called *local norms*. Local norms are helpful in making intraschool comparisons and in providing information that is useful for student placement in appropriate classes. These different types of norms make it very important for you to examine standardized test reports and know the type of norm that is used to determine percentile rank and standard scores.

Teacher's Corner

Arleen Reinhardt

National Board Certified High School English Teacher

The Stanford 9 was a test that my county used to give that enabled me to understand more fully the reasons for a student's difficulty. I was able to help my parents and students understand why they struggled more in one area than in another. As a result, I was able to suggest strategies and use strategies in my classroom that helped me individualize instruction for students more quickly. Although this test was, of course, only one type of assessment, it offered a good starting point for me to better understand my students' strengths and weaknesses.

When comparing an individual's performance to the norm group, the overall competence of this group is critical in determining relative position. Ranking high with a low-performing group may indicate, in an absolute sense, less competence than ranking low in a high-performing group. Thus, the exact nature of the norming group is important, and several types of norms can be used.

Some tests, such as the Metropolitan Achievement Tests, the Stanford Achievement Tests, the *TerraNova*, and the California Achievement Tests, have diagnostic batteries. These batteries have more items in each area than the survey forms of the tests. Each battery is identified with a descriptive title, such as *spelling*, *punctuation*, *letter recognition*, *fraction computations*, *graphs*, and so on, but the best way to be sure about the match between what the battery says it is testing and your learning targets or standards is to examine the objectives and the type of test items that are used.

Aptitude Tests.   Standardized **aptitude tests** measure a student's cognitive ability, potential, or capacity to learn. This ability is determined by both in-school and out-of-school experiences. Thus, aptitude tests are less specifically tied to what is taught in school than are achievement tests.

It's important to remember that aptitude tests provide a measure of *current* developed ability, not innate capacity that cannot change. This level of ability is helpful in planning instruction in two ways: knowing the general capabilities students bring to the class in different areas and knowing the discrepancies between aptitude and achievement.

An understanding of the general ability levels of your students will help you design instructional experiences and group students appropriately. Suppose one class has an average aptitude score of 83 (below average) and another a score of 120 (above average). Would you use the same teaching materials and approaches in each of these classes? Similarly, would you give the same assignments to individual students who differ widely in ability? Student achievement is maximized when the method of instruction or learning activity matches the aptitude. For example, low-ability students may need remediation, and high-ability students would benefit most from enrichment activities.

Aptitude tests are also used for determining expected learning by examining any discrepancy between ability and achievement. If there is a large discrepancy and if other information is consistent, a student may be an underachiever. Many standardized test services provide a report that includes both aptitude and achievement test score results and presents predicted scores. This makes the determination of discrepancy easier.

Readiness Tests.   **Readiness tests** are actually a specialized type of aptitude test. However, readiness tests, because of the high number of items from specific skill areas, can also be used diagnostically to determine the skills students need to improve if they are to be successful in school. Thus, readiness tests both predict achievement and diagnose weaknesses.

Most readiness tests are used in early elementary grades and for reading. The tests are helpful in identifying particular skills and knowledge to plan instruction and in designing remedial exercises. For example, the *Boehm Test of Basic Concepts*, Third Edition, assesses student comprehension of the basic verbal concepts that are needed for comprehension of verbal communication (e.g., concepts such as many, smallest, nearest). Reading readiness tests are helpful in identifying skills that need to be mastered, such as visual discrimination of letters, auditory discrimination, recognition of letters and numbers, and following instructions. Readiness tests should not be used as the sole criterion for determining whether a child has the skills and knowledge to begin kindergarten or first grade. Scores from these tests should always be used with other information to provide a comprehensive evaluation of readiness.

Understanding and Interpreting Standards-Based and Standardized Test Scores

When you first look at test score reports they may seem to be very complicated and difficult to understand, particularly for standardized tests with norms. This is because they are typically designed to provide as much information as possible on a single page. For a comprehensive battery, scores are often reported for each skill as well as each subskill. The best approach for understanding a report is to consult the test manual and find examples that are explained. Most test publishers and states do a very good job of explaining the meaning of each part of the report.

Test Score Report Formats

There are also many different types of reports. Each test publisher or state has a unique format for reporting results and usually includes different kinds of scores. In addition, there are different formats to report the same scores. Thus, the same battery may be reported as a list of students in your class, the class as a whole, a skills analysis for the class or individual student, individual profiles, profile charts, growth scale profiles, and other formats. Some reports include only scores for major tests; others include subskill scores and item scores. Different norms may be used. All of this means that each report contains somewhat different information, organized and presented in dissimilar ways. You need to first identify what type of report you are dealing with, then find an explanation for it in an interpretive guide. After you have become acquainted with the types of standardized tests and reports used in your school, you will be in a position to routinely interpret them in accurate and helpful ways.

In our brave new world of technology, many digital options are available for standards-based reports, often in files that can be massaged and downloaded. Reports are highly customized, depending on whether you want school, district, or different groups of students, grade level, subject, year, and type of score (e.g., numbers and percentages of students proficient). If benchmark tests are used, you will probably see results by item for each student. You will need to read each item to make judgments about whether students were taught what was tested and did or did not understand.

Interpreting Standards-Based and Standardized Scores

Once you get the scores you obviously need to make some sense of them so that they provide you with accurate and helpful information. Here you'll make professional judgments about what the scores mean and how they can be used. Several types of scores can be reported, and a good understanding of fundamental descriptive statistics is essential (see Appendix A). For standards-based tests, one type of report includes the percentage of students who have achieved the various levels described by the state system (e.g., 40 % adequate, 60% advanced). In addition, there will be frequency and percentage correct information, and more complex scale scores that have a unique meaning, based on how the number of correct answers is represented on a different numerical scale (see Appendix A for an explanation). Standardized tests rely heavily on scaled scores (e.g., SAT 200-800; ACT 1-36) that convert to percentile rank.

There is one somewhat technical concept related to interpretation that is critical. It is called *standard error of measurement*. It's related to reliability/precision. We'll consider this first, followed by a discussion of alignment and other factors that need attention to make appropriate interpretations.

Standard Error of Measurement.   As I have stressed throughout this text, every test score has some degree of error. Chapter 3 introduced the relationship between error and reliability/precision. Basically, as error increases, reliability/precision decreases. But reliability/precision indices only reflect error within a test; we cannot know what type or amount of other sources of error have influenced a student's score. Therefore, we estimate the degree of error that is probable, given the reliability/precision estimate of the test. This degree of error is estimated mathematically and is reported as the **standard error of measurement (SEM)**.

If a student took a test many times, the resulting set of scores would look like a normal distribution. That is, sometimes the student would get a "good" error and get a higher score, and sometimes the student would get a "bad" error, resulting in a lower score. If we assume that the student's *true* score is the mean of this hypothetical distribution, then we can use this as a starting point for estimating the *actual* true score. Standard error of measurement creates an interval, and it is within this interval that we can be confident that the student's true score lies. Intervals can be thought of as *confidence bands* or a *margin of error*. Of course, we do not know *where* in the interval the true score lies, so we are most accurate in interpreting the performance as described by the interval, not as a single score.

The idea of interpreting single scores as a band or interval has important implications. If you are drawing a conclusion about the performance of a single student, your thinking should be something like this: "Trevor's performance in mathematics places him between the 86th and 94th percentiles," rather than,

"Trevor's score is at the 90th percentile." This will give you a more realistic and accurate basis for judging Trevor's real or actual level of performance. When comparing two scores from the same standardized test battery, a meaningful difference in performance is indicated only when the intervals, as established by one standard error of measurement, do not overlap. Thus, it would be wrong to conclude that a student's language achievement score of 72 is higher than the reading score of 70 if the confidence bands overlap. The same logic is needed for comparing ability with achievement or for comparing the scores of different individuals on the same test. That is, if the bands do not overlap, then you should conclude that there is probably a meaningful difference between the scores.

For standards-based test scores there is also a SEM, at least for the individual score. That is, if a student obtained a score of 400, which places him in the "proficient" category, his or her *actual* proficiency is somewhere around 400. It could be 390 or 405. If the student's real proficiency is 390 and the cutoff for being proficient is 400, he or she would be misclassified, in this case a false positive. In the world of standards-based testing, there are always a number of students whose real or actual proficiency doesn't match the test result and accompanying identified level. In Virginia, for example, it's not unusual to have 4%–8% of the students misclassified on a single test administration (that number is reduced dramatically with repeated testing, though obviously the false positives don't need to retest).

Fortunately, test publishers report standard errors of measurement to help you interpret the scores properly, and often they are displayed visually in the form of a shaded band or line surrounding the score. Unfortunately, there is usually a slightly different standard error of measurement for each subtest and for different ranges of scores.

Alignment.   As pointed out in Chapter 3, one of the most critical aspects of interpreting standardized test scores is to determine the extent to which the test content is aligned with the curriculum, with your teaching, and with your classroom assessments.

If the content, emphasis, and cognitive level of the standardized or standards-based test match well with your instruction, the curriculum, and classroom assessment, then there is strong alignment. With strong alignment, the test scores serve as a check on the effectiveness of the instruction. With weak alignment, scores on standardized tests have some implications, but because of a lack of emphasis on the same content and cognitive level, these implications are not as clear. For example, if we know that there is a good match and the scores are low, there is reason to learn why. High test scores with a good match are validation that students are indeed learning the content as intended.

Figure 7.4 illustrates the degree of alignment that can be expected from different types of assessments. You will see that standards aptitude tests are least aligned with what you teach, and classroom assessments are most aligned. So *your classroom assessments* (as long as they are good) say the most about what students are learning and the effectiveness of your teaching. At least this is my belief! What students demonstrate on progressively more general assessments is influenced by

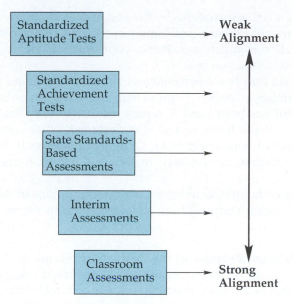

FIGURE 7.4   Alignment of Various Types of Assessments with Student Learning and Motivation

other factors, while your classroom assessments are tightly aligned to learning targets and instruction.

Standards-Based Interpretations.   As previously discussed, standards-based interpretations compare student performance to established standards rather than to other students. These tests are designed to provide a valid indication of skills and knowledge in specific areas. (Most norm-referenced tests also provide standards-referenced information by indicating the number of items answered correctly in specific areas, but because the primary purpose of these tests is to compare individuals, they typically do not provide information as meaningful as from standards-based tests.)

It is important for each skill or area for which a score is reported to be described in detail. With delimited and well-defined learning targets, the score can more easily be interpreted to suggest some degree of mastery. Your judgment concerning the degree of a student's mastery is usually based on the percentage of correctly answered items that measure a specific target. The meaning that is given to the percentage of correct answers is generally based on a review of the definition of the target and the difficulty of the items. An important aspect of making this decision is having a sufficient number of items to adequately measure the trait.

One approach to sound interpretation is to set in your mind a group of "minimally competent" students in reference to the target, then see how many items these students answer correctly. If the mean number of correct answers is, say, 7 of 10, then your "standard" becomes 70% of the items. It may be that the level is set in relation to a goal for students by the end of the year, or you may set standards based on how others have performed in the past. Regardless of the approach, the interpretation is largely a matter of your professional judgment, so think carefully about the criteria you use.

In state tests you will simply see percentages of students obtaining proficient or passing marks. Obtaining a "pass" or "proficient" score is standards-based in the sense that a standard has been used to report results. To fully interpret the results, teachers need to know how the test was designed, what subscales are used, and how the standard was determined. Disaggregating results to specific targets provides information most likely to be used by teachers in their instruction.

With these recommendations, keep the following suggestions in mind when making standards-based interpretations from standardized tests (summarized in Figure 7.5):

1. Determine the Primary Purpose of the Test—Is It Norm- or Standards-Based? Standards-based tests are designed for standards-based interpretations. As long as the descriptions of the traits match your learning targets, these types of tests will provide helpful information, usually more helpful than norm-referenced tests because they are better aligned with instruction. Be wary of using norm-referenced tests for standards-based interpretations.

2. Examine the Clarity and Specificity of the Definitions and Traits Measured. For each score that is reported, there needs to be an adequate definition of what is being measured. Norm-referenced tests tend to define what is measured more broadly, standards-based tests more specifically. You may need to consult the technical manual to get sufficient detail of the definition to make a valid judgment about the match between what the test says it is measuring and what you want measured. There should be good content-related evidence of validity to demonstrate an adequate sampling of content or skills from a larger domain.

3. Be Sure There Is a Sufficient Number of Items to Make a Valid Decision. The general rule is to have four to six different test items for each target. For learning targets that are less specific, more than 10 items may be needed. In some norm-referenced tests you may see skills listed with as few as three or four items. This is too few for making definite conclusions, though the results may suggest a need for further investigation.

FIGURE 7.5   Checklist for Making Standards-Based Interpretations

✓ Is the primary purpose of the test norm- or criterion-referenced/standards-based?
✓ Are measured targets delimited and clearly defined?
✓ Are there enough items to measure each target adequately?
✓ Is the difficulty level of the items matched with the learning targets?
✓ Does the sample of items represent the larger domain of interest?
✓ Are scores disaggregated by group?

4. Examine Item Difficulty and Match to Your Standards. Norm-referenced tests may not use easy items because easy items do not discriminate students as well as difficult items, whereas standards-based tests tend to have some easy items so that most students will do reasonably well. This means that the difficulty of the items may differ considerably with the same definition for the target. Inspect the items carefully and use your knowledge of their difficulty in setting standards.

5. Examine a Sample of Items from a Larger Domain. Standards-based scores are usually reported in categories or subscales as well as for the total test, and these groupings of items refer to student performance in the corresponding domains of knowledge and skills. Although some standards-based test reports show results for each item, it is not what the individual items measure but what is represented by the items as a group that is most important. As discussed earlier, the tests sample from the larger content domains. Thus, it is important to generalize from the group of items to the standards they represent.

An example of the kind of data that can be provided is illustrated in Table 7.1 for eighth-grade science on Virginia's 2012–2013 Standards of Learning test. You will see that there were five reporting categories (subscales) on the test. Each reporting category was represented by specific standards, and there were a few items that measure each reporting category. There was also alignment information with sixth-grade standards that covered prerequisite content. You will also see that the number of items was for the *reporting category*, not for a specific *standard*. That means that in a given year it is possible that some standards are not tested at all!

6. Disaggregate Scores by Groups of Students. Scores should be disaggregated, if possible, by groups of students. This allows for more specific probing of certain students to confirm what is suggested by the results. It's best to keep interpretations at the level of groups of students rather than individuals, unless there are unusually high or low scores.

In Figure 7.6, I have shown a sequence of steps you need to take to make appropriate interpretations from both year-end and benchmark standards-based tests, since these are the scores you'll most likely be provided. What you want to ensure when you receive the results is that your interpretations of the scores are valid. That way, when you use those interpretations to modify instruction or give students feedback, it's much more likely to be on target and helpful.

Establishing the credibility of the scores involves examination of test items for quality and level of difficulty, knowing from test blueprints how the sampling of standards was completed and how subscale scores were formed, noting reliability and standard error of measurement, and having some indication of student effort. The test blueprint is your very best friend! It will show you, as in Table 7.1, which specific subareas have been assessed. The second step I like to call "instructional dosage." What was the alignment between what students were taught and what was tested? Scores on subscales covering content that was not taught are pretty meaningless. If possible, it's very helpful to break out results by subgroups of students, by subscales (e.g., high-achieving students on other measures of

TABLE 7.1   **Example of State Standards-Based Test Blueprint**

Grade 8 Science Test Blueprint Summary Table

Reporting Category	Grade 6 Standards of Learning	Life Science Standards of Learning	Physical Science Standards of Learning	Number of Items
Assessed with Other SOL	6.1j	LS.1j	PS.1n	
Scientific Investigation	6.1a–i	LS.1a–i	PS.1a–m	10
Force, Motion, Energy, and Matter	6.2a, e 6.4a–g 6.5a–b 6.6a		PS.2a–f PS.3a–b PS.4a–c PS.5a–c PS.6a–b PS.7a–d PS.8a–d PS.9a–e PS.10a–d PS.11a–d	15
Life Systems		LS.2a–d LS.3a–b LS.4a–d LS.5a–c LS.12a–f LS.13a		7
Ecosystems	6.7a–g	LS.6a–d LS.7a–b LS.8a–e LS.9a–c LS.10a–c LS.11a–e		7
Earth and Space Systems	6.2b–d 6.3a–e 6.5c–f 6.6b–f 6.8a–i 6.9a–d	LS.13b–c		11
Excluded from Testing	None			
Number of Operational Items				50
Number of Field Test Items*				10
Total Number of Items on Test				60

Source: Virginia Students of Learning Assessments Test Blueprint Grade 8 Science. Richmond, VA: Virginia Department of Education; accessed August 11, 2016, from http://www.doe.virginia.gov/testing/sol/blueprints/science_blueprints/2010/2010_blueprint_science_8.pdf

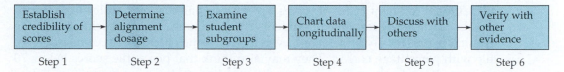

| Establish credibility of scores | Determine alignment dosage | Examine student subgroups | Chart data longitudinally | Discuss with others | Verify with other evidence |
| Step 1 | Step 2 | Step 3 | Step 4 | Step 5 | Step 6 |

FIGURE 7.6   **Steps to Ensure Valid Interpretations from Year-End and Benchmark Standards-Based Tests.**

achievement in one group and low achievers in another group). It's really helpful to graph data longitudinally to look for trends over time—trends are typically more powerful than what you learn from a single year.

The fifth step is to take the results and join in a collaborative effort with others to determine what it all means. This can be extremely helpful. Tentative interpretations can then be verified with other student performance evidence, from classroom tests, homework, and other assessments. Once verified, you're ready to draw conclusions and use the data for instructional adjustments.

Interpreting Test Reports for Parents

Most teachers interpret the results of standardized and standards-based tests for parents. Because you are in contact with students daily and are aware of their classroom performance, you are in the best position to communicate with parents regarding the results of standards-based and standardized tests. You can determine what level of detail to report and how the results coincide with classroom performance. This is done most effectively face-to-face in the context of a teacher–parent conference, though many schools distribute or make available reports without scheduling a conference. In such a conference, you can point out important cautions and discuss the results in a way that will make sense. Before the conference, you should review available information and prepare it to show student progress and areas of strength and weakness that may need specific action at home and school. This should include other examples of student work, in addition to the test results, to lessen the tendency to place too much value on test scores.

In preparing for the conference, keep in mind that most parents are interested in particular types of information. These include some indication of relative standing, growth since earlier testing, performance compared to standards, weaknesses, and strengths. For each of these areas you should present the relevant numbers, but be sure to include a clear and easy-to-understand narrative—using plain, everyday language—that explains the numbers. You should always include some explanation of norms, standards, and the standard error of measurement. It is important for parents to realize that, for most reports, the scores do not represent comparisons with other students in the class. Parents obviously don't need an extended explanation of error, but it's important for them to understand that the results represent *approximate* and not absolute or precise performance.

Of the different types of scores to report to parents, percentiles from norm-referenced tests (percentage of students from the norm group scoring below the result) are most easily understood, even though some parents will confuse percentile with percentage correct. They may also think that percentile scores below 70 are poor because they are accustomed to grading systems in which 70 or below may mean failure. In fact, for most standardized tests, students will score in the average range if they answer 60%–70% of the items correctly.

Many states will provide help in interpreting their state standards-based reports to parents. You need to check the appropriate website to obtain helpful information and tips.

In summary, the following suggestions will help you interpret standardized and standards-based test reports confidently and in a way that will accurately inform parents and help the student:

1. **Understand the Meaning of Every Score Reported to Parents.** It is embarrassing, not to mention unprofessional, not to know how to interpret each score on the report.

2. **Examine Individual Student Reports Comprehensively Before a Conference with Parents.** This will prevent you from trying to understand and explain at the same time.

3. **Gather Evidence of Student Performance in the Classroom That Can Supplement the Test Scores.** This demonstrates your commitment to the preparation and careful analysis of each student's performance, and it provides more concrete examples of performance that parents can easily understand.

4. **Be Prepared to Address Areas of Concern Most Parents Have, Such as Standing, Progress, Performance Compared to Standards, Strengths, and Weaknesses.** This may require you to review the student's previous performance on other standardized tests.

5. **Be Prepared to Distinguish Between Ability and Achievement.** Many parents want to know whether their child is performing "up to their ability." You might even have a short written description of the difference to supplement your verbal explanation.

6. **Explain the Importance of Norms and Error in Testing for Proper Interpretation.** This could include your knowledge of any extenuating circumstances that may have affected the student's performance.

7. **Summarize Clearly What the Scores Mean.** Don't simply show the numbers and expect the parents to be able to understand. You will need to summarize in language that the parents can comprehend.

8. **Try to Create a Discussion with Parents, Rather Than Making a Presentation to Them.** Ask questions to involve parents in the conference and to enhance your ability to determine whether they in fact understand the meaning of the scores.

Preparing Students to Take Standards-Based and Standardized Tests

You want your students to perform as well as possible on standards-based and standardized tests, especially since the stakes are high, both for students and teachers. This is accomplished if students are properly prepared before taking the test.

One area to address is making sure that students have good test-taking skills. These skills, introduced in the previous chapter, help familiarize students with item formats and give them strategies so that the validity of the results is improved. Students should be proficient with the test-taking skills listed in Table 7.2.

TABLE 7.2   Test-Taking Skills and Strategies

Skill or Strategy	Description	Purpose	Components
Tuning In	Using and following oral directions	To listen for rules and directions To hear the time limits	Be alert for a cue to begin listening Stop what you are doing Look at the speaker Tune in to the directions Concentrate, focus, listen Follow directions
Following Written Directions	Learning to read, interpret, and do	To know what to do To know steps and procedures To understand the task To gather instructions	Read all directions thoroughly and carefully Check, highlight, underline, or circle the words that tell you what to do Number the directions Visualize the steps Go over directions again when the task is completed
Bubbling In	Learning to fill in the answer sheet quickly and accurately	To know how to fill in a small circle correctly that matches the right answer for each question To be sure the test is scored accurately To allow you to show what you know	Use a number two pencil Using the hand you do not write with, point to the correct answer on your test booklet so that you don't lose your place Use other hand to fill in the bubble next to the correct number on the answer sheet Fill in completely Stay inside the bubble Erase all marks outside the bubble

(Continued)

TABLE 7.2 (*Continued*)

Skill or Strategy	Description	Purpose	Components
Know and Go	Learning to trust your instincts about an answer and move on	To recognize the "aha" or intuitive feeling when you know the answer To learn to mark the answer quickly and move on To avoid analyzing a question too much	Read the question Read the answers If you know an answer is right, mark it If you know it, do not change your answer Move on to the next question
Be Back	Learning to answer easy questions first and mark difficult ones to revisit later	To answer all the questions you know first To answer easy questions first and quickly To prevent you from getting "stuck" on an item To know to return to a question if there is time	Answer questions and move on If the answer does not come quickly, think "I'll be back" If permitted, jot down the numbers of any items you want to check Return to marked items and complete the test Guess if there is no penalty for guessing
When in Doubt, Try It Out	Learning to make educated guesses	To consider each choice as the correct answer To eliminate incorrect answers To narrow your choices to two possible answers To mark one answer when you are in doubt	Read questions carefully Eliminate clearly wrong answers Try out remaining answers For math questions, first try the middle option as correct Make smart guesses and move on If you have no idea which answer is correct, guess
Take a Double Take	Learning to check your work and avoid careless errors	Find and correct mistakes To realize that if you know the answer but accidentally fill in the wrong circle, you lose points To remember to always check your work To be sure you don't lose points for a simple error	Quickly review each answer, testing it against the question See if the number of the response matches the question Look for spaces not completed, then guess the answers Scan the answer sheet for stray marks and erase as needed

TABLE 7.2 *(Continued)*

Skill or Strategy	Description	Purpose	Components
Set the Pace	Learning to control the time spent on each task	To develop an awareness of time segments for pacing To adjust the speed of your work To know when to use fast versus slow reading To develop a feel for pacing To keep from running out of time	When starting a question, decide if it is easy or hard Speed up for easy questions Slow down for hard questions Adjust reading speed to the purpose Practice fast-pace tips such as knowing facts, formulas, and terms; how to read graphs and charts; knowing when to use a calculator; knowing when to move on (after 2 minutes)
Keep On Keeping On	Learning to try different approaches and be persistent	To get past difficult spots and do your best To avoid wasting time To learn to apply different approaches or strategies for difficult questions	Try educated guesses when the answer is unknown Read the passage for thorough understanding Try various strategies to answer the question Keep working in each section until finished Use deep breathing if feeling frustrated, defeated, or hopeless

Source: Based on Chapman and King (2009).

You also want to set an appropriate classroom climate or environment for taking the test. This begins with your attitude toward the test. If you convey to students that you believe the test is a burden, an unnecessary or even unfair imposition, then students may also adopt such an attitude and may not try their best. Be happy with the test; convey an attitude of challenge and opportunity. Discuss with your students the purpose and nature of the test. Emphasize that it is most important for students to try to do their best, not just to obtain a high score. Tell the students how the tests will be used in conjunction with other information; this will reduce anxiety. You want to enhance student confidence by giving them short practice tests. These tests help to acquaint students with the directions and the types of items they will answer. Also provide students opportunities for instruction and assessment that is different from the specific test format. Using "varied-format" preparation increases overall knowledge and improves performance (Popham, 2017).

Student motivation is a key factor in obtaining valid results from large-scale testing (Wise & Smith, 2016). Motivate your students to put forth their best effort by helping them understand how the results from the test will benefit them. Show

how incorrect answers can be used to improve learning and essential life skills, their knowledge of themselves, and planning for the future. Avoid comments that might make students concerned or anxious.

Reassure your students that some anxiety is normal and can provide energy to help them perform better. Some of your students may be so anxious about the test that their anxiety seriously interferes with their performance. If you suspect that a student's performance is adversely affected by test anxiety, after you have done all you can to alleviate the fears, then you may want to have the student visit with a school counselor to determine the extent of the problem. If necessary, appropriate counseling and desensitization exercises can be explored. At the very least, incorporate your awareness of the anxiety when interpreting the results of the test (see Cizek & Burg, 2006, for further detail on test anxiety).

Emphasize the importance of a good night's sleep and a healthy breakfast or lunch to students to stay alert and at their best for the test. Of course, be sure that the physical environment for taking the test is appropriate. There should be adequate work space and lighting as well as good ventilation. Like classroom summative assessments, the room should be quiet, without distractions, and the test should be scheduled to avoid events that may disturb the students. Students should be seated to avoid distractions and cheating. Morning testing is preferred. One of the important ways to prepare students for testing is to do everything you can to make students comfortable, self-confident, and in control. Students need to be familiar with the nature of the test and know what to expect. Likewise, teachers need to be confident about the way students will perform on the test. This is communicated to students when the teacher knows directions, guidelines, and procedures and demonstrates confidence by being calm and business-like (Flippo, 2008). It is best to remove any visual aids that could assist students and as indicated in Chapter 6, to place a sign on the outside of the door, such as Testing—Do Not Disturb.

The key to successful student performance on standards-based and standardized tests is to focus more on the standards and student learning than on test performance. This requires an in-depth understanding of the nature of the standards and the kind of mental operations needed to answer test questions. Teachers achieve this in-depth understanding by "unpacking" standards, breaking them down to know the specific levels of knowledge and skills that are required (Tileston & Darling, 2008). Is the knowledge declarative or procedural? Is the emphasis on knowing, applying, or problem solving? What mental operation is needed to answer the types of questions on the standards-based tests?

It is particularly important to maximize teaching time and learning and familiarize students with the test format and item type just enough to help them develop the self-confidence they need to be successful. The worst practice, seen more and more with standards-based education, is to drill students over and over by taking tests similar to the standards-based ones. There is no compelling evidence that such strategies improve test scores. Some familiarity is important, but in many schools there is simply way too much time taken to test, test, and then test some more, often only with multiple-choice type items that are commonly used in large-scale tests.

FIGURE 7.7   Do's and Don'ts of Standardized and Standards-Based Test Preparation

Do	Don't
Improve student test-taking skills	Use the standardized test format for classroom tests
Establish a suitable environment	
Motivate students to do their best	Characterize tests as an extra burden
Use released items	Tell students important decisions are made solely on the basis of test scores
Explain why tests are given and how results will be used	Use previous forms of the same test
Give practice tests	Teach the test
Tell students they probably won't know all the answers	Have a negative attitude about the test
	Use items with a format that is identical to the test
Tell students not to give up	
Allay student anxiety	Limit instruction and classroom
Have a positive attitude about the test	assessments to be aligned only with the test

Poor test performance is caused by many different factors, though the following are most prevalent (Chapman & King, 2009):

- Distractions that prevent clear thinking, caused by lack of sleep, noise, hunger, physical discomforts, interruptions, teacher pressure
- Inadequate preparation, caused by poor study and test-taking skills, inattention, lack of confidence, unfamiliarity with the test format and procedures
- Lack of internal readiness, promoted by negative self-talk, fear of failure, panic, low motivation, nervousness
- Confusion, caused by unfamiliarity with types of items, unclear directions, lack of strategies for completing the test (p. 90)

Figure 7.7 lists some do's and don'ts regarding test preparation practices.

Administering Standards-Based and Standardized Tests

Because most standardized and standards-based tests are given in the classroom, you will most likely be responsible for administering them to your students. The most important part of administering these tests is to *follow the directions carefully and explicitly*. This point cannot be overstated. You must adhere strictly to the instructions that are given by the test publisher. The procedures are set to ensure standardization in the conditions under which students in different classes and schools take the test. The directions indicate what to say, how to respond to student questions, and what to do as students are working on the test. Familiarize yourself with the directions before you read them to your students, word for word as specified. Don't try to paraphrase directions or recite them from memory, even if you have given the test many times.

During the test you may answer student questions about the directions or procedures for answering items, but you should not help students in any way with an answer or what is meant by a question on the test. Although you may be tempted to give students hints or tell them to "answer more quickly" or "slow down and think more," these responses are inappropriate. You need to essentially suspend your role as classroom teacher for a while and assume the role of test administrator.

While observing students as they take the test you may see some unusual behavior or events that could affect the students' performance. It is best to record these behaviors and events for use in subsequent interpretation of the results. Interruptions should also be recorded.

Summary

The purpose of this chapter was to introduce you to the principles of standards-based and standardized testing to enable you to make reasonable interpretations of and use of your students' scores. The results of these tests, when used correctly, provide helpful information concerning the effectiveness of your instruction and the progress of your students. Since standards-based test results will be available to parents, you need to be knowledgeable and confident in your discussions with them about the meaning of the scores. Important points in the chapter include the following:

- Standardized tests have set procedures for administration and scoring.
- Standards-based tests are criterion-referenced, determining whether students have achieved targeted performance levels.
- Standards-based assessments include state, national, and benchmark tests.
- Norm-referenced standardized tests provide informative "external" measures and help identify student relative strengths and weaknesses.
- Different types of norms, such as national norms, special group norms, or local norms, influence the reported percentile ranks and other comparative scores.
- Proper interpretation of scores from norm-referenced standardized tests depends on the nature of the norm group.
- Norms are not standards or expectations; they should be recent, appropriate to your use, and based on good sampling.
- Aptitude (ability) and readiness standardized tests measure capacity to learn.
- Standard error of measurement (SEM) expresses the degree of error to be expected with individual test scores; test results are best interpreted as intervals defined by the SEM.
- Alignment of the content, emphasis, and cognitive level of a test with instruction is needed for proper interpretation; classroom assessments are best aligned, and aptitude tests are worst aligned.

- Good standards-based judgments depend on well-defined targets and a sufficient number of test items to provide a reliable result.
- Standardized test reports vary in format and organization; consult the interpretive guide to aid in understanding.
- Prepare students for taking standardized tests by establishing a good environment, lessening test anxiety, motivating students to do their best, avoiding distractions, and giving students practice test items and exercises.

Introductory Case Study Answer

The letter appropriately conveyed to parents the purpose of the benchmark test, but it did not contain information about how teachers prepared students for the test. The letter attempted to explain conclusions about student performance that could be made and instructional adjustments that would be made based on scores. However, parents are left with some important questions:

- The letter contained information about the computer adaptive format and technology-enhanced items, but did not explain these terms to parents.
- The letter says the test is an achievement, not ability, test, but doesn't elaborate on the difference.
- The letter contained a percentage score, but did not indicate a proficient and advanced level of mastery nor did it provide information about interpreting the percentage score.
- The letter stated that teachers would adjust their instruction, but it did not indicate that this would be done through individual/small-group remediation and/or whole-class review of specific content.

Suggestions for Action Research

1. Observe a class in which students take a standards-based or standardized test. If possible, take a copy of the test administration guidelines with you and determine how closely the teacher follows the directions. What has the teacher done to motivate the students and set a proper environment? Observe the students as they are taking the test. Do they seem motivated and serious? How quickly do they work?

2. Sit in on two or three teacher–parent conferences that review the results of standardized tests. Compare what occurs with the suggestions in the chapter. How well, in your opinion, does the teacher interpret the scores? Is the teacher accurate?

3. Interview some parents about standards-based or standardized tests. What did they get from the reports? Which types of scores were most meaningful to them? Did the results surprise them? Were the results consistent with other performance, such as grades?

4. Interview some teachers about state standards-based testing. Ask them how they use the results of these tests to improve their instruction. Ask them to recall situations in which parents did not seem to understand the results of the test very well. Looking back, what could the teacher have done differently to enhance parent understanding?

MyEdLab Self-Check 7.1

MyEdLab Self-Check 7.2

MyEdLab Self-Check 7.3

MyEdLab Self-Check 7.4

MyEdLab Application Exercise 7.1   Interpreting Standardized Test Reports

MyEdLab Application Exercise 7.2   Interpreting Test Results for Parents

Selected-Response Assessment: Multiple-Choice, Binary-Choice, and Matching Items

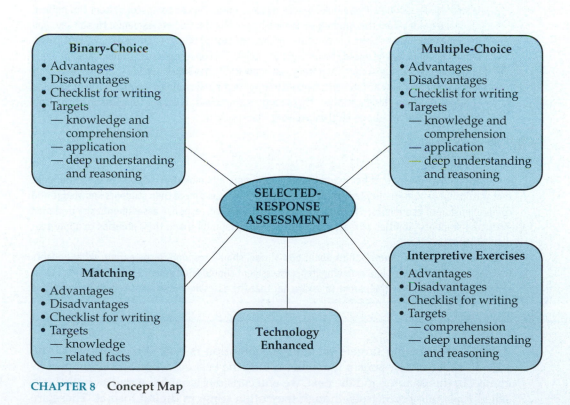

Binary-Choice
- Advantages
- Disadvantages
- Checklist for writing
- Targets
  — knowledge and comprehension
  — application
  — deep understanding and reasoning

Multiple-Choice
- Advantages
- Disadvantages
- Checklist for writing
- Targets
  — knowledge and comprehension
  — application
  — deep understanding and reasoning

SELECTED-RESPONSE ASSESSMENT

Matching
- Advantages
- Disadvantages
- Checklist for writing
- Targets
  — knowledge
  — related facts

Technology Enhanced

Interpretive Exercises
- Advantages
- Disadvantages
- Checklist for writing
- Targets
  — comprehension
  — deep understanding and reasoning

CHAPTER 8 Concept Map

Learning Outcomes

After reading this chapter, you should be able to:

8.1 Recognize the advantages and disadvantages of using different selected-response type items, including multiple-choice, binary-choice, and matching.

8.2 Identify best practices in the construction of selected-response items.

8.3 Be able to construct sound selected-response items that match the nature of the learning target that is assessed.

8.4 Understand the nature of interpretive exercises and technology-enhanced items.

Introductory Case Study

How Should Miriam Respond to the Parent?

On Tuesday, Miriam, a high school economics teacher, received an email from a parent.

> It said: Hi, Mrs. Jones. I was looking over my son's grades in the computer system and noticed all of the grades from this grading period are from computerized assessments. My son says you prefer using these because the computer grades the test so students quickly know their grade. While I am glad for the speedy turnaround of grades, I'm concerned that students are not given any short-answer questions where they can show what they know outside of memorized facts and vocabulary. How are students demonstrating their application to the real world or showing you that they can think critically? My son enjoys your class, but I am concerned that he isn't being prepared for college-level coursework. Please advise.
>
> Sincerely,
> Mrs. Baker

Miriam was aware that her graded assessments were all computerized, but she felt confident that the design of high-quality test items allowed for her to assess more than students knowledge and comprehension of economics. She firmly believed the selected-response assessments she designed evaluated students' abilities to reason using deeper understanding and their abilities to apply economic concepts.

As you read this chapter, think about how Miriam should respond to the parent. What benefits to using a multiple-choice and matching items assessment should Miriam share with the parent? What can Miriam tell and show the parent to assure her that the assessments evaluate students' ability to apply and show deeper reasoning?

With learning targets established, attention is now directed toward the kind of assessment that will provide the best evidence of student performance. In this chapter and the next, we will consider what have traditionally been called *paper-and-pencil* tests, though they often come in digital format. These are assessments that have been used for decades for measuring student achievement. This chapter is concerned with selected-response assessment items that direct students to select a correct answer from two or more possible answers that are provided. Although we have all taken selected-response tests, familiarity does not mean that these items are not challenging to construct! The principles, guidelines, and examples that are presented will help you write high-quality selected-response items and evaluate the ones you may use from online databases. We'll begin with the ubiquitous multiple-choice format.

Multiple-Choice Items

As you are well aware, multiple-choice items are used widely in schools. This is because they efficiently provide a direct assessment of many types of learning targets, including the ability to recognize correct choices to assess knowledge, comprehension, computation, interpretation of information, application of knowledge to new examples, and, to a lesser extent, reasoning. They also provide an *indirect* assessment of recall knowledge, comprehension with the use of examples, and the ability to construct answers. And, of course, they are the primary type of item used in accountability and other standardized tests.

Multiple-choice questions offer several advantages but also have disadvantages (see Table 8.1). Like other selected-response items, they can provide a broad sampling of knowledge. Scoring is quick, easy, and objective, and it doesn't hurt to give students practice on the type of items they are likely to encounter on high-stakes tests (as long as you still use other types of assessments!). Now that digital items are commonplace, scoring can be immediate. Compared with binary-choice items, multiple-choice are typically more reliable, less prone to guessing the correct answer. Multiple-choice items have diagnostic power because selection of certain distractors can pinpoint an error in knowledge or misconception. Because

TABLE 8.1   Advantages and Disadvantages of Multiple-Choice Items

Advantages	Disadvantages
Can assess a variety of learning targets	Time-consuming to write
Efficient and easy to score and grade	Difficult to write good items
Scoring is objective	Provides limited feedback to students
Provides wide content sampling and coverage	Tends to focus on lower level cognitive skills
Gives students practice for standardized tests	Influenced by reading ability and testwiseness
Can provide diagnostic information about student misunderstandings	Unable to measure some types of targets
	Encourages guessing

students don't write out answers, it's more difficult to finesse a correct answer by bluffing or being more elaborate, and writing skill is not needed to demonstrate knowledge and understanding.

There are also disadvantages. It is relatively difficult to write multiple-choice items, especially good distractors. Many teachers find that it isn't too hard to come up with one or two good distractors, but the third or fourth ones are often giveaways to students. This increases the probability that students will guess the right answer. It is especially difficult to write good items that assess deep understanding and reasoning targets. As a result, you will be challenged to write multiple-choice items that do more than assess simple recall knowledge. It's easy to pick out trivial facts for the items, rather than big ideas or themes.

Students learn that the way to study for multiple-choice items is to read and reread the material to focus on recognition. Thus, like other selected-response items, the type of mental preparation prompted by taking multiple-choice items may not be consistent with more contemporary theories of learning and cognition. Rather than learning to construct meaning, students are encouraged to guess correct answers. More complicated items demand good reading skills, which may favor higher-ability students. Students who have test-wise skills also have an advantage. Finally, it's easy to simply use too many multiple-choice tests, especially when research indicates that constructed-response items provide more information about what students understand and can do. You will probably find that constructed-response answers, not those provided by selecting correct answers, provide more complete information about student understanding.

The format of multiple-choice items is easily recognized. The item begins with a **stem**, in the form of a question or incomplete statement, and three or more **alternatives**. The alternatives contain one correct or best answer and two or more **distractors**. It is usually best to use a question as the stem and to provide one correct answer, especially when assessing knowledge. A direct question is preferred for several reasons: It is easier to write, it forces you to state the complete problem more clearly in the stem, its format is familiar to students, it avoids the problem of grammatically tailoring each alternative to the stem, and questions place less demand on reading skills to understand the problem. Questions are clearly better for younger students. Items that assess the "best" answer allow for greater discrimination and are very effective for measuring understanding. In this type of item, each alternative may have some correct aspect, but one answer is better than the others.

Suggestions for writing multiple-choice items are summarized in the following points. These guidelines are also helpful when you review, evaluate, and select questions from an item bank. When you write the items, begin with the stem, then the correct response, and finally the distractors. Once you have developed good items (you know about how good an item is only after students answer it and you can analyze their responses), make sure you keep good items secure so you can use them again with other students—you don't want to write all new items for each new or different group of students. This doesn't mean that you keep giving the same test to every class every year, or to each secondary class the same year! You want to establish a bank of good items that you can choose from, add new ones as needed, and make minor changes in items, such as the order of the alternatives or wording. The bank also provides items that can be used as a pretest.

1. Write the Stem as a Clearly Described Question or Task. You want the stem to be meaningful by itself. It should clearly and succinctly communicate what is expected. If the stem makes sense only by reading the responses, it is poorly constructed. It is best, then, to put as much information as possible in the stem and not the responses, as long as the stem does not become too wordy or complex. The general rule is this: *Use complete stems and short responses.* This reduces the time students need to read the items and reduces redundant wording in each alternative. Of course, you do not want to include words in the stem that are not needed; the stem is longer than the alternatives but is still as succinct as possible. The exception to this general rule is testing definitions. For definitions, it's best to put the word in the stem. In the end, a good indicator of an effective stem is if students have a tentative answer in mind quickly, before reading the options.

Examples

Poor: The legislative branch of the federal government
  a. has term limits of 6 years.
  b. is used to determine if laws are consistent with the Constitution.
  c. carries out the laws of the land.
  d. makes laws.

Improved: Which branch of the federal government is responsible for making laws?
  a. Judicial.
  b. Legislative.
  c. Executive.
  d. Legal.

The alternative should be ordered in a logical, meaningful way.

Poor: What is the length of the table?
  a. 1 foot
  b. 24 inches
  c. 15 inches
  d. 2 feet

Improved: What is the length of the table in feet?
  a. 1
  b. 2
  c. 3
  d. 4

2. Avoid the Use of Negatives in the Stem. Using words such as *not* and *except* may confuse students, create anxiety, and lead to frustration. This lessens reliability/precision. Often students simply overlook the negative valence. It also takes longer to respond to such items. In cases in which knowing what not to do is important, as in knowing rules of the road for driving, the negative stem is fine as long as the negative word is emphasized by boldface or underlining.

Examples

Poor: Which of the following is not a mammal?
  a. Dog
  b. Spider
  c. Horse
  d. Wolf
  e. Cat

Improved: Which of the following is a mammal?
  a. Shark
  b. Frog
  c. Bear
  d. Snake
  e. Lizard

   3. Write the Correct Response with No Irrelevant Clues. There should not be any difference between the wording of the correct answer and distractors that would clue the student to respond on some basis other than the knowledge being tested. Common mistakes include making the correct response longer, more elaborate or detailed, more general, more technical, the one that is grammatically correct, or the one that repeats wording in the stem.

Examples

Poor: In an experiment the independent variable
  a. nonmanipulated.
  b. is the manipulated variable controlled by the experimenter.
  c. confounded.
  d. extraneous.

Improved: In an experiment the independent variable is
  a. the one that has at least three levels.
  b. usually continuous.
  c. manipulated by the experimenter.
  d. controlled so that it is not a confounded variable.

Poor: What is the education department responsible for?
  a. Making policies about education.
  b. Enforcing health rules.
  c. Carrying out the policies of the governor.
  d. Forcing colleges to balance their budgets.

4. Do Not Use Verbatim Correct Responses. Avoid using the same language or wording as in textbooks or handouts as the correct response. This is because a sentence out of context loses meaning, and rote memorization is encouraged. Move beyond recall knowledge to comprehension by changing the wording.

5. Write the Distractors to Be Plausible Yet Wrong. Distractors are useless if they are so obviously wrong that students do not even consider them as possible answers. The intent of a multiple-choice item is to have students *discriminate* among what they see as possible correct answers. Distractors should appear to be plausible to poorly prepared students. A good approach to establishing plausible yet incorrect distractors is to identify common misunderstandings or errors by students and then write distractors that appeal to students who have the misunderstandings. When students select these types of distractors it helps pinpoint feedback. Other ways to write good distractors include the use of words that have verbal associations with the stem, important words (e.g., *enduring, major, noteworthy*), length and complexity that matches the stem, and the use of qualifiers such as *generally* and *usually*. Poor distractors contain content that is plainly wrong, grammatical inconsistencies, or qualifiers such as *always* and *never*, or they state the opposite of the correct answer.

Examples

Poor: Which of the following is the largest city in the United States?
  a. Michigan
  b. London
  c. New York
  d. Berlin

Improved: Which of the following is the largest city in the United States?
  a. Los Angeles
  b. Chicago
  c. New York
  d. Miami

The number of distractors depends on several factors. Most multiple-choice items have two, three, or four distractors. Other things being equal, an item with two or three distractors is best. Interestingly, research has shown that using two distractors produces about the same results as three (Rodriguez & Haladyna, 2013), so don't be shy about not coming up with a third distractor. More questions are possible with only two distractors, which may provide better content coverage. Questions for young children often have only two distractors, which is fine. One thing for sure: Don't add obviously wrong distractors just to get to three or four.

Once you have had some experience with writing distractors, you can determine whether the distractors are being used with approximately equal frequency. If a particular distractor is rarely selected, then the next time it is used it should be modified to be more plausible. This process is part of what is called item analysis. **Item analysis** is collecting and using information about the way students have responded. Along with providing frequencies of responses to distractors, item analysis is done to determine the difficulty of the item (the percentage of students answering correctly), and whether the item *discriminates* between high and low performers on the test (i.e., whether most high performers answered it correctly and most low performers missed it, which is the pattern you want.)

6. Avoid Using "All of the Above," "None of the Above," or Other Special Distractors. These phrases are undesirable for a number of reasons. "All of the above" is the right answer if all the options are correct, and some students may select the first item that is correct without reading the others. Only when students need to know what *not* to do would "none of the above" be appropriate. Be sure to avoid options such as "A and C but not D" or other combinations. Items with this type of response tend to measure reasoning ability as much as knowledge, and, especially for measuring knowledge, the items take far too long to answer. If you're like me, these items can also create negative affect, confusion, and even bewilderment. Lower ability students are quickly turned off.

7. Use Each Alternative as the Correct Answer About the Same Number of Times. If you have four possible choices, about 25% of the items should have the same letter as the correct response (20% if there are five choices). This avoids a pattern that can increase the chance that students will guess the correct answer. Perhaps you have heard the old admonition from test-wise students, "when in doubt, pick C." There is some truth to this for test writers who are not careful to use all the responses equally as the correct one.

Figure 8.1 summarizes these suggestions for writing effective multiple-choice items.

FIGURE 8.1   Checklist for Writing Multiple-Choice Items

✓ Is the stem stated as clearly, directly, and simply as possible?
✓ Is the problem self-contained in the stem?
✓ Does the stem avoid the use of negatives?
✓ Is there only one correct or best answer?
✓ Are all the alternatives parallel with respect to grammatical structure, length, and complexity?
✓ Are irrelevant clues avoided?
✓ Are the alternatives short?
✓ Are complex alternatives avoided?
✓ Are alternatives placed in logical order?
✓ Are the distractors plausible to students who do not know the correct answer?
✓ Are correct answers spread equally among all the choices?

Assessing Knowledge and Comprehension

Knowledge and comprehension targets are important in all subjects. Declarative knowledge of terminology and facts is effectively assessed with multiple-choice items, as is procedural knowledge. Here are some examples of good items for measuring terminology:

Examples

Which of the following best defines *reliability/precision*?
   a. Consistency of scores
   b. Accuracy of scores
   c. Fairness of the assessment
   d. Test specifications

What is the best definition of *validity*?
   a. The consistency of scores.
   b. The reasonableness of the inferences made from test scores.
   c. Whether a test measures what it purports to measure.
   d. The extent to which the scores are free from error.

Knowledge of facts builds an important foundation for other kinds of learning, such as application, deep understanding, and reasoning. We normally think about facts as the four *Ws*—what, where, when, and who. The following items illustrate the assessment of specific facts:

Who was the first president of the United States?
   a. Thomas Jefferson
   b. John Adams
   c. George Washington
   d. Benjamin Franklin

What was the name of the general in the Civil War who later became president?
   a. Andrew Jackson
   b. Abraham Lincoln
   c. William Tecumseh Sherman
   d. Ulysses Grant

Multiple-choice items are also useful for measuring knowledge of principles, for example:

Which of the following is the best description of the principle of supply and demand?
   a. As supplies go up, prices go up.
   b. As supplies go down, prices go down.
   c. As prices go up, supplies go up.
   d. As supplies go up, prices go down.

Comprehension is demonstrated when students understand the essential meaning of a concept, principle, or procedure. They show this by identifying explanations and examples, by converting and translating, and by interpreting and predicting.

Test items that assess knowledge can be changed easily to assess comprehension. For instance, simply change the words used to describe or define something so that it is not verbatim from the instructional materials. Higher levels of comprehension require more work. Suppose that as a student you have learned that "photosynthesis is the process by which plants use light to make glucose." The following example shows how to measure this as comprehension.

Which of the following is most consistent with the process of photosynthesis?
- **a.** Plants that get light do not need to make glucose.
- **b.** Plants that get less light make less glucose.
- **c.** Glucose is produced from plants before photosynthesis.
- **d.** Energy is stored in plants as glucose.

Assessing Application

Understanding is demonstrated through application when students are able to *use* what they know to solve problems in a *new* situation or context. This is a more sophisticated type of understanding than comprehension, and it includes the ability to interpret new information with what is known and to apply rules, principles, and strategies. Obviously, this is a very important type of learning target, because we want students to apply what they learn in school to new situations outside school. Knowing something well enough to apply it successfully to new situations is called *learning for transfer*. The goal is to have sufficient understanding to transfer what is known to different situations.

Perhaps the best example of learning for application is mathematics. At one level, students can memorize the steps for solving certain kinds of math problems—that is, what to do first, second, and so forth. They may even show some comprehension by being able to explain the steps in their own words. But if they cannot apply the steps to new problems and get the right answer, we conclude that they really don't *understand* the process. That's why we give math tests with new problems. Likewise, much of what we do in language arts instruction is focused on understanding at the application level. Students learn rules for grammar, sentence structure, to write drafts before final copy, and reading skills. We conclude that they actually understand how to read and write by demonstrating their skill with new material.

Your goal in assessing application is to construct items that contain new data or information that students work with to obtain the answer, and to create new problems in which students extend what they know in a novel way. The extent of newness determines, to some extent, item difficulty and degree of understanding demonstrated. Items that contain completely new or unfamiliar material are generally more difficult than items in which there are only small differences between what was learned and the content of the question. This is why students may be able to solve new mathematics computational problems well but have trouble applying the same procedures to word problems that put the question in a new context.

The key feature of application items, then, is presenting situations that the students have not previously encountered. There are several strategies for constructing such items. One approach is to present a fictional problem that can be solved by applying appropriate procedural knowledge. For example, if students have learned about electricity and resistance, the following objective questions would test at the application level.

Examples

Application

1. Shaunda has decided to make two magnets by wrapping wire around a nail and attaching the wires to a battery so that the electric current can create a magnetic force. One magnet (A) uses thin wire, and one magnet (B) uses thick wire. Which magnet will be the strongest?
   a. A
   b. B
   c. A and B will be the same
   d. Cannot be determined from the information provided

2. A researcher investigated whether a new type of fertilizer would result in greater growth of corn plants. What is the independent variable?
   a. Growth of corn plants
   b. The researcher
   c. Type of fertilizer
   d. Amount of sunlight

3. William is given a $2.00 allowance each week. He wants to save enough money to go to the movie, which costs $4.00, and buy some candy and a soft drink at the movie. The candy will cost $1.50 and the drink will cost $2.50. How many weeks will William have to wait before he can go to the movie and buy the candy and soft drink?

   a. 2
   b. 3
   c. 4
   d. 5

Assessing Reasoning and Deep Understanding

As previously pointed out, each of the assessment methods discussed in this text can be used to measure most learning targets. Reasoning can be measured by selected-response items, and knowledge can be evaluated in student essays or performance products. Also, when we assess reasoning, we are often measuring how much students understand. This is clearly illustrated in the scoring criteria for many essay items, in which students are graded for demonstrating an understanding of certain concepts or principles. But there is an important trade-off. Items that assess reasoning and deep understanding well cannot begin to sample the *amount* of knowledge and understanding that can be tested with relatively straightforward multiple-choice items.

Single multiple-choice items can be used to assess reasoning in two ways. One way is to focus on a particular skill to determine whether students are able to recognize and use that skill. A second use is to assess the extent to which students can use their knowledge and skills in performing a problem-solving, decision-making, or other reasoning task. The first use is illustrated with the following examples:

Examples

(Distinguishing fact from opinion) Which of the following statements about our solar system is a *fact* rather than an *opinion*?
  a. The moon is made of attractive white soil.
  b. Stars can be grouped into important clusters.
  c. A star is formed from a white dwarf.
  d. Optical telescopes provide the best way to study the stars.

(Identifying assumptions) When Patrick Henry said "give me liberty or give me death," his assumption was that:
  a. everyone would agree with him.
  b. Thomas Jefferson would be impressed by the speech.
  c. if he couldn't have freedom he might as well die.
  d. his words would be taught to students for years.

(Recognizing bias) Peter told the group that "the ill-prepared, ridiculous senator has no business being involved in this important debate." Which words make Peter's statement biased?
  a. Important, senator
  b. Important, business
  c. Ill-prepared, ridiculous
  d. Debate, involved

(Comparison) One way in which insects are different from centipedes is that:
  a. they are different colors.
  b. one is an arthropod.
  c. centipedes have more legs.
  d. insects have two body parts.

(Analysis) Reginald decided to go sailing with a friend. He took supplies with him so he could eat, repair anything that might be broken, and find where on the lake he could sail. Which of the following supplies would best meet his needs?

   a. Bread, hammer, map
   b. Milk, bread, screwdriver
   c. Map, hammer, pliers, screwdriver
   d. Screwdriver, hammer, pliers

(Synthesis) What is the main idea in the following paragraph?

Julie picked a pretty blue boat for her first sail. It took her about an hour to understand all the parts of the boat and another hour to get the sail on. Her first sail was on a beautiful summer day. She tried to go fast but couldn't. After several lessons, she was able to make her boat go fast.

   a. Sailing is fun
   b. Julie's first sail
   c. Sailing is difficult
   d. Going fast on a sailboat

The next few examples show how multiple-choice items can be used to assess the students' ability to perform a reasoning task.

Examples

(Hypothesizing) If there were a significant increase in the number of hawks in a given area,

   a. the number of plants would increase.
   b. the number of mice would increase.
   c. there would be fewer hawk nests.
   d. the number of mice would decrease.

(Problem solving) Farmers want to be able to make more money for the crops they grow, but too many farmers are growing too many crops. What can the farmers do to make more money?

   a. Try to convince the public to pay higher prices
   b. Agree to produce fewer crops
   c. Reduce the number of farmers
   d. Work on legislation to turn farmland into parks

(Critical thinking) Peter is deciding which car to buy. He is impressed with the sales representative for the Ford, and he likes the color of the Buick. The Ford is smaller and gets more miles to the gallon. The Buick takes larger tires and has a smaller trunk. More people can ride in the Ford. Which car should Peter purchase if he wants to do everything he can to ensure that his favorite lake does not become polluted?

   a. Ford
   b. Buick

    c. Either car
    d. Can't decide from the information provided

(Predicting) Suppose that the midwest United States, which grows most of the country's corn, suffered a drought for several years and produced much less corn than usual. What would happen to the price of corn?

    a. The price would rise.
    b. The price would fall.
    c. The price would stay the same.
    d. People would eat less corn.

Binary-Choice Items

When students select an answer from only two response categories, they are completing a **binary-choice item**. This type of item may also be called *alternative response*, *alternate response*, or *alternate choice*. The most popular binary-choice item is the true/false question; other types of options can be right/wrong, correct/incorrect, yes/no, fact/opinion, agree/disagree, and so on. In each case, the student selects one of two options.

Binary-choice items are constructed from propositional statements about knowledge. A *proposition* is a declarative sentence that makes a claim about content or relationships among content. Simple recall propositions include the following:

Los Angeles is the capital of California.
Peru is in the southern hemisphere.
The area of a square is found by squaring the length of one side.

These propositions provide the basis for good test items because they capture an important thought or idea. Once the proposition is constructed, it is relatively easy to keep it as is, rephrase and keep the same meaning, or change one aspect of the statement and then use it for a binary-choice test item. As such, the items provide a simple and direct measure of one's knowledge of facts, definitions, and the like, as long as there is no exception or qualification to the statement. That is, one of the two choices must be *absolutely* true or false, correct or incorrect, and so on. Some subjects, such as science and history, lend themselves to this type of absolute proposition better than others.

Using binary-choice items has several advantages. First, the format of such questions is similar to what is asked in class, so students are familiar with the thinking process involved in making binary choices. Second, short binary items allows extensive sampling of knowledge because students are able to answer many items in a short time (five to eight items per minute). Third, these items can be written in short, easy-to-understand sentences. Compared to multiple-choice items, binary-choice questions are relatively easy to construct, and scoring is objective and quick.

The major disadvantage of binary-choice items is that they are susceptible to guessing, particularly if the items are poorly constructed, and often more test-wise

FIGURE 8.2   Checklist for Writing Binary-Choice Items

✓ Does the item contain a single proposition or idea?
✓ Is the type of answer logically consistent with the statement?
✓ Are the statements succinct?
✓ Is the item stated positively?
✓ Is the length of both statements in an item about the same?
✓ Do the correct responses have a pattern?
✓ Are unequivocal terms used?
✓ Does the item try to trick students?
✓ Is trivial knowledge being tested?
✓ Are about half the items answered correctly with the same response?

students are able to score higher. Thus, a combination of some knowledge, guessing, and poorly constructed items that give clues to the correct answer will allow some students to score well, even though their level of knowledge is weak.

Assessing Knowledge and Comprehension

Writing good binary-choice items begins with propositions about major knowledge targets. In converting the propositions to test items, you will need to keep the items short, simple, direct, and easy to understand. This is best accomplished by avoiding ambiguity and clues to the correct answer. The following suggestions, summarized in Figure 8.2, will help accomplish this.

1. Write the Item So That the Answer Options Are Consistent with the Logic in the Sentence. The way the item is written will suggest a certain logic for what type of response is most appropriate. For example, if you want to test spelling knowledge, it doesn't make much sense to use true/false questions; it would be better to use correct/incorrect as options.

2. Include a Single Fact or Idea in the Item. For assessing recall knowledge, avoid two or more facts, ideas, or propositions in a single item. This is because one idea or fact may be true and the other false, which introduces ambiguity and error.

Examples

Poor: T F California is susceptible to earthquakes because of the collision between oceanic and continental plates.

Improved: T F Earthquakes in California are caused by the collision between oceanic and continental plates.

3. Avoid Long Sentences. Try to keep the sentences as concise as possible. This allows you to include more test items and reduces ambiguity. Longer sentences tend to favor students who have stronger reading comprehension skills.

Examples

> *Poor:*   T   F   A cup with hot water that has a spoon in it will cool more quickly than a similar cup with the same amount of hot water that does not have a spoon in it.
> *Improved:*   T   F   Hot water in a cup will cool more quickly if a spoon is placed in the cup.

4. Avoid Insignificant or Trivial Facts and Words. It is relatively easy to write "tough" binary-choice items that measure trivial knowledge. Avoid this by beginning with what you believe are the most significant learning targets.

Examples

> *Poor:*   Charles Darwin was twenty-two years old when he began his voyage of the world.
> *Poor:*   An elephant spends about fifteen hours a day eating and foraging.

5. Avoid Negative Statements. Statements that include the words *not* or *no* are confusing to students and make items and answers more difficult to understand. Careful reading and sound logic become prerequisites for answering correctly. If the knowledge can be tested only with a negatively worded statement, be sure to highlight the negative word with boldface type, underlining, or all caps.

Examples

> *Poor:*   United States senators are not elected to six-year terms.
> *Improved:*   United States senators are elected to six-year terms.

6. Avoid Clues to the Answer. Test-wise students will look for specific words that suggest that the item is false. When adjectives and adverbs such as *never, all, every, always,* and *absolutely* are used, the answer is usually false. Also, avoid any kind of pattern in the questions that provides clues to the answer, such as all true items being longer, alternating true and false answers, tending to use one type of answer more than the other, or all the items being either true or false. It is best to write questions so that about 50% of the answers are true.

7. Do Not Try to Trick Students. Items that are written to "trick" students by including a word that changes the meaning of an idea or by inserting some trivial fact should be avoided. Trick items undermine your credibility, frustrate students, and provide less valid measures of knowledge.

8. Avoid Using Vague Adjectives and Adverbs. Adjectives and adverbs such as *frequent, sometimes, occasionally, typically,* and *usually* are interpreted differently by each student. It is best to avoid these types of words because the meaning of the statement is not equivocal.

Assessing Application

Assessing application with binary-choice items is essentially the same process as is used with multiple-choice items. Knowledge needs to be used to answer questions that present novel situations. For example, the following questions would test what students have learned about electricity and resistance at the application level.

Examples

1. T   F   Other things being equal, an electric stove with greater resistance will be hotter than a stove with less resistance.

2. T   F   Jon is building a new electric motor. His decision to use thicker wire results in less resistance.

Assessing Reasoning and Deep Understanding

Binary-choice items can be used to assess reasoning skills in several different ways. Students can be asked to indicate whether a statement is a fact or an opinion:

Examples

If the statement is a fact, circle F; if it is an opinion, circle O.

F   O   Literature is ancient Rome's most important legacy.

F   O   The word *Mississippi* has 11 letters.

F   O   The best way to wash a car is with a sponge.

Additional reasoning skills can be assessed using the same approach by developing some statements that are examples of the skill and some statements that are not examples. This can be done with many of the critical thinking skills (e.g., identifying stereotypes, biased statements, emotional language, relevant data, and verifiable data).

Examples

If the statement is an example of a stereotype, circle S; if it is not a stereotype, circle N.

S   N   Mexican Americans are good musicians.

S   N   Women live longer than men.

If emotional language is used in the statement, circle E; if no emotional language is used, circle N.

E   N   Health insurance reform is needed so that poor people with serious injuries will be able to lead productive lives.

E   N   Health insurance is going to cost a lot of money.

Logic can be assessed by asking if one statement follows logically from another:

> *Example*
>
> If the second part of the sentence explains why the first part is true, circle T for true; if it does not explain why the first part is true, circle F for false.
>
> T F   Food is essential *because* it tastes good.
>
> T F   Plants are essential *because* they provide oxygen.
>
> T F   Reggie is tall *because* he has blue eyes.

Matching Items

Matching items effectively and efficiently measure the extent to which students know related facts, associations, and relationships. Some examples of such associations include terms with definitions, persons with descriptions, dates with events, and symbols with names.

The major advantage of matching is that the teacher can efficiently obtain a good sampling of a large amount of knowledge. Matching is easily and objectively scored. Constructing good matching items is not as difficult as preparing multiple-choice items. However, poor matching items are constructed when there is insufficient material to include in the item and irrelevant information is added that is unrelated to the major topic that has been targeted for assessment.

In a matching item, the items on the left are called the *premises*. In the right-hand column are the *responses*. The student's task is to match the correct response with each of the premises. As long as the suggestions listed next are followed, matching items are excellent for measuring knowledge that includes associations.

1. Make Sure Directions Are Clear to Students. Even though matching items are familiar to students, it is helpful to indicate in writing (or orally for young students) the basis for the matching and where and how student responses should be recorded. Generally, letters are used for each response in the right-hand column, and students are asked to write the selected letter next to each premise. Younger students can be asked to draw lines to connect the premises to the responses. It is important in the directions to indicate that *each response may be used once, more than once*, or *not at all*. This lessens the probability that, through a process of elimination, guessing will be a factor in the results.

2. Include Homogeneous Premises and Responses. Avoid putting information from different lessons in the same matching item. You wouldn't want to include recent scientists, early U.S. presidents, and sports figures in the same item. Even though what is considered "homogeneous" varies among teachers, this principle is the one most violated. For example, it makes good sense to use matching to test student knowledge of important dates during the Civil War. It would not be a good idea to contain both dates and men's names as responses. Testing homogeneous material with matching is effective for fairly fine discriminations among facts. For example, matching dates with events in one of the Civil War battles provides greater discrimination than matching dates with major battles.

3. Use Four to Eight Premises. You do not want to have too long a list of premises. A relatively short list will probably be more homogeneous and will be perceived by students as more fair.

4. Keep Responses Short and Logically Ordered. Usually the responses include a list of one- or two-word names, dates, or other terms. Definitions, events, and descriptions are in the premise column. Students will be more accurate in their answers if the responses are in logical order. Thus, if responses are dates, they should be rank ordered by year; words or names should be alphabetized. Like premises, keep the number of responses to 8, 10 at the most. Longer lists waste students' time and contribute to error by including reasoning abilities as part of what is needed to answer the item correctly.

5. Avoid Grammatical Clues to Correct Answers. As with completion items, you need to be careful that none of your matches are likely because of grammatical clues, such as verb tense agreement.

6. Put Premises and Responses on the Same Page. You don't want students to have to flip back and forth between two pages to answer the items. This is distracting and only contributes to error.

7. Use More Responses Than Premises. Using more responses than premises provides greater coverage of information and is a better indicator of knowledge by reducing guessing of some correct answers that occurs if the same number of premises and responses are used and each response is used only once.

Example

The following is an example of a good matching item. Notice the complete directions, responses on the right in logical order, and homogeneous content (achievements of early presidents).

Directions: Match the achievements in column A with the names of presidents in column B. Write the letter of the president who had the achievement on the line next to each number. Each name in column B may be used once, more than once, or not at all.

Column A	Column B
_____ **1.** Second president	**A.** John Adams
_____ **2.** President when there were no severe external threats to the country	**B.** John Quincy Adams
_____ **3.** Declined to run for a third term	**C.** Andrew Jackson
_____ **4.** Wrote the Declaration of Independence	**D.** Thomas Jefferson
	E. James Madison
_____ **5.** Last of the presidents from Virginia	**F.** James Monroe
	G. George Washington

Suggestions for writing matching items are summarized in Figure 8.3.

Selected-Response Interpretive Exercises

The interpretive exercise consists of some information or data, followed by several selected-response type questions. The information or data are typically in the form of maps, paragraphs, charts, figures, a story, a table of data, or pictures. The form of the question makes it possible to assess interpretation, analysis, application, critical thinking, and other reasoning skills, as well as comprehension.

Selected-response interpretive exercises have four major advantages over other types of items. First, because there are several questions about the same information, it is possible to measure more reasoning skills in greater depth. Second, because information is provided, it is possible to separate the assessment of the reasoning skills from content knowledge of the subject. If content is not provided in the question, as is the case with most multiple-choice items, then a failure to provide a good answer could be attributed to either the student's lack of knowledge or lack of reasoning skill. In the interpretive exercise, students have all or most of the information needed as part of the question, so successful performance provides a more direct measure of reasoning skill. Clearly, the intent of the exercise is to assess how students use the information provided to answer questions. If

FIGURE 8.3   Checklist for Writing Matching Items

✓ Is it clear how and where students place their answers?
✓ Is it clear that each response may be used once, more than once, or not at all?
✓ Is the information included homogeneous?
✓ Are there more responses than premises?
✓ Are the responses logically ordered?
✓ Are grammatical clues avoided?
✓ Is there only one feasible answer for each premise?
✓ Is the set of premises or responses too long?
✓ Are premises and responses on the same page?

students know ahead of time that the information will be provided, then they can concentrate their study on application and other uses of the information.

A third advantage of the interpretive exercise is that it is relatively famliar material that students encounter in everyday living, such as maps, newspaper articles, and graphs. Consistent with constructivist learning theory, this connects the material better with the student, increasing meaningfulness and relevance. Finally, because interpretive exercises provide a standard structure for all students, the results tend to be more reliable. Students are unable to select a reasoning skill they are most proficient with, as they can do with essay questions. They must use the one called for in each question.

Interpretive exercises have three limitations. First, they are time consuming and difficult to write. Not only do you need to locate or develop the information or data that will be new for the students and at the right difficulty level, which could take considerable time, but you also need to construct the questions. The information you first identify may need to be modified, and most teachers are not accustomed to writing several questions for a single passage or example.

A second limitation is that you are unable to assess how students organize their thoughts and ideas or to know whether they can produce their own answers without being cued. Third, many interpretive exercises rely heavily on reading comprehension. This puts poor readers at a distinct disadvantage. It takes them longer to read the material for understanding, let alone reason with it. This disadvantage holds for other types of items that require extensive reading as well, but it is especially troublesome for interpretive exercises.

Whether you develop your own interpretive exercises or use ones that have already been prepared, the following suggestions will help ensure high quality (see Figure 8.4 for a checklist summary).

1. Identify the Comprehension and Reasoning Skills to Be Assessed Before Selection or Development of the Interpretive Exercise. The sequence you use is important because you want the exercise to fit your learning targets, not have learning targets determined by the interpretive exercise. This is especially important given the number of different conceptualizations of thinking and reasoning skills. What may be called "critical thinking" or "analysis" in a teacher's manual may not coincide with what you think the target is. You need to have a clear idea of the skill to be assessed and then select or develop the material that best fits your definition.

FIGURE 8.4   Checklist for Writing Interpretive Exercises

✓ Are reasoning targets clearly defined before writing the exercise?
✓ Is introductory material brief?
✓ Is introductory material new to the students?
✓ Are there several questions for each exercise?
✓ Does the exercise test deep understanding and reasoning (and not just simple understanding)?

2. Keep Introductory Material as Brief as Possible. Keeping the introductory material brief minimizes the influence of general reading ability. There should be just enough material so that the students can answer the questions.

3. Select Similar but New Introductory Material. Deep understanding and reasoning skills are best measured with material that is mostly new to the students. If the material is the same as that covered in class, you will measure rote memory or simple understanding rather than reasoning. The goal is to find or develop examples that are similar to what students have already studied. The material should vary slightly in form or content, but it should not be completely new. A good strategy to use to accomplish this is to take passages, examples, and data students have been exposed to and alter them sufficiently so that correct answers cannot be given by memory.

4. Construct Several Test Items for Each Exercise. Asking more than one question for each exercise obtains a better sample of their understanding and the proficiency of students' reasoning skills. It would be particularly inefficient to have a very long introductory passage and a single question.

5. Construct Items to Require Understanding and Reasoning. You do not want to use questions that can be answered without even reading the introductory material. This happens when students' general knowledge is such that they can determine the correct answer from the question alone.

Assessing Comprehension

The most common type of selected-response interpretive exercise is in the area of reading comprehension. A reading passage is presented, followed by several questions that test the student's comprehension.

Selected-response interpretive exercises are illustrated in the following four examples. Note that many different formats can be used for the items. The reasoning skills that are assessed in Examples 2, 3, and 4 are indicated in parentheses next to each example number.

Example 1.

Hummingbirds

The hummingbird is amazing! Its wings flap so fast that they are a blur, flapping as much as 80 times a second. The flapping wings also make a soft buzzing sound, which is why it is called a humming bird. The fast flapping wings are used to go straight up or down, sideways, backward, or upside down.

The hummingbird eats the sugary juice of flowers, which is called nectar. It hovers in the air while it is eating with its long, thin bill. Much energy is needed by the hummingbird, so that it eats about every 10 minutes and travels to about 1,500 different flowers each day.

1. Which of the following best describes nectar?
    a. Food that comes from insects
    b. Sweet food from flowers
    c. Food found in flower petals
    d. Food that is found in small pools of water

2. What is the main idea in the second paragraph?
    a. Hummingbird wings flap very fast.
    b. Hummingbirds have narrow bills to suck out nectar.
    c. Hummingbirds are small.
    d. Hummingbirds go up or down.

3. Why do hummingbirds need to eat all the time?
    a. To obtain nectar
    b. To provide energy needed to fly
    c. To fly up or down
    d. To eat sugar

4. T   F   Nectar is a sweet kind of food.

Assessing Reasoning and Deep Understanding

Interpretive items are especially good at assessing reasoning and critical thinking skills.

Example 2. (drawing inferences, analyzing perspectives)

Two citizens spoke at the city council meeting. Here are their statements. Use the information to help you answer the questions.

CITIZEN A: The Bower House should be restored and used as a museum. A museum would help the people of the community learn about their heritage and would attract tourists to Grenville. We should not sell the property to the Opti Company. Grenville has grown too quickly, and a factory would bring even more people into the area. In addition, a factory's industrial waste would threaten the quality of our water.

CITIZEN B: Grenville needs the Opti factory. The factory would provide needed jobs. The tax money it would bring into the community would help improve our streets, schools, and other city services. A museum, on the other hand, would hurt our local economy. Taxes would have to be raised to pay for the restoration of the Bower House. A museum would not create enough jobs to solve our unemployment problem.

Write the letter A next to each statement that Citizen A would most likely agree with.

Write the letter B next to each statement that Citizen B would most likely agree with.

_____ **(10)** Jobs are the foundation of a community.

_____ **(11)** Pollution problems will multiply.

_____ **(12)** We are in danger of losing the history of our community.

_____ **(13)** Hanging on to the past hurts the future.

Example 3.   (*recognizing the relevance of information*)

Sally lost her pencil on her way to school. It was red and given to her by her grandmother. She wanted the teacher to ask the class if anyone found the pencil.

Circle *yes* if the information in the sentence will help the class find the pencil.

Circle *no* if the information in the sentence will not help the class find the pencil.

yes   no   **1.** The pencil was new.

yes   no   **2.** Sally rides the bus to school.

yes   no   **3.** The pencil is red.

yes   no   **4.** The pencil was a present from Sally's grandmother.

yes   no   **5.** The pencil had a new eraser.

yes   no   **6.** The teacher knows Sally's grandmother.

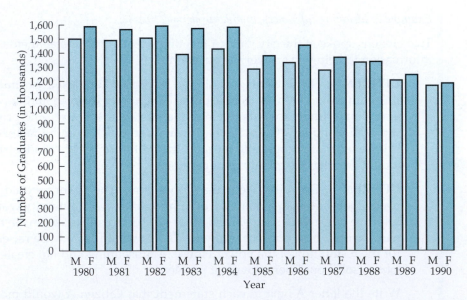

FIGURE 8.5   Number of Male and Female Students Graduating from High School in the United States

Source: U.S. Department of Education, Office of Educational Research and Improvement. (1994). *Digest of Education Statistics*, p. 188.

Teacher's Corner

Stephanie Stoebe

Texas Round Rock Independent School District Teacher of the Year

I have found different types of selected-response items to be effective in different situations, but I try to make sure the questions zone in on the standards that I want to gather student data on. I think that true/false questions are best for ensuring that a basic understanding of the material has been attained, and I am then comfortable to move to deeper instruction. When I use true/false questions, I will design them so that students must support their answers. In the directions, I write that after choosing true or false, students must tell me why they chose that answer. The strategy of rationalizing often results in higher level thinking, showing me that the student knows much more than simple recall of facts. (Sometimes students have even disputed that the question may be *both* true and false.) It takes a lot of time for me to make effective multiple-choice questions; I don't want to give the answers away or be too obscure in my responses. When they are available, I will use selected multiple-choice answers that have been generated from outside sources. I put a few of these questions on assessments because students do need practice in choosing answers where information is presented in different forms. Matching can be effective if there are more answer choices in one column. Then students who struggle to recall have a "bank" of answers. Also, it is not as common for a student to miss one question and then actually get two answers marked wrong. I do not have to wonder: "Do I have to reteach plot and setting then, or just plot?"

Example 4. (*analysis, inference, error analysis*)

Based on Figure 8.5, circle T if the statement is true and F if the statement is false.

T   F   In 1990, more female than male students graduated from high school.

T   F   From 1980 to 1990, the percentage of female students graduating from high school increased gradually.

T   F   Overall, the best year for graduating students was 1987.

T   F   From 1980 to 1990, more female than male students graduated from high school.

Notice in the Teacher's Corner how Stephanie Stoebe uses true/false, multiple-choice, and matching formats for her high school students.

Technology-Enhanced Selected-Response Items

With advances in technology there are new possibilities for creating selected-response items that are exciting in how they can improve assessment, yet at the same time daunting in how they are constructed, administered, and scored.

There is significant research and development in **technology-enhanced** (or *technology-adapted*) items, those that are presented and answered digitally. The capability of the technology is used to design items that are relevant and engaging, measuring more than knowledge in an efficient manner that can be objectively scored. Digital media is utilized in the form of graphics, audio and video clips, and presentations. There can be simulations and scenarios, passages and speeches. Suppose I wanted to test your understanding of the basics of sailing. Think how much better it would be for you to view boats actually sailing as the stimulus, then answer questions, rather than take a written test. The test questions could be based on what is viewed in the video clip and could be answered online. For example, the video could show a group of boats sailing different points from the wind, and you could be asked to identify which are beating, reaching, and running by dragging the number of each boat to the right box (one for beating, one for reaching, and one for running). Or, students could be asked to draw a diagram that would change a tack from a beat to a reach. As another kind of example, students can be given data and asked to draw a graph online. Selected-response technology-enhanced items ask students to select from possible answers that are presented or to identify specific aspects of a written passage. For example, a student may be asked to identify all the nouns and verbs from a specific passage by using a red highlight for nouns and a yellow highlight for verbs, or students could be given a list of words to drag into one of two boxes, one for nouns and one for verbs. In other items, students can be asked to classify, to reorder text or steps in a procedure, or to identify the main idea of a story. For a geometry item, students can be asked to drag examples of shapes to correct categories (e.g., rectangle, square, triangle).

The allure of technology-enhanced items is great, but designing them for online use and scoring is difficult, not something most teachers would have the time or expertise to do. But, increasingly, you will find them on standardized tests, online test item databases, and testing apps, as illustrated in Chapter 7.

Summary

This chapter has examined the nature of selected-response assessments, including multiple-choice, binary-choice, matching, interpretive exercises, and technology-enhanced items. It was shown how these formats can be used for different types of learning targets. Suggestions for writing each type, with examples, were summarized. Major points include the following:

- Multiple-choice items consist of a stem, correct answer, and distractors.
- It is best to format the stem in a multiple-choice item as a question.
- Multiple-choice items can be used for efficient assessment of a large domain of knowledge, generally provide reliable scores, and are easily and objectively scored.

- Multiple-choice items are difficult to write, especially for deep understanding and reasoning targets.
- The use of negatives in multiple-choice item stems should be avoided.
- For multiple-choice items, it is better to have longer stems than alternatives.
- Multiple-choice items are effective if they are clearly and directly stated with one correct answer, include plausible distractors, and do not provide clues to the correct answer.
- Multiple-choice items can be used to assess specific reasoning skills or to use reasoning in problem solving.
- Binary-choice items, such as true/false items, are effective if they are clearly, succinctly, and positively stated as single propositions or statements.
- Matching items are effective for assessing simple understanding of related facts or concepts as long as responses are short, premises and responses are homogeneous, lists are logically ordered, no grammatical clues are given, and no more than 10 premises are in one matching item.
- Selected-response interpretive exercises include information and/or data, followed by several questions.
- Interpretive exercises are effective for assessing comprehension, application, and reasoning skills and can reflect real-life situations, contexts, and issues.
- Interpretive exercises are effective if learning targets are clearly defined, if introductory material is new to students, and if they are not too long.

Introductory Case Study Answer

Miriam should share with the parent that there are more benefits than just fast grading. The scoring is objective, allows her to assess more content than she could with fewer open-ended questions, gives students immediate feedback on their misunderstandings, and provides practice for standardized tests.

Miriam should show the parent examples of questions that assess economic content application, deeper understanding, and reasoning. These questions should show the parent that by containing new situations not encountered in class, they require students to use skills such as comparing, analyzing, and hypothesizing. Miriam could also show the parent questions that require students to determine whether a statement is or is not an example and expose the parent to selected-response interpretive exercises where students must use the real-world information provided in the question to select their answers.

Suggestions for Action Research

1. Collect some examples of selected-response test items. Analyze the items and the format of the test in relation to the suggestions provided in the chapter. Show how you would improve the items and format of the test.

2. With another student, make up a knowledge test of each of the three types of selected-response items of the content of this chapter that could be taken in 1 hour. Begin with a table of specifications or outline and indicate the learning targets. Give the test to four other students for their critique, and then revise the test as needed. Show the original test and the revised one to your supervisor or teacher for his or her critique and further suggestions. Keep a journal of your progress in making up the test. What was difficult? How much time did it take? What would have made the process more efficient?

MyEdLab Self-Check 8.1

MyEdLab Self-Check 8.2

MyEdLab Self-Check 8.3

MyEdLab Self-Check 8.4

MyEdLab Application Exercise 8.1   Binary-choice Items

MyEdLab Application Exercise 8.2   Multiple-choice Item Construction

---

Constructed-Response Assessment: Completion, Short-Answer, and Essay Items

Completion

- Strengths
- Weaknesses
- Checklist for writing
  — verbatim language avoided
  — format
  — verbal cues avoided
  — single answer
- Objectively scored

CONSTRUCTED-RESPONSE ASSESSMENTS

Short-answer

- Strengths
- Weaknesses
- Checklist for writing
  — single correct answer
  — format
  — concise
  — appropriate difficulty
- Mostly objective scoring

Essay

- Strengths
- Weaknesses
- Restricted- or extended-response
- Checklist for writing
  — clarity of task
  — time frame for answering
- Scoring
  — subjective
  — criteria
  — holistic or analytical
  — procedures

CHAPTER 9 Concept Map

Learning Outcomes

After reading this chapter, you should be able to:

9.1   Know the guidelines for writing and/or selecting effective completion, short-answer, and essay type items.

9.2   Understand the advantages and disadvantages of using different types of constructed-response items.

9.3   Understand how to score constructed-response items.

9.4   Be able to construct effective completion, short-answer, and essay type items, and scoring criteria.

Introductory Case Study

What Should Barry Include in His Presentation?

Barry, a fourth-grade teacher, was exceptional at tailoring his instruction to meet his students' needs. His students' end-of-year standardized test scores indicated that his students had mastery in all subject areas, yet his grade book, which contained numerous assessments, contained only noncomputerized assessments. When asked by colleagues about his theory on assessment, he explained that he felt students should do computerized assessments for practice, but that he relied more heavily on other forms of assessments to understand students' learning. Non-selected-response assessments helped him understand individual students' needs at a deeper level, so he used them to drive his remediation and enrichment efforts.

Since the school district was concerned with standardized end-of-year testing, most curriculum materials contained selected-response style computerized assessments, and Barry had been creating from scratch his own constructed-response assessments. Even though the district pushed for teachers to give computerized selected-response assessments, the principal of Barry's school, Edgebrook Elementary, believed that teachers should incorporate both the computerized and alternative forms of assessments into their instructional practices. She believed the latter could help teachers in determining at a deeper level what students know, understand, and can do. She believed that successfully designed alternative assessments could equally impact learning. So, in an effort to move teachers forward with this notion, the principal asked Barry if he would provide a 20-minute professional development session at the next faculty meeting. Barry's focus should be on the nuts-and-bolts of creating constructed-response assessments. She told Barry to keep his information applicable to all subject areas and to focus on constructed-response assessments; other forms of assessment such as performance assessments would be presented by other teachers at future faculty meetings.

As you read this chapter, think about the most important elements Barry should include in his presentation. Barry tells teachers that three principles should guide their decision in what type of constructed-response questions to use. What are those principles? What should Barry include on his continuum to demonstrate the benefits and trade-offs of using each type of item? When teachers ask Barry what are a few of the nuts-and-bolts that they should remember when writing constructed-response questions, what should he advise?

Constructed-response assessment (also called *supply-type*) has been and continues to be a mainstay testing tool of teachers. When students are able to recall answers to direct questions without cues to the correct answer you are able to clearly determine if students have a thorough understanding, can apply knowledge to solve problems, and can reason. Teachers also use constructed responses, whether provided in writing or orally, continually in a formative manner. That's because, in the main, more is learned about what students know, understand, and can do with constructed-response items than with selected-response items.

Choosing the Right Type of Constructed-Response Item

As a teacher you will use constructed-response items, probably extensively, so the real question is which types to use and when to use them. The choice depends on three primary considerations: (a) the nature of the targets; (b) the importance of "objective" scoring; and (c) the effects on student studying and motivation. These considerations can be summarized by thinking about the relative complexity of different types of constructed-response items—from very short and simple to very long and complex (see Figure 9.1). Sentence completion and fill-in-the-blank type items are the shortest. They are best for measuring knowledge and simple understanding targets, and they can cover more content compared to more complex constructed-response items. They have the most objective scoring. However, they may also encourage students to memorize material.

Short-answer items provide less coverage of content, are somewhat more subjective in how they are scored, and promote more understanding and application of knowledge. While essays can cover much content and encourage deep understanding and reasoning, grading can be very subjective. The most complex types of constructed-response items, such as papers, projects, and performance assessment, cover the least amount of content but can emphasize application, deep understanding, and reasoning.

Each type of constructed-response item affects students differently in how they prepare for the test. The more complex the task, the greater the effort, intrinsic motivation and studying of organization, patterns, and applications. So there is a trade-off—is it more important to stress higher levels of thinking or obtain

FIGURE 9.1 **Considerations for Using Different Types of Constructed-Response Items**

Completion Fill-In	Short Answer	Essay	Papers, Performances, Projects
Short, simple responses	←	→	Long, complex responses
Objective scoring	←	→	Subjective scoring
Encourages recall knowledge	←	→	Encourages complex thinking
Encourages memorization	←	→	Encourages application and transfer

objectively scored results quickly that cover more knowledge? Note in the first teacher's corner in this chapter how a high school teacher balances these considerations using short-answer and essay items. Mostly, as I've already emphasized, you'll need a mix of these different types of constructed-response items.

We will consider three types of constructed-response items—completion, short answer, and essay—then examine more complex constructed-response assessments—performance assessments—in the next chapter.

Completion Items

The most common and effective way to assess knowledge is simply to ask a question and require the students to answer it from memory. With **completion items** (some actually call them objective because there is typically only one correct answer), students are presented with an incomplete sentence with one or two blanks and write words as their answer(s) in the blanks.

The completion item offers the least freedom of student response, calling for one or two answers at the end or middle of a sentence. Responses may be in the form of words, numbers, or symbols. If properly constructed, completion items are excellent for measuring how well students can recall facts because of these strengths: (a) they are easy to construct, (b) their short response time allows a good sampling of different facts, (c) guessing contributes little to error, (d) scorer reliability is high, (e) they can be scored more quickly than short-answer or essay items, and (f) they provide more valid results than a test with an equal number of selected-response items (e.g., multiple-choice). There are only two limitations of using completion items to measure knowledge. The first is in the time needed for scoring. When compared to selected-response items, they take a little longer to score. Second, if the sentence is not well constructed, more than one answer may be possible for each blank, which reduces validity.

Completion items should be used almost exclusively for assessing simple declarative or procedural knowledge. The following suggestions for constructing completion items use examples that measure these types of knowledge. The suggestions are also helpful in evaluating the quality of constructed-response items that are provided from test banks or online services.

1. Paraphrase Sentences from Textbooks and Other Instructional Materials. It is tempting to lift a sentence verbatim from materials the students have studied and replace a word or two with blanks. However, statements in textbooks or online materials, when taken out of context, are often too vague or general to be good completion items. Also, you don't want to encourage students to memorize phraseology. Consistent with constructivistic learning principles, you want students to connect what they learn with what they already know, even when it is recall. Thus, you want to paraphrase or restate facts in words that are different from those the students have read and studied.

Examples

The textbook statement is "James Buchanan, elected president in 1856, personally opposed slavery."

Poor: James Buchanan, elected president in 1856, personally opposed _____.

Improved: The name of the president who was elected in 1856, and who thought slavery was *not* right, was _____.

2. Word the Sentence So That Only a Single Answer Is Correct. The greatest error in writing completion items is to use sentences that can be correctly completed with more than one response. This occurs if the sentence is too vague or open-ended.

Examples

Poor: Columbus first landed on "America" _____.

Improved: Columbus first landed on "America" in _____.

Better: Columbus first landed on "America" in the year _____.

In the first example, students could logically provide correct answers having nothing to do with the year. In the improved version an answer like "a boat" would be correct.

3. Place Blanks at the End of the Sentence. If blanks are placed at the beginning or in the middle of the sentence, it may be more difficult for students to understand what response is called for. It is easier and more direct to first read the sentence and then determine what will complete it correctly. There are some instances when it makes sense to put blanks somewhere in the middle of the sentence, as you'll see in suggestion 5.

Examples

Poor: In 1945, _____ decided to have the atomic bomb dropped on Japan.

Improved: The name of the president who decided to have the atomic bomb dropped on Japan in 1945 was _____.

You also will not want to use more than two blanks in a single sentence. This will confuse students and measure reasoning skills as much as, if not more than, knowledge.

Example

Poor: The name of the _____ who decided to have the _____ _____ dropped on _____ in 1945 was _____.

4. If Answered in Numerical Units, Specify the Unit Required. For completion items that require numerical answers, the specific units or the degree of precision should be indicated.

Examples

> *Poor:* The distance between the moon and the earth is _____.
>
> *Improved:* The distance between the moon and the earth is _____ miles.

5. Avoid Clues to the Correct Answer. Students will look for clues in the way sentences are worded and the length of blanks that may indicate a correct answer. The most common wording errors are using single or plural verbs and wording the sentence so that the blank is preceded by "a" or "an." These clues can be eliminated by avoiding verb agreement with the answer, by using "a(an)," and by making all blanks the same length. Students also use varied lengths of blanks as clues to the correct answer.

Examples

> *Poor:* The two legislative branches of the United States federal government are the _____ and the _____ _____ _____.
>
> *Improved:* The two legislative branches of the United States federal government are the _____ and the _____.

6. The suggestions for writing and selecting effective completion items are summarized in the form of a checklist in Figure 9.2.

Short-Answer Items

Short-answer items, in which the student supplies an answer consisting of one word, a few words, or a sentence or two, are generally preferred to completion items for assessing knowledge targets. First, this type of item is similar to how

FIGURE 9.2 **Checklist for Writing/Selecting Completion Items**

✓ Is verbatim language from instructional materials avoided?

✓ Is knowledge being assessed?

✓ Is a single, brief answer required?

✓ Is the blank at the end of the sentence?

✓ Is the length of each blank the same?

✓ Is the precision of a numerical answer specified?

✓ Is it worded to avoid verbal clues to the right answer?

teachers phrase questions and direct student behavior during instruction. This means that the item is more natural for students. Students are familiar with answering questions and providing responses to commands that require knowledge (e.g., "Write the definition of each of the words on the board"). Completion items require students to interpret the question from the sentence. This step is avoided with direct questions. Second, it is easier to write these items.

Assessing Knowledge and Comprehension

Short-answer items are best stated in the form of a question (e.g., "Which state is surrounded by three large bodies of fresh water?"). They can also be stated in general directions (e.g., "Define each of the following terms"), and they can require responses to visual stimulus materials (e.g., "Name each of the countries identified with arrows A–D").

Like completion items, short-answer items are good for measuring knowledge because students can respond to many items quickly, a good sample of knowledge is obtained, guessing is avoided, scoring is fairly objective, and results are generally more valid than those obtained from selected-response formats. The main disadvantage of short-answer items is that scoring takes longer and is more subjective than completion or selected-response items. The following suggestions will help you write and select good short-answer items.

1. **State the Item So That Only One Answer Is Correct.** Be sure that the question or directions are stated so that what is required in the answer is clear to students. If more than one answer is correct, the item is vague and the result is invalid. If you are expecting a one-word answer, use a single short blank.

Examples

Poor: Where is the Eiffel Tower located? _____

Improved: In what country is the Eiffel Tower located? *or* Name the country in which the Eiffel Tower is located: _____

Obviously, in the first item students could give several responses—Europe, Paris, France—each of which would be technically correct.

2. **State the Item So That the Required Answer Is Brief.** Remember that short-answer items of knowledge have answers that are *short!* Keep student responses to a word or two, or a short sentence, or two or three sentences if necessary, by properly wording the item, offering clear directions, and providing space or blanks that indicate the length of the response. In the directions, state clearly that students should not repeat the question in their answer.

Examples

> *Poor:*   What does the term *reptile* mean? _____
>
> _____
>
> *Improved:*   Name three characteristics of reptiles.
>
>   **1.** _____
>
>   **2.** _____
>
>   **3.** _____

Examples

List three ways the recession of the 1980s was like the depression of the 1920s.

>   **1.** _____
>
>   **2.** _____
>
>   **3.** _____

How does a pine tree differ from an oak tree? _____

Name one difference between vertebrate and invertebrate animals.
_____

3. Do Not Use Questions Verbatim from Textbooks or Other Instructional Materials. Most textbooks include review questions and questions for study. You don't want to use these same questions, or really anything verbatim for that matter, on tests because it gives clues to the correct answer and encourages rote memorization.

4. Designate Units Required for the Answer. Students need to know the specific units and the degree of precision that should be used in their answer. This will avoid the time students may take to try to figure out what is wanted—such as asking a question for clarification during the test—and it will mitigate scoring difficulties.

Examples

> *Poor:*   When was President John F. Kennedy killed? _____
>
> *Improved:*   In what year was President John F. Kennedy killed? _____

5. State the Item Succinctly with Words Students Understand. It is best to state questions or sentences as concisely as possible and to avoid using words or phrases that may be difficult for some students to understand.

Examples

Poor: What was the name of the extraordinary president of the United States who earlier had used his extensive military skills in a protracted war with exemplary soldiers from another country? _____

Improved: What United States general defeated the British and later became president? _____

Assessing Reasoning and Deep Understanding

Short-answer items can assess deep understanding as long as the response that is required is brief. Students are required to use their knowledge, not simply recall it. Here are examples of short-answer items that assess deep understanding:

Examples

What are two different points of view about whether it is best to have nationalized medicine?

1. _____

2. _____

What is the implication for the environment of using more nuclear power to provide electricity?

_____

_____

_____

_____

How would the validity of an assessment be judged if the teacher used multiple-choice items rather than essay items to test student knowledge?

_____

_____

_____

_____

Short-answer items can assess reasoning skills when students are required to supply a brief response to a question or a situation that can be understood only by using the targeted thinking skills.

Examples

(Deductive Reasoning): Coach Greene substitutes his basketball players by height, so that the first substitute is the tallest player on the bench, the next substitute is the next tallest, and so forth. Reginald is taller than Sam, and Juan is taller than Reginald. Which of these three players should Coach Greene play first? _____

(Credibility of a Source): The principal needs to decide if the new block schedule allows teachers to go into topics in greater detail. He can ask a parent, a teacher, or a principal from another school. Whom should he ask to get the most objective answer? Why?

_____

_____

(Analysis/Prediction): People want health insurance, but they don't want to be forced to buy it from a company in their community. The law says that a person must buy health insurance from a company in his or her community. What action by the people is most likely?

_____

_____

_____

_____

(Analysis/Prediction): Explain how a plant, a mouse, a snake, and a human can be part of a food chain.

_____

_____

_____

_____

An effective approach for fostering deep understanding is to ask students to justify and explain their answers. This is best accomplished by providing opportunities for them to examine different responses and evaluate these responses according to scoring criteria and/or a rubric. Students can be asked to determine which criteria are met, and they can examine inadequate responses and explain why. By critiquing responses and making suggestions for improvements, understanding is richer and more complete (Parke, Lane, Silver, & Magone, 2003).

An example of an interpretive item that assesses deep understanding in mathematics is illustrated in Figure 9.3. The target is student understanding of the concept "average." Students know in advance that they will need to explain their answer.

Figure 9.4 summarizes suggestions for writing and selecting short-answer items.

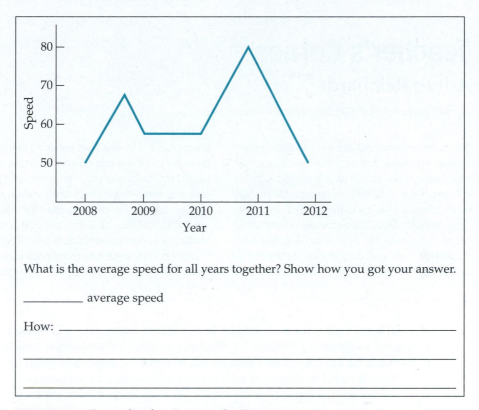

What is the average speed for all years together? Show how you got your answer.

_____ average speed

How: _____

_____

_____

FIGURE 9.3   **Example of an Interpretive Item**

Essay Items

Essays can tap complex thinking by requiring students to organize and integrate information, interpret information, give arguments, give explanations, evaluate the merit of ideas, and conduct other types of reasoning. Although more objective formats are clearly superior for measuring knowledge, the essay is an excellent way to measure deep understanding and mastery of complex information. Research on

FIGURE 9.4   **Checklist for Writing/Selecting Short-Answer Items**

✓ Is only one answer correct?

✓ Are questions from textbooks avoided?

✓ Is it clear to students that the answer is brief?

✓ Is the precision of a numerical answer specified?

✓ Is the item written as succinctly as possible?

✓ Is the space designated for answers consistent with the length required?

✓ Are words used in the item too difficult for any students?

Teacher's Corner

Arleen Reinhardt

National Board Certified High School English Teacher

I use short-answer questions when I want students to give me quick and accurate responses that might apply information or analyze content. For example, I might ask students to apply the content of their reading to the stages of plot structure. Thus, students would have to know the definition of the stages of plot to do so. If my objective is for students to analyze and synthesize information—to use critical thinking skills—I will use essay questions. In this way, I am requiring students to show their thinking skills. Students cannot simply memorize information but must compare/contrast, show cause/effect relationships, interpret, or discuss; and all ideas must be substantiated with details from the content studied. Students are often asked to relate new information to other course content or to previous knowledge in order to make the new ideas relevant for them.

student learning habits shows that when students know they will face an essay test they tend to study by looking for themes, patterns, relationships, and how information can be organized and sequenced. In contrast, when studying for objective tests students tend to fragment information and memorize each piece.

There are two types of essay items, depending on the length and complexity of the answers. In a *restricted-response* essay item (also called *short essay*) the answer is relatively short and simple, while in an *extended-response* essay item the answers are longer and more complex. The restricted-response type item is typically used when more content is covered and students are asked to use deep understanding and application to draw conclusions, explain, interpret, state assumptions, and perform similar cognitive tasks. Extended-response essay items are used to assess organization, integrated learning from several sources, original ideas, reasoning, critical thinking, and evaluation of data, content, or ideas. There is a more holistic and individualized response, sometimes with many different appropriate and even excellent responses. With restricted-type items there tends to be a single correct answer. However, while different types of learning are targeted, the length of the answer does not necessarily indicate the type of target being measured.

Examples: Restricted-Response Essay Items

Write a brief explanation of why hurricanes are more likely to strike Florida than California.

Why are tomatoes better for your health than potato chips?

What is the effect on inflation when the prime interest rate is raised?

Examples: Extended-Response Essay Questions

> Explain how the fertilizer farmers use to grow crops—how much and what type—may pollute our lakes and streams.

> Describe the major events that led to the beginning of the Civil War, showing how the events are related.

> Give an example, new to me and not one from class, of how the law of supply and demand would make prices of some products increase. Explain why.

As I've already emphasized, major advantage of using essay questions is that deep understanding, complex thinking, and reasoning skills can be assessed. Essays motivate better study habits and provide students with flexibility in how they wish to respond. Written responses allow you to evaluate the ability of students to communicate their reasoning through writing. Compared to developing selected-response items that measure reasoning, essay items are less time consuming to construct. However, constructing a *good* essay question may take considerable time.

The major disadvantages of essay items are related to scoring student responses. Reading and scoring answers is very time consuming, especially if done conscientiously so that meaningful feedback is given to students. From a practical standpoint, most teachers find that they can give only a few essay items. Scoring essays is also notoriously unreliable. It is not uncommon for different teachers to grade the same essay quite differently.

You will probably be the only one to judge your students' answers to essay questions, and variations in your mood, halo effects, your expectations, the order in which students are evaluated, and other factors affect your professional judgments. This is not meant to imply that it is inappropriate to use subjective judgments in scoring. You *want* to be able to make judgments; that's one reason for using the essay format. When done appropriately, these judgments are professional, not arbitrary. Another shortcoming of essay items is that they do not provide for very good sampling of content knowledge. The essay cannot sample well because relatively few questions are asked. Sampling is also limited to the reasoning skills that are assessed. For example, a single extended-response essay item that asks students to make a decision based on information provided may give you a good indication of one or two reasoning skills, but several shorter items could sample different types of skills.

Finally, there's the issue of student writing skills. While many essays are intended to evaluate writing, those that are focused more on content and reasoning skills are confounded with students' abilities to write. This is a function of both quality and quantity of answers. Better writers are simply able to express themselves more clearly and are able to write more quickly, often resulting in more complete responses. As the grader, you need to be careful not to let length of answer equate to depth of understanding. You also need to provide sufficient time to write the answers so that writing skill is less of a factor.

FIGURE 9.5   Checklist for Writing/Selecting Essay Items

✓ Is the targeted reasoning skill measured?

✓ Is the task clearly specified?

✓ Is there enough time to answer the questions?

✓ Are choices among several questions avoided?

See Figure 9.5 for a checklist of what to consider when writing/selecting essay items.

Constructing/Selecting Essay Items

In this section we'll review suggestions for writing and selecting effective essay items. Then we'll turn to scoring students' responses.

1. **Construct the Item to Elicit Skills Identified in the Learning Target.** Once the thinking targets are identified, the wording in the question needs to be such that the specific skill(s) will need to be used to answer the question. This is easier with restricted-response items that focus on a single thinking skill. With extended-response items, the scoring criteria can be matched to the skills assessed. A good

Teacher's Corner
Stephanie Stoebe
Texas Round Rock Independent School District Teacher of the Year

I am all about working smarter, not harder, especially when you teach English and have 180 students. Short-answer questions must be able to let students demonstrate a high level of understanding in a relatively easy way to grade. Students are often able to show me their comprehension on different levels with the same question. For example, in one of my classes, we read Amy Tan's "The Rules of the Game" and I wanted to know if my students could identify the theme of the short story, a standard in the freshman English Language Arts curriculum here in Texas. When I asked the question, "What theme of the story would you consider the most relevant?" I was asking for demonstration of a standard, but also giving students the opportunity to synthesize and produce responses on a higher level. Essays give students a chance to really explore a topic and test different hypotheses. On the first draft, I NEVER concentrate on grammar or spelling. Using essays, in my opinion, is for synthesizing and evaluating. It is only in the final edit that we as a class focus on the lower-level items that make a published work complete.

way to begin writing the item to match the target is to start with existing items, such as those in Figure 9.6.

2. Write the Item to Clarify the Specific Task. After reading an essay item, students ask, "What does the teacher want in my answer?" If the question or prompt is described ambiguously, so that students interpret what is called for in the answer differently, many responses will be off target. Such responses lead to flawed, invalid interpretations by teachers. When students misinterpret the task, you don't know if they have the targeted skill or not.

FIGURE 9.6   Sample Item Stems for Assessing Thinking Skills

Skill	Stem
Inference	• Based on the cases presented, what is likely to occur in three years? • What can you infer about attitudes toward religion from these posters?
Justification	• Which option would you select? Why do you think it's the best one? • Why is it better to travel to this city by train rather than by automobile?
Comparison	• Describe the similarities and differences between the Japanese and American systems of public education. • How are the following alike, and how are they different?
Generalization	• Use the following data to suggest what is likely to occur to similar towns. • Do the results from this research have implications for what should be done in the next town?
Application	• Examine this example of a new business. What is being done right and what is being done wrong? • Use the equation for calculating standard deviation to describe the variability of these sample data.
Analysis	• Describe the most important facts in this story that lead to the conclusion that there was a murder. • Identify the unstated assumptions in this argument.
Synthesis	• Examine the interview data from five persons and summarize the main message that is communicated. • What is the main idea that is being communicated by these articles?
Evaluation	• How would you evaluate the following example of research? What would be your overall judgment of its credibility, and why? • Give me your judgment about the merit and worth of using computerized instruction outlined in this article.
Creativity	• What are some new ways cell phones could be used to ensure children's safety?

To clearly set forth the nature of the task, try to make the essay question as specific as possible. Don't be hesitant about explicitly stating the nature of the desired response.

Examples

Poor: Why do Haitian farmers have trouble making a living?

Improved: Describe how the weather, soil, and poverty in Haiti contribute to the plight of farmers. Indicate which of these three factors contributes most to the difficulties farmers experience, and give reasons for your selection.

Poor: How was World War I different from World War II?

Improved: How were the social and political factors leading up to World War I in Germany different from those leading up to World War II? Focus your answer on the 10-year period that preceded the beginning of each war.

You can see that each of the "poorly" worded items gives students too much freedom to write about any of a number of aspects of either Haiti or differences between the wars.

Another way to clarify to students the nature of the task is to indicate the criteria for scoring their answer in the question. This can be labeled a *scoring plan*, *scoring criteria*, *rubric*, or *attributes to be scored*. It essentially tells the students what you will be looking for when grading their answers. This is particularly important if the organization of the response or writing skills are included as criteria.

Examples of Scoring Criteria

(*For Scoring Writing Skills*)

- Organization
- Clarity
- Appropriateness to audience
- Mechanics

(*For Scoring an Argument*)

- Distinguishing between facts and opinions
- Judging credibility of a source
- Identifying relevant material
- Recognizing inconsistencies
- Using logic

(*For Scoring Decision Making*)

- Identifying goals or purpose
- Identifying obstacles
- Identifying and evaluating alternatives
- Justifying the choice of one alternative

3. Indicate Approximately How Much Time Students Should Spend on Each Essay Item. You should have some idea of how much time students will need to answer each item, whether by hand or computer. For restricted-response questions, the amount of time needed is relatively short and easy to estimate. For extended-response items, determining a reasonable estimate is more difficult. You can get some idea by writing draft answers, and as you gain more teaching experience, the responses of previous students to similar questions will be helpful. Take into consideration the writing abilities of your students and, as indicated previously, be sure that even your slowest writers can complete their answers satisfactorily in the time available. Be careful as well to make sure that, when answers are completed electronically, each student has sufficient typing and computer use skills so that a lack of such skills will not impact the answers. The bottom line is, unless you want to measure writing and computer skills, don't allow them to be confounded with student understanding and thinking skills. If you are unsure about the time needed, err by providing more time than is needed rather than less time.

4. Avoid Giving Students Options as to Which Essay Questions They Will Answer. Many teachers offer students a choice of questions to answer. For example, if there are seven questions, the teacher may tell students to answer their choice of three. Students (probably including yourself as a student), love such questions because the selected items are the ones they believe they are best prepared for. Your students will really like this approach if they know *before* taking the test that they will have a choice. Then they can restrict their study to part of the material, rather than to all of it (you can avoid this by telling students *you* will select the items they will write on).

Giving students a choice of questions, however, means that each student may be taking a unique test. Differences in the difficulty of each question are probably unknown. This makes scoring more problematic and your inferences of student knowledge and understanding less valid. It is true that you can't measure every important target, and giving students a choice does provide them an opportunity to do their best work. However, this advantage is usually outweighed by difficulties in scoring and making sound inferences.

Scoring Essays

Scoring essay question responses is difficult because each student writes a unique answer and because many distractions affect scoring reliability/precision. Obviously scoring is subjective, so it is important to practice a few procedures to ensure that the professional judgments are accurate.

The following guidelines will help (see Figure 9.7).

1. Outline What Constitutes a Good or Acceptable Answer as a Scoring Key. This should be completed before administering or scoring student responses. If done before the test is finalized, an outline provides you with an opportunity to revise the stem or question on the basis of what you learn by delineating the response. It's important to have the points specified before reading student

FIGURE 9.7   Checklist for Scoring Essays

✓ Is the answer outlined before testing students?

✓ Is the scoring method—holistic or analytic—appropriate?

✓ Is the role of writing mechanics clarified?

✓ Are items scored one at a time?

✓ Is the order in which the papers are graded changed?

✓ Is the identity of the student anonymous?

answers so that you are not unduly influenced by the initial answers you read. These answers can set the standard for what follows. The scoring key provides a common basis for evaluating each answer. An outline lessens the influence of other extraneous factors, such as vocabulary or neatness.

2. Select an Appropriate Scoring Method. Essays are scored in two ways: holistically or analytically. In **holistic** scoring, the teacher makes an overall judgment about the answer, giving it a single score or grade. The score can be based on a general single judgment, often accomplished by placing essays in designated piles that represent different degrees of quality, or by grading several specific scoring criteria to come up with a single score for each essay. The holistic method is most appropriate for extended-response essays (in which the responses are not limited and are generally long). Figure 9.8 shows an example of a holistic scoring guide for an extended-response essay item.

FIGURE 9.8   Example of Essay Holistic Scoring Guide

Item: Compare and contrast the first and second Iraq wars. Show how they were similar and how they were different along geographic, political, and natural resource dimensions.

Level of Performance	Description
Exceptional (5)	Thorough and detailed understanding of both wars; provides justifications for all points; complete listing of similarities and differences for all dimensions; provides additional insights
Excellent (4)	Complete understanding of both wars; justifications for most points; lists similarities and differences for all dimensions
Very Good (3)	Mostly complete understanding of both wars; justifications for some points; lists most similarities and differences for two dimensions
Acceptable (2)	Incomplete understanding of one or both wars; justifications provided for some points though incomplete; similarities and differences listed with some attention to dimensions
Poor (1)	Incomplete understanding of both wars; justifications inadequate or not present; similarities and differences not correct

Analytic scoring is achieved by awarding each of the identified criteria separate points. Thus, there would be several scores for each essay (and probably a total score that results from adding all the component scores). Analytic scoring is preferred for restricted-response questions (for which there is a limit to the amount of response the student provides). The advantage of analytic scoring is that it provides students with more specific feedback, though this should not replace individualized teacher comments. However, analytic scoring can be very time consuming, and sometimes adding scored parts does not do justice to the overall student response. To avoid excessive attention to specific factors, keep the number of features to be scored analytically to three or four. The holistic scoring guide used in Figure 9.8 is transformed into an analytic guide in Figure 9.9.

3. **Clarify the Role of Writing Mechanics.** Suppose you are a biology teacher and you use essay questions. Does it matter if students spell poorly or use bad sentence structure? Such writing mechanics can certainly influence your overall impression of an answer, so it is important to decide early about whether, and to what extent, these factors are included as scoring criteria. Regardless of how you

FIGURE 9.9   Example of Essay Analytic Scoring Guide

Item: Compare and contrast the first and second Iraq wars. Show how they were similar and how they were different along geographic, political, and natural resource dimensions.

Facet	Inadequate	Adequate	Very Good	Excellent	Points
	1	*2*	*3*	*4*	
Understands both wars	Clearly does not understand	Demonstrates minimal understanding	Demonstrates complete understanding of most aspects	Demonstrates complete understanding of all aspects	
Similarities	Does not address	Shows one correct similarity	Shows two correct similarities	Shows at least three correct similarities	
Differences	Does not address	Shows one correct difference	Shows two correct differences	Shows at least three correct differences	
Inclusion of dimensions	Fails to include any dimensions	Includes one correct dimension	Includes two correct dimensions	Includes at least three correct dimensions	
TOTAL POINTS					

decide to incorporate writing mechanics, it is generally best to give students a separate score for these skills.

4. Score One Item at a Time. When faced with a pile of papers to grade, it's tempting to simply start with the first paper, grade all the questions for that student, and then go on to the next student. To lessen the influence of order of student work and your own fatigue, however, it is best to score one item at a time for all students, and to change the order of the papers for each question. Reliability/ precision will increase if you read all responses to question 1 in one order, all responses to question 2 in a different order, and so on. This avoids the tendency to allow the answer a student gives to the first question to influence the subsequent evaluation of question 2, and so forth for the remaining questions. It is also best to score all answers to each item in one sitting, if possible. This helps you to be consistent in applying criteria to the answers. If you try to grade too much at one time you'll be susceptible to *rater drift*, a scorer's worst nightmare, by interpreting differently over time or overlooking criteria to become more strict or lenient.

5. If Possible, Keep the Identity of the Student Anonymous. It is best not to know whose answer you are grading. This avoids the tendency to be influenced by impressions of the student from class discussion or other tests (*halo effect*). This source of error, which is probably the most serious one that influences results if answers are hand-written, is difficult to control because most teachers get to know the writing patterns and styles of their students. You can have students put their names on the back of the papers, or use typed answers, but the best guard is to be consciously aware of the potential bias to keep it minimized.

Technology-Enhanced Scoring of Constructed-Response Items

Considerable effort being placed by testing experts on developing software that will take the subjectivity out of scoring written answers to constructed-response items, quickly, generating feedback to the student. While most of the development of technology-enhanced scoring is being done for large-scale testing, there is software that you can use in your classroom. The programs can provide prompts, have students generate responses, and then have the students submit the responses for immediate scoring and feedback. As indicated in Chapter 7, some state accountability tests now include completion items and grade responses electronically. For simple constructed-response items this is a very effective, objective way of scoring. The issue is how this gets translated for you in your classroom, with your students. It is now common for teachers to access banks of technology-enhanced constructed-response items, and with software downloaded on your server or computer you'll be able to administer and score very efficiently. And someday I imagine you'll be able to design your constructed-response items and your own protocols for grading, all completed electronically.

Summary

This chapter focused on three types of constructed-response assessment items—completion, short answer, and essay, and briefly discussed technology-enhanced constructed-response items. The following points summarize the chapter:

- Completion items require a constructed response, usually in a space at the end of a sentence.
- Completion items are good for assessing facts and essential knowledge. They are easy to construct with objective scoring. Verbatim language from learning materials should be avoided.
- Short-answer items, typically written as questions that are new for students, are best for assessing knowledge, comprehension, and some reasoning skills.
- Assessment of deep understanding with short-answer questions shows how students can use their knowledge.
- The scoring of short-answer items should be fairly objective, with single correct answers.
- Short-answer interpretive exercises, with graphs, data, and other information, are excellent for assessing understanding and thinking skills.
- Essay items are used primarily for assessing deep understanding, complex thinking, and reasoning skills.
- Essay items allow students to show their understanding and reasoning skills by organizing their thoughts and constructing an answer.
- Extended-response essays are best for assessing complex reasoning skills such as decision making and problem solving, and restricted-response items are better for assessing specific thinking skills, comprehension, and application.
- The major disadvantage of essays is in the scoring, which is time consuming and fraught with many potential sources of error.
- Good essays clearly define the task to students, specifically in terms of the skills that will be assessed. Students should know about how much time to spend on each essay item, and the option to choose items should be avoided.
- The scoring of essays is enhanced when an outline of an acceptable answer is made before testing students; when the correct method of scoring is used (holistic or analytical); when the scoring is done by question, not by student; when the order of papers is changed; and when answers are anonymous.
- Technology-enhanced constructed-response items offer great promise for more efficient and less subjective scoring of student answers.

Introductory Case Study Answer

Barry should be sure that teachers understand that their choice of type of constructed-response items should be dependent on the learning targets, the importance of objective scoring, and the effects on student studying and motivation. Barry's continuum should mark each constructed-response item type with regard to the following:

1. Required level of knowledge, understanding, and application

2. Ease of construction of items

3. Amount of content coverage

4. Reliability of scoring

5. Ease and speed of scoring

6. Length of student responses

7. Objectivity of scoring

8. Validity of scoring

9. Impact on student preparation for assessment

10. Level of student thinking required

Barry should advise teachers that when writing constructed-response items they should be mindful of the following:

1. Avoid verbatim language from instructional materials.

2. Avoid wording that provides verbal clues.

3. Be precise when numerical answers are required.

4. Use age-appropriate language.

5. Use an appropriate question-stem for assessing a specific skill.

6. Avoid giving students options for which questions to answer.

7. Ensure procedures are in place for scoring.

Suggestions for Action Research

1. Write an essay question with criteria for analytic or holistic scoring and examples of responses that would be graded A, B, and C. Give the question, scoring criteria, and examples of responses with grades deleted to four other students for them to grade. Compare their judgments with the grades you assigned.

2. Examine two or three textbooks written for the area in which you wish to teach, either teacher's editions or the ones students use, and identify examples of constructed-response test items. Critique two completion, short-answer, and essay items.

3. Ask a teacher how he or she uses short-answer and essay items. Obtain examples of each and evaluate them according to the checklists presented in the chapter.

4. Observe some students as they take a constructed-response test that assesses deep understanding. How long does it take them to formulate an answer? How much time does it take to write an answer? If possible, examine their responses. How would you evaluate their work?

MyEdLab Self-Check 9.1

MyEdLab Self-Check 9.2

MyEdLab Self-Check 9.3

MyEdLab Self-Check 9.4

MyEdLab Application Exercise 9.1   Advantages/Disadvantages of Constructed-Response Items

MyEdLab Application Exercise 9.2   Scoring Rubric for Essay Items

Performance Assessment

Characteristics
- Strengths
  — authentic
  — sustained work
  — uses reasoning skills
  — engaging
  — no single correct answer
  — specific criteria
- Limitations
  — reliability/precision
  — sampling
  — time

PERFORMANCE ASSESSMENT

Performance Tasks and Contexts
- Restricted
- Extended
- Description
- Question or prompt
- Suggestions
  — essential
  — authentic
  — engaging
  — feasible
  — open
  — constraints

Scoring and Evaluating
- Checklists
- Rating scales
- Rubrics
  — holistic
  — analytic
- Developing rubrics
  — steps
  — focus
  — match with purpose
  — observable
  — understandable
  — clear
  — minimize error
  — feasible

Learning Targets
- Deep understanding
- Reasoning
- Skills
  — communication and presentation
  — psychomotor
- Products
  — papers
  — reports
  — projects
  — presentations

CHAPTER 10   Concept Map

Learning Outcomes

After reading this chapter, you should be able to:

10.1   Identify the essential characteristics of performance assessments and under what circumstances it would be appropriate to use a performance assessment to measure student proficiency. Know the strengths and limitations of performance assessments.

10.2   Write both restricted and extended performance tasks that are consistent with needed elements of effective tasks.

10.3   Understand the differences between checklists, rating scales, and rubrics; know when it is best to use each type, and be able to identify effective and ineffective rubrics.

10.4   Know the steps that are needed to develop effective rubrics; generate an example of how each step was utilized in a novel rubric.

Introductory Case Study

How Would You Evaluate the Performance Task?

Brittany, a fifth-grade teacher, wanted to collaborate with Betty, the school librarian, on an integrated science/language arts unit. Brittany's learning targets included specifics in reading (research), writing (computer product) and oral language (presentation) skills. Students had briefly studied tornados, but the unit was cut short due to snow days. Betty proposed the following performance task:

> Last year there was a tornado that hit in our town. The mayor knows that you have been studying tornadoes this year in fifth grade, and he wants you to work in teams of two to educate students at your school on characteristics of a tornado, and what to do if a tornado occurs. First, use computer and book resources to research information on tornados. Second, use the information to create a PowerPoint or Prezi presentation for students in second grade. Third, create a brochure or flyer that can be sent home with these students. You will present your information to students on the state-wide tornado drill day.

Brittany and Betty determined that students would come to the library for three class periods to do their research. For the following week during reading class, while Brittany was working with reading groups, students would work independently on laptops to create their presentation. The technology resource teacher would then work with students on their flyer/brochure product during three computer lab sessions.

As you read this chapter, evaluate the performance task. Which categories of learning targets did the performance assessment evaluate? What is the weakest aspect of this performance task? How could all three approaches to scoring be used to evaluate Brittany's learning targets?

In Chapters 8 and 9, we examined what are often called conventional *paper-and-pencil* methods of assessment. These techniques effectively assess knowledge and understanding targets and, to a lesser extent, reasoning and skill targets. We now turn to assessments that engage students in activities and tasks that require application of knowledge and skills through the construction of products. This kind of "alternative" assessment is consistent with current theories of learning and motivation and has seen a resurgence of interest with the importance of inculcating 21st-century skills and project-based approaches to teaching.

What Is Performance Assessment?

Simply put, a **performance assessment** involves a student's demonstration of a skill or competency in creating a product, constructing a response, or making a presentation (Lane, 2010). Rather than ask questions about how to do something, students actually perform the skill or behavior. The term *performance* is shorthand for *performance-based* or *performance-and-product*. The idea is that students use their knowledge and skills to construct something. This can be as simple as showing keyboard skills in typing, or as complex as creating a remote-controlled machine. The emphasis is on the students' ability to perform tasks by producing their own work with their knowledge and skills. In some cases, this is a presentation, such as singing, playing the piano, or performing gymnastics. In other cases, this ability is expressed through a product, such as a completed paper, project, or video.

Performance assessment is simply applying the teaching/learning methods used successfully for years in the adult world. Musicians, artists (like my son Jon), athletes, architects, and doctors all learn by getting feedback on what they have constructed and demonstrated in practice. This same approach can be applied to learning all content areas, targeting important skill outcomes.

Figure 10.1 illustrates characteristics of effective performance assessments, most of which are typically present to some extent. But be careful. Because the term *performance assessment* is now so popular (again actually, it was quite the rage a couples decades ago), test publishers and some educators have come to use it as a label for constructed-response, interpretive exercises, and essay items. It's as though there is an ideal for what a performance assessment should look like, and many variations in practice.

Other terms, such as *alternative assessment* and *authentic assessment*, are sometimes used interchangeably with performance assessment, but they actually mean something different. An **alternative assessment** is any method that differs from conventional paper-and-pencil tests, most particularly objective tests. Examples of alternative assessments include observations, exhibitions, oral presentations, experiments, portfolios, interviews, and projects. (Some think of essays as a type of alternative assessment because they require students to construct responses.)

Authentic assessment involves the direct examination of a student's ability to use knowledge to perform a task that is like what is encountered in real life or

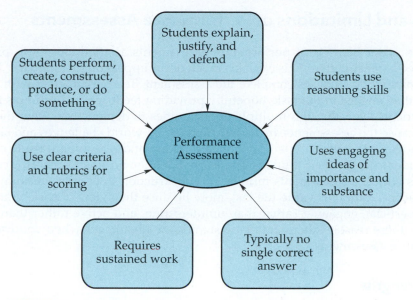

FIGURE 10.1   **Characteristics of Performance Assessments**

in the real world. Authenticity is judged in the nature of the task completed and in the context of the task (e.g., in the options available, constraints, and access to resources). Authentic classroom assessment is excellent for motivating students—it gets them engaged and requires application thinking skills. But like the term performance assessment, what constitutes authentic assessment varies. Frey, Schmitt, and Allen (2012) reviewed of over 100 sources claiming to be about authentic assessment and found that there are many different conceptualizations. They discovered that while the idea of having a realistic, real-world (outside the classroom) task is essential,, the literature stresses eight additional characteristics:

1. A performance-based task
2. A cognitively complex task
3. A defense of an answer or product
4. Formative
5. Includes collaboration with others
6. Known scoring criteria
7. Use of multiple indicators for scoring
8. A mastery, criterion-referenced orientation

This list shows how for some authentic assessment includes both performance assessment and formative assessment. The reality is that the extent to which these characteristics are present varies considerably, and for your teaching you need to decide which of these is needed.

Strengths and Limitations of Performance Assessments

The major benefits of performance assessments are tied closely to providing effective instruction. This explains much of the appeal of the approach. Learning occurs while students complete the assessment. Teachers interact with students as they engage in the task, hopefully providing feedback and prompts that help students learn through multiple opportunities to demonstrate what their skills. Because the assessments are usually tied to real-world challenges and situations, students are better prepared for such thinking and reasoning outside of school. Students justify their thinking and learn that often no single answer is correct. In this way, the assessments influence the instruction to be more meaningful and practical. Students value the task more because they view it as rich rather than superficial, engaging rather than uninteresting, and active rather than passive. For these reasons, there are many significant advantages when you use performance assessments.

Strengths

Performance assessments are better suited to measure complex thinking targets than are selected-response tests or simple constructed-response items. Students are more engaged in active learning as a part of the assessment because they need to be engaged to perform successfully. Since the emphasis is on what students *do*, skills are more directly assessed, and there are more opportunities to observe the process students use to arrive at answers or responses. Students who traditionally do not perform well on paper-and-pencil tests have an opportunity to demonstrate their learning in a different way.

Another advantage of performance assessments is that multiple, specific criteria for judging success are identified. You should share these criteria with students before the assessment so that the students can use them as they learn. In this way, students learn how to evaluate their own performance through self-assessment. They learn how to ask questions and, in many assessments, how to work effectively with others.

Finally, performance assessment motivates educators to explore the purposes and processes of schooling. Because of the nature of the assessments, teachers revisit their learning goals, instructional practices, and standards. They explore how students will use their classroom time differently and whether there are adequate resources for all students.

Limitations

The limitations of using performance assessment lie in three areas: reliability/precision, sampling, and time. Unfortunately, performance assessments are subject to considerable measurement error, which lowers reliability/precision. Like essay items, the major source of measurement error with performance assessments is with scoring. Because scoring requires professional judgment, usually by only one person, there will be variations and error due to bias and other factors, similar to what affects evaluating essay answers. Although procedures exist that can minimize scoring error—such as carefully constructed criteria, tasks, and scoring rubrics; systematic scoring procedures; and using more than one rater—reliability/precision is likely to be lower than what is achieved with other types of assessment. Inconsistent student performance also contributes to error. That is, student performance at one time may differ noticeably from what the student would demonstrate at another time (this might occur, for example, if on the day of the performance the student is ill).

Because it takes considerable time for students to do performance assessments, you will have relatively few samples of student proficiency. Furthermore, we know that performance on one task may not provide a very good estimate of student success on other tasks. This means that if you intend to use the results of performance assessment to form conclusions about capability in a larger domain of learning targets, you need to accumulate information from multiple tasks. It also helps to select tasks that can optimize generalization to the learning targets. Suppose the learning target is concerned with skills associated with making a PowerPoint presentation. If the task is relatively restricted (e.g., using only a few PowerPoint features with a short presentation, making a 2-minute speech), generalization is more limited than when the task encompasses additional skills (e.g., the PowerPoint is longer and contains many features, making a 15-minute speech). Your choice, then, is to use many restricted tasks or few tasks to reach the same level of generalizability.

The third major limitation of performance assessment concerns time. First, it is very time consuming for teachers to construct good tasks, develop scoring

Teacher's Corner

Patricia Harris

National Board Certified Elementary Art Teacher

As I develop a lesson, I first create a sample of the lesson artwork so that I can analyze the experience of what the student will need to know and encounter and what the potential learning and product results will be. Specifically, in developing my fifth-grade animation art unit, I created scoring criteria and a rubric based on my experience in analyzing the lesson as well as adjustments that I have made in reflecting on my past teaching of this unit.

I established a point scale for varying levels of accomplishment and weighted the different criteria according to what was most valuable to the students' success. I also created a bonus points category, awarding special independently created "aha moments" to further encourage students to be independent thinkers and innovators. The students work collaboratively throughout this unit and use the rubric as a guide during the creation of their animation movies as well as a collective assessment tool to gauge their success when they view their and fellow students' animation movies.

TABLE 10.1   **Strengths and Weaknesses of Performance Assessments**

Strengths	Weaknesses
Integrates assessment with instruction.	Reliability/precision may be difficult to establish.
Learning occurs during assessment.	
Provides opportunities for formative assessment.	Measurement error due to subjective nature of the scoring may be significant.
Tends to be more authentic than other types of assessments.	Inconsistent student performance across time may result in inaccurate conclusions.
More engaging; active involvement of students.	Few samples of student achievement.
Provides additional way for students to show what they know and can do.	Requires considerable teacher time to prepare and student time to complete.
Emphasis on reasoning skills.	Difficult to plan for amount of time needed.
Forces teachers to establish specific criteria to identify successful performance.	Limited ability to generalize to a larger domain of knowledge.
Encourages student self-assessment.	
Emphasis on application of knowledge.	
Encourages reexamination of instructional goals and the purpose of schooling.	

criteria and rubrics, administer the task, observe students, and then apply the rubrics to score the performance or product. For performances that are difficult to score at the time of the performance, such as when a student makes a speech, adequate time needs to be taken with each student as he or she performs the task. Second, it is difficult, in a timely fashion, to interact with all students and give them meaningful feedback as they learn and make decisions. Finally, it is difficult to estimate the amount of time students will need to complete performance assessments, especially if the task is one you haven't used previously and if students are unaccustomed to the format and/or expectations.

The strengths and weaknesses of performance assessments are summarized in Table 10.1. The weaknesses are usually outweighed by the strengths, but only if your approach is thoughtful, reflective, and rigorous. Performance assessment is complex and demanding. Time, energy, and resources must be invested to meet goals identified in the strengths listed.

Learning Targets for Performance Assessments

Performance assessments are primarily used for four types of learning targets—deep understanding, reasoning, skills, and products. Deep understanding and reasoning involve in-depth, complex thinking about what is known and application of knowledge and skills in novel and more sophisticated ways. Skills include student proficiency in reasoning, communication, and psychomotor tasks. Products are completed works, such as term papers, projects, and other assignments in which students use their knowledge and skills.

Deep Understanding

The essence of performance assessment includes the development of students' deep understanding of something. The idea is to involve students meaningfully in hands-on activities for extended periods of time so that their understanding is richer and more extensive than what can be attained by more conventional instruction and traditional paper-and-pencil assessments. Deep understanding in performance assessments focuses on the *use* of knowledge and skills. Student responses are constructed in unique ways to demonstrate depth of thought and subtleties of meaning in novel situations. Students are asked to demonstrate what they understand through the application of knowledge and skills.

Reasoning

Like deep understanding, reasoning is essential with most performance assessments. Students will use reasoning skills as they demonstrate skills and construct products. Typically, students are given a problem to solve or are asked to make a decision or other outcome, such as a letter to the editor or school newsletter, based on information that is provided. They use cognitive processes such as analysis, synthesis, critical thinking, inference, prediction, generalizing, and hypothesis testing.

Skills

In addition to reasoning skills, students are required to demonstrate communication, presentation, and/or psychomotor skills. These targets are ideally suited to performance assessment. We'll consider each one.

Communication and Presentation Skills. Learning targets focused on communication skills involve student performance of reading, writing, speaking, and listening. For reading, targets can be divided into process—what students do before, during, and after reading—and product—what students get from the reading. Reading targets for elementary students progress from targets such as phonemic awareness skills (e.g., decoding, phonological awareness, blending), to skills needed for comprehension and understanding (such as discrimination, contextual cues, inference, blending, sequencing, and identifying main ideas). For effective performance assessment, each of these areas needs to be delineated as a specific target. For instance, a word identification target may include naming and matching uppercase and lowercase letters, recognizing words by sight, recognizing sounds and symbols for consonants at the beginnings and ends of words, and sounding out three-letter words. For older students, reading targets focus on comprehension products and strategies and on reading efficiency, including stating main ideas; identifying the setting, characters, and events in stories; drawing inferences from context; and reading speed. More advanced reading skills include sensitivity to word meanings related to origins, nuances, or figurative meanings; identifying contradictions; and identifying possible multiple inferences. All reading targets should include the ability to perform a specific skill for novel reading materials. A variety of formats should also be represented.

Writing skill targets are also related to a student's grade level. The emphasis for young students is on their ability to construct letters and copy words and simple sentences legibly. For writing complete essays or papers, elaborate delineations of skills have been developed. Typically, important dimensions of writing are used as categories, as illustrated in the following writing targets:

Purpose	Clarity of purpose; awareness of audience and task; clarity of ideas
Organization	Unity and coherence
Details	Appropriateness of details to purpose and support for main point(s) of writer's response
Voice/tone	Personal investment and expression
Usage, mechanics, and grammar	Correct usage (tense formation, agreement, word choice), mechanics (spelling, capitalization, punctuation), grammar, and sentence construction

Other dimensions can be used when the writing skill being measured is more specific, such as writing a persuasive letter, a research paper, or an editorial. Writing targets, like those in reading, should include the ability to perform the skill in a variety of situations or contexts. That is, if students have been taught persuasive writing by developing letters to editors, the student may write a persuasive advertisement or speech to demonstrate that he or she has obtained the skill.

Oral communication skill targets can be generalized to many situations or focused on a specific type of presentation, such as giving a speech, singing a song, speaking a foreign language, or competing in a debate. When the emphasis is on general oral communication skills, the targets typically center on the following three general categories (Russell & Airasian, 2012):

Physical expression	Eye contact, posture, facial expressions, gestures, and body movement
Vocal expression	Articulation, clarity, vocal variation, loudness, pace, and rate
Verbal expression	Repetition, organization, summarizations, reasoning, completeness of ideas and thoughts, selection of appropriate words to convey precise meanings

A more specific set of oral communication skill targets is illustrated in the following guidelines for high school students[1]:

A. Speaking clearly, expressively, and audibly
  1. Using voice expressively
  2. Speaking articulately and pronouncing words correctly
  3. Using appropriate vocal volume

   B. Presenting ideas with appropriate introduction, development, and conclusion
     1. Presenting ideas in an effective order
     2. Providing a clear focus on the central idea
     3. Providing signal words, internal summaries, and transitions

   C. Developing ideas using appropriate support materials
     1. Being clear and using reasoning processes
     2. Clarifying, illustrating, exemplifying, and documenting ideas

   D. Using nonverbal cues
     1. Using eye contact
     2. Using appropriate facial expressions, gestures, and body movement

   E. Selecting language to a specific purpose
     1. Using language and conventions appropriate for the audience

For specific purposes, the skills are more targeted. For example, if a presentation involves a demonstration of how to use a microscope, the target could include such criteria as clarity of explanations, understanding of appropriate steps, appropriateness of examples when adjustments are necessary, dependency on notes, and whether attention is maintained, as well as more general features such as posture, enunciation, and eye contact.

Psychomotor Skills. There are two steps in identifying psychomotor skill learning targets. The first step is to describe clearly the physical actions that are required. These may be developmentally appropriate skills or skills that are needed for specific tasks. I have divided the psychomotor area into five categories in Table 10.2 to

TABLE 10.2 **Examples of Psychomotor Skills**

Fine Motor	Gross Motor	Complex	Visual	Verbal and Auditory
Cutting paper with scissors	Walking	Perform a golf swing	Copying	Identify and discriminate sounds
Drawing a line	Jumping	Operate a computer	Finding letters	Imitate sounds
Tracing	Balancing	Drive a car	Finding embedded figures	Pronounce carefully
Eye–hand coordination	Throwing	Dissect a frog	Identifying shapes	Articulate
Penmanship	Skipping	Perform backwalkover on balance beam	Discriminating on the basis of attributes such as size, shape, and color	Blend vowels
Coloring	Pull-ups			Use proper lip and tongue placement to produce sounds
Drawing shapes	Hopping	Operate a microscope		
Connecting dots	Kicking	Sail a boat		
Pointing		Operate a drill press		
Buttoning				
Zippering				

help you describe the behavior: fine-motor skills (such as holding a pencil, meas-uring chemicals, and using scissors), gross-motor actions (such as jumping and lifting), more complex athletic skills (such as shooting a basketball or playing golf), some visual skills, and verbal/auditory skills for young children.

The second step is to identify the level at which the skill is to be performed. One effective way to do this is to use an existing classification of the psychomotor domain. This system is hierarchical. At one level there is *guided response*, which essentially involves imitating a behavior or following directions. At higher levels students show more adaptability and origination, a greater ability to show new actions and make adjustments as needed.

Products

Performance assessment products are completed works. For years, students have done papers, reports, and projects. What makes these products different when used for performance assessment is that they are more engaging and authentic, and they are scored more systematically with clear criteria and standards. For example, rather than having sixth graders report on a foreign country by summa-rizing the history, politics, and economics of the country, students write promo-tional materials for the country that would help others decide if it would be an interesting place to visit. In chemistry, students are asked to identify an unknown substance. Why not have them identify the substances from a local landfill, river, or body of water? In music, students can demonstrate their proficiency and knowl-edge by creating and playing a new song. Table 10.3 presents some other exam-ples, varying in authenticity.

As a learning target, each product needs to be clearly described in some detail so that there is no misunderstanding about what students are required

TABLE 10.3 Performance Products and Skills Varying in Authenticity

Relatively Unauthentic	Somewhat Authentic	Very Authentic
Indicate which parts of a garden design are accurate.	Design a garden.	Create a garden.
Write a paper on zoning.	Write a proposal to change fictitious zoning laws.	Write a proposal to present to city council to change zoning laws.
Answer a series of questions about what materials are needed for a trip.	Defend the selection of supplies needed for a hypothetical trip.	Plan a trip with your family, indicating needed supplies.
Explain what you would teach to students learning to play basketball.	Show how to perform basketball skills in practice.	Play a basketball game.
Listen to a tape and interpret a foreign language.	Hold a conversation with a teacher in a foreign language.	Hold a conversation with a person from a foreign country in his or her native language.

to do. It is insufficient to simply say, for example, "Write a report on one of the planets and present it to the class." Students need to know about the specific elements of the product (e.g., length, types of information needed, nature of the audience, context, materials that can be used, what can be shown to the audience) and how they will be evaluated. One effective way to do this is to show examples of completed projects to students. These are not meant to be copied, but they can be used to communicate standards and expectations. If the examples can demonstrate different levels of proficiency, so much the better. A good way to generate products is to think about what people in different occupations do. What does a city planner do? What would an expert witness produce for a trial? How does a mapmaker create a map that is easy to understand? What kinds of stories does a newspaper columnist write? How would an advertising agent represent state parks to attract tourists?

Constructing Performance Tasks

Once learning targets have been identified and you have decided that a performance assessment is the method you want to use, three steps will guide you in constructing the complete performance task. The first is to identify the performance task in which students will be engaged; the second is to develop descriptions of the task and the context in which the performance is to be conducted; the third is to write the specific question, prompt, or problem the students will receive (Figure 10.2).

Step 1: Identify the Performance Task

The performance task is what students are required to do in the performance assessment, either individually or in groups. The tasks can vary by subject and by level of complexity. Some performance tasks are specific to a content area, and others integrate several subjects and skills. With regard to level of complexity, it is useful to distinguish two types: restricted and extended.

Restricted- and Extended-Type Performance Tasks.   **Restricted-type tasks** target a narrowly defined skill and require relatively brief responses. The task is structured and specific. These tasks may look similar to short essay questions and interpretive exercises that have open-ended items. The difference is in the relative emphasis on characteristics listed in Figure 10.1. Often the performance task is

FIGURE 10.2   **Steps in Constructing Performance Tasks**

structured to elicit student explanations of their answer. Students may be asked to defend an answer, indicate why a different answer is not correct, tell how they did something; draw a diagram, construct a visual map, graph, or flowchart, or show some other aspect of their reasoning. In contrast, short essay questions and interpretive exercises are designed to infer reasoning from correct answers. Although restricted-type tasks require relatively little time for administration and scoring in comparison with extended-type tasks (providing greater reliability and sampling), it is likely that fewer of the important characteristics of authentic performance assessments are included. Many publishers provide performance assessments in a standardized format, and most of them contain restricted-type tasks. Further examples of restricted-type performance tasks are listed in Table 10.4.

Extended-type tasks are more complex, elaborate, and time consuming. Extended-type tasks often include collaborative work with small groups of students. The assignment usually requires that students use a variety of sources of information (e.g., observations, library, interviews). Judgments will need to be made about which information is most relevant. Products are typically developed

TABLE 10.4   Examples of Restricted- and Extended-Type Performance Assessment Tasks

Restricted-Type	Extended-Type
Construct a bar graph from data provided.	Construct a PowerPoint presentation.
Talk in French about what is on a menu.	Design a playhouse and estimate the cost of materials and labor.
Read an article from a newspaper and answer questions.	Plan a trip to another country; include the budget and itinerary.
Review a zoning map of a city and indicate changes that would encourage more commercial development.	Conduct a historical reenactment (e.g., Boston Tea Party, the Lincoln–Douglas debates).
Flip a coin 10 times. Predict what the next 10 flips would be. Explain why.	Diagnose and repair a car problem.
Listen to Fox News and explain whether you believe the stories are biased.	Design an advertising campaign for a new or existing product.
Construct a poster that explains the parts of flowers.	Publish a newspaper.
Sing a song.	Design a park.
Type at least 35 words a minute with five or fewer mistakes.	Create a commercial.
Using scissors, cut outlined figures from a page.	Write and perform a song.
Recite a poem.	Prepare a plan for dealing with waste materials.
Write a paper about the importance of protecting forests from being converted to farmland.	Design and carry out a study to determine which grocery store has the lowest prices.
Write examples of good and poor multiple-choice questions.	Plan and install a new car radio stereo system.
	Design a computer simulation.

over several days or even weeks, with opportunities for revision. This allows students to apply a variety of skills and makes it easier to integrate different content areas and reasoning skills.

It is not too difficult to come up with ideas for what would be an engaging extended-type task. As previously indicated, one effective approach is to think about what people do in different occupations. Another way to generate ideas is to check curriculum guides and teacher's editions of textbooks because most will have activities and assignments that tap student application and reasoning skills. Perhaps the best way to generate ideas is by brainstorming with others, especially members of the community. They can be particularly helpful in thinking about authentic tasks that involve reasoning and communication skills. Some ideas that could be transformed into extended-type tasks are included in Table 10.4. Once you have a general idea for the task, you need to develop it into a more detailed set of specifications.

Step 2: Prepare the Task Description

The performance task needs to be specified so that it meets the criteria for good performance assessment and is clear to students. This is accomplished by preparing a *task description*. The purpose of the task description is to provide a blueprint or listing of specifications to ensure that essential criteria are met, that the task is reasonable, and that it will elicit desired student performance. The task description is not the same as the actual format and wording of the question or prompt that is given to students; it is more like a lesson plan. The task description should include the following:

> Content and skill targets to be assessed
> Description of student activities
> > Group or individual
> > Help allowed
> Resources needed
> Teacher role
> Administrative process
> Scoring procedures

It is essential to clearly describe the specific targets to be assessed to make certain that the activities and scoring are well matched to ensure both valid and practical assessments. Think about what students will actually do to respond to the question or solve the problem by specifying the context in which they will work:

> Will they consult other experts, use library resources, do experiments?
> Are they allowed to work together, or is it an individual assignment?
> What types of help from others are allowed?
> Is there sufficient time to complete the activities?

Once the activities are described, the resources needed to accomplish them can be identified.

> Are needed materials and resources available for all students?
> What needs to be obtained before the assessment?

It will be helpful to describe your role in the exercise.

> Will you consult your students or give them ideas?
> Are you comfortable with and adequately prepared for what you will do?
> What administrative procedures are required?

Finally, identify scoring procedures.

> Will scoring match the learning targets?
> Is adequate time available for scoring?
> Do you have the expertise needed to do the scoring?
> Is it practical?

One effective way to begin to design the task is to think about what has been done instructionally The assessment task should be structured to mirror the nature of classroom instruction so that what you are asking students to do is something that they are already at least somewhat familiar with. Once the task description is completed and you are satisfied that the assessment will be valid and practical, you are ready to prepare the specific performance task question or prompt.

Step 3: Prepare the Performance Task Question or Prompt

The actual question, problem, or prompt that you give to students will be based on the task description. It needs to be stated so that it clearly identifies what the final outcome or product is, outlines what students are allowed and encouraged to do, and explains the criteria that will be used to judge the product. A good question or prompt also provides a context that helps students understand the meaningfulness and relevance of the task.

It's often best to use or adapt performance tasks that have already been developed. Several professional organizations have organized networks and other resources for developing performance tasks. Many subject-oriented professional organizations, such as the National Council of Teachers of Mathematics, have good resources for identifying performance tasks, and the Internet can be used to tap into a vast array of examples. Just Google "performance assessment" with your area of teaching and grade level and lots of ideas will pop up.

Whether you develop your own tasks or use intact or modified existing ones, you will want to evaluate the task on the basis of the following suggestions (summarized in Figure 10.3).

FIGURE 10.3 **Checklist for Writing Performance Tasks**

✓ Are multiple, essential targets included?
✓ Are multiple correct responses possible?
✓ Is the task authentic?
✓ Is the task rich?
✓ Is the task clearly defined?
✓ Is the task challenging and engaging, fostering perseverance?
✓ Are criteria for scoring shared with the task?
✓ Are conditions for completing the task included?
✓ Does the task involve interaction with others?
✓ Is the task biased for some students?

1. The Performance Task Should Integrate the Most Essential Aspects of the Content Being Assessed with the Most Essential Skills. Performance assessment is ideal for focusing student attention and learning on the "big ideas" of a subject, the major concepts, principles, and processes that are important to a discipline. If the task encourages learning of peripheral or tangential topics or specific details, it is not well suited to the goal of performance assessment. Tasks should be broad in scope. Similarly, reasoning and other skills essential to the task should represent essential processes. The task should be written to integrate content with skills. For example, it would be better to debate important content or contemporary issues rather than something relatively unimportant. A good test for whether the task meets these criteria is to decide if what is assessed could be done as well with more objective, less time-consuming measures.

Examples

> *Poor:* Estimate the answers to the following three addition problems. Explain in your own words the strategy used to give your answer.
>
> *Improved:* Sam and Tyron were planning a trip to a nearby state. They wanted to visit as many different major cities as possible. Using the map, estimate the number of major cities they will be able to visit on a single tank of gas (14 gallons) if their car gets 25 miles to the gallon.

2. The Task Should Be Authentic. This suggestion lies at the heart of authentic performance assessment. As indicated earlier, authentic tasks are relevant to real-world and real-life contexts (Groeber, 2007), though as I have pointed out, research has shown that many have a broader view of what constitutes authenticity (Frey, Schmitt, & Bowen, 2009). If the task is rich, it will raise other questions and lead to other inquiry. Grant Wiggins developed a set of six standards for judging the degree of authenticity in an assessment task (Wiggins, 1998). He suggests that a task is authentic if it:

A. *Is realistic.* The task replicates the ways in which a person's knowledge and abilities are "tested" in real-world situations.

B. *Requires judgment and innovation.* The student has to use knowledge and skills wisely and effectively to solve unstructured problems, and the solution involves more than following a set routine or procedure or plugging in knowledge.

C. *Asks the student to "do" the subject.* The student has to carry out exploration and work within the discipline of the subject area, rather than restating what is already known or what was taught.

D. *Replicates or simulates the contexts in which adults are "tested" in the workplace, in civic life, and in personal life.* Contexts involve specific situations that have particular constraints, purposes, and audiences. Students need to experience what it is like to do tasks in workplace and other real-life contexts.

E. *Assesses the student's ability to efficiently and effectively use a repertoire of knowledge and skill to negotiate a complex task.* Students should be required to integrate all knowledge and skills needed, rather than to demonstrate competence of isolated knowledge and skills.

F. *Allows appropriate opportunities to rehearse, practice, consult resources, and get feedback on and refine performances and products.* Rather than rely on secure tests as an audit of performance, learning should be focused through cycles of performance-feedback-revision-performance, on the production of known high-quality products and standards, and learning in context. (pp. 22, 24)

Examples

Poor: Compare and contrast different kinds of literature.

Improved: You have been asked to make a presentation to our school board about different types of literature. Prepare a PowerPoint presentation that you would use to explain different types of literature, including poems, biographies, mysteries, and fictional novels. Provide examples of each type, explain the characteristics of each, and explain why you like some better than others. Create charts or figures as part of your presentation, which should be no longer than 15 minutes.

3. **Structure the Task to Assess Multiple Learning Targets.** As pointed out in the first suggestion, it is best if the task addresses both content and skill targets. Within each of these areas there may be different types of targets. For instance, assessing content may include both knowledge and understanding and, as in the preceding example, both reasoning and communication skills. It is also common to include different types of communication and reasoning skills in the same task (e.g., students provide both a written and an oral report or need to think critically and synthesize to arrive at an answer).

4. **Structure the Task So That You Can Help Students Succeed.** Good performance assessment involves the interaction of instruction with assessment. The task needs to be something that students learn from, which is most likely when there are opportunities for you to increase student proficiency by asking

questions, providing resources, and giving feedback. In this kind of active teaching you are intervening as students learn, rather than simply providing information. Part of teachability is being certain that students have the needed prerequisite knowledge and skills to succeed.

5. Think Through What Students Will Do to Be Sure That the Task Is Feasible. Imagine what you would do if given the task. What resources would you need? How much time would you need? What steps would you take? It should be realistic for students to implement the task. This depends both on your own expertise and willingness and on the costs and availability of equipment, materials, and other resources so that every student has the same opportunity to be successful.

6. The Task Should Allow for Multiple Solutions. If a performance task is properly structured, more than one correct response is not only possible but desirable. The task should not encourage drill or practice for which there is a single solution. The possibility of multiple solutions encourages students to personalize the process and makes it easier for you to demand that students justify and explain their assumptions, planning, predictions, and other responses. Different students may take different paths in responding to the task.

7. The Task Should Be Clear. An unambiguous set of directions that explicitly indicates the nature of the task is essential. If the directions are too vague, students may not focus on the learning targets or may waste time trying to figure out what they should be doing. A task such as "Give an oral report on a foreign country" is too general. Students need to know the reason for the task, and the directions should provide sufficient detail so that students know how to proceed. Do they work alone or with others? What resources are available? How much time do they have? What is the role of the teacher? Here is an example of a clearly defined task:

> Your assignment is to construct an original experiment that will show what causes objects to sink. Your answer should include examples that illustrate three characteristics. In demonstrating your answer you will have five minutes to show different objects sinking in water, accompanied by explanations of how each characteristic is important.

8. The Task Should Be Challenging and Stimulating to Students. One of the things you hope for is that students will be motivated to use their skills and knowledge to be involved and engaged, sometimes for many days or weeks. You also want students to monitor themselves and think about their progress. This is more likely to occur when the task is something students can get excited about or can see some relevance for, and when the task is not too easy or too difficult. Persistence is fostered if the task is interesting and thought provoking. This is easier if you know your students' strengths and limitations and are familiar with what kinds of topics would motivate them. One approach is to blend what is familiar with novelty. Tasks that are authentic are not necessarily stimulating and challenging.

Teacher's Corner

Elizabeth O'Brien

National Board Certified Middle School Mathematics Teacher

In my geometry classes, when studying volume I have students bring in products from home that come in double containers. For example, toothpaste comes in a tube and then is packaged in a box, and most pills come in a bottle and then are packaged in a box. Students are asked to find the volume of the outer package using the formulas we have studied, and then find the volume of the inner package by displacement. When they find the difference between the volumes we discuss how companies could save money on packaging and why they might use the double package method. To conclude the unit, students are asked to write a letter to the manufacturer of the product describing their findings and what and why they think changes should be made.

Overall, students enjoy this project. It allows them to use geometry for something they see as useful. They also love taking a side and using their data to argue for or against a change. The letters allow me to see a depth of understanding a typical problem does not allow for.

9. **Include Explicitly Stated Scoring Criteria.** By now you are familiar with this admonition. Specifying criteria helps students understand what they need to do and communicates learning priorities and your expectations. Students need to know about the criteria *before* beginning work on the task. Sometimes criteria are individually tailored to each task; others are more generic for several different kinds of tasks. What is shared with students as part of the task, however, may not be the same instrument or scale you use when evaluating their work. The identification of criteria, and how you translate those criteria into a scale for evaluation, is discussed in the next section. From a practical perspective, the development of the task and scoring criteria is iterative: One influences the other as both are developed.

10. **Include Constraints for Completing the Task.** It's best if the performance is done under constraints that are defined by context, rules, and regulations. According to Borich and Tombari (2004), these constraints include the following:

Time. How much time should a learner or group of learners have to plan, revise, and finish the task?

Reference material. What resources (dictionaries, textbooks, class notes, CD-ROMs) will learners be able to consult while they are completing the assessment task?

Other people. Will your learners be able to ask for help from peers, teachers, and experts as they take a test or complete a project?

Equipment. Will your learners have access to computers, calculators, spell checkers, or other aids or materials as they complete the assignment?

Scoring criteria. Will you inform your learners about the explicit standards that you use to evaluate the product or performance? (p. 220)

The intent of considering such constraints is to define in a more realistic way the nature of the situation in which the performance or product is demonstrated.

Performance tasks will vary, depending on your style of teaching, learning targets, students, and context. Most of the variance will be contained in the following:

Is the task individual, small group, or large group?
Does the task focus on process or product, or both?
Is the task short or long?
Is the task contained in the classroom or will it require activities outside of class?
What modalities for presentation are used—oral, written, or psychomotor?

Performance Criteria

After students have completed the task, will then review their work and make a professional judgment about its quality. Rather than relying on unstated rules for making these judgments, performance assessments include *performance criteria*, what you call on or use to determine student proficiency. Performance criteria, then, serve as the basis for evaluating the quality of student work.

Performance criteria (or *scoring criteria* or simply *criteria*) are what you look for in student responses to evaluate their progress toward meeting the learning target. In other words, performance criteria are the dimensions or traits in products or performance that are used to illustrate and define understanding, reasoning, and proficiency. Explicitly defined performance criteria help to make what is a subjective process clear, consistent, and defensible.

To establish good criteria, you should begin with identification of the most important dimensions or traits of the performance or product. This is a summary of the essential qualities of student proficiency. These dimensions should reflect your instructional goals as well as teachable and observable aspects of the performance. Ask yourself this question: "What distinguishes an adequate from an inadequate demonstration of the target?"

One of the best ways to identify criteria is to work backward from examples of student work. These examples (or *exemplars*) are analyzed to determine what traits or dimensions distinguish them and are used as the basis for concluding that one student's work meets a specific standard or target. The dimensions become criteria. For example, for evaluating a speech, dimensions could include content, organization, and delivery. Delivery may be composed of additional criteria, such as posture, gestures, facial expressions, and eye contact. For a singing performance, you could include pitch, rhythm, diction, and tone quality as criteria, then determine additional criteria for each of these four. As you might imagine, you can go into great detail describing dimensions. But to be practical, you need to balance specificity with what is manageable.

The following is an example of reasonable criteria for a specific learning target.

Learning target: Students will be able to write a persuasive paper to encourage the reader to accept a specific course of action or point of view.

Criteria: Appropriateness of language for the audience.
Plausibility and relevance of supporting arguments.
Level of detail presented.
Evidence of creative, innovative thinking.
Clarity of expression.
Organization of ideas.

Scoring and Evaluating

The second essential part of evaluating performance assessments is to have a well-developed, clear approach to scoring and evaluating the extent to which different levels of the criteria are demonstrated. There are three common approaches to this scoring—checklists, rating scales, and rubrics (see Figure 10.4).

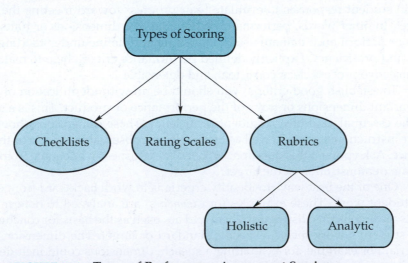

FIGURE 10.4   Types of Performance Assessment Scoring

FIGURE 10.5   **Checklist for Evaluating a PowerPoint Presentation**

Yes	No	
_____	_____	1. The topic has been extensively and accurately researched.
_____	_____	2. A storyboard, consisting of logically and sequentially numbered slides, has been developed.
_____	_____	3. The introduction is interesting and engages the audience.
_____	_____	4. The fonts are easy to read and point size varies appropriately for headings and text.
_____	_____	5. The use of italics, bold, and underline contributes to the readability of the text.
_____	_____	6. The background and colors enhance the text.
_____	_____	7. The graphics, animation, and sounds enhance the overall presentation.
_____	_____	8. Graphics are of proper size.
_____	_____	9. The text is free of spelling, punctuation, capitalization, and grammatical errors.

Checklists

A checklist is a simple listing of the criteria or dimension, and you will simply check whether or not each criterion was met or each dimension demonstrated. It is a yes/no type of decision. Checklists are good for evaluating a sequence of steps that are required. For example, it would make sense to use a checklist to evaluate whether a student followed the proper steps in using a microscope or diagnosing a rough-sounding motor. Figure 10.5 shows an example of a checklist that could be used to evaluate a PowerPoint presentation.

Rating Scales

A rating scale is used to indicate the degree to which a particular dimension is present, beyond a simple yes/no. It provides a way to record and communicate qualitatively different levels of performance. Several types of rating scales are available; we will consider three: numerical, qualitative, and numerical/quantitative combined.

The *numerical scale* uses numbers on a continuum to indicate different levels of proficiency in terms of frequency or quality. The number of points on the scale can vary, from as few as 2 to 10 or more. The number of points is determined on the basis of the decision that will be made. If you are going to use the scale to indicate low, medium, and high, then 3 points are sufficient. More points on the scale permit greater discrimination, provide more diagnostic information, and permit more specific feedback to students.

Here are some examples of numerical scales:

Complete Understanding of the Problem	5 4 3 2 1	No Understanding of the Problem
Little or No Organization	1 2 3 4 5 6 7	Clear and Complete Organization
Emergent Reader	1 2 3	Fluent Reader

A *qualitative scale* uses verbal descriptions to indicate student performance. There are two types of qualitative descriptors. One type indicates the different gradations of the dimension:

Minimal	*Partial*			
Never	*Seldom*	*Occasionally*	*Frequently*	*Always*
Consistently	*Sporadically*	*Rarely*		
Complete understanding	*Nearly complete understanding*	*Some understanding*	*Limited understanding*	
Uses capital letters appropriately most or all of the time	*Uses capital letters appropriately some of the time*	*Rarely uses capital letters appropriately*		
Always speaks clearly	*Speaks clearly most of the time*	*Speaks clearly some of the time*	*Rarely speaks clearly*	

A second type of qualitative scale includes gradations of the criteria and some indication of how the performance compares to established standards. This is the most frequently used type of rating scale for performance assessments. Descriptors such as the following are used:

novice	*emergent*	*proficient*	*advanced*
inadequate	*needs improvement*	*good*	*excellent*
excellent	*proficient*	*needs improvement*	
absent	*developing*	*adequate*	*fully developed*
limited	*partial*	*thorough*	
emerging	*developing*	*achieving*	
not there yet	*shows growth*	*proficient*	

Rubrics

Rubrics are the most common and most effective way to score performance assessments (Lane, 2013). A **rubric** is a scoring guide that includes a scale that spans different levels of competency. This scale is used with the criteria to establish a two-dimensional table, with the criteria on one side and the scale on the other. Within the table are descriptions of how teachers differentiate between different scale points for each criterion. That is, a rubric uses descriptions of different levels of quality on each of the criteria.

The rubric organizes and gives more detail to the criteria. They are worded in ways that communicate to students how their teacher evaluates the essence of what is being assessed. Wiggins (1998) uses the following questions to help understand the function of rubrics:

By what criteria should performance be judged?
What should we look for to judge performance success?

What does the range in the quality of the performance look like?

How should the different levels of quality be described and distinguished from one another?

For example, if a teacher is evaluating the logic of an argument, one of the criteria could be the trustworthiness and relevance of supporting facts. Different levels of quality for those criteria could be expressed as follows:

No supporting facts

Facts presented have weak trustworthiness and relevance

Facts presented have acceptable trustworthiness or relevance

Facts presented are clearly trustworthy and relevant

The goal of having rubrics, then, is to communicate your standards-based judgments so that it is clear how your judgments will be made. By doing this, students are informed about specific strengths and deficiencies. An example of an excellent rubric is shown in Figure 10.6.

Developing Rubrics   Rubrics are best developed by combining several different procedures (Gallavan, 2009; Schwartz & Kenney, 2008). It is helpful to begin by clarifying how the discipline defines different levels of performance. This will give you an idea of the nature and number of gradations that should be used. It is also

FIGURE 10.6   **Example of Rubric for Essay Response to Policy Recommendation Article**

Criteria	Needs Improvement	Proficient	Advanced
Summary	Main idea not clearly identified	Incomplete summary or simple repeating of article	Main idea clearly summarized in own words
Focus of agreement/disagreement	Incomplete, unclear agreement/disagreement not related to author's argument	Agreement/disagreement stated but incomplete or somewhat unclear; related to author's argument but not specifically	Clear, specific indication of what is in agreement and/or disagreement directly related to author's argument
Support for agreement/disagreement	Lack of clear support for agreement/disagreement	Specious analysis with generalized arguments of support mostly consistent with what is in the article	Analysis of the author's argument included with examples
Style and coherence	Serious errors in usage, grammar, mechanics, and/or coherence	Acceptable coherence and well organized with noticeable errors in usage, grammar, or mechanics	Clearly organized, appropriate style, no major errors in usage, grammar, or mechanics

helpful to obtain samples of how others have described and scored performance in the area to be assessed.

Another approach, alluded to earlier, is to gather performance samples and determine the characteristics of the works that distinguish effective from ineffective ones. The samples could be from students as well as so-called experts in the area. You could start by putting a group of student samples into three qualitatively different piles to indicate three levels of performance. Then examine the samples to see what distinguishes them. The identified characteristics provide the basis for the dimensions of the rating scale. At this point, you can review your initial thinking about the scale with others to see whether they agree with you. With feedback from others, you can write the first draft of the descriptors at each point of the rating scale.

Use the first draft of the rubric with additional samples of student work to verify that it functions as intended. Revise as needed, and try it again with more samples of student work until you are satisfied that it provides a valid, reliable/precise, and fair way to judge student performance. Don't forget to use student feedback as part of the process.

Holistic or Analytic?   An important decision is whether the rubric will be *holistic* or *analytic*. A **holistic rubric** is one in which each category of the scale contains several criteria, yielding a single score that gives an overall impression or rating. Advantages of using a holistic rubric are its simplicity and the ability to provide a reasonable summary rating. All the traits are efficiently combined, the work is scored quickly, and only one score results. For example, in gymnastics, my daughter received a single holistic score between 1 and 10, in which separate judgments for various dimensions (flexibility, balance, position, etc.) are combined. The disadvantage of a holistic score is that it reveals little about what needs to be improved. Thus, for feedback purposes, holistic scores provide little specific information about what the student did well and what needs further improvement.

When the purpose of the assessment is summative, at the end of a unit or course, a holistic rubric is appropriate. But even when used summatively, holistic scales can vary greatly in the specificity of what is used in the judgments. For example, the following holistic rubric for reading is rather skimpy; very little is indicated about what went into the judgment.

> Level 4: *Sophisticated* understanding of text indicated with constructed meaning.
> Level 3: *Solid* understanding of text indicated with some constructed meaning.
> Level 2: *Partial* understanding of text indicated with tenuous constructed meaning.
> Level 1: *Superficial* understanding of text with little or no constructed meaning.

Popham (2007) refers to this type of holistic rubric as *hypergeneral.* Such rubrics are so general and limited that there is little indication of the criteria that should be used to make judgments about student proficiency. This does not provide much instructional guidance or student awareness of criteria. Contrast this rubric with the one in Figure 10.7, which is also concerned with reading. It is obvious that this more developed and specific rubric provides a detailed explanation of how the reading was judged and why each level was assigned. Even with this more specific scale, however, how do you judge a student who showed multiple connections between the text and the reader's ideas/experiences but had interpretations that were not directly supported by appropriate text references? This kind of problem, in which the traits being assessed do not all conform within a single category, is almost certain to exist with holistic scales for some students.

Another example of a holistic rubric is illustrated in Figure 10.8 for graphing data. Note how several criteria are included in each of the three levels.

FIGURE 10.7   Example of Holistic Rubric

Reading Rubric

Rating Scale	Evaluative Criteria
4	There is clearly a sophisticated understanding of the text with substantial evidence of constructed meaning from the text. Text references were used to support meaningful interpretations. There is evidence of connections between the text and the reader's ideas/experiences. There is evidence that the reader takes a critical stance (e.g., analyzes the author's style of writing, questions the text, provides alternative interpretations, views the text from different perspectives).
3	A solid though not sophisticated understanding of the text is demonstrated. There is adequate evidence of constructed meaning. Some but not many connections are made between the text and the reader's ideas/experiences. Interpretations are generally supported by appropriate text references. There is some evidence of a critical stance toward the text.
2	Only a partial understanding of the text is demonstrated with incomplete evidence of constructed meaning. While some connections are made between the text and the reader's ideas/expressions, these connections are superficial and not well developed. Interpretations are lacking or not supported by appropriate text references. There is little or no evidence of taking a critical stance toward the text.
1	A poor, superficial understanding of the text is demonstrated with very limited evidence of constructed meaning. There is no evidence of connections between the text and the reader's ideas/experiences, and there are no interpretations or evidence of a critical stance.

Source: Based on McTighe and Ferrara (1998).

FIGURE 10.8 Holistic Rubric for Graphic Display of Data

3 Points	The graph contains all data accurately (placed correctly). All units of measurement are correctly labeled. The graph is appropriately scaled. The title is clear and appropriate. The graph is neat and easy to understand.
2 Points	Some or most data are accurately graphed with some errors. Units of measurement are for the most part correct but contain minor errors. The scale is appropriate and does not contain awkward jumps in value. The title generally tells what the data show but could be improved. The graph is generally neat and easy to read but could be improved.
1 Point	Some or most of the data are inaccurately represented, contain major errors, or are missing. Only some parts of the graph are correctly labeled or labels are missing. The scales are inappropriate or contain awkward jumps in value. The title does not reflect what the data show. The graph is sloppy and difficult to understand.
0 Points	No data presented or mostly missing. Lack of labeling or mostly incorrect labeling. Scales are missing or mostly incorrect. Title is missing. Graph cannot be understood.

Source: Based on McTighe and Wiggins (2004).

An **analytic rubric** (or *analytic-trait rubric*) is one in which each criterion receives a separate score. If analytic scoring were used in gymnastics, each criterion such as flexibility, balance, and position would be scored separately. This kind of rubric provides much better diagnostic information and feedback for the learner, and is more useful for formative assessment. Students are able to see their strengths and weaknesses more clearly. They are able to connect their preparation and effort with each evaluation. However, analytic rubrics take longer to create and score.

In general, to the extent possible based on practical constraints, it is best to use analytic rubrics. Like other good assessment techniques, once established, good analytic rubrics, with appropriate modifications, will serve you well for many years. An analytic rubric is illustrated in Figure 10.9. This rubric transforms the holistic one in Figure 10.8 about graphing data into an analytic one. In this example four criteria are evaluated separately—title, labels, accuracy, and neatness. The rubric also shows the weight that each criterion will have in determining the overall score. Actually, an analytic rubric can be as simple as a numerical scale that follows each criterion, such as the following, which could be used to evaluate creative writing:

Criterion	Outstanding		Competent		Marginal
Creative ideas	5	4	3	2	1
Logical organization	5	4	3	2	1
Relevance of detail	5	4	3	2	1
Variety in words and sentences	5	4	3	2	1
Vivid images	5	4	3	2	1

FIGURE 10.9   Example of Analytic Rubric for Graphic Display of Data

Criteria	Score				Weight
	0	1	2	3	
Title	Missing title	Missing or does not reflect data	Title included though only a general indication of data	Title included that clearly tells what the data show	10%
Labels	Labels missing	Labels included only for some parts of the graph	Labels included, though some are incorrect	Labels accurately included for all parts of the graph	20%
Scales	No scales	Scales are graphed but incorrectly	Scales are adequate with some errors	Scales are appropriate	20%
Accuracy	Data missing	Data are missing, inaccurate, or contain major errors	Data are included, though with some errors	Data are accurately included for all parts of the graph	30%
Legibility	Unable to understand	Graph is sloppy and difficult to understand	Graph is generally legible and readable	Graph is very neat, legible, and easy to read	20%

Source: Based on McTighe and Wiggins (2004).

However, such rubrics still do not indicate much about why ideas were "competent" and not "outstanding" or why vivid images were rated "marginal." Analytic rubrics use language that is as descriptive as possible about the nature of the criterion that differentiates it from one level to the next. It will be much more helpful, for example, for students to know that "eye contact with the audience was direct and sustained for most of the presentation," rather than receiving feedback such as "excellent" or "completely." The difference between holistic and analytic rubrics is illustrated in Figure 10.10.

The following suggestions, summarized in Figure 10.11, will provide further help as you develop rubrics.

1. **Be Sure the Criteria Focus on Important Aspects of the Performance.** There are many ways to distinguish between different examples of student work. You want to use those criteria that are essential in relation to the learning targets you are assessing. Because it is not feasible to include every possible way in which performances may differ, you need to identify those that are most important. For example, if you are making judgments about writing and use mechanics as one of the criteria, it would not be practical to include every grammatical rule in characterizing the descriptions. Rather, you need to select the few most important aspects, such as tense formation, agreement, and punctuation.

2. **Match the Type of Rating with the Purpose of the Assessment.** If your purpose is more global and you need an overall judgment, a holistic scale should be

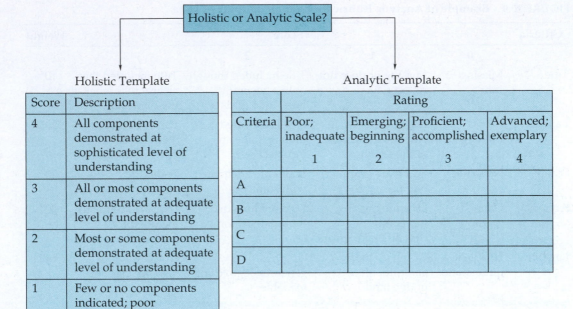

FIGURE 10.10 **Differences Between Holistic and Analytic Rubrics**

used. If the major reason for the assessment is to provide feedback about different aspects of the performance, an analytical approach would be best.

3. Descriptions of the Criteria Should Be Directly Observable. Try to keep the descriptions focused on behaviors or aspects of products or skills that you can observe directly. You want to use clearly visible, overt behaviors for which relatively little inference is required (e.g., behaviors such as loudness, eye contact, and enunciation are easily and reliably observed). It is best to avoid high-inference criteria that are judged on the basis of behavior, such as attitudes, interests, and effort, because the behaviors are easily faked and are more susceptible to rater error and bias. This means that when the target is a disposition or affective in nature, the focus needs to be on behaviors that can be directly observed. Avoid the

FIGURE 10.11 **Checklist for Writing and Implementing Rubrics**

✓ Do criteria focus on important aspects of the performance?
✓ Is the type of rating matched with the purpose?
✓ Are the traits directly observable?
✓ Are the criteria understandable?
✓ Are the traits clearly defined?
✓ Is scoring error minimized?
✓ Is the scoring system feasible?

use of adverbs that communicate standards, such as *adequately*, *correctly*, and *poorly*. These evaluative words should be kept separate from what is observed.

Examples

> *Poor:*   Demonstrates a positive attitude toward learning keyboarding skills.
>
> *Improved:*   Voluntarily gives to the teacher or other students two reasons why it is important to learn keyboarding skills.

4. Criteria Should Be Written So That Students, Parents, and Others Understand Them. Recall that you should share criteria with students before instruction. The purpose of this is to encourage students to incorporate the descriptions as standards in doing their work and to self-monitor. Obviously, if the descriptions are unclear, students cannot apply them to their work, and the meaningfulness of your feedback is lessened. Consequently, pay attention to wording and phrases; write so that students easily comprehend the criteria. A helpful approach to ensure understanding is simple but often overlooked—ask the students! It is also helpful to provide examples of student work that illustrate different descriptions. Notice in Elizabeth Shanahan's Teacher's Corner how she worked to make her rubric accessible to students.

5. Characteristics and Traits Used in the Scale Should Be Clearly and Specifically Defined. You need to have sufficient detail in your descriptions so that the criteria are not vague. If a few general terms are used, observed behaviors are open to different interpretations. The wording needs to be clear and unambiguous.

Teacher's Corner
Elizabeth Shanahan

Los Reyes Texas Elementary School

Our district has developed an excellent rubric used throughout the district. The language within the rubric is formal and specific. However, a problem developed when actually using the rubric: the *kids* could not understand it. Consequently, understanding errors, setting goals, and striving for higher writing grades became frustrating for my students. My solution? I used the district writing rubric as a prototype to develop a student-friendly rubric. I also made it a point to *teach* the rubric at the beginning of the school year, so kids would be able to understand my expectations. More importantly, my students discovered they could use the student-friendly rubric as a tool to improve their own writing. The result was a newfound confidence and passion for writing. Student learning improved, self-confidence improved, and test scores improved.

Examples (wood shop assignment to build a letter holder)

> *Poor:*   Construction is sound.
>
> *Improved:*   Pieces fit firmly together; sanded to a smooth surface; glue does not show; varnish is even.

Note the clarity and specificity of the analytic scale illustrated in Figure 10.12. This is an example of an excellent rubric, in this case for writing a persuasive essay.

6. Take Appropriate Steps to Minimize Scoring Error. The goal of any scoring system is to be objective and consistent. Because performance assessment involves professional judgment, some types of errors in particular should be avoided to achieve objectivity and consistency. The most common errors are associated with the *personal bias* and *halo effects* of the person who is making the judgment. Personal bias results in three kinds of errors. **Generosity error** occurs when the teacher tends to give higher scores; **severity error** results when teachers use the low end of the scale and underrate students' performances. A third type of personal bias is **central tendency error**, in which students are rated in the middle.

As explained earlier, the **halo effect** occurs when the teacher's general impression of the student affects scores given on individual traits or performances. If the teacher has an overall favorable impression, he or she may tend to give ratings that are higher than what is warranted; a negative impression results in the opposite. The halo effect is mitigated if the identity of the student is concealed (though this is not possible with most performance assessments), by using clearly and sufficiently described criteria, and by periodically asking others to review your judgments. Halo effects can also occur if the nature of a response to one dimension, or the general appearance of the student, affects your subsequent judgments of other dimensions. That is, if the student does extremely well on the first dimension, there may be a tendency to rate the next dimensions higher, and students who look and act nice may be rated higher. Perhaps the best way to avoid the halo effect is to be aware of its potential for affecting your judgment and monitoring yourself so that it doesn't occur. Other sources of scoring error, such as order effects and rater exhaustion, should also be avoided.

To be consistent in the way you apply the criteria, rescore some of the first products scored after finishing all the students, and score one criterion for all students at the same time. This helps avoid order and halo effects that occur because of performance on previous dimensions. Scoring each product several times, each time on a different criterion, allows you to keep the overall purpose of the rubric in mind.

7. The Scoring System Needs to Be Feasible. There are several reasons to limit the number and complexity of criteria that are judged. First, you need to be practical with respect to the amount of time it takes to develop the scoring criteria and do the scoring. Generally, five to eight different criteria for a single product are

FIGURE 10.12 Example of an Elementary Persuasive Essay Rubric

	4	3	2	1
Opinions and Reasons	Opinion is clearly stated with at least two detailed supportive reasons.	Opinion stated with one or two reasons that may be unclear.	Opinion stated but unclear; reasons are weak; may not stay on subject.	Opinion not stated; reasons not stated, confusing, or unclear.
Organization	Interesting lead paragraph with a clear middle and end; sequence logical; paragraphs have clear main ideas, topic sentences, and closing sentences.	While the paper has a clear beginning, middle, and end, the sequence could be clearer; paragraphs may not contain all elements.	The beginning, middle, and end sections are not clear; some ideas may be placed inappropriately; considerable problems with paragraphs.	There are no sections in the paper; ideas strung together loosely; paragraphs problematic.
Voice	The writing style effectively communicates writer engagement and caring about the topic.	The writing clearly communicates ideas without passion; voice not consistent.	The style is relatively void of emotion, feeling, or enthusiasm, communicating little writer engagement.	The writing style is insipid, with no emotional engagement.
Sentence structure	All sentences are clear, begin in a variety of ways, and contain appropriate subject–verb agreement.	Most sentences are clear and begin appropriately; most subject–verb agreement is correct.	There are many unclear or incomplete sentences, with some run-on sentences; some subject–verb agreement problems; considerable revisions needed.	So many of the sentences are not clear, incomplete, or contain subject–verb agreement problems that the story is difficult to read; extensive revision needed.
Mechanics	Spelling, capitalization, punctuation, and grammar are all correct with little or no editing needed.	Spelling, capitalization, punctuation, and grammar are mostly correct; some editing needed.	Considerable mechanical mistakes; much editing needed.	The mechanics are very poor, with the need for extensive editing and revisions.

Source: Based on Andrade, H. L., Du, Y., and Wang, X. (2008). Putting rubrics to the test: The effect of a model, criteria generation, and rubric referenced self-assessment on elementary school students' writing. *Educational Measurement: Issues and Practice, 27*(2), 3–13.

sufficient and manageable. Second, students will be able to focus only on a limited number of aspects of the performance. Third, if holistic descriptions are too complex, it is difficult and time consuming to keep all the facets in mind. Finally, it may be difficult to summarize and synthesize too many separate dimensions into a brief report or evaluation.

One last suggestion will be helpful as you design effective rubrics. Because performance assessment is well established, there are numerous examples of rubrics for every subject and grade level. Along with many books and guides, just like finding performance tasks, the Internet can be used to access all kinds of rubrics (like all material on the Internet, the quality of these examples will vary, so be a critical consumer!).

Summary

This chapter introduced performance assessment as an excellent approach to measuring behavior, thinking skill, and product learning targets. Important points made in the chapter include the following:

- In contrast to paper-and-pencil tests, performance assessment requires students to construct an original response (performance or product) to a task that is scored with teacher judgment.
- Authentic assessment involves a performance task that approximates what students are likely to have to do in real-world settings.
- Performance assessment integrates instruction with evaluation of student achievement and is based on constructivist learning theory. Multiple criteria for judging successful performance are developed.
- Effective performance assessment engages students in meaningful activities that enhance their thinking skills and demonstrate their ability to apply what they have learned.
- Limitations of performance assessments include the resources and time needed to conduct them, bias and unreliability in scoring, and a lack of generalization to larger domains of knowledge.
- Performance assessment is used most frequently with deep understanding, reasoning, skill, and product learning targets.
- Communication skill targets include reading, writing, and speaking.
- Psychomotor skill targets consist of physical actions—fine motor, gross motor, complex athletic, and visual, and verbal/auditory.
- Product targets are completed student works, such as papers, written reports, and projects.
- Presentation targets include oral presentations and reports.
- The performance task defines what students are required to do.
- Restricted-type tasks target a narrowly defined skill and have a brief response.

- Extended-type tasks target complex tasks and have extensive responses. These may take several days or even weeks to complete.
- The task description needs to clearly indicate the target, student activities, resources needed, teacher role, administrative procedures, and scoring procedures.
- Effective tasks have multiple targets that integrate essential content and skills, are grounded in real-world contexts, rely on teacher help, are feasible, allow for multiple solutions, are clear, are challenging and stimulating, and include scoring criteria.
- Criteria are narrative descriptions of the dimensions used to evaluate the students.
- Scoring performance assessment is done with checklists, rating scales, and rubrics.
- Rating scales are used to indicate different levels of performance.
- Holistic rubrics contain several dimensions together; analytic rubrics provide a separate score for each dimension.
- Complete scoring rubrics include both descriptions and evaluative labels for different levels of the dimension.
- Scoring criteria are based on clear definitions of different levels of proficiency and samples of student work.
- High-quality scoring criteria focus on important aspects of the performance, match the type of rating (holistic or analytical) with the purpose of the assessment, are directly observable, are understandable, are clearly and specifically defined, minimize error, and are feasible.

Introductory Case Study Answer

This task evaluated all four learning target categories. The task evaluated students' (a) deep understanding of tornados; (b) reasoning abilities of analysis and synthesis of researching information; (c) skills in research, communication, and presentation; and (d) authentic computer products.

The weakest aspect of the performance task is that it does not include explicit scoring criteria to determine student proficiency.

The performance task lends itself to developing three different types of scoring approaches.

- For part 1, a rating scale could be included so that students were evaluated on the amount and quality of resources used and information included. This would help evaluate whether the reading (research) learning targets were met.
- For part 2, a rubric could be used to evaluate students' mastery of the oral language (presentation) learning targets.
- For parts 2 and 3, a checklist could be integrated to ensure that students included each criterion that was important for evaluating whether students met the writing (computer product) learning targets.

Suggestions for Action Research

1. Identify a teacher who is using performance assessments and observe students during the assessment. Are they actively involved and on task? Do they seem motivated, even eager to get feedback on their performance? How "authentic" is the task? Can there be more than one correct answer? Is instruction integrated with the assessment? If possible, interview some students and ask them how they react to performance assessments. What do they like and dislike about them? How do they compare to more traditional types of assessment? How could they be more effective?

2. Devise a performance assessment for some aspect of this chapter. Include the performance task and scoring rubric, using the criteria in Figures 10.3 and 10.11. Critique the assessments through class discussion.

3. Try out some scoring rubrics with teachers. You will need to formulate learning targets and the performance task. Construct exemplars of student work that illustrate different scores. Ask the teachers to give you some feedback about the rubric. Is it reasonable? Does it allow for meaningful differentiation between important dimensions of the task? Is it practical? Would students understand the rubric? How could the scoring rubric be improved?

4. In a small group with other students, do some research on three examples of performance tasks in your field. Do they appear to meet the criteria in Figure 10.3? How could they be improved? Be prepared to present your findings to the class for discussion.

MyEdLab Self-Check 10.1

MyEdLab Self-Check 10.2

MyEdLab Self-Check 10.3

MyEdLab Self-Check 10.4

MyEdLab Application Exercise 10.1   Performance Task Assessment

MyEdLab Application Exercise 10.2   Steps to Develop a Rubric

---

Endnote

1. Based on District 214's speech assessment rating guide. (n.d.). Arlington Heights, IL: Township High School District 214.

Portfolios: Paper and Digital

Characteristics
- Clear purpose
- Systematic and organized sample of work
- Preestablished guidelines
- Student selection of some content
- Student self-reflection
- Documented progress
- Clear scoring criteria
- Conferences
- Advantages/ disadvantages

Digital
- Characteristics
- Requirements
- Advantages
- Disadvantages
- Examples

Implementing
- Review nature of portfolios with students
- Supply content
- Include right number of entries
- Include table of contents
- Include student self-evaluation guidelines

PORTFOLIO ASSESSMENT

Teacher Evaluation
- Checklist of contents
- Portfolio structure
- Individual entries
- Entire contents
- Written comments
- Student–teacher conference

Types
- Documentation
  — Celebration
  — Competence
  — Project
- Growth

Planning
- Identify learning targets and standards
- Identify use
- Identify structure
- Determine content
- Determine self-reflection guidelines
- Determine scoring criteria

CHAPTER 11   **Concept Map**

Learning Outcomes

After reading this chapter, you should be able to:

11.1 List the essential characteristics of an effective portfolio and what steps are needed to implement portfolio assessment.

11.2 Identify the advantages and disadvantages of using portfolios and determine if portfolios would be useful in your teaching.

11.3 Distinguish among different types of documentation portfolios and contrast with growth portfolios. Know when it is appropriate to use each type and align with learning targets.

11.4 Recognize the advantages of using digital rather than paper portfolios; be able to identify a possible digital platform that could be used for your grade level and subject.

Introductory Case Study

What Is Wrong with Khalil's Thinking?

One of Woodgrove School District's requirements was for teachers to ensure students maintained a writing portfolio to show student growth. The number of writing pieces to be included was flexible, but teachers were mandated to illustrate a variety of styles of writing. The students' portfolio would go home with report cards, and at the end of the year, they would be given to the next year's teachers so that teachers could see individual student growth and know where to begin writing instruction. As a new seventh-grade English teacher, Khalil was excited about putting together his students' portfolios and felt confident in his abilities since he had completed an Eportfolio of his student teaching experiences.

In November, Khalil started looking at the writing pieces he had collected on each student. Since Khalil knew he would be documenting student competence in the portfolio, he had copied students' work before commenting on it earlier in the grading period. As he reviewed each students' work and selected pieces that demonstrated mastery of seventh-grade writing standards, he pulled out the clean copies and wrote the English standard number for which the student showed mastery. He also decided against including student drafts and his scoring rubric scoring forms to limit the quantity of paper in the folder and not show students' grades. He wanted the portfolio to highlight his students' excellent writing.

As Khalil was putting together the portfolios, he decided that no expository writing pieces would be included. When he looked at students' writings, he wasn't confident that students had mastered their persuasive and descriptive writing skills. Thus, Khalil decided the best plan for systemically deciding what to include would be to pick a writing style focus for each grading period. He thought it best to include only fictional narrative pieces from the first grading period, the second grading period would include expository pieces, the third grading period would have personal narrative writings, and the fourth grading period products would be authentic real-world pieces such as letters to congressmen.

Once Khalil finalized his student portfolios, he gave them out to students and asked students to self-reflect on their writing and to make a list of what they felt they did well. He then provided students with an exemplar paper that demonstrated mastery of the set writing goals for the next grading period and asked students to determine how they would accomplish these writing goals. When students were finished, they put this self-evaluation in their portfolio and took their portfolios home for signatures.

As you read this chapter, decide what is wrong, if anything, with Khalil's thinking. Did Khalil err when developing his students' writing portfolios? How?

This chapter shows how to use collections of evidence of student performance that can effectively portray student learning, motivate students, and promote important cognitive skills and dispositions. Portfolios were rather popular in the 1990s but, because of reliability/precision issues and the growing importance of selected-response assessments for large-scale accountability tests, their use diminished, much like performance assessments. Now they are making a comeback! In addition to exciting and engaging digital possibilities for portfolios, in our current environment of increased scrutiny on basing teacher evaluation on students' academic progress portfolios may become the best way to document student learning.

What Are Portfolios?

In many professions, *portfolio* is a familiar term. Portfolios have constituted the primary method of evaluation in fields such as art, architecture, modeling, photography, and journalism. These professions have realized the value of documenting proficiency, skill, style, and talent with examples of actual work. In education, a **portfolio** can be defined as a purposeful, systematic process of collecting and evaluating student formative and/or summative assessments to document progress toward the attainment of learning targets or show evidence that learning targets have been achieved. Whether paper-based or digital, portfolios are limited, meaningful collections of student work, typically illustrated by presenting and reflecting on different assessments. They usually include specific and predetermined guidelines for the selection of contents, criteria for scoring, and evidence of student self-reflection on what has been accomplished.

An effective portfolio has several essential characteristics (Figure 11.1). First, a portfolio is *purposeful*. There is a clear reason why certain works would be included and how the portfolio is to be used and a rationale for why a portfolio is better than other types of assessment. Second, the portfolio represents a *systematic* and *well-organized* collection of materials that make up a meaningful *sample* of student work. It is not designed as a comprehensive or exhaustive collection of assessments. Third, *preestablished guidelines* are set up so that it is clear what materials should be included. Fourth, students are engaged in the process by *selecting some of the materials* and by continually evaluating and *reflecting* on their work. Fifth, effective portfolios are designed to engage and motivate students, and allow

FIGURE 11.1 **Characteristics of Effective Portfolios**

- Clearly defined purpose aligned with learning targets, standards, and 21st-century skills
- Systematically organized collection of student work products
- High student engagement and motivation
- Individualized student artifacts
- Preestablished guidelines used to establish contents
- Some student selection of contents
- Student self-reflection
- Clear and appropriate criteria for evaluating student products
- Conferences held between students and teachers to review and evaluate

them to individualize their submissions. Sixth, based on clear and well-specified *scoring criteria, progress* is documented with the evaluations. Finally, *conferences* are held between teacher and student to review progress, identify areas that need further improvement, and facilitate student reflection.

Although the precise nature of what is called a portfolio will be unique to a particular setting, there are two major types—the *documentation* or the *growth* portfolio. **Documentation portfolios** show student work that illustrates achievement, often aligned to learning standards. These include the *celebration* or *showcase* portfolio, in which a student selects his or her best work, what he or she is most proud of, or to show results of a project. Because the student chooses the work, each profile of accomplishment is unique, resulting in individual profiles. This encourages self-reflection and self-evaluation, but makes scoring more difficult and time consuming because of the unique structure and content of each portfolio.

The *competence* or *standards-based* portfolio is structured to provide evidence that a targeted level of proficiency has been achieved. For this kind of portfolio, the criteria for determination of mastery or competence need to be clearly defined. The focal point of *project* portfolios is on a single example or illustration of the competence of the student. These can be very engaging, especially in a digital format. Typically, there is documentation of reaching each important target.

The **growth portfolio** reveals change in student proficiency over time. Selections of student work are collected at different times to show how skills have improved. Most of the examples are selected by teachers or are predetermined. Growth portfolios are excellent for documenting progress and providing concrete examples that show changes over time. Table 11.1 shows examples of each of these types of portfolios.

Regardless of the specific type or label, portfolios have advantages and disadvantages that determine whether you will find them useful. Portfolios combine the strengths of performance assessments with the ability to provide a continuous record of progress and improvement, and include student goal-setting and self-assessment. The advantages are compelling reasons to use portfolios if needed resources are provided. Like any method of assessment, portfolios have limitations and trade-offs.

TABLE 11.1 Different Types of Portfolios

Type	Description	Examples
Documentation *Celebration*	Shows student's best work	Highest scored test Highest graded paper Best project
Competence	Shows levels of achievement reached in relation to learning targets	Mastery of each competency needed to do electrical work
Project	Illustrates competence on completion of a single task	History unit final presentation Small-group project on identifying chemicals in a water sample
Growth	Shows improvement of student competence over time	Examples of writing that show differences in skill Drawings from the first part of the semester to the last week of the semester

Advantages

Perhaps the most important advantage of using portfolios is that students are actively involved in self-evaluation and self-reflection (Belgrad, 2013; Borich & Tombari, 2004). Students become part of the assessment process and function as self-directed learners. They reflect on their performance and accomplishments, critique themselves, and evaluate their progress. This leads to setting goals for further learning. Students learn that self-evaluation is an important part of self-improvement; portfolios encourage and support critical thinking through student self-reflection (Kingore, 2008). Students also apply decision-making skills in selecting certain works to be included and providing justifications for inclusion. In this sense, portfolios are open and always accessible to the student.

Closely related to self-assessment is the notion that portfolios involve *collaborative assessment*. Students learn that assessment is most effective when it is done with others. In addition to self-reflection, students learn from peer reviews and teacher feedback. They may evaluate the work of others and interact with teachers to come to a better understanding of the quality of their performance.

Another important advantage of portfolios is that they promote an ongoing process wherein students demonstrate performance, evaluate, and revise to learn and produce improved work. Assessment is continuous and integrally related to learning. Often formative as well as summative assessments are included. With portfolios, well-developed criteria are used to continually evaluate student progress and provide meaningful, targeted feedback.

Because most portfolios contain samples of student work over time, they focus on self-improvement rather than comparison with others. This reinforces self-referencing. When each student has a unique set of materials in his or her portfolio, assessment and learning are individualized. Thus, even though the overall learning targets are the same, portfolios easily accommodate individual differences among students and can show unique capabilities and accomplishments. As we will see, however, this is a disadvantage when it comes to scoring.

Motivation is enhanced as students see the link between their efforts and accomplishments and as they exert greater control over their learning. They become more engaged in learning because both instruction and assessment shift from being completely externally controlled by the teacher to a mix of external and internal control. A sixth-grade teacher relates this kind of impact on students (Martin-Kniep & Cunningham, 1998): "With this portfolio, I saw better work than I had in the past. Students were more excited than they had ever been in my class.

Teacher's Corner

Ann Marie Seely

National Board Certified High School English Teacher

Portfolio assessment works only when students understand where they are, where they need to go, and are provided with instruction to support the journey. Often, teachers see storing a student's writing in a folder as "portfolio assessment." They create a check sheet for each item that should be in the folder and grade based on completion. True portfolio assessment is personal, and it has to have an element of choice by the person being assessed. In order for students to choose the best pieces to represent their growth as writers, they need to know what constitutes success. Personal goal-setting based on clear criteria for success is important to the portfolio process as is frequent reflection on those goals. At the beginning of the year, students begin their portfolios with a writing sample. That sample is scored based on the rubric we will use throughout the year, but it is not graded. After students see the score, they are asked to write a reflection about their areas of strength and areas for improvement. This reflection becomes part of the portfolio. As students move through instruction and learn how to improve their writing, they revisit the samples in their portfolio and reflect on their growth. Finally, students are asked to select several pieces of writing that show their growth as writers. Students are allowed to revise those pieces and/or add outside writing—such as poems, short stories, other academic writing, and so on—in order to demonstrate their growth. Their final piece of the portfolio is a personal reflection. While this reflection might take the form of an essay, it might also be done orally (through a podcast, perhaps). Portfolio assessment takes time and dedication on the part of the teacher, but when implemented correctly, it can truly show individual student growth.

They were thrilled about what they had accomplished" (p. 60). As pointed out by Borich and Tombari (2004), this enables teachers to focus on students' persistence, effort, and willingness to change.

A hallmark of portfolios is that they contain examples of student products. This emphasis on products is helpful in several ways. First, products reinforce the importance of performance assessment to students and parents. Products provide excellent evidence to help teachers diagnose learning difficulties, meet with students, and provide individualized feedback. The concrete examples provided are very helpful in explaining student progress to parents. It is much easier to clarify reasons for your evaluations when you have a set of examples in a parent conference. These products can also be aligned to standards, showing how the work relates to levels of proficiency.

Finally, portfolios are flexible, especially digital ones. They can be adapted to different ages, subjects, types of products, abilities, interests, and learning styles. There is no single set of procedures, products, or grading criteria that must be used. You have the opportunity to customize your portfolio requirements to your needs and capabilities, to different learning targets, to available resources, and, most important, to differences among the students.

Disadvantages

There are some important limitations to using portfolios. Like other performance assessments, scoring is the major drawback. Not only is scoring time consuming, but research on the reliability/precision of scoring contents has shown that it is also difficult to obtain high inter-rater reliability. Inconsistent scoring results from criteria that are too general and can be interpreted differently, from such detailed criteria that raters are overwhelmed, or from the inadequate training of raters. Usually, criteria are too general, and raters have not received much training.

A second disadvantage is that effective portfolio assessment takes considerable time and resources. Many hours are needed to design the portfolios and scoring criteria, or learn the digital platform, and many more hours will be spent reviewing, scoring, and conferencing with students and parents. Additional time may be needed to obtain the training to feel confident and to implement the portfolios properly. You need to decide if this amount of time is worth the effort. Let me emphasize that time and resources are needed to do portfolio assessment *correctly*. It's not the same as simply producing a folder of student work. Effective portfolio assessment is very demanding; it requires time, expertise, and commitment.

A final disadvantage to consider is the potential for limited generalizability. With portfolios, you generalize from a sample of the examples and demonstrated performance according to the criteria to broader learning targets. In doing this, you will need to be careful that the generalization is justified, that what is in the portfolio provides each student with a fair opportunity to demonstrate his or her level of competency on the general learning target. For example, if you are making

FIGURE 11.2 Advantages and Disadvantages of Portfolio Assessment

Advantages	Disadvantages
• Promotes student self-assessment	• Scoring difficulties may lead to low reliability
• Promotes collaborative assessment	• Teacher training needed
• Enhances student motivation	• Time consuming to develop criteria, score, and meet with students
• Systematic assessment is ongoing	
• Focus is on improvement, not comparisons with others	• Students may not make good selections of which materials to include
• Focus is on students' strengths—what they can do	• Sampling of student products may lead to weak generalization
• Assessment process is individualized	• Parents may find portfolios difficult to understand
• Allows demonstration of unique accomplishments	
• Provides concrete examples for parent conferences	
• Products can be used for individualized teacher diagnosis	
• Flexibility and adaptability	

judgments about the ability of a student to communicate by writing and the only types of writing in the portfolio are creative and expository, then the validity of the conclusion about writing more generally is weak. Figure 11.2 summarizes the advantages and disadvantages of portfolio assessment.

Planning for Portfolio Assessment

The process of planning and implementing portfolio assessment is illustrated in Figure 11.3. Suggestions for planning are presented in the form of a checklist in Figure 11.4.

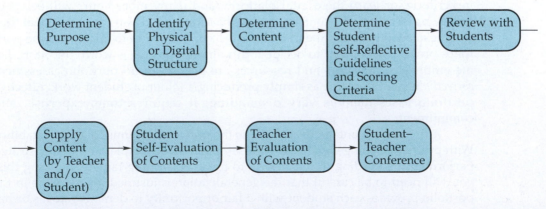

FIGURE 11.3 Steps for Planning and Implementing Portfolio Assessment

FIGURE 11.4   Checklist for Planning Portfolio Assessment

- Are learning targets clear?
- Are uses of the portfolio clear?
- Is the physical structure for holding materials in a paper portfolio adequate and easily accessed?
- Are technical resources and student computer skills adequate for digital portfolios?
- Are procedures for selecting the content clear?
- Does the nature of the content match the purpose?
- Are student self-reflective guidelines and questions clear?
- Are scoring criteria established?

Purpose

Designing a portfolio begins with a clear idea about the purpose of the assessment. This involves both the specific learning targets and the proposed use of the portfolio contents (Seitz & Bartholomew, 2008).

Learning Targets and Standards.   Portfolios are ideal for assessing product, skill, and reasoning targets, and for enhancing desired student dispositions. This is especially true for multidimensional skills such as writing, reading, and problem solving. With extensive self-reflection, critical thinking is an important target. Students also develop metacognitive and decision-making skills. In our standards-based education culture, it will probably be necessary to align the portfolio to content-area standards. Because standards are typically broader than learning targets, the alignment is made for the contents of the portfolio as a whole. Both with respect to cognitive skills required for completing work and for the level of proficiency demonstrated, the contents need to be matched to the standards. Effective portfolios are usually easily matched with many 21st-century skills and dispositions.

Uses.   The purpose of the portfolio will influence the contents and the criteria used for evaluation. For example, if the primary purpose is to document typical student work and progress, the portfolio will be highly individualized. It will tend to be a relatively loosely organized collection of samples selected by both the teacher and the student, accompanied by both student and teacher evaluations. There are many entries, representing different levels of performance, because the goal is to show what is typical, not necessarily the student's best work. If the portfolios are used primarily for demonstrating competence on state standards, there will be greater standardization about what to include and how the portfolios are reviewed, and most samples are selected by the teacher.

If the primary purpose is to illustrate what students are capable of doing, then the orientation is more toward a celebration type of portfolio. Only the student's best work is included. The emphasis is on student selection, self-reflection, and self-assessment, rather than on standardization for evaluation. This approach uses the portfolio to showcase what each individual has achieved. There may or may not be much indication of progress, but the emphasis is clearly on what has been accomplished rather than on improvement. This type of portfolio is ideal for project-based learning and instruction.

In a growth portfolio, improvement over time is shown by comparing early artifacts with later ones. A good example could be a persuasive letter to the editor. At the beginning of the semester students write such a letter. Later in the semester, after learning about what is needed to be persuasive, another letter is written. Growth is demonstrated by comparing the two products, using the same criteria.

Some portfolios are used to show parents and others what students have achieved. If this is the primary purpose, more attention needs to be given to what will make sense to parents, with somewhat less attention to student self-reflection. In contrast, if portfolios are used primarily diagnostically and with students to help them progress, then more time is spent with student–teacher conferences during the school day. If the purpose is to help students self-reflect or peer review, then structure and support for these activities need to be provided.

Portfolios are usually implemented for multiple purposes. Because your time and energy are limited, try to identify a *primary* purpose and design the portfolio based on that purpose. Wiggins (1998) points out that portfolio assessment is often implemented without sufficient attention to purpose. He indicates, for example, that portfolios can primarily serve as instruction or assessment tools, focus on documentation or evaluation, be controlled by the teacher or student, and contain a sample of best work or show change over time. The specific nature of portfolio assessment differs depending on the importance of these various purposes. As a consequence, determining primary purpose with clarity is critical.

Identify Physical and/or Digital Structure

Once your purpose has been determined, you need to think about some practical aspects of the portfolio. What will it look like? Paper-based portfolio content is printed and put in envelopes or folders. How large do the folders need to be? Where are they stored so that students can have easy access to them? Do you have boxes to put them in? Commonly used containers include cardboard boxes, file folders, file cabinets, cereal boxes, and accordion files. Putting folders on shelves where they are visible and accessible tells students they are important and should be used continuously. Your choices for these containers will influence to some extent what will be put in the portfolios. In addition, you will need to think about the actual arrangement of the documents in the portfolio. Is it done chronologically, by subject area, or by type of document? What materials will be needed to separate the documents?

Digital structure is varied, depending on whether you use an established platform or program, or if you design your own. Typically, the structure is either contained in an app or software program, with links to various artifacts, and often will be stored in a cloud or online with the company that provides the format. Larger data dashboards can be integrated electronically and allow you link the portfolio to grade reporting and other forms of assessment. Blogs, easily designed by teachers, can also be used for digital portfolios. Digital formats will continue to evolve, with increasingly sophisticated and adaptable structures that will better align portfolio assessment with standards, other assessments, and reports to parents.

Determine Nature of the Content

The content of a portfolio consists of work samples and student and teacher evaluations. Work samples are usually derived directly from instructional activities. The range of work samples is often extensive, determined to some extent by the subject. For example, in language arts you could use entries from student journals, book reports, audiotapes of oral presentations, workbook assignments, and poetry. In science, you might include lab reports, questions posed by students for further investigation, drawings, solutions to problems, videos, and pictures of projects.

Select categories of samples that will allow you to meet the purpose of the portfolio. If you need to show progress, select tasks and samples that can show improvement, such as initial drafts, rewritten drafts, and final papers. If you need to provide feedback to students on the procedures they use in putting together a report, be sure to include a summary of that process as part of the portfolio. Use work samples that capitalize on the advantages of portfolios, such as flexibility, individuality, and authenticity. The categories should allow for sufficient variation so that students can show individual work. This often means giving students choices about what they can include.

Figure 11.5 shows examples of the types of work samples that can be included.

Determine Student Self-Reflective Guidelines and Scoring Criteria

You need to establish guidelines for student self-reflection and the scoring criteria you will use when evaluating student performance. This should be done so that both the guidelines and criteria can be explained to students *before* they begin their work. In many cases, students can be involved in the development of self-reflective guidelines and scoring criteria, much as pointed out in the next chapter for self-assessment. By working on these together, students will develop greater ownership of the process and will have experience in working collaboratively with you. However, keep in mind that you have ultimate responsibility to control the process to ensure integrity and high quality.

Implementing Portfolio Assessment

Planning is complete. Now you begin the process of actually using the portfolios with your students. This begins with explaining to students what portfolios are and how they will be used. The checklist in Figure 11.6 summarizes the suggestions for effective implementation and use.

Secondary Writing Portfolio

- Initial draft of essay demonstrating your ability to argue a position.
- Final draft of essay demonstrating your ability to argue a position.
- Brief report prepared for a class project or presentation.
- Your best example of writing based on library research.
- An example of correspondence, such as a letter or email message.
- An example of an essay examination answer.
- An example of creative writing.
- Reflection indicating how you have improved your writing.

Secondary Geometry Portfolio

- Quizzes and chapter tests.
- Drawings that represent at least 10 different geometric shapes.
- Brief report of the use of geometry in two daily newspapers.
- List of geometric terms with definitions.
- Identify three different business logos using circles and identify essential geometric elements.
- Identify and illustrate three types of bridges that represent different geometric shapes.
- Find a newspaper or online ad that illustrates the effective use of triangles.
- Reflection indicating what you have learned about the use of geometric shapes.

Secondary History Portfolio

- Quizzes and chapter tests.
- Annotated bibliography of sources describing the Revolutionary War.
- Research report on the contributions of a major figure in the Revolutionary War.
- Map of Revolutionary War battles and movement of troops.
- Video reenactment of a historical event.
- Essay indicating what lessons were learned in the Revolutionary War that may have relevance today.
- A multimedia presentation on a selected significant event of the Revolutionary War.
- Journal entries from trip to Williamsburg, VA.
- Reflection indicating what products and activities about the Revolutionary War have had the greatest meaning to you.

Elementary Language Arts Portfolio

- Homework, quizzes, and chapter tests.
- Summary of the main ideas of three different types or genres of books.
- Completion of Reading Checklist indicating number of different types of articles and books read.
- Examples of initial and final drafts of two fictional short stories.
- Research paper on the lives of three children's books authors.
- An example of a poem.
- Log of reactions to reading books.
- Reflection indicating what reading and writing products and activities have had the greatest meaning to you.

FIGURE 11.5 **Examples of Portfolio Contents**

Source: Based on Burke, 2009.

FIGURE 11.6   Checklist for Implementing and Using Portfolios

✓ Are students knowledgeable about what a portfolio is and how it will
   be used?
✓ Do students know why portfolios are important?
✓ Do students have the necessary technical skills to use a digital portfolio?
✓ Are students responsible for or involved in selecting the content?
✓ Are there a sufficient number of work samples but not too many?
✓ Is a table of contents included?
✓ Are specific self-evaluation questions provided?
✓ Is the checklist of contents complete?
✓ Are scoring criteria for individual items and entire contents clear?
✓ Are individualized teacher-written comments provided?
✓ Are student–teacher conferences included?

Review with Students

Because many students will not be familiar with portfolios, you will need to
explain carefully what is involved and what they will be doing. Begin with your
learning targets, show examples, and give students opportunities to ask questions. Try to provide just enough structure so students can get started without
telling them exactly what to do. Put yourself in the student's place—if you had to
do this new thing, what would be your response and what would you like to
know?

Supplying Portfolio Content

Who selects the content of the portfolio—the student, teacher, or both? If both the
student and teacher supply samples, what should the proportions be? Are the
entries prescribed? Answers to these questions depend on the age and previous
experience of students and the purpose of the portfolio. For obvious reasons, preschool and primary students shouldn't assume sole responsibility for selecting all
the samples for their portfolios, although they certainly can be consulted and play
an active role in selection. Older students should assume more responsibility for
selection, although even older students who are inexperienced with portfolios
will initially need considerable structure. Even if students are primarily responsible for selecting the contents, it will be helpful to provide guidelines about the
nature of the works to be included.

   When deciding who will select the content you need to consider somewhat
conflicting goals. On the one hand, you want to foster student ownership and
involvement, which is enhanced when students have input into what to include.
On the other hand, you will probably need some degree of standardization so that
equitable evidence of student performance toward achieving standards is provided. This is best accomplished with greater teacher control. One effective compromise is for students and teachers to decide together what to include. For

example, students can select, in consultation with the teacher, three pieces they believe demonstrate their writing ability and progress for a semester. Another approach is to give students some restrictions and include student explanations of the choices. The teacher might prescribe the categories of writing samples, such as poem, persuasive essay, and technical report, and students would select within each of these categories. Regardless of who makes the selections, however, there need to be clear guidelines for what is included, when it should be submitted, and how it should be labeled (Green & Johnson, 2010).

Questions about the number of samples of student work also need to be answered. You will find that too many indiscriminate samples become overwhelming and difficult to organize, but too few items may not provide enough information. A portfolio with more complex products that takes a longer time to create will have fewer samples than one that illustrates the growth of a number of relatively simple skills. A general rule of thumb for a documentation portfolio is to add one artifact every week or two, for a total of 10 to 15 different items for the year. For showcase portfolios, as few as three samples may be sufficient (a final project may be represented with one). Some teachers differentiate between a *working* portfolio, in which students keep most of their work, and a *display* or *final* portfolio, in which selections are made from the working portfolio. Haertel (1990) suggests a value-added approach, in which students include only those samples that contribute to understanding how the student has improved or progressed. That is, the student or teacher might ask, "What value is added by each piece of evidence?" If a piece doesn't contribute something new, it's not included.

To organize the portfolio, it is best to include a table of contents that can be expanded with each new entry. The table, which should be located at the beginning, should include a brief description, date produced, date submitted, and date evaluated. A sample table can be provided, but ownership is enhanced if students have some flexibility to develop their own table or overview. Directions to students could be something like, "What do you need to tell your parents so they can understand what is in your portfolio and what it means?"

Student Self-Reflection

One of the most challenging yet rewarding aspects of using portfolios is getting students to the point where they are comfortable, confident, and accurate in analyzing and criticizing their own work. These *reflective* or *self-evaluation* activities need to be taught. Most students have had little experience with reflection, so one of the first steps in using a portfolio is getting students comfortable with simple and nonthreatening forms of self-reflection. One useful strategy to accomplish this is to begin with teacher modeling and critiques. Once students understand what is involved by seeing examples (e.g., using an overhead of work from previous, unnamed students), they can begin to engage in their own reflections orally with each other. After they have engaged in these elementary forms of reflection, are they prepared to proceed to more complex self-evaluations? This can take several weeks. A good way to introduce students to self-reflection is to have them label various pieces as "Best Work," "Most Creative," "Most Difficult," "Most Effort," "Most Fun," "Most Improved," and so on.

The next step could be the use of specific items to structure student evaluations. For example:

This piece shows that I've met the standard because _____
This piece shows that I really understand the process because _____
If I could show this piece to anyone, I would pick _____ because _____
The piece that was my biggest challenge was _____ because _____
One thing that I have learned from doing this piece is that I _____

Finally, questions can be asked to give students less structure in how to respond:

What did you learn from writing this piece?
What would you have done differently if you had had more time?
What are your greatest strengths and weaknesses in this sample?
What would you do differently if you did this over?
What problems or obstacles did you experience when doing this? How would you overcome these problems or obstacles next time?
Is this your best work? Why or why not?
What will you do for your next work?
If you could work more on this piece of writing, what would you do?
Which sample would you say is most unsatisfying? Give specific reasons for your evaluation. How would you revise it so that it would be more satisfying?
How did your selection change from rough draft to final copy?

Self-reflection responses are insights into how involved students have been in reaching the learning target, what the students perceive to be their strengths, and how instruction can be tailored to meet needs (sometimes a student's perceived strengths are inaccurate and need to be corrected). Figures 11.7 and 11.8 present examples of student responses to self-reflective prompts. In Figure 11.7, students were asked to select a piece of writing that "is important to them," and explain why they made the selection. In this example, the responses from the same three students are indicated, appearing in the same order. The answers, although varied, illustrate what students think about themselves and what they believe they need to work on in the future. Figure 11.8 shows how younger students, in this case third graders, can be involved in self-reflection.

Some portfolios include peer evaluations. These can be very helpful, especially when students are beginning to get used to the idea of self-reflection and you are trying to establish a trusting environment. The focus of peer evaluations is on analysis and the constructive, supportive criticism of strategies, styles, and other concrete aspects of the product.

The most comprehensive reflection is done on all the contents of the portfolio at the end of the semester or year. This evaluation focuses much more on the

FIGURE 11.7 Middle and High School Student Responses to Self-Reflection Questions

---

Why did you select this particular piece of writing?

"This is my best piece of the year, clearly the strongest."
"I put more effort into this paper than any of the others."
"You can see how much detail is included and how many references I used."

What do you see as the special strengths of this paper?

"It shows that I am able to write a good piece that is unique to me."
"The use of many references."
"The correct use of grammar."

What was especially important when you were writing this piece?

"I wanted to write a piece that people would find different and interesting."
"To give it my best shot, to really try hard."

What have you learned about writing from your work on this piece?

"That I might begin writing one thing and end up writing something else."
"Writing like this is not as hard as I thought it would be."
"I learned that it's important to check back even when you think it's good."

If you could go on working on this piece, what would you do?

"I think I would add some information to make my case stronger."
"Give more detail."
"I might explain more about why the students decided to go to the game."

What kind of writing would you like to do in the future?

"I think more creative short stories would be great."
"Maybe it would be fun to write a murder mystery."

---

overall learning target. Here are some examples of questions to ask for this more comprehensive self-reflection.

> How do you think your writing has changed this year?
> What have you learned this year about how to write?
> What new things did you learn this year about writing?
> What pieces of work show how much better you write now compared to the start of the year?

Student self-reflection can also include comments or a review by parents. One of the advantages of using portfolios is that they are well suited to parent involvement. At the beginning of the year, you will need to inform parents about what portfolios are and how they can actively participate to be helpful. Students can consult their parents when selecting work samples, and parents can help students reflect on their work. Informally, parents can continuously provide advice and encouragement. More formally, parents can complete a form or answer a

LANGUAGE ARTS PORTFOLIO
STUDENT REFLECTION

Name: _Patricia_ _____   Date: _____

This piece was selected because:

I was very happy with it
My handwritting is good.

This piece is good because:

It shows that I can
write.

One thing I learned from doing this piece was that:

If I try harder I can
do well.

What I would do to make the piece better:

Make it longer.

FIGURE 11.8   Elementary Student Self-Reflection

specific set of questions. Students can then incorporate parent comments and suggestions into their own reflection.

Teacher Evaluation and Feedback

Teachers evaluate the contents of a portfolio with checklists of contents, evaluations of the overall quality of how well the portfolio has been put together, evaluations of individual entries, and overall evaluations of learning targets and standards. We'll consider each of these types.

Checklists of Contents.   A summary to ensure that the contents of the portfolio are complete is often provided in the form of a simple checklist. The checklist can vary according to the level of specificity desired and by the audience. Some checklists are relatively brief, and others are long and detailed. Others can be designed for teachers, administrators, or parents. Student checklists tend to be brief, but those for teachers and schools are typically more comprehensive.

Portfolio Structure Evaluation.   Portfolios can be evaluated according to how well students have demonstrated skill in completing the structural requirements, such as the selection of samples, thoroughness, appearance, self-reflection, and organization. These aspects can be evaluated by assigning points to each aspect according to a scale (e.g., 5 = excellent, 1 = poor), by making written comments, or both. When evaluating selections, consider the diversity of the samples, the time periods represented, and overall appropriateness. The quality of student reflection can be judged by the clarity and depth of thought, the level of analysis, and the clarity of communication. Organization can be evaluated by using a checklist to indicate whether required components are included, properly sequenced, and clearly labeled.

Evaluations of Individual Entries.   The evaluation of each individual entry in the portfolio can be accomplished with the scoring criteria and rubrics that were discussed in Chapter 10, albeit with much less standardization. Many teachers find that more individualized, informal feedback on work samples is effective and efficient, particularly when many items are included in the portfolio. Furthermore, it is likely that not every entry will be evaluated in the same way. However, it is important to provide sufficient feedback so that students know what has been done well and what needs to be improved.

Evaluation of Entire Contents.   The learning targets and standards for the portfolio as a whole are not the same as those for individual entries. The language of the evaluation reflects the more general nature of the target or standard. The words used may emphasize the developmental nature of learning when the purpose is to focus on student improvement and progress. Thus, phrases such as "students demonstrate the ability to understand increasingly complex software programs," "a greater number of self-evaluative criteria applied," "increased understanding of," or "increased ability to" are used. You will also want to be sure to include individualized written comments for each student. This descriptive summary of performance and progress should highlight changes that have occurred, strengths, and areas that need improvement. It's usually best to point out the strengths and improvements first and then use language to address weaknesses about what needs improvement. Words such as *improving*, *developing*, *partial*, and even *novice* are better than *unacceptable* or *inadequate*.

Student–Teacher Conferences

The final step in implementing portfolios is conducting a conference with each student to review the contents, student reflections, and your evaluations of individual

FIGURE 11.9   Documentation Portfolio Implementation Timelines

Unit	Semester	Yearlong
• Collect contents for three or four weeks. • Reflect on contents two weeks prior to the end of the unit. • Conduct conferences and grade in the last week.	• Collect contents for the entire semester. • Review contents at the end of each quarter. • Select seven to ten products three to four weeks before the end of the semester. • Allow one week for students to reflect on contents. • Conduct conferences and grade in the last week.	• Collect contents over the entire year. • Review contents at the end of each quarter. • Student reflections conducted at the end of each quarter. • Select final contents four weeks before the end of school. • Conferences held last three weeks of the year. • Grade last week of the year.

items and all of the work together as related to learning targets. Conferences with students should be scheduled throughout the year; some suggest having one conference each month at the elementary level. Early in the year the conferences can be used to clarify purposes and procedures, answer questions, and establish trust.

It is best if students are given some guidelines to prepare for each conference. During the conference, allow the student to do most of the talking. Have students compare their reflections with your evaluations and make plans for subsequent work. Although weaknesses and areas for improvement need to be covered, show students what is possible and their progress, rather than dwelling on what is wrong. Make sure that at the end of the conference there is a plan of action for the future. Limit the conference to no more than 10 or 15 minutes. You may want to have students take notes about what was discussed in the conference and make your own brief notes. Focus on one or two major topics or areas at each conference. This helps ensure a full and thoughtful discussion, rather than a superficial treatment of several areas.

Figure 11.9 summarizes steps in the implementation of portfolio assessment, with an emphasis on when activities take place and time needed for completion.

Digital Portfolios

An increasingly popular approach to portfolio assessment is to create, store, and report materials electronically. A **digital portfolio** (or *eportfolio*) is a dynamic, changing electronic collection of evidence, typically stored and managed online or with software apps and programs. This type of portfolio can have the same purposes as a hard-copy file, but it allows for some additional features to further extend learning, and encourages individualized, engaged, self-directed learning on more authentic topics. As illustrated in Figure 11.10, a digital format can be used to focus on new learning targets. Students and teachers are able to do more with the results and relate what is stored to other learning activities and goals. Students are encouraged to analyze information, to connect information in new ways, and to collaborate with

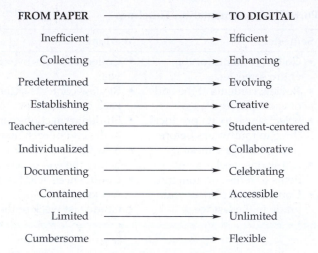

FROM PAPER		TO DIGITAL
Inefficient	⟶	Efficient
Collecting	⟶	Enhancing
Predetermined	⟶	Evolving
Establishing	⟶	Creative
Teacher-centered	⟶	Student-centered
Individualized	⟶	Collaborative
Documenting	⟶	Celebrating
Contained	⟶	Accessible
Limited	⟶	Unlimited
Cumbersome	⟶	Flexible

FIGURE 11.10   Added Benefits of Digital Portfolios
Source: Based on Barrett (2007).

others in ways that result in more revision of initial work (Beckers, Dolmans, & van Merrienboer, 2016). A large amount of information can be stored efficiently and securely, organized in meaningful ways. Students are able to add examples, reflect, draw conclusions on an ongoing basis, and use their portfolios for several years. When used correctly, then, digital portfolios encourage students to be active participants in authentic learning, stressing individuality, creativity, and use of their own voice. Each student can incorporate their own style and individuality. Often portfolios become compelling stories of students' journeys. Digital portfolios, unlike hardcopy portfolios, are easily accessible and transportable. Most can be accessed anytime, anywhere. This promotes greater parental involvement in student work that can improve their understanding of learning and achievement.

An obvious advantage of having an electronic portfolio is that it encourages and makes possible the use of multimedia elements. This feature is very motivating for students. It promotes the use of unique materials that reflect students' individual voices. There is more student ownership, with opportunities to build self-efficacy and pride. Adding links to websites, videos, other students' work, voice recordings, photographs, blogs, audio recordings, and scanned documents, and the ability to synthesize evidence from a variety of sources, engages students in ways that are difficult to achieve with traditional paper-based portfolios. Hyperlinks can be used to quickly access additional material. Students are able to store, refine, and reuse the evidence. How better to show progress in reading than to include videos of a student reading a passage from one month to the next? Each clip could be included in the portfolio. How students progress in their drawing can be captured by taking photos of increasingly complex drawings during the year. They can be easily loaded into a digital portfolio. Speaking a foreign language can be recorded at the beginning of the semester and again at the end, stored digitally, and compared to show growth. The possibilities are endless!

Electronic portfolios are excellent in showcasing student thinking and creativity for college admissions or selection into specialty high schools. For example, in 2016 a "senior portfolio" was used by Northridge Academy High School, in California, containing 13 sections:

1: Letter of Introduction to the readers of the portfolio
2: My certificates, scholarships, awards, and report card copies
3: Resume
4: Brag Sheet
5: Letters of recommendation
6: Autobiographical incident essay
7: Post-secondary plan
8: UC, CSU, private, community college or post-secondary program application/s
9: Proof of filing FAFSA
10: Four pieces of my quality work with a reflection
11: Service learning project
12: Job application
13: "My Journey" PowerPoint

Similarly, electronic portfolios are excellent for student projects. Here are a few examples:

Is running harmful or helpful?
How films are made.
The psychosocial challenges of single parent homes.
The effect of music on learning.
Art therapy for children.
Cybersecurity and individual rights.
The decline of religion in America.
Homelessness in America.
You are what your read and listen to.
Breaking the cycle of poverty.

It's not hard to imagine how multimedia could be used for each of these and how students could be very engaged and motivated in creating the pieces for the portfolio. This shows how digital portfolios can take both teaching and assessment to a higher level.

Some apps, such as FreshGrade, allow teachers to record students, upload to tablets or mobile devices, and incorporate into a structured digital portfolio. The portfolios show each student's work, allow filtering by product, subject, date, and other delimiters, and provide a means for the teacher to respond electronically with feedback. GoogleApps can be used for digital portfolios by integrating Google Notebook, GoogleDocs, PhotoBooth, YouTube, Picasa, iMovie, and Garage Band into a portfolio stored on a local server or cloud-based. Often blogs are utilized. Figure 11.11 illustrates the use of Kidblog to create a science portfolio.

Overview

As a new project in science class we will be using KidBlog and (**Mr. Clauset's Class Blog**) to create digital portfolios for our work in science.

Each student has a blog page that will be used to document his or her tech projects. The blog will handle videos, animations, audio podcasts, pictures, and articles. You get to design your own blog page, create your own title, choose your own topics, and use the software of your choice.

Possible topics include: Weather, NASA satellites and remote sensing, Space, Astronomy, Mars probes and robots, Earth's Interior, Pangaea, Continental Drift, Dinosaurs, Earthquakes, Tsunamis, Volcanoes, Density, Climate Change, Geologic Time, Geology, Planetary Change Over Time, & Software Screencasts.

Thirty-eight percent (38%) of your grade in science will come from the QUANTITY of digital artifacts that you personally produce each month and describe on your Kidblog section to showcase what you have learned in science or what you are interested in, based on the above list of acceptable science topics that tie in with our curriculum.

We'll devote each Friday of class time to working on these projects. Projects are due at the end of each month. Grades are determined by the QUANTITY of videos, podcasts, articles, animations, blog posts, etc. that you produce and describe or include on your blog page. You can create videos, podcasts, comics, blog entries, Google Sites webpages, or screencasts of project software.

Possible applications include: Audioboo (Internet-based & iOS free app), iMovie (Mac OS & iPad), Photo Story 3 (Microsoft free download), Google Sites (Internet-based webpage development), Explain Everything (iPad), Audacity (open source on all platforms)/Goldwave (class editing), Kidblog (use your Moodle password), Animation software (your choice), or Screencasting software (like Screencast-O-Matic).

FIGURE 11.11   **Example of Use of Blog for Creating a Portfolio.**

Source: Accessed August 26, 2016 from http://www.tclauset.org/c5/media/digital-portfolios/

Note how each student designs their own portfolio and the range of artifacts that can be included. You will easily find digital portfolio platforms for your grade level and subject by searching the Internet, though it's probable that your school system and/or colleagues have had experience and offer products to get you started.

Of course, using electronic portfolios depends on having sufficient hardware and/or online access, adequate teacher and student competence in using computer-based information, and adequate technical support. Storage could be on a network server, tablet, cloud, or on classroom computers. There are also a number of options for electronic formats, digitizing, and platforms for presentation of results (Worcester, 2009). With the Internet, Web 2.0 tools, and social media, the possibilities for engaging, efficient, and impactful eportfolios are immense (Belgrad, 2013). It is probably just a matter of time before digital formats will replace traditional physical folders.

Although there may be a learning curve for both teachers and students (often more for teachers!) to have the skills necessary to digitize portfolios, electronic formats can be powerful in enhancing student engagement and learning. And, you may well find that using portfolios will impact your teaching in significant ways. Teachers who use portfolios report increased use of formative assessment, authentic assessment, greater differentiation of instruction, more individualization, and greater emphasis on 21st-century skills (McLeod & Vasinda, 2009).

Summary

The essence of portfolios is to gather and evaluate student work products that demonstrate progress toward specified learning targets and attainment of learning standards. By combining principles of performance assessment with student self-reflection, portfolios and eportfolios can be powerful tools to improve student learning. With the flexibility inherent in portfolios, it is possible to individualize assessment so that you can maximize meaningful feedback to each student. Other major points in the chapter include the following:

- Portfolio assessment is systematic and purposeful.
- Portfolio assessment includes student selection of contents and student self-reflection.
- Different types of portfolios include documentation (celebration, competence, project) and growth.
- Portfolios integrate assessment with instruction by focusing on improvement and progress.
- Portfolios are adaptable to individual students.
- Limitations include reliability/precision of scoring and time for preparation and implementation.

- Portfolios may result in limited generalizability.
- Planning for portfolio assessment includes the identification of learning targets and uses, physical structures, content, guidelines for student self-reflection, and scoring criteria.
- Implementing portfolio assessment includes reviewing with students, supplying content, student self-evaluations, teacher evaluations, and student–teacher conferences.
- Students should be meaningfully involved in the selection of work samples.
- Just enough work samples need to be included to meet the purpose of the portfolio.
- A table of contents should be included in the portfolio.
- Student self-evaluation needs to be taught. Students progress to eventually become skilled at analyzing and critiquing their own and others' works.
- The teacher evaluates checklists of contents, the student's ability to put together the portfolio, individual items, and the content as a whole with scores from rubrics and written comments.
- Student–teacher conferences should be held throughout the year to review progress and establish plans.
- Digital portfolios offer extensive opportunities to extend and showcase student learning.

Introductory Case Study Answer

Khalil erred by not being aware of the characteristics of effective portfolios:

1. By including only summative assessments (not formative assessments), he used a documentation of mastery, not a growth perspective. The writing pieces in the portfolios do not compare early products with later ones. The students' portfolios did not reveal student proficiency over time, but rather demonstrated accomplishment at one point in the year.
2. Khalil selected the pieces instead of allowing for some student choice.
3. The writing pieces selected for the portfolio were not aligned with specific learning targets, but rather instead with styles of writing.
4. Khalil did not include his evaluation of students' writing.
5. The portfolios were maintained by Khalil, not the students.
6. Students' self-evaluation of their writing occurred at the end of the grading period rather than being a continuous process over time.
7. Khalil did not teach students how to self-evaluate and provided no structure for student self-evaluation efforts.
8. Khalil set the students' writing goals instead of students' self-reflection leading to goals.
9. Khalil's focus was on comparing students' writing to others instead of focusing on individual improvement.
10. Khalil did conduct student-teacher conferences to review the contents or students' self-evaluations.

Suggestions for Action Research

1. Locate two or three examples of digital portfolios that are used by different teachers. Review the contents of the portfolios carefully, looking for characteristics that have been discussed in this chapter. How are the portfolios alike, and how are they different? Are they being used for different purposes? Is the structure and content appropriate for the intended use? Are they structured to engage students and allow for individualized work?

2. Interview students who have had some experience with portfolios. Ask them what they like and don't like about doing portfolios, how much time it takes them to complete their work, and what the teacher does to help them. Focus on student self-reflection. Ask the students how they have self-evaluated themselves and what they think they have learned from the process.

3. Visit two or three classrooms and see how portfolios are used. If possible, talk with the teachers to get their views about how to organize portfolios so that they are efficient.

4. Devise a digital student portfolio assignment for students. Include each of the steps in Figure 11.3, and include examples where possible. Then ask two or three teachers to review your assignment and give you feedback on how it could be improved, how much time it would take to implement, how realistic it would be, and what students would probably get out of it.

MyEdLab Self-Check 11.1

MyEdLab Self-Check 11.2

MyEdLab Self-Check 11.3

MyEdLab Self-Check 11.4

MyEdLab Application Exercise 11.1   Portfolio Assessment: Purpose

MyEdLab Application Exercise 11.2   Portfolio Assessment for Problem-Based Learning (PBL)

Assessing "Noncognitive" Dispositions and Skills

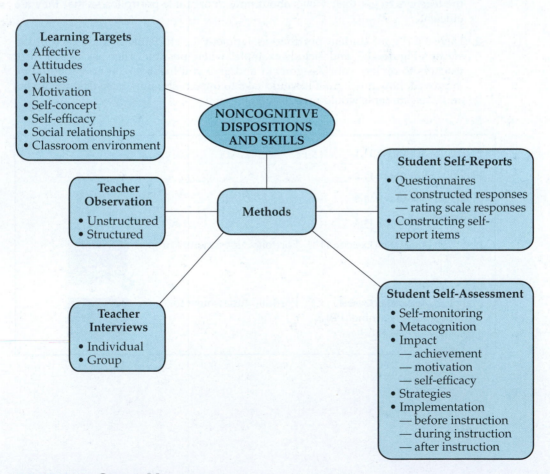

Learning Targets
- Affective
- Attitudes
- Values
- Motivation
- Self-concept
- Self-efficacy
- Social relationships
- Classroom environment

NONCOGNITIVE DISPOSITIONS AND SKILLS

Methods

Teacher Observation
- Unstructured
- Structured

Teacher Interviews
- Individual
- Group

Student Self-Reports
- Questionnaires
  — constructed responses
  — rating scale responses
- Constructing self-report items

Student Self-Assessment
- Self-monitoring
- Metacognition
- Impact
  — achievement
  — motivation
  — self-efficacy
- Strategies
- Implementation
  — before instruction
  — during instruction
  — after instruction

CHAPTER 12   Concept Map

Learning Outcomes

After reading this chapter, you should be able to:

12.1   Understand the nature of noncognitive dispositions and trait targets, including definitions of different attributes such as attitudes, self-concept, values, and student self-assessment.

12.2   Identify what is needed for effective assessment of noncognitive dispositions and traits. Specifically, know what is what is needed to assure reliable/precise and valid scores.

12.3   Be able to design questions for student self-reports of noncognitive dispositions and traits, including question stems and response scales for both selected- and constructed-response formats, that are appropriate for a specified grade level.

12.4   Understand how student self-assessment is a key element of learning. Identify how to address the improvement of self-assessment before, during, and after instruction, and what strategies can be used to measure self-assessment.

Introductory Case Study

How Should Miguel Evaluate Each Disposition?

At Miguel's mid-year evaluation, his principal, Cindy said, "Miguel, based on your students' midterm exam scores, I believe your students are mastering the cognitive learning targets for AP calculus. However, do you know if your students are developing positive noncognitive dispositions towards learning calculus?" Miguel looked confused.

Cindy elaborated explaining to Miguel that "positive noncognitive dispositions support and influence learning. They maximize students' motivation to learn, enhance students' beliefs that they can learn, and ultimately lead to effective student learning." Cindy provided Miguel with a list of noncognitive disposition traits and asked him to pick three he thought would be most appropriate to assess for his AP calculus students. Miguel picked interest in mathematics, self-efficacy, and altruism.

Cindy then challenged Miguel to determine how he would assess these noncognitive learning targets, and provide data to her regarding each target. Cindy encouraged him to use three different assessment methods—one for each disposition.

As Miguel walked out of his evaluation he was perplexed, so he went to his collaborating teacher and asked for help. The collaborating teacher, Josie, asked Miguel to explain why he picked these three dispositions.

Miguel said he first picked *interest* in math because he believed if he knew which students were not interested in math, he might be able to work with these students to help them see the applicability of math to their future careers. This might increase their motivation to learn. Second, Miguel said he picked *self-efficacy* to determine students' self-perceptions of their capabilities to learn calculus. Miguel believed strongly that students' beliefs about their abilities to be successful in calculus were directly linked to their success. He knew he might need to provide more targeted feedback to those with less self-efficacy. Lastly, Miguel commented that he picked *altruism* because students' willingness to help each other on calculus problems led to effective student learning. Miguel knew students who could explain calculus to others had a better grasp than those who couldn't explain. Knowing who was willing to help others might give him information regarding students' mastery of cognitive learning targets.

As you read this chapter, think about how Miguel should evaluate each disposition. Which disposition would be best evaluated using teacher observations, teacher interviews, and self-report questionnaire/survey? What is the purpose of student self-assessments? If Miguel incorporated these into his class, how would students benefit? What does Miguel need to be aware of if he decides to incorporate self-assessments?

C hapters 8 to 11 focused on what have traditionally been called *cognitive* learning targets and skills. We now turn to a set of student attributes that quite frankly are equally important, especially with the new emphasis on 21st-century dispositions. These traits are often referred to as either *"affective," "social-emotional,"* or *"noncognitive,"* mostly to distinguish them from so-called cognitive targets such as knowledge, understanding, and thinking skills such as critical thinking and reasoning. Cognitive targets are relatively easy to identify and specify; everything not captured by assessment of achievement and aptitude defaults to the catchall noncognitive (though as we'll see what is called noncognitive includes thinking!). Regardless of how they are labeled, these dispositions and traits must be appreciated and attended to, and occasionally systematically assessed by teachers. In this chapter the terms *disposition* and *trait* refer to attitudes, beliefs, grit, mindset, self-control, goal orientation, and values that are part of a student's character and personality. Skills in this context are both interpersonal and intrapersonal (such as self-regulation and recognizing one's own emotional state). We'll first consider some reasons why these types of targets are essential for success in school and life.

Are "Noncognitive" Disposition and Skill Targets Important?

The simple answer is *absolutely*. There is no question that positive noncognitive dispositions and skills are essential to be successful in school, career, and life (West, Kraft, Finn, Martin, Duckworth, Gabrieli, & Gabrieli, 2016). Students need traits such as being responsible, having integrity, being able to self-monitor, work collaboratively with others, persevere in the face of obstacles, and a host of other attitudes, personality characteristics, values, and skills. In addition, much research has established clear linkages between affect and learning (Ormrod, 2011; Popham, 2009; Rivers, Hagelskamp, & Brackett, 2013; Stiggins, 2007). Students are more proficient at problem solving when they enjoy what they are doing and see a value in the outcomes, and will be more motivated to exert maximum effort on assessments (Wise & Smith, 2016). Students who are in a good mood and emotionally involved are more likely to pay attention to information, remember it, rehearse it meaningfully, and apply it. Too much anxiety interferes with learning and test-taking; an optimum level of arousal is needed for maximum performance. Classrooms with more positive "climates" foster student engagement and learning much more than do classrooms with negative climates. Furthermore, longitudinal research has shown that such qualities predict economic, social, psychologic, and physical well-being (Duckworth & Yeager, 2015). From practical experience, teachers know that students who are confident about their ability to learn, who like the school subjects they study, who have a positive attitude toward learning, who respect others, and who show a concern for others are much more likely to be motivated and involved in learning. Every good teacher knows the value of noncognitive attributes, with good reason.

So why aren't these kinds of traits normally considered specific learning targets for which instruction is focused, and why are they rarely systematically assessed? Four reasons seem likely. First, especially in the higher grades, schooling is organized by subject matter. Cognitive subject matter targets have always mattered most (as evidenced by high-stakes accountability testing and teacher evaluation based on measures of student growth in achievement), and there are some who believe that the development of attitudes and values should be a home and family responsibility. Second, defining traits such as attitudes, interests, self-concept, grit, perseverance, adaptability, and integrity is difficult. Each of them is abstract and sometimes "fuzzy." It's hard to get consensus about the nature of each trait.

Third, the assessment of noncognitive dispositions and skills, which often depends on student self-reports, is fraught with difficulties. The many potential sources of error in measuring these traits often result in low reliability/precision and little evidence of validity. Student motivation is a primary concern. Students need to take such assessments seriously to provide accurate results, yet many may be inhibited if their responses are not anonymous. Students find it easy to fake responses on self-report instruments if the results are to be used for grading or some other purpose. They may want to please the teacher with positive responses. Another source of error is that many dispositions are easily influenced by momentary or temporary moods. This is especially true for younger students. Teacher bias can also have a significant influence on what may be recorded or perceived.

Fourth, because of differences brought about by context, backgrounds, and culture, students and teachers have a different frame of reference about how to understand and report on different traits. A perception about what constitutes self-efficacy may vary systematically for students at different ability levels or different cultures. For high-achieving students, self-efficacy related to math may be low if they are struggling, despite the fact that they are in an honors math class. It's all a matter of perspective, which often depends on your frame of reference.

What cannot be disputed is that many "noncognitive" traits, in the form of attitudes, self-beliefs, and values, are inexorably intertwined with achievement and student performance. Table 12.1 shows the close relationships between achievement and affect. Students who do well are more positive about themselves

TABLE 12.1   Relationships Between Learning Success and Affect

Successful Learning	Unsuccessful Learning
Hopeful	Hopeless
Optimistic	Pessimistic
Feels positive	Feels negative
Wants more success	Wants to avoid further failure
Seeks challenges	Avoids challenges
Seeks and uses feedback	Sees feedback as criticism
Empowered	Embarrassed
Confident	Unsure
Engaged	Disengaged
Positive attitudes	Negative attitudes
Values learning	Avoids learning
Seeks new ideas	Avoids new ideas

Source: Based in part on Stiggins (2007).

and what they are learning, whereas struggling students tend to have negative affect. As you can no doubt surmise, these "feelings" affect student engagement, student motivation, and subsequent achievement, which in turn promote certain emotional responses to perceived success and failure. Students with positive affective reactions are less deterred when they don't do well and are motivated to learn from feedback. Those with negative emotional responses will be less inclined to use their performance and feedback in meaningful ways.

What are the advantages, then, for you to systematically setting and assessing noncognitive disposition and skill targets? Positive noncognitive dispositions and skills are essential for:

- Effective learning
- Being an involved and productive member of our society
- Preparing for occupational and vocational satisfaction and productivity (e.g., work habits, a willingness to learn, interpersonal skills)
- Maximizing the motivation to learn now and in the future
- Preventing students from dropping out of school
- Enhancing students' beliefs that they are capable of learning (self-efficacy)
- Enhancing perseverance in the face of difficulty
- Enhancing students' altruism

Virtually all schools' and school districts' mission statements include noncognitive outcomes, and teachers constantly assess affect informally during instruction. The following sections discuss suggestions and techniques for taking noncognitive outcomes to a more serious level. What better way can you signal to students that these traits are critical to their future success than by talking about and measuring them? We'll begin by considering more specifically the nature of some noncognitive targets, then look at how to assess them.

What Are Dispositional Traits and Learning Targets?

Dispositions consist of a range of intrapersonal attitudes, interests, values, character, and personality traits. As mentioned, many use the term *affective* to refer to noncognitive traits. *Affect*, however, has a technical meaning that is rather restrictive: the emotions or feelings we have toward someone or something. Since attitudes, values, self-concept, citizenship, and other noncognitive traits involve thinking and beliefs, they involve more than emotion or feelings. Nevertheless, the literature refers to a range of possible outcomes as affective (including the *Taxonomy of Educational Objectives: Handbook II: Affective Domain* [Krathwohl, Bloom, & Masia, 1964]). I have summarized many noncognitive traits and skills in Table 12.2. Although there isn't space to consider each of these in detail, I do want to look at a few of the more important ones. Because of the general nature of the term

TABLE 12.2   Noncognitive Traits and Skills

Trait	Definition
Attitudes	Predisposition to respond favorably or unfavorably to specified situations, concepts, objects, institutions, or persons
Interests	Personal preference for certain kinds of activities
Values	Importance, worth, or usefulness of modes or conduct and end states of existence
Self-Monitoring	Conscious awareness of being on-track, on-task, and evaluating work
Integrity	Honesty and truthfulness of one's actions
Motivation	Desire and willingness to be engaged in behavior and intensity of involvement
Self-Efficacy	Self-perceptions of capabilities to learn
Self-Esteem	Attitudes toward oneself; degree of self-respect, worthiness, or desirability of self-concept
Adaptability	Ability and willingness to cope with changing conditions
Interpersonal Relationships	Nature of interpersonal interactions and functioning in group settings
Altruism	Willingness to help others
Perseverance	Willingness to continue trying in the face of difficulties or barriers
Grit	Perseverance of effort to achieve long-term goals in the face of obstacles and challenges

noncognitive, it is best to use these more specific dispositions and skills when developing your learning targets.

Attitude Targets

Attitudes are internal states and beliefs that vary from positive to negative. The internal state is some degree of positive/negative or favorable/unfavorable reaction toward an object, situation, issue, activity, person, group of objects, general environment, or group of persons. Thus, we typically think about attitudes *toward* something. In schools, that may be learning, subjects, teachers, other students, homework, tests, and other referents. Usually, then, you can identify the positive or negative attitudes that you want to foster or at least monitor. Some examples are:

A Positive *Attitude Toward*

Learning
School
Math, Science, English, and other subjects
Homework
Classroom rules
Teachers
Working with others
Staying on task
Mistakes
Taking responsibility for one's acts

A Negative *Attitude Toward*

Cheating
Drug use
Fighting
Skipping school
Dropping out

Attitudes consist of three elements or contributing factors:

1. An *affective* component of positive or negative feelings
2. A *cognitive* component describing worth or value
3. A *behavioral* component indicating a willingness or desire to engage in specific actions

The *affective* component consists of the emotion or feeling associated with an object or a person (e.g., good or bad feelings, enjoyment, likes, comfort, anxiety). When we describe a student as "liking" math or "enjoying" art, we are focusing on the affective component. The *cognitive* component is an evaluative belief (such as thinking something is valuable, useful, worthless, etc.). In school, students can think history is useless and mathematics is valuable. The *behavioral* component is actually responding in a positive way. A strong and stable attitude is evidenced when all three components are consistent. That is, when Liam reacts positively to science assignments, thinks it's important, and reads *National Geographic* at home, he has a very strong positive attitude toward science. But it's likely that for many students these components will contradict one another. Louise may not like English very much but think that it's important.

This tripartite conceptualization has important implications for identifying attitude targets. Are you interested in feelings, thoughts, or behaviors? If you want to have a learning target such as "students will have a positive attitude toward school," you need to include all three components in your assessment because the general nature of the target would need to be consistent with the assessment. However, if your target is "students will like coming to school," then the assessment should focus on the affective component.

Value Targets

Values generally refer either to desirable end states of existence or to modes of conduct (Rokeach, 1973). End states of existence are conditions and aspects of ourselves and our world that we want, such as a safe life, world peace, freedom, happiness, social acceptance, and wisdom. Modes of conduct are reflected in what we believe is appropriate and needed in our everyday existence, such as being honest, cheerful, ambitious, loving, responsible, and helpful. Each of these values can be placed into categories consistent with different areas of our lives. Thus, you can think about moral, political, social, aesthetic, economic, technological, and religious values.

I recommend that you stick with values that are relatively noncontroversial and that are clearly related to academic learning and school and district goals. Popham (2017) has suggested some values as being sufficiently meritorious and noncontroversial:

- *Honesty.* Students should learn to value honesty in their dealings with others.
- *Integrity.* Students should firmly adhere to their own code of values, for example, moral or artistic beliefs.
- *Justice.* Students should subscribe to the view that all citizens should be the recipients of equal justice from governmental law enforcement agencies.
- *Freedom.* Students should believe that democratic nations must provide the maximum level of freedom to their citizens.

Other relatively noncontroversial values include kindness, generosity, perseverance, loyalty, respect, courage, compassion, and tolerance. Popham also suggests, and I agree, that you should limit the number of affective traits targeted and assessed. It is better to do a sound job of assessing a few important traits than to try to assess many traits superficially.

Motivation Targets

In the context of schooling, motivation can be defined as the extent to which students are involved in trying to learn. This includes the students' initiation of learning, their intensity of effort, their commitment, and their persistence. In other words, *motivation* is the purposeful engagement in learning to master knowledge or skills; students take learning seriously and value opportunities to learn. There are two factors that influence motivation: expectations of success and value of the activity. Expectations refer to the *self-efficacy* of the student, the student's self-perception of his or her capability to perform successfully (more on self-efficacy below). Values are self-perceptions of the importance of the performance. That is, does the student see any value in the activity? Is it intrinsically enjoyable or satisfying? Will it meet some social or psychological need, such as self-worth, competence, or belonging, or will it help the student to attain an important goal? Your students will see the relevance of your assessments. Those that connect with them will be taken seriously, those that don't not so much.

Students who believe that they are capable of achieving success and that the activity holds value for them will be highly motivated to learn. If they value the outcome but believe that no matter how hard they try they probably won't be successful, their motivation will be weak. Similarly, we see many very capable students who are unmotivated because the activity holds no importance for them.

Like attitudes, using the general definition of motivation as an outcome is too vague because you are unable to pinpoint the source of the lack of effort and involvement. I suggest that you focus motivation targets on self-efficacy and value, differentiated by academic subject and type of learning (e.g., knowledge, understanding, reasoning). Here are some examples:

- Students will believe that they are capable of learning how to multiply fractions. (self-efficacy)
- Students will believe that it is important to know how to multiply fractions. (value)
- Students will believe that they are able to learn how bills are passed in the U.S. Senate. (self-efficacy)
- Students will believe that it is important to know how bills are passed in the U.S. Senate. (value)

Another important consideration in assessing motivation is knowing why students are learning, the reasons they give for their actions. When students do something because it is inherently interesting, enjoyable, or challenging, they are *intrinsically* motivated. In contrast, *extrinsic* motivation is doing something because it leads to a separate outcome (e.g., reward or punishment; Ryan & Deci, 2000). Students who are motivated by a need to understand and master the task (mastery orientation) demonstrate more positive behavior and thinking than students who are doing something for the result or outcome (performance orientation).

Mastery orientation students are more engaged, have a natural inclination to generate solutions to difficulties, display better persistence, and generate more positive attributions to success and failure (success attributed to ability and moderate effort; failure to lack of effort).

Self-Concept Targets

There is an extensive literature on self-concept and its cousin, self-esteem. Many educators refer to these characteristics when discussing students who have problems with school and learning (e.g., "Sam has a low self-concept," "Adrianne has a low opinion of herself"). There is no question that these beliefs are important, even with the controversy over whether self-concept and self-esteem precedes or results from academic learning (I think mostly performance precedes and influences self-concept, not the other way around—what do you think?).

For setting targets, it is helpful to remember that self-concept and self-esteem are multidimensional (Marsh & Craven, 1997). There is a bodily self, an athletic self, a mathematics self, a social self, and so forth. Each of us has a self-description in each area, which is our self-concept or self-image. In addition, we also have a sense of self-regard, self-affirmation, and self-worth in each area (self-esteem). Thus, a student can have a self-concept that he is tall and thin, but feel very comfortable with that and accept this description. Another student can have the same self-concept but feel inferior or inadequate.

I suggest staying away from global self-concept and self-esteem targets, as well as those that do not differentiate between a self-description and an evaluation of that description. Like attitudes and motivation, measuring general self-concept is simply not that helpful. This is because much of what makes up general self-concept comes from areas not directly related to academic learning and schooling. By specifying *academic* self-concept, or self-concept of academic ability, you will obtain a more valid indication of what students think about themselves as learners. If you set targets that are specific to subject areas, the resulting information will be more useful. Also, it's helpful to know where students draw the line between descriptions of themselves and whether they like those descriptions. From the standpoint of more serious mental or emotional problems, a general measure may be needed, but it's best to leave that to a school psychologist or counselor.

Self-Efficacy Targets

Self-efficacy is a student's belief that he or she is capable of learning a specific task or area of knowledge (Bandura, 2006). These are self-perceptions of the degree of confidence they have of reaching learning targets. Students estimate what they think they are able to accomplish and the likelihood of success if they exert sufficient effort. Students with a positive self-efficacy are more likely to persist and remain engaged in learning, whereas students with a low self-efficacy tend to give up or avoid what they believe are difficult tasks. They are skilled at knowing when they are learning, the degree of effort required for further learning, when they are right or wrong, and which strategies for learning are needed. They are better at knowing when they have mastered the learning target and tend to attribute their success to their ability and effort. These attributions help students have positive self-expectancies about learning in the future. Self-efficacy is focused on what *can* be achieved, not what *will* be achieved, (Bandura, 2006), and is conceptually different from self-concept, self-esteem, and outcome expectations (which are driven but what occurs).

It turns out that self-efficacy is at the heart of learning and motivation. It is well established that a positive self-efficacy is critical to future learning and related to the development of many 21st-century skills. Like self-concept, self-efficacy is task-specific, pertaining to different domains of functioning. That is, we can have a positive self-efficacy in learning math but a weak sense of confidence that we can do well in English. For example, you may be sure about learning to drive, but unsure about learning to scuba dive.

Interpersonal Skill Learning Targets

Interpersonal skills involve the nature of social relationships that students have with one another and with the teacher. They constitute a complex set of interaction skills, including the identification of and appropriate responses to social cues. Peer relations, friendship, functioning in groups, assertiveness, cooperation, collaboration, prosocial behavior, empathy, taking perspective, and conflict resolution are examples of the nature of social relationships that can be specified as targets. Social interaction is a key element of knowledge construction, active learning, and deep understanding (Borich & Tombari, 2004). As interaction occurs, students are forced to adjust their thinking to accommodate alternative viewpoints, to defend their ideas, and to debate their opinions. These processes encourage a deep, rather than superficial, understanding and keep students engaged. Also, interaction can promote good reasoning and problem-solving strategies through observation and the give-and-take that ensues.

For each of these broad social relationship areas, specific targets need to be identified. For example, a target concerned with peer relationships might include showing interest in others, listening to peers, sharing, and contributing to group activities. Cooperative skills could include sharing, listening, volunteering ideas and suggestions, supporting and accepting others' ideas, taking turns, and criticizing constructively.

Collaborative skills needed to work in small groups could include four components: (a) basic interaction, (b) getting along, (c) coaching, and (d) fulfilling particular roles (Borich & Tombari, 2004). Skills for each of the components are summarized in Table 12.3.

My recommendation for identifying interpersonal skill targets is that it is necessary to be very specific about what is emphasized. A general target about

TABLE 12.3   A Taxonomy of Collaborative Skills

Component	Definition	Skills
Basic Interaction	Students like and respect each other.	Listening Making eye contact Answering questions Using the right voice Making sense Apologizing
Getting Along	Students sustain their respect and liking for one another.	Taking turns Sharing Following rules Assisting Asking for help or a favor Using polite words
Coaching	Students both give and receive corrective feedback and encouragement.	Suggesting an action or activity Giving and receiving compliments or praise Being specific Giving advice Correcting and being corrected
Role-Fulfilling	Fulfilling specific roles creates positive interdependency and individual accountability.	Summarizer Checker Researcher Runner Recorder Supporter Troubleshooter

Source: Based on Borich and Tombari (2004).

"improved social relationships" or "improved collaboration skills" simply does not provide the level of specificity needed to focus your instruction and assessment. Here are some examples of possible social relationship targets:

- Students will contribute to small-group discussions.
- Students will have sustained friendships with two or more other students.
- Students will demonstrate skills in helping other students solve a problem.
- Students will demonstrate that they are able to negotiate with others and compromise.

Social relationships are also important for establishing the "climate" of your classroom. If you have been in many classrooms, you know that each one has a unique feel to it; it's as though you can sense the degree to which a class is comfortable, relaxed, and productive, and whether students seem happy, content, and serious. Some classes are warm and supportive, and others seem very cold and rejecting, even hostile. Together, such characteristics make up what is called class-room environment, classroom climate, or classroom culture. Obviously, a positive climate promotes learning, so a reasonable noncognitive target would be to estab-lish student relationships that encourage and support feelings, relationships, and beliefs that promote this kind of environment.

Classroom environment is made up of a number of characteristics that can be used as targets, most of which are influenced by social relationships. These include:

Affiliation—the extent to which students like and accept each other
Involvement—the extent to which students are interested in and engaged in learning
Task orientation—the extent to which classroom activities are focused on the completion of academic tasks
Cohesiveness—the extent to which students share norms and expectations
Competition—the emphasis on competition between students
Favoritism—whether each student enjoys the same privileges
Influence—the extent to which each student influences classroom decisions
Friction—the extent to which students bicker with one another
Formality—the emphasis on enforcing rules
Communication—the extent to which communication among students and with the teacher is genuine and honest
Warmth—the extent to which students care about one another and show empathy

These dimensions arise primarily from the nature of student relationships and their abilities to cooperate, trust another, listen, and collaborate.

Methods of Assessing "Noncognitive" Dispositions and Skills

Keep three considerations in mind whenever you assess noncognitive targets. First, emotions and feelings can change quickly, especially for young children and during early adolescence. This suggests that to obtain a valid indication of an indi-vidual student's emotion or feeling, it is necessary to conduct several assessments over a substantial length of time. What you want to know is what the dominant or prevalent disposition is, and if you rely on a single assessment, there is a good chance that what you measure is not a good indication of the trait.

Second, try to use different approaches to measuring the same target. For example, if you use only student self-reports, which are subject to social desirabil-ity and faking, these limitations may significantly affect the results. However, if student self-reports are consistent with your observations, then a stronger case can be made.

Finally, decide if you need individual student or group results. This is related to purpose and will influence the method that you should use. If your purpose is to use assessment for making reports to parents, then obviously you need information on each student. In this case, you should use multiple methods of collecting data over time and keep records to verify your judgments. If the assessments will be used to improve instruction, then you need results for the group as a whole. This is the more common and advisable use of affective assessment, primarily because you can rely more on anonymous student self-reports (Popham, 2017).

There are really only three feasible methods of assessing students' noncognitive dispositions and skills: teacher observation, teacher interviews, and student self-reports. Student self-assessment, while perhaps technically a form of self-report, is considered separately since it is different from traditional measures of attitudes and beliefs. We will start with teacher observation, something you will obviously do; the focus here is on observation to assess noncognitive targets.

Teacher Observation

The first step in using observation is to determine in advance how specific behaviors relate to the target. This begins with a clear definition of the trait, followed by lists of student behaviors and actions that correspond to positive and negative dimensions of the trait. Let's consider attitudes. We can identify the behaviors and actions initially by considering what students with positive and negative attitudes do and say. If we have two columns, one listing behaviors for positive attitudes and one listing behaviors for negative attitudes, we define what will be observed. Suppose you are interested in attitudes toward learning. What is it that students with a positive attitude toward learning do and say? What are the actions of those with a negative attitude? Table 12.4 lists some possibilities. These behaviors provide a foundation for developing guidelines, checklists, or rating scales. The ones in the positive column are referred to as *approach* behaviors; those in the negative column as *avoidance* behaviors. Approach behaviors result in more direct, frequent, and intense contact; avoidance behaviors are just the opposite, resulting in less direct, less frequent, or less intense contact. These dimensions—directness, frequency, and intensity—are helpful in describing the behaviors that indicate positive and negative attitudes.

How do you develop these lists of positive and negative behaviors? I have found that the best approach is to find time to brainstorm with other teachers. Published instruments are available that may give you some ideas, but these won't consider the unique characteristics of your school and students. The following behaviors were brainstormed by teachers in one of my classes to indicate a positive student attitude toward school subjects (e.g., mathematics, science, English):

Seeks corrective feedback
Asks questions
Helps other students
Prepares for tests
Reads about the subject outside class

TABLE 12.4   Student Behaviors Indicating Positive and Negative Attitudes Toward Learning

Positive	Negative
rarely misses class	is frequently absent
rarely late to class	is frequently tardy
asks lots of questions	rarely asks questions
helps other students	rarely helps other students
works well independently without supervision	needs constant supervision
laughs	little response to humor
is involved in extracurricular activities	is not involved in extracurricular activities
says he or she likes school	says he or she doesn't like school
comes to class early	rarely comes to class early
stays after school	rarely stays after school
volunteers to help	doesn't volunteer
completes homework	often does not complete homework
tries hard to do well	doesn't care about bad grades
completes extra credit work	never does extra credit work
completes assignments before they are due	never completes assignments before the due date
rarely complains	complains
is rarely off-task	sleeps in class
rarely bothers other students	bothers other students
eyes on work	stares out window

Asks about careers in the subject
Asks about colleges strong in the subject
Asks other students to be quiet in class
Is concerned with poor performance
Joins clubs
Initiates activities
Stays alert in class and on task

Once a fairly complete list of behaviors is developed, you will need to decide if you want to use an informal, unstructured observation, or one that is more formal and structured. These types differ in preparation and what is recorded.

Unstructured Observation.   Unstructured (anecdotal) observation is much like what was discussed in Chapter 4. An unstructured observation is usually open ended; typically there is no checklist or rating scale for recording what is observed. However, you do know what trait you are focused on, and you have at least generated some guidelines and examples of behaviors that indicate the trait. In that sense, you have determined in advance what to look for, but you also need to be open to other actions that may reflect on the trait.

During the observation period, or just after it, record behaviors that reflect the trait. Some of what you record may correspond to the guidelines or a list of possible behaviors, but record other actions also—anything that may have relevance to the target. Keep your interpretations separate from descriptions of the behaviors. Take brief anecdotal notes and then make sense of them at a later time. Actually, this is what teachers do regularly in their heads in a way that is even less systemic than these unstructured observations. The difference is in whether there is any predetermined list of behaviors, and whether the teachers record their observations.

It's best if you can avoid making conclusions or inferences in what you record. You want to describe what you saw or heard, but not what that may mean. Words such as *unhappy, frustrated, sad, motivated,* and *positive* are your interpretations of observed behaviors. It is better to stick to simple descriptions, such as *frowned, asked question, stared out window,* and *kept writing the entire time.* Look for both positive and negative actions. The tendency is to be more influenced by bad or negative behavior, especially if it interferes with other students. Once descriptions from several different times are recorded, then you can look over all of them and come to conclusions about the affective trait. Don't rely on a single observation.

The advantage of the unstructured observation is that it occurs naturally and you are not constrained by what is in a checklist or rating scale. There is no problem if specific behaviors aren't displayed, and behaviors that were not previously listed can be included. A disadvantage is that it is not practical to record much about student behavior on a regular basis. It's hard to find even 15 or 20 minutes at the end of the day, and it is virtually impossible to find any time during the school day.

Structured Observation. A structured observation differs in the amount of preparation needed and the way you record what is observed. In structured observation, more time is needed to prepare a checklist or rating form that is to be used for recording purposes. This form is generated from the list of positive and negative behaviors to make it easy and convenient for you to make checks quickly and easily.

The format of the checklist is simple and straightforward. The behaviors are listed, and you make a single check next to each behavior to indicate frequency. Frequency can be indicated by answering yes or no, observed or not observed; by the number of times a behavior occurred; or by some kind of **rating scale** (*always, often, sometimes, rarely, never, occasionally, consistently*). Rating scales are used to describe behavior over an extended period of time.

Two examples of checklists are illustrated in Figure 12.1 for assessing attitude toward reading. The first, labeled *frequency*, would be used to record the number of times each behavior was observed. The second type is a *rating* in which

FIGURE 12.1   Checklists for Structured Observations of Reading Behavior

Frequency Method

Student Name: _____   Date: _____   Time Frame: _____

Number of Occurrences	Behavior
	1. Tells others that a book was good
	2. Reads for at least five minutes continuously
	3. Asks questions about what is read
	4. Goes through books on the table

Rating Method

Student Name: _____   Date: _____   Time Frame: _____

Behavior	Never	Rarely	Sometimes	Most of the Time	Almost Always
Tells others that a book was good					
Reads for at least five minutes continuously					
Asks questions about what is read					
Goes through books on the table					

the teacher estimates how often each behavior occurs as defined by a set scale. Another example is shown in Figure 12.2 (page 343). In this example, the targeted trait is participation. A holistic rating scale is used to describe qualitatively different levels of participation. Notice that several behaviors are included in scores 2–5. This type of rating scale is helpful in providing a general overview of the trait being measured.

Your choice of using a frequency checklist or rating scale depends on the time frame (ratings are better for longer periods of time) and the nature of the behavior. Some behaviors are better suited to a simple checklist, such as "follows instructions" and "completes homework." My experience is that a simple scale,

FIGURE 12.2   Scoring Criteria for Participation

Participation in Class

Student: _____ Date: _____ Lesson: _____

Criteria	Score
Always listens to instructions. Very actively involved from the beginning. Obviously intent on learning the skill. Leads others. Shares thoughts and ideas.	5
Listens to instructions. Once started, actively involved. Usually intent on learning the skill. Rarely distracted from the task. Often shares thoughts and ideas. Does not usually lead others.	4
Sometimes needs clarification about directions. Hard to get started and stay involved. More passive than active. Sometimes distracted from the task. Rarely shares thoughts and ideas.	3
Does not pay attention to instructions. Distracts others. Needs reminders to stay on task. Passive. Rarely shares thoughts and ideas.	2
Did not participate.	1

with only three descriptors to indicate frequency (e.g., *usually*, *sometimes*, *rarely*), is sufficient. Additional rating scales are illustrated in Figure 12.3. If there is a large number of behaviors, organize them into major categories. This will make it easier to record and draw inferences from the results. Other suggestions are listed in Figure 12.4.

Teacher Interviews

The most direct way students self-report their affect, beliefs, and social-emotional traits is in the context of a personal conversation or interview. Teachers can use different types of personal communication with students, such as individual and group interviews, discussions, and casual conversations, to assess noncognitive traits. In some ways, this is like an observation, but because you have an opportunity to be directly involved with the students it is possible to probe and respond to better understand.

An important prerequisite for getting students to reveal their true feelings and beliefs is establishing trust. Without a sense of trust, students may not be comfortable expressing their feelings. They will tend to say what they think their teachers want to hear, say what is socially acceptable or desirable, or say very little, if anything. Younger students are usually pretty candid about themselves; older students may be more reserved. You enhance trust by communicating warmth, caring, and respect and by listening attentively to what the students communicate.

FIGURE 12.3   Examples of Rating Scales

Class Social Skills Observational Ratings

Date(s) _____

Class _____

Ratings:

+ Often or Always   ✓ Sometimes   —Rarely   ✗ Not observed

Student	Takes turns	Listens to others	Thanks others	Helps others	Comments
Ryann	✓	+	✓	+	
Dylan	+	—	—	✓	
Liam	+	✓	✓	✓	
Ryan	✓	✓	—	—	Needs improvement

Student Observational Rating

Student name: Katherine Mathis _____

Date(s): Sept. 10–20 _____

Location(s): Robious Middle School _____

Observer(s): Ms. Chandler and Ms. Dunlap _____

	Often	Some-times	Rarely	Not observed	Comments
Social Skills					Ryann works very well with others; others like her
Listens	✓				
Helps others		✓			
Cooperative		✓			
Polite	✓				
Work Habits					Has difficulty following through with some assignments
Perseveres			✓		
Works hard		✓			
Organized			✓		
On time			✓		
Emotional Skills					Appropriate self-awareness and control
Expresses feelings		✓			
Understands others' feelings	✓				
Controls anger				✓	
Non-aggressive		✓			

Next Steps: Work with Katherine to help her understand effort needed to complete her work accurately

Other Comments:

FIGURE 12.4   Checklist for Using Teacher Observation to Assess Affect

✓ Determine behaviors to be observed in advance.
✓ Record student name, time, date, and location.
✓ Write brief descriptions of observed behavior.
✓ Keep descriptions separate from interpretations.
✓ Record positive and negative behaviors.
✓ Make several observations of each student.
✓ Record as soon as possible following the observation.
✓ Use a simple and efficient system, using preprinted forms.

Source: Based on Costa and Kallick (2004).

An advantage of interviewing is that you can clarify questions, probe where appropriate to clarify responses, and note nonverbal behavior. Students have an opportunity to qualify or expand on previous answers. These procedures help avoid ambiguity and vagueness, problems often associated with measuring dispositions.

It is difficult for some students, even when there is a trusting relationship, to articulate their feelings in a one-on-one interview. They may simply be unaccustomed to answering questions about attitudes and values. A group discussion or group interview is a good alternative for these students. People generally open up more in a group setting, as long as peer pressure and cliques don't interfere. Another advantage of using groups is that it is much more efficient than individual interviews. Also, feelings and beliefs can become clearer as students hear others talk. You can use students as leaders of group interviews. They may be able to probe better because they are familiar with the language and lifestyles of their classmates. Be prepared to record student responses and your interpretations. During an interview, it is difficult to write very much, and it's not practical to tape-record, transcribe, and analyze the transcription. I suggest that you prepare a brief outline of the major areas that will be covered, leaving space to make brief notes as you interview. As soon as possible after the interview, go back over your notes and fill in enough detail so that what the student said and communicated is clearly indicated. Like observation, be careful to keep your descriptions separate from your interpretations.

Student Self-Report Questionnaires and Surveys

You have probably completed many self-report attitude questionnaires or surveys, so you have a general idea what they are like. With self-reports, there is no question that cognitions are used to generate responses. According to Duckworth and Yeager (2015), the process involves five steps, as illustrated in Figure 12.5 for responding to this question used to assess attitudes toward math: "How often do you feel you will do well on your math tests?" You can see that this student first needs to determine what "doing well" means. Once that is established, relevant information is recalled and integrated into a summary judgment. In the fourth

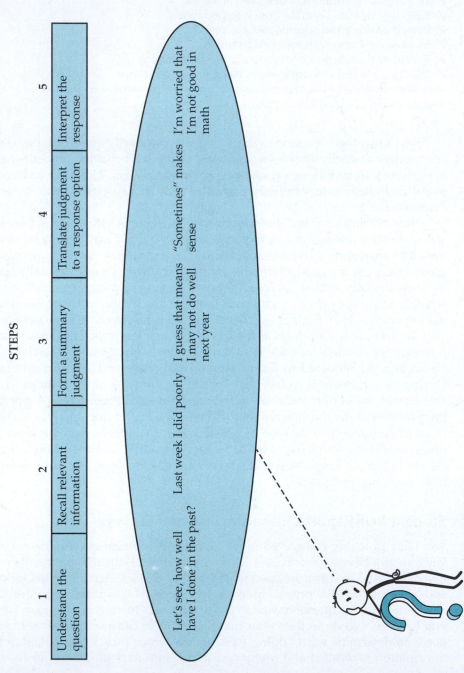

STEPS

1	2	3	4	5
Understand the question	Recall relevant information	Form a summary judgment	Translate judgment to a response option	Interpret the response

Let's see, how well have I done in the past?

Last week I did poorly

I guess that means I may not do well next year

"Sometimes" makes sense

I'm worried that I'm not good in math

FIGURE 12.5 Steps students take in responding to self-report questions. (Based on Duckworth and Yeager, 2015).

step, the judgment is applied to the response scale, with subsequent feelings and thoughts about what it means.

According to Stiggins (2008), one key to the successful use of student self-reports is to get students to take the questionnaires seriously. This will happen if students see that what you are asking about is relevant to them and that actions are taken as a result of the findings. You want to help students understand that they have nothing to lose and something to gain by being cooperative. This may be especially important for students with English language learning difficulties and those from various cultures.

Another key is using questions to which students are willing and able to provide thoughtful responses. This is accomplished if the wording of the questions is precise, if the format is easy to understand and respond to, and if the response options make sense. The questions can use either a constructed-response or selected-response format.

Constructed-Response Formats.   A straightforward approach to asking students about their attitudes, feelings, and beliefs is to have them respond to a simple statement or question. Often, incomplete sentences can be used.

Examples

> I think mathematics is …
> When I have free time, I like to …
> The subject I like most is …
> What I like most about school is …
> What I like least about school is …
> Science is …
> I think I am …

Essay items can be used with older students. These items provide a more extensive, in-depth response than incomplete sentences.

Example

> Write a paragraph on the subject you like most in school. Tell me why. Comment on what it is about the subject and your experience with it that leads you to like it the most. Describe yourself as a student. Are you a good student? What are you good at? How hard do you try to get good grades? Does learning come easy or hard for you?

An advantage of the incomplete sentence format is that it taps whatever comes to mind from each student. You are not cuing students about what to think or suggesting how they should respond, so what you get is what is foremost and most salient in the student's mind. Of course, students need to be able to read and write and take the task seriously. If you use this method, be sure to give students enough time to think and write and encourage them to write as much as they can think about for each item.

Teacher's Corner

Elizabeth O'Brien

National Board Certified Middle School Mathematics Teacher

In the beginning of the year I always have students write a "mathography." I ask them to write about themselves and their history and relationship with math. I learn a tremendous amount about my students that I would never learn otherwise. This helps to explain some students' attitudes and approaches to the material. It also enables me to understand the situations that students have dealt with in the past, which often affect how they deal with material in the present.

In addition, I do a learning style inventory in the beginning of the year with students. I do this as much for them as for myself. Many students have not given any thought to how they learn best or why they often do better for one type of teacher versus another. This instrument allows me and the students to get a better picture of my classroom and the students in it and how I should adapt my teaching to them.

There are two disadvantages to constructed-response formats. One is that even if you tell students that their answers are anonymous, they may think you'll recognize their handwriting; hence, faking is a concern. Second, scoring the responses takes time and is more subjective than more traditional objective formats. Overall, though, this approach offers an excellent way to get a general overview of student perspectives, feelings, and thoughts.

Selected-Response Formats. There are many different types of selected-response formats to choose from when assessing noncognitive targets. We will look at a few commonly used scales. When you decide to create your own instrument and wonder which of these response formats would be best, try to match the format with the trait. There is no single best response format. Some work better with some traits, and some work better with others, depending on the wording and the nature of the trait. Your job will be to make the best match.

Most selected-response formats create a scale that is used with statements concerning the trait. A widely used format to assess attitudes, for example, is the **Likert scale** (pronounced Lí kert). This scale is very versatile; it can be adapted to almost any type of noncognitive trait. Students read statements and then record their agreement or disagreement with them according to a five-point scale (*strongly agree, agree, undecided, disagree, strongly disagree*). The statements are generated from your list of positive and negative behaviors or beliefs and are put in a form that makes sense for the response scale. The statements contain some indication of the direction of the attitude, as illustrated in the following examples. The response scale indicates intensity.

Examples

Mathematics is boring.
It is important to get good grades in school.
It is important to complete homework on time.
Class discussion is better than lectures.
School is fun.
I enjoy reading.
Science is challenging.
Science is difficult.

An advantage of this format is that many such statements can be presented on a page or two to efficiently assess a number of different attitudes (see Figure 12.6). Note that some negatively worded statements are included in the example. These should be used sparingly with younger children, with words such as *not*, *don't*, and *no* appropriately highlighted or underlined.

The responses to the Likert scale are scored by assigning weights from 1 to 5 for each position on the scale so that 5 reflects the most positive and 1 the most negative (SA = 5, A = 4, NS = 3, D = 2, SD = 1). The scores from all the items assessing the same trait are then totaled, though the percentage of responses to each position is probably more important than summary statistics. In other words, you

FIGURE 12.6   Likert Scale for School Attitudes

Student Opinion Survey

Directions: Read each statement carefully and indicate how much you agree or disagree with it by circling the appropriate letter(s) to the right.

Key: SA – Strongly Agree
    A – Agree
   NS – Not Sure
    D – Disagree
  SD – Strongly Disagree

		1	2	3	4	5
1.	Science class is challenging.	SD	D	NS	A	SA
2.	Reading is important.	SD	D	NS	A	SA
3.	I like coming to school.	SD	D	NS	A	SA
4.	I like doing science experiments.	SD	D	NS	A	SA
5.	Homework is hard for me.	SD	D	NS	A	SA
6.	Cheating is very bad.	SD	D	NS	A	SA
7.	Learning about circles and triangles is useless.	SD	D	NS	A	SA
8.	I do *not* like to work in small groups.	SD	D	NS	A	SA
9.	Doing well in school is important.	SD	D	NS	A	SA
10.	I believe that what I learn in school is important.	SD	D	NS	A	SA

wouldn't add the scores from items 1, 7, and 8 in Figure 12.6 because they address different traits, though you could add items 3, 9, and 10, which deal with attitudes toward school. When adding items and obtaining average scores of statements that are worded so that a "disagree" response refers to a more positive attitude or belief, the scoring needs to be reversed. Thus, the scoring for items 1, 5, 7, and 8 in Figure 12.5 should be reversed (SD = 5, D = 4, A = 2, SA = 1).

Reliability/precision is higher if several items assessing the same trait can be added together. This needs to be balanced with the practical limitation on the total number of items in the questionnaire and with the response of students who feel that they don't need to be answering questions that are just about the same as items they have already responded to.

You can use the principle of the Likert scale to construct any number of different response formats. For younger children, for example, the five-point scale is usually truncated to three responses (*agree, unsure, disagree*), or even two (such as *agree* or *disagree, yes* or *no, true* or *not true*). Many self-report instruments use a Likert-type scale that asks students to indicate *how often* they have engaged in specific behaviors or had particular thoughts, as alluded to in Figure 12.5. These scales are easier to respond to because they are less abstract. They are best for behaviors and cognitive components of attitudes.

Examples

How often do you believe that most of what you learn in school is important?
   a. Always
   b. Frequently
   c. Sometimes
   d. Rarely
   e. Never

How frequently do you *dislike* coming to this class?
   a. All the time
   b. Most of the time
   c. Sometimes
   d. Rarely
   e. Never

How often do you find the classroom activities interesting?
   a. Almost always
   b. Often
   c. Occasionally
   d. Rarely if ever

Another frequently used variation of the Likert scale is to ask students whether something is true for them. This can be a simple dichotomous item, such as a true/false statement, or you can use a scale.

Examples

How true is each statement for you?

If I want I can get good grades in science.
   a. Very true
   b. Somewhat true
   c. Not at all true

When I really try hard I can do well in school.
   a. True
   b. Untrue

Students try hard to do better than each other in this class.
   a. True
   b. False

I am a good student.
   a. Yes
   b. No

In assessing self-efficacy it is common to ask students *how certain* they are that they can do certain things, such as learn science, take good notes in class, organize work, understand if they study, or learn English. A scale to record responses could be from 1 (Not at all certain) to 10 (Very certain).

In some questionnaires, there are different scales for different items. In these types of formats, the scales are dependent on the terminology and intent of each item. Sometimes the nature of the trait is named in the item; then the scale gives students choices. For other items, the scale defines the trait being measured.

Examples

How important is it for you to be a good reader?
   a. Extremely important
   b. Very important
   c. Somewhat important
   d. Not important

Science is:
   a. interesting.
   b. dull.
   c. difficult.

Indicate how you feel about your performance on the test.

| _____ | _____ | _____ | _____ |
| Immense pride | Some pride | Some failure | Immense failure |

_____	_____	_____	_____
Very happy	Somewhat happy	Somewhat sad	Very sad

Indicate the extent to which you believe your performance on the project was a success or failure.

    a. Extreme success
    b. Somewhat successful
    c. Failure
    d. Extreme failure

Circle the statement that best describes your interest in learning _most of the time._

    a. I am pretty interested in what we learn.
    b. This class is somewhat interesting, but I find my mind wandering sometimes.
    c. I often find this class pretty boring.

For young students, the response format is often in the form of faces rather than words.

Examples

Learning about science

Reading books

For classroom climate and value targets, self-report questionnaires often ask students to select from several options. The options refer to different traits or values, rather than showing a range of the same trait.

Examples

I did well on this test because I:

    a. studied hard.
    b. got lucky.

Select one of the following:

    a. Students in this class like to help each other out.
    b. There is a lot of bickering between students in this class.

Select the statement that you agree with the most.

   a. People should be required to volunteer to help those less fortunate.

   b. People who find a wallet should give it to the police.

Interests are efficiently measured with checklists, ranking, or simple dichotomous choices.

Examples

Indicate whether you are interested (I) or uninterested (U) in learning about each of the historical topics listed.

_____ **a.** Vietnam War

_____ **b.** World War II

_____ **c.** Holocaust

_____ **d.** Depression

_____ **e.** Stock market crash

Rank the following from most liked (1) to least liked (5).

_____ History

_____ Sports

_____ Science

_____ Music

_____ Art

An advantage of selected-response formats is that they make it easy to ensure anonymity. Anonymity is important when the traits are more personal, such as values and self-concept. It is also an efficient way of collecting information. However, you don't want to ask too many questions just because it is efficient. It's best to keep self-report questionnaires short. Although you need more than a single item to reliably assess an affective trait, if you have too many items, students may lose concentration and motivation. Select only those traits that you will take action on; don't use items simply because it would be interesting to know what students think.

If you need to develop your own self-report items to assess noncognitive targets, begin by listing the behaviors, thoughts, and feelings that correspond to each trait, similar to what I suggested earlier for observations. Once you select a response format, write sentences that are clear and succinct, and write direct statements that students will easily understand. Keep items simple and short. You may find that published instruments will give you some good ideas for how to word items, set up response formats, and in general lay out a questionnaire. You may find an existing instrument that meets your purpose very well.

In wording the items, avoid the use of negatives, especially double negatives.

Examples

Poor: There isn't a student in this class who does not like to work with others.

Improved: Students in this class like to work with each other.

If you are interested in present self-perceptions, which is usually the case, avoid writing in the past tense.

Examples

> *Poor:*   I have always liked science.
>
> *Improved:*   I like science.

Avoid absolutes such as *always, never, all,* and *every* in the item stem. These terms, because they represent an all-or-none judgment, may cause you to miss the more accurate self-perception.

Examples

> *Poor:*   I never like science.
>
> *Improved:*   I rarely like science.

Avoid items that ask about more than one thing or thought. Double-barreled items are difficult to interpret because you don't know which of the two thoughts or ideas the student has responded to.

Examples

> *Poor:*   I like science and mathematics.
>
> *Improved:*   I like science.

These and other suggestions presented in this section are summarized in Figure 12.7. I should point out, however, that classroom teachers rarely have an opportunity to develop sophisticated instruments with strong and well-documented technical qualities. Thus, locally developed items and instruments should be used cautiously and in conjunction with other evidence.

Student Self-Assessment

What is self-assessment? Simply put, student **self-assessment** is a process in which students *monitor* and *evaluate* their learning and performance. Monitoring is

FIGURE 12.7   Checklist for Using Rating Scales to Assess Noncognitive Targets

✓ Keep measures focused on specific traits.
✓ Match response format to the trait being assessed.
✓ Ensure anonymity if possible.
✓ Keep questionnaires brief.
✓ Keep items short and simple.
✓ Avoid negatives and absolutes.
✓ Write items in present tense.
✓ Avoid double-barreled items.

Teacher's Corner

Arleen Reinhardt

National Board Certified High School English and Special Education Teacher

Noncognitive assessments help me to determine how effective my activities are, how clear my objectives are, whether students are treated fairly, and whether the classroom environment is conducive to student learning. At the end of each semester, I give students a questionnaire that asks them to evaluate what they have learned, to offer suggestions for my improvement, and to comment upon how they feel while in the class.

Most students give sincere and helpful comments. In fact, I often learn that students take their learning and time spent in school very seriously. I often use these comments to plan future lessons and to help me build stronger relationships with individual students. Student comments help me to become a better teacher because they force me to reflect upon my teaching.

an awareness of the thinking and learning strategies that are needed and actual performance. Evaluation involves making a judgment about the quality of their work and their progress toward targeted performance. That is, self-assessment engages students deeply in self-observations and making judgments about their work, identifying discrepancies between current and desired performance (McMillan & Hearn, 2008; Ross, 2006). This aligns closely to what is emphasized in standards-based education because such thinking implies an understanding of performance targets and the criteria that are used to indicate success.

Self-assessment is an excellent strategy for formative assessment since students give themselves immediate feedback, based on specific aspects of their performance according to standards and criteria, and make adjustments to how and what they are learning (Crooks, 2007). They improve their performance by taking responsibility for their own learning, gaining an understanding of their strengths and weaknesses. It empowers students to independently guide their own learning by using internal feedback to determine whether and when to seek assistance, when to keep moving forward, and when to adapt new learning strategies to reach learning targets (Heritage & Anderson, 2009; Heritage, 2013).

Successful student self-assessment has a multitude of positive benefits. Perhaps most important, research suggests that self-assessment contributes to higher achievement, especially when students receive direct instruction on self-assessment procedures (Black & Wiliam, 1998; Brown & Harris, 2013; Ross, 2006; Sadler & Good, 2006). The purpose of self-assessment is to involve students deeply in the evaluation of their work so that immediate feedback can be incorporated and used to improve learning. The emphasis is on progress and mastery of knowledge and understanding, which increases confidence and motivation. Students learn to use assessment information to set performance goals, to make decisions about how to improve, to describe quality work, to communicate their progress toward meeting learning targets, and to develop metacognitive skills (Chappuis & Stiggins, 2002). Self-assessment enhances students' internal sense of control and fosters attributions to effort that strengthen persistence and perseverance.

Theories from three areas of study provide support for self-assessment as a powerful source of learning: cognitive theories of motivation and learning, meta-cognition theory, and self-efficacy theory (McMillan & Hearn, 2008). Cognitive and constructivist theories of learning stress the importance of connecting new learning to what they already know and understand. Self-assessment helps this process by providing students with meaningful feedback that is based on criteria they have internalized. Rather than learning in a rote manner, students learn by constantly comparing their understandings with desired learning outcomes. The knowledge that is constructed is meaningful in the sense that it is in the context of students' existing knowledge.

A good example that shows how student self-assessment can improve learning is reported by Frederiksen and White (2004). In their work, students use a process the researchers called *reflective assessment*. The purpose of reflective assessment is to develop students' metacognitive science inquiry knowledge. Students were taught to evaluate their work according to criteria representing "higher-level" cognitive skills, such as reasoning, being inventive, and being systematic. Students evaluated the scientific research they had conducted using these criteria on a five-point scale. They also wrote justifications for their ratings. Based on this approach, experiments comparing students using reflective assessment to a control group showed that reflective assessment was effective in developing the students' thinking skills and in providing higher quality products.

From a motivational perspective, self-assessment is key to establishing a mastery goal orientation. This type of motivation is based on improving knowledge, understanding, and skill, rather than on simply being successful with the outcome. Mastery goals require, to at least some extent, an internal processing of information, whereas for performance goal orientation the monitoring and evaluation are external. Self-assessment contributes to a mastery type of motivation by enabling students to know their progress toward full understanding.

Metacognition involves skills that are directly influenced by self-assessment. Both self-monitoring and self-evaluation are important metacognitive skills. Students learn to manage learning activities and time, check their understanding, and switch to different approaches to learning. They are taught to constantly monitor their progress as well as what is influencing their learning. Students learn how to form internal questions about their learning and performance, to make decisions about what other learning is needed, and to be aware if projected learning plans are not resulting in satisfactory improvement. The emphasis, then, is on *self-directed* learning, which has powerful implications for motivation and positive attitudes toward learning. Figures 12.8 and 12.9 illustrate rubrics that can be used periodically to remind students about the metacognitive skills they should be using.

FIGURE 12.8   **Rubric for Metacognition and Self-Monitoring**

Criteria	Score			
	1	**2**	**3**	**4**
Goal setting	Minimal or no goals set	Some goals set though not comprehensive or realistic	Adequate goals set with reminders	Sets realistic and appropriate goals independently
Expectations	Does not set expectations	Expectations unrealistic	Mix of realistic and unrealistic expectations	Mostly or completely realistic expectations
Monitoring	Is not aware of progress toward reaching goals	Requires reminders to make changes in activities to meet goals	Adequate evidence that the student is aware of progress of most goals	Extensive evidence that the student is aware of progress toward goals
Understanding	Is not aware of whether or not information is understood	Requires frequent reminders to check for understanding	Requires some or minimal reminders to check for understanding	Independently is able to check for understanding
Process	Is not aware of what process is best for attaining understanding	Requires frequent reminders to think about processes for attaining understanding	Requires some or minimal reminders to think about processes for attaining understanding	Independently is able to monitor processes required to attain understanding
Reflection	Shows no or minimal evidence of reflection on thinking processes, understanding, and goal attainment	Shows some evidence of reflection on thinking processes, understanding, and goal attainment	Shows adequate evidence of reflection on thinking processes, understanding, and goal attainment	Reflects extensively on thinking processes, understanding, and goal attainment

A key element in self-assessment is the development of students' self-reflective habits and skills. This is best accomplished with a clear idea of what the habits and skills are and specific instruction in these dispositions. You will need to be very clear to students about your expectations for them to monitor their work and thinking and to be reflective about their work, describing what you expect them to do in terms they can understand. Examples that illustrate the dispositions are helpful. This may need to be very simple. For example, students can be introduced to self-assessment by asking them to say whether answers to questions are

FIGURE 12.9   Checklist for Metacognitive Skills

Metacognitive Skill	I *Rarely* Do This	I Do This *Some* of the Time	I Do This *Most* of the Time	I *Always* Do This
I make sure I know the criteria for judging my performance before I begin.				
I am willing to share with others and the teacher when I don't understand something.				
I learn from my mistakes.				
I strive for more learning.				
I check my work for mistakes and completeness.				
I know how to evaluate the work of other students.				
I think about what I need to do to perform better.				

correct or incorrect, then answering: Why is the answer incorrect? What tells you specifically that it is incorrect? What can be done to have a correct answer? As students respond to these questions, your focus should be on whether their answers reflect a willingness to apply what they know, so simply showing this kind of engagement needs to be recognized and rewarded.

The goal of self-assessment is to empower students so that they can guide their own learning and internalize the criteria for judging success. This occurs when students first understand the criteria and then evaluate their progress toward attainment of specific achievement targets, as they learn, and know what further learning is needed to reach the targets. Students give themselves meaningful formative feedback during instruction. This process is individualized for each student, allowing students to obtain specific information rather than relying on general evaluative feedback for the class as a whole. Assessment is integrated with learning as well as with instruction, and when students are judging their own performance the responsibility for learning lies more with them than with the teacher.

Self-Assessment Strategies.   There are many approaches to address students' self-assessment. Some examples are summarized, which list the activities by when they occur—either before, during, or after instruction (Chappuis & Stiggins, 2002; Costa & Kallick, 2004; Stiggins, 2008).

Before *Instruction, Students*

- Review with the teacher the table of specifications to discuss what it means.
- Examine samples of student performance in the past to show how criteria can be used to evaluate the samples with reference to the learning goals.
- Suggest how samples of student performance could be improved to meet the targeted performance.
- Share scoring criteria with exemplars of student work illustrating different levels of performance.
- Analyze examples of student work using the scoring criteria.
- Develop a table of specifications.
- Develop assessments and scoring criteria.
- Develop practice test items.
- Match test items to the table of specifications.
- Transform criteria into checklists and other methods of keeping track of progress.
- Practice self-assessment with familiar tasks and easily understood criteria.

During *Instruction, Students*

- Keep track of the match between what is covered and target criteria.
- Keep a log of growth toward meeting the target.
- Signal teacher when milestones are accomplished.
- Indicate level of understanding using cards or electronic clickers.
- Evaluate their own and others' work at the end of each day and show progress toward meeting the target.
- Make predictions about how well they will perform in the summative assessment.
- Ask questions that encourage self-evaluation (e.g., How does your work compare to the exemplars? Have you met the target completely? What additional learning is needed? What can you do to improve your learning? Are you sure that is correct? How do you know? What areas are you having

trouble learning? What rating do you deserve? Why? How much more time will be needed to reach this target? What are some ways you can learn to reach the target? What do you need to work on?)

- Rate each other during discussions.
- Predict how well they will perform and the areas in which they will need further learning.
- Identify targets that have been difficult to learn.
- Self-evaluate understanding every 15 to 20 minutes.
- Engage in peer tutoring.
- Maintain learning portfolios.
- Check work in progress.
- List the steps needed to learn the material.

After *Instruction, Students*

- Design practice tests.
- Evaluate the quality of practice test items.
- Participate in scoring the assessments.
- Make suggestions about how to improve the assessment.
- Construct test items and justify how they will measure student performance in relation to learning targets.
- Evaluate their own work and/or others' work according to provided criteria.
- Rate themselves and others.
- Interview each other to judge performance.
- Conduct student-led parent–teacher conferences.
- Provide their own explanations for grades they have received.

Although you won't be able to use all these suggestions, the important point is that you need to find and be comfortable using activities that will use and promote student self-assessment. It's largely a matter of the commitment you make to self-assessment and whether it's something that you are aware of when planning and carrying out instruction and assessment.

Student self-assessment is not without limitations. Perhaps the biggest challenge is to get students used to doing it. This will take time because most students are accustomed to receiving only teacher feedback and appraisal. Some students will self-assess better than others, which will require some individual attention by the teacher. It may also be so time-consuming to have students involved in self-assessment that valuable instructional time is lost. Finally, you may need to develop a strong rationale for using student self-assessment if this is new for your school or department. With the current trend toward standardization of both assessment and instruction, your use of student self-assessment may not fit well with what is required or encouraged.

It will be helpful to students if you provide them with worksheets, checklists, sentence completion, rating scales, and other prepared material to provide

FIGURE 12.10   Student Self-Assessment Rating Form

Student Name: _____ Teacher: _____ Date: _____

Scientific Method
The student will understand the essential characteristics of experiments.

Area	Got It—Test Me	Got Most of It—Just Some Fine-Tuning Needed	Got Some of It—Further Work Needed	Don't Get It at All—Help, Please
Independent and dependent variables				
Researcher control of variables				
Random assignment of subjects				
Control group				
Confounding variables				

FIGURE 12.11   Self-Assessment Rating Form for Reading

Reading Progress Report

Student Name: _____ Teacher Name: _____ Date: _____

I am able to:

	Yes, Let's Go On	Not Quite Yet	Not Yet
Explain the author's purpose			
Pick out fact from fantasy			
Describe how the setting is important to the story			
Describe how the language used is important to the story			
Pick out the main characters of the story			

structure to self-assessment. Especially for younger students, concepts such as self-assessment, self-monitoring, and self-rating are abstract and difficult to comprehend. Figures 12.10 and 12.11 are examples of the kinds of forms you can prepare and use with your students.

Which Method or Combination of Methods Should I Use?

We have covered three approaches to measuring noncognitive dispositions and beliefs—observation, student self-report, and student self-assessment—and each method has advantages and disadvantages. Your choice of which of these to use depends on a number of factors. Consider the type of trait or belief you want to assess. You can get a pretty good idea of a student's general reaction to something or someone through observation, but to diagnose attitude components you'll need a self-report of some kind. Checklists are effective for self-assessment. Observation is best to get at socially oriented affect and skills. If you are interested in group responses and tendencies, which is generally recommended, then a selected-response self-report is probably best because you can ensure anonymity, and it is easily scored. Finally, you need to take into consideration the use of the information. If you intend to use the results for grading (which I do not recommend), then multiple approaches may be needed, and you'll need to be especially careful about faking on self-reports and even peer judgments. In the end, the choice of method depends most on your context, nature of students, targets, and level of comfort in using any particular approach.

Summary

This chapter considered student noncognitive dispositions and traits, important but often neglected outcomes. Sound assessment of these noncognitive outcomes begins with clear and specific targets. Suggestions were made for conceptualizing traits that most would consider essential for successful learning. Three methods are used most frequently for measuring noncognitive outcomes: teacher observation and interviewing, student self-reports, and student self-assessment. Observation can be structured or unstructured, and there are many different formats for self-reports and self-assessments. My suggestion is to pick a few most important traits, do a good job of assessing them, and then use the results to improve instruction. Other essential points made in the chapter include the following:

- Positive noncognitive traits influence motivation and cognitive learning.
- The term *affect* refers to emotions and feelings.
- Attitudes are predispositions to respond favorably or unfavorably. They include cognitive, affective, and behavioral components.
- Values are end states of existence or desired modes of conduct.

- Motivation is the purposeful engagement to learn. It is determined by self-efficacy (the student's beliefs about his or her capability to learn) and the value of learning.
- Academic self-concept is the way students describe themselves as learners. Self-esteem is how students feel about themselves. (It's best to avoid general measures of self-concept or self-esteem.)
- Social relationship targets involve interpersonal interaction and competence.
- Classroom environment is the climate established through factors such as affiliation, involvement, cohesiveness, formality, friction, and warmth.
- Teacher observation can be structured or unstructured. Several observations should be made; recording of behavior should occur as soon as possible after the observation. Inferences are made from what was observed.
- Student self-reports include questionnaires and surveys. Most use scaled responses.
- Interviews allow teachers to probe and clarify to avoid ambiguity, though they cannot be anonymous and are time consuming.
- Questionnaires are time efficient and can be anonymous. Proper student motivation to take the questions seriously is essential.
- Constructed-response questions tap traits without cuing students, which indicates what is most salient to students.
- Rating scale formats, such as the Likert scale, are very common. They are efficient to score and can be anonymous when assessing groups.
- In constructing student surveys, keep them brief, write in the present tense, and avoid negative and double-barreled items.
- Student self-assessment consists of self-monitoring and self-evaluation.
- Students who self-assess have better achievement, more positive motivation, and a stronger self-efficacy.
- Self-assessment skills can be taught and implemented before, during, or after instruction.
- There is greater error in measuring noncognitive traits and dispositions than achievement and aptitude.

Introductory Case Study Answer

Student interest in calculus would be best evaluated using a self-report questionnaire. Student self-efficacy in calculus would be best evaluated with teacher interviews. Student altruism in calculus would be best evaluated using teacher observations/interviews. With self-assessments students monitor and evaluate their learning and performance. By completing self-assessments, students develop an awareness of their learning and evaluate their work towards meeting the targeted objectives. Students take responsibility for their learning by giving themselves feedback and making decisions to adjust their learning. By incorporating self-assessments into his class, Miguel's students may

1. gain and understanding of their strengths and weaknesses,
2. be empowered to independently guide their learning,

3. use internal feedback to determine if they need assistance,
4. increase their achievement,
5. develop metacognitive skills,
6. from reflective habits and skills,
7. have greater motivation for learning, and
8. develop stronger self-efficacy beliefs.

Miguel should be aware of the following when implementing self-assessments:

1. Students need direct instruction on self-assessment procedures.
2. Students are accustomed to receiving mostly teacher feedback, so self-assessment can be challenging to get students used to doing it.
3. The process can be time consuming.
4. Students will benefit from teacher-provided materials that provide structure for self-assessment.

Suggestions for Action Research

1. Identify some noncognitive disposition and skill targets for students and construct a short questionnaire to assess the targets. If possible, find a group of students who could respond to the questionnaire. After they answer all the questions, ask them about their feelings toward the questions and the clarity of the wording. What do the results look like? Would the teacher agree with the results? How difficult was it to develop the questionnaire?

2. Interview several teachers about noncognitive targets in the classroom. Ask them how they arrived at their targets and whether there is any systematic approach to assessing them. Ask what the advantages and disadvantages would be to using different kinds of assessment techniques, such as observation and student self-reports.

3. Ask a group of students about self-assessment. What do they think about the idea? Do they think it would motivate them? Give them some specific examples of student self-assessment materials. Would they be interested in doing it? What do students see as strengths and weaknesses? Do they think they have the skills to do self-assessment?

MyEdLab Self-Check 12.1

MyEdLab Self-Check 12.2

MyEdLab Self-Check 12.3

MyEdLab Self-Check 12.4

MyEdLab Application Exercise 12.1   Effective Assessment of Noncognitive Dispositions and Traits

MyEdLab Application Exercise 12.2   Student Self-Assessment

Assessment for Students with Exceptional Needs

with Serra De Arment, Amy Hutton, and Yaoying Xu

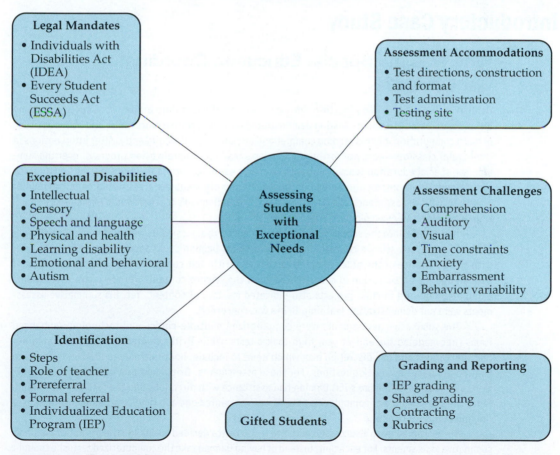

Legal Mandates
- Individuals with Disabilities Act (IDEA)
- Every Student Succeeds Act (ESSA)

Assessment Accommodations
- Test directions, construction and format
- Test administration
- Testing site

Exceptional Disabilities
- Intellectual
- Sensory
- Speech and language
- Physical and health
- Learning disability
- Emotional and behavioral
- Autism

Assessing Students with Exceptional Needs

Assessment Challenges
- Comprehension
- Auditory
- Visual
- Time constraints
- Anxiety
- Embarrassment
- Behavior variability

Identification
- Steps
- Role of teacher
- Prereferral
- Formal referral
- Individualized Education Program (IEP)

Gifted Students

Grading and Reporting
- IEP grading
- Shared grading
- Contracting
- Rubrics

CHAPTER 13 Concept Map

Learning Outcomes

After reading this chapter, you should be able to:

13.1   Understand the essential legal mandates for educating students with special needs and how those mandates influence assessment.

13.2   Understand the basic elements of identification for special needs students, the sequence of steps taken, and the role of the classroom teacher in that process.

13.3   Understand why assessment accommodations are needed to ensure fair and accurate assessment, as well as grading and reporting, for students with learning difficulties as well as gifted and talented students.

13.4   Know assessment difficulties for students with special needs, and be able to identify assessment accommodations that are needed for each difficulty.

Introductory Case Study

Why Was the Special Education Coordinator Concerned?

Damian, a student in Britta's fourth-grade class, was identified in third grade with a specific learning disability in reading. Damian's testing demonstrated normal cognitive functioning and above aptitude in math computation, but his reading comprehension skills lagged significantly. After interventions in the regular classroom were not furthering Damian's reading comprehension progress, over the summer, the special education team, along with Damian's parents, rewrote Damian's IEP for fourth grade to include pull-out instruction in reading. Instruction in other subject areas would be in the regular classroom with the assistance of a classroom aide. Britta, Damian's teacher, would implement instructional and assessment accommodations.

Two months into the school year, Damian's summative assessments were not indicating mastery of the fourth-grade science content. During instruction, Damian could answer questions orally and, with the assistance of the aide, complete activities. Britta felt confident from her observations of Damian and his participation in class that he knew the science content. Her formative assessments using diagrams and in-class projects also indicated mastery of content. Yet, his summative assessments were not demonstrating learning. Britta was concerned.

The summative assessments were computerized multiple-choice and technology-enhanced items that modeled the end-of-year high-stakes tests. While Britta created the tests to match her learning targets and had discretion over which items to include, her principal required all teachers to use the provided test-bank questions. For these assessments, Britta had provided the accommodations as indicated in Damian's IEP. Damian had assistance with directions and the test was read aloud. Since the assessment was computerized, items were presented one at a time, and Damian could skip or flag questions for review.

Since Damian wasn't successful with the tests, Britta decided to change the format of Damian's summative assessments. For each unit, instead of having Damian take the computerized test, she thought it might be best to provide an alternative assessment in which Damian could show his knowledge. She would provide Damian with a list of keywords/concepts for the unit, and Damian would create a concept map of his knowledge. The aide would monitor Damian while he was completing the assessment and provide guiding questions and statements such as "You might need to define that word" or "Consider telling when you should use that concept." Damian would be allowed to include pictures, diagrams, short phrases, or definitions. Britta would ensure that the list of keywords/concepts she gave Damian included the same content as the questions in the computerized assessment. She would also develop a rubric for grading Damian's concept map that included only scores related to content, not effort, creativity, or handwriting.

Before implementing these changes, Britta needed approval from her school's Special Education Coordinator. When Britta explained her idea, the coordinator's response was not what Britta expected. Britta thought she would be pleased and excited that she was implementing adjustments so that Damian's summative assessments and grades would demonstrate his level of learning. Instead, the coordinator's face showed concern.

As you read this chapter, think about why the coordinator was concerned with Britta's proposal. Were Britta's changes to Damian's summative assessments accommodations or modifications? Why do you believe the coordinator was concerned? Is Britta's alternative assessment appropriate?

Increasingly, students with exceptionalities are taught in general education classrooms. Teachers are responsible for gathering assessment information when a disability is suspected and to inform special education eligibility decisions. Once special education services are in place, appropriate assessment accommodations are necessary for students with disabilities to ensure fairness and accuracy in gathering evidence of their learning. Assessing students with exceptional needs can be challenging, largely due to the highly individualized nature of gathering assessment information and the need to provide assessment accommodations. In this chapter we will consider assessment for students with identified disabilities who are likely to receive instruction in general education classrooms. More likely than not, that will include your classroom. A review of important legal mandates is included to provide a context for providing assessment accommodations.

Legal Mandates

In 1975, the Education for All Handicapped Children Act, Public Law 94-142, was passed to provide free appropriate public education (FAPE) for school-aged individuals with special needs in the least restrictive environment (LRE). The act, which was updated in 1990 as the Individuals with Disabilities Education Act (IDEA; P.L. 101-476, and reauthorized in 1997), requires states to establish procedures to ensure that students with special needs are educated, to the maximum extent possible, with students who are not disabled, that is, in the least restrictive environment. The most common procedure for meeting this mandate has been to "mainstream" students with special needs by placing them in general education classes with appropriate instructional support. Later the term **inclusion** has been used to mean that students with disabilities are served primarily in the general education classroom with individual supports as needed, under the responsibilities of the general education teacher (Mastropieri & Scruggs, 2013). In fact, students can be removed from general classes only when the severity of the disability prevents satisfactory instruction and learning progress. As a result, most classroom teachers must now be familiar with how students are identified as having "special needs" and how assessment procedures used in the course of general education classroom instruction need to be modified to ensure that these students are evaluated fairly.

One of the most important new provisions under IDEA 1990 was that the law recognized that most students with disabilities spent all or most of their school time in general education settings, so it included a provision requiring that a general education teacher become a member of the team for the student's individualized education program (IEP). The trend is toward increasing governmental involvement in protecting the rights of individuals with disabilities, and as a general education teacher you will be responsible for adhering to these regulations with students in inclusive settings.

The most recent reauthorization of IDEA, P.L. 108-446, the Individuals with Disabilities Education Improvement Act, or IDEIA, was passed in 2004 to provide more educational opportunities for students with disabilities in general education settings (Pierangelo & Giuliani, 2012). According to P.L. 94-142, and later IDEA, classroom teachers are responsible for gathering and providing the information used to identify students who may become eligible for special education services and for developing and implementing an **individualized education program (IEP)**. The IEP is a written plan that serves as a legal document. It is developed by a team of individuals (IEP committee) that specifies the present level of the student's knowledge and skills, annual goals, short-term learning objectives, the initiation and duration of special services, evaluation procedures, and the educational program for the student (Spinelli, 2002). Later in the chapter you learn more about the details of this individualized planning document for students with disabilities.

The 2004 reauthorization of IDEA, or IDEIA, restated the importance of identifying the student's present level of educational performance, but made it more explicit with both academic and nonacademic achievements. The IEP document must include a statement of the student's present levels of "academic achievement and functional performance," documenting how the disability affects the student's involvement and progress in the general education curriculum (34 CFR Part 300, §300.320). This most recent version of special education law emphasizes:

- The option for schools to use the Response to Intervention (RTI) approach to determining eligibility for special education services.
- State alignment of accountability systems for students with disabilities to the current federal education law, the Every Student Succeeds Act of 2015, which requires all students to be taught to high academic standards that will prepare them for success in college and careers.
- IEPs specifically address academic achievement of students with disabilities.

- Individual accommodations for testing and alternative statewide assessments and justification for participating in alternative assessments specified in IEPs.

For identification purposes, IDEA requires that the selection and administration of materials and procedures used for evaluation and placement must be **nondiscriminatory**. At a minimum, the law requires that:

1. Trained personnel administer validated tests and other evaluation materials and provide and administer such materials in the child's native language or other mode of communication, whenever feasible.
2. Tests and other evaluation materials include those tailored to assess specific areas of educational need and not merely those designed to provide a single general intelligence quotient.
3. Trained personnel select and administer tests to reflect accurately the child's aptitude or achievement level without discriminating against the child's disability.
4. Trained personnel use no single procedure as the sole criterion for determining an appropriate educational program for a child.
5. A multidisciplinary team assesses the child in all areas related to the suspected disability. (Wood, 2002, p. 11)

Additionally, IDEA requires that information provided by parents and other informal assessment measures must be considered. The IEP team must determine that the deficits are not due to the lack of instruction in reading or math or English proficiency. The classroom teacher needs to address and document how to enable the student with special needs to participate and progress in the general education curriculum (Smith, Polloway, Patton, & Dowdy, 2012). Figure 13.1 provides an example of what this documentation may look like.

Essentially, these provisions mean that assessment must be planned and conducted so that the disability does not contribute to the score or result. That is, it would be unfair to use a test written in English to determine that a student whose primary language is Spanish has an intellectual disability, just as it would be unfair to conclude that a student with a fine-motor disability did not know

FIGURE 13.1 **Example of Student Progress in the General Education Curriculum**

Nesha's learning disability affects her problem-solving capabilities in math. Nesha has difficulty independently solving multi-step word problems. By breaking lengthier word problem into several separate steps, Nesha has much greater success. She has not yet shown that she can successfully separate word problems into distinct steps on her own, but this is a skill we are working on through repeated practice. It helps if Nesha can refer to a list of brief reminders for how to solve multi-step word problems. She enjoys working on word problems the most when she can collaborate with a peer study buddy.

the answer to an essay question because there was insufficient time to write the answer.

Ultimately, teachers are responsible for ensuring that the student will participate in regular classroom activities to the maximum extent possible. This includes both formal and informal classroom assessments. Here, your understanding of what is required with each type of assessment and your knowledge of the specific disabilities of the students are used to ensure that, whenever possible, assessment procedures do not need to be modified.

Exceptional Disabilities

Every student identified with a disability will have different strengths and needs, necessitating a variety of accommodations for multiple children within a single classroom. Further, a single student receiving special education services may have more than one identified disability. It is important to be aware of the main characteristics of disabilities as part of assessment for special education services, as well as the educational implications of disabilities for informing classroom assessment practices.

Special education law (IDEA) specifies 13 disability categories as guidance for identifying students as eligible to receive special education services (autism, deafness, deaf-blindness, emotional disturbance, hearing impairment, intellectual disability,[1] multiple disabilities, orthopedic impairment, other health impairment, specific learning disability, speech or language impairment, traumatic brain injury, and visual impairment). This section will provide you with insight into disabilities you are most likely to encounter in a general education setting and how they might impact your assessment practices.

Intellectual Disability

Students are identified as having an **intellectual disability** on the basis of low scores on a standardized intelligence test and consistent deficits in one or more *adaptive behaviors* that adversely affect educational performance for their age and/or grade. **Adaptive behaviors** are those that are needed for normal functioning in daily living situations, for example, expressive and receptive communication, daily living skills such as personal hygiene and eating habits, coping skills, and motor skills. The extent of the intellectual disability is indicated in degrees: mild, moderate, and severe. Typically, students with mild intellectual disabilities are served within the general education classroom.

Although school psychologists will take care of the IQ testing, you may need to provide information regarding a student's adaptive behaviors. Often, you

---

[1]Note that the most recent iteration of IDEA (2004) originally used the term *mental retardation* among the 13 disability categories. However, *Rosa's Law*, signed by President Obama in 2010, requires that the term be replaced with *intellectual disability* in federal health, education, and labor policy.

accomplish this with the help of established adaptive behavior scales, such as the *Vineland Adaptive Behavior Scale*, the *Adaptive Behavior Scale*, and the *Adaptive Behavior Inventory for Children*. Teachers, as well as primary caregivers, are interviewed to document the student's behavioral competencies. In addition, it is important for you to confirm findings from these instruments through observations of the student's adaptive behaviors within the classroom.

You need to keep two cautions in mind when assessing adaptive behavior. First, no single adaptive behavior instrument covers all areas of adaptive skills, and the data for these instruments are gathered from third-party observers. Thus, it is important to select the instrument that will provide the most valid inferences for the situation and to keep in mind that third parties may be biased in their interpretation of the information you and the student's primary caregiver(s) provide about the student. Second, you need to be careful that a student's cultural or linguistic background does not influence the assessment of adaptive behavior. Some students may have difficulty functioning in the classroom because of these differences. Within their home and community environments they may not exhibit adaptive skill deficits. Thus, adaptive behavior is best evaluated relative to the context in which it occurs (Witt, Elliott, Daly, Gresham, & Kramer, 1998).

Sensory Impairments

Students who have vision or hearing deficits may be identified as sensory impaired. This could include vision difficulties, with or without correction, including acuity and eye–hand coordination; or a hearing deficit that interferes with educational performance. When you notice a student is experiencing learning difficulty, an important first step is to assess that student's vision and hearing. A school nurse can complete these assessments formally, but within the classroom, your close observation can provide clues about the presence of these sensory impairments.

Speech and Language Disorders

Students who demonstrate difficulty with communication or a voice impairment are eligible for special education services under the category of speech and language impairment. Communication deficits may include stuttering, impaired articulation, or difficulties expressing or understanding verbal language. Students with voice impairments have problems with the sound quality of their voices such that communication is adversely affected.

Physical and Health Impairments

Students may be diagnosed with physical limitation, or orthopedic impairment, that limits their ability to physically move or engage with the classroom learning environment. This may include limitations such as limb amputation or cerebral palsy. Unless concurrently diagnosed with another disability or condition, orthopedic impairments typically do not limit a student's intellectual functioning.

However, accommodations may be necessary to support a student's physical access to learning experiences and assessments.

Other health impairments are generally less overtly obvious and may include diagnoses of epilepsy, diabetes, or muscular dystrophy, to name a few. Students with attention deficits are also typically considered eligible for special education services under the category of *other health impairment*. These students have difficulty focusing and staying focused on tasks and learning activities. When inattention and/or hyperactivity-impulsivity is/are sustained (for at least 6 months) in different environments and is inconsistent with age-appropriate behavior of the student, three presentations of attention deficit hyperactivity disorder (ADHD) can occur (American Psychiatric Association, 2013).

- **Predominantly Inattentive Presentation.** These students are often unable to sustain attention, are easily distracted, have difficulties organizing, make careless mistakes, tend to lose things, and may be forgetful (McLoughlin & Lewis, 2007). Although standardized instruments are used to confirm the presence of these disorders, teacher observations are essential.
- **Predominantly Hyperactive-Impulsive Presentation.** Students who fidget excessively, have difficulty sitting, appear restless, and are constantly "on the go" may be identified as **hyperactive**. A related disability, **impulsivity**, occurs when a student has difficulty waiting in turn, "blurts" out answers, and constantly interrupts others. As with attention-only deficits, hyperactivity must interfere to a significant extent with the ability of the student to learn and demonstrate what he or she understands.
- **Combined Presentation.** When a student demonstrates a significant number of behaviors characterizing both inattentive and hyperactive-impulsive subtypes, the student shows a combined presentation of ADHD. This means that the student may not only have difficulty sustaining attention and focusing on academic work; such a student is also likely to be very active and may act without thinking.

Specific Learning Disability

The IDEA definition of specific learning disability (SLD) has remained constant for many years:

> "Specific learning disability" means a disorder in one or more of the basic psychological processes involved in understanding or using language, spoken or written, which may manifest itself in an imperfect ability to listen, think, speak, read, write, spell, or to do mathematical calculations. (*Federal Register*, 1977, p. 65, 083)

To qualify for special education services under this disability category, the student must have an average or above-average intelligence and nonetheless exhibit difficulties with academic tasks manifested through difficulties in listening, thinking, or speaking. The real problem is how to operationalize this definition. That is, how "imperfect" must the student's ability be in order to be identified as having an SLD? For the three decades before IDEA of 2004, a discrepancy approach was applied to answer this question. Under the discrepancy model, a severe discrepancy between the student's ability (intelligence) and performance (achievement) must be demonstrated to qualify for special education services under the category of SLD. This approach was criticized because an IQ-achievement discrepancy cannot be reliably assessed until a student enters the third grade (Shaywitz, Fletcher, Holahan, & Shaywitz, 1992; Stuebing et al., 2002). In other words, educators had to wait for some young students to fail before they could reliably detect a specific learning disability.

In response to this criticism, IDEA 2004 no longer requires the use of discrepancy models for determining SLD (Harris-Murri, King, & Rostenberg, 2006). As an alternative approach, the Response to Intervention (RTI) model was proposed to determine eligibility for special education services. One of the fundamental differences between the RTI and the discrepancy model is in early intervention. Unlike the discrepancy model, which is primarily an assessment system for eligibility requirement, RTI is an intervention delivery system that is provided for all students (Burke, 2010). Instead of looking for within-child deficits as evidence of a disability, RTI targets a broader and more contextual analysis by considering day-to-day interpersonal and institutional factors that may affect student achievement and behavior (Harris-Murri, King, & Rostenberg, 2006).

Emotional and Behavioral Disorders

Also called an *emotional disturbance* by IDEA, or, in some states, an *emotional disability*, a student identified with an **emotional** or **behavioral disorder** consistently exhibits one or more of the following characteristics to a marked degree that clearly interferes with learning:

- poor academic performance not due to other disabilities
- poor interpersonal relationships
- inappropriate behaviors or feelings in normal circumstances
- extreme unhappiness, melancholy, or depression
- unfounded physical symptoms or fears associated with school or personal problems

You will need to make systematic observations of a student who may be classified under the category of emotional disturbance. These could include, for example, noting each time the student displays inappropriate behavior, such as crying or yelling, in normal circumstances for no apparent reason. When the inappropriate behavior continues for an extended time, under different conditions, a serious emotional problem may be found. However, final diagnosis will require consultation with a specialist, such as a counselor or school psychologist.

Autism

Autism is a complex yet increasingly prevalent disability, where students present certain characteristics along a continuum, or spectrum, of severity. Like ADHD, autism is primarily diagnosed according to criteria established in the *Diagnostic and Statistical Manual of Mental Disorders (DSM-V)* (American Psychiatric Association, 2013). However, the IDEA definition pertains to functioning within educational contexts. Students with autism demonstrate significant challenges with verbal and nonverbal communication and social interaction that negatively impact their academic performance. Usually identified before age 3, these students often engage in repetitive behaviors, have difficulty with change, and atypically perceive sensory information (such as light, sound, touch, and taste). Students presenting with milder forms of autism, indicated by verbal capabilities and achievement at or above grade level are typically taught in the general education classroom.

Children over the age of three can be identified as having autism as well as long as they meet the criteria outlined by the law. Given the problematic behaviors associated with autism, you will need to closely observe a student's behavior and complete a behavior checklist as part of the process of identification.

Identifying Students for Special Education Services

The steps leading to identifying a student as having one or more of the 13 disabilities specified by IDEA that qualifies him or her to receive special education services are summarized in Figure 13.2.

Identification must adhere to legal requirements and include a multidisciplinary evaluation conducted by a multidisciplinary team (MDT) (Salvia & Ysseldyke, 2001). Under IDEA 2004, the MDT must include at least one teacher or specialist with knowledge in the area of the suspected disability. The MDT often consists of individuals with a variety of perspectives and expertise, including:

- General education teacher
- Special education teacher

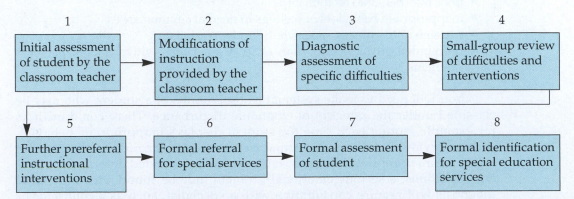

FIGURE 13.2   Steps for Identifying Students for Special Education Services

- School psychologist
- Speech and language specialist
- Parents
- Medical personnel whenever appropriate
- Social worker
- School/guidance counselor
- School nurses
- Occupational and/or physical therapists

To examine your role as a teacher in this process, as related to assessment, there are two major categories of steps: those done before identification and the actual identification of various disabilities.

Initially, students are observed and evaluated with intervention strategies to see if these changes are sufficient for improving student performance. In effect, you need to be certain that relatively simple changes in teaching methods or materials are not sufficient to improve the student's performance. If the student continues to have difficulties, the next step is to more closely analyze the student's ability to perform as expected. This usually includes the diagnostic assessment of specific learning difficulties or deficits using routine, teacher-made assessments. An analysis of errors may pinpoint these difficulties and suggest specific remediation strategies that can also be tried.

Prereferral

Some schools have a formal process of prereferral review for students with continuing difficulties. This may be called the *prereferral committee*, the *child study team*, the *student assistance team*, or *prereferral intervention team* (PIT). The purpose of this group is to provide an external review of your tentative diagnosis and feedback concerning instructional interventions that have been tried. The team's responsibilities may include reviewing information provided in the initial referral, collecting additional information such as school history, previous evaluation results, observations and interviews, and generating suggestions to address the student's difficulties and needs (Smith et al., 2012). The prereferral intervention is often implemented by the classroom teacher who indicates that a classroom-based learning or behavioral problem exists after the student does not respond to scientifically based instruction or behavioral interventions. Sometimes members of the committee observe the student in class or conduct individual assessments. Often the committee will recommend additional interventions that may effectively address the problem, or a specific plan will be developed. In the event that the student still struggles, a comprehensive educational assessment is completed.

As a prereferral approach, RTI has been used at different levels prior to a referral for special education services. Through this model teachers can determine if a student responds to scientific, research-based interventions within the general education classroom. The implementation of research-based instructional and/or behavioral supports with closely monitored progress are essential elements of the pre-referral process. For students who do not respond to the intervention, a more individualized and intensive instruction is provided before the formal referral for special education services is made.

The focus of RTI as a prereferral approach is to identify students who are experiencing academic and/or behavioral difficulties in early grades, and to provide effective interventions before they fall further behind. RTI is also referred to as *tiered instruction* because of its different levels of intervention. Emerging from prereferral intervention models, the problem-solving approach of RTI requires a team of teachers and other school personnel to identify strategies for adapting instruction and/or the classroom environment to increase the success of students who had academic or behavioral difficulties, prior to referring the student for special education evaluation (Fuchs, Mock, Morgan, & Young, 2003; Graner, Faggella-Luby, & Fritschmann, 2005).

Most school districts that are using RTI have implemented a three-tier intervention process. Tier 1 refers to high-quality instructional and behavioral supports for all children in general education settings by measuring the rate of academic growth of all students in comparison to other classes in the school or district or nation. Curriculum-based measurement (CBM) would be used to determine the overall achievement level and growth in achievement for the classroom of the struggling student. When students' rate of progress and performance lag behind those of their grade-level peers, these students will receive more specialized prevention or remediation at the Tier 2 level. Interventions at Tier 2 are still provided within general education settings. If students are not making satisfactory performance with the more intensive, specialized intervention, they will be moved to the Tier 3 level, which is an even more individualized intervention, but not yet special education and related services. This intervention level could occur within the general education curriculum, but also in a setting outside the classroom that is more appropriate for individualized instruction.

The continuous monitoring of progress (often weekly), measuring how adequately students respond to an intervention, is particularly important in an RTI model. Instead of a fixed period of time for a student staying in a specific tier level, most programs use the rate of progress as a means of determining whether a student should move from one tier to the next. For example, in moving a student from Tier 2 to Tier 3, instead of a 15-week fixed schedule, the student may be moved to a Tier 3 intervention after the ongoing documentation shows consistent nonresponsiveness of the student to a scientific, research-based intervention. After Tier 3, the nonresponsiveness could be cause to suspect that a student has a disability and should be referred for a comprehensive special education evaluation.

Formal Referral

Formal referral is a serious step because it suggests that the student may be eligible for special education services. A referral for a comprehensive special education evaluation marks the official beginning of the special education process. Once a student is formally referred, specific timelines and procedures must be followed to comply with federal and state laws. The initial phases of the special education processes include formal referral and determination of eligibility, submission of evidence of the severity and duration of the identified problem, and formation of the IEP team. Consequently, you will need to have specific documentation of the learning or behavior difficulties, interventions that have been tried, and the results of these interventions. It would be inadequate to simply say, for example, "Derek is always causing trouble in class. He likes to bother other students by poking and provoking them. We have tried several different approaches with Derek, each with limited success. He has a lot of trouble with mathematics." Rather, the information needs to be specific. For example:

> Derek physically touched, hit, or poked other students an average of 15 times per day in a way that disturbed or bothered the students. He talks without raising his hand in class discussions 75% of the time. Time out, individual contracts, and sessions with the counselor have been used with limited success that soon dissipates. Derek has turned in homework only 20% of the time. In class, he is unable to complete mathematics assignments that deal with the addition and subtraction of complex fractions. He is off task with mathematics assignments 50% of the time.

A screening committee will review the written referral, and the student's parents will be contacted. Suggestions for additional instructional interventions may be made. If the committee concludes that a formal assessment is needed, parental permission is secured, and a comprehensive evaluation begins. This process includes the multidisciplinary assessment of all areas of suspected disability, which is administered and interpreted by specialists in different areas as part of the multidisciplinary team (e.g., a school psychologist to administer intelligence, personality, and projective tests; a physical therapist to evaluate gross-motor skills; and an audiologist to evaluate hearing acuity). Students are tested by a variety of methods, which may include additional informal observation by the general education teacher. It is essential that the general education teacher document that the student is not making adequate progress over a period of time despite the additional opportunities and instruction being provided. In any event, identification is confirmed when classroom teacher evaluations and those of the specialists coincide.

Following formal assessment, the student may be identified as having one or more of the specific educational disabilities outlined by IDEA. Tables 13.1 and 13.2 summarize the teacher's role in the assessment and identification process.

Your role in this process involves not only using the assessment information, but also gathering and sharing the assessment information with other team members, including parents, and developing multiple classroom-based assessment instruments. It is important that you ask questions and encourage family participation throughout the process of assessment and intervention. While your input is critical to the accurate evaluation of your student, be aware of possible bias. It is best to use assessments for collecting objective information instead of confirming observations or conclusions about a student's difficulties.

TABLE 13.1 **Classroom Teacher's Role in the Assessment Process**

Steps in the Assessment Process	Classroom Teacher's Role
Prereferral	✓ Recognize areas where intervention is necessary using informal assessment methods ✓ Implement educational interventions, potentially using a response-to-intervention framework ✓ See if these interventions are successful in making the necessary improvements ✓ Document all interventions and the student's response or lack thereof to those interventions
Prereferral committee	✓ Recognize behaviors and specific disability indicators that may warrant a special education referral, versus those more related to cultural and linguistic differences ✓ Consult with committee members ✓ Implement interventions, as recommended by the committee
Formal Referral	✓ Document educational strengths, limitations, and needs through data collection of student work samples, behavioral observations, teacher-made tests, and other informal measures ✓ Consult with committee members and parents ✓ Complete needed referral forms ✓ Attend child study committee meeting and present data on student progress and behaviors ✓ Participate during development and implementation of IEP for students in the general education setting
Post-Assessment (if student is found eligible for special education services)	✓ Participate in development and implementation of IEP ✓ Accommodate students, as required by the IEP, and provide progress reports ✓ Collaborate with special education teachers, as needed

Source: Based on Wood (2006).

In order to determine eligibility, a comprehensive evaluation process must be used with the selection of assessment measures and procedures that are appropriate for the student's age, grade level, cultural background, and development. Once data are collected from various sources with multiple measures, the team will determine whether a disability exists and if so, whether the student needs special education and related services because of the identified disability.

Individualized Education Programs (IEPs)

Once a student is identified as having a disability that adversely affects educational performance and requires specialized instruction, the student is provided with an individualized education program (IEP). The IEP is a written plan that

TABLE 13.2   Classroom Teacher's Role in the Identification Process

Disability	Teacher's Role	Questions
Intellectual disability	Document adaptive behaviors; meet with child study committee	How well does the student function with daily life skills? Do deficits in daily living skills affect academic performance? Does cultural or linguistic background contribute to deficits in daily living skills?
Sensory impairment	Document visual or auditory; meet with child study committee	Can the student see well enough? Is there adequate eye–hand coordination? Is there a problem with the student's hearing?
Speech impairment	Document articulation and/or communication behaviors; meet with child study committee	Is there a speech problem of some kind?
Physical disability	Observe effect of disability on academic performance; meet with the child study committee	Does the disability adversely affect academic performance?
Learning disability	Document learning problems and achievement; interpret information in the cumulative folder; meet with child study committee	Is the student responding to a scientifically based instruction/intervention? Is the student's nonresponsiveness related to environmental factors, cultural situation, or language proficiency?
Emotional and behavioral disorders	Document inappropriate behaviors and feelings; meet with child study committee	Does the student have average or above-average intelligence? Is the behavior extreme for the circumstances? Is the behavior fleeting or consistent? Are any other disabilities responsible for the poor performance? How well does the student interact with others? Is the student unhappy, depressed, or withdrawn much of the time?
Attention deficit hyperactivity disorder	Observe and record instances of failing to pay attention, inappropriate hyperactivity and impulsivity; meet with child study committee	Does the student repeatedly, in many circumstances, demonstrate significant inattention? Is the student easily distracted? Does the student make careless mistakes? Is the student constantly restless? Does the student fidget excessively? Is the student always on the go or "wired"?
Autism	Observe communication, social interactions, and associated behaviors; meet with child study committee	Does the student have poor social and communication skills? Is the student overly focused on certain objects, subjects, or routines? Does the student have limited problem-solving skills and motivation?

serves as legal document. The key word is *individualized*, so two students identi-fied with the same disability may have different learning goals and accommoda-tions. The IEP is developed by a team of individuals (IEP team) who specify the present level of the student's knowledge and skills, annual goals, short-term learning objectives, the initiation and duration of special services, evaluation pro-cedures, and the educational program for the student (Spinelli, 2012).

Together with the special education teacher, the classroom teacher plays a major role in both determining and implementing the IEP, and in monitoring progress toward mastery of the goals and objectives. Assessments used by teachers provide the information necessary to determine whether students are making satisfactory progress toward meeting learning targets as specified in the IEP.

With respect to writing and implementing the IEP, teachers have several responsibilities. As a member of an IEP committee, you provide important infor-mation because the plan must be based on a clear and accurate documentation of the present level of academic achievements and functional performance of the student. This includes identification of a student's strengths as well as needs.

The IEP document must include a summary of the student's strengths, limitations, and needs, written to address each identified need, and be reviewed at least annually. Another teacher responsibility is setting short- and long-term learning targets and specifying the criteria and evaluation procedures that will be used to monitor progress toward meeting the targets (McLoughlin & Lewis, 2008). Here, it is important to set *individualized* targets. Every student needs a customized set of realistic targets that takes into account identified strengths and needs and preferred learning modes and styles. Appropriately delineated evaluation criteria and procedures need to reflect the degree of difficulty in the tasks, the variety of methods that should be employed, and a reasonable timetable.

Finally, teachers are responsible for ensuring that the student will partici-pate in regular classroom activities to the maximum extent possible. This includes both formal and informal classroom assessments. Here, your understanding of what is required with each type of assessment and your knowledge of the specific disabilities of the students are used to ensure that, whenever possible, assess-ment procedures do not need to be modified.

We have included an example of a hypothetical student IEP in Appendix B. That will give you a better sense of what is included and the considerations that lead to assessment accommodations.

Assessment Challenges for Students with Exceptional Needs

Your goal in assessing student learning is to obtain a fair and accurate indication of performance. Because disabilities may affect test-taking ability, you will need to make accommodations, or changes, in assessments when needed to ensure valid inferences and consequences. There are many justifiable ways to alter assessments

TABLE 13.3   **Problems Encountered by Students with Special Needs That Impact Classroom Assessment**

Problem	Impact on Assessment
Comprehension difficulties	Understanding directions; completing assessments requiring reasoning skills
Auditory difficulties	Understanding oral directions and test items; distracted by noises
Visual difficulties	Understanding written directions and test items; decoding symbols and letters; visual distractions
Time constraint difficulties	Completing assessments
Anxiety	Completing assessments; providing correct information
Embarrassment	Understanding directions; completing assessments
Variability of behavior	Completing assessments; demonstrating best work

for students with special needs. Before we consider these, it will be helpful to review the difficulties encountered by students with disabilities in testing situations. These difficulties are summarized in Table 13.3.

Comprehension Difficulties

Many students with mild disabilities have difficulty with comprehension. This means that they may struggle to understand verbal or written directions. If there is a sequence of steps in the directions, they may not be able to remember all the steps, particularly if the directions are verbal. Lengthy written directions may be too complicated, and the reading level may be too high. There may be words or phrases that the student does not understand. If the directions include several different operations, the student may be confused about what to do. Obviously, without a clear understanding of how to proceed, it will be difficult for these students to demonstrate their knowledge or skills.

Students with mild disabilities have even more difficulty understanding directions or test items that require reasoning skills. These students may respond well to knowledge and understanding questions and deal well with concrete ideas, but they may not respond very well to abstractions. For example, it would be relatively easy for such students to respond to a straightforward short-answer question such as, "What are the characteristics of a democratic government?" but much harder to respond to a more abstract question such as "How is the government of the United States different from a socialist government?"

Auditory Difficulties

Students with auditory disabilities have trouble processing information they hear quickly and accurately. This makes it especially hard for these students to follow and understand verbal directions. These students may also be sensitive to auditory distractions in the classroom. This could include sound from the hallway or an adjoining classroom, talking among students, outside noise, desk movement, pencil sharpening, questions asked by students, teacher reprimands, school announcements, and so on. Although these sounds may seem "normal" and do not bother most students, those with auditory disabilities will be distracted, and their attention will be diverted from the task at hand.

Visual Difficulties

Students with visual disabilities have difficulty processing what they see. These students may copy homework assignments or test questions from the board incorrectly by transposing numbers or interchanging letters. Often the student has difficulty transferring information to paper. A cluttered board that requires visual discrimination may also cause problems. Visual disabilities also pose challenges on some handwritten tests if the test is not legible and clearly organized. Some students with a visual disability have difficulty decoding certain symbols, letters, and abbreviations, such as +, −, *b* and *d*, < and >, and *n* and *m*. One symbol may be confused with another, and test problems with many symbols may take a long time for these students to understand.

Some types of objective test items are a problem because of visual perceptual difficulties. For example, lengthy matching items pose particular problems because the student may take a long time to peruse the columns, searching for answers and identifying the correct letters to use. Multiple-choice items that run responses together on the same line make it hard to discriminate among the possible answers.

Visual distractions can also interfere with test taking. For some students, a single visual cue—such as students moving in the classroom when getting up to turn in papers, student gestures, teacher motions, or something or someone outside—disrupts their present visual focus and makes it difficult to for them to maintain concentration.

Time Constraint Difficulties

Time can pose a major problem for many students with disabilities. Frequently visual, auditory, motor coordination, and reading difficulties make it hard for some students to complete tests in the same time frame as other students. Thus, these students should not be penalized for being unable to complete a test, especially timed tests that are constructed to reward speed in decoding and understanding questions and writing answers.

Anxiety

Although most students experience some degree of anxiety when completing tests, students with disabilities may be especially affected by feelings of anxiety because they fear that their disability will make it difficult to complete the test.

Some students are simply unable to function very well in a traditional test setting because the length or format of the test overwhelms them.

One general strategy to reduce unhealthy anxiety is to make sure that students have learned appropriate test-taking skills (detailed in Chapter 7). They need to know what to do if they do not fully understand the directions and how to proceed in answering different types of items (e.g., looking for clue words in multiple-choice, true/false, and completion items; crossing out incorrect alternatives in multiple-choice items; crossing out answers used in matching items). They also need to know to flag and skip difficult items and then come back to them when they have answered all other questions.

Embarrassment

Students with disabilities may be more sensitive than other students to feelings of embarrassment. They often want to hide or disguise their problems so that they are not singled out or labeled by their peers. As a result, they may want to appear to be "normal" when taking a test by not asking questions about directions and handing in the test at the same time as other students do, whether or not they are finished. They don't want to risk embarrassment by being the only one to have a question or by being the last one to complete their work. Students with special needs may also be embarrassed if they take a different test than others.

Variability of Behavior

The behavior of students with disabilities may vary considerably. This means that their disabilities may affect their behavior one day and not the next, and it may be difficult to predict this variability. This is especially true for students with emotional disturbances. For example, a student with a conduct disorder may be very disruptive one day and very on-task the next. Consequently, you will need to be tolerant and flexible in your assessments, realizing that on a particular day the disability may pose increased difficulties for the student.

Assessment Accommodations

An *assessment accommodation* refers to a change in testing materials or testing procedures provided to students to result in a valid indication of their knowledge, understanding, and skill (Salvia, Ysseldyke, & Bolt, 2013). When you develop your intervention strategies, you need to include accommodations in your planning, and, if necessary, the modifications as well. Accommodations are different from modifications. Accommodations do not substantially change the content of the curriculum, the difficulty level of instruction, or the assessment criteria. Modifications may involve more significant changes in the assessment criteria, curriculum content, or level of instruction and learning (Smith et al., 2012). Once you understand how disabilities can interfere with valid assessment, you can take steps to adapt the test or other assessment to accommodate the disability. Thurlow, Lazarus, Thompson, and Morse (2005) reported that all states most commonly allowed accommodations in the areas of presentations, equipment/materials, response, scheduling and timing, and setting. These accommodations can be grouped into three major categories: adaptations in test construction, test administration, and testing site (Wood, 2002).

You may feel pressured or challenged to provide accommodations to meet individual needs in a large general education or inclusive classroom. One option is to develop tests that are accessible to all your students in the same setting, using **universally designed assessments** (UDA). UDA refers to assessments that are designed to allow participation for the widest possible range of students (Spinelli, 2012). The concept of UDA is to meet the needs of all students in a diverse setting through a universally accessible design instead of through individualized accommodations. In this way, teachers thoughtfully design assessments from the outset to be clear and appropriate for all diverse learners in the classroom rather than adjusting or accommodating existing assessments to meet some students' needs after the fact (Thurlow, Lazarus, Christensen, & Shyyvan, 2016).

Adaptations in Test Directions, Construction, and Format

The first component to adapt is directions for the test. You can do this for all students, or you can provide a separate set of directions for students with disabilities. Here are some ways to modify test directions:

1. Read written directions aloud, slowly, and give students ample opportunity to ask questions about the directions. Reread directions for each page of questions.
2. Keep directions short and simple.
3. Give examples of how to answer questions.
4. Focus attention by underlining verbs.
5. Provide separate directions for each section of the test.
6. Provide one direction for each sentence (list sentences vertically).
7. Check students' understanding of the directions.
8. During the test, check the students' answers to be sure they understand the directions.
9. When reading is not the testing purpose, adjust the reading level of the items, or provide assistance with reading if necessary (Mastropieri & Scruggs, 2013).

The general format of the test should be designed to simplify the amount of information that is processed at one time. Accomplish this by leaving plenty of white space on each page so that students are not overwhelmed. The printing should be large, with adequate space between items; this results in a smaller number of items per page. The test should be separated into clearly distinguished short sections, and only one type of question should be on each page. The printing should be dark and clear. If bubble sheets are used for objective items, use larger

Teacher's Corner

Susan Pereira

National Board Certified Elementary Teacher

It is critical that the general education teacher work in collaboration with the special education teacher when assessing children with special needs. The regular education teacher should communicate to the special education teacher the objective or standard that is to be evaluated and, collectively, develop a tool to measure appropriately. Sometimes an evaluation can be used with just a few minor accommodations, perhaps giving the evaluation in a one-on-one setting or asking just a few questions at a time. In order to determine the most effective and appropriate assessment tool, the teacher must look at the child as an individual, keeping in mind the goals and accommodations set forth in the child's individualized education program.

bubbles or transcribe students' answers to a bubble sheet for them. Be sure multiple-choice items list the alternatives vertically, and do not run questions or answers across two pages. Number each page of the test. Some students may be aided by a large sheet of construction paper that they can place below the question or that has a cut-out window to allow a greater focus on a particular section of the test. If possible, design the format of an adapted test to look as much like the test for other students as possible (Salend, 2009).

Other accommodations to the format of the test depend on the type of item.

Short-Answer and Essay Items. Students with disabilities may have difficulty with constructed-response items because of the organization, reasoning, and writing skills required. For these reasons, complicated essay questions requiring long responses should be avoided. If you use an essay question, be sure students understand terms such as *compare*, *contrast*, and *discuss*. To help students better understand your expectations, it is important to define command words and provide examples to demonstrate what you expect for the test items. Use a limited number of essay questions, and allow students to use outlines for their answers. Some students may need to audio record their answer rather than writing it; all students will need to have sufficient time.

Example

Poor: Compare and contrast the Canadian and U.S. governments.

Improved: *Compare* and *contrast* the Canadian and U.S. governments.

   I. *Compare* by telling how the governments are *alike*. Give two examples.
   II. *Contrast* by telling how the governments are *different*. Give two examples.

If the short-answer question focuses on recall, you can adapt it in ways that will help students to organize their thoughts and not feel overwhelmed.

> *Example (adapted from* Creating a Learning Community at Fowler High School, *1993)*
>
> *Poor:*
>
> Directions: On your own paper, identify the following quotations. Tell (1) who said it, (2) to whom it was said or if it was a soliloquy, (3) when it was said, and (4) what it means.
>
> But soft, what light through yonder window breaks?
> It is the east, and Juliet is the sun.
> Arise, fair sun, and kill the envious moon.
> (Include a series of several more quotes.)
>
> *Improved:*
>
> Directions: In the space provided, identify the following for each quotation.
>
> Tell   **1.** Who said it
>   **2.** To whom it was said or if it was a soliloquy
>   **3.** When it was said
>   **4.** What it means
>
> | *Who said it; to whom it was said* | *When it was said* |
> |---|---|
> | Juliet | When Tybalt kills Mercutio |
> | Romeo | When Juliet waits for news from Romeo |
> | Paris | The balcony scene |
> | Mercutio | When Paris discusses his marriage with Friar Laurence |
> | The Prince | |
>
> **1.**   But soft, what light through yonder window breaks?
>   It is the east, and Juliet is the sun.
>   Arise, fair sun, and kill the envious moon.
>
> | *Who said it* | *To whom* | *When* | *What it means* |
> |---|---|---|---|
> | _____ | _____ | _____ | _____ |
> | _____ | _____ | _____ | _____ |
> | _____ | _____ | _____ | _____ |

Multiple-Choice Items. If the test contains multiple-choice questions, have students circle the correct answer rather than writing the letter of the correct response next to the item or transferring the answer to a separate sheet. Arrange response alternatives vertically, and include no more than four alternatives for each question.

Keep the language simple and concise, and as indicated earlier, avoid wording such as "a and b but not d," or "either a or c," or "none of the above" that weights the item more heavily for reasoning skills. Limit the number of multiple-choice items, and give plenty of time to complete the test. Other students may easily be able to answer one or more items per minute, but it will take students with special needs longer. Follow the suggestions listed in Chapter 8, and realize that poorly constructed and formatted items are likely to be detrimental to students with disabilities.

Binary-Choice Items.   True/false and other binary-choice items need to be stated clearly and concisely. Answers should be circled. Negatively stated items should be avoided. Students could be confused when asked to choose "false" for a negative statement, for example, "The office of president is not described in the Constitution" (Salend, 1995). Sometimes students are asked to change false items to make them true, but this is not recommended for students with disabilities. Limit the number of items to 10 to 15.

Completion Items.   These items can be modified to reduce the student's dependence on structured recall by providing *word banks* that accompany the items. The word bank is a list of possible answers that reduces dependence on memory. The list can be printed on a separate sheet of paper so that the student can move it up and down on the right side of the page. Also, provide large blanks for students with motor control difficulties.

Performance Assessments.   Performance assessments are especially helpful when testing students who may have word-finding (retrieval) problems, communication disorders, or other skills that limit their verbal communication (Mastropieri & Scruggs, 2013). The first accommodation to performance assessments may need to be in the directions. Students with disabilities need directions that clearly specify what is expected, with examples, and a reasonable time frame. Because these assessments involve thinking and application skills, it is important to be certain that students with disabilities are able to perform the skills required. The steps may need to be clearly delineated.

First, determine exactly what you want your students to be able to do after the instructional unit. Then set up the materials and provide opportunities for students to perform on the test. Finally, score students' performance by using a scoring rubric that clearly lists test items and scoring criteria (Mastropieri & Scruggs, 2013). To score the test item objectively, the scoring rubric needs to be developed with clear and specific criteria, as illustrated in Figure 13.3.

Obviously, if some aspect of the performance requires physical skills or coordination that the disability prevents or makes difficult, assistance will need to be provided. If the performance requires group participation, you will need to closely monitor the interactions.

Portfolios.   In some ways, this type of assessment is ideal for students with disabilities because the assignments and products can be individualized to show

FIGURE 13.3   **Example of Scoring Criteria**

Draw a picture of an ecosystem. Label all parts.

Score	Scoring Criteria
3	Picture with living and nonliving things that appear to interact in some general way. Living and nonliving things labeled.
2	Picture of living and nonliving things not labeled, or labeled living things, or labeled nonliving things.
1	One of the above or general relevant comment.
0	Nothing relevant.

Source: Based on Mastropieri & Scruggs, 2013.

progress. This means that you may need to adapt the portfolio requirements to fit well with what the student is capable of doing. In the portfolio you could include your reflection of how the student made progress and how the student was responsible for success.

Portfolio assessment may lack standardization and objectivity; therefore, teachers need to ensure that grades or judgments based on portfolio products are reliable/precise and valid (Gelfer, Xu, & Perkins, 2004; Mastropieri & Scruggs, 2013). The following strategies can help with the reliability/precision and validity of a portfolio assessment:

1. Use multiple measures of the same skills or products.
2. Have multiple individuals independently assess portfolio products.
3. Make comparisons with more traditional measures (e.g., standardized tests, criterion-referenced measurement, or direct observation).

Adaptations in Test Administration

Adaptations during test administration involve changes in procedures that lessen the negative effect of disabilities while the student is taking the test. Most of these procedural accommodations depend on the nature of the disability or difficulty, as summarized in Figure 13.4. Do note that this is not an exhaustive list, nor are the suggestions exclusive to the identified problem area. You may find that some adjustments to test administration are universally beneficial for students and do not compromise the integrity of the test.

These accommodations are also based on common sense. For example, if the student has a visual problem, you need to give directions orally and check carefully to determine whether he or she has understood the questions. For students who are hindered by time constraints, provide breaks and make sure they have sufficient time to complete the test. It may be best to divide a long test into sections and spread the testing over several days, though unlimited time to complete tests

FIGURE 13.4   Adaptations in Test Administration

Comprehension	• Present test directions orally and in writing. • Double-check student understanding. • Let students audio record responses. • Correct open-ended responses for content and not spelling or grammar. • Read the test aloud. • Provide an outline for essay responses. • Use objective test items. • Use task analysis to separate a larger task into smaller or simpler steps. • Provide an audio recording of directions and test items that students can replay as needed.
Auditory Difficulties	• Use written instead of oral directions and questions. Supplement with visuals or pictures. • Go slowly when presenting tests orally; enunciate words distinctly. • Seat students in a quiet place for testing. • Stress the importance of being quiet to all students.
Visual Difficulties	• Present test directions orally and in writing. • Provide an audio recording of directions and test items. • Allow student to provide verbal rather than written responses. • Seat student away from visual distractions; use a study carrel or adjust desk placement. • Provide test questions section by section instead of all at once. • Keep additional distractions to a minimum: avoid having students submit papers during the test; meet classroom visitors at the door and talk in the hallway.
Time Constraints	• Provide plenty of time to complete the test; avoid timed tests when possible. • Offer breaks during tests or split the test across two days. • Audio record or allow verbal response for students with slow writing skills.
Anxiety	• Provide study guides and practice test items or practice tests. • Plan for several small tests instead of a few large or lengthy tests. • Use criterion-referenced instead of norm-referenced assessments. • Refrain from placing additional pressure on students' test performance by emphasizing negative or dire consequences for poor performance. • Allow retesting. • Prompt anxiety reducing strategies during the test (deep breaths, positive self-talk).
Embarrassment	• Avoid singling out students with disabilities during testing; offer help and confer about accommodations privately. • Monitor all students the same way during testing. • Model modified or accommodated tests after the original version so they are visually similar; provide the same cover sheet.
Variable Behavior	• Allow retesting and rescheduling of test to a different day. • Monitor student closely to determine if problem behavior is interferring with test performance.

Source: Based on Salend (2011) and Wood (2002).

should be avoided. A good rule of thumb is to provide students with disabilities 50% additional time to complete a test (Reynolds, Livingston, & Willson, 2008).

In general, it is best to place a "Testing—Do Not Disturb" sign on your classroom door to discourage visitors and other distractions. You will need to monitor students with special needs closely as they take the test and encourage them to ask questions. It is also helpful to encourage them to use dark paper to underline the items they are currently working on (Lazzari & Wood, 1994).

Adaptations in Testing Site

You may find it necessary to allow students with special needs to take the test in a different location than the general education classroom. This alternative test site is often the resource room in the school or some other room that is quiet with fewer distractions than the general education classroom. Also, as long as someone can monitor the testing, the student will have more opportunities to ask questions and feel less embarrassed when asking for clarification or further explanation.

If you are unsure about how you should accommodate a student with special needs, revisit the IEP and also check with the student's assigned special education teacher. This individual can help you more fully understand the student's strengths and limitations, as well as the appropriateness of specific adaptations.

Grading and Reporting Accommodations

For students with special needs in inclusive settings it is necessary to consider some adaptations to the grading procedures to make sure that disabilities do not unfairly influence the determination of the grade. This may present a dilemma for you. On the one hand, is it fair to use different grading standards and procedures for some students? On the other hand, is it fair to possibly penalize students by forcing an existing grading scheme on them that may have detrimental impacts? The ideal solution would be to keep the grading system for students with special needs the same as that used for other students and be sure that appropriate accommodations have been made in the assessment strategies to ensure that the information on which the grade is determined is not adversely affected by the disability. However, depending on the student's IEP, it may be necessary to adapt the grading system that is used. While grading is considered in more detail in Chapter 15, here we will consider some principles for special needs students.

Grading Accommodations

Several types of grading accommodations are appropriate for students with special needs. These include IEP grading, shared grading, and contract grading.

IEP Grading.   The IEP grading system bases grades on the achievement of the goals and objectives explicitly stated in the student's IEP. The criteria needed to obtain satisfactory progress are stated in the IEP. It is problematic, however, to translate success in reaching IEP objectives to grades. One approach is to use the school district's performance standards to determine grades. For example, if the student has performed at the 90% proficiency level, as required by the IEP to demonstrate competence, and 90% translates to a B letter grade, then the student is assigned a B for that assessment. Another approach is to review the criteria in the IEP and match levels of performance with what other students need to demonstrate for different grades. If you decide, for instance, that the level of mastery a student with special needs demonstrates by achieving but not exceeding all IEP objectives is about the same level as that demonstrated by other students receiving Cs, then the grade for the student with special needs would also be a C. If the student exceeds stated IEP objectives, then a B or A may be appropriate.

Because the goal of inclusion is to make the educational experience of students with disabilities like that of other students, it is best if the grading procedures reflect the same criteria. You should avoid a process whereby the grade is determined merely on the percentage of IEP objectives obtained, because there is a tendency to inadvertently set low or easier objectives to help students obtain good grades (Cohen, 1983).

Shared Grading. In shared grading, the general education and special education or resource room teachers determine the grade together. The weight that each teacher provides for the grade should be agreed on at the beginning of the marking period. This usually reflects the extent to which each teacher is responsible for different areas of learning. Typically, the classroom teacher will have the most influence on the grades.

One advantage of this type of grading is that the special education or resource room teacher may be able to provide some insight that helps explain poor grades and other mitigating circumstances related to the student's disability. Using this team approach also helps the classroom teacher determine appropriate criteria and standards for grading.

Contracting. A contract is a written agreement between the general education teacher and the student that specifies the nature of the work that the student must complete to achieve a particular grade. Teachers frequently use contracts for students with special needs because they can integrate IEP objectives and clearly state for the student and parents the type and quality of work to be completed. For older students, the contract should include options for achieving different grades. Contracts for elementary-level students should be simpler, with more general outcomes at a single level, as illustrated in Figure 13.5. Several components should be included in a contract, such as:

- A description of the work to be completed
- A description of criteria by which work will be evaluated
- Signatures of the student, teacher, and other involved parties
- A timeline for completion of the work

FIGURE 13.5   Sample Contract for Elementary-Level Students

I will receive a "plus" for work in class today as long as I:

- Take belongings from my backpack and put them in my desk *without being asked*,
- Join my reading group the first time it is called,
- Clean off my desk after snack and put all the garbage in the trash can,
- Raise my hand each time I want to answer a question,
- Put all my finished papers in the "done" basket before lunch,
- Line up on the playground immediately *the first time the whistle is blown*,
- Put all the classroom supplies back in the supply boxes after project time,
- Put all my finished papers in the "done" basket before I go home,
- Put my homework papers in my portfolio and take them home, and
- Put my belongings in my backpack, get my coat from the cubby, and line up to leave school *before my bus is called*.

_____   _____   _____
Student   Teacher   Date

Source: Based on Wood (2002).

Rubrics.   A rubric is used with standards-based grading with an established guideline or planned set of criteria documenting what is expected for a specific assignment (Spinelli, 2012). A well-developed rubric should always include clear, specific, and explicit criteria that students are expected to achieve at different levels. This is especially helpful for students who have difficulty understanding expectations. With a clearly structured rubric students can self-evaluate their performance during the task completion process. Table 13.4 lists the characteristics of a high-quality rubric.

Reporting Accommodations

Regardless of the grading system that you use, it will probably be necessary to supplement the regular progress report with additional information. This is typically done as a checklist or a narrative summary that interprets achievement in

TABLE 13.4   Characteristics of High-Quality Rubrics for Students with Special Needs

Characteristics	Description
Relevant	All requirements are directly related to the assignment.
Explicit	The expectations are clearly stated for each criterion.
Specific	Each criterion is clearly described with measurable terms.
Fair	The rubric includes universally designed assessments or accommodations for students with special needs.
Valid	The contents to be measured are relevant to the materials taught.
Focused	The focus is on the target skills instead of the procedures.

light of the student's disability. A checklist is convenient for showing progress in developmentally sequenced courses and can easily integrate the IEP with course objectives to give a more complete report. The checklist states the objectives, and the teacher indicates if each has been mastered or needs further work.

A narrative summary helps you to give the student a still more personalized evaluation. Although such a report takes some time, it more fully explains why you believe the student demonstrated certain skills, which skills were not mastered, and which need special attention. The narrative can also be used to report on behavioral performance, emotions, and interpersonal skills, as well as academic performance. Specific incidents or examples can be described. The following is an example of a progress report for an eighth-grade student with a learning disability (Mehring, 1995). Notice that the teacher has indicated areas of improvement, accommodations (typing), and areas that will be stressed in the future.

> Alphonso has improved his ability to recognize and correct spelling errors. He has mastered the recognition and capitalization of proper nouns, names, titles, and buildings. He is not yet consistent in his capitalization of cities. Punctuation, especially the use of commas, is also an area in which Alphonso needs improvement. He has been using the computer to prepare drafts of his written products. This has made it easier for him to edit since his handwriting is laborious and illegible at times. The overall quality and length of his creative writings has improved significantly since the last reporting period. We will continue to focus on capitalization and punctuation throughout the next grading period. In addition, we will begin working on recognizing and correcting sentence problems (fragments, run-ons, unclear pronoun reference, and awkward sentences). (Mehring, 1995, p. 17)

By focusing a supplemental progress report on the learning process, students will have a better idea about how they need to change to improve their performance. Students and parents need to know if a specific approach to learning needs to be modified or if something else needs to be further investigated.

Another way to report the progress of students with disabilities is to graph the student's performance throughout the reported period. Graphs such as bar charts are considered one of the most effective and efficient ways to demonstrate students' learning because they include the most information with the least explanation, and they are easy for everybody to understand. See Figure 13.6 as an example of using a bar chart to illustrate a student's progress.

Gifted Students

Though you may not think of these students as having "special needs," students with identified gifts and talents are also thought of as exceptional learners. Due to their high achievement potential and need for services and activities outside of what are offered in the typical classroom, assessment accommodations may be needed. Many of the principles of assessment discussed throughout this chapter

FIGURE 13.6   Mike's Reading Comprehension Throughout 9 Weeks

apply to the identification and classroom assessment of gifted students. For these students, supplemental services and supports help them to further develop their unique capabilities. Gifted students may have general high achievement potential, particular areas of strength (such as in math or arts), or be identified as *twice exceptional*. **Twice exceptional** students are those who have been identified as gifted but also have an identified disability.

As is the case with assessing students for special education eligibility, assessing students for gifted educational programming is multifaceted. Assessment often occurs through a two-stage process where by students are screened using an achievement or intelligence test, and then assessed in specific areas relative to suspected strengths, motivation, and persistence (Friend, 2014). Authentic assessments may be used to provide students the opportunity to show what they know in a real-world, or authentic, way. These types of assessments may include portfolios, written essays, or instances of problem solving (Worrell & Erwin, 2011). Because teachers must use a combination of objective assessment tools and subjective judgment of students' overall profiles in order to identify students as gifted, it is essential that efforts be made to ensure equity and minimize bias (Council for Exceptional Children, 2015; National Association for Gifted Children, 2010).

Within the classroom, teachers should similarly use a variety of assessment practices with students identified as gifted. Twice exceptional students will likely require specific testing accommodations, but as suggested previously, teachers can universally design assessments in an effort to appropriately assess all students without the need for further individualized accommodations.

Summary

The purpose of this chapter was to introduce you to the assessment adaptations needed to accommodate students with exceptional needs in inclusive settings. Overall, suggestions made in other chapters apply to these students, but you need to keep some additional considerations in mind. In general, it is important to make sure that a student's disability does not unfairly influence his or her performance on tests and other types of assessments. Major points in the chapter include the following:

- Legal mandates in IDEA require educational experiences, including assessment, to take place in the least restrictive environment.
- Regular classroom teachers are responsible for gathering information to identify students for special education services.
- The reauthorization of the Individuals with Disabilities Education Act (IDEA) of 1990 required that a general education teacher become a member of the IEP team.
- The evaluation of students for identification must be nondiscriminatory—in the student's native language and not racially or culturally biased.
- The most recent reauthorization of the Individuals with Disabilities Education Act (IDEA) of 2004 proposed the response to intervention (RTI) model as an alternative approach to determining eligibility for special education services.
- Teacher observation is a major component in identification and writing the student's IEP.
- Teachers are responsible for setting individualized learning targets with appropriate assessments and for providing specific assessment information for referral and possible identification.
- Students are identified as having one or more educational disabilities, based in part on careful teacher observation.
- Teachers are responsible for assessing the adaptive behaviors of students referred and identified as having intellectual disability.
- Comprehension difficulties require adaptations in test directions.
- Auditory and visual difficulties require a minimum of distractions.
- Time constraint difficulties require longer testing time and frequent breaks in testing.
- Anxiety and embarrassment need to be minimized for students with special needs.
- The behavior of students with disabilities varies from day to day; this variation needs to be considered when observing and evaluating student behavior.
- Adaptations may need to be made to test directions, the format of the test, and the construction of different types of items.
- Adaptations may be needed during test administration and to the testing site.
- Grading students with special needs should include consideration of IEP objectives, opinions of other teachers working with the student, and contracting.
- Gifted students are similarly considered exceptional learners, and many assessment techniques and accommodations discussed are relevant for meeting their needs as well.

Introductory Case Study Answer

Britta's changes were assessment accommodations. Assessment accommodations can include changes in testing materials to result in a valid indication of a student's knowledge, understanding, and skills. An accommodation does not substantially change the content, level of difficulty, or assessment criteria. Britta's alternative assessment covered the same level and amount content and she proposed scoring it based on content knowledge that was similar to other students' summative assessments. An assessment modification would involve changes in the assessment criteria, curriculum content, and/or level of learning.

The coordinator was most likely concerned because Britta had not tried other, less substantial assessment accommodations. Since Damian is required to take the end-of-year high-stakes assessment, it is critical that Damian get practice throughout the school year. Thus, while Britta was providing the minimal accommodations as described in Damian's IEP, she should observe Damian's response to other accommodations when given the high-stakes testing format. Such accommodations might include:

a) giving Damian the same computerized assessment as a paper-pencil assessment;
b) allowing Damian to take the assessment in another environment with fewer distractions;
c) provide Damian with similar practice items from the test bank prior to the assessment;
d) allow for retesting;
e) modify the wording of questions so that the wording is simple and distracters/extra information is eliminated;
f) ensure that Damian has extra time to complete the test without fear of missing out on classroom activities;
g) provide extensive modeling in testing strategies; and
h) orally double-checking his understanding of each question before allowing him to answer it.

Britta's adjusted assessment is appropriate because, while it appears to be very different from other students' summative assessment, it assesses the same content. The goal of assessing student learning is to obtain a fair and accurate indication of performance. Because Damian's disability affects his test-taking skills, appropriate assessment accommodations to ensure fairness and accuracy in gathering evidence of his learning are necessary. By changing the format of Damian's assessment, Britta can ensure her inferences about his knowledge are valid. Adjustments will also ensure that his grade is not adversely affected by his disability.

Suggestions for Action Research

1. Interview two or three regular classroom teachers about the accommodations they make for students with exceptional needs who are in their classes. Ask about their experience in gathering information for identification and setting learning targets, as well as about the assessment accommodations they have made. Compare their responses to suggestions in the chapter.

2. Interview two special education teachers. Ask them what they believe regular classroom teachers need to know to accommodate students with special needs in inclusive settings. In their work with regular classroom teachers, what do they see as the teachers' greatest weaknesses when making assessment accommodations?

3. In a team with one or two other students, devise a plan for how you would accommodate the assessment of one or two students with special needs who have been placed in general education classrooms. You will need as much information about the students as possible, and it would be best if you could observe the students. Once the plan is complete, review it with the students' teacher(s) for feedback and suggestions.

MyEdLab Self-Check 13.1

MyEdLab Self-Check 13.2

MyEdLab Self-Check 13.3

MyEdLab Self-Check 13.4

MyEdLab Application Exercise 13.1   Identifying Students with Special Needs

MyEdLab Application Exercise 13.2   Assessment Accommodations

Assessment for Culturally and Linguistically Diverse Students

with Amy Hutton

Who are CLD students?

- English language learners
- English as a second language students
- Culturally diverse students

Summative Assessment Accommodations

- Preparation
- Direct translation
- Portfolios
- Accommodation options
- Grading

Embedded Formative Assessment Accommodations

- Observations
- Nonverbal behavior and vocal cues
- Informal oral questioning
- Code-switching
- Summative-based formative
- Assessments

Assessment for CLD Students

Acculturation

- Stages
- Assessment
  - Embedded informal
  - Formal

Impact on Classroom Assessment

- Language and literacy
- Educational background
- Cultural factors

Challenges in Content-Area Assessment

- Comprehension
- Expression
- Lack of knowledge
- Unfamiliarity
- Stress
- Bias and sensitivity

CHAPTER 14 Concept Map

Learning Outcomes

After reading this chapter, you should be able to:

14.1 Understand the characteristics of CLD students, as well as the potential impact these characteristics could have on both the nature of classroom assessments and interpretations of student work.

14.2 Know the steps involved in acculturation and how acculturation is an important influence on CLD student assessment.

14.3 Know how assessment should be modified to accommodate CLD student cultural, language, educational, and socioeconomic differences.

14.4 Be able to give examples of formative and summative assessments that have been modified to accommodate CLD students.

14.5 Know the key features of effective assessment of CLD students.

Introductory Case Study

Why Make These Specific Adaptations?

Aaron, a third-grade teacher, was hosting a student teacher, Kayla, during his science unit on animal adaptations. Aaron's summative assessment on the terms *hibernation*, *migration*, and *camouflage* was to be given on Friday. It included students (a) writing the definition of each science term, (b) giving two examples of animals that use each adaptation, and (c) writing three sentences explaining an adaptation the student would want to have for himself if he were on a deserted island and why that specific adaptation.

As Aaron was looking over the assessment, he told Kayla that he would need to adapt it for his student, Eduardo, an English language learner who had immigrated to America last year. He explained that he would make the following changes:

1. He will write the three terms on a sheet of paper, say them aloud, and then have Eduardo draw a picture to explain what he knows about each term.
2. He will have six cards with pictures of animals. Each animal card will clearly display one adaptation. He will say a term and have Eduardo find at least one of the two cards that display that adaptation.
3. He will eliminate the writing section for Eduardo. Instead, he will have Eduardo tell him orally which adaptation he wished he could have and give one reason why. Aaron will also give Eduardo an example.

Kayla admitted that she had not been exposed to teaching culturally and linguistically diverse students; she wanted to learn more. She asked Aaron to explain his reasoning behind each of the assessment changes.

Aaron started with the statement, "When Eduardo came to America, he spoke no English and had not had formal schooling during the previous year. Eduardo is still is a Level 1 on a scale of 1–5 in regard to his reading and writing abilities, but he is a Level 3 for speaking and listening. From my observations, informal oral questioning, partner activities, and other formative assessments this week, I believe Eduardo understands the difference between the three adaptations. Now I want to formally assess his knowledge. Since assessment is a form of communication, I want Eduardo to communicate to me what he knows about adaptations. If I give him the same summative assessment as my other students, he may not be able to accurately demonstrate his knowledge. The changes to the assessment don't alter the purpose of the assessment and assess the same learning objectives for Eduardo as my other students, they just do it in an alternative manner that reduces the language barrier."

As you read the chapter, think about why Aaron made these specific adaptations for Eduardo. What does Aaron know about the impact that Eduardo's language and literacy skill factors (reading, writing, listening, speaking) could have on his assessment of the science content? Explain why each assessment adaptation may or may not be appropriate for Eduardo.

An undeniable fact about our schools is that the student population is becoming increasingly diverse. In fact, by 2050 it is estimated that white school-aged children will comprise between 25% and 40% of the total student population (Gottlieb, 2016; Herrera, Murry & Cabral, 2014). The trend is not confined to urban settings—suburban and rural areas also see significance growth in nonmajority children. Since you know from previous chapters that high-quality assessment needs to be appropriate and fair for all students, it is imperative to understand how this diversity needs to be considered in your assessments. Consider the following questions from teachers:

- It's the sixth week of class and Ramon has not shown any desire to show what he has learned on either his homework or tests. Why is that?
- From my observations Maryna has learned how to multiple. Why are her test scores so low?
- Why doesn't Yaoying ask more questions in class?
- Even when I used the Spanish version of the test Manuel did poorly. Why didn't he do better on the assessment?

These kinds of questions address what we'll cover in this chapter. First, we'll consider just what is meant by "culturally and linguistically" different, then examine the process of acculturation of these students. In the final sections, assessment strategies are reviewed that accommodate these differences to promote more accurate recording of achievement and promotion of student learning.

Who Are "Culturally and Linguistically" Diverse Students?

In the context of this chapter, we use the term *culturally and linguistically diverse* (CLD) learners to describe students whose culture or language differs from that of the dominant culture. You might think of the "dominant" culture as the one that has traditionally been associated with white students from relatively well-educated, financially stable families that are comfortable in their environment. CLD children, in contrast, have characteristics that are qualitatively different from those in the dominant culture, so how they understand, process, and react to both instruction and assessment differs from those from the majority culture. This is because CLD children have learned, through immersion in the nondominate culture, to approach learning and interaction with others in a manner that is consistent with their family and community norms, not what they may experience in a traditional classroom.

What kind of CLD child first comes to your mind? It's very possible that it could be English language learners (ELL), English as a second language (ESL) students, or limited English proficiency (LEP) students. For these students, English is their second language; they may also be called limited English proficiency (LEP) students. Other related acronyms are also used, such as EL (English learners), or ESOL (English for speakers of other languages), as are other descriptive terms such as *language-minority students*, *heritage language learners*, *language learners*, *nonnative English speakers*, or *bilingual students*. The proliferation of terms can be confusing, to say the least. Just be sure to know what is meant by the term or acronym in your particular setting. Regardless of the label used, which will vary across school districts, schools, and even teachers within the same school, the dominant feature is that these students are unable to communicate in English with sufficient fluency to learn effectively (Solano-Flores, 2016). The difficulties in understanding English, the language used for instruction, essentially puts "limits" on their capacity to learn. These limitations apply to assessment as well.

English language learners represent numerous nationalities, socioeconomic backgrounds, cultures, and ethnicities. While Latino families represent a large percentage of LEP students in America, followed by Asian students, increasing immigration of families from a wide range of countries is diversifying the range of different non-English languages. Those not as easily distinguishable are second-generation students, whose parents may have immigrated and still speak a second language at home. Many other types of culturally and linguistically diverse learners exist, such as indigenous populations, transnational students, and those from communities with heavy influences of nondominant culture. Any of these backgrounds could influence the way a child learns and whether or not they are able to successfully participate in an English-dominant classroom.

What about students whose primary language is English, but are still different from those in the dominant culture? These are individuals who are essentially at a cultural disadvantage, not because of the dominant language, but because of other characteristics that contribute to difficulties learning in a majority culture. These are often minority students living in poverty in urban, rural, and even suburban areas. Children of unauthorized parents, even if they do speak English, would be included in this group, as would, to some extent, English-speaking students from different countries. Poverty, of course, has significant deleterious impacts on children due to family isolation, frequent moves from one "home" to another, single parenting, lack of resources, and other factors. These influences may result in a cultural deprivation that results in characteristics at odds with the mainstream culture.

We prefer the use of CLD because it is more inclusive, capturing a range of linguistic and cultural differences that need to be understood, appreciated, and attended to in both instruction and assessment. It certainly includes children whose dominate language is not English, but even English-speaking, culturally different students need appropriate assessment accommodations. As we will see, making those appropriate accommodations can be challenging. Many of the challenges faced by CLD students are very similar to those faced by students with special needs, sometimes resulting in inappropriate labeling (see Chapter 13).

Acculturation

In this section two important aspects of what CLD students experience as they accommodate to the dominant culture are discussed. First, acculturation is defined, with examples, then we look at how acculturation can be assessed.

Understanding Acculturation

Acculturation is a process of assimilation into a different culture. It refers to how an individual adopts the norms, behaviors, and traditions of a culturally different group. Children initially adopt the values and language appropriate to their dominant context (enculturation). When students are placed in an environment with a different culture, they must make behavioral and psychological changes to cope with and do well in the "new" setting. They are, in a sense, "acculturating," and their journey on this process can greatly impact their academic performance (Van de Vijver, 2016). That is, learning, as demonstrated on assessments, may well be overshadowed by the process of acculturation. What children become accustomed to with respect to patterns of response and other behavior that has "worked" becomes a filter through which new demands and actions are understood and acted on. This is where the teacher, who may be used to interpreting behavior from one lens (his or her own, consistent with the dominant culture), may misunderstand and make inaccurate conclusions. For instance, in some cultures it may be perfectly normal for children to believe that their role as a learner is to receive and understand information, that the learning process is primarily one in which information is provided by the teacher and received by the student. This may result in the student's lack of appreciation for participation, which could be interpreted as being disengaged, uninterested, or not trying. Knowing a student's level of acculturation can help you to more accurately assess that student's knowledge. While acculturation occurs gradually, at a different rate for every student, most students will experience four phases (Herrera, Murray, & Cabral, [2014]; see Figure 14.1):

1. *Euphoria*: There is curiosity and enthusiasm about the host culture.
2. *Culture shock*: Novelty gives way to reality. Irritability, anger, grief, and sometimes depression ensue.
3. *Anomie*: The individual begins to understand and sort out his or her role in each culture. Frequently, however, the individual feels he or she is in a cultural "no man's land," estranged from the home culture but not yet accepted

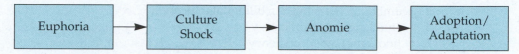

FIGURE 14.1   **Stages of Acculturation**

into the mainstream of the host culture. This period can be short-lived or persist throughout an individual's lifetime. Anomie is often associated with negative overall socialization. By contrast, the ability to adapt to the norms of the new culture while retaining affiliation with the old correlates with much more positive acculturation.

4. *Adoption/Adaptation*: The individual may fully adopt the new culture as a replacement for the primary culture (assimilation) or adapt to it in a manner that allows him or her to function authentically within both (integration).

These stages are influenced by the extent to which there are differences between the cultures. As differences increase, some stages may take longer, with a greater level of intensity of culture shock. For instance, with dramatic changes in language for some immigrants, there is also the loss of friends, familiar settings, and community. Family routines, financial security, social isolation, and other changes can prolong the process of acculturation and challenge teachers to understand the depth of influence of these factors. Also, it is important to understand that most students will want to continue to value and experience the norms and activities of their original culture (Van de Vijver, 2016).

Acculturation is a complex process, and it will require you to pay attention to the process to understand and work with students in the most effective manner, including how they are assessed. CLD students may need individualized accommodations on assessments based upon their specific background and level of acculturation.

Assessment of Acculturation

As has been stressed more than a few times in this book, good assessment involves the use of multiple, ongoing types of assessment. This is particularly true for measuring acculturation. The multiple approaches at your disposal include formal and informal embedded assessments.

Formal Assessment.   There are many available tools that can be used to formally assess acculturation. A popular instrument is the *Acculturation Quick Screen* (AQS). It measures the extent to which a student is acculturating into the school culture. It can also be used to make decisions about what assessment accommodations will be necessary. In addition, it provides a baseline from which acculturation can regularly be assessed. The instrument includes the following factors:

1. Number of years in United States/Canada
2. Number of years in school district

3. Number of years in ESL/bilingual education
4. Home language proficiency
5. School language proficiency
6. Bilingual proficiency
7. Ethnicity/nation of origin
8. Percentage in school speaking student's language/dialect

The AQS provides an indication of how quickly students will acculturate. Administering this assessment regularly can identify CLD students who might have other challenges, such as learning disabilities, as these students may not acculturate at the expected rate. The AQS also provides a foundation for whether or not CLD students should be given assessment accommodations. A low AQS score may suggest that students with lower levels of acculturation should not be assessed using standardized assessments without case-specific modifications. The AQS is a useful tool for distinguishing between students struggling with acculturation and CLD students who might need special education interventions (Collier, 2004). Other measures of acculturation focus on specific populations, mostly for Asian and Hispanic students (Herrera, Murry, & Cabral, 2014).

Informal Assessment.   Most classroom teachers will primarily use informal assessments of acculturation. As you interact with CLD students on a daily basis, it is important to informally assess level of acculturation on a continuing basis. These more informal approaches include the following:

- Home visits: Although this is not always feasible, home visits can provide extensive information, offering insights that other assessments are not able to capture. In a home visit, you will have an opportunity to observe the student, his/her caregivers, and any other family members. Seeing some of the daily life of the student and the challenges that life contains can provide beneficial information for assessing acculturation and what accommodations might be necessary in order to help that student succeed.
- Observations: It is important to observe CLD students carefully to assess the acculturation challenges they are facing. You can readily observe communication with English-speaking peers, whether the student chooses to interact with English speakers or their native language speakers, how well the student participates in large and small groups, and other preferences the student may show in the classroom. These choices help to quickly assess how well the student is acculturating. Developing a rubric of observations, specific to your classroom, can allow you to assess students' acculturation progress across time in a more objective way.
- Creative activities: Activities can help provide understanding about a student's background, as well as their acculturation. Activities could center around family information, cultural background, family customs, ancestors, and other dimensions of their dominant culture. These types of activities can allow students to get to know each other, while providing you with insight

into the CLD student and how his/her background might influence future learning. Note in following example how valuable information can be obtained with a "creative" activity.

Have the students present to the class information about a tradition that is important to their family. Examples could include special events or holidays their family celebrates, recipes that have been passed down from ancestors, or cultural traditions. This exercise would provide information about what their family considers to be important. Here's an example of what could be communicated:

In my family, an annual tradition is to make Pfeffernusse cookies during the Christmas holiday season. The recipe for these cookies has been in my family for many generations. Every member of the family is trained on the multi-day process of making these cookies. These cookies are quite different from those typically found in American grocery stores, as they are much harder and are not covered in powdered sugar. They were passed down through the Socolofsky side of my family. I'm not sure when the Socolofsky family came to the United States, but its roots are in Switzerland and Slovakia.

Other creative forms of data collection could include the use of identity puzzles into one for the entire class, constructing a place of origin map with discussions, a cultural quilt or mosaic, and a heritage paper that includes ancestral ties and previous places of residence.

CLD Student Assessment

This section examines how characteristics of CLD students may influence the assessment experience, and specific aspects of assessment that need to be considered as you design, administer, and interpret results.

CLD Student Characteristics Influencing Assessment

Although a variety of factors affect CLD students' performance on assessment, four are most important: language and literacy skills, educational background, socioeconomic status, and culture (Durán, 2008; Educational Testing Service, 2009). Let's look at each of these in greater detail.

Language and Literacy Skills.   Assessment in content-area courses is heavily language dependent and integrated, which makes it difficult to separate language and content knowledge. It is very likely that the difficulty of CLD students' English language skills will mask their content knowledge, which weakens the validity of the assessments. For example, research has shown that as the linguistic demands of math questions increases, students with weak dominant culture language perform less well than on math problems that are not as strongly loaded with language (e.g., story problems) (Van de Vijver, 2016).

CLD students' language proficiency is typically identified by ESL specialists through a state- or school district-mandated English language proficiency test, and a home language survey. There is a wide range of English language proficiency. Some students are nearly fluent, whereas others do not know the alphabet and basic sounds. It is also noteworthy that students who communicate fairly well may struggle with academic English language presented in classes and texts. Furthermore, some CLD students' abilities in speaking, listening, reading, and writing have not developed evenly. As a consequence, students who are seemingly fluent in listening and speaking may have difficulty in reading and writing, whereas other show quite opposite strengths and weaknesses.

Unfortunately, many schools deny CLD students the opportunity to learn and/or be assessed in their native language, even while those students are moving through the acculturation process. This lack of native language support impairs the education of the student and makes it more difficult for teachers to know how to differentiate learning, as they cannot tell if it is a language barrier or a content issue. It is important to include instructional practices in the classroom that allow the student to learn the content with as little language impairment as possible. Assessments may need to be tailored so that CLD students can demonstrate content knowledge.

Educational Background.   Another factor that makes a significant impact on CLD students' learning and assessments is their prior schooling experience (Thomas & Collier, 2002). CLD students have a wide array of schooling experiences. For those from outside the United States, some received education equivalent to their native English-speaking counterparts, whereas other students are not only far behind in terms of content knowledge but also are not familiar with various school functions, including methods of assessment. CLD students who have a general education schooling experience with solid grade-level content knowledge in their home countries generally acculturate and do well on tests. For CLD students native to the United States, their parents might not have the educational backgrounds to effectively support to their children, and the language spoken at home could have a negative impact on how well the student can perform on tests. Homes and neighborhoods in which few adults are college educated may not inculcate the values and attitudes needed for students to be motivated to learn and give appropriate effort to homework and in-class assessments. As has been discussed in Chapter 12, such "noncognitive" factors influence students' perceptions of assessment and how seriously they take challenges, being wrong, and feedback.

Socioeconomic Status.   Socioeconomic status is comprised of family and immediate community levels of income, education, and job status. Students living in poverty, mostly but not exclusively in urban or rural areas, have the trifecta—low income, little parental education, and low job status. There may also be a high level of single-parent homes, and racial and ethnic concentrations of groups of people. Other students have mixed or high socioeconomic status. Low socioeconomic students, as a result, come from a culture with different experiences and values compared to middle and high socioeconomic students. In recent decades in the United States, these differences have been exacerbated, making it increasingly difficult for low socioeconomic students to acculturate into a culture dominated by higher socioeconomic mores and values. These culturally, if not linguistically different, students experience some of the same limitations as those immigrating from different countries.

Cultural Factors. The degree of familiarity with the mainstream culture can have an effect on CLD students' performance on tests, whether classroom or large-scale assessments. Students who are familiar with the norms for taking standardized tests, for instance, will be more comfortable with such assessments. Some cultures may emphasize competition and doing well in tests, but others may not. Different cultures promote dissimilar perceptions of plagiarism and cheating. In some non-Western cultures "intelligence" includes social behaviors, such as obedience, unlike the cognitive emphasis in the United States. Table 14.1 describes some further cultural differences and potential implications for classroom assessment (Hoover, 2009).

Classroom Assessment Difficulties

There is no question that cultural and language differences impact students' performances on and reactions to assessments, whether formative or summative, classroom-based or large-scale. Your challenge is to understand and account for these barriers to performance to enable an accurate understanding of what

Teacher's Corner
Stephanie Stoebe
Texas Teacher of the Year

Two of the most effective formative assessments for teaching students who are learning English or who have special needs involve the use of nonlinguistic representations and active note taking. A graphic organizer can help put dates, events, and ideas in order, showing me if the students have a clear understanding of the skill we are learning. Since many graphic organizers call for single words, short phrases, or simple sentences, struggling students are not overwhelmed and I get to see if how concepts are being mastered. Is there a narrow margin of understanding or are details being supplied to indicate a more advanced level? Both English language learners and students with special needs also benefit specifically from note-taking techniques that keep them actively engaged in the classroom. My students soon learn that while I do want them to remain focused on their learning, note-taking strategies help them identify the most crucial elements of the lesson. If I want my students to learn, I have to make them aware of their metacognitive processes.

TABLE 14.1 **Cultural Differences and Their Implications for Assessment**

Examples of Cultural Differences	Description	Implications for Assessment
Cooperative vs. Competitive Learning	Some cultures teach children to be self-reliant and work independently, whereas others encourage sharing and cooperation.	For cultures that emphasize sharing, what we consider to be copying or cheating may be something that is encouraged. For cultures emphasizing independence and competition, students may not know how to effectively work with other students.
Active and Passive Learning	Passive learners are taught to be quiet, attentive, and only respond when called upon.	Teachers may misinterpret a student's passiveness as laziness, shyness, or insecurity. These students may need help to become active learners, especially to take ownership of their own learning, versus relying solely on the teacher. For assessments, they might require extra encouragement to try hard and demonstrate knowledge.
Motivation	A student's motivation can be related to cultural values and norms. Some cultures teach that certain subjects are only meant for men or for women, but not both, leading to more or less motivation, depending on the subject.	Students may need to be encouraged and taught that it's okay to pursue certain subjects, as equal opportunity may be a new concept. Doing well on assessments in these areas should be encouraged for all students.
Locus of Control	Some cultures believe that certain things are out of their control (controlled by external forces), whereas other things can be controlled by the person. For instance, some students might believe that they don't have any control over their success or future.	Teachers should assist students in developing an internal locus of control, encouraging them to set achievement goals and work to reach them.
Teaching/ Learning Style Compatibility	Students may not be used to a particular teaching style, leading to them having difficulty learning.	Teachers should use a variety of teaching techniques to see what is effective with CLD students. Then, teachers should work with CLD students to develop skills to learn from the teaching styles with which they have difficulty. Different types of assessments may be necessary.
Time	Many cultures view time differently. In some, time is very structured, whereas others time is not driven by a clock, but more by life events and needs. For instance, in some cultures, arriving late for an event is perfectly acceptable.	Students may need instruction on time expectations, so that they can be successful in their studies.

Source: Based on Hoover (2009).

students know and can accomplish. Typical difficulties that CLD students experience in assessments stem from (a) difficulty in comprehension of test language, (b) difficulty in expressing what they know, (c) lack of content and cultural knowledge in test items, (d) unfamiliarity of test types, and (e) emotional stress.

Difficulty Comprehending Test Language. CLD students may struggle with understanding assessment terms and language, especially complex sentence structures, idiomatic expressions, jargon and technical terms, double negatives, and unclear organization. These factors can make it more difficult for CLD students; mainstream students will be less affected. Alvermann and Phelps (2005) suggest teachers review test item readability for CLD students by checking the following:

- Vocabulary is at the intended grade level.
- Sentence complexity is at the intended grade level.
- Sentences are clearly and logically connected.
- Definitions and glossaries are used to facilitate comprehension.
- Content of the test items is linked to students' experiences and prior knowledge.
- Organization of each test item is clear and easy to follow.
- Clear examples are provided.
- Test items include questions of higher-order and critical thinking skills (not just recall).
- Test directions are precise, explicit, and understandable.
- Options of multiple-choice items are reasonable and balanced.

Difficulty Expressing What Is Known. CLD students' difficulties in expressing what know may be evident in multiple ways, such as poor spelling, poor grammar, improper word choice, lack of variety in expressions, and poor organization. In general, it takes a considerable amount of time for second language learners to gain sophisticated expressive skills (speaking and writing). Because English is not a phonemic language, spelling and sound don't always match. As a result, poor spelling does not necessarily indicate CLD students' lack of comprehension skills. Similar logic applies to grammar, word choice, and organization of writing. Furthermore, it is difficult for CLD students to respond to long essay questions demanding sophisticated persuasive writing.

Lack of Content and Cultural Knowledge in Test Items. Lack of grade-level content knowledge in test items negatively affects CLD students' ability to understand and respond to questions. Some CLD students, especially those who have little or interrupted schooling, have poor or different conceptions of content knowledge. Also, CLD students may have an adequate foundation in content knowledge but are unable to do well on formal tests that are designed for native speakers. Culturally assumed but not explicitly taught knowledge in the test items can interfere with CLD students' assessment performance. It is best, then, to provide culturally neutral content contexts in test items.

Unfamiliarity with Test Formats.   CLD students may not be familiar with commonly used test formats. For example, students required to complete science lab reports who are not familiar with this type of task may not understand the level of independent work required or time constraints. Writing tasks, such as explaining how to reach conclusions in problems, writing math problems, writing essays conveying students' own points of view, or conducting research to gather information, may be unfamiliar to some CLD students.

Emotional Stress.   It is possible for CLD students' emotional stress to have a negative impact on testing. Because it may take considerable effort to process information in a second language, timed tests can cause stress, resulting in a short attention span, fatigue, anxiety, and frustration. Unhealthy test anxiety can lead to debilitating stress and fear.

Bias and Sensitivity

As pointed out in Chapter 3, bias causes serious problems with fairness. Bias can have a significant impact on the effective assessment of CLD students. CLD students may come from cultures where logic, linearity, and verbal skills were not emphasized like they are in the United States.

It's easy for teachers to universalize their experiences and assume cross-cultural similarity. For instance, a test item that includes examples from the culturally dominant country (e.g., baseball or football in the United States), may make it more difficult for CLD students to be successful. High-stakes, standardized tests are scrutinized to prevent cultural biases; however, assessments developed by a classroom teacher do not receive the same level of review. Given the diversity of current classrooms, it can be difficult if not impossible to develop tests that are free of bias for all students, but test items and directions should always be reviewed to eliminate potential biased language and examples. The following questions can help you to identify bias in your assessments (adapted from Herrera, Murray, & Cabral, [2014]).

1. Is the content of the assessment linked to known student experiences outside of the classroom?
2. Is experience from prior schools necessary to answer the questions?
3. Have cultural values and practices been considered for their impact on student responses?
4. Does the assessment match the developmental level(s) of the students?
5. Do the language demands match the level(s) and proficiency(ies) of the students?
6. What prerequisite skills are necessary to complete the assessment? Are they related to the content-area being measured?
7. Are the accommodations employed during assessment consistent with those used during content-area instruction?
8. Has the assessment process and product been reviewed by others for sources of potential bias?

9. Are the criteria for responses or goal attainment clearly defined?
10. How has rater and inter-rater reliability been addressed (e.g., "blind" grading)?

The following is an example of a biased and insensitive assessment.

> In an elementary classroom, the Ms. Lane wants to assess the students' comfort with basic addition and subtraction. She decides to use this short quiz:
>
> Please answer the following questions with a scalar.
>
> 1. T'shai has twelve pops. Jeanne drinks six of T'shai's pops. How many pops does T'shai have left?
> 2. In a vaudeville show, five actors are in blackface and seven are not. How many actors are there?
> 3. Bob pays forty bucks for two movie tickets. Judy pays twenty dollars for one movie ticket. How much total money did Bob and Judy spend on movie tickets?

This quiz contains both biased and insensitive items. First, the instructions use the word "scalar." It is likely that CLD students would not know that a scalar is a single number. A more appropriate term should be used in the instructions. In the first question, students learning English may not know how to read names with apostrophes in them. Using a simpler name places the focus back on the content, not on a student's ability to read the name. In addition, students may not realize that soda is called "pop" in some places. They may only be familiar with the verb, pop, which would be confusing. Using a more universal name for soda helps prevent misunderstandings. The second question talks about vaudeville. This term is likely above the reading level of the students in this class. In addition, CLD students probably are not familiar with vaudeville. Since using the word *vaudeville* is not necessary to assess addition and subtraction skills, removing it is the best option. In addition, the word "blackface," although historical, is culturally insensitive. The final question assumes that students know that bucks and dollars are the same thing. If they don't know that, students might wonder why the question is asking about male deer and money. Using dollars consistently across the question places the emphasis back on the content.

Here are three revised questions for the quiz that are much less likely to penalize CLD students:

> Please answer the following questions with a single number.
>
> 1. Joy has twelve sodas. Jeanne drinks six of Joy's sodas. How many sodas does Joy have left?
> 2. In a show, five actors are female and seven are male. How many actors are there?
> 3. Bob pays forty dollars for two movie tickets. Judy pays twenty dollars for one movie ticket. How much total money did Bob and Judy spend on movie tickets?

Let's take this a step further. We have addressed several issues with these changes. However, even these adjusted questions still are assessing more than addition and subtraction. They're assessing the reading skills of the students. For CLD students, who may be struggling with reading English, errors on the assessment may be due to their reading levels, not math proficiency. Assessment of the math skills could be constructed without language:

Please answer the following:

1. $12 - 6 =$ _____
2. $5 + 7 =$ _____
3. $40 + 20 =$ _____

While word problems can and should have a place in a mathematics assessment, CLD students might require accommodations to be sure that math, not other skills, is being tested.

Assessment Accommodations

In this section, we'll examine additional ways you can make accommodations in your assessments of CLD students. We'll start with embedded formative assessment.

Embedded Formative Assessment

Because embedded formative assessment is less structured and depends heavily on how students react to feedback, it is subject to considerable influence based on CLD student characteristics and their level of acculturation. As described in Chapter 4, embedded formative assessment is an on-going, on-the-fly process of gathering evidence of student learning and providing feedback to students. For CLD students, the process needs to be appropriately differentiated.

Learning Targets and Criteria.   One of tenets of formative assessment is that students understand the nature of learning targets and criteria. This is important because it helps students know what needs to be accomplished to close the gap between current proficiency and the target or standard. For CLD students it is especially important to check with them to be sure they understand the targets and criteria. This may require an individual conference, translation, and examples that they can understand and relate to. To avoid embarrassment, CLD students may signal that they understand, but not actually have a solid understanding. It's important for you to check the level of understanding.

Observations.   Observations are key to implementing effective embedded formative assessment for CLD students. It can provide very helpful insight into why a student is struggling or behaving in a particular manner. Both anecdotal and more systematic observations are helpful. Keep in mind that your objective in observing is to obtain valid indicators of what students may be thinking or feeling. These interpretations will depend not only on the veracity of your observing, it will also depend on how well you understand the characteristics of the CLD students. Being clear about what a student does or looks like is only part of the process. You also need to interpret in light of what behavior may mean in the student's native culture. Building off a CLD student's native strengths can help build their confidence and encourage them to take risks.

Assessing Nonverbal Behavior and Vocal Cues.   Given the difficulties CLD students face with communicating in a new language, nonverbal cues can provide important clues for when a student is struggling with due to language. Nonverbal behavior can quickly show when a particular task is ineffective for CLD students, allowing you to make adjustments for that student. Gestures and body language can help CLD students clarify meaning or demonstrate understanding of content. However, you need to be aware that nonverbal behavior can mean different things to different cultures. Even relatively minor things, like table manners, can differ greatly from one country to another. Something that is considered proper in one country can be improper in another. Voice-related cues also provide insight into the assessment of CLD students. The presence of pauses, speed in responding, and voice volume of the CLD student may indicate a lack of understanding or language difficulty or may be expected in their native culture.

Informal Oral Questioning.   Questioning during instruction is a great way to assess student understanding. The types of questions asked also demonstrates how students should prepare for more formal assessments. CLD students, especially those who are not confident in their language abilities, may be less inclined to answer questions, especially in front of their peers. If a precedent of asking questions of a variety of students is established, CLD students will have a greater opportunity to provide an answer. In addition, CLD students typically require more time to process language, often not responding as quickly to a question. It is important to allow CLD students with sufficient time to process the question and compose an answer. Open-ended questions may also be more difficult for CLD students than close-ended questions, so it is important to tailor the question to the language level of the student. Native-language support may also be necessary for CLD students until their language acquisition improves.

Code-Switching.   As CLD students become more comfortable with the new language, it is likely that they will *code-switch*, which means they alternate between two languages during conversation. They can alternate between sentences and even within the same sentence. Although this may seem like a problem, code-switching can improve the demonstration of ability. It shows that students understand the similarities and differences between the two language and can more easily switch between them. Code-switching does not mean that students are confused. Sometimes, it is simply easier for the student to express a thought in native language. This means that you need to value and accept code-switching, especially as students acculturate.

Summative-Based Formative Assessment

Like embedded formative assessment, changes in summative-based formative assessment are needed to most effectively improve CLD learning and motivation.

Structured Exercises and In-Class Assignments.   These exercises allow the teacher to observe the student in the context of a specific task. Teachers may design an activity that all students complete or provide different activities, depending on the individual student. For CLD students, you might design an exercise for the entire class but provide language and other modifications for students who are still learning English. For example, math word problems could be matched to the students' native language and/or culture. The content of the items or tasks would align to what students could more easily process. You could also pair CLD students with English-speaking partners or small-group members, which provides them with a less threatening opportunity to use their language skills. In-class assignments will provide an excellent opportunity to provide feedback in an individualized way that allows the student some level of privacy. By being able to ask questions quietly and give suggestions to an individual student, you are able to tailor your comments to the students' CLD characteristics. The CLD student may be more willing to ask questions and respond when it's not public.

Pretests.   Pretests can be especially stressful for CLD students, especially if there are no accommodations or changes in test format that allow the students to perform the skill or demonstrate the knowledge. Even the idea of giving a pretest could be unique, causing confusion and stress. Students from nondominant cultures may have difficulty understanding the purpose of pretests and find poor performance especially demoralizing. Like structured exercises, pretests can be matched to native characteristics and culture, though this takes time and energy. Remember to use the pretest results in conjunction with other sources of information about student competency.

Homework.   Homework provides one of your best opportunities to plan formative assessment that accommodates CLD students' characteristics and culture, though CLD students may not have the same support at home as their native English-speaking peers. Parents of CLD students may not speak English or may come from a culture unfamiliar with homework, or may simply be in a situation in which support cannot be provided. This suggests that CLD students may need more direct attention, patience, and feedback from teachers on their homework. In addition, language can continue to be a barrier and cause homework to take significantly more time for CLD students. Accommodations such as structuring additional support, shortening assignments, providing language alternatives, or creating alternate assignments, can be helpful.

Quizzes, Unit Tests, and Interim Assessments.   Quizzes, unit tests, and interim test results may be used formatively with CLD students, but accommodations already mentioned are important for making accurate conclusions about student proficiency. Much like homework and seatwork, quizzes can be easily modified for CLD students. Changing unit and common tests is more difficult; interim tests may not allow any changes. However, even modified quizzes and unit tests can be stressful for CLD students if they are unfamiliar with testing and/or are in the process of acquiring English language skills. CLD students need ample time to summative-based assessments, often needing more time than their peers. It is very important to provide specific, individualized feedback for CLD students that distinguishes a lack of content knowledge from a language barrier. And, of course, results from quizzes, unit tests, and interim tests should be combined with other evidence of knowledge and skills.

Digital Formats.   Technology can be uniquely situated to meet the needs of CLD learners by providing additional support in the student's native language. There may be programs matched to your grade level and content area that will allow assessment modifications such as providing translations, bilingual dictionaries, and audiovisual presentations of prompts.

Summative Assessment

Some of the modifications for formative assessment are also appropriate for summative assessment. Other strategies can be employed as well, as summarized in Table 14.2.

Preparing CLD Students for Summative Assessments.   CLD students who come from a different "assessment" culture may not be familiar with testing strategies or the types of items that appear on tests. They may need training on how to complete summative assessments. This could include giving students examples of directions, items, and time frames for completion, as well as test-taking strategies (see Chapter 7). Creating a test vocabulary handbook, with both visual and written documentation in appropriate languages, can be helpful. The best preparation is to have CLD students complete part of a sample assessment under low-stakes testing conditions. This experience can be discussed to improve their familiarity with what will be required.

Direct Translation?   It can be tempting, especially with available technology, to directly translate assessments into a student's native language. However, if the student did not receive the content instruction in their native language and may not possess sufficient literacy skills in that language, translation alone does not necessarily improve performance. In addition, the quality of a translation is dependent upon the competence of the translator, and, especially for customized classroom assessments, there are strong limits to having personnel to do the translations. It is more appropriate for the student to be assessed in the language in

TABLE 14.2   Accommodation Options for CLD Students

Accommodation	Description
Exemptions/ Alternative Assessments	Students with lower levels of acculturation may not be prepared to take "regular" assessments. Exemptions or alternative assessments might be necessary. But, as a student's level of acculturation increases, the amount of exemptions and alternate assessments should decrease.
Extra Time	CLD students may require more time to comprehend the question being asked on an assessment before they can answer the question. Providing extra time can help relieve the burden of comprehending the test question.
One-on-One Teacher Assistance	Students with lower acculturation levels may need help understanding what is being asked. The opportunity to ask clarifying questions can allow CLD students to better demonstrate their knowledge, without being impaired by not understanding the prompt.
Oral Question Prompts	If a CLD student has better speaking and listening skills than written/ reading skills, a teacher could read the question prompts. This would allow the student to demonstrate his/her knowledge without the added confusion of having to read the prompts and write the answers.
Translator/Bilingual Tests	Since CLD students typically don't receive instruction in their native language, providing a translator or bilingual test for assessment purposes is generally not recommended.
Dictionary/List of Terms	Depending on the type of test, a bilingual dictionary could be useful. Another option would be to provide a list of terms used in the question prompt, along with the definitions in the student's native language. However, an accurate comparison of terms is necessary. A better option would be to keep the language of the question prompt simple when designing an assessment.

which they received their instruction, with appropriate accommodations (see Table 14.2).

Summative Assessment Formats.   As you know, summative assessments can come in a variety of designs and formats. The unique features of each of these will need to be considered with CLD students, and accommodations matched to the type of assessment. The first consideration is the extent of experience with a particular type of assessment, and whether the nature of that experience is different from what will be used in your classroom. Expectations for completing essay items in one culture may be quite different from those in another culture.

For constructed-response items, it will be especially important for CLD students to know the nature of the answer that needs to be provided. This is best accomplished by providing examples. It is also important to allow sufficient time for CLD students to record their answers. It is beneficial to allow students to submit graphic organizers or outlines as alternative ways to demonstrate their understanding, especially when students' English skills are minimal.

Teachers may also want to consider providing ELL students with a word bank. Note in the following example how prompts are used to simplify the nature of the required response.

> Write a character description of two of the following characters based on the novel *Nothing but the Truth*:
>
> Philip Malloy   Dr. Seymour
> Miss Narwin   Mr. Malloy
>
> Philip Malloy is _____. I know this because he _____. I think he would be a _____ friend because in the story he _____. He can also be _____. For example, in the story he _____.

Another example is a science lab report prompt that offers clear directions, along with a word bank.

> Please write a conclusion for each experiment. The conclusion needs to have three parts:
>
> 1. Answer the problem stated at the beginning of the experiment.
> 2. Accept or reject the hypothesis.
> 3. Summarize the data collected and explain the results.
>
> Word bank: hypothesis, materials, procedure, data, accept, reject, graph, chart, diagram, summarize, conclusion

For selected-response items, CLD students may need dictionaries, glossaries, or other supplemental materials to be able to understand each question and alternative. Like essay items, multiple-choice testing may be different in various cultures. Limit the number of alternatives, simplify distractors, and avoid potentially confusing words such as *always* and *never*. Digital formats may need to be accompanied by explicit directions, and, again, examples and practice items are needed. For all formats, it's important to have simple, clear, and comprehensible directions.

Performance assessments and portfolios can be used very effectively with CLD students. This is primarily because CLD students are able to individualize and customize some performances, if allowed, and their portfolios, to reflect strengths associated with their dominant culture. With less acculturation, limited formal schooling experience, and/or lower levels of English proficiency, it is best to use more structured portfolios (Gottlieb, 2016). Initially, you will want to work closely with CLD students on their portfolio choices and self-reflections. More freedom can be provided with experience.

Doing effective, fair summative assessment of CLD students in your classroom will require a number of appropriate practices. A checklist of those practices is shown in Figure 14.2.

FIGURE 14.2   Checklist for Effective Assessment of CLD Students

---

✓ Understand CLD student characteristics, native culture, and level of acculturation.
✓ Provide multiple pathways for CLD students to demonstrate proficiency.
✓ Provide visual and graphic support.
✓ Be attuned to potential cultural, linguistic, and socioeconomic bias.
✓ Individualize assessments as appropriate to features of the CLD student's dominant culture.
✓ Provide flexible scheduling and extended time to complete assessments.
✓ Provide dictionaries, glossaries, word banks, and other supplemental materials to aid comprehension of English.
✓ Provide examples of appropriate answers for constructed-response items, performance assessments, and portfolios.

Grading CLD Students

Determining grades for all students, as you will see in Chapter 15, is anything but a simple process. For CLD students, grading takes on a new level of complexity. The primary purpose of grading is to provide an indicator of student proficiency on the content knowledge and skills being taught. Since assessment performance and your evaluation of student work is confounded by CLD characteristics and acculturation, grades may not accurately reflect the actual level of knowledge and skill of the student.

While grades have traditionally been based on both norm-referenced and criterion-referenced approaches, with CLD students it is best to focus grades on progress toward individualized learning goals and proficiency on state standards. The challenge is to find in your assessments sufficiently valid information to determine both progress and absolute proficiency compared to desired standards. Most teachers use nonacademic factors in grading, such as effort and participation. With CLD students you need to be careful to not stress these types of indicators too much. It's easy to justify using them, which makes matters more difficult.

Your goal, then, is to base grading on indicators of actual knowledge and skills. This is accomplished by using appropriate assessment accommodations to make sure that native language, culture, and level of acculturation is not unduly effecting student performance. We recommend greater weight to assessments that minimize the influence of CLDs native culture and language. It is also helpful to provide separate grades, when possible, for English language learners that show their progress in English language. That allows interpretation of grades in relation to English proficiency. Grades can also be separated for what is shown in the native language as well as English. For example, a reporting card can indicate achievement in English as well as in the primary language. The best way to use grades is to be sure they clearly indicate a single meaning. An overall semester grade in social studies is less clear than grades on individual assessments that can be meaningfully related to English language or cultural limitations. More descriptive grading schemes, such as the use of rubrics, can be adapted quite nicely for CLD students.

Summary

The purpose of this chapter was to introduce you to the assessment adaptations needed to accommodate culturally and linguistically diverse students in inclusive settings. Overall, suggestions made in other chapters apply to these students, but you need to keep some additional considerations in mind. In general, it is important to fully understand CLD student characteristics and level of acculturation, and make sure that a student's native culture or language limitations do not unfairly influence performance on tests and other types of assessments. Major points in the chapter include the following:

- The number and percentage of CLD students in U.S. classroom is growing rapidly.
- CLD students are characterized by innate cultural and language traits that are significantly different from a new school and classroom culture.
- CLD students include those who have different linguistic backgrounds, such as English language learners, as well as English-speaking students from different cultures.
- Acculturation is the process through which students progress to be assimilated into a dominant culture from one that is different.
- Acculturation involves four sequential steps: euphoria, culture shock, anomie, and assimilation/adaptation.
- Factors that influence the assessments of CLD students include language and literacy skills, educational and socioeconomic background, and culture.
- Most assessments are heavily language dependent and language integrated, making the distinction between content and language difficult.
- Formative assessment strategies need to incorporate CLD student characteristics and perspectives so that student verbal and nonverbal behavior is appropriately understood and feedback can be individualized.
- CLD students experience difficulty in classroom-based assessments due to their lack of comprehension, unfamiliarity with different types of assessments, and emotional stress.
- Assessment modifications for CLD students include extra time, simplifying and clarifying test language, use of visual aids, models, examples, prompts and glossaries of terms, graphic organizers, and outlines.
- Alternative assessments, such as performance and portfolio assessments can provide ELL students with better opportunities to demonstrate their knowledge, understanding, and skills.
- Assessment of CLD students is more effective when individualized and placed in the context of cultural and linguistic differences and level of acculturation.
- Grading CLD students needs to include multiple, measures of knowledge and skills, sometimes demonstrated in both native and English languages, with careful attention to bias.

Introductory Case Study Answer

Aaron knows that Eduardo's language and literacy skill factors (reading, writing, listening, speaking) will impact his science assessment capabilities. Assessment in science is heavily language dependent, which makes it difficult to separate language and content knowledge. Since Eduardo's language factors have not developed evenly, his assessment needed to be tailored so that he could demonstrate content-knowledge using his strengths of speaking and listening.

The assessment adaptations are appropriate for Eduardo for these reasons:

- Reading aloud the terms ensures Eduardo's reading skills do not impact his assessment. Aaron is ensuring that Eduardo knows specifically which term Eduardo needs to explain.
- Drawing what Eduardo knows about each term allows Eduardo to express what he learned from listening without the impact of writing specific definitions.
- Allowing Eduardo to match pictures of animals and reducing the requirement from two to one animal reduces the bias of the assessment based on Eduardo's lack of educational background that could impact his knowledge of animal names.
- By having Eduardo orally explain which adaptation he would like to have and why, Aaron is using Eduardo's strength of speaking and eliminating the need for Eduardo to write, his weakness.
- By changing the prompt that Eduardo needs to answer in part three of the assessment, Aaron is ensuring that he is not introducing the confounding variable of "deserted island," a concept not explained in the unit that may be unfamiliar to Eduardo.
- Aaron knows that English language learners may need examples in order to know what is expected because culturally linguistic and diverse learners often have difficulty comprehending test language. By providing an example, Aaron believe Eduardo will know what is expected and still be able to compete this creative and higher-level thinking assessment component.

Suggestions for Action Research

1. Gather a small group of CLD students together and explore with them the difficulties they have with taking assessments. Probe to determine why. Also ask the students to give suggestions for what they think will be assessments that will be a more accurate measure of what they know and can do.

2. Observe a class that has CLD students. Note the nature of the interaction between the teacher and these students, and compare these interactions with those of other students. Look for any signs of differences. From a formative assessment perspective, see if you observe feedback. Is it about the same level and degree of helpfulness? Is more or less feedback provided to these students?

3. Discuss with a teacher who has CLD students in his/her class how the teacher modifies, if at all, the assessments of these students. Ask what specific changes are made, and why. Probe to see if the teacher believes that these accommodations result in a more accurate, fair description of what the student(s) know and can do.

MyEdLab Self-Check 14.1

MyEdLab Self-Check 14.2

MyEdLab Self-Check 14.3

MyEdLab Self-Check 14.4

MyEdLab Self-Check 14.5

MyEdLab Application Exercise 14.1   Acculturation

MyEdLab Application Exercise 14.2   Formative Assessment
Modifications to Accommodate CLD Students

Grading and Reporting Student Performance

with Jesse Senechal and Divya Varier

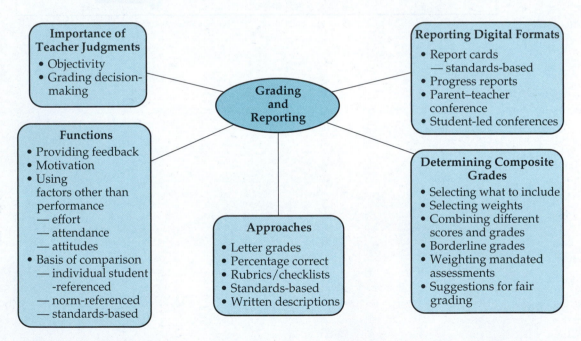

Importance of Teacher Judgments
- Objectivity
- Grading decision-making

Reporting Digital Formats
- Report cards
  — standards-based
- Progress reports
- Parent–teacher conference
- Student-led conferences

Grading and Reporting

Functions
- Providing feedback
- Motivation
- Using factors other than performance
  — effort
  — attendance
  — attitudes
- Basis of comparison
  — individual student -referenced
  — norm-referenced
  — standards-based

Approaches
- Letter grades
- Percentage correct
- Rubrics/checklists
- Standards-based
- Written descriptions

Determining Composite Grades
- Selecting what to include
- Selecting weights
- Combining different scores and grades
- Borderline grades
- Weighting mandated assessments
- Suggestions for fair grading

CHAPTER 15 Concept Map

Learning Outcomes

After reading this chapter, you should be able to:

15.1 Understand that while the goal of grading is to provide an objective recording of student achievement, teacher professional judgment is essential to the process. Being clear and explicit about such judgment will enhance the validity of grades.

15.2 Know how to use different approaches to grading, including letter grades, percentage correct, rubrics, and standards.

15.3 Understand that grading is a process of comparison, either with prior achievement (showing progress), other students, or standards.

15.4 Know the functions of grading, including the impact of grades on student motivation and how grades communicate important information to parents.

15.5 Be able to construct a grading plan that includes factors other than achievement, such as effort, attendance, and improvement, and devise a strategy for combining individually graded products into an appropriately weighted composite score.

15.6 Know the essential best practices for communicating with parents about students' grades.

Introductory Case Study

What are the Strengths and Weaknesses of This Grading Plan?

In August, during teacher preparation week, the teachers in Dana's high school history department were tasked with creating a common grading plan that all teachers would implement for the upcoming year. This stemmed from last year's parents complaining to the principal that teachers' grading practices differed greatly. An "A" in one teacher's class wasn't equivalent to an "A" in another teacher's class because of what was included in a final grade. The parents argued that grades played a vital role in students' GPA, class ranking and college admissions. They felt that the differing grading practices were leading to unfair advantages for some students. To determine if there was truth to the claim, the principal reviewed the teachers' electronic grade books over the summer and became aware of the significant differences between teachers. The principal believed the department could devise a grading plan that would be more equitable for students and would help guide the two new faculty members joining the department this year.

As the department chair, Dana had the task of getting a consensus for a grading plan. She knew it would be difficult, so at the beginning of the work session she gave everyone a sheet of paper with the school district's grading philosophy: Grades should provide an accurate representation of student learning and grading practices should enhance student motivation for the purpose of increasing student learning. She asked each person to repeatedly remind themselves of this statement during the work session and to remember that use of the district's ten-point grading scale was mandated.

At the end of the session, Dana was frustrated. The agreed upon a grading plan included the following policies:

1. Grades will be based primarily on academic performance.
2. Grades should come from summative assessments and not formative assessments.
3. Teachers will include a maximum of four grades from tests (so as to minimize testing time and maximize instructional time).
4. Only one project and one essay should be included in the final grade.
5. Teachers will include the district's end-of-grading period benchmark as a grade.
6. Homework should be graded once every other week during the grading period.
7. Essays and projects will require teacher feedback. Tests will not receive feedback.
8. Students who are borderline between letter grades may be bumped up using effort as the determinate.
9. When a later assessment of the same material indicates greater student mastery, the previously graded assignment should be dropped.
10. Students caught cheating will have no penalty on the graded assessment.

Dana felt that there were some merits to the grading plan, but she was also concerned that many aspects were in conflict with the district's philosophy. She also worried about what the grading plan conveyed to students and parents.

As you read this chapter, think about the grading plan's strengths and weaknesses. What aspects of the grading plan support the district's grading philosophy? Which aspects are in conflict?

In the past few chapters we have seen how teachers can assess students on a variety of learning targets with different types of assessments. As was pointed out in the model of classroom assessment presented in Chapter 1, now you need to do something with the assessment results. Specifically, you will need to make professional judgments about the quality of student work and translate that into grades and reports. We begin this chapter with a discussion about the importance of a teacher's professional judgment in grading, then consider the functions of grading, specific approaches to grading, considerations for grading group work, ideas for determining composite (report card) grades, and finally, a discussion of strategies for reporting progress to students and parents.

Teachers' Judgments in Grading

The evaluating and grading process requires you to make many professional judgmental decisions. These decisions are based on your personal value system on a number of different issues. It's important to understand the nature of this judgment process, beginning with what you will want to keep foremost in mind: objectivity.

Objectivity

You have plenty of experience with grading, and you probably would want more objectivity than subjectivity in this process. This is consistent with best practice—grades should be primarily an "objective" measure of student performance. When a student receives an A for a course, an objective conclusion is that he or she has mastered the course content, whereas an F represents the student's failure to achieve a minimum level of proficiency. There is the expectation that the teacher would be able to produce documentation, in the form of a gradebook or a portfolio of student work, to objectively justify the grade. In fact, in certain cases justifying grades becomes a legal requirement (McElligott & Brookhart, 2009). The preference for objectivity in grading is important because these marks have important uses. School class placements, college admissions, and scholarship awards rely heavily on grades. Grades also affect individual students' perceptions of themselves as learners, and they affect student motivation. We depend on our grading systems to indicate fairly and accurately the status of the student. Objectivity helps grading meet these goals, but how much "objectivity" is there in grading?

While objectivity is a great goal, you simply can't eliminate your professional judgments in the process of grading. Judgments are made before assessment (e.g., the difficulty of test items, what is covered on the assessment, whether extra-credit items will be included), as well as after assessments are completed (e.g., scoring short-answer and essay items). Further judgments are made about how scores of different assessments are combined to determine final grades (e.g., how assessments are weighted, how to handle borderline scores). Here are some typical questions teachers ask related to assessment and grading that are answered by using their professional judgment:

> Are my grades supposed to mean the same thing as other teachers' grades?
> Am I grading students too hard or too easy?
> Should effort and improvement be included in the grade?
> Should student participation be included in the grade?
> How should different assessments be weighted and combined?
> How should I assign grades to individual students based on group work?
> What distribution of grades should I end up with?
> What do I do if most of my students fail the test?
> What do I do with students who test well but don't hand in homework?

There are no straightforward or correct answers to these questions. Although guidelines for grading may be established by school or district policy—the scope and rigidity of which vary widely, sometimes even within a school—it is ultimately the classroom teachers who must use their judgment to interpret these guidelines within their discipline, grade level, and unique learning context. And even when you come to an understanding of how these questions should be answered, there are always individual student situations that demand flexibility. Consider the following scenarios:

In your tenth-grade math class final grades are based on homework, tests, and a project, which counted 30%. One of your more competent students, Jerome, gets an A on homework and every test, but does not turn in the project.

You are a high school social studies teacher. Your second-period class consists of students with a fairly wide range of ability. You give a midterm and final exam. Sophie gets a B on her midterm and an A on the final exam.

What grades would you give? Should Jerome get a low final grade because of the zero obtained for not turning in the project, even though he scores so high on tests of content knowledge? Should Sophie get an A because she showed improvement?

In some schools, there is substantial dialogue around these value systems. For example, the professional learning community model encourages groups of teachers to develop common understandings of what it means to grade fairly (Vescio, Ross, & Adams, 2008; DuFour, DuFour, Eaker, & Many, 2010). For advocates of standards-based grading highly structured district guidelines are recommended (Marzano, 2006; O'Connor, 2009). Some school districts may allow teachers some discretion about grading practices. Whether it is in the context of district guidelines or in a collaborative or individual setting, as a teacher you will ultimately develop a personal philosophy of grading that translates into what you do. To develop your grading plan, then, you need to consider and answer the following questions, as illustrated in Figure 15.1.

These questions are best answered when they are based on an understanding of the different purposes or functions that grades serve and the types of

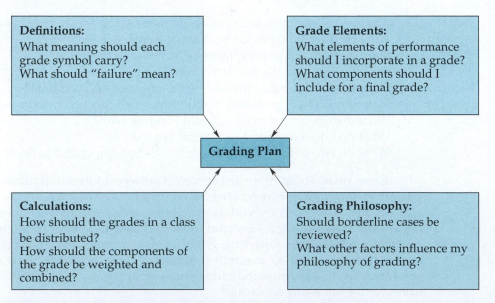

FIGURE 15.1   Questions to Consider in Developing a Grading Plan

comparison standards that are used. In the end, you need to use methods and comparisons that best meet your major purpose. As we will see later in this chapter, grades often serve several purposes, which makes matters more complicated.

We need to make an important point concerning professional judgments. These judgments are *subjective* and *intuitive* in the sense that there is no single correct procedure or set of rules that standardize professional decision making. You may use a grading scale, score student tests and performances, then mathematically calculate grades, but this is not a procedure that is necessarily correct because it appears to be objective. Think for a moment about a physician making a decision about whether a patient is sufficiently strong to endure an operation. In a sense, this is like grading. The doctor takes many measures, then examines them *in the light of his or her experience and knowledge* before giving a yes or no judgment. Could two physicians differ in their opinions about whether to operate, given the same information? Absolutely. Likewise, two teachers can differ on the meaning of students' performances. You might look at the tests and conclude that the student has mastered a skill, whereas a colleague might conclude the opposite. In reality, there is a wide range of factors that may influence your judgment about grades, including your teaching experience, your understanding of the learning context, your knowledge about your subject area, and your personal value system. To be an effective teacher, you need to understand the issues, make some informed judgments, and then be willing to have confidence in your decisions (Guskey & Bailey, 2010).

Teachers' Grading Decision Making

In Chapter 1 it was pointed out that teachers' assessment and grading decisions are heavily influenced by teacher beliefs and values about enhancing student learning, and that these beliefs and values often conflict with external pressures such as mandated statewide testing, parental concerns, and district policies (Bonner, 2016; McMillan, 2002b, 2003; McMillan & Workman, 1999). In fact, the recent push toward centralized systems of assessment and accountability has led to tension between the value of objective grading practices and teachers' subjective professional judgment.

Recent studies of the ethical dilemmas of assessment show that teachers, in making grading decisions, often negotiate between several conflicting demands (Pope, Green, Johnson, & Mitchell, 2009). For example, it is common in the age of high-stakes tests for teachers to experience pressure to adopt certain grading practices that focus on auditing and reporting student achievement, rather than supporting the teacher's values of promoting learning. Teachers need "objective" evidence of student performance to defend grades to parents, and district policies may restrict the nature and use of different grading procedures. However, the easily audited measures that these pressures require are not always in sync with what teachers know to be quality assessment. Practical constraints such as these limit what teachers can realistically accomplish. Although it might be best to use many different samples of student performance for grades, it might not be feasible in light of other instructional needs. It is best to consider these external factors in light of your own beliefs and values about teaching and learning. Recognize that tension may exist, but, in the end, keep your grading decision making based primarily on what is best for student learning and motivation.

We maintain that taking account of teacher internal values and beliefs is essential because they provide a rationale for using grading practices that are most consistent with what is most important in the teaching/learning process. Thus, because teachers want all students to succeed, they may give extra credit to enable students to "pull up" low grades. Because of individual differences in students, teachers may use different types of assessments so everyone has a chance of obtaining a good grade. Performance assessments may be used because they motivate and engage students more effectively than multiple-choice tests and allow teachers to grade participation. Note in the following teacher responses how grading decisions are based on their more encompassing beliefs and values about learning:

- To me grades are extremely secondary to the whole process of what we do. I have goals for what I want to teach, and I use assessment so that I know what I need to work on, what students have mastered, and what they haven't.
- I'm always trying to find some ways so that all the children can find success, not just Johnny and Suzy getting the A but also Sally and Jim can get an A.
- Then I generally think of their effort, whether I feel they've really tried and whether they've turned in all their work. If they tried to make an effort to improve, I won't give them an F.
- When it's borderline, how hard has the child worked during the year?

Functions of Marking and Grading

Why do we grade at all? What do you want your grades to mean to your students? How do you want students to be affected? What might students' grades mean to other stakeholders such as parents or school officials? Although at a basic level all teachers want marks and grades to have a positive impact on student learning and motivation, the reality is that grades have various intended and unintended impacts. For example, suppose Mr. Wren decides to be "fair" to students by using the top score on a test as 100 and adjusts the percentage correct for all other students accordingly. Would it be fair if the class happened to have one or two exceptionally bright students? What might happen to student motivation in that class? This is one of many factors that will determine how grades are interpreted and thus affect students. Some other important influences include the level of feedback communicated in the grade or mark about the student performance, whether grades are being used to compare students, how grades motivate students, and whether factors other than performance should be included. In this section, we will explore these various functions and effects of grading.

Providing Feedback

One of the most difficult professional decisions you will have to make about grading students is the nature and amount of feedback they will receive about their performance. Let's examine a couple of examples to illustrate this point.

When Ryann McMillan was in the sixth grade a few years ago (actually more than a few), she spent several weeks putting together a report on Italy. In looking over the report, her father thought she did an excellent job (of course, there may be just a little bias here!). She got the paper back with a B+ on it and a short comment, "Good work." She was somewhat disappointed, but more important, she didn't know why she did not get a higher grade. There was no information about how the teacher had come to this conclusion. How did this affect her? She was sad and bewildered, in general a negative effect, even though she had done well. An alternative could have been for the teacher to provide her with a detailed summary of how the teacher evaluated each section of the paper, so that she could better understand its strengths and weaknesses.

However, from another perspective, we can say that it is simply not possible for you to give detailed comments to every graded assignment or test. For example, say a high school English teacher assigns a three-page paper to five junior-level American literature classes. Over 100 papers need to be graded. Does the teacher spend a scant 5 minutes grading and commenting on each paper? If so, that's still over 8 hours of work, and that is for just one assignment. Practically, teachers must make important judgments about what assessments to target for intensive feedback. There is also the issue of what forms of feedback are most useful to students. Some papers could be marked up and commented on extensively, but not in a way that is useful for students. In fact, it has been shown that some forms of feedback can have negative effects on student achievement (Marzano, 2006; Brookhart, 2013). This feedback could be vague or unclear. Additionally, it is easy to understand how "too much red ink"—just like not enough—might discourage students and have a negative effect on motivation.

These examples demonstrate not only the importance of providing appropriate feedback, but also the challenges of doing so. This is another instance when your sound and reasoned professional judgment as a teacher is essential. We know from Chapters 4 and 5 that, in general, more detailed, individualized feedback has a positive effect on motivation, and it allows students to make more accurate connections between how they studied or prepared and their performance. Through experience, effective teachers learn to give students this consistent, detailed, and useful feedback in ways that are realistic, considering the practical constraints of time and workload.

Basis of Comparison

A second, related function of grading, is to provide a basis of comparison to something, some kind of referent. There are three forms of comparison, each of which may influence the way grading decisions are made: **individual student-referenced**,

norm-referenced, and **standards-based**. Basically, this distinction boils down to the question: "When we assign grades, what exactly are we comparing?" This is an important distinction because it has significant implications not only for how teachers teach and students learn, but also for the issues of educational equity.

Individual Student-Referenced Comparison.   Giving a grade to a student based on comparison with the student's prior performance or aptitude is referred to as *individual student-referenced* or *self-referenced* grading (Brookhart, 2009). The two considerations for student-referenced comparison—prior performance and aptitude—are based on distinct ideas about the function of grading. Both also present some problems.

Grading with consideration of prior performance is grounded in the idea that if learning is defined as a change in performance, why not measure how much students know before and then after instruction? Students who show the most improvement, hence learning, would get the highest grades. One grading technique based on this logic is the use of *personal best goals* (Liem, 2012), where students' best performance on a given task is always the measure of comparison. However, there are some serious limitations to this approach. What happens when students score high in the beginning, on the pretest, and don't have an opportunity to show much improvement? What about student faking, in which students intentionally receive a low score on the pretest to more easily show improvement? Keeping track of pre- and post-instruction scores for *each* student for each learning target would not be very practical. Nonetheless, improvement can be a positive motivator for borderline situations.

Regarding aptitude, the argument goes something like this: If we can tailor assignments and grading to each student's potential, all students can be motivated and all students can experience success. Rather than grading only on achievement, which favors students who bring higher aptitude for learning, grades reflect how well each student has achieved in relation to his or her potential. High-aptitude students will be challenged, and low-aptitude students will have realistic opportunities for good grades.

An example of this style of grading, as pointed out in Chapters 13 and 14, would be the accommodations and modifications made for students with special needs (Jung, 2009) and English language learners (Sampson, 2009). In these cases, there is a recognition that students from these populations may come with a lack of requisite skills and knowledge (aptitude), and that to be fair, certain adjustments through scaffolding of standards need to occur.

However, there are also many problems related to the idea of grading in comparison to individual aptitude. First, this argument is based on knowing what aptitude is and being able to assess it. There has never been an agreed-upon definition of aptitude, though it often is used synonymously with general intelligence. Work by Sternberg (1986) and Gardner (1985) has challenged traditional definitions of intelligence and has shown that we are still a long way from adequately understanding something as complex as aptitude for learning. Second, measuring aptitude is fraught with difficulties, not the least of which concerns cultural bias. Even if we had a proper definition and a good measure, there are insurmountable practical difficulties in trying to assess aptitude for each student and grade accordingly.

Thus, although there is no question that students do have different levels of ability, and you need to use this knowledge in instruction and for giving students feedback, you don't want to factor it into grades and marks. The only exception—aside from special education and ELL (as discussed above)—might be for border-line situations when giving semester grades. Even then, it would be better to use prior achievement than to use aptitude. Using prior achievement avoids the conceptualization and measurement problems associated with aptitude.

Norm-Referenced Grading.   Grading by comparison to the achievement of other students is referred to as *norm-referenced* or *relative* grading. In the classroom, this means that grades indicate how the student performed in comparison with the other students in the class (or several classes in middle and high schools). This method has been known as *grading on the curve*. In this approach, certain proportions of students are given designated grades, pretty much regardless of the level of performance of the students, or higher grades are only given to students who outperform others. That is, sometimes a certain percentage of the class will receive As, Bs, Cs, Ds, and Fs. There is no indication of how much students master or what percentage of test items were answered correctly. A student can answer 70% of the items on one test correctly, and if that is the highest score, it will be an A. On another test, a 70 might be relatively low, receiving a C or D. It's also possible for a student to get a C for getting a 95 on a test if others received even higher scores.

Although norm-referenced grading has fallen out of fashion both among the educational research community (Guskey, 2009; Marzano, 2006; O'Connor, 2009), and in practice, it is clear that it has had a significant and lasting impact on the way grading occurs. Because norm-referenced grading is based on comparing students to each other, its major function is to differentiate the highest- or best-performing students from others. In this sense, it provides the conceptual basis for the way our schools sort students. Indeed, a definition of grades that includes C as "average" and B as "above average" is a norm-referenced type of comparison. We can also see its influence in how we adjust curves based on student ability (e.g., honors-track classes have a higher percentage of As than general-track classes), by how difficult teachers make their tests, and by how tough teachers are in grading papers, projects, and other products.

An undesirable outcome of relative grading is that it fosters student competitiveness. It is clear that when students know that their grade is dependent on how others perform, a very competitive environment is created. This usually has a negative impact on student effort, motivation, interpersonal relationships, and teacher communication. The motivation of students who continually score near the bottom is undermined. Student cooperation is reduced. For these reasons, as well as the capriciousness with which some teachers set curves (Jon [McMillan's son] had a teacher who set the curve by designating the highest score an A—please don't do that!), most grading has moved away from comparisons with others and toward systems that are based on absolute level of student performance.

Standards-Based Grading.   Grading that is determined by what level of performance is obtained is now typically called *standards-based* or *standards-referenced* (in prior years called **criterion-referenced**). In this method, there is no comparison with other students; rather the basis of comparison is a predetermined standard of performance. This could be as simple as a percentage-based scale of items that must be answered correctly, or as complex as a detailed rubric that presents an analysis of student progress based on a list of various content-specific performance standards. Currently, as previously stressed, there is not only a proliferation of national, state, and district standards, but also pressure to close the achievement gaps between different racial and socioeconomic groups. In this context, the idea of standards-based grading is appealing. When done well, it lays out specific criteria for performance and holds open the possibility that all students can meet those goals.

The most common and traditional method of using absolute levels of performance is called *percentage-based* grading. This is typically used for objective tests, for which teachers assign a grade to a specific percentage of items answered correctly. Usually the school system establishes the scale, such as the following:

A	90–100	% correct
B	80–89	% correct
C	70–79	% correct
D	66–69	% correct
F		below 66 % correct

The criterion is supposedly set by the percentage of correct items for each grade. Thus, a scale in which 94–100 is an A is often regarded as more stringent or tough than a scale with an A range of 90–100. Some school systems have periodic debates about the relative worth of more stringent versus more lax grading scales. However, the importance of this debate is mitigated by the pressure schools feel to sort students, combined with the variability in difficulty on any two assessments of the same thing. Simply put, a score of 70 on a hard test means something different from a 70 on an easier test. Consequently, what is important is not only the percentage correct, but also how hard it is to get those items correct! Two teachers, given the same learning target, can easily come up with different assessments that are not the same in terms of difficulty.

Using forms of standards-based grading that move away from single grades or percentages on assignments provide more specific feedback about various dimensions of student performance (Guskey, 2009; Marzano, 2006, 2010; Marzano & Heflebower, 2011; O'Connor, 2009). In this model of grading, teachers, schools, and districts develop assessments that spell out in some detail the specific behaviors (standards) students must perform to obtain each letter grade. The assessments use some form of rubric to indicate achievement on specific skills addressed in a given assignment. The scoring rubric and exemplars define the levels of mastery for specific skills, and, on the basis of the teacher's observations, a grade is assigned to indicate what level of performance was demonstrated. Because standards-based grading usually relies on rubrics that give a detailed breakdown of student performance by standard, it is a system that provides a high degree of feedback to the student without being an overly time-intensive method for teachers.

Figure 15.2 shows an example of a standards-based assessment rubric for fifth-grade writing. The rubric is based on Iowa state standards, and connects each aspect of the assessment to specific state standards. A grade may be assigned to different levels, but it is more common to simply indicate how consistently a student demonstrates each skill. As we will see in a later section, standard-based grading leads to a dramatically different type of reporting system from letter grades. It is perhaps because of this shift away from familiar methods of reporting student achievement that districts have been slow to fully adopt this reform.

FIGURE 15.2   Standards-Based Assessment Rubric

Source: Area Education Agency (AEA), https://www.aea267.k12.ia.us/iowa-core/resources/rubrics-learning-progressions/standards-based-rubrics/fifth-grade-rubrics/

5th Grade Writing Rubric

Student Name: _____   Date: _____

Teacher Name: _____

Writing Skill	Almost Never 1	Rarely 2	Occasionally 3	Frequently 4	Almost Always 5
Text Types and Purposes					
1. **Write** opinion pieces on topics or texts, supporting a point of view with reasons and information. **(W.5.1.)(DOK 3,4)**					
a. **Introduce** a topic or text clearly, **state** an opinion, and **create** an organizational structure in which ideas are logically grouped to support the writer's purpose.					
b. **Provide** logically ordered reasons that are supported by facts and details.					
c. **Link** opinion and reasons using words, phrases, and clauses (e.g., *consequently, specifically*).					
d. **Provide** a concluding statement or section related to the opinion presented.					

(Continued)

FIGURE 15.2 *(Continued)*

Writing Skill	Almost Never 1	Rarely 2	Occasionally 3	Frequently 4	Almost Always 5
2. **Write** informative/explanatory texts to examine a topic and convey ideas and information clearly. **(W.5.2.)(DOK 3,4)**					
a. **Introduce** a topic clearly, **provide** a general observation and focus, and **group** related information logically; include formatting (e.g., headings), illustrations, and multimedia when useful to aiding comprehension.					
b. **Develop** the topic with facts, definitions, concrete details, quotations, or other information and examples related to the topic.					
c. **Link** ideas within and across categories of information using words, phrases, and clauses (e.g., *in contrast, especially*).					
d. **Use** precise language and domain-specific vocabulary to **inform** about or **explain** the topic.					
e. **Provide** a concluding statement or section related to the information or explanation presented.					

Note. The table shows only a small part of the original rubric that can be retrieved from the source link above. Retrieved May 15, 2016 from Area Education Agency (AEA), https://www.aea267.k12.ia.us/iowa-core/resources/rubrics-learning-progressions/standards-based-rubrics/fifth-grade-rubrics/.

Table 15.1 summarizes differences between individual student-referenced, norm-referenced, and standards-based approaches for marking and grading students. As you probably sensed, we believe that standards-based grading is the most effective way of structuring a grading system that is designed to improve teaching and learning. This preference not only reflects the consensus of assessment experts, but also the trends in school districts across the country. Nonetheless, it is important to understand the logic and the forms of individual student-referenced and norm-referenced grading because they still have a strong influence on the way many of us think about grading.

TABLE 15.1 **Characteristics of Individual Student-Referenced, Norm-Referenced, and Standards-Based Grading**

	Individual Student-Referenced	Norm-Referenced	Standards-Based
Interpretation	Scores compared to student prior performance or aptitude	Score compared to the performances of other students	Score compared to predetermined standards and criteria
Nature of Score	Percentage correct; levels of mastery set on individual basis	Percentile rank; standard scores; grading curve	Percentage correct; descriptive performance standards
Difficulty of Test Items	Items are gauged to individual ability or prior performance	Uses average to difficult items to obtain spread of scores; very easy and very difficult items not used	Uses average to easy items to result in a high percentage of correct answers
Use of Scores	To measure individual growth	To rank order and sort students	To describe the level of performance obtained
Effect on Motivation	Challenges students to improve individual performance	Dependent on comparison group; competitive	Encourages students to focus on meeting learning goals and fosters a growth mindset over fixed mindset
Strengths	Results provide good formative feedback to students	Results in more difficult assessments that challenge students; effective means of sorting students	Matches student performance to clearly defined learning targets; lessens competitiveness
Weaknesses	A common measure of performance is lost; aptitude and prior performance are hard to assess	Grades determined by comparison to other students; some students are always at the bottom	Establishing clearly defined learning targets and setting standards that include mastery is difficult

Motivation

A third primary function of grading is to motivate students. One way or another, your grading practices will enhance or lessen student motivation. Recent research in student motivation highlights a few key factors that are significant for enhancing student motivation; some of these have been discussed in earlier chapters (Brookhart, 2004; Marzano, 2006).

It is well established that student motivation is enhanced when students believe that their success is due to internal, controllable attributions or beliefs about what caused the success (Covington, 1992; Weiner, 1974, 1985). Did they succeed because of something they did (e.g., effort) that can be controlled by them in the future? Or, was success due to something that they can't control, such as luck or help from others? Teachers can help students see the connection between their efforts and the grades they receive (whether good or bad) to reinforce their reasoning that their grade was due to effort, something they control. This helps establish a belief that they are able to accomplish learning tasks (self-efficacy), which is important for motivation and learning.

Standards-based grading lends itself well to fostering student thinking and motivation toward effort and taking ownership for performance (Vatterott, 2015). For example, take the case of a student who focused a lot of effort on some parts of an assignment but failed to meet all its requirements. Giving a low grade may lessen the student's motivation, and giving a high grade based on effort may be misinterpreted as adequate performance. Using a checklist or rubric to substantiate a grade based on performance could help the student make connections between effort and performance. Similarly, learning tasks need to be moderately challenging so that grades are not simply a verification of already established self-perceptions about ability with little new information to improve. Grades on very easy tasks result in lower motivation (Bong, 2001). The old adage of "making sure students work for their grades" to motivate them is supported by research. Furthermore, effort is more important than ability. Let's look at this more closely.

Research on mindset has had a major impact on how we perceive student's motivation and goal orientation toward learning. Dweck (2008) describes two mindsets that determine student effort and, subsequently, learning. Individuals with a *fixed* mindset believe intelligence or ability is not malleable to effort, whereas individuals with a *growth* mindset believe that intelligence or ability grows as a result of appropriate effort. The purpose of considering mindset in motivation is not to label the causes of student's success and failures, but to find ways to help students develop a growth mindset. The implication of mindset on grading is for you to reflect on how your communication about grading and feedback might affect students' perception of their ability. While providing corrective feedback on student work, are you using words that encourage students to overcome learning difficulties? Does your feedback include strategies or next steps for students to improve their work? How do you respond to a student who says they failed because they are not good at something? Consider grading and feedback as opportunities to orient students toward a growth mindset. Use language that communicates to students that learning is process that takes time and hard work, but also that mistakes, failures, and difficulties are part of the learning process (McMillan, forthcoming). For example, instead of saying "you did your best" on a sincere effort but subpar performance, say "I see you worked hard on this" and follow up with a question or strategy that will focus their effort on making improvements.

Closely related to mindset is the importance of motivation goals. The role of goals in motivating students is also well established (Ames, 1992; Elliot & Thrash, 2001; Senko, Hulleman, & Harackiewicz, 2011). Students tend to have one of two types of goals—mastery or performance. As previously discussed, **mastery goals** involve students' conceptions of their competence about performing a task or completing a test. The focus is on self-improvement, on being able to demonstrate successfully the knowledge, understanding, or skill. There is an intrinsic reason for learning, for wanting to learn because demonstrating the knowledge or skill is what is important. Students with a mastery goal orientation learn more, prefer more challenging tasks, have more positive attitudes, become more success oriented (rather than failure avoiding), and believe that success depends on internal attributions such as effort and ability (Brookhart, 2012). **Performance goals** are divided into two types: performance-approach goals and performance-avoidance goals (Cury, Elliot, Sarrazin, Da Fonseca, & Rufo, 2002; Elliot & Church, 1997; Elliot, McGregor, & Gable, 1999). Students with performance-approach goals are inclined to take on new tasks and outwardly demonstrate their ability for tasks. Students who hold performance-avoidance goals are motivated to *avoid* novel or challenging tasks for fear of revealing incompetence (Ames, 1992; Elliot & Church, 1997; Maehr & Zusho, 2009). With both types of performance goal, students are motivated not because of learning for its own sake, but for getting a high grade, passing the test, or scoring higher than other students. The motivation is to do well to achieve an extrinsic reward, regardless of the learning that occurs. Good grades are used to impress others, avoid failure, or obtain privileges. Additionally, such goals have been found to be maladaptive for other academic outcomes such as risk taking and stress, particularly when performance-oriented students encounter failure (Robins & Pals, 2002). Recent research suggests that students may not be solely mastery or performance oriented (McMillan & Turner, 2014); rather, they may approach tasks differently based on interest and other motivational factors (Senko et al., 2011). Recognizing maladaptive approaches to learning and using feedback to help a student to develop a mastery approach can enhance motivation.

As a classroom teacher, you have a critical role in using grades to relate to mastery goals, especially with the recent emphasis on high-stakes accountability tests and the school culture these tests create. If the meaning of the grade is mostly about "getting a good score" rather than "demonstrating understanding," motivation is transient and less powerful. When grades indicate feedback related to learning, intrinsic motivation is enhanced. The implication for grading is that giving grades without accompanying feedback information fosters extrinsic motivation. Grades need to be accompanied by specific feedback—whether in the form of teacher comments, student–teacher conferences, or rubric checklists—that students can use to both verify learning and further develop their knowledge, understanding, or skill.

Finally, grades affect motivation most when they are presented *while* students learn (formatively), not just *after* learning (summatively). When grades are used to support formative feedback, students are encouraged to be *self-monitoring* and *self-reflecting*, which enhances self-efficacy and intrinsic motivation (Marzano, 2006; McMillan, 2009; Zimmerman, 2001). When grades are used as a summative judgment, the function tends to focus on extrinsic rewards and management of student behavior (compliance).

Using Factors Other Than Academic Performance

Many studies have documented that teachers tend to award "hodgepodge" grades that reflect both academic and nonacademic factors that are related to achievement (e.g., effort, attitudes) (Brookhart, 1993; Cross & Frary, 1999; D'Agostino & Welsh, 2007; McMillan, 2001, 2002a; McMillan, Myran, & Workman, 2002). Although most assessment experts agree that nonacademic indicators should have little or no bearing on the academic performance grade, it is common for teachers to use them in their grading practice (Brookhart et al., 2016). Nonacademic factors have also been recognized, in national reports by the business community, as important qualities for the preparation of the workforce (Marzano, 2006)—back again to 21st-century dispositions! For this reason, a look at several of these factors is warranted. Let's begin with the most important one mentioned earlier, student effort.

Effort.   There is a commonsense logic to why student effort should be considered when grading. Aren't students who try harder learning more, even if it doesn't show up on a test, paper, or project? Isn't it good to reward low-achieving students who try hard? Don't we need to find something to praise low-achieving students for to keep them engaged? Isn't it true that we value effort in the workplace and as a society, so children should learn the importance of effort by seeing it reflected in their grades? Doesn't rewarding effort help students understand that effort is a key, internally controllable factor in determining success?

While these may be compelling reasons to include effort in determining grades, there are a number of difficulties. First, different teachers operationalize effort differently, so it is something that varies from one teacher to another. It's true that we could define effort as "completing homework" or "participating in class discussion" or "being on task," but each of these definitions is problematic. Second, we don't have a satisfactory way to measure effort. Something that could

Teacher's Corner

Terri Williams

National Board Certified Elementary Special Education Teacher

When determining students' grades, I often consider effort, participation, and improvement. If, when calculating student grades, the numerical percentage is a point or two closer to the next highest letter grade, I consider adding the necessary points to raise that student's grade. Students who put forth effort, participate in class, are motivated, and show improvement over time deserve the better grade. These students often need the extra positive reinforcement to maintain their effort and motivation. Adding the extra points to a final grade increases the chances that motivation and effort will continue.

be easily and accurately measured, completing homework, could also be considered pretty shallow. Participation in class discussion is influenced by many factors, only one of which is controlled by each student. How do you know if a student is on-task? Sometimes it seems obvious, though students can fake this pretty well, and most of the time we either can't tell or can't systematically observe and record sufficiently to get a good measure. If students know they will be graded on effort, will they try to make you think that they are trying by how they act, when in fact it's a bluff and they really aren't trying?

Third, does including effort tend to favor more assertive students? What about students who are quiet? Could gender or racial/ethnic characteristics be related to the value of effort or expectations about showing effort? Certainly we would not want our grades to be affected by these characteristics. Fourth, how much would effort count? What amount of a grade or percentage of a score would be reasonable? How would you know and keep track of the level of contribution for each student? Finally, are we sending students the wrong message if they learn that they can get by just by trying hard, even if the performance is less than satisfactory?

There seem to be some pretty good reasons for and against including effort (see Table 15.2). This is one of those areas of professional judgment you'll need to make decisions about. But we do have some suggestions. If you want to include effort in the determination of grades, use it for borderline cases. Never allow effort to become a major part of a mark or score. Second, report effort separately from performance. Do this often, and allow students opportunities to disagree with your assessment. Try to define effort as clearly as possible and stick to your definition. This definition should be shared with students with examples. If you include effort for one student, it's only fair to include it for all students. Even if effort is not a part of your grading, remember that effort attributions related to performance should still be emphasized.

Attendance.   Many schools have specific guidelines related to attendance and grades. That is, in certain schools and districts students become ineligible for credit,

TABLE 15.2   **Arguments for and Against Using Effort in Grading**

For	Against
• Students who try hard learn more	• Teachers operationalize effort differently
• Rewards motivation and engagement	• Hard to define and measure
• Rewards lower-achieving students for something	• Can be faked
• Rewards an internal attributional factor that is in control of the student	• Favors more assertive students
• Leads to higher grades	• Lack of consistency in how effort is weighted
	• Teaches students that they can get by with effort and not performance
	• Takes focus away from performance

or "automatic failures" when they miss a certain number of classes (McElligott & Brookhart, 2009). On a certain level this makes sense. To learn, students need to be in class. If a student misses 15 or 20 classes in a semester, no matter what the reason, it seems that it would be hard to justify giving a passing grade. And similar to the argument for factoring in effort, school should, as a preparation for the workplace, hold students accountable for their attendance. However, if we punish students academically for nonacademic issues, we risk losing focus on the essential purpose of grades. When grades become too closely related to attendance expectations, "just showing up" becomes some students' argument for why they should pass! A better solution for the student with attendance problems would be for the school to develop ways of creating attendance-related consequences, for example, making up class time after school or on Saturdays.

Attitudes.   Another factor to consider in classroom grading and marking is student attitudes. Shouldn't students with a positive attitude be rewarded? Suppose two students perform about the same and both are equally borderline between an A and a B. If one student has a very positive attitude, would that mean that he or she should get an A, while the other student with a negative attitude would get a B? Like student effort, attitudes are important, and it might be helpful if we could efficiently and accurately include this in grading. The reality is that attitudes are difficult to define and measure and are susceptible to student faking. So, like the other "nonacademic" factors we have considered, it is generally not a good idea to try to use attitudes in grading. It is best if grades and marks are predominately determined by student performance in relation to learning targets. If other factors are included, their influence should be minimal.

Group Work

If grading individual work has its challenges and subjectivity, grading group work only adds more complexity to a teacher's grading practices. But a major characteristic of 21st-century learning, as explained in Chapter 2, is the development of collaborative skills. While you may be familiar with group work in a general sense, the term *cooperative learning* is often associated with activities that promote students' communication and interpersonal skills. Cooperative learning refers to purposeful activities that provide students opportunities to work with classmates in small groups by sharing assigned tasks to achieve learning goals for the group but based on individual accountability. Although there are several models of cooperative learning, there are two key components: (1) students work together toward a common goal; and (2) students are held accountable for each other's learning rather than making a final group product (Slavin, 2010). There is evidence that cooperative learning benefits all students and results in desirable motivational outcomes in addition to achievement gains.

But how does a teacher include group work in grading? Should teachers assign "cooperation" grades to the whole group or to individual students? Experts in cooperative learning strongly advise against assigning group grades. While

Teacher's Corner

Jenny Smith

Middle School Teacher

On Grading Group Work

I provide a rubric for the assignment beforehand and walk students through it to ensure that expectations are clear. I give groups the opportunity to revise their work if they receive a low grade. I include an individual component, usually a reflection on how the group worked together, summary of learning, etc. I also give groups the opportunity to grade themselves on how they worked together and provide examples. I stay present and observe as groups are working and intervene if a group is struggling to work together or struggling with the content. Grading group work adds legitimacy to the idea that it's important to be able to work with and learn from others. The challenge of course is that students are likely to be vocal about how they feel about who they're working and they need to be taught how to work as a group, how to listen, compromise, share ideas, etc. I feel like this has to be in place before I am comfortable grading group work.

there are some strategies that you can use, it's far from an exact science (Brookhart, 2013). It is helpful to clarify and make a distinction between learning skills that should be graded compared to skills that are important to assess but not grade. Creating rubrics and reflection prompts to assess participation and explaining them to students prior to group work clarifies expectations. Using peer review to evaluate each member's contribution is another strategy that works in combination with teachers' own observations. In assessing learning outcomes (for each individual student!), separate rubrics, reflection prompts, or a test at the end of the project that target learning goals can facilitate individual grading. The key to successful group work (and grading group work) is to clearly articulate the need for group work, intended learning outcomes (aligned with standards), and criteria for assessing and grading prior to implementing.

Approaches to Marking and Grading

There are several ways to mark and grade student performance. Each has advantages and disadvantages (see Table 15.3), which relate to a number of issues, including (a) the degree to which the approach allows for adequate feedback, (b) the flexibility of the approach to various forms of assessment, and (c) the practicality of the approach considering constraints such as limited teacher time. We will consider the most common types of symbols or scores that are used, including letter grades, percentage correct, rubrics (checklists), standards-based grades, and written descriptions. Most teachers use a combination of these in the classroom

TABLE 15.3   Comparison of Different Types of Grading

Approach	Degree of Feedback	Flexibility to Forms of Assessment	Practical Constraints (Time and skill needed to implement)
Letter Grades	Used alone, provides little feedback to student beyond single indicator of relative performance	Can be adapted for use with multiple forms of assessment	Clarifying meaning of letter grades to students may take time and skill
Percentage Correct	Used alone, provides little feedback to student beyond single indicator of relative performance	Tends to favor assessments that have clearly defined right and wrong answers	Easy to calculate and combine scores; developing appropriate assessments may take some time
Rubrics/Checklists	Gives high degree of feedback related to rubric dimensions; combined dimension scores give feedback for overall performance	Can be adapted for multiple forms of assessment	Developing rubrics takes time; once developed, grading with rubrics is relatively quick
Standards-Based	Gives high degree of feedback related to the identified performance standards	Can be adapted for multiple forms of assessment	Determining appropriate performance standards may be difficult and time consuming; once measures are developed, grading is relatively quick
Written Descriptions	Allows a high level of personalized feedback; however, when used alone does not give students measure of relative performance	Designed for qualitative, open-ended forms of assessment; not as appropriate for objective tests with right and wrong answers	Time-intensive grading; not practical for use with all assignments

with the hope of trying to achieve a balance between consistency in grading practice and adaptability to a variety of assessments, student learning styles, and school contexts.

Letter Grades

Perhaps the most common way of marking student performance is to give a letter grade. Traditionally, letter grades correspond to different adjectives, such as excellent or outstanding, good, average or acceptable, poor, and unsatisfactory. Often plus and minus symbols are used to provide finer distinctions. Letter grades provide a convenient, concise, and familiar approach to marking. In addition, grades are readily understood by students and parents to provide an overall indication of performance.

The major limitation of letter grades is that they provide only a general indication of performance. There is nothing wrong with giving students an overall, summary judgment in the form of a grade. However, such a general mark, by itself, does not indicate what was done correctly or incorrectly. Strengths and limitations are not communicated. There is also a tendency for teachers to be influenced by factors other than performance in coming up with a grade, especially on papers, projects, and presentations (e.g., effort, work habits, attitude). Furthermore, because teachers differ in their value systems, the proportion of students getting each grade can vary. In one class, most students can get As and Bs, whereas in another class, most students receive Bs and Cs.

What you need to make clear to your students about grades is what each letter means, so that their interpretation is accurate, appropriate, and helpful. Does getting an A mean that a student did outstanding work, or does it mean best in the class? Does it mean that the teacher thinks the student worked hard on this or that it was done really well? Does getting a C mean about as well as most students or satisfactory work? There are a number of possible interpretations, depending on how much factors other than performance are included and the basis of comparison (individual student referenced, norm-referenced, or standards-based). Critics of traditional grading methods suggest doing away with such "omnibus" grades (Marzano & Heflebower, 2011).

If you are clear about what each letter grade means, first to yourself and then to your students, it makes letter grading a much more effective means of enhancing student achievement. Table 15.4 presents different interpretations of letter grades.

Notice that it is possible to combine or mix norm- and standards-based approaches (Terwilliger, 1989). What often occurs is that the higher grades tend to be norm-referenced and the lower ones tend to be standards-based. That is, to get an A, students need to perform better than most, but a failure judgment tends to be based on absolute standards. If a purely relative scale were used and the norming group were the class itself, some students would always fail, despite what might be a high level of performance, and that occurs rarely if at all (a better procedure is to use data from previous classes to set the norm from a larger group). Also, some students would always succeed. It is only with absolute scales that all students can either succeed or fail.

Percentage Correct

For objective tests, the most common approach to reporting performance is to indicate the percentage of items answered correctly, then convert that to a grade. Thus, we often characterize our achievement as, say, getting a 75 or a 92 on a test. These numbers refer to the percentage of items or points obtained out of a

TABLE 15.4   Different Interpretations of Letter Grades

Grade	Standards-Based	Norm-Referenced	Combined Norm-Referenced and Standards-Based	Based on Improvement
A	Outstanding or advanced: complete knowledge of all content; mastery of all targets; exceeds standards	Outstanding: among the highest or best performance	Outstanding: very high level of performance	Outstanding: much improvement on most or all targets
B	Very good or proficient: complete knowledge of most content; mastery of most targets; meets most standards	Very good: performs above the class average	Very good: better than average performance	Very good: some improvement on most or all targets
C	Acceptable or basic: command of only basic concepts or skills; mastery of some targets; meets some standards	Average: performs at the class average	Average	Acceptable: some improvement on some targets
D	Making progress or developing: lacks knowledge of most content; mastery of only a few targets; meets only a few standards	Poor: below the class average	Below average or weak: minimum performance for passing	Making progress: minimal progress on most targets
F	Unsatisfactory: lacks knowledge of content; no mastery of targets; does not meet any standards	Unsatisfactory: far below average; among the worst in the class	Unsatisfactory: lacks sufficient knowledge to pass	Unsatisfactory: no improvement on any targets

possible 100. These scores are easy to calculate, record, and combine at the end of the grading period. Usually, letter grades are associated with ranges of scores, so it's really a letter grade system that gives students a somewhat finer discrimination in their performance. It is possible, if not very common, to grade everything with percentage correct, even papers and essay items.

There are a number of limitations to using the percentage correct in marking and grading. The first problem is that with a percentage there is still only a general indication of performance communicated. With a single percentage, it is very difficult to understand student performance on specific skills. A second limitation is the tendency to equate percentage of items correct with percent mastered. As we have pointed out, items can differ tremendously in level of difficulty, so when students obtain a high percentage of correct answers, mastery may or may not be demonstrated, depending on the difficulty level of the assessment (Marzano & Heflebower, 2011). Thus, it is probably incorrect to conclude that when a student obtains a 100, he or she knows 100% of the learning targets, or that a score of 50 corresponds to mastery of half of the targets.

Another disadvantage is that the discriminations that are suggested by a scale from 1 to 100 are much finer than what can be reliably assessed. Because of error in testing, there is usually no meaningful difference between scores differentiated by one or two points. That is, scores of 92 and 93 suggest the same level of student performance. In other words, the degree of precision suggested by percentage correct is not justified given the error that exists.

Finally, it has also been pointed out that the 100-point scale has a natural bias because typically three-fifths of the scale—from 0 to 60—represent failing grades. With this type of scale, the averaging in of "catastrophically" low grades, such as zeros, gives an unfair assessment of student achievement and has the potential to demotivate students (Guskey, 2002; Marzano & Heflebower, 2011; Wormeli, 2006). This issue has led to minimum grading policies in some districts that pull zero grades up to 50 (Carey & Carifio, 2012).

Rubrics/Checklists

A variation of the proficient/not proficient approach is to give students a rubric or a checklist to indicate their performance on each aspect of the learning target, then convert each point on the rubric to a grade. The rubric has two or more categories. In a simple dichotomous rubric, the teacher might prepare a series of statements that describe aspects of the performance that the students need to include and places a check mark next to each one the teacher judges to be demonstrated.

A more elaborate approach provides students with scales of performance with detailed descriptions of each step of the scale. The teacher makes checks on the scale to indicate the level of performance. The rubric that describes the scoring is used as the checklist. The advantage of this type of grading is that the students receive detailed feedback about what they did well and what needs improvement. The detail in the rubric helps students understand more precisely where they need to improve. An additional benefit is that when rubrics are presented at the beginning of an assignment, they give students a specific idea of what they need to do to get the grade they want.

The difficulty of this approach is developing the rubrics and keeping the system practical. However, once you develop detailed lists, they are fairly efficient because you only make check marks. This can be done efficiently, even if there are several such statements for each student product. It is certainly more efficient than writing comments on papers, though some individualized comments are important as well.

Standards-Based

Standards-based grading has emerged as a relatively new and highly effective form of grading that provides meaningful feedback to students and parents (Guskey, 2009; Guskey & Jung, 2013; Marzano, 2006; O'Connor, 2009). Guskey and Bailey (2001) have identified four steps in the development of standards-based grading:

1. Identify major learning targets and standards.
2. Establish performance indicators for the standards.

3. Identify benchmarks that indicate graduated levels of proficiency.
4. Develop reporting forms that indicate progress and final achievement toward meeting the standards.

As discussed earlier, and pointed out by Brookhart (2009), standards-based grading is a direct descendant of criterion-referenced grading. Both emphasize the idea of an absolute, established level of performance in a carefully defined domain. In standards-based grading, however, the "criterion" refers to specific content-based learning targets that are established for all students. Typically, these targets reflect learning outcomes that are determined by the state for each grade level that provide information on the content to be learned at each level. Consequently, a standards-based grade typically represents a student's knowledge of content as related to one or several standards.

The challenge with the first step of identifying the standards is to get them at the right level of specificity. Having too many standards can indicate a broad but insufficient depth of coverage of content. Standards that are too detailed make reporting cumbersome and time consuming for teachers and too complex for parent understanding. They also tend to orient assessments—and hence teaching— toward narrowly defined standards, rather than integrated and connected educational outcomes. On the other hand, standards that are too general do not provide enough information to show strengths or weaknesses. One effective approach to get standards at the right level is to begin with broad ones (often these are required) and provide more specific targets under each one. This may involve reframing the language of the curriculum standards to be broader to enable effective and meaningful communication so that parents as well as students can see overall performance and areas of strength and weakness (Guskey & Bailey, 2010). Figure 15.3 provides an example of a broad learning goal defined as a student demonstrating scientific reasoning. More specific criteria are listed to "unpack" the standard (Marzano & Haystead, 2008) to reveal components that represent the demonstration of the learning goal (see Chapter 2). The language in the individual standards clearly indicates what the student should be able to do: *distinguish*, *state*, *communicate*, etc.

The performance indicators are descriptors that indicate the status of student achievement in relation to the standard. In addition, they describe to what extent or how consistently a student demonstrated the learning target in an assessment. At one time this was simply the idea of pass/fail. Today, the most common form is to use descriptors such as *beginning*, *progressing*, *proficient*, and *exceptional*.

It is important for the descriptors to show benchmarks that indicate graduated levels of proficiency to facilitate reporting progress as well as current performance level. Descriptors that indicate how often the standard was reached, such as *seldom*, *sometimes*, *frequently*, or *consistently*, could be used (Marzano & Haystead, 2008). By indicating progress with performance indicators, students and parents will be able to gauge the amount of learning that has been demonstrated over the marking period. It also provides information on areas for improvement. As we will discuss later in the chapter, the advocates of standards-based grades

FIGURE 15.3   Elementary Reporting Form Illustrating a Grade for the Overall Standard with Separate Process Skill Indicators

Key to Process Skill Grades:

4 = Consistently and accurately
3 = Often and usually accurate
2 = Occasionally with some inaccuracies
1 = Seldom or rarely with many inaccuracies

Standard: Demonstrate Scientific Reasoning	Overall Grade: B
Process Skill Indicators	
Distinguishes between observations, conclusions, and inferences	3
States appropriate hypotheses	4
Communicates data with simple graphs and pictures	2
Simple models are used to explain results	3
Variables are identified	3
Appropriate conclusions are drawn from the data	2

have suggested the reworking of the traditional report card to reflect the standards-based methodology (Marzano, 2006; Welsh & D'Agostino, 2008; Guskey & Bailey, 2010).

A major premise of standards-based grading is that students take more responsibility for their learning (Vatterott, 2015). One way to support the use of standards-based grading that can help with student motivation is to prefix "I can" to the learning targets. School districts and states many provide such tools for student self-evaluation along with grading rubrics. Standards, therefore, can serve as self-assessment tools that can reinforce standards-based teaching and learning. As we will discuss later in the chapter, the advocates of standards-based grades have suggested the reworking of the traditional report card to reflect the standards-based methodology (Marzano, 2006; Welsh & D'Agostino, 2008; Guskey & Bailey, 2010).

Written Descriptions

An alternative to giving only a grade or score is to mark students' work with written descriptions. The advantage of this approach is that the comments can be highly individualized, pointing out unique strengths and weaknesses, and can focus attention on important issues. Students appreciate the effort of teachers who take the time to make these comments. Of course, the time needed to do this is a major disadvantage. Many secondary teachers simply do not have sufficient time to give this level of feedback. Then there is the added complication of converting the descriptions into grades or scores for report cards. Here the advantage from one perspective becomes a disadvantage from another because the uniqueness of the descriptions makes it difficult to grade consistently and fairly. In a strict system of written descriptions, the function of grades as a basis of comparison is lost.

Determining Report Card (Composite) Grades

Despite the movement toward standards-based grading and the critique of the single "omnibus" grade (Marzano & Heflebower, 2011), we are still far from doing away with the end of unit and semester grades that are given by teachers to provide a single indicator of student performance in each academic area. Recognizing that professional judgment is essential for determining final grades, as well as marks and grades for individual assessments, you will make some important decisions about how to calculate final grades. These decisions can be summarized in the form of three steps:

1. Select what to include in the final grade.
2. Select weights for each individual assessment.
3. Combine weighted scores to determine a single grade.

Before examining these steps, keep in mind that electronic grading systems, which you will probably use, will influence how the grades are combined. These systems essentially open up grading to students and parents. While the transparency of these systems may be in line with the idea of providing ongoing formative feedback, as well as summative information, they may restrict your ability to make changes when calculating final grades. This will be discussed in some detail later in the chapter.

Select What to Include in the Final Grade

Generally, this is where you may have a fair amount of leeway. To some extent, it is up to you to determine which assessments will contribute to the final grade. As we have already suggested, it is best if you base final grades primarily on academic performance. But which performances should be included? Tests? Participation in class? Papers? Quizzes? Homework? Before selecting the assessments, think again about your overall learning goals. Your selection of what goes into the final grade should provide the most accurate information in relation to these goals. If you have done a good job of basing your formal assessments on the learning targets, then each of these assessments will contribute meaningfully to the grade. It is less clear if pop quizzes, participation, and homework should be included.

On the one hand, pop quizzes, participation, and homework do focus on student performance, but can they legitimately serve as documentation of student learning and understanding? If they are primarily formative in nature to give students practice and feedback, they may be viewed more as instruction than assessment and should not be included in a final grade. Proponents of standards-based grading recommend against using homework and practice assessments in a final grade (Vatterott, 2015). Some teachers argue that pop quizzes are not fair to students, and some also contend that homework may not have been completed by the student. Many teachers realize that participation in class is influenced by group dynamics and personality. Other teachers view pop quizzes, participation, and homework as indicators of how much students are paying attention and learning in class and will use them to calculate final grades. A recommended strategy is to minimize the number of tasks that are graded to allow for more feedback, using ungraded tasks that can support mastery-oriented grading (Nagel, 2013). The choice of whether to include these student performances is yours, and either choice is legitimate. Just be sure to make clear to students and parents what is going into the grade and why it is fair.

As discussed earlier, you will want to be especially careful in considering factors such as attendance, effort, and personal/social characteristics such as cooperativeness, participation, and work habits in determining grades. You don't want nonacademic factors to have much influence on the final grade.

We believe the best rule on these matters is this: If a grade is for academic performance in areas such as reading, science, mathematics, history, and the like, then the grade should be determined primarily by student academic performance on major assessments. In a standards-based grading system, the student's last, best performance most accurately reflects learning and should be heavily weighted (Nagel, 2015). This is essentially a matter of maintaining appropriate validity so that your inferences about academic performance are reasonable. If cooperativeness and participation are important targets, consider separate grades for each.

Finally, in selecting the assessments that you will include, carefully consider how many are needed to give an accurate overall judgment of each student's performance. Would it be reasonable to base a semester grade on a single exam? How about a 9-week grade—would two tests and a paper be sufficient? Probably most would agree that a single assessment alone is definitely not sufficient. In the words of Grant Wiggins, "A single grade hides more than it reveals" (1998, p. 248). Three assessments for a 9-week grade is much better, but even that may not be sufficient. Often schools using online grade books are able to keep track of the number of assessments teachers record and set guidelines for a minimum number. The rule of thumb with respect to the number of assessments needed is the more, the better (Marzano, 2006). However, there is also the risk that too much assessment takes away important instructional time. This is especially true in the current landscape of high-stakes standardized assessment. Many school divisions have mandated quarterly standardized assessments on top of the state tests (or even more frequently). There are cases when those mandated assessments are not well designed or well aligned with the curriculum of your course. In that case, they should not be factored in, and other teacher-developed assessments need to be used to determine final grades. The danger, then, is overtesting the students. Overtested students may become bored or apathetic about the process of testing, which introduces significant error into the assessment. Once again, your professional judgment is needed to negotiate the challenges of using grades in ways that promote authentic learning.

Select Weights for Each Assessment

You will need to decide how much each assessment will count in the final grade. Obviously, more important assessments are given greater weight. What determines if an assessment is important? You probably guessed it—more professional judgment! The most significant assessments are those that (a) correspond most closely to the learning goals and targets (content-related evidence for validity), (b) reflect instructional time, (c) are most reliable, and (d) are most current.

Because there are multiple learning targets in a unit or semester, you need to break out the percentage that each target contributes to the whole. We have illustrated this in Figure 15.4 in the form of a pie chart for a unit on the animal kingdom. You can see that different percentages correspond to each topic. In this case, the overall goal is determined mostly by vertebrate animal characteristics and behaviors. Now you need to weigh your assessments to match these percentages so that the final grade reflects the relative contribution of each topic. This will provide good content-related evidence for validity, which is a primary concern. In this example, about 50% of what determines the final grade should be the assessments on vertebrates. This percentage is independent of the length of the book chapters, or assessments, or the instructional time devoted to each topic. What you are determining is solely the value of each of the topics.

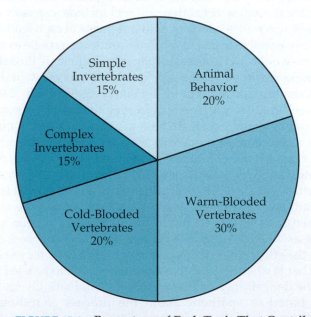

FIGURE 15.4   Percentage of Each Topic That Contributes to the Final Grade

Even though instructional time is not a factor in the first consideration of weights, it's still an important barometer of the amount of emphasis given to each topic. For this reason, we think it's only fair to take time devoted to instruction as a factor.

As we have already emphasized, students need to know before an assessment is taken what will be covered. This may include topics or concepts that have not been discussed in class. Although there is nothing wrong with testing students on material that wasn't covered in class, it's best if the weights reflect instructional focus. If you spent 50% of your 9 weeks studying simple invertebrates, it probably wouldn't be fair to weight this topic at only 15%. Similarly, you might determine that you *intend* to weight vertebrates at 50%, but when you look back over the weeks, you figure that only 25% of the students' time was spent learning about vertebrates. This would suggest that a more appropriate weight would be 30%–35%, at most. Obviously, you don't know for sure how much time you take until the instruction is completed. Although it is good to have guidelines to share with students at the beginning of an instructional unit, your final determination of weights needs to be determined close to the end of instruction. For this reason, weights should not be set in stone at the beginning of the unit. Ideally, you should have guidelines to share with students at the beginning of terms, but then hold off your final determination of weights until close to the end of instruction. However, this principle of grading comes into some conflict with the open online grading systems that allow students and parents to track all of their assignments and grade totals through the semester. In this case, making changes to assignment weights at the end of the semester might seem unfair to the students.

Reliability/precision is a factor in weighting. Other things being equal, it is best to put more weight on more accurate assessments. This will reduce the overall amount of error that is included in determining the grade. Generally, reliability/precision increases with a greater number of items for each target and for objective items. But the most important concern is validity; highly reliable/precise scores from assessments should never be given more weight than is appropriate, given the validity of the assessment.

If you test the same content more than once, as you would with a cumulative final exam, put more weight on the most recent assessment. In fact, a later assessment on the same material might mean that the earlier assessment should be dropped. Although there is a bias toward averaging in most grading systems, it doesn't always make sense pedagogically, and advocates of standards-based grading have argued against it (Marzano, 2006; O'Connor, 2009). After all, if your goal is to communicate accurately the nature of a student's current performance, wouldn't the more recent assessment be better? From a practical standpoint, however, you'll find that it's difficult to simply discard an earlier test score. The best compromise is to weight the cumulative exam more than each of the preceding ones so that final performance outweighs what students demonstrate at the beginning or middle of the unit.

Given these considerations, you now need to combine the assessments properly to obtain the final grade.

Combining Different Scores and Grades

Over the past 10 years, most schools and districts have moved toward using electronic grading systems. These systems can take the form of stand-alone gradebook software programs that are used on teachers' individual computers, or web-based programs that can be accessed online by teachers, administrators, students, and parents. Schools and school districts may specific grading requirements and weighting formulae beforehand for teachers. The two main advantages of the software-based systems are that you can work offline, and they are quicker for entering grades and making calculations. Another important advantage of the online systems is the high degree of on-demand communication they allow both within the school and between teachers, students, and parents. Both systems not only save time by allowing teachers to avoid tedious and complex calculations, but also give multiple opportunities for increasing grade feedback with the students and parents.

Teacher's Corner

Rebecca Field

High School Teacher

The electronic grading system that I use lets me weight different categories, for example, classroom projects and research are weighted more than objective tests and homework in my class because I think they are more important. The grading system has lots of room to be flexible within the parameters that I place within my gradebook. Each teacher is allowed to change the gradebook to suit his/her classroom and teaching philosophy. As for the perceived impersonal nature of electronic grading, I actually think the grading system has become MORE personal. I receive emails from students much more frequently and students seem to be more aware of the connection between their work and the grade they earn. I am able to keep track of how students are doing, not just in my class, but in all classes. It helps me to notice if a child is struggling just in my class, and I can investigate further or meet with school counselors if a student's grades are dropping dramatically in other classes. I can communicate with parents in a more efficient way because I do not have to spend time on the phone, and parents are more informed of progress and improvement. I do not have to worry about calculating my own grades, which saves a huge amount of time for me personally. I can print or save reports that help me to look at growth, and I can see easily if I need to adjust grades for the entire class. Because students can see grades updated live, I can easily motivate student to turn in work quickly because if I enter a zero into the grade book, students usually respond immediately. Students have access to their grades all the time. Parent involvement has advantages and disadvantages. The number of emails and calls that I receive from parents and students has increased dramatically because of the immediacy of grade updates. I do not think using a digital gradebook has affected the way I teach, my assignments, or the relationships that I make with my students. Like all 21st-century additions to my classroom, it is simply a tool that I use that has required some adaptations.

Guskey (2002) points out that the mathematical precision that is achieved with electronic grading systems does not necessarily bring greater objectivity, accuracy, or fairness. He points out that these programs do not lessen the challenges teachers face when making decisions about what will be included and how each score or grade contributes to the final grade (e.g., how to handle zeros, averaging, improvement). Professional judgment is still key. In this section, we will give a brief overview of what options for combining grades are available when working within a gradebook program and then discuss the importance of incorporating the intangibles of teacher judgment. Figures 15.5 and 15.6 illustrate examples of formats that are used with electronic gradebooks.

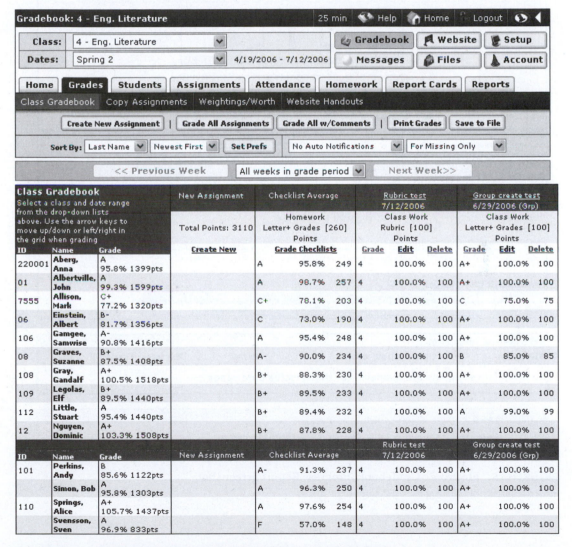

FIGURE 15.5   Grading Page Screenshot of an Electronic Gradebook

Source: Courtesy of Blue Pegasus LLC Copyright 2016.

GradeBookWizard.com
Blue Pegasus

E30058 Nguyen, Dominic
Student Progress Report
Grade Period: 1st nine weeks

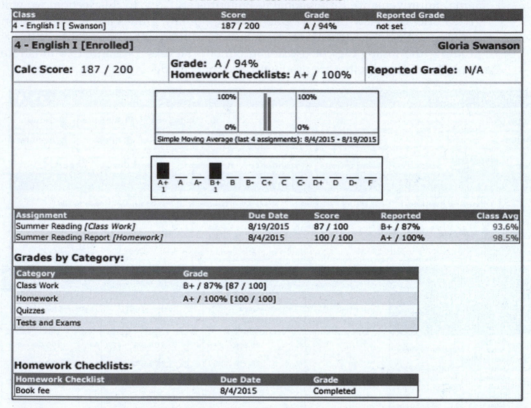

Class	Score	Grade	Reported Grade
4 - English I [Swanson]	187 / 200	A / 94%	not set

4 - English I [Enrolled]   **Gloria Swanson**

Calc Score: 187 / 200   **Grade:** A / 94%   **Reported Grade:** N/A
Homework Checklists: A+ / 100%

Simple Moving Average (last 4 assignments): 8/4/2015 - 8/19/2015

| A+ | A | A- | B+ | B | B- | C+ | C | C- | D+ | D | D- | F |
| 1 | | | 1 | | | | | | | | | |

Assignment	Due Date	Score	Reported	Class Avg
Summer Reading [Class Work]	8/19/2015	87 / 100	B+ / 87%	93.6%
Summer Reading Report [Homework]	8/4/2015	100 / 100	A+ / 100%	98.5%

Grades by Category:

Category	Grade
Class Work	B+ / 87% [87 / 100]
Homework	A+ / 100% [100 / 100]
Quizzes	
Tests and Exams	

Homework Checklists:

Homework Checklist	Due Date	Grade
Book fee	8/4/2015	Completed

Attendance Incidents

Absent:	Excused Absence:	Tardy:	Excused Tardy:

No attendance records are available for the selected date range

Discipline Log

No discipline records are available for the selected date range

FIGURE 15.6   Electronic Gradebook, Progress Report Screenshot
Source: Courtesy of Blue Pegasus LLC Copyright 2016.

Weighted Categories Versus Total Points Methods.   Traditionally there are two systems for combining grades and computing totals. In the **weighted categories method**, assessments that use different types of scores and grades and tests with different numbers of items are scaled and combined to produce a composite grade. For example, homework assignments, which may be graded on a check plus/check/check minus scale; projects, graded using a rubric; and exams that follow a 100-point objective scale can be weighted by category and combined to develop a final grade. The advantage of the percent correct method is that it allows for some flexibility in the weighting process.

With the **total points method**, the teacher gives each assessment a number of points that reflects its weight. The final grade is simply the total points of all assessments added. For example, homework assignments may only count for 5 or 10 points, whereas a test may be weighted 50 points. The advantage of the total points method is that because the weight is worked into the point value of an assignment, it clearly lets students know the importance of an assignment toward the final grade. The disadvantage of this approach is that the teacher must adjust the number of items to equal the points each assessment should provide, or change the score of an assessment to reflect the points. In most cases this is pretty cumbersome, so if the total points method is used, the assessments are carefully designed to avoid the recalculation of any individual assessment so that they can simply be added. This may constrain the nature of the assessments. Rather than have the method of combining scores drive the assessments, let each assessment be constructed to provide the best measure of student performance, and then combine. In our opinion, the weighted categories approach is much better than total points for this reason. However, in most gradebook programs there is a choice when setting up a class between these two methods.

Using Judgment When Combining Grades.   Whether you use the weighted categories or total points method, you are essentially taking the average of results from many different assessments. Although averaging is justified as a way to include all the assessments (and keep students motivated), there is a danger that *mindless* averaging, as we have noted, will distort the students' true capabilities (e.g., using zeros). For this reason, it is always important to look at the practice of combining grades as more than just a cold computation. For example, when a student evaluation system is designed to move students from novice to expert on an appropriate skill continuum, it may not make good sense to average performances during the entire period of learning (Wiggins, 1998). If a student begins as a novice and obtains a low score, should that score be averaged with a final "expert" performance to result in an average grade? What is critical is reporting student attainment of the skill in relation to the rubric and scoring criteria at the time of the report, regardless of earlier performances. Obviously, this is an instance where adjustments need to be made. This could take the form of shifting weights to emphasize more recent work. Regardless, it is important for teachers to always think critically about the effect of their grading systems.

Consider a less systematic approach to combining grades: the *eyeball method.* With the eyeball method, the teacher simply reviews the scores and grades and estimates an average for them, without performing any calculations, to come up with what seems to be the correct grade. This has obvious disadvantages and the method isn't generally recommended, but it does have one redeeming quality. With eyeballing, the teacher asks, "All things considered and looking at the whole as more than the sum of each part, what is the most valid grade for this student?" The notion that it's important to consider everything together has some merit because it recognizes that teacher professional judgment is needed to give grades.

At the other extreme, there are teachers who mindlessly calculate averages without any consideration of factors that might be important, such as student absenteeism, effort, and possible testing error. Just because a numeric average comes up with a certain grade doesn't mean that that grade is a valid indicator of student achievement. In some cases, eyeballing grades might be a good first step. The eyeballed grades could then be compared to calculated percentages. This might help teachers identify the inclinations and biases they have that are the root of some of their professional decisions. Another idea is to ask for eyeball grades from students. That is, pass out student portfolios, have students review them, and then ask, "Based on what you see in front of you, what grade do you think you deserve? Justify your answer." These student-eyeballed grades not only give teachers many insights into the individual students' self-perception as learners, they also lead to very entertaining discussions!

Cheating.   Another issue is the lowering of grades in response to student cheating (Cizek, 1999, 2003). Obviously, cheating is a very serious offense, and appropriate disciplinary action is warranted. However, lowering grades may not be appropriate discipline if there is an extreme negative impact on the grade. Suppose you give a zero to a student when he or she is caught cheating on a major test. Does this score accurately represent the student's knowledge and performance? Here you are using grades to punish the student. It would be better to find another kind of punishment and retest the student.

Assessing the Weight of Mandated Assessments.   As noted above, there has been a consistent push over the last decade to increase the number of mandated

Teacher's Corner

Tami Slater

National Board Certified Elementary Reading Specialist Teacher

I do not use zeros in calculating final grades. Students in elementary school do not get enough grades in one subject, and averaging in a zero as a grade would bring their average down so low, the student would not recover from it. A zero averaged in a final grade would not show a true reflection of what the student can do, and that is what I believe grades need to show.

assessments given by teachers. In many cases, end-of-year state standardized assessments have been supplemented by division-level 9-weeks tests and, in certain cases, biweekly common assessments developed at either the division or the school level. The question is, should these assessments be incorporated into the final grade? In certain cases, division or school policy might dictate this decision; however, if teachers are allowed judgment on this issue, they should carefully assess both the quality and alignment of the assessments to their course curriculum.

Recognizing Teacher Fallibility.   One of the most difficult challenges teachers face, especially when they first start to teach and test students, is to write tests at the appropriate level of difficulty and emphasis. Suppose you prepare a test and the majority of students do very poorly. There are two primary considerations here. One is that the students just didn't get it, didn't understand. The other is that the test is unfair—that the emphasis on some areas does not match instruction. Sometimes when students do poorly it reflects more on inadequacies of your teaching than it does on student achievement! You need to be open to this possibility and make appropriate changes to reflect student achievement more fairly. One option is to give an improved makeup test.

Finally, it's important to be willing to change grades when justified. In the first place, mistakes are made in hand-calculated grades. A possible hint of this occurs when a final grade for a student just doesn't seem right. In this circumstance, go back over the calculations to be sure there are no mistakes. Second, students sometimes have legitimate arguments about a grade. It is possible to overlook things. In fact, this is probable when you grade a lot of assessments. Be willing to admit that you were wrong and record the best, most accurate score or grade.

See Table 15.5 for a summary of what to do and what not to do for effective grading practices.

Teacher's Corner

Brian Letourneau

National Board Certified Teacher, High School History

When grading my AP U.S. History unit tests, any student may take a retake of the summative assessment; it does not matter whether the student got at 91% or a 71% on the original test. If a student is unhappy with his or her performance, the student has their parents sign the original test so the parent is in the loop and nothing is hidden. I then meet individually with the student and have a conversation about the gaps in their learning to help the student focus their studying. The student then takes another version of the original test. The number of questions and links to essential questions is the same; the actual questions differ.

I believe that students learn at different paces and some students just need more learning time. So after taking the second test, the student's better grade is the one recorded. I don't average the two or have a maximum grade allowed; I simply record the highest demonstration of a student's learning.

TABLE 15.5   Do's and Don'ts of Effective Grading

Do	Don't
Use well-thought-out professional judgments	Depend entirely on number crunching
Try everything you can to score and grade fairly	Allow personal bias to affect grades
Grade according to preestablished learning targets and standards	Grade on the curve using the class as the norm group
Clearly inform students and parents of grading procedures at the beginning of the semester	Keep grading procedures secret
Base grades primarily on student performance	Use effort, improvement, attitudes, and motivation for borderline students
Rely most on current information	Penalize poorly performing students early in the semester
Mark, grade, and return assessments to students as soon as possible and with as much feedback as possible	Return assessments weeks later with little or no feedback
Review borderline cases carefully; when in doubt, assign the higher grade	Be inflexible with borderline cases
Convert scores to the same scale before combining	Use zero scores indiscriminately when averaging grades
Weight scores before combining	Include extra-credit assignments that are not related to the learning targets
Use a sufficient number of assessments	Rely on one or two assessments for a semester grade
Be willing to change grades when warranted	Lower grades for cheating, misbehaving, tardiness, or absence

Reporting Student Progress to Parents

An important function of marks and grades is to provide information that can be shared with parents. Parents are critical to student learning, and effectively reporting student progress can help them better understand their children and know what they can do to provide appropriate support and motivation. Reporting to parents can take many forms, including weekly or monthly grade reports, phone calls, emails, letters, newsletters, conferences, and of course, report cards. Online gradebooks have also become important for reporting and communicating about progress. Although report card grades are the most common way by which parents keep abreast of student progress, what those grades communicate is usually limited and needs to be supplemented with additional information.

Report Cards

The foundation for most reporting systems is the report card. The "card" is constructed to communicate to parents the progress of their children. Typically, report cards provide little more than a series of letter or percentage grades for subject areas, along with a few teacher comments. For report cards to be effective, parents must be able to understand what the grades and comments mean. The information needs to be accurately interpreted, and parents need to learn enough to guide improvement efforts.

For this reason, there has been a push among proponents of standards-based grading to develop standards-based report cards that provide more precise information to students and parents about student learning (Azwell & Schmar, 1995; Brookhart, 2009; Guskey & Bailey, 2010; Wiggins, 1998). Standards-based report cards break subject-area grades down into more specific standards-based measures and show both the student's growth and level of mastery of the standard. However, a standards-based report card could include several pages of detailed data about student learning, leaving students and parents confused and unsure about the final or "real" grade. The biggest challenge to using of standards-based report cards is a general resistance to changing the familiar format. The resistance is perhaps due to familiarity and the simplicity of letter grades in conveying student performance. Educating parents about standards-based grading, its purpose, and how it differs from traditional grading could alleviate some of the resistance. Walking parents through both traditional and standards-based reports can help them appreciate the improved depth of information in a standards-based report card (Guskey & Jung, 2013).

Progress Reports

One approach to communicating student progress is to provide some type of ongoing report. This could be done weekly, biweekly, or monthly, or even in real time. The advantage of progress reports is not only that they help ensure that there are no surprises at the end of the semester, but they have also been shown to have a significant and positive effect on student learning (Marzano, 2006). With electronic gradebooks, it is now possible to quickly create progress grade reports for entire classes (see Figure 15.6). These reports can be customized by the teacher to show not only student grades on class assignments and averaged totals, but also summaries of performance by category, graphs, connections between assignments and standards, and student attendance information. Additional information you may want to include would be learning targets for the period, copies of rubrics and scoring criteria, descriptions of student motivation and affect, and written suggestions for helping the student. You will want to be sure to include some positive comments. It may be helpful to identify two or three areas that the parents could focus on until the next report. If possible, provide specific expectations for what you want parents to do at home to help. Be clear in asserting that parents need to be partners in the learning process. If these expectations can be individualized for each student, so much the better, but even a standard list of expectations is good.

Another type of progress report is the informal note or letter. Taking only a minute or two to write a personal note to parents about their child is much appreciated. It shows concern and caring. Begin such a note with something positive, then summarize progress and suggest an expectation or two for improvements.

Parent–Teacher Conferences

The parent–teacher conference is a common way for teachers to communicate in person with parents about student progress. This is typically a face-to-face discussion, though phone conferences and calls can also be used. In fact, brief phone calls by the teacher to talk with parents, like informal notes, are very well received and appreciated, especially when the calls are about positive progress and suggestions rather than for disciplinary or other problems.

There are two types of parent–teacher conferences, each based on a different primary purpose. Group conferences, such as what occurs at back-to-school or open-house nights, are conducted to communicate school and class policies, class content, evaluation procedures, expectations, and procedures for getting in touch with the teacher. Individual conferences are conducted to discuss the individual student's achievement, progress, or difficulties. Parent–teacher conferences may be initiated by either the teacher or the parent, based on these purposes.

Parent–teacher conferences are required in most schools. Although the formats for middle and high school conferences are different from those for elementary school because of the number of students, the goals are basically the same. Whether the conference is in the context of a one-on-one meeting or a back-to-school night, most of the suggestions in Figure 15.7 apply.

It is essential to plan the conference and to be prepared. This means having all the information well organized in advance and knowing what you hope to

FIGURE 15.7 **Checklist for Conducting Parent–Teacher Conferences**

✓ Plan each conference in advance.
✓ Conduct the conference in a private, quiet, comfortable setting.
✓ Explain how to interpret standards-based report cards
✓ Begin with a discussion of positive student performances.
✓ Establish an informal, professional tone.
✓ Encourage parent participation in the conference.
✓ Be frank in reviewing student strengths and weaknesses.
✓ Review language skills.
✓ Review learning targets with examples of student performances that show progress.
✓ Avoid discussing other students and teachers.
✓ Avoid bluffing.
✓ Identify two or three areas to work on in a plan of action.

achieve from the conference. This will probably include a list of areas you want to cover and some questions to ask parents. If possible, you may be able to find out what parents would like to review before the conference. Examples of student work should be organized to show progress and performance in relation to learning targets. The conference is an ideal time for pointing out specific areas of strength and weakness that report card grades cannot communicate.

You want the conference to be a conversation. Listening to parents will help you understand their child better. Even though it is natural to feel anxious about meeting with parents, it's important to take a strong, professional stance. Rather than being timid, be modest but take charge. This should be done with a friendly and informal tone that encourages parents to participate. You'll want to be positive, but you need to be direct and honest about areas that need improvement. Keep the focus on academic progress rather than student behavior.

We think it's always important to discuss student performance in reading, writing, and speaking, regardless of the subject matter of the class. These language skills are essential and should be reviewed. Avoid discussing other students or teachers, and be willing to admit that you don't know an answer to a question. By the end of the conference you should identify, in consultation with the parents, a course of action or steps to be taken at home and at school.

Student-Led Conferences

A relatively new kind of reporting to parents involves students as the leader in their own conferences (Stiggins, 2008b). In a student-led conference, students lead parents through a detailed and direct review of their work. Teachers take the role of facilitator by creating a positive environment in which the conferences can take place, and by preparing students. For students to take responsibility for leading a conference with their parents, they need to have reflected on and evaluated their performance. In preparing for the conference, students must learn to describe and evaluate their work. This self-reflection promotes additional learning (Marzano, 2006) and gives students confidence that they are able to understand their capabilities and achievements. A sense of pride and ownership is developed in the student. In a student-led conference, students are essentially telling a story about their learning. This helps parents see progress over time from the perspective of the student. In addition to promoting student responsibility, in the student-led conference parents tend to be more involved.

Summary

This chapter stressed the importance of a teacher's professional judgment when implementing a grading and reporting system. There is no completely objective procedure for grading. Grading is professional decision making that depends on the teacher's values and beliefs, experience, external pressures, and best subjective judgments, as well as school and district policies. We reviewed the different functions of marking and grading and took a close look at how factors other than academic performance affect grades. The chapter examined the basis of comparison used in grading, as well as approaches to marking and grading. Approaches to combine assessments were presented, along with reporting procedures to parents. Important points include the following:

- An important function of marking and grading is to provide students with feedback about their academic performance.
- Although teachers should strive for a high degree of objectivity in grading, it is important to understand the role of professional judgment.
- When grading, teachers negotiate between external constraints (e.g., grade policies, limited time) and their professional values related to assessment.
- Teachers need to provide a sufficient level of detail for marking to be informative for students.
- In general, use nonacademic factors such as effort, attendance, student aptitude, improvement, and attitudes for borderline cases.
- Grades communicate comparison between student performance and an individual's prior performance or aptitude (individual student-referenced), between student performance and the performance of other students (norm-referenced), or between student performance and predetermined standards (standards-based).
- Percent correct is the most common type of standards-based grading. Percentage correct depends on item difficulty.
- Motivation is enhanced when grades are used formatively as well as summatively to communicate internal attributions, self-efficacy, progress on mastery goals, and intrinsic value.
- Clarifying the need or purpose for a group activity and establishing clear learning targets and grading criteria can facilitate effective group work as well as fair grading.
- Approaches to grading include using letters, percent correct measures, rubrics, checklists, standards-based, and written descriptions.
- Determining report card grades requires professional decisions about what to include, how to weight each assessment, and how weighted assessments are combined.
- Provide a sufficient number of assessments to obtain a fair and accurate portrait of the student.
- Weight each assessment by the contribution to the goal, instructional time, and reliability. Give more recent, comprehensive assessments more weight.
- Be flexible with borderline cases; don't let numbers make what should be professional decisions, subjective decisions.
- Do not use zeros indiscriminately when averaging scores.
- Grades should be changed when warranted to reflect the most fair and accurate record of student performance.

- Reporting student progress to parents can be done through online grading programs, by phone, email, with written materials, and in teacher–parent conferences.
- Reports to parents should be well prepared with samples of student work to illustrate progress and areas that need further attention.
- Teacher–parent conferences are informal, professional meetings during which teachers discuss progress with parents and determine action steps to be taken.
- Student-led conferences with parents promote student self-evaluation and parent involvement.

Introductory Case Study Answer

The grading plan items of 1, 8, 9, and 10 support the district's grading philosophy. Items 2, 3, 4, 5, 6, and 7 are in conflict with the district's grading philosophy.

1. Academic performance should be the primary influence in grading. Teachers should use grades to indicate mastery of learning targets. This will indicate to students areas for further learning.

2. Grades impact motivation the most when they are presented while students learn, not just after learning. Formative assessments can and should be used as grades so students understand areas for further learning prior to a summative assessment.

3. Instructional time should be maximized, but a predetermined number of test grades may not allow for accurate alignment in assessing teachers' learning targets. A small number of assessments may not be sufficient to provide a fair and accurate portrait of students' learning.

4. Students often are motivated by performance assessments. Limiting the number may limit student motivation for learning.

5. Using a benchmark as a grade should only be done if the assessment clearly aligns with a teacher's instruction and students are provided a blueprint prior to the assessment.

6. Teachers should be cautious when grading homework. If the purpose of homework is to be primarily formative, to give students feedback, it is more of an instructional tool than an assessment.

7. Students should receive feedback on all assessments in order to plan subsequent learning goals.

8. Effort and other nonacademic factors should only be used in borderline cases.

9. Final grades should communicate accurately the nature of a student's current learning; the most recent assessment is a better indicator.

10. Lowering grades is not appropriate because grades should accurately represent the students' knowledge and performance.

Suggestions for Action Research

1. Create a grading plan that would make sense for a class you plan to teach. Include a statement of purpose and explain what would be included, how weights would be established, and the final grading scale. Then give the plan to other students and ask them to critique it. If possible, give the plan to a classroom teacher and see how realistic it is.

2. Interview teachers on the subject of grading. Do they use an individual student-referenced, norm-referenced, or standards-based approach, or a combination? Ask them about the areas that require professional judgments, like what to do with borderline students, how zeros are used, how group work is graded, how to apply extra credit, and the like. Ask them how they use grades to motivate students. Have them tell the story of some especially difficult professional judgments they had to make.

3. Observe a class when graded tests or papers are returned to students. What is their reaction? What do they seem to do with the information? If possible, speak with the students afterwards and ask them how they feel about the grading.

4. Conduct an experiment by giving some students just grades and other students grades with comments and suggestions for improvement. See if the students react differently. Interview the students to determine if the nature of the feedback affected their motivation.

5. Talk with some parents about their experiences with parent–teacher conferences. What did they get out of it? How could it have been improved? Were the suggestions in Figure 15.7 followed?

6. Write a personal history of your experiences of being graded as a student. Discuss a time that you felt you were graded unfairly. Tell the story of a teacher who you thought did a good job encouraging learning through good grading practices.

7. For two assignments that are evaluated using standards-based rubrics, discuss the rubric with students prior to one assignment but not the other. Explain the components of the rubric, encourage students to discuss and provide feedback on the grading criteria, and provide strategies to successfully complete the assignment. Ask students how they approached each assignment, and examine whether there is a difference in the quality of student work in both assignments while grading.

MyEdLab Self-Check 15.1

MyEdLab Self-Check 15.2

MyEdLab Self-Check 15.3

MyEdLab Self-Check 15.4

MyEdLab Self-Check 15.5

MyEdLab Self-Check 15.6

MyEdLab Application Exercise 15.1   Rubrics for Grading

MyEdLab Application Exercise 15.2   Grading Plan

Fundamental Descriptive Statistics and Scaled Scores

Descriptive Statistics

Descriptive statistics are used to summarize a larger number of scores to better understand them "at a glance." The nature of the description can be in the form of a single number, such as an average score, a table of scores, or a graph. You have seen and read many of these kinds of descriptions (e.g., the average rainfall for a month, the median price of new homes, a baseball batting average). Descriptive statistics efficiently portray important features of a group of scores to convey information that is essential for understanding what group and individual scores mean, how they should be interpreted. For standardized tests, descriptive statistics are used as the basis for establishing, reporting, and interpreting scores, and for accumulating evidence for validity and reliability/precision.

Frequency Distributions

The first step in understanding important characteristics of a large set of test scores is to organize them into a frequency distribution. This distribution simply indicates the number of students who obtained different scores on the test. In a simple **frequency distribution**, the scores are ranked, from highest to lowest, and the number of students obtaining each score is indicated. If the scores are organized into intervals, a *grouped frequency distribution* is used. Suppose, for example, that a test had 80 items. Figure A.1 illustrates the scores received by 20 students, as well as simple and grouped frequency distributions that show the number of students obtaining each score or interval of scores.

Often the scores are presented graphically as a frequency polygon or histogram to more easily display important features (Figures A.2a and A.2b). The **frequency polygon** is a line graph, which is formed by connecting the highest frequencies of each score. The **histogram** is formed by using rectangular columns to represent the frequency of each score.

For a relatively small number of scores, a frequency polygon is usually jagged, as shown in Figure A.2a. For a large number of scores and test items, the line looks more like a smooth curve. The nature of the curve can usually be described as being

FIGURE A.1 Frequency Distributions of Test Scores

Student	Score	Simple Frequency Distribution		Grouped Frequency Distribution	
		Score	f	Interval	f
Austin	96				
Tyler	94	96	1	92–96	3
Tracey	92	94	1	86–91	4
Karon	90	92	1	80–85	7
Hannah	90	90	2	74–79	3
Lanie	86	86	2	68–73	3
Allyson	86	84	3		
Felix	84	80	4		
Tryon	84	78	1		
Freya	84	74	2		
Mike	80	70	2		
Mark	80	68	1		
Ann	80				
Kristen	80				
Laura	78				
Megan	74				
Michelle	74				
Kathryn	70				
Don	70				
Jim	68				

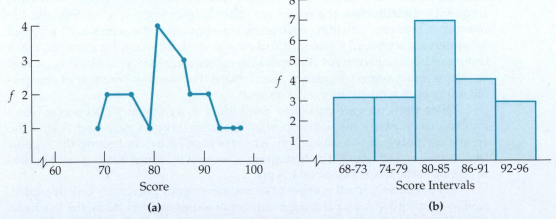

FIGURE A.2 Frequency Polygon of Scores (a) and Histogram (b) from Figure A.1

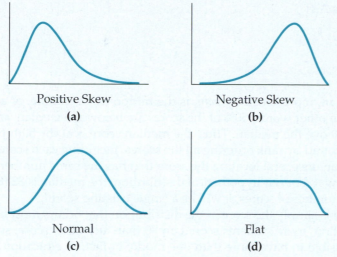

Positive Skew
(a)

Negative Skew
(b)

Normal
(c)

Flat
(d)

FIGURE A.3   Types of Frequency Distributions

normal, positively skewed, negatively skewed, or *flat.* Typically, for standardized tests, the curve very closely approximates a normal distribution (a symmetrical, bell-shaped curve) for a large group of students (e.g., for the norming group). If the distribution is **positively skewed**, or skewed to the right, most of the scores are piled up at the lower end, and there are just a few high scores. For a **negatively skewed** distribution, it is just the opposite—most of the scores are high with few low scores (skewed to the left). In a flat distribution, each score is obtained with about the same frequency. Figures A.3a–A.3d illustrate each of these types of curves.

Measures of Central Tendency

A measure of central tendency is a single number that is calculated to represent the average or typical score in the distribution. There are three measures of central tendency commonly used in education: the mean, median, and mode. The **mean** is the arithmetic average. It is calculated by adding all the scores in the distribution and then dividing that sum by the number of scores. It is represented by $\overline{X}$ or M. For the distribution of scores in Figure A.1 the mean is 82.

$$\overline{X} = \frac{\sum X}{N}$$

where

$\overline{X}$ = the mean
$\sum$ = the sum of (indicates that all scores are added)
X = each individual score
N = total number of scores

For Figure A.1:

$$\overline{X} = \frac{1,640}{20}$$

$$\overline{X} = 82$$

The **median**, represented by *mdn*, is the midpoint, or middle, of a distribution of scores. In other words, 50% of the scores are below the median, and 50% of the scores are above the median. Thus, the median score is at the 50th percentile. The median is found by rank ordering all the scores, including each score even if it occurs more than once, and locating the score that has the same number of scores above and below it. For our hypothetical distribution, the median is 82 (84 + 80/2; for an uneven number of scores, it will be a single existing score).

The **mode** is simply the score in the distribution that occurs most frequently. In our distribution, more students scored an 80 than any other score, so 80 is the mode. It is possible to have more than one mode; in fact, in education, distributions are often described as *bimodal*.

In a normal distribution, the mean, median, and mode are the same. In a positively skewed distribution, the mean is higher than the median (hence, skewed positively), and in a negatively skewed distribution, the mean is lower than the median. This is because the mean, unlike the median, is calculated by taking the value of every score into account. Therefore, extreme values affect the mean, whereas the median is not impacted by an unusual high or low score.

Measures of Variability

A second type of statistic that is important in describing a set of scores is a measure of variability. Measures of *variability*, or *dispersion*, indicate how much the scores spread out from the mean. If the scores are bunched together close to the mean, then there is little or a small amount of variability. A large or great amount of variability is characteristic of a distribution in which the scores are spread way out from the mean. Two distributions with the same mean can have very different variability, as illustrated in Figure A.4.

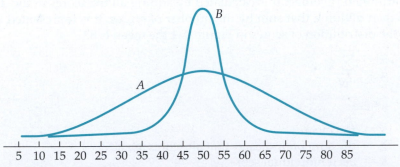

FIGURE A.4   Distributions with the Same Mean, Different Variability

To more precisely indicate the variability, two measures are typically used—the range and standard deviation. The **range** is simply the difference between the highest and lowest score in the distribution (in our example 28; 96 − 68). This is an easily calculated but crude index of variability, primarily because extremely high or low scores result in a range that indicates more variability than is actually present in the group as a whole.

A more complicated but much more precise measure of variability is *standard deviation*. The **standard deviation** (*SD*) is a number that conceptually indicates the *average* deviation of the scores from the mean. It is calculated by employing a formula that looks difficult but is relatively straightforward. These are the essential steps:

1. Calculate the mean of the distribution.
2. Calculate the difference each score is from the mean (these are called deviation scores).
3. Square each difference score (this makes all the deviation scores positive).
4. Add the squared difference scores.
5. Divide by the total number of scores in the distribution.
6. Calculate the square root of the result of step 5.

These steps are illustrated with our hypothetical set of test scores in Figure A.5. Essentially, you simply calculate the squared deviation scores, find the "average" squared deviation score, and then take the square root to return to the original unit of measurement. In this distribution, one standard deviation is equal to 7.92. Unless you are using a normative grading procedure, standard deviation is not very helpful for classroom testing. However, because of the relationship between standard deviation and the normal curve, it is fundamental to understanding standardized test scores.

With a standardized test, the frequency distribution of raw scores for the norming group will usually be distributed in an approximately normal fashion. In a normal distribution, the meaning of the term *one standard deviation* is the same in regard to percentile rank, regardless of the actual value of standard deviation for that distribution. Thus, +1*SD* is always at the 84th percentile, +2*SD* is at the 98th percentile, −1*SD* is at the 16th percentile, and −2*SD* is at the 2nd percentile in every normal distribution. This property makes it possible to compare student scores to the norm group distribution in terms of percentile rank and to compare relative standing on different tests. For instance, suppose a norm group took a standardized test, and on the basis of their performance a raw score of 26 items answered correctly was one standard deviation above the mean for the norm group (84th percentile). When a student in your class gets the same number of items correct (26), the percentile reported is the 84th. Obviously, if the norm group was different and 26 items turned out to be at +2*SD*, then the student's score would be reported at the 98th percentile. You would also know that a score at one standard deviation on one test is the same in terms of relative standing as one standard deviation on another test. Most important for standardized tests, standard deviation is used to compute standard scores and other statistics that are used for interpretation and analysis.

FIGURE A.5   Steps in Calculating Standard Deviation

	(1)	(2)	(3)	(4)	(5)
Score	Deviation Score	Deviation Score Squared	Squared Deviation Scores Added	Added Scores Divided by N	Square Root
96	$96 - 82 = 14$	$14 \times 14 = 196$	$+196$		
94	$94 - 82 = 12$	$12 \times 12 = 144$	$+144$		
92	$92 - 82 = 10$	$10 \times 10 = 100$	$+100$		
90	$90 - 82 = 8$	$8 \times 8 = 64$	$+64$		
90	$90 - 82 = 8$	$8 \times 8 = 64$	$+64$		
86	$86 - 82 = 4$	$4 \times 4 = 16$	$+16$		
86	$86 - 82 = 4$	$4 \times 4 = 16$	$+16$		
84	$84 - 82 = 2$	$2 \times 2 = 4$	$+4$		
84	$84 - 82 = 2$	$2 \times 2 = 4$	$+4$		
84	$84 - 82 = 2$	$2 \times 2 = 4$	$+4$		
80	$80 - 82 = -2$	$-2 \times -2 = 4$	$+4$		
80	$80 - 82 = -2$	$-2 \times -2 = 4$	$+4$		
80	$80 - 82 = -2$	$-2 \times -2 = 4$	$+4$		
80	$80 - 82 = 2$	$-2 \times -2 = 4$	$+4$		
78	$78 - 82 = -4$	$-4 \times -4 = 16$	$+16$		
74	$74 - 82 = -8$	$-8 \times -8 = 64$	$+64$		
74	$74 - 82 = -8$	$-8 \times -8 = 64$	$+64$		
70	$70 - 82 = -12$	$-12 \times -12 = 144$	$+144$		
70	$70 - 82 = -12$	$-12 \times -12 = 144$	$+144$		
68	$68 - 82 = -14$	$-14 \times -14 = 196$	$+196$	$1{,}256/20 = 62.8$	$\sqrt{62.8} = 7.92$
			$= 1{,}256$		

Standard Scores

Standard or scaled scores are derived from raw scores in units based on the standard deviation of the distribution. They are obtained by using a linear transformation, which simply changes the value of the mean and one standard deviation, or a nonlinear, normalizing transformation based on the percentiles of the normal curve. Most standard scores reported with standardized tests are normalized. The term *standard* in this context does not mean a specific level of performance or expectation. Rather, it refers to the standard normal curve as the basis for interpretation. Standard scores have equal units between different values, which allows for additional statistical procedures.

Z-Score.   The simplest and most easily calculated standard score is the *z*-**score**, which indicates how far a score lies above or below the mean in standard deviation units. Because $1SD = 1$, a *z*-score of 1 is one standard deviation unit above the mean. The formula for computing *z*-scores is relatively straightforward if you know the value of one standard deviation:

$$z\text{-score} = \frac{X - \overline{X}}{SD}$$

where

X = any raw score
$\overline{X}$ = mean of the raw scores
SD = standard deviation of the raw score distribution

For example, a *z*-score for 90 in our hypothetical distribution would be 1.01(90 – 82/7.92). If the raw score is less than the mean, the *z*-score will be negative (e.g., the *z*-score for 70 in our distribution of 20 students would be −1.01(70 − 82/7.92).

If the *z*-score is a linear transformation, the distribution of *z*-scores will be identical to the distribution of raw scores. It is also possible to normalize the raw score distribution when converting to *z*-scores. This transforms the distribution to a normal one, regardless of what the raw score distribution looked like. If the raw score distribution is normal, then using the formula will also result in a normal distribution of *z*-scores. For most standardized tests, the standard scores are normalized. Thus, a *z*-score of 1 is at the 84th percentile, a *z*-score of 2 is at the 98th percentile, and so forth.

Because the *z*-score distribution has a standard deviation equal to 1, these scores can easily be transformed to other standard scores that will only have positive values.

Normal Curve Equivalent.   The **normal curve equivalent (NCE)** is a normalized standard score that has a mean of 50 and a standard deviation of 21.06. The reason for selecting 50 for the mean and 21.06 for the standard deviation was so that NCE scores, like percentiles, would range from 1 to 99. The percentiles of 1, 50, and 99 are equivalent to NCEs of 1, 50, and 99. However, at other points on the scale, NCEs are not the same as percentiles. For example:

NCE	Percentile
90	97
75	88
25	12
10	3

It is fairly easy to confuse NCEs with percentiles because they convert the same range of scores (1–99), especially for someone who is not familiar with measurement principles. Thus, you need to be careful when explaining what NCEs mean to parents. So why are NCEs used at all? Because they are standard scores (percentiles are not), they can, like other standard scores, be used statistically for research and evaluation purposes.

Stanines.   A **stanine** indicates about where a score lies in relation to the normal curve of the norming group. Stanines are reported as single-digit scores from 1 to 9. A stanine of 5 indicates that the score is in the middle of the distribution; stanines 1, 2, and 3 are considered below average; 7, 8, and 9 are above average; and stanines of 4, 5, and 6 are about average. Although there is a precise, statistically determined procedure for determining stanines, it is practical to use the range from 1 to 9 as a simple, easily understood way to indicate relative standing. Each stanine covers a specific area of the normal curve in terms of percentiles:

Stanine	*Percentile Rank*	*Stanine*	*Percentile Rank*
9	96 or higher	4	23 to 39
8	89 to 95	3	11 to 22
7	77 to 88	2	4 to 10
6	60 to 76	1	Below 4
5	40 to 59		

Notice that there is a different percentage of scores in stanines 5, 6, 7, 8, and 9. This is because the width of the stanine is the same in relation to the curve of the normal distribution. Another way you can think about stanines is that they have a mean of 5, with a standard deviation of 2. Because they are normalized, stanines from conceptually similar but different tests can be compared, such as aptitude and achievement tests. Remember that meaningful differences in performance are indicated when the scores differ by at least two stanines.

A disadvantage of the stanine is that even though you know the area of the normal curve the score lies in, you don't know what part of this area the score is in. In this sense, stanines are less precise than percentile rank. For example, percentile scores of 42 and 58 have the same stanine score of 5. However, when stanine scores differ by more than 1, it is probable that there is a meaningful difference between achievement in those areas. That is, if the reading stanine score is 5 and the mathematics stanine is 7, the student is demonstrating stronger achievement in mathematics.

Scaled Score.   Most standardized achievement tests use what is called a **scaled score** (also called the *scale level*, or *growth score*) to show year-to-year progress in achievement and to compare different levels of the same test. Each test publisher uses a different scale. Higher scores are associated with higher grade levels, which provide anchors against which a student's progress can be compared. This makes it possible to use developmental standard scores to plot performance from year to year.

Deviation IQ Scores. For many years, the results of IQ and general ability testing have been reported on a scale that has a mean of 100 and a standard deviation of 15 or 16. Originally, IQ scores were actual intelligence quotients, calculated by dividing mental age by chronological age and multiplying this ratio by 100. Today, IQ scores are determined like other derived standard scores. For each age group in a norming sample, the raw scores are converted to z-scores, then to deviation IQ scores by multiplying the z-score by 15 or 16 and adding that product to 100. Most test publishers refer to the student's "ability," "aptitude," or to "standard age" scores rather than IQ because *intelligence* today refers to many other traits besides academic ability or reasoning.

Other Standard Scores. The advantage of standard scores—being able to convert raw scores to scores directly related to the normal curve and percentile rank—is also a disadvantage from the standpoint that there are so many different standard scores. Once you understand the nature of the scores, you can readily interpret the results. For example, in Virginia, a unique scale of 0–600 is used for reporting results, even though there are only about 50 questions on each test. For year-end accountability tests the standard scores are typically converted to provide a range of scores that fall within one of the major levels of the test (e.g., proficient, needs improvement, advanced). In Virginia, most standard scores above 400 indicate proficiency. Unlike scaled scores that are reported for many standardized achievement tests, usually you are not able to compare students' standard scores on a state accountability test from year-to-year.

The key step for you to fully understand standard scores is go online and investigate the test, scores, and reporting. All standardized tests, including state accountability tests, will have information online that is essential for appropriate interpretation and use of the scores.

Measures of Relationship

It is often helpful, even necessary, to know the degree to which two scores from different measures are related. Typically, this degree of relationship is estimated by what is called a *correlation coefficient.* Correlations are reported in standardized test technical manuals for validity and reliability/precision. Also, an important principle in interpreting test scores introduced in Chapter 7, standard error of measurement, is determined from correlation.

Scatterplot. The **scatterplot**, (*scattergram* or *scatter diagram*), is a graphic representation of relationship. When used in education, a scatterplot can give you a descriptive picture of relationship by forming a visual array of the intersections of students' scores on two measures. As illustrated in Figure A.6, each measure is rank ordered from lowest to highest on a different axis. The two scores from each student are used to establish a point of intersection. When this is completed for all students, a pattern is formed that provides a general indication of the direction and strength of the relationship. The direction of the pattern indicates whether

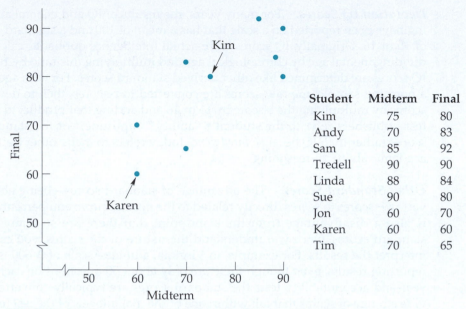

Student	Midterm	Final
Kim	75	80
Andy	70	83
Sam	85	92
Tredell	90	90
Linda	88	84
Sue	90	80
Jon	60	70
Karen	60	60
Tim	70	65

FIGURE A.6   **Scatterplot of Relationship Between Two Tests**

there is a positive, a negative, a curvilinear, or no relationship. It is positive if scores on one variable increase with increases in the other scores, and it is negative (inverse) if scores on one variable increase as scores on the other measure decrease. If the pattern looks like a U shape, it is curvilinear; and if it is a straight line or no particular pattern at all, there is little if any relationship.

Scatterplots help to identify intersections that are not typical, which lower the correlation coefficient, and to identify curvilinear relationships. However, these scatterplots are rarely reported in standardized test manuals. Typically, these manuals report the correlation coefficients.

Correlation Coefficient.   The **correlation coefficient** is a number that is calculated to represent the direction and strength of the relationship. The number ranges between -1 and $+1$. A high positive value (e.g., $+0.85$ or $+0.90$) indicates a high positive relationship, a low negative correlation (e.g., -0.10 or -0.25) represents a low negative relationship, and so forth. The *strength* of the relationship is independent from the *direction*. Thus, a positive or negative value indicates direction, and the value of the correlation, from 0 to 1 or from 0 to -1, determines strength. A perfect correlation is designated by either $+1$ or -1. As the value approaches these perfect correlations from zero, it becomes stronger, or higher. That is, a correlation is stronger as it changes from 0.2 to 0.5 to 0.6, and also as it changes from -0.2 to -0.5 to -0.6. A correlation of -0.8 is stronger (higher) than a correlation of $+0.7$.

Four cautions need to be emphasized when interpreting correlations. First, correlation does not imply causation. Just because two measures are related, it rarely means that one *caused* the other. Other factors may be involved in causation, and the direction of the cause may not be clear. Second, be alert for curvilinear relationships, because most correlation coefficients assume that the relationship is linear. Third, also be alert to what is called **restricted range**. If the values of one measure are truncated, with a small range, it will in all likelihood result in a low correlation. Given a full range of scores, the correlation would be higher. Fourth, relationships expressed as correlation coefficients generally are less precise than the number would suggest. That is, a "very high" correlation of 0.80 does not mean that 80% of the relationship is accounted for. If you think of correlation as predicting one score from another score, you will see how relatively imprecise this can be. Examine the scatterplots of various correlations in Figure A.7. You will see

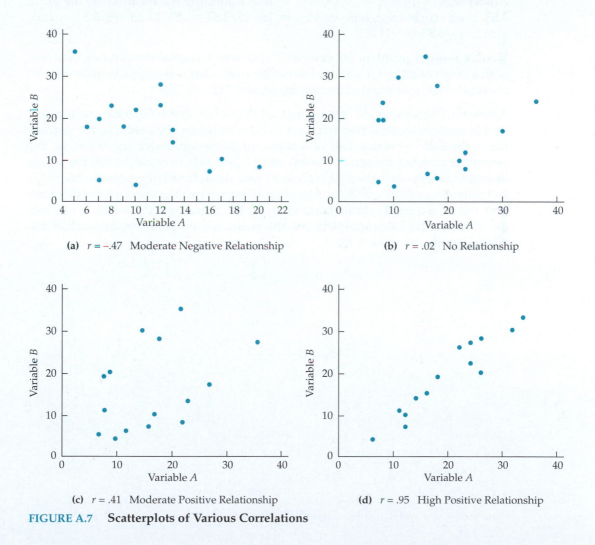

(a) $r = -.47$ Moderate Negative Relationship

(b) $r = .02$ No Relationship

(c) $r = .41$ Moderate Positive Relationship

(d) $r = .95$ High Positive Relationship

FIGURE A.7   Scatterplots of Various Correlations

that in a moderate relationship (c), if you try to predict the value of variable B on the y axis, say, from a score of 10 for variable A, a range of approximately 5 to 20 is predicted.

Practice and Review

As practice and review, calculate the mean, median, and standard deviation from the following set of scores.

Also determine linear z-scores for 18, 20, and 11. 10, 17, 18, 15, 20, 16, 15, 21, 12, 11, 22.

Answers: $\overline{X} = 161/11 = 16.09$; $mdn = 16\ x$. Rounding the mean to 16, the SD is 3.83. The z-scores are as follows: 18: $z = 18-16/3.83 = .53$; 20: $20-16/3.83 = 1.05$; 11: $11-16/3.83 = -1.31$.

Here is another problem for review: If you have a normal distribution of scores with a mean of 80 and a standard deviation of 6, what is the approximate percentile rank of the following scores: 86; 68; 83; and 71?

Answers: The score of 86 is one standard deviation above the mean, so the percentile is the 84th; 68 is two standard deviations below the mean, so the percentile is the 2nd; 83 is one half of a standard deviation above the mean, so the percentile rank is between 50 (mean) and 84 (one SD); because 34% of the scores lie in this range, one half of 34 is 17, so 83 is at about the 67th percentile (50 + 17) (actually it would be a little greater than 17 because of the curve of the distribution, but 67 is a good approximation); using the same logic, 71, which is one and one-half standard deviations below the mean, would be at approximately the 8th percentile (50 − 34 + 8).

Example of Student Individualized Education Program (IEP)

Individualized Education Program

Student Name __Shaneka Rose__   Student ID Number __012345__   Grade _8_

DOB _8/30/2002_ Age _14_ Disability(ies) __Intellectual Disability/Other Health Impaired__

Parent(s) Name __Mr. and Mrs. Rose__   Email __rose@email.com__

Home Address __1234 Maple Lane__   Primary (555)123-4567

Date of IEP meeting	01/10/2015
Date parent notified of IEP meeting	12/10/2014
This IEP will be reviewed no later than	1/10/2016
Most recent eligibility date	07/01/2013
Next re-evaluation, including eligibility, must occur before	06/08/2016

Copy of IEP given to parent __Mrs. Rose__ Case Manager __Barbara Jones__ On (Date) __01/10/2015__

IEP Teacher/Manager __Barbara Jones__ Phone Number (555) 765-4321

The Individualized Education Plan (IEP) that accompanies this document is meant to support the positive process and team approach. The IEP is a working document that outlines the student's vision for the future, strengths and needs. The IEP is not written in isolation. The intent of an IEP is to bring together a team of people who understand and support the student in order to come to consensus on a plan and an appropriate and effective education for the student. No two teams are alike and each team will arrive at different answers, ideas, and supports and services to address the student's unique needs. The student and his/her family members are vital participants, as well as teachers, assistants, specialists, outside service providers, and the principal. When all team members are present, the valuable information shared supports the development of a rich student profile and education plan.

PARTICIPANTS INVOLVED:
The list below indicates that the individual participated in the development of this IEP and the placement decision; it does not authorize consent.

NAME OF PARTICIPANT	POSITION
Mr. and Mrs. Rose	Parents
Shaneka Rose	Student
Mrs. Edwards	General Education Teacher
Mrs. Jones	Special Education Teacher
Mrs. Baker	Administrator

Factors for IEP Team Consideration

During the IEP meeting, the following factors must be considered by the IEP team. Best practice suggests that the IEP team document that the factors were considered and any decision made relative to each. The factors are addressed in other sections of the IEP if not documented on this page (for example: see Present Level of Academic Achievement and Functional Performance).

1. Results of the initial or most recent evaluation of the student; __see present level of performance__
2. The strengths of the student; __see present level of performance__
3. The academic, developmental, and functional needs of the student; __see present level of performance__
4. The concerns of the parent(s) for enhancing the education of their child; __see present level of performance__
5. The communication needs of the student; __Shaneka speaks English and requires no communication device to clearly communicate.__
6. The student's needs for benchmarks or short-term objectives; __Shaneka demonstrates a need for benchmarks and short-term objectives to monitor her performance.__
7. Whether the student requires assistive technology devices and services. __Shaneka utilizes read aloud and text to speech software when working on the computer, in class she utilizes a slant board during handwriting tasks.__
8. In the case of a **student whose behavior impedes his or her learning or that of others**, consider the use of positive behavioral interventions, strategies, and supports to address that behavior; __Shaneka's behavior does not, at this time, impede her learning or that of others.__

9. In the case of a **student with limited English proficiency**, consider the language needs of the student as those needs relate to the student's IEP; This does not apply to Shaneka.

10. In the case of a **student who is blind or is visually impaired**, provide for instruction in Braille and the use of Braille unless the IEP team determines after an evaluation of the student's reading and writing skills, needs, and appropriate reading and writing media, including an evaluation of the student's future needs for instruction in Braille or the use of Braille, that instruction in Braille or the use of Braille is not appropriate for the student. This does not apply to Shaneka.

11. In the case of a **student who is deaf or hard of hearing**, consider the student's language and communication needs, opportunities for direct communications with peers and professional personnel in the student's language and communication mode, academic level, and full range of needs, including opportunities for direct instruction in the student's language and communication mode. This does not apply to Shaneka.

Present Level of Academic Achievement and Functional Performance

The Present Level of Academic Achievement and Functional Performance summarize the results of assessments that identify the student's interests, preferences, strengths, and areas of need, including assistive technology and/or accessible materials. It also describes the effect of the student's disability on his or her involvement and progress in the general education curriculum, and for preschool children, as appropriate, how the disability affects the student's participation in appropriate activities. This includes the student's performance and achievement in academic areas such as writing, reading, mathematics, science, and history/social sciences. It also includes the student's performance in functional areas, such as self-determination, social competence, communication, behavior, and personal management. Test scores, if included, should be self-explanatory or an explanation should be included, and the Present Level of Academic Achievement and Functional Performance should be written in objective measurable terms, to the extent possible. There should be a direct relationship among the desired goals, the Present Level of Academic Achievement and Functional Performance, and all other components of the IEP. For Sheneka, this is what was summarized as her present level of achievement and functioning:

> Shaneka is a delightful young lady who tends to be very positive and upbeat. She is very social and has a wide circle of friends, many of whom she eats lunch with. Shaneka participates in the recreational league cheerleading in the Fall and has been participating since Kindergarten. Shaneka reports that she does not enjoy school, that her classes are too hard. Parents report that Shaneka often complains about school and requests to go shopping or practice cheerleading instead.

Shaneka was found eligible for special education services as a student with an Intellectual Disability and an Other Health Impairment. At her last eligibility, cognitive functioning scores were found to in the extremely low range. She has a demonstrated strength in reading but conceptual math is difficult for her. On the Brigance Inventory of Basic Skills, Shaneka's scores were 3.6 grade equivalent on Word Recognition and 3.0 grade equivalent on Vocabulary Comprehension. In math Shaneka scored a 1.8 grade equivalent on Computational Skills and 1.2 grade equivalent in the area of Problem Solving. When given writing tasks, she rarely composes full sentences and she prefers to tell you rather than write a response.

This year has been very difficult for Shaneka. She received services primarily in the collaborative classroom setting and she struggled with the content demands. Modifications were made to the curriculum in Science and Social Studies in order to meet Shaneka's need for exploration and repetition. Her parents report that they would be made aware that modifications would result in less depth and breadth of State Standards content and could possibly impact her eligibility for a standard or advanced standard diploma. At this time, Shaneka continues to have significant deficiencies in reading and math resulting in the content and pacing in the general curriculum to be overwhelming.

When asked, Shaneka indicated she would like to work with animals, specifically dogs after high school. Her parents report the family has two dogs which Shaneka assists in the care of. Her parents routinely take her to the local pound where Shaneka enjoys donating supplies and playing with dogs as a volunteer. This area of interest should be explored during transition planning. Shaneka's parents want their daughter to successfully complete high school and go on to become independent through working and living on her own. Their greatest concern is Shaneka's continued progress towards this goal.

Measurable Annual Goal

 # 1   MEASURABLE ANNUAL GOAL:

Given reading instruction, Shaneka will be able to identify the main idea of a passage and analyze the author's purpose for writing it.

The IEP team considered the need for short-term objectives/benchmarks.

 X **Short-term objectives/benchmarks are included for this goal.**
 ☐ **Short-term objectives/benchmarks are not included for this goal.**

How will progress toward this annual goal be measured? (check all that apply)

___ Classroom Participation	_X_ Observation	_X_ Criterion-referenced test: ___
_X_ Checklist	___ Special Projects	___ Norm-referenced test: ___
___ Class work	_X_ Tests and Quizzes	___ Other: ___
___ Homework	___ Written Reports	

Services – Least Restrictive Environment – Placement Accommodations/Modifications

This student will be provided access to general education classes, special education classes, other school services and activities including nonacademic activities and extracurricular activities, and education related settings:

__ with no accommodations/modifications   _X_ with the following accommodations/modifications

Accommodations/modifications provided as part of the instructional and testing/assessment process will allow the student equal opportunity to access the curriculum and demonstrate achievement. Accommodations/modifications also provide access to nonacademic and extracurricular activities and educationally related settings. Accommodations/modifications based solely on the potential to enhance performance beyond providing equal access are inappropriate. Accommodations may be in, but not limited to, the areas of time, scheduling, setting, presentation and response including assistive technology and/or accessible materials. The impact of any modifications listed should be discussed.

ACCOMMODATIONS/MODIFICATIONS (list, as appropriate)

Accommodation(s)/ Modification(s)	Frequency	Location (name of school *)	Instructional Setting	Duration m/d/y to m/d/y
Slant board during assignments requiring writing	Daily – as assigned	Everywhere USA	General education	1/10/2015 to 1/9/2016
Read aloud software – during computer instruction	Daily – as assigned	Everywhere USA	General education Resource class	1/10/2015 to 1/9/2016
Text to speech software – during computer instruction	Daily – as assigned	Everywhere USA	General education Resource class	1/10/2015 to 1/9/2016
Teacher check of completed agenda	Daily by class	Everywhere USA	General Education	1/10/2015 to 1/9/2016

* IEP teams are required to identify the specific school site (public or private) when the parent expresses concerns about the location of the services or refuses the proposed site. A listing of more than one anticipated location is permissible, if the parents do not indicate that they will object to any particular school or state that the team should identify a single school.

Supports for School Personnel: (Describe supports such as equipment, consultation, or training for school staff to meet the unique needs for the student) **Shaneka has utilized these accommodations independently and should require only start up assistance. Consultation with the division AT specialist may be helpful for staff who are unfamiliar with these programs/devices.**

Participation in the State and Divisionwide Accountability/ Assessment System

This student's participation in state and district-wide assessments must be discussed annually. During the duration of this IEP:

Will the student be at a grade level or enrolled in a course for which the student must participate in a state and/or division-wide assessment? *If yes, continue to next question.*	X Yes ☐ No
Based on the Present Level of Academic Achievement and Functional Performance, is this student being considered for participation in the *State Standardized Assessment (select appropriate content area)* ☐ Reading ☐ Math ☐ Science ☐ History/Social Science ☐ Grade 8 Writing	☐ Yes X No
Based on the Present Level of Academic Achievement and Functional Performance, is this student being considered for participation in the State Alternate Assessment Program, which is based on Aligned State Standards? *If yes, complete the "Alternate Assessment Participation Criteria".*	X Yes ☐ No
Does the student meet Alternate Assessment participation criteria?	X Yes ☐ No

If "yes" to any of the above, check the assessment(s) chosen and attach (or maintain in student's educational record) the assessment page(s), which will document how the student will participate in State's accountability system and any needed accommodations and/or modifications.

__ State Assessments ☐ Reading ☐ Math ☐ Science ☐ History/Social Science ☐ Grade 8 Writing

_X_ State Alternate Assessment Program

☐ **District-Wide Assessment (list):**

PARTICIPATION IN STATEWIDE ASSESSMENTS

Test	Assessment Type* (State Assessment, Alternate Assessment)	Accommodations**	If yes, list accommodation(s)
Reading	X __ Reading 8 Alternate Assessment ☐ Not Assessed at this Grade Level	X Yes ☐ No	Text to speech dictation
Math	X __ Math 8 Alternate Assessment___ ☐ Not Assessed at this Grade Level	X Yes ☐ No	Read aloud software Text to speech dictation

(Continued)

Test	Assessment Type* (State Assessment, Alternate Assessment)	Accommodations**	If yes, list accommodation(s)
Science	X __ Science 8 Alternate Assessment___ ☐ Not Assessed at this Grade Level	XYes ☐ No	Read aloud software Text to speech dictation
History/SS	X __ Civics 8 Alternate Assessment ___ ☐ Not Assessed at this Grade Level	XYes ☐ No	Read aloud software Text to speech dictation
Writing	X __ Writing 8 Alternate Assessment ___ ☐ Not Assessed at this Grade Level	XYes ☐ No	Read aloud software Text to speech dictation

* Students with disabilities are expected to participate in all content area assessments that are available to students without disabilities. The IEP Team determines how the student will participate in the accountability system.

** Accommodation(s) must be based upon those the student generally uses during classroom instruction and assessment, including assistive technology and/or accessible materials.

☐ **District-Wide Assessment (list):** _____

EXPLANATION FOR NON-PARTICIPATION IN REGULAR STATE OR DIVISION-WIDE ASSESSMENTS

If an IEP team determines that a student must take an alternate assessment instead of a regular state assessment, explain in the space below why the student cannot participate in this regular assessment; why the particular assessment selected is appropriate for the student, including that the student meets the criteria for the alternate assessment; and how the student's nonparticipation in the regular assessment will impact the child's promotion; or other matters.

    ☐ Alternate/Alternative Assessments Participation Criteria is attached or maintained in the student's educational record

Least Restrictive Environment (LRE)

When discussing the least restrictive environment and placement options, the following must be considered:

- To the maximum extent appropriate, the student is educated with children without disabilities.
- Special classes, separate schooling or other removal of the student from the regular educational environment occurs only when the nature or severity of the disability is such that education in regular classes with the use of supplementary aids and services cannot be achieved satisfactorily.

- The student's placement should be as close as possible to the child's home and unless the IEP of the student with a disability requires some other arrangement, the student is educated in the school that he or she would attend if he or she did not have a disability.
- In selecting the LRE, consideration is given to any potential harmful effect on the student or on the quality of services that he/she needs.
- The student with a disability shall be served in a program with age-appropriate peers unless it can be shown that for a particular student with a disability, the alternative placement is appropriate as documented by the IEP.

Free Appropriate Public Education (FAPE)

When discussing FAPE for this student, it is important for the IEP team to remember that FAPE may include, as appropriate:

- Educational Programs and Services
- Proper Functioning of Hearing Aids
- Assistive Technology and/or accessible materials
- Transportation
- Nonacademic and Extracurricular Services and Activities
- Physical Education
- Extended School Year Services (ESY)
- Length of School Day

Services:

Identify the service(s), including frequency, duration, and location that will be provided to or on behalf of the student in order for the student to receive a free appropriate public education. These services are the special education services and as necessary, the related services, supplementary aids and services based on peer-reviewed research to the extent practicable, assistive technology and/or accessible materials, supports for personnel*, accommodations and/or modifications* and extended school year services* the student will receive that will address area(s) of need as identified by the IEP team. Address any needed transportation and physical education services including accommodations and/or modifications. * These services are listed on the "Accommodations/Modifications" page and "Extended School Year Services" page, as needed.

Service(s)	Frequency	**School/location Instructional Setting (classroom)	Duration m/d/y to m/d/y	Disability Service Area: Primary, Secondary, Tertiary ***	Percentage Special Education Service by Disability Category
Reading	5x per week; 5 hours total	Resource room	1/10/2015 to 1/9/2016	Intellectual Disability	14%

Service(s)	Frequency	**School/location Instructional Setting (classroom)	Duration m/d/y to m/d/y	Disability Service Area: Primary, Secondary, Tertiary ***	Percentage Special Education Service by Disability Category
Writing	5x per week; 2.5 hours total	General Education classroom	1/10/2015 to 1/9/2016	Other Health Impairment	7%

** IEP teams are required to identify the specific school site (public or private) when the parent expresses concerns about the location of the services or refuses the proposed site. A listing of more than one anticipated location is permissible, if the parents do not indicate that they will object to any particular school or state that the team should identify a single school.

*** Not required for the IEP-may be included for data collection purposes. The total percent of services for the primary, secondary, and tertiary disabilities cannot exceed 100. **To calculate the percentage of special education services, the amount of time required to provide all special education services described in the IEP is divided by the length of the standard instructional day multiplied by 100.**

Placement

No single model for the delivery of services to any population or category of children with disabilities is acceptable for meeting the requirement for a continuum of alternative placements. All placement decisions shall be based on the individual needs of each student. The team may consider placement options in conjunction with discussing any needed supplementary aids and services, accommodations/ modifications, assistive technology and/or accessible materials, and supports for school personnel. In considering the placement continuum options, check those the team discussed. Then, describe the placement selected in the **PLACEMENT DECISION** section below. Determination of the Least Restrictive Environment (LRE) and placement may be one or a combination of options along the continuum.

PLACEMENT CONTINUUM OPTIONS CONSIDERED: (check all that have been considered):	*PLACEMENT DECISION: (select the appropriate placement option)
☐ X general education class(es) ☐ X special class(es) ☐ special education day school ☐ state special education program / school ☐ Public residential facility ☐ Private residential facility ☐ Homebound ☐ Hospital ☐ Other _____	☐ X Inside regular class at least 80% of time ☐ Inside regular class 40% to 79% of time ☐ Inside regular class less than 40% of time ☐ Public separate school (day) facility ☐ Private separate school (day) facility ☐ Public residential facility ☐ Private residential facility ☐ Homebound ☐ Hospital ☐ Other _____

*To calculate the percentage of time in the regular class, the amount of time spent in the regular classroom is divided by length of the entire school day multiplied by 100.

Based upon identified services and the consideration of least restrictive environment (LRE) and placement continuum options, describe in the space below the placement. Additionally, summarize the discussions and decision around LRE and placement. This must include an explanation of why the student **will not** be participating with students without disabilities in the general education class(es), programs, and activities.

Explanation of Placement Decision:

Shaneka will spend most of the school day receiving instruction within the general education classroom. Due to the nature of her disability and needs in reading comprehension, she will receive special education services within a special education environment 14% of the day. This placement represents Shaneka's least restrictive environment.

Self-Instructional Review Exercises

Chapter 1

Each chapter contains self-instructional exercises. They are intended to check your understanding of the content of the chapter. An answer key is provided at the end of the text to give you immediate feedback. You will learn most if you don't look at the key before you answer the question!

1. What is the relationship between teacher decision making, complex classroom environments, and assessment?
2. What does it mean when we say that assessment is not just an "add-on" or "end-of-instruction" activity?
3. What is the difference between a *test* and an *assessment*?
4. Refer to Table 1.2. Identify each of the following examples as preassessment (P), formative assessment (F), or summative assessment (S).
   a. Giving a pop quiz
   b. Giving a cumulative final exam
   c. Praising students for correct answers
   d. Using homework to judge student knowledge
   e. Reviewing student scores on last year's standardized test
   f. Changing the lesson plan because of student inattention
   g. Reviewing student files to understand students' cultural backgrounds
5. Identify each of the following quotes as referring to one of the four components of classroom assessment: purpose (P), measurement (M), interpretation (I), and use (U).
   a. "Last week I determined that my students did not know very much about the Civil War."
   b. "This year I want to see if I can assess student attitudes."
   c. "The test helped me to identify where students were weak."
   d. "I like the idea of using performance-based assessments."
   e. "I intend to combine several different assessments to determine the grade."
6. How do assessments communicate expectations for student learning?
7. Why, according to recent research on learning, is performance assessment well suited to effective instruction?

Chapter 2

1. Identify each of the following as a goal (G), standard (S), or learning target (LT):
   a. Students will identify three different types of rocks from a display of 15 rocks and place them in like piles.
   b. Students will be familiar with global geography.
   c. Students will be able to write creative passages and critique other students' creative passages.
   d. Students will answer 10 of 12 questions about ancient Egypt in 15 minutes without use of notes.
2. What does the term *criteria* have in common with behavioral objectives? How is it different from what is contained in objectives?
3. Suppose a teacher pulls out a graded paper that was handed in by a student from a previous year's class and distributes it to the class. What would the paper be called in relation to assessment?
   a. Rubric
   b. Anchor
   c. Scoring criteria
   d. Performance criteria
4. Give at least three reasons why using public criteria that are shared with students before instruction is an effective teaching/learning tool for evaluating student work.
5. Why is it important to include criteria in learning targets and standards?
6. Identify each of the following as a knowledge target (K) or a deep understanding/reasoning target (DU).
   a. Recalling historical facts from the Revolutionary War
   b. Comparing vertebrates to invertebrates
   c. Identifying the organs in a dissected frog
   d. Explaining how and why recent U.S. recessions affected the world economy
7. Why may Bloom's original taxonomy of educational objectives *not* be the best source for identifying classroom learning targets?
8. Give original examples of at least one knowledge and one deep understanding learning target that could be stated for you concerning the content of this chapter.
9. What is the primary difference between content and performance standards?
10. Identify each of the following descriptions as declarative (D) or procedural (P) and as knowledge (K) or understanding (U).
    a. Define procedural knowledge.
    b. What is the sequence of steps in preparing an objective test?
    c. Give an example of a multiple-choice item that measures application.
    d. List three suggestions for constructing matching items.
    e. Predict whether students will have questions about how to answer the items in the test.
    f. Review the strategy a teacher has used to construct binary-choice test items to determine if they can be improved.

11. Identify the thinking or reasoning skill illustrated by each of the following examples, using this key:

A Analysis   P Problem solving

S Synthesis   I Inference

C Critical thinking   E Evaluation

D Decision making

a. Suppose you were President Trump and had to decide whether to send more troops to Afghanistan. What would you do? Why would you do it?

b. State your reasons for agreeing or disagreeing with the following statement: Religious people are more likely to help others.

c. Given what you know about sailing, what would most likely occur if a novice sailor tried to sail directly into the wind?

d. Examine three different human cultures. What is common in all three cultures, and what principle about being human does this suggest?

e. Examine four recent presidential speeches. Is any part of the speeches the same?

f. How can the United States reduce the rate of teenage pregnancies?

g. Suppose you had to choose between increasing taxes to reduce the U.S. budget deficit or decreasing federal spending to reduce the deficit. Which would you choose? Why? How would your choice affect retired persons?

h. Examine the data on birth rates. What is likely to happen to the birth rate by the year 2020? Why?

Chapter 3

1. Should teachers be concerned about relatively technical features of assessments such as validity and reliability/precision? Why or why not?

2. Match the description with the type of assessment.

_____ (1) Based on verbal instruction   a. Selected
                                                                               response

_____ (2) Made up of questionnaires and surveys   b. Essay

_____ (3) Selection or supply type   c. Performance

_____ (4) Constructs unique response to demonstrate skill   d. Oral question

_____ (5) Either restricted- or extended-constructed   e. Observation
             response

_____ (6) Used constantly by teachers informally   f. Self-assessment

3. For each of the following situations or questions, indicate which assessment method provides the best match (selected response, S; essay, E; performance, P; oral question, OR; observation, OB; and self-report, SR).

a. Mrs. Keen needs to check students to see if they are able to draw graphs correctly like the example just demonstrated in class.

   b. Mr. Garcia wants to see if his students are comprehending the story before moving to the next set of instructional activities.
   c. Ms. Powell wants to find out how many spelling words her students know.
   d. Ms. Tanner wants to see how well her students can compare and contrast the Vietnam War with World War II.
   e. Mr. Johnson's objective is to enhance his students' self-efficacy and attitudes toward school.
   f. Mr. Greene wants to know if his sailing clinic students can identify different parts of a sailboat.

4. Which of the following statements is correct, and why?
   a. Validity is impossible without strong reliability/precision.
   b. A test can be reliable/precise without validity.
   c. A valid test is reliable/precise.

5. Mr. Nelson asks the other math teachers in his high school to review his midterm to see if the test items represent his learning targets. Which type of evidence for validity is being used?
   a. content-related
   b. criterion-related
   c. consequential

6. The students in the following lists are rank ordered, based on their performance on two tests of the same content (highest score at the top, next highest score second, etc.). Do the results suggest a reliable/precise assessment? Why or why not?

Test A	Test B
Germaine	Ryann
Cynthia	Robert
Ryann	Steve
Steve	Germaine
Robert	Cynthia

7. Which aspect of fairness is illustrated in each of the following assessment situations?
   a. Students complained because they were not told what to study for the test.
   b. Students studied the wrong way for the test (e.g., they memorized content).
   c. The teacher was unable to cover the last unit that was on the test.
   d. The story students read, the one they would be tested on, was about life in the northeast during winter. Students who had been to that part of the country in winter showed better comprehension scores than students who had rarely even seen snow.
   e. Students complained that most of what was taught was not on the test.

8. Is the following test item biased? Why or why not?

   Ramon has decided to develop a family budget. He has $2,000 to work with and decides to put $1,000 into the mortgage, $300 into food, $200 into transportation, $300 into entertainment, $150 into utilities, and $50 into savings. What percent of Ramon's budget is being spent in each of the categories?

9. Why is it important for teachers to consider practicality and efficiency in selecting their assessments, as well as more technical aspects such as validity and reliability/precision?

Chapter 4

1. Identify each of the following examples of body language as an emblem (E), illustrator (I), affect display (AD), regulator (R), or adapter (A).
   a. Student leans toward you and raises both hands immediately after you ask a question.
   b. Student points to the pencil sharpener as if to ask, "May I sharpen my pencil?"
   c. Mary is sitting upright in her chair, arms on desk, chin up, with an expectant expression on her face.
   d. Sam uses his hands to show how large the fish was.
2. Match the messages most likely to be conveyed with the descriptions provided. Each message may be used once, not at all, or more than once.

_____ (1) Pauses when speaking; eyes downcast	**A.** Confident
_____ (2) Eyebrows uplifted; speaks fast; raises hand	**B.** Nervous
_____ (3) Looks around room; slumped in chair with head resting in one hand	**C.** Angry
_____ (4) Direct eye contact; speaks clearly with few pauses; uses variety in tone	**D.** Defensive
_____ (5) Enlarged pupils; chin up; arms open	**E.** Bored
_____ (6) Taps pencil; rigid body; pupils contracted	**F.** Frustrated
_____ (7) Loud; eyebrows lowered; hands make fists	**G.** Happy
_____ (8) Arms and legs crossed; leans away	**H.** Interested

3. Mr. Bush had observed Trent carefully over the past few days because he was concerned that Trent would revert to his old pattern of cheating by looking at others' papers. What observation error is Mr. Bush most susceptible to, and why?
4. Mrs. Greene saw Renee staring out the window, obviously not concentrating on her work. Because Renee is a good student and this is not very typical of her, Mrs. Greene ignores the behavior. What type of observation error was Mrs. Greene careful _not_ to make in this situation? What error is possible in her interpretation?
5. Why is it important to match the type of question you ask students in class with your learning targets?
6. How would a teacher preface a question to make sure students took sufficient time to think about the answer before responding?
7. What type of question—convergent or divergent—would be best to determine whether students knew how to find the area of a rectangle?

8. Identify each of the following examples as self-referenced (SR), target-referenced (TR), or standards-based (SB) feedback.
   a. Louise, your work is consistent with the progress you need to make to show proficiency on the state test at the end of the year.
   b. Reggie, the homework you did shows that you understand most of what is needed to do well on our upcoming quiz later this week.
   c. Maxine, compared to your earlier paper, this revision is much improved, with better grammar and punctuation, and greater clarity.
   d. John, when you are able to use that flip of your wrist, when shooting a free throw, rather than keep it straight, you'll make a greater percentage of shots.

9. Which of the following is a characteristic of effective feedback?
   a. Emphasize internal attributions for being right and wrong.
   b. Use phrases that are essentially the same for all students.
   c. Wait as long as possible before giving feedback.
   d. Target feedback to refer to students' progress.
   e. Use different feedback for different students.
   f. Make feedback actionable.

Chapter 5

1. Indicate whether each of the following describes a pretest (PT), structured exercise (SE), homework (H), or seatwork (S).
   a. Students are asked to define and give examples in new sentences of five new vocabulary terms.
   b. Students start a new lesson by taking 15 minutes to answer seven constructed-response items about the Civil War, in preparation for a new unit on middle 19th-century US history.
   c. An elementary teacher asks students to write a paragraph about their most interesting summer experience.
   d. At the end of the day the teacher gives students 10 new math problems that will be checked first thing the next day.
   e. The Lincoln Consolidated School District decides to prepare and administer the same 30-item test to all fifth graders during the first week of school.

2. Which of the following are characteristics of an interim test?
   a. Given at the end of the school year.
   b. Typically contains less than 10 items.
   c. Is intended to be used to assess student progress toward achieving outcome standards.
   d. Is administered a few times a year.
   e. Shows what a teacher may need to emphasize in instruction for selected students.

3. Which of the following is an example of effective feedback that follows from a summative-based assessment?
   a. "Sally, I can see from your test score that you are really good in math!"
   b. "Jeff, this quiz shows that you need to practice your b's to make a straighter line, not so much of a loop."

    c. "Jon, I can see by your interim test score that you're on target to do well on the year-end test."

    d. "Maxine, you did better than anyone else on this homework assignment."

4. How would you suggest improving the following feedback:

"Robert, you have a good report. Your grammar is excellent, although you have some problems with sentence structure. The conclusion is incomplete. Work harder on providing more detail."

5. Identify each of the following as an effective (E) or ineffective (IE) instructional adjustment.

    a. Mr. Nail decided to give a struggling student a new app to focus on mastering the third stage of a geometry learning progression.

    b. Ms. Hernandez instructed three of her students who did not understand noun–verb agreement to review both appropriate and inappropriate example sentences and identify why each was correct or incorrect.

    c. Mr. Cotter decided to form six small groups of students and give each group a challenging problem that matched their current level of understanding.

    d. Mr. Xu saw that some of his students did not fully comprehend macro economic theory and indicated that they needed to study harder.

Chapter 6

1. Indicate which of the following characteristics of assessments would be summative (S) and which would be formative (F):

    a. To certify student learning

    b. Structured

    c. Mastery oriented

    d. After instruction

    e. Student feedback

    f. Individualized

2. Under what circumstances would it be reasonable to use summative assessments for instructional planning?

3. Match the descriptions in column A with the criteria for constructing summative assessments in column B. Each criterion may be used once, more than once, or not at all.

Column A	Column B
_____ **(1)** Revision of a test provided in instructional materials	**a.** Representative sampling
_____ **(2)** Use of test blueprint	**b.** Length of assessment
_____ **(3)** Teaching test-taking skills	**c.** Number of assessments
_____ **(4)** Using an adequate number of items for each area	**d.** Use of publisher's test
_____ **(5)** Providing time for student questions	**e.** Preparing students
_____ **(6)** Chapter review	**f.** Scheduling assessments

4. Indicate whether each of the following practices is desirable (D) or undesirable (U) in putting summative tests together.
   a. Plan on students completing at least four multiple-choice questions per minute.
   b. Tell students to work as quickly as possible.
   c. Arrange items so that the most difficult are first.
   d. Keep items with the same format together.
   e. Be sure to keep white space on pages to a minimum.

Chapter 7

1. Which of the following are considered standardized tests?
   a. Common Core State Standards assessments
   b. Iowa Test of Basic Skills
   c. Essay test given in Mrs. Brown's class
   d. Nine weeks test given in Hanover County Public Schools to all ninth graders
   e. Dunlap Test of Mental Abilities
2. What is standard error of measurement most related to?
   a. validity
   b. reliability/precision
   c. fairness
   d. alignment
3. What kind of information would lead one to conclude that a student has clear weaknesses in a particular skill?
4. How is it possible for all school districts in a state to be above the 50th percentile on a standardized norm-referenced test?
5. Indicate whether each of the following characteristics refers to a norm-referenced (NR), standards-based (SB), or aptitude (A) test. More than one may apply to each characteristic.
   a. Compares score results from different subjects
   b. Shows capacity to learn in the future
   c. Reports percentage of students at prespecified levels of achievement
   d. Uses proficiency ratings
   e. Readiness test
   f. Criterion-referenced scores
   g. Uses norms
6. Indicate whether each of the following is a norm-referenced (NR) or standards-based (SB) interpretation.
   a. Sally was at the advanced proficient level in social science.
   b. John scored "needs to improve" on the test.
   c. Micha did better than most who took the test.
   d. Uses percentile scores.
   e. Uses percentage of item correct scores.
   f. On the basis of the benchmark test results it looks like most students are doing well.

7. Indicate whether each of the following suggested activities help or hinder student performance on a standardized test.
   a. Tell students their futures depend on their scores.
   b. To avoid making students anxious, do not tell them very much about the test.
   c. Make sure the room temperature is about right.
   d. Arrange desks so that students face each other in groups of four.
   e. Give students a practice test that is very similar in format.
   f. Tell students they probably won't be able to answer many of the questions.
   g. Teach to the test.
   h. Tell students you think the test is taking away from class time and student learning.

Chapter 8

1. Match the suggestions or descriptions from column A with the type(s) of objective items in column B. Each type of item may be used once, more than once, or not at all; each suggestion or description may have more than one correct match.

   Column A

   _____ **(1)** Generally more time consuming to construct

   _____ **(2)** Effectively measures relations

   _____ **(3)** Conveniently constructed from instructional materials

   _____ **(4)** Responses ordered logically

   _____ **(5)** Correct answers spread equally among all possible choices

   _____ **(6)** Verbatim language from textbooks is avoided

   _____ **(7)** Uses clear, concise statements

   Column B

   a. Matching

   b. Binary-choice

   c. Multiple-choice

2. Using the checklist for writing matching items, evaluate each of the following items and revise them so that they will be improved.
   1. Match the states with the characteristics.

   _____ Florida

   _____ New York

   _____ Michigan

   _____ Colorado

   _____ Iowa

   _____ Texas

   _____ Utah

   _____ Illinois

   _____ Virginia

   _____ North Carolina

   a. St. Augustine

   b. Bordered by Missouri and Minnesota

   c. Alamo

   d. Jamestown

   e. Outer Banks

   f. Lincoln

   g. Largest city

   h. Great Lake State

   i. Great Salt Lake

   j. Denver

2. T   F   Students do not construct their own answers to every type of item except multiple choice.
3. Circle the best answer.
Michigan is a(n) (a) Great Lake State, (b) state in which the Rocky Mountains are located, (c) example of a state that is west of the Mississippi, (d) none of the above.
4. Circle the correct answer.
Biodegradable substances are
   a. nonrenewable resources.
   b. materials that can be broken down into substances that are simpler and do not result in environmental pollution.
   c. becoming less popular.
   d. like fossil fuels.

Chapter 9

1. Indicate whether each of the following would be best measured by a short-answer item (SA), an interpretive exercise (I), or an essay question (E).
   a. Discerning the meaning of a series of pictures
   b. Asking students about the validity of an argument used in a debate tournament
   c. Analyzing a passage to identify irrelevant information and opinions
   d. Being able to construct a logical argument
   e. Knowing the sequence of steps involved in problem solving
   f. Giving examples of the principle of tropism
   g. Being able to distinguish critical thinking from decision-making
   h. Determining whether Michelangelo would be regarded as a great artist if he lived today and, if so, why
   i. Identifying several valid generalizations from the data presented
2. Evaluate the following interpretive exercise. Is it clear? How could the format be improved? What cognitive skills are assessed?

   Directions: Based on the food web presented in Figure 9.10, answer these questions:

   1. What do mice eat to get energy from the sun?
   2. What happens to snakes if the grass is killed by poison?
   3. What happens to the hawk population if grass is excessively fed by fertilizer?
   4. What happens to the population of snakes if all the crickets die?

3. Evaluate the following essay question. What learning targets does it appear to assess? How could it be improved?

   Do you think freedom of the press should extend to the irresponsible sensationalism of Hearst during the era of the Spanish-American War? Justify your answer.

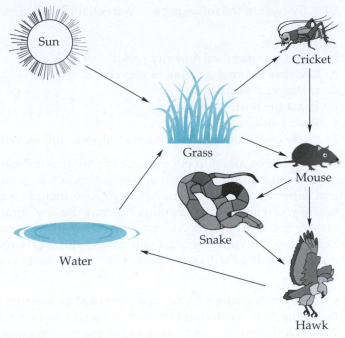

FIGURE 9.10   Food Web

Chapter 10

1. How does authentic assessment differ from performance assessment?
2. Explain how each of the following words is important in describing the nature of performance assessment: *explain, reasoning, observable, criteria, standards, engaging,* and *prespecified.*
3. Identify each of the following as an advantage (A) or disadvantage (D) of performance assessment.
   a. Resource intensive
   b. Integrates instruction with assessment
   c. Student self-assessment
   d. Scoring
   e. Reasoning skills
   f. Active learning
   g. Use of criteria
   h. Length
4. Identify each of the following skills as fine motor (FM), gross motor (GM), or complex (C).
   a. Making up new dives
   b. Tracing a picture of a lion just as the teacher did
   c. Making cursive capital letters easily
   d. Changing running stride to accommodate an uneven surface

5. Classify each of the following as a restricted (R) or extended (E) performance task.
   a. Tie shoes
   b. Prepare a plan for a new city park
   c. Construct a building from toothpicks
   d. Interpret a weather map
   e. Enact the Boston Tea Party
   f. Read a tide table
6. Evaluate the following performance task description. What is missing?

   You have been asked to organize a camping trip in North Dakota. There are seven campers. Indicate what you believe you will need for a three-day trip and provide reasons for your answer. Also include a detailed itinerary of where you will go while camping. You may use any library resources that you believe are helpful, and you may interview others who have had camping experience. As your teacher, I will answer questions about how you gather information, but I will not evaluate your answer until you have something to turn in.

7. Create a scoring rubric for the task presented in question 6. Show how each of the elements of writing and implementing scoring criteria presented in Figure 10.11 is followed in your answer. Include reasoning skills in your rubric.

Chapter 11

1. Indicate whether each of the following is an advantage (A) or disadvantage (D) of using portfolio assessment:
   a. Collaboration between student and teacher
   b. Student selection of contents
   c. Scoring
   d. Continuous monitoring of student progress
   e. Training teacher to do portfolios
   f. Generalizability
   g. Student self-evaluation
2. Indicate whether it would be best to use a celebration (CE), competence (CO), growth (G), or project (P) portfolio for each of the following purposes:
   a. To show examples of a student's work
   b. For the student to demonstrate his or her best work
   c. To show what students in a class are capable of doing
   d. To indicate the progress of the class on an important target
   e. For grading
   f. To show a student's progress
3. Evaluate the planning that is illustrated by the teacher in the following example. Is what she has planned consistent with what a portfolio is all about? Why or why not? Is her planning adequate? What else does she need to do?

Ms. Taylor has decided to implement a mathematics portfolio in her sixth-grade classroom. She believes the portfolios will increase student learning. She provides manila folders for the students and tells them that they will keep all their math worksheets and tests in them. She tells the students that they will be talking to her periodically about what is in the folder.

4. Match the description or example with the appropriate step in implementing portfolio assessment. Each step can be used more than once or may not be used at all:

_____ **a.** Rubric used to evaluate the sixth writing sample   **A.** Review with students

_____ **b.** Mr. Lind meets with students once a week   **B.** Supply content

_____ **c.** Students ask questions about how to self-reflect   **C.** Student self-reflection

_____ **d.** Teacher prepares an overhead that outlines the basics of portfolio assessment   **D.** Teacher evaluation

_____ **e.** Table of contents is prepared   **E.** Student–teacher conference

_____ **f.** Students select three work samples

_____ **g.** A checklist includes outline and self-reflection categories

5. The following scenario describes how a middle school social science teacher goes about implementing portfolio assessment in his class. After reading the scenario, review the checklist in Figure 11.6. Use this checklist as criteria to evaluate how well Mr. Trent does in using portfolios.

Gary Trent has read a lot lately about portfolios and decides to use them with his seventh-grade social studies classes. He spends the last week before school fine-tuning what he hopes his students can learn from doing the portfolios. Although he thinks he must give grades to ensure student motivation, he plans to use the portfolios to demonstrate to other teachers what his students are capable of achieving.

Gary decides to ask his students to bring something to class to hold the materials that will go in the portfolio. He explains to his students that they will be selecting one example each week from their work in his class that shows their best effort. Every month students meet with each other to critique what was included, and after the meeting students complete a self-evaluation worksheet. Throughout the semester, Gary plans to talk with each student at least once about his or her portfolio.

Near the end of the semester, Gary collects all the portfolios, grades them, and returns them to his students. He makes sure that each student receives individualized comments with the grade.

Chapter 12

1. What are some reasons that most teachers don't systematically assess noncognitive disposition and trait targets?

2. Match the nature of the learning with the target. Each target may be used more than once or not at all.

_____ **(1)** Cooperation and conflict resolution	**a.** Attitude
_____ **(2)** Student views of themselves	**b.** Value
_____ **(3)** Honesty and integrity	**c.** Motivation
_____ **(4)** Character education	**d.** Self-concept
_____ **(5)** Cognitive and affective components	**e.** Social relationships/ collaboration
_____ **(6)** Student expectations to do well	**f.** Classroom environment
_____ **(7)** Warmth in the classroom	**g.** Self-efficacy
_____ **(8)** Thinking math is important but not liking it	
_____ **(9)** Engagement and involvement	
_____ **(10)** Kindness, respect, tolerance	

3. Critique the efforts of the teachers in the following two scenarios to assess noncognitive dispositions. What have they done well and how could they improve?

   Scenario 1: Mr. Talbot

   Mr. Talbot decided that he wanted to assess his fifth graders on their attitudes toward social studies. He asks students to complete the sentence, "Social studies is. . . ." Also, at the end of each week he summarizes how much students have liked the social studies units. He writes a brief description for each student, then gives each a rating of 1 to 5.

   Scenario 2: Ms. Headly

   Ms. Headly teaches art to middle school students. Because all the students in the school come through her class, she wants to be sure that students leave the class with a positive attitude toward art and strong aesthetic values. She decides to develop and administer a survey of art attitudes and values at the beginning and end of each semester. She consults other teachers to generate a list of thoughts and behaviors that are positive and negative. She uses a response format of "like me" and "not like me" with the 50 items. Ms. Headly instructs the students not to put their names on the surveys.

4. Identify each of the following as a characteristic of observation (O), interview (I), constructed-response self-report (CRSR), or rating scale self-report (RSSR).
   a. Can take into account nonverbal behaviors
   b. Relatively easy to administer but more difficult to score
   c. Subject to teacher bias
   d. Can be anonymous

    e. Very time consuming to gather data

    f. Student explanations for answers can be provided

    g. The method of choice for assessing self-monitoring

    h. Can be done without students' knowledge or awareness

5. What are strengths and limitations of student self-assessment?

Chapter 13

1. According to P.L. 94-142, what are the two essential responsibilities of regular classroom teachers concerning the assessment of students with special needs who are in inclusive settings?

2. What was one of the most important new provisions added to IDEA 1990 regarding general education teachers' responsibilities?

3. Indicate whether each of the following statements represents nondiscriminatory assessment (Y for yes, N for no):

    a. A single procedure may be used for identification.

    b. Assessment is conducted by a multidisciplinary team.

    c. Assessments are conducted in English.

    d. The disability may not affect the scores students receive.

    e. Racial and cultural discrimination must be avoided.

4. True or False: IDEA 2004 required that response to intervention (RTI) be used to replace the discrepancy approach to identifying a student with specific learning disability.

5. Read the following scenario and indicate whether the teacher has properly followed the steps necessary to refer a student for identification.

Mrs. Albert was immediately suspicious of Jane, thinking that she might have a learning disability. Jane did not achieve very well on written tests and seemed to have trouble concentrating. She was also distracted very easily. Mrs. Albert tried Jane in another reading group, but this did not seem to help. After looking at Jane's previous test scores, Mrs. Albert decided to refer her for identification.

6. Indicate whether each of the descriptions listed is characteristic of students with intellectual disability (ID), emotional or behavioral disorder (EBD), sensory impairment (SI), speech and language impairment (SLI), physical impairment (PI), attention deficits (AD), hyperactivity (H), or learning disability (LD).

    a. Diabetes

    b. Language deficit

    c. Discrepancy between ability and achievement

    d. Poor adaptive behaviors

    e. Poor eyesight

    f. Slow learning

    g. Restless

    h. Easily distracted

7. Indicate whether each of the difficulties listed is characteristic of students with comprehension difficulties (C), sensory difficulties (SD), time constraint difficulties (TCD), anxiety (A), embarrassment (E), or behavior variability (BV).
   a. Gets sequence of steps wrong
   b. Worries excessively about performance
   c. Hands in an incomplete test with other students
   d. Has trouble one day finishing a test, no trouble the next day
   e. Takes longer to complete the test

8. Indicate whether each of the following test administration adaptations is considered good practice (Y for yes, N for no).
   a. Making tests with fewer items
   b. Closely monitoring students while they are taking a test
   c. Modifying tests
   d. Giving special attention when handing out tests
   e. Using norm-referenced testing
   f. Emphasizing internal attributions
   g. Giving practice tests
   h. Allowing students to take a written test orally
   i. Using objective rather than essay items
   j. Using normal seating arrangements
   k. Checking student understanding of directions

9. Read the following scenario and indicate what was correct and what was incorrect or lacking in the teacher's assessment accommodations.

   Mr. Calder was careful to read all the directions aloud, and he gave examples of how the students should answer each item. He prepared a separate set of directions for his students with special needs. He designed the test to make sure as many questions as possible were included on each page. He underlined key words in the short-answer questions and wrote objective items so that the students corrected wrong answers. Mr. Calder did not permit questions once students began the test. He told students that they had to complete the test in 30 minutes, and he placed a sign on the door indicating that testing was taking place.

10. Ms. Ramirez has a student with a learning disability in her classroom. His name is Tyron. Ms. Ramirez has decided to use a contract grading procedure, and she wants to be able to report progress on the contract to Tyron's parents. How would Ms. Ramirez begin to develop her contract, and how would she report progress to his parents?

Chapter 14

1. Which of the following are steps in the acculturation process?
   a. enculturation
   b. anomie
   c. integration
   d. culture shock

2. Teacher often assess students formatively on the basis of participation in daily classroom activities, seatwork assignments, and questioning. What are three steps teachers can take so that these types of informal assessments of CLD students are valid?

3. Indicate whether each of the following assessment adaptations for CLD students is considered good practice (Y for yes, N for no).
   a. Making tests with fewer items for CLD students
   b. Closely monitoring students while they are taking a test
   c. Providing dictionaries
   d. Giving special attention when handing out tests
   e. Using norm-referenced testing
   f. Using oral question prompts
   g. Giving practice tests
   h. Allowing students to take a written test orally
   i. Using objective rather than essay items
   j. Using normal seating arrangements
   k. Checking student understanding of directions
   l. Giving CLD students extra time to complete a test

4. Indicate whether each example characteristic is referring to a language or literacy skill (LLS), educational background (EB), socioeconomic status (SES), or cultural factor (CF).
   a. Highest parents' level of education
   b. Growing up in a bilingual home
   c. Coming to class with virtually no ability to speak English
   d. Valuing cooperativeness more than competitiveness
   e. Learning how to multiply in a different way
   f. Having a high paying job
   g. Not understanding test directions

5. Indicate which of the following does **not** help ELL students comprehend test language.
   a. Use simple sentences over complex sentences.
   b. Provide definitions or dictionaries.
   c. Present both oral and written forms.
   d. Avoid test questions containing double negatives, *always,* and *never.*
   e. Avoid jargon and technical terms.
   f. Use idiomatic expressions.
   g. Provide visual images explaining relationships and concepts of test items.
   h. Provide native language translation.

6. Indicate which of the following does **not** help CLD students demonstrate what they already know.
   a. Allow graphic organizers.
   b. Allow outlining or classifying.
   c. Allow illustrations or pictures.
   d. Allow oral responses.
   e. Performance in front of class.

    f. Reduce the length of paper in essay questions.

    g. Provide examples or models.

    h. Provide a word bank and key expressions in essay questions.

7. Mr. Green, an eighth-grade math teacher, did not realize Mei was an ELL student until she failed word problems completely. He was puzzled over why Mei did not do well in word problem questions, but she excelled in computation skills. Mei speaks English fluently enough without much difficulty. Mr. Green wonders what he needs to do to help Mei perform better in the math word problems. Discuss the ways that Mr. Green can accommodate Mei's needs in word problems.

8. Ms. Smith is a fifth-grade reading teacher. She noticed that her ELL student, Maria, who seemingly speaks fluently without accent, makes spelling and grammar errors in her writing. Although Maria seems to comprehend grade-level stories quite well, her writing falls short of fifth-grade-level work. Ms. Smith feels torn in grading her writing—on the one hand, Maria's idea presented in writing is excellent and deserves an "A," but her poor spelling and grammar are weak. What is the best way to grade Maria's writing?

Chapter 15

1. Indicate whether each of the following refers to individual student-referenced (ISR), norm-referenced (NR), or standards-based (SB) grading.

    a. based on the idea that some students will fail

    b. measures the growth of particular students

    c. average test scores are typically lower

    d. easily adapted from scoring rubrics

    e. uses percentile rank

    f. uses percent correct

    g. gives all students an opportunity to succeed

    h. factors in student ability

    i. fosters student competitiveness

2. In what ways is teacher professional judgment important in determining the actual standard employed in grading and marking students?

3. What major limitation do most approaches to grading have in common? What can teachers do to avoid this limitation?

4. Shaunda is a sixth grader. She is the oldest in a low-income family of six. Because her parents are not home very much, Shaunda takes on responsibilities with her brothers and sisters. The family lives in a small home, so it's hard for Shaunda to get the privacy she needs to do her homework. Consequently, she often does not hand in any homework. She has a very positive attitude toward school, and she is very attentive in class and tries hard to do well. Your class uses the following grading policy: in-class work accounts for 25% of the final grade; homework, 25%; and 50% for tests and quizzes. The grading scale in the school is 95–100, A; 85–94, B; 75–84, C; 65–74, D; <65, F. Shaunda's averages are in-class work, 85%; homework, 30%; and tests and quizzes, 70%. What overall composite percent correct would Shaunda have? What grade

would you give her? Does the grade reflect her academic performance? Should the grading policy be changed?

5. Suppose Greg is a very capable student who does very well on tests (e.g., 95s) but very poorly on homework. He just doesn't want to do work he sees as boring. His homework scores pull his test scores down so that the overall average is B–. What final grade would you give? How is motivation affected?

Answers to Self-Instructional Review Exercises

Chapter 1

1. Complex classroom contexts that are different for each teacher influence the nature of instructional decision making, and information from assessment tailored to the context is needed to make good decisions.
2. "Add-on" means assessment that occurs at the end of an instructional unit, for example, the midterm or final exam. However, the teacher also assesses students before and during instruction. Assessment should not be thought of as testing only at the end of instruction; it is conducted continuously as students learn.
3. A test is only one part of assessment. Assessment refers to measuring something, evaluating what is measured, and then using the information for decision making. A test is one way to measure.
4. a. F, b. S, c. F, d. F, e. P, f. F, g. P.
5. a. I, b. P, c. I, d. M, e. U.
6. Expectations are set by the nature of the standards and criteria used in the assessments and the way teachers provide feedback and otherwise respond to students.
7. Recent learning research has shown the importance of connecting new to existing information, of applying knowledge, and developing thinking skills. Performance assessments foster these skills by relating content and processes to problem solving in meaningful contexts.

Chapter 2

1. a. LT, b. G, c. S, d. LT.
2. Criteria are part of what would be included in a behavioral objective. Criteria, in contrast to objectives, contain descriptions of different levels of performance.
3. b.
4. Could have selected from several reasons: communicating goals and different levels of work to parents, documenting judgments, helping students evaluate their own work, motivating students, providing targeted feedback.
5. Criteria are needed to completely understand the nature of the target and what it takes to achieve different levels of performance. Without criteria,

targets are statements similar to simple behavioral objectives (without conditions, criteria, and audience).

6. a. K, b. DU, c. K, d. DU.
7. Bloom's taxonomy is not aligned very well with more recent research on learning and motivation.
8. For example,

    Knowledge: Students are able to recall and write accurately 80% of the definitions of key terms in the chapter.

    Deep Understanding and Reasoning: Students are able to analyze five examples of learning targets and modify them in writing so that they correspond better to the criteria in the chapter.
9. Content standards describe the nature of the material that is to be learned, whereas performance standards indicate levels of achievement on the content that must be met.
10. a. DK, b. PK, c. DU, d. DK, e. DU, f. PU.
11. a. D, b. C, c. I, d. S, e. A, f. P, g. C, h. I.

Chapter 3

1. Yes, but not in the way psychometricians do with published, standardized tests. Validity and reliability/precision are essential to fairness, being aware of potential error, proper interpretation of assessments, and teacher decision-making. Both validity and reliability/precision for classroom assessments are best estimated by teacher judgment and logical analysis, not statistically. With the growing use of standardized testing understanding of validity and reliability/precision is essential to test interpretation.
2. (1) d, (2) f, (3) a, (4) c, (5) b, (6) e.
3. a. OB, b. OR, c. S, d. E, e. SR, f. S.
4. a. Yes; if the score is not consistent or stable, with much error, the inference will be inaccurate and invalid. b. Yes; a measure of the circumference of your big toe is very reliable/precise but not very valid for measuring your ability to read. c. No; tests are not valid or invalid, only inferences from scores are. It would be better to say "A valid inference is based on reliable/precise scores."
5. a.
6. Not very reliable/precise. Germaine scored highest on Test A but near the bottom on Test B; Robert scored at the bottom on Test A but near the top on Test B. A reliable/precise assessment would result in nearly the same rank ordering for both tests.
7. a. Student knowledge of assessment. b. Student knowledge of assessment. c. Opportunity to learn. d. Biased content. e. Alignment.
8. Probably not. In this example, a minority group name is used, but it would be unlikely to elicit negative affect from Hispanic members of the class. There is no content that is clearly biased.

9. Because the time you have is limited, and priorities need to be set so that you balance instruction with assessment.

Chapter 4

1. a. R, b. E, c. AD, d. I.
2. (1) F, (2) H, (3) E, (4) A, (5) A, (6) B, (7) C, (8) D.
3. Mr. Bush is using previous behavior to motivate his informal observations, so his initial impressions may distort what he finds (primacy effect). He may also have a preconceived idea about what Trent would do (observer bias).
4. At least Mrs. Greene did not commit the error of unrepresentative sampling, because this was not a common occurrence. However, her interpretation that Renee was not thinking about her lesson may not be accurate. If this type of behavior became frequent and extensive, Mrs. Greene would want to ask Renee to get her perspective.
5. Matching questions with targets (a) helps to clarify to students what is important, (b) allows you to check student understanding of targets, (c) reinforces learning, and (d) balances emphasis given to each target.
6. The easiest way is the most direct—simply tell the students to wait a certain number of seconds before answering (e.g., 15 or 30 seconds). You can also ask them to write their answer, then think about it, before responding orally.
7. Convergent; only one or two possible ways are correct.
8. a, SB; b, TR; c, SR; d, SR
9. a, d, e, f.

Chapter 5

1. a, SE; b, PT; c, S or SE; d, H; e, PT.
2. c, d, e.
3. b.
4. This feedback seems okay at first; you may well have received something like this many times. But when you look closely at what is said, the feedback is weak. The teacher does not indicate how Robert can improve nor does the teacher identify Robert's specific mistakes or problems in sentence structure, conclusion, or providing detail. The teacher has indicated there is "improvement," but this is not clear indication of progress. The teacher also does not say how Robert can improve his difficulties, only that he has them.
5. a) E
   b) E
   c) E
   d) IE

Chapter 6

1. (a) S, (b) S, (c) F, (d) S, (e) F, (f) F.
2. It would be appropriate to use summative assessments if the scores were disaggregated to show specific strengths and weaknesses, were clearly

related to subsequent learning, and were confirmed by other sources of information.

3. (1) d, (2) a, (3) e, (4) a, (5) b, (6) e.
4. (a) U, (b) U, (c) U, (d) D, (e) U.

Chapter 7

1. a, b, d, e.
2. b—a large standard error of measurement means less reliable, a small standard error of measurement means more reliable.
3. When the information from several different sources suggests the same conclusion, when there is a pattern of performance for several years, and when your own informal assessment coincides with what is in school records.
4. Because norms are established in one year (e.g., 2014) and then used for several more years, and current scores (e.g., 2066) are compared to the 2014 norms. Before new norms are established, all the school districts may target skills assessed on the test.
5. a. NR and A; b. A; c. SB; d. SB; e. A; f, SB; g. NR and A.
6. a. SB, b. SB, c. NR, d. NR, e. SB, f. SB.
7. a. hinder, b. hinder, c. help, d. hinder, e. help, f. hinder, g. help, h. hinder.

Chapter 8

1. 1. c, 2. a, 3. b, 4. a, c, 5. c, 6. a, b, c, 7. a, b, c.
2. (1) There are probably too many items in one list. Additional responses should be included as distractors. Better to have states listed on the right. Directions are inadequate. Format is difficult to score. Premises are not homogeneous and are on the wrong side. Do not mix cities with historical figures, geographic descriptions, and state mottoes.

Revision: On the line next to each number in column A, write the letter of the state from column B that matches the geographic descriptions. Each state may be used once, more than once, or not at all.

Column A	Column B
_____ (1) Is bordered by three Great Lakes	a. New York
_____ (2) Contains part of the Rocky Mountains	b. Virginia
_____ (3) Has an upper and lower peninsula	c. Ohio
_____ (4) Is bordered by the Ohio and Mississippi rivers	d. Michigan
_____ (5) Contains the Blue Ridge Mountains	e. Texas
	f. Colorado
	g. Illinois
	h. Maryland
	i. North Carolina

(2) The negatives in this item make it very hard to understand. State more directly the proposition to be tested. Directions need to be included.

Revision: If the statement is true, circle T; if it is false, circle F.
T F Students construct answers to multiple-choice items.

(3) The directions should indicate "correct" answer, not "best" answer. The alternatives should be listed vertically under the stem. The stem should be long, the alternatives short. Option (c) does not fit grammatically and is not concise. "None of the above" should be avoided. It would be better to use a question.

Revision: Circle the correct answer.
Which of the following is a characteristic of Michigan?

   a. It is surrounded by the Great Lakes.
   b. It contains the Rocky Mountains.
   c. It is a single peninsula.
   d. It borders the Atlantic Ocean.

(4) The correct answer, b, is because of the complexity of the sentence in relation to the others. Fossil fuels are also biodegradable, so more than one correct answer is possible. The stem is short and the correct alternative long. It is more clearly stated as a question.

Revision: Circle the correct answer.
What type of material is broken down by decomposers into simpler substances that do not pollute the environment?

   a. Nonrenewable
   b. Biodegradable
   c. Fossil fuel
   d. Decomposition

Chapter 9

1. a. I; b. I or E; c. I; d. E; e. SA; f. E; g. SA; h. E; i. I.
2. The general format of the question is appropriate, and it is good to have several questions about the material presented. Introductory information is kept to a minimum. Presumably students have been studying food chains or webs; this one should be new. Clearly the questions cannot be answered correctly unless the student understands the food web. The format of the questions could be improved so that students check or circle correct answers rather than taking time to write their answers (e.g., What must the hawks do to get energy generated from the sun? a. live in warmer areas, b. eat more crickets, c. get more exercise, d. eat more mice). This would reduce the time students need to answer the questions and the time needed for scoring. The reasoning target assessed by the question is primarily inference and deductive reasoning.

Application and understanding targets are also assessed. The assessment could be improved by asking additional "what-if" questions, especially about things that indirectly affect the food web (e.g., What if there is cloudy weather? What would happen to the amount of grass if a herd of cows was added?).

3. This essay question assesses evaluation and critical thinking skills. A decision must be made with reasonable justification. It also assesses constructing support and deductive reasoning. The item could be improved by indicating how much time students should take in answering it, by indicating scoring criteria, and by providing more specific information about what is expected. Including the word *irresponsible* gives students a clear tip to what the teacher is looking for. Phrases such as *justify your answer* give students some direction but are vague. What level of detail is expected? How many reasons are adequate? What is meant by *justify?* There should also be an indication of the total points for the item.

Chapter 10

1. Authentic assessment refers to the nature of the task that approximates what is done in the real world. Performance assessment involves the construction of responses by students—it may or may not be authentic.

2. Students are required to *explain* their responses as well as to produce them; *reasoning* targets are usually assessed, students use *reasoning* skills to demonstrate their proficiency; student performance is judged by what is directly *observable*; *criteria* are used to judge the adequacy of the performance on the basis of *prespecified standards* that relate a description of the performance to a statement of worth; good performance tasks are those that are *engaging* for students.

3. a. D, b. A, c. A, d. D, e. A, f. A, g. A, h. D.

4. a. C, b. FM, c. FM, d. GM, adaptation.

5. a. R, b. E, c. E, d. R, e. E, f. R.

6. As a performance prompt, this isn't too bad, but as a performance task description it could be improved considerably. There is no indication of the targets, whether this is an individual or group project, the administrative process, and, most important, no indication of the scoring criteria. It is a fairly authentic task and integrates different subjects. It does say something about the role of the teacher and resources, but more detail on both of these aspects could be provided.

7. There will be individual answers to this question, so you'll need to review one another's work by applying the questions in Figure 10.11. I would begin with an analysis of the essential understandings and skills needed to plan the trip. This would comprise the dimensions that are evaluated (e.g., the ability to use maps, the ability to understand the impact of terrain and time of year on what will be needed, the extent to which plans follow from assumptions, the logic and soundness of reasons stated). I would then employ a scale to indicate the extent to which each of these dimensions is present (e.g., inadequate, adequate, more than adequate, or absent; developing, proficient, advanced). For example, for the extent to which plans follow from assumptions, you might note the following:

Absent	There is no indication of assumptions or how plans are based on assumptions.
Developing	Assumptions are not clearly stated but implied; plans are not explicitly related to assumptions but are implied.
Proficient	Some assumptions are clearly stated and plans are explicitly related to the assumptions.
Advanced	A comprehensive and well-thought-out list of assumptions is used; assumptions are explicitly related to plans.

Chapter 11

1. a. A; b. A or D (a disadvantage if students are not provided sufficient direction and supervision); c. D; d. A; e. D; f. D; g. A.
2. a. all; b. CE; c. CO or P; d. G; e. CE; f. G.
3. This is not really portfolio assessment, at least not in the way portfolios have been discussed in this chapter. Neither the teacher nor the students select anything (everything is included), and there is no indication that any performance products are included. There is a lack of specification about the purpose of the portfolio. Folders will be used, but we don't know where they will be placed. There is no indication that student self-reflection guidelines and scoring criteria have been developed.
4. a. D, b. E, c. C, d. A, e. B, f. B, g. D.
5. Gary does something right in using portfolios but needs to be more specific and systematic in a number of areas. It's good that he takes time to plan what he wants to do. However, the stated purpose is not one of the major reasons that portfolios should be used. There is only a brief reference to learning targets and no indication that he has prepared specific scoring criteria or student self-reflection guidelines. Simply asking students to select one example of their work per week is probably too vague. Gary needs to be more specific about what kinds of work should be included and about the physical structure of the portfolio. Because he has several classes, it may not be feasible to store each portfolio in the room. It's not clear that students know enough about portfolios for the procedure to work. It's good that students select the content, and Gary is on target in emphasizing student self-reflection. One problem may be that there will be too many work samples by the end of the semester, making Gary's grading process difficult. It might be better to have students select one work example per week and then at the end of the semester choose a few items from these to demonstrate achievement. Gary's plan to meet with students at least once informally is okay, but there is no provision for a more formal conference near the end of the semester. It's good that he includes individualized written comments.

Chapter 12

1. Three reasons were given in the chapter: Noncognitive takes second seat to cognitive outcomes; assessing dispositions is difficult to do well; and teachers do not want to put up with controversy.

2. (1) e, (2) c, (3) b, (4) b, (5) a, (6) g, (7) f, (8) a, (9) c, (10) b or e.
3. *Scenario 1.* On the positive side, Mr. Talbot has used more than one method to assess attitudes, and he has a fairly narrow trait in mind. It's good that he isolates the affective component of attitudes (likes) and that his observation notes are brief. On the negative, though, his sentence is too broad and may not give him much information about attitudes. There is no indication that he has generated examples of approach and avoidance behaviors. Students could easily respond with answers such as "short" or "in the morning," which wouldn't be much help. He should try to summarize more frequently than once a week, even though trying to write descriptions for each student will take a lot of time. He records his interpretations rather than student behavior.

   Scenario 2. For the most part, this is an example of good assessment. Ms. Headly took the time to first list behaviors, then establish a response format that would work, then develop the items. She ensured anonymity, and she looked at attitudes and values before and after her course. However, the survey is pretty long, and she is dependent on a single assessment method. It is possible that her bias would be perceived by students, and it might encourage them to provide positive answers at the end of the semester.
4. a. O and I; b. PR; c. O and I and CRSR; d. RSSR; e. O and I; f. CRSR; g. RSSR; h. O.
5. Strengths: promotes better student understanding of learning targets and scoring criteria; promotes student self-reflection and self-evaluation; provides immediate, specific, and individualized feedback; leads to an awareness of progress; increases motivation; enhances self-efficacy. Limitations: self-assessment skills need to be taught; time is needed for self-evaluation; differences between students requires individualized instruction; may not be supported because of other initiatives or alignment requirements; instructional time may be lost.

Chapter 13

1. Gathering information for identification and implementing the IEP.
2. One of the most important new provisions added to IDEA 1990 was that the law recognized that most students with disabilities spend all or most of their school time in general education settings, and so it included a provision requiring that a general education teacher become a member of the team for the IEP.
3. a. N, b. Y, c. N, d. Y, e. Y.
4. False. IDEA 2004 *proposed* Response to Intervention (RTI) as an alternative approach to determining eligibility for special education services. Many states have adopted RTI as an alternative approach under which a severe discrepancy between IQ and achievement was no longer required. However, IDEA did not require that RTI be the only approach.
5. Mrs. Albert did some things right but in general did not do enough to justify formal referral. She seems to have targeted behaviors that are characteristic

of students with a learning disability, and she did try one instructional intervention. However, more instructional interventions are needed to be sure that the problems could not be ameliorated in the class without referral. There is no indication that the teacher made any more structured, diagnostic assessments, and there is no evidence of any type of prereferral review. A serious oversight is that Mrs. Albert has not requested that outsiders review the situation.

6. a. PI, b. LD, c. LD, d. MR, e. SI, f. none, g. H, h. AD.
7. a. C, b. A, c. E, d. VB, e. TCD.
8. a. N, b. Y, c. Y, d. N, e. N, f. Y, g. Y, h. Y, i. Y, j. N, k. Y.
9. Correct procedures included reading the directions aloud, giving examples, underlining key words, and placing a sign on the door. Incorrect procedures, from an adaptation perspective, included giving students with disabilities a separate set of directions (which may cause embarrassment), putting too much on each page of the test, asking students to correct wrong answers for objective items, not permitting questions during the test, and giving students what seems like a short time limit.
10. It would be best to begin with a clear indication of the work to be completed and how different grades will be assigned. A specific time line for completing the work should be included. Signatures of the student and parents are needed to ensure that all understand. The teacher's report should not simply indicate what grades are achieved, but should also include some personalized comments and suggestions.

Chapter 14

1. b, c, d.
2. Make sure students understand the nature of learning targets and criteria; observe students carefully; alter questioning to allow students ample time to process and answer the question.
3. a, N; b, Y; c, Y; d, N; e, N; f, Y; g, Y; h, Y; i, N; j, N; k, Y; l, Y.
4. a, SES; b, LLS; c, LLS; d, CF; EB; f, SES; g, LLS.
5. f.
6. e.
7. There is a widespread misconception that math is an universal language and, therefore, ELLs will not experience much difficulty. However, word problems and context-based questions contain inseparable language components, which creates difficulties in understanding questions. Therefore, Mr. Green can simplify test language and/or provide customized glossaries. If possible, using graphs and visual images explaining relationships also helps ELLs demonstrate their math knowledge effectively.
8. First, ELLs do not develop reading and writing skills evenly in an equal pace. Reading is a receptive skill, which is developed prior to writing (expressive) skills. Furthermore, Maria's different native language background, in which spelling and sound match and pronouns are not often used as they are in the English language, precludes Maria's writing from being error-free. Given this,

Ms. Smith should weigh spelling and grammar errors low or not at all, unless her intention is to measure students' correct usage of grammar and spelling. Creating a specific analytic scoring rubric will also guide both teacher and students clearly in evaluating her response.

Chapter 15

1. a. NR, b. ISR, c. NR, d. SB, e. NR, f. SB, g. SB, h. ISR, i. NR.
2. The standard is set by how difficult the teacher makes the assessment items; scores essay, short-answer, and performance-based assessments; and sets the criterion level (e.g., the percentage correct).
3. The major limitation of letter grades, percent correct, and pass–fail approaches is that they provide only a general overview of performance. Supplemental information that details the strengths and weaknesses of the students is needed.
4. Shaunda's composite score would be figured as $(85 \times .25) + (30 \times .25) + (70 \times .5) = 21.25 + 7.5 + 35 = 63.75$. According to the grading scale, she would receive an F. This reflects the relatively high contribution of homework and the fact that she was not able to get much of it finished. However, her classwork and performance on tests tell a different story, and a more accurate grade would be a D. Suppose homework was 10% instead of 25% and classwork was 40%. Then her composite would be a 72, almost 10 points higher. Given her home situation, she certainly should not fail, and the grading scale needs to be changed to put more weight on academic performance. The relatively high percentage for in-class work, 25%, is subject to teacher bias and should be reduced.
5. Actual test performance should not be affected negatively by nonacademic factors such as effort and compliance. We suggest a policy that homework won't hurt a grade, but could improve it, and give the student an A. Motivation is negatively affected because homework is obviously too easy and does not help Greg learn. The final grade has little meaning with respect to his self-efficacy. The goal orientation is on performance rather than mastery, and the final grade of B– does not accurately indicate his level of competence. There is no indication that grades have been used formatively.

Glossary

Achievement test battery a series of standardized achievement tests with common norms for interpretation.

Acculturation process of assimilation into a new culture.

Adaptive behavior being able to meet independence and social responsibility expectations for the age and context in which the behavior occurs.

Adequate yearly progress (AYP) a provision of NCLB legislation requiring schools to show improvements each year in student participation and performance.

Alignment extent to which instructional activities and classroom assessments cover tested material.

Alternative assessment refers to a number of different kinds of assessments that are not traditional paper-and-pencil tests, such as performance and portfolio assessments.

Alternatives refers to possible answers in a multiple-choice item.

Analytic rubric type of scoring in which separate scores are provided for each criterion used.

Anchor examples of student responses, products, and performances that illustrate specific points on a scoring criteria scale.

Anecdotal observation brief written notes or records of student behavior.

Aptitude test type of standardized test that measures cognitive ability, potential, or capacity to learn.

Assessment the process of gathering, evaluating, and using information.

Assessment accommodation modified testing for students with special needs.

Attention deficit disorder (ADD) a classification of special needs in which the student is unable to sustain attention while being easily distracted.

Attention deficit hyperactivity disorder (ADHD) a classification of special needs in which the student is inattentive, hyperactive, and/or impulsive.

Attitude a predisposition to respond favorably or unfavorably to something; consists of affective, cognitive, and behavioral components.

Authentic assessment assessments that mirror tasks carried out in actual, naturally occurring settings.

Autism verbal, nonverbal and social interaction challenges that significantly interfere with learning.

Behavioral disorder *see* Emotional disorder.

Benchmark test *see* Interim test.

Binary-choice item type of selected-response item in which the respondent selects one of two possible answers.

Blueprint *see* Test blueprint.

Central tendency error scoring bias in which students tend to be rated in the middle of the evaluation scale.

Classroom assessment the collection, evaluation, and use of information for teacher decision making.

515

Common assessment same assessment used across teachers, departments, and districts to measure several weeks of learning.

Completion item a type of constructed-response item in which students write words to complete a prompt or sentence.

Computer adaptive test digital test containing multiple-choice items with increasing levels of difficulty.

Consequential validity type of validity evidence related to how assessment impacts both intended and unintended impacts from the results.

Constructed-response format type of item in which students create or produce their own answer or response.

Content-related evidence type of evidence for validity in which judgments are made about the representativeness of a sample of items from a larger domain.

Criteria categories of specific behaviors or dimensions used to evaluate students.

Criterion-referenced type of test score interpretation in which performance is compared to established levels of competence.

Criterion-related evidence type of evidence for validity in which scores from an assessment are related to other measures of the same trait or future behavior.

Digital portfolios systematic collection of student performance built and stored electronically.

Dispositions attitudes, interests, values, and character, personality, and affective traits.

Distractors incorrect alternatives in a multiple-choice item.

Documentation portfolio used to show what students' performance on identified learning standards.

Educational goal indicator of relatively broad student outcomes.

Educational objective a relatively specific statement of what students should know and be capable of doing at the end of an instructional unit.

Embedded formative assessment ongoing evaluation of student performance with appropriate feedback during instruction.

Emotional disorder consistent, inappropriate behaviors and feelings not attributed to other disabilities that interfere with academic work.

Essay type of item in which students provide an extended or restricted written response to a question.

Exemplar *see* Anchor.

Extended-type task a performance assessment task that may last days or weeks in which students provide extensive answers.

Fair assessment assessments that are free from bias and other factors that mask actual student knowledge and performance capabilities.

Feedback indicating verbally or in writing the correctness of an action, answer, or other response.

Formative assessment assessment that occurs during and after instruction to provide feedback to teachers and students.

Generosity error scoring bias in which teachers rate students higher than their performance deserves.

Goal *see* Educational goal.

Growth portfolio systematic collection of materials that shows how much progress students have accomplished.

Halo effect general impression influences scores or grades on subsequent assessments.

High-stakes tests tests that students must perform adequately on for graduation, promotion in grade, school accreditation, and other important implications.

Holistic rubric type of scoring in which a single score is given for overall performance.

Hyperactive excessively active behavior sustained in many situations.

Impulsivity   responding quickly, without time for reflection.

Inclusion   educational approach in which students with disabilities are taught in classrooms with students who do not have disabilities.

Individual student referenced   a type of grading in which the grade is based on comparisons with prior achievement and aptitude.

Individualized education program (IEP)   plan for providing appropriate services to students with disabilities.

Intellectual disability   significantly low mental ability and weak adaptive behavior.

Instructional validity   judgment of the extent of the match between what is taught and what is assessed.

Interim test   regular testing of students during the school year to monitor progress toward achieving end-of-year state standards.

Item analysis   review of pattern of responses to an objective item to determine the quality of distractors, discrimination, and difficulty.

Learning disability   mental processing deficit that manifests as a significant discrepancy between aptitude and achievement.

Learning goal   student desire to understand and learn with positive self-conceptions of competence.

Learning progressions   a sequence of steps in learning that describes progressively more sophisticated understanding.

Learning target   a description of performance that includes what students should know and be able to do and what criteria are used to judge the performance.

Likert scale   rating scale in which a respondent indicates the extent to which there is agreement or disagreement to a series of statements.

Mastery goal   *see* Learning goal.

Measurement   a systematic process of differentiating traits, characteristics, or behavior.

Nondiscriminatory   assessment and related actions that result in scores that are not unduly affected by a disability.

Norm-referenced   a type of test interpretation in which relative standing is identified by comparing performance to how others (norm group) performed.

Objective   *see* Educational objective or Teaching objective.

Oral questioning   type of assessment in which the teacher asks questions orally.

Performance assessment   type of assessment in which students perform an activity or create a product.

Performance criteria   *see* Criteria.

Performance goal   motivation for doing well is to pass or obtain a score rather than primarily to understand.

Portfolio   a systematic collection of student products to assess progress.

Preassessment   gathering information about students prior to instruction.

Pretest   assessment administered prior to instruction in the content and skills that will be taught.

Rating scale   a scale that contains gradations of the trait being assessed.

Readiness test   type of standardized aptitude test that identifies strengths and weaknesses of specific skills.

Reasoning   mental operation in which cognitive skills are combined with knowledge to solve a problem, make a decision, or complete a task.

Reliability/precision   the consistency, stability, and dependability of scores; an estimate of amount of error.

Restricted-type task   performance assessment task in which the student provides a limited response to a task that is completed within a day, hour, or minutes.

Rubric a scoring guide that uses criteria to differentiate between levels of student proficiency on a rating scale.

Selected-response format type of item for which students select a response from possible responses that are provided.

Self-assessment students' self-report evaluations of their work.

Self-efficacy a belief about one's capability to learn.

Severity error scoring bias in which teachers rate students lower than they should.

Speeded tests type of test in which students have a set amount of time to answer all questions.

Standardized tests large-scale tests that are administered and scored the same way.

Standards statements of expected student outcomes.

Standards-based instructional and assessment approaches that use standards to establish learning expectations.

Stem question or phrase in a multiple-choice item that is answered by selecting from given alternatives.

Standard error or measurement a quantitative estimate that shows the band of likely scores if a person takes a test multiple times.

Student self-assessment see Self-assessment

Summative assessment assessment that occurs at the end of an instructional unit to document student learning.

Summative-based formative assessment use of results of summative assessments to provide feedback and instruction that improves learning.

Table of specifications see Test blueprint.

Target see Learning target.

Teacher observation method of gathering assessment information in which the teacher systematically or informally observes students.

Teaching objective a description of the instructional plan.

Technology-enhanced a type of electronic test item that requires manipulation of information to provide answers.

Test blueprint systematic presentation of the learning targets and nature of items in an assessment.

Testwiseness knowledge and skills about item format and characteristics that are used to help identify correct answers.

Total points method approach to grading in which points for each product are summed.

Twice exceptional gifted students with disabilities.

Universally designed assessments (UDA) assessments that are structured to be used for all students to the greatest extent possible, without the need for specialized adaptations or accommodations.

Validity the appropriateness and legitimacy of the inferences, claims, and uses made from scores that result from an assessment.

Values end states of existence or desirable modes of conduct.

Weighted categories method approach to grading in which each product is assigned an emphasis toward the final grade.

References

Abrams, L. M., & McMillan, J. H. (2012). The instructional influence of interim assessments. In R. Lissitz (Ed.), *Informing the practice of teaching using formative and interim assessment: A systems approach* (pp. 103–130). Charlotte, NC: Information Age Publishing.

Abrams, L. M., Wetzel, A., & McMillan, J. H. (2010, May). *Teachers' formative use of benchmark test data.* Paper presented at the annual meeting of the American Educational Research Association, Denver.

Achieve. (2015). The role of learning progressions in competency-based pathways. Retrieved July 18, 2016 from http://achieve.org/files/Achieve-LearningProgressionsinCBP.pdf

Alonzo, A., & Gearhart, M. (2006). Considering learning progressions from a classroom assessment perspective. *Measurement: Interdisciplinary Research and Perspectives 14* (1–2): 99–126.

Alvermann, D. E., & Phelps, S. F. (2005). Assessment of students. In P. A. Richard-Amota & M. A. Snow (Eds.), *Academic success for English language learners: Strategies for K–12 mainstream teachers* (pp. 311–340). White Plains, NY: Longman.

American Educational Research Association. (2003). Standards and tests: Keeping them aligned. *Research Points, 1*(1), 1–4.

American Psychiatric Association. (2013). *Diagnostic and statistical manual of mental disorders* (5th ed.). Arlington, VA: Author.

Ames, C. (1992). Classrooms: Goals, structures, and student motivation. *Journal of Educational Psychology, 84*(3), 261–271.

Anderson, L. W., & Krathwohl, D. R. (2001). *A taxonomy for learning, teaching, and assessing: A revision of Bloom's taxonomy of educational objectives.* New York: Longman.

Andrade, H. (2013). Classroom assessment in the context of learning theory and research. In J. H. McMillan (Ed.), *SAGE Handbook of research on classroom assessment* (pp. 17–34). Thousand Oaks, CA: Sage

Andrade, H., & Brookhart, S. M. (2016). The role of classroom assessment in supporting self-regulated learning. In D. Laveault & L. Allal (Eds.), *Assessment for learning: Meeting the challenge of implementation* (pp. 293–310). Heidelberg: Springer.

Arter, J. A. (1996). Establishing performance criteria. In R. E. Blum & J. A. Arter (Eds.), *Handbook for student performance assessment in an era of restructuring* (pp. VI-1:1–VI-2:8). Alexandria, VA: Association for Supervision and Curriculum Development.

Azwell, T., & Schmar, E. (1995). *Report card on report cards: Alternatives to consider.* Portsmouth, NH: Heinemann.

Bandura, A. (2006). Guide for constructing self-efficacy scales. In T. Urdan and F. Pajares (Eds.), *Self-efficacy beliefs of adolescents.* Charlotte, NC: Information Age Publishing.

Barrett, H. C. (2007). Researching electronic portfolios and learning engagement: The REFLECT initiative. *Journal of Adolescent & Adult Literacy, 50*(6), 436–449.

Beckers, J., Dolmans, D., & van Merrienboer, J. (2016). E-portfolios enhancing students' self-directed learning: A systematic review of influencing factors. *Australian Journal of Educational Technology, 32*(2), 32–46.

Belgrad, S. F. (2013). Portfolios and e-portfolios: Student reflection, self-assessment, and goal setting in the learning process. In J. H. McMillan (Ed.), *Sage handbook of research on classroom assessment* (pp. 331–346). Thousand Oaks, CA: Sage Publications.

Bennett, R. E. (2011). Formative assessment: A critical review. *Assessment in Education: Principles, Policy & Practice, 18*(1), 5–25.

Bennett, R. E. (2015). The changing nature of educational assessment. *Review of Research in Education, 39*(1), 370–407. doi: 10.3102/0091732X14554179

Billups, L. H., & Rauth, M. (1987). Teachers and research. In V. Richardson-Koehler (Ed.), *Educator's handbook.* White Plains, NY: Longman.

Black, P., & Wiliam, D. (1998). Assessment and classroom learning. *Assessment in Education, 5*(1), 103–110.

Black, P., & Wiliam, D. (2004). The formative purpose: Assessment must first promote learning. In M. Wilson (Ed.), *Towards coherence between classroom assessment and accountability.* 103rd Yearbook of the National Society for the Study of Education. Chicago: University of Chicago Press.

Black, P., Wilson, M., & Yao, S. Y. (2011). Road maps for learning: A guide to the navigation of learning progressions. *Measurement: Interdisciplinary Research and Perspectives, 9*(2–3), 71–122.

Bloom, B. S. (Ed.). (1956). *Taxonomy of educational objectives: The classification of educational goals. Handbook 1. Cognitive domain.* New York: David McKay.

Bocala, C., & Boudett, K. P. (2015). Teaching educators habits of mind for using data wisely. *Teachers College Record, 117*(4), 1–20.

Bong, M. (2001). Academic motivation in self-efficacy, task value, achievement goal orientations, and attributional beliefs. *Journal of Educational Research, 97*(6), 287–298.

Bonner, S. M. (2013). Validity in classroom assessment: Purposes, properties, and principles. In J. H. McMillan (Ed.), *Sage handbook of research on classroom assessment* (pp. 87–106). Thousand Oaks, CA: Sage.

Bonner, S. M. (2016). Teachers' perceptions about assessment: Competing narratives. In G. T. L. Brown & L. R. Harris (Eds.), *Handbook of human and social conditions in assessment* (pp. 21–39). New York: Routledge.

Borich, G. D., & Tombari, M. L. (2004). *Educational assessment for the elementary and middle school classroom* (2nd ed.). Upper Saddle River, NJ: Pearson Education.

Brookhart, S. M. (1993). Teachers' grading practices: Meaning and values. *Journal of Educational Measurement, 30*, 123–142.

Brookhart, S. M. (2004). *Grading.* Upper Saddle River, NJ: Pearson Education.

Brookhart, S. M. (2005, April). *Research on formative classroom assessment: State-of-the-art.* Paper presented at the annual meeting of the American Educational Research Association, Montreal.

Brookhart, S. M. (2007). Expanding views about formative classroom assessment: A review of the literature. In J. H. McMillan (Ed.), *Formative classroom assessment: Theory into practice.* New York: Teachers College Press.

Brookhart, S. M. (2008). *How to give effective feedback to your students.* Alexandria, VA: Association for Supervision and Curriculum Development.

Brookhart, S. M. (2009). *Grading* (2nd ed.). New York: Merrill.

Brookhart, S. M. (2011). Educational assessment knowledge and skills for teachers. *Educational Measurement: Issues and Practice, 30*(1), 3–12.

Brookhart, S. M. (2013a). Classroom assessment in the context of motivation theory and research. In J. H. McMillan (Ed.), *Sage handbook of research on classroom assessment* (pp. 35–54). Thousand Oaks, CA: Sage.

Brookhart, S. M. (2013b). *Grading and group work.* Alexandria, VA: Association for Supervision and Curriculum Development.

Brookhart, S. M. (2014). *How to design questions and tasks to assess student thinking.* Association for Supervision & Curriculum Development.

Brookhart, S. M. (2015). *How to make decisions with different kinds of student assessment data.* Alexandria, VA: Association for Supervision & Curriculum Development.

Brookhart, S. M., Guskey, T., Bowers, A., McMillan, J., Smith, J., Smith, L., Stevens, M., & Welsh, M. (2016). A century of grading research: Meaning and value in the most common educational measure. *Review of Educational Research 86*(4), 803-848.

Brown, G. T. L., & Harris, L. R. (2013). Student self-assessment. In J. H. McMillan (Ed.), *Sage handbook of research on classroom assessment* (pp. 367–394). Thousand Oaks, CA: Sage.

Burke, K. (2009). *The mindful school: How to assess authentic learning* (5th ed.). Thousand Oaks, CA: Corwin Press.

Burke, K. (2010). *From standards to rubrics in six steps: Tools for assessment student learning, K–8* (3rd ed.). Thousand Oaks, CA: Corwin Press.

Campbell, C. (2012). Research on teacher competency in classroom assessment. In J. H. McMillan (Ed.), *Sage handbook of research on classroom assessment* (pp. 71–84). Thousand Oaks, CA: Sage.

Carey, T., & Carifio, J. (2012). The minimum grading controversy: Results of a quantitative study of seven years of grading data from an urban high school. *Educational Researcher, 41*(6), 201–208.

Chapman, C., & King, R. (2009). *Test success in the brain-compatible classroom* (2nd ed.). Thousand Oaks, CA: Corwin Press.

Chappuis, J. (2012). "How am I doing?" *Educational Leadership, 70*(1), 36–41.

Chappuis, S., & Stiggins, R. J. (2002). Classroom assessment for learning. *Educational Leadership, 60*(1), 40–44.

Cizek, G. J. (1999). *Cheating on tests: How to do it, detect, and prevent it.* Mahwah, NJ: Erlbaum.

Cizek, G. J. (2003). *Detecting and preventing classroom cheating: Promoting integrity in assessment.* Thousand Oaks, CA: Corwin Press.

Cizek, G. J., & Burg, S. S. (2006). *Addressing test anxiety in a high-stakes environment: Strategies for classrooms and schools.* Thousand Oaks, CA: Corwin Press.

Cohen, S. B. (1983). Assigning report card grades to the mainstreamed child. *Teaching Exceptional Students, 15*, 86–89.

Collier, C. (2004). Assessment of Acculturation. In G. B. Esquivel, E. C. Lopez & R. M. Cabral (Eds.), *Handbook of Multicultural School Psychology* (pp. 353–380). Mahwah, NJ: Lawrence Erlbaum Associations, Inc.

Costa, A. L., & Kallick, B. (2004). *Assessment strategies for self-directed learning.* Thousand Oaks, CA: Corwin Press/Sage Publications.

Council for Exceptional Children. (2015). *What every special educator must know: Ethics, standards, and guidelines* (7th ed.). Arlington, VA: Author.

Covington, M. V. (1992). *Making the grade: A self-worth perspective on motivation and school reform.* New York: Cambridge University Press.

Crooks, T. (2007, April). *Key factors in the effectiveness of assessment for learning.* Paper presented at the Annual Meeting of the American Educational Research Association, Chicago.

Cross, L. H., & Frary, R. B. (1999). Hodgepodge grading: Endorsed by students and teachers alike. *Applied Measurement in Education, 12*, 53–72.

Cury, F., Elliot, A., Sarrazin, D., Da Fonseca, D., & Rufo, M. (2002). The trichotomous achievement goal model and intrinsic motivation: A sequential mediational analysis. *Journal of Experimental Social Psychology, 38*, 473–481.

D'Agostino, J., & Welsh, M. (2007). *Standards-based progress reports and standards-based assessment score convergence.* Paper presented at the annual meeting of the American Education Research Association, Chicago.

DiRanna, K., Osmundson, E., Topps, J., Barakos, L., Gearhart, M., Cerwin, K., Carnahan, D., & Strang, C. (2008). *Assessment-centered teaching: A reflective practice.* Thousand Oaks, CA: Corwin Press.

Doyle, W. (1986). Classroom organization and management. In M. C. Wittrock (Ed.), *Handbook of research on teaching* (3rd ed.). New York: Macmillan.

Duckworth, A. L., Yeager, D. S. (2015). Measurement matters: Assessing personal qualities other than cognitive ability for educational purposes. *Educational Researcher, 44*(4), 237–251.

DuFour, R., DuFour, R., Eaker, R., & Many, T. (2010). *Learning by doing: A handbook for professional learning communities at work.* Solution Tree Press.

Durán, P. R. (2008). Assessing English language learners' achievement. *Review of Research in Education, 32,* 292–327.

Dweck, C. S. (2008). *Mindset: The new psychology of success.* New York: Ballantine Books.

Educational Testing Service. (2009). *Guidelines for the assessment of English language learners.* Retrieved June 1, 2009, from http://www.ets.org/Media/About_ETS/pdf/ELL_Guidelines.pdf

Ekman, P., & Friesen, W. V. (1969). The repertoire of nonverbal behavior: Categories, origins, usage, and coding. *Semiotica, 69,* 49–97.

Elliot, E., & Church, M. A. (1997). A hierarchical model of approach and avoidance achievement motivation. *Journal of Personality and Social Psychology, 72*(1), 218–232. doi: 10.1037/0022-3514.72.1.218

Elliot, A., McGregor, H. A., & Gable, S. (1999). Achievement goals, study strategies, and exam performance: A mediational analysis. *Journal of Educational Psychology, 91*(3), 549–563.

Elliot, A. J., & Thrash, T. M. (2001). Achievement goals and the hierarchical model of achievement motivation. *Educational Psychology Review, 13*(2), 139–156.

Federal Register. (1977, December 29). *Procedures for evaluating specific learning disabilities.* Washington, DC: Department of Health, Education, and Welfare.

Flippo, R. F. (2008). *Preparing students for testing and doing better in school.* Thousand Oaks, CA: Corwin Press.

Frederiksen, J. R., & White, B. Y. (2004). Designing assessments for instruction and accountability: An application of validity theory to assessing scientific inquiry. In M. Wilson (Ed.), *Toward coherence between classroom assessment and accountability.* 103rd Yearbook of the National Society for the Study of Education. Chicago: University of Chicago Press.

Frey, B. B., Schmitt, V. L., & Allen, J. P. (2012). Defining authentic classroom assessment. *Practical Assessment, Research & Evaluation, 17*(2). Available online: http://pareonline.net/getvn.asp?v=17&n=2

Frey, B. B., Schmitt, V. L., & Bowen, A. (2009, April). *Dimensions of authenticity in authentic assessment.* Paper presented at the Annual Meeting of the American Educational Research Association, San Diego.

Friend, M. (2014). *Special education: Contemporary perspectives for school professionals.* Boston: Pearson.

Fuchs, D., Mock, D., Morgan, P. L., & Young, C. I. (2003). Responsiveness intervention: Definitions, evidence, and implications for the learning disabilities construct. *Learning Disabilities Research & Practice, 18*(3), 157–171.

Furtak, E. M. (2009). *Formative assessment for secondary science teachers.* Thousand Oaks, CA: Corwin Press.

Gagne, E. D., Yekovich, C. W., & Yekovich, F. R. (1993). *The cognitive psychology of school learning* (2nd ed.). New York: HarperCollins.

Gallavan, N. P. (2009). *Developing performance-based assessments: Grades 6–12.* Thousand Oaks, CA: Corwin Press.

Gardner, H. (2011). *Frames of mind: The theory of multiple intelligences* (3rd ed.). New York: Basic Books.

Gelfer, J. I., Xu, Y., & Perkins, P. (2004). Developing portfolios to evaluate teacher performance in early childhood education. *Early Childhood Education Journal, 32*(2), 63–68.

Goertz, M. E., Olah, L., & Meggan, M. (2009). *From testing to teaching: The use of interim assessments in classroom instruction* (CPRE Research Report #RR-65). Philadelphia: University of Pennsylvania, Graduate School of Education.

Good, T. L., & Brophy, J. E. (2008). *Looking in classrooms* (10th ed.). Upper Saddle River, NJ: Pearson Education.

Gottlieb, M. (2016). *Assessing English language learners: Bridges to educational equity* (2nd ed.). Thousand Oaks, CA: Corwin.

Graner, P. S., Faggella-Luby, M. N., & Fritschmann, N. S. (2005). An overview of responsiveness to intervention: What practitioners ought to know. *Topics in Language Disorders, 25*(2), 93–105.

Green, S. K., & Johnson, R. L. (2010). *Assessment is essential.* Boston: McGraw-Hill.

Groeber, J. F. (2007). *Designing and using rubrics for reading and language arts, K–6* (2nd ed.). Thousand Oaks, CA: Corwin Press.

Gronlund, N. E., & Brookhart, S. M. (2009). *Gronlund's writing instructional objectives* (8th ed.). New York: Macmillan.

Guskey, T. R. (2002). Computerized gradebooks and the myth of objectivity. *Phi Delta Kappan, 83*(1), 775–780.

Guskey, T. R. (2007). Formative classroom assessment and Benjamin S. Bloom: Theory, research, and practice. In J. H. McMillan (Ed.), *Formative classroom assessment: Theory into practice.* New York: Teachers College Press.

Guskey, T. R. (2009). *Practical solutions for serious problems in standards-based grading.* Thousand Oaks, CA: Corwin Press.

Guskey, T. R., & Bailey, J. M. (2010). *Developing standards-based report cards.* Thousand Oaks, CA: Corwin Press.

Guskey, T.R., & Jung, L.A. (2013). *Answers to essential questions about standards, assessments, grading, & reporting.* Thousand Oaks, CA: Corwin Press.

Haertel, E. (1990). *From expert opinions to reliable scores: Psychometrics for judgment-based teacher assessment.* Paper presented at the annual meeting of the American Educational Research Association, Boston.

Harlen, W. (2003). *Enhancing inquiry through formative assessment.* San Francisco, CA: Institute for Inquiry, Exploratorium.

Harris-Murri, N., King, K., & Rostenberg, D. (2006). Reducing disproportionate minority representation in special education programs for students with emotional disturbances: Toward a culturally responsive response to intervention model. *Education and Treatment of Children, 29*(4), 779–799.

Hattie, J. (2008). *Visible learning: A synthesis of over 800 meta-analyses relating to achievement.* London: Routledge.

Hattie, J., & Timperley, H. (2007). The power of feedback. *Review of Educational Research, 77,* 81–112.

Heritage, M. (2007). Formative assessment: What do teachers need to know and do? *Phi Delta Kappan, 89*(2), 140–145.

Heritage, M. (2008). *Learning progressions: Supporting instruction and formative assessment.* Los Angeles, CA: National Center for Research on Evaluation, Standards, and Student Testing.

Heritage, M. (2013). Gathering evidence of student understanding. In J. H. McMillan (Ed.), *Sage handbook of research on classroom assessment* (pp. 179–196). Thousand Oaks, CA: Sage.

Heritage, M., & Anderson, C. (2009, April). *Laying the groundwork for formative assessment.* Paper presented at the 2009 Annual Meeting of the American Educational Research Association.

Herrera, S. G., Murry, K. G., & Cabral, R. M. (2012). *Assessment accommodations for classroom teachers of culturally and linguistically diverse students* (2nd ed.). Upper Saddle River, NJ: Pearson.

Hill, B. C., Ruptic, C., & Norwick, L. (1998). *Classroom-based assessment.* Norwood, MA: Christopher-Gordon.

Hill, D. (2007). *Emotionomics.* Edina, MN: Beavers Pond Group.

Hoover, J. J. (2009). *Differentiating learning differences from disabilities: Meeting diverse needs through multi-tiered response to intervention.* Upper Saddle River, NJ: Pearson.

Horowitz, F. D., Darling-Hammond, L., Bransford, J., Comer, J., Rosebrock, K., Austin, K., & Rust, F. (2005). Educating teachers for developmentally appropriate practice. In L. Darling-Hammond & J. Bransford (Eds.), *Preparing teachers for a changing world.* Hoboken, NJ: Wiley.

Jackson, P. W. (1990). *Life in classrooms.* New York: Holt, Rinehart, and Winston.

Jimerson, S. R., Burns, M. K., & VanDreHeyden, A. M. (2015). *Handbook of response to intervention: The science and practice of multi-tiered systems of support.* New York: Springer.

Jung, L. A. (2009). The challenges of grading and reporting in special education: An inclusive grading model. In T. R. Guskey (Ed.), *Practical solutions for serious problems in standards-based grading.* Thousand Oaks, CA: Corwin Press.

Kane, M. T. (2016). Explicating validity. *Assessment in Education: Principles, Policy & Practice, 23*(2), 198–211.

Kendall, J. (2011). *Understanding common core state standards.* Alexandria, VA: ASCD.

Kingore, B. (2008). *Developing portfolios for authentic assessment, pre-K–3: Guiding potential in young learners.* Thousand Oaks, CA: Corwin Press.

Kluger, A. N., & DeNisi, A. (1996). The effects of feedback interventions on performance: A historical review, a meta-analysis, and a preliminary feedback intervention theory. *Psychological Bulletin, 119*(2), 254–284.

Knapp, M. L., & Hill, J. A. (2013). *Nonverbal communication in human interaction* (8th ed.). Florence, KY: Wadsworth Cengage Learning.

Krathwohl, D. R., Bloom, B. S., & Masia, B. B. (1964). *Taxonomy of educational objectives, handbook II: Affective domain.* New York: David McKay.

Lane, S. (2010). *Performance assessment: The state of the art* (SCOPE Student Assessment Series). Stanford, CA: Stanford University, Stanford Center for Opportunity Policy in Education.

Lane, S. (2013). Performance assessment. In J. H. McMillan (Ed.), *Sage handbook of research on classroom assessment* (pp. 313–329). Thousand Oaks, CA: Sage.

Lazzari, A. M., & Wood, J. W. (1994). *Test right: Strategies and exercises to improve test performance.* East Moline, IL: LinguiSystems.

Leathers, D. G., & Eaves, M. H. (2008). *Successful nonverbal communication: Principles and applications* (4th ed.). New York: Macmillan.

Liem, G. A. (2012). Personal best goals and academic and social functioning: A longitudinal perspective. *Learning and Instruction, 22*(3), 222–230.

Maehr, M. L., & Zusho, A. (2009). Achievement goal theory: The past, present, and future. In K. Wentzel & A. Wingfield (Eds.), *Handbook of motivation at school* (pp. 77–104). New York: Routledge.

Mandinach, E., Friedman, J. M., & Gummer, E. (2015). How can schools of education help to build educators' capacity to use data? A systemic view of the issue. *Teachers College Record, 117*(4), 1–50.

Marsh, H. W., & Craven, R. (1997). Academic self-concept: Beyond the dustbowl. In G. D. Phye (Ed.), *Handbook of classroom assessment: Learning, adjustment, and achievement.* San Diego, CA: Academic Press.

Marsh, J., Pane, J., & Hamilton, L. (2006). *Making sense of data-driven decision making in education: Evidence from recent RAND research.* Washington, DC: RAND Corporation.

Martin-Kniep, G. O., & Cunningham, D. (1998). *Why am I doing this? Purposeful teaching through portfolio assessment.* Portsmouth, NH: Heinemann.

Marzano, R. J. (2006). *Classroom assessment and grading that work.* Alexandria, VA: ASCD.

Marzano, R. J., & Haystead, M. W. (2008). *Making standards useful in the classroom.* Alexandria, VA: Association for Supervision and Curriculum Development.

Marzano, R. J., & Heflebower, T. (2011). Grades that show what students know. *Educational Leadership, 69*(3), 35–39.

Marzano, R. J., & Kendall, J. S. (2007). *The new taxonomy of educational objectives* (2nd ed.). Thousand Oaks, CA: Corwin Press.

Mastropieri, M. A., & Scruggs, T. E. (2013). *The inclusive classroom: Strategies for effective instruction* (5th ed.). Upper Saddle River, NJ: Pearson/Merrill Prentice Hall.

Mayer, R. E. (2002). *The promise of educational psychology: Vol. II. Teaching for meaningful learning.* Upper Saddle River, NJ: Merrill/Prentice Hall.

McElligott, J., & Brookhart, S. M. (2009). Legal issues of grading in the era of high stakes accountability. In T. R. Guskey (Ed.), *Practical solutions for serious problems in standards-based grading.* Thousand Oaks, CA: Corwin Press.

McLeod, J. K., & Vasinda, S. (2009). Electronic portfolios: Perspectives of students, teachers and parents. *Education and Information Technologies, 14*(1), 29–38

McLoughlin, J. A., & Lewis, R. B. (2007). *Assessing students with special needs* (7th ed.). Upper Saddle River, NJ: Pearson Education.

McMillan, J. H. (2001). Secondary teachers' classroom assessment and grading practices. *Educational Measurement: Issues and Practice, 20*(1), 20–32.

McMillan, J. H. (2002a). Elementary school teachers' classroom assessment and grading practices. *Journal of Educational Research, 95*(4), 203–214.

McMillan, J. H. (2002b). *The impact of high-stakes external testing on classroom assessment decision-making.* Paper presented at the annual meeting of the American Educational Research Association, New Orleans.

McMillan, J. H. (2003). Understanding and improving teachers' classroom assessment decision making. *Educational Measurement: Issues and Practices, 22*(4), 34–43.

McMillan, J. H. (2008). *Assessment essentials for standards-based education.* Thousand Oaks, CA: Corwin Press.

McMillan, J. H. (2009). Synthesis of issues and implications for practice. In T. Guskey (Ed.), *Practical solutions for serious problems in standards-based grading* (pp. 105–120). Thousand Oaks, CA: Corwin Press.

McMillan, J. H. (2010). The practical implications of educational aims and contexts for formative assessment. In H. L. Andrade & G. J. Cizek (Eds.), *Handbook of formative assessment* (pp. 41–58). Oxford, England: Routledge.

McMillan, J. H. (2016). Section discussion: Student perceptions of assessment. In G. T. L. Brown & L. R. Harris (Eds.), *Handbook of Human and Social Conditions in Assessment* (pp. 221–243). New York: Routledge.

McMillan, J. H. (forthcoming). *Using students' assessment mistakes and learning deficits to enhance motivation and learning.* New York: Routledge.

McMillan, J. H., & Hearn, J. (2008). Student self-assessment: The key to stronger student motivation and higher achievement. *Educational Horizons, 87*(1), 40–49.

McMillan, J. H., Myran, S., & Workman, D. (2002). Elementary teachers' classroom assessment and grading practices. *Journal of Educational Research, 95*(4), 203–213.

McMillan, J. H., & Tierney, R. D. (2009). *Reconceptualizing fairness for classroom assessment.* (Unpublished manuscript).

McMillan, J. H., & Turner, A. B. (2014). *Understanding student voices about assessment: Links to learning and motivation.* Paper presented at the annual meeting of the American Educational Research Association, Philadelphia.

McMillan, J. H., & Workman, D. (1999). *Teachers' classroom assessment and grading practices: Phase 2.* Richmond, VA: Metropolitan Educational Research Consortium.

McTighe, J., & Ferrara, S. (1998). *Assessing learning in the classroom.* Washington, DC: National Education Association.

McTighe, J., & Wiggins, G. (2004). *Understanding by design: Professional development workbook* (2nd ed.). Alexandria, VA: Association for Supervision and Curriculum Development.

Mehrabian, A. (1981). *Silent messages* (2nd ed.). Belmont, CA: Wadsworth.

Mehring, T. A. (1995). Report card options for students with disabilities in general education. In T. Azwell & E. Schmar (Eds.), *Report card on report cards: Alternatives to consider.* Portsmouth, NH: Heinemann.

Miller, M. D., Linn, R. L., & Gronlund, N. E. (2013). *Measurement and assessment in teaching* (11th ed.). Upper Saddle River, NJ: Pearson Education.

Moss, C. M., & Brookhart, S. M. (2009). *Advancing formative assessment in every classroom: A guide for instructional leaders.* Alexandria, VA: ASCD.

Mottet, T. P., & Richmond, V. P. (2000). *Student nonverbal communication and its influence on teachers and teaching: A review of literature.* Paper presented at the annual meeting of the National Communication Association.

Nagel, D. (2015). *Effective grading practices for secondary teachers: Practical strategies to prevent failure, recover credits, and increase standards-based/referenced grading.* Thousand Oaks, CA: Sage Publications.

National Association for Gifted Children. (2010). *Pre-K–grade 12 gifted programming standards.* Washington, DC: Author.

National Center on Response to Intervention. (2010). *Essential components of RTI: A closer look at response to intervention.* Retrieved September 2, 2012, from http://www.rti4success.org/pdf/rtiessentialcomponents_042710.pdf

National Council on Measurement in Education. (1995). *Code of professional responsibilities in educational measurement.* Washington, DC: Author.

Nichols, S. L., & Harris, L. R. (2016). Accountability assessment's effects on teachers and schools. In G. T. L. Brown & L. R. Harris (Eds.), *Handbook of human and social conditions in assessment* (pp. 40–56). New York: Routledge.

Nilsen, B. A. (2008). *Observation and assessment.* Clifton Park, NY: Thompson Delmar Learning.

Nolen, S. B., Haladyna, T. M., & Haas, N. S. (1989). *A survey of Arizona teachers and administrators on the uses and effects of state-mandated standardized achievement testing* (Tech. Rep. No. 89–2). Phoenix, AZ: Arizona State University, West Campus.

O'Conner, K. (2010). *A repair kit for grading: 15 fixes for broken grades* (2nd ed.). Portland, OR: Educational Testing Service.

O'Connor, K. (2009). *How to grade for learning k–12.* Thousand Oaks, CA: Corwin Press.

O'Malley, J. M., & Pierce, L. V. (1996). *Authentic assessment for English language learners: Practical approaches for teachers.* White Plains, NY: Longman.

Ormrod, J. E. (2011). *Human learning* (11th ed.). Upper Saddle River, NJ: Merrill/Prentice Hall.

Parke, C. S., Lane, S., Silver, E. A., & Magone, M. E. (2003). *Using assessment to improve middle-grades mathematics teaching and learning: Suggested activities using QUASAR tasks, scoring criteria, and students' work.* Reston, VA: National Council of Teachers of Mathematics.

Parkes, J. (2013). Reliability in classroom assessment. In J. H. McMillan (Ed.), *Sage handbook of research on classroom assessment* (pp. 107–124). Thousand Oaks, CA: Sage.

Partnership for Assessment of Readiness for College and Careers (PARCC). (2016). *The PARCC tests.* Retrieved from http://www.parcconline.org/about/the-parcc-tests

Pellegrino, J. W., & Hilton, M. L. (Eds.). (2012). *Education for life and work: Developing transferable knowledge and skills in the 21st century.* Washington, DC: National Research Council.

Penuel, W. R., & Shepard, L. A. (2016). Assessment and teaching. In D. H. Gitomer & C. A. Bell (Eds.), *Handbook of research on teaching* (5th ed.) (pp. 787–850). Washington, DC: American Educational Research Association.

Perie, M., Marion, S., & Gong, B. (2009). Moving toward a comprehensive assessment system: A framework for considering interim assessments. *Educational Measurement: Issues and Practice, 28*(3), 5–13.

Pierangelo, R., & Giuliani, G. A. (2012). *Assessment in special education: A practical approach* (4th ed.). Boston: Pearson.

Pintrich, P. R., & Schunk, D. H. (2013). *Motivation in education: Theory, research, and applications* (4th ed.). Upper Saddle River, NJ; Columbus, OH: Merrill/Prentice Hall.

Pope, N., Green, S. K., Johnson, R. L., & Mitchell, M. (2009). Examining teacher ethical dilemmas in classroom assessment. *Teaching and Teacher Education, 25,* 778–782.

Popham, W. J. (2007). The lowdown on learning progressions. *Educational Leadership, 64*(7), 83–84.

Popham, W. J. (2009). Assessing student affect. *Educational Leadership, 66*(8), 85–86.

Popham, W. J. (2011). *Transformative assessment in action: An inside look at applying the process.* Alexandria, VA: ASCD.

Popham, W. J. (2014). Right test for the wrong reason, *Phi Delta Kappan, 96*(1), 47–52.

Popham, W. J. (2017). *Classroom assessment: What teachers need to know* (8th ed.). Boston: Pearson Education.

Quellmalz, E. S., Davenport, J. L., Timms, M. J., DeBoer, G. E., Jordan, K. A., Huang, C. W., & Buckley, B. C. (2013). Next-generation environments for assessing and promoting complex science learning. *Journal of Educational Psychology, 105*(4), 1100–1114. doi:10.1037/a0032220

Reynolds, C. R., Livingston, R. B., & Willson, V. (2008). *Measurement and assessment in education* (2nd ed.). Boston: Pearson Education.

Rivers, S. E., Hagelskamp, C., & Brackett, M. A. (2013). Understanding and assessing the social-emotional attributes of classrooms. In J. H. McMillan (Ed.), *Sage handbook of research on classroom assessment* (pp. 347–366). Thousand Oaks, CA: Sage.

Robins, R. W., & Pals, J. L. (2002). Implicit self-theories in the academic domain: Implications for goal orientation, attributions, affect, and self-esteem change. *Self and Identity, 1*(4), 313–336.

Rodriguez, M. C., & Haladyna, T. M. (2013). Writing selected-response items for classroom assessment. In J. H. McMillan (Ed.), *Sage handbook of research on classroom assessment* (pp. 293–311). Thousand Oaks, CA: Sage.

Rokeach, M. (1973). *The nature of human values.* New York: Free Press.

Ross, J. A. (2006). The reliability, validity, and utility of self-assessment. *Practical Assessment, Research & Evaluation, 11*(10). Available online at http://pareonline.net/getvn.asp?v=11&n=10

Roth, W. M. (2001). Gestures: Their role in teaching and learning. *Review of Educational Research, 71*(3), 365–392.

Rothman, R. (2012). How we got here: The emergence of the Common Core State Standards. *State Education Standard, 12*(2), 4–8.

Ruiz-Primo, M. A., & Furtak, E. M. (2007). Exploring teachers' informal formative assessment practices and students' understanding in the context of scientific inquiry. *Journal of Research in Science Teaching, 44*(1), 57–84.

Ruiz-Primo, M. A., & Li, M. (2013). Examining formative feedback in the classroom context: New research perspectives. In J. H. McMillan (Ed.), *Sage handbook of research on classroom assessment* (pp. 215–232). Thousand Oaks, CA: Sage.

Russell, M. K., & Airasian, P. W. (2012). *Classroom assessment: Concepts and applications* (7th ed.). New York: McGraw-Hill.

Ryan, A. M., & Deci, E. L. (2000). Self-determination theory and the facilitation of intrinsic motivation, social development, and well-being. *American Psychologist, 55,* 68–78.

Sadler, P. M., & Good, E. (2006). The impact of self- and peer-grading on student learning. *Educational Assessment, 11,* 1–31.

Salend, S. J. (1995). Modifying tests for diverse learners. *Intervention in School and Clinic, 31,* 84–90.

Salend, S. J. (2009). *Classroom testing and assessment for ALL students: Beyond standardization.* Thousand Oaks, CA: Corwin Press.

Salend, S. J. (2011). Addressing test anxiety. *Teaching Exceptional Children, 44*(2), 58–68.

Salvia, J., & Ysseldyke, J. E. (2001). *Assessment* (8th ed.). Boston: Houghton Mifflin.

Salvia, J., Ysseldyke, J. E., & Bolt, S. (2013). *Assessment in special and inclusive education.* Belmont, CA: Wadsworth.

Sampson, S. O. (2009). Assigning fair, accurate, and meaningful grades to students who are English language learners. In T. Guskey (Ed.), *Practical solutions for serious problems in standards-based grading.* Thousand Oaks, CA: Corwin Press.

Schunk, D. H. (1991). Self-efficacy and academic motivation. *Educational Psychologist, 26,* 207–231.

Schwartz, J. L., & Kenney, J. M. (2008). *Tasks and rubrics for balanced mathematics assessment in primary and elementary grades.* Thousand Oaks, CA: Corwin Press.

Seitz, H., & Bartholomew, C. (2008). Powerful portfolios for young children. *Early Childhood Education Journal, 36,* 63–68.

Senko, C., Hulleman, C. S., & Harackiewicz, J. M. (2011). Achievement goal theory at the crossroads: Old controversies, current challenges, and new directions. *Educational Psychologist, 46*(1), 26–47.

Shaywitz, B. A., Fletcher, J. M., Holahan, J. M., & Shaywitz, S. E. (1992). Discrepancy compared to low achievement definitions of reading disability. *Journal of Learning Disabilities, 25*, 639–648.

Shepard, L. A. (2004). Curricular coherence in assessment design. In M. Wilson (Ed.), *Towards coherence between classroom assessment and accountability.* 103rd Yearbook of the National Society for the Study of Education. Chicago: University of Chicago Press.

Shepard, L. A. (2009). Commentary: Evaluating the validity of formative and interim assessment. *Educational Measurement: Issues and Practice, 28*(3), 32–37.

Shute, V. J. (2008). Focus on formative feedback. *Review of Educational Research, 78*(1), 153–189.

Slavin, R. E. (2010). Co-operative learning: What makes group-work work? In H. Dumont, D. Istance, and F. Benavides (Eds.), *The nature of learning: Using research to inspire practice* (pp. 161–178). Paris, France: OECD.

Smarter Balanced Assessment Consortium. (2016). *Smarter assessments.* Retrieved July 26, 2016, from http://www.smarterbalanced.org/assessments/

Smith, T. E. C., Polloway, E. A., Patton, J. R., & Dowdy, C. A. (2012). *Teaching students with special needs in inclusive settings* (6th ed.). Upper Saddle River, NJ: Pearson Education.

Smith, J. K., Smith, L. F., & DeLisi, R. (2011). *Natural classroom assessment.* Thousand Oaks, CA: Corwin Press.

Solano-Flores, G. (2016). *Assessing English language learners: Theory and practice.* New York: Routledge.

Spinelli, C. G. (2002). *Classroom assessment for students with special needs in inclusive settings.* Upper Saddle River, NJ: Merrill/Prentice Hall.

Spinelli, C. G. (2012). *Classroom assessment for students in special and general education* (3rd ed.). Upper Saddle River, NJ: Pearson Education.

Sternberg, R. J. (1986). The future of intelligence testing. *Educational Measurement: Issues and Practice, 5*, 19–22.

Stiggins, R. J. (2002). Assessment crisis: The absence of assessment for learning. *Phi Delta Kappan, 83*(10), 758–765.

Stiggins, R. J. (2007). Assessment through the student's eyes. *Educational Leadership, 64*, 22–26.

Stiggins, R. J. (2008). *A call for the development of balanced assessment systems.* Princeton, NJ: Educational Testing Service.

Stiggins, R. J., & Chappuis, J. (2011). *Student-involved assessment FOR learning* (6th ed.). Upper Saddle River, NJ: Pearson Merrill Prentice Hall.

Stiggins, R. J., Arter, J. A., Chappuis, J., & Chappuis, S. (2009). *Classroom assessment for student learning: Doing it right-using it well.* Upper Saddle River, NJ: Pearson.

Stuebing, K. K., Fletcher, J. M., LeDoux, J. M., Lyon, G. R., Shaywitz, S. E., & Shaywitz, B. A. (2002). Validity of IQ-discrepancy classifications of reading disabilities: A meta-analysis. *American Educational Research Journal, 39*, 469–518.

Terwilliger, J. S. (1989). Classroom standard setting and grading practices. *Educational Measurement: Issues and Practice, 8*(2), 15–19.

Tierney, R. D. (2013). Fairness in classroom assessment. In J. H. McMillan (Ed.), *Sage handbook of research on classroom assessment* (pp. 125–144). Thousand Oaks, CA: Sage.

Thomas, W., & Collier, V. (2002). *A national study of school effectiveness for language minority students' long-term academic achievement.* Santa Cruz, CA: Center for Research on Education, Diversity and Excellence.

Thurlow, M. L., Lazarus, S. S., Christensen, L. L., & Shyyan, V. (2016). *Principles and characteristics of inclusive assessment systems in a changing assessment landscape* (NCEO Report 400). Minneapolis, MN: University of Minnesota, National Center on Educational Outcomes.

Thurlow, M. L., Lazarus, S. S., Thompson, S. J., & Morse, A. B. (2005). State policies on assessment participation and accommodations for students with disabilities. *Journal of Special Education, 38*, 232–240.

Tileston, D. W., & Darling, S. K. (2008). *Teaching strategies that prepare students for high-stakes tests.* Thousand Oaks, CA: Corwin Press.

Tomlinson, C. A. (2014). *The differentiated classroom: Responding to the needs of all learners* (2nd ed.). Alexandria, VA: ASCD.

Tomlinson, C. A., & Moon, T. R. (2013a). Differentiation and classroom assessment. In J. H. McMillan (Ed.), *Sage handbook of research on classroom assessment* (pp. 415–430). Thousand Oaks, CA: Sage.

Tomlinson, C. A., & Moon, T. R. (2013b). *Assessment and student success in a differentiated classroom.* Alexandria, VA: ASCD.

Van de Vijver, F. J. R. (2016). Assessment in education in multicultural populations. In G. T. L. Brown & L. R. Harris (Eds.), *Handbook of human and social conditions in assessment* (pp. 436–453). New York: Routledge.

Vatterott, C. (2015). *Rethinking grading: Meaningful assessment for standards-based learning.* Alexandria, VA: Association for Supervision and Curriculum Development.

Vescio, V., Ross, D., & Adams, A. (2008). A review of research on the impact of professional learning communities on teaching practice and student learning. *Teaching and Teacher Education, 24*(1), 80–91.

Wayman, J., & Cho, V. (2009). Preparing educators to effectively use student data systems. In T. Kowalksi & T. Lasley II (Eds.), *Handbook of data-based decision making in education* (pp. 89–104). New York: Routledge.

Weiner, B. (1974). *Achievement motivation and attribution theory.* Morristown, NJ: General Learning Press.

Weiner, B. (1985). An attributional theory of achievement motivation and emotion. *Psychological Review, 92*(4), 548–573.

Welsh, M. E., & D'Agostino, J. V. (2008). Effective standards-based progress report grading. In T. R. Guskey (Ed.), *Practical solutions for serious problems in standards-based grading* (pp. 75–104). Thousand Oaks, CA: Corwin Press.

West, M. R., Kraft, M. A, Finn, A. S., Martin, R. E., Duckworth, A. L., Gabrieli, C. F. O., & Gabrieli, J. D. E. (2016). Promise and paradox: Measuring students' non-cognitive skills and the impact on schooling. *Educational Evaluation and Policy Analysis, 38*(1), 148–170.

Wiggins, G. P. (1998). *Educative assessment: Designing assessments to inform and improve student performance.* San Francisco: Jossey-Bass.

Wiggins, G. (2012). Seven keys to effective feedback. *Educational Leadership, 70*(1), 10–17.

Wiggins, G. P., & McTighe, J. (2005). *Understanding by design* (2nd ed.). Washington, DC: Association for Supervision and Curriculum Development.

Wiggins, G. P., & McTighe, J. (2011). *The understanding by design guide to creating high-quality units.* Alexandria, VA: ASCD.

Wiliam, D. (2010). An integrative summary of the research literature and implication for a new theory of formative assessment. In H. L. Andrade & G. J. Cizek (Eds.), *Handbook of formative assessment* (pp. 18–40). New York: Routledge.

Wiliam, D. (2011). *Embedded formative assessment.* Bloomington, IN: Solution Tree Press.

Wiliam, D., & Leahy, S. (2007). A theoretical foundation for formative assessment. In J. H. McMillan (Ed.), *Formative classroom assessment: Theory into practice.* New York: Teachers College Press.

Wiliam, D., & Leahy, S. (2015). *Embedding formative assessment: Practical techniques for K-12 classrooms.* West Palm Beach, FL: Learning Sciences International.

Wilson, M., & Bertenthal, M. (Eds.). (2005). *Systems for state science assessment.* Washington, DC: National Academies Press.

Wise, S. L., & Smith, L. F. (2016). The validity of assessment when students don't give good effort. In G. T. L. Brown & L. R. Harris (Eds.), *Handbook of human and social conditions in assessment* (pp. 204–220). New York: Routledge.

Witt, J. C., Elliott, S. N., Daly, E. J., III, Gresham, F. M., & Kramer, J. J. (1998). *Assessment of at-risk and special needs children* (2nd ed.). Boston: McGraw-Hill.

Wood, J. W. (2002). *Adapting instruction to accommodate students in inclusive settings* (4th ed.). Upper Saddle River, NJ: Prentice Hall.

Worcester, T. (2009). *Portfolio planning sheet.* Accessed September 29, 2009, from http://www.tammyworcester.com/TWHandouts/HandoutsPresentationsTW/Entries/2022/1/1_Electronic_Portfolios_files/electronicportfolio.pdf

Wormeli, R. (2006). *Fair isn't always equal: Assessing & grading in the differentiated classroom.* Portland, ME: Stenhouse Publishers.

Worrell, F. C., & Erwin, J. O. (2011). Best practices in identifying students for gifted and talented education programs. *Journal of Applied School Psychology, 27,* 319–340.

Zimmerman, B. J. (2001). Theories of self-regulated learning and academic achievement: An overview and analysis. In B. J. Zimmerman, & D. H. Schunk (Eds.), *Self-regulated learning and academic achievement: theoretical perspectives* (2nd ed.) (pp. 1–38). Mahwah, NJ: Erlbaum.

Index